HEALTH AND HUMAN DEVELOPMENT

SOCIAL AND CULTURAL PSYCHIATRY EXPERIENCE FROM THE CARIBBEAN REGION

HEALTH AND HUMAN DEVELOPMENT

JOAV MERRICK - SERIES EDITOR –
NATIONAL INSTITUTE OF CHILD HEALTH
AND HUMAN DEVELOPMENT,
MINISTRY OF SOCIAL AFFAIRS, JERUSALEM

Adolescent Behavior Research: International Perspectives
Joav Merrick and Hatim A. Omar (Editors)
2007. ISBN: 1-60021-649-8

Complementary Medicine Systems: Comparison and Integration
Karl W. Kratky
2008. ISBN: 978-1-60456-475-4

Pain in Children and Youth
Patricia Schofield and Joav Merrick (Editors)
2008. ISBN: 978-1-60456-951-3

Challenges in Adolescent Health: An Australian Perspective
*David Bennett, Susan Towns, Elizabeth Elliott
and Joav Merrick (Editors)*
2009. ISBN: 978-1-60741-616-6 (Hardcover)
2009. ISBN: 978-1-61668-240-8 (E-book)

Behavioral Pediatrics, 3rd Edition
*Donald E. Greydanus, Dilip R. Patel,
Helen D. Pratt and Joseph L. Calles, Jr. (Editors)*
2009. ISBN: 978-1-60692-702-1 (Hardcover)
2009. ISBN: 978-1-60876-630-7 (E-book)

**Health and Happiness from Meaningful Work:
Research in Quality of Working Life**
Søren Ventegodt and Joav Merrick (Editors)
2009. ISBN: 978-1-60692-820-2

Obesity and Adolescence: A Public Health Concern
*Hatim A. Omar, Donald E. Greydanus,
Dilip R. Patel and Joav Merrick (Editors)*
2009. ISBN: 978-1-60456-821-9

Poverty and Children: A Public Health Concern
Alexis Lieberman and Joav Merrick (Editors)
2009. ISBN: 978-1-60741-140-6

Living on the Edge: The Mythical, Spiritual, and Philosophical Roots of Social Marginality
Joseph Goodbread
2009. ISBN: 978-1-60741-162-8

Alcohol-Related Cognitive Disorders: Research and Clinical Perspectives
Leo Sher, Isack Kandel and Joav Merrick (Editors)
2009. ISBN: 978-1-60741-730-9 (Hardcover)
2009. ISBN: 978-1-60876-623-9 (E-book)

Child Rural Health: International Aspects
Erica Bell and Joav Merrick (Editors)
2010. ISBN: 978-1-60876-357-3

Advances in Environmental Health Effects of Toxigenic Mold and Mycotoxins- Volume 1
Ebere Cyril Anyanwu
2010. ISBN: 978-1-60741-953-2

Children and Pain
Patricia Schofield and Joav Merrick (Editors)
2009. ISBN: 978-1-60876-020-6 (Hardcover)
2009. ISBN: 978-1-61728-183-9 (E-book)

Conceptualizing Behavior in Health and Social Research: A Practical Guide to Data Analysis
Said Shahtahmasebi and Damon Berridge
2010. ISBN: 978-1-60876-383-2

Chance Action and Therapy. The Playful Way of Changing
Uri Wernik
2010. ISBN: 978-1-60876-393-1

Adolescence and Chronic Illness. A Public Health Concern
Hatim Omar, Donald E. Greydanus, Dilip R. Patel and Joav Merrick (Editors)
2010. ISBN: 978-1-60876-628-4 (Hardcover)
2010. ISBN: 978-1-61761-482-8 (E-book)

Adolescence and Sports
Dilip R. Patel, Donald E. Greydanus, Hatim Omar and Joav Merrick (Editors)
2010. ISBN: 978-1-60876-702-1 (Hardcover)
2010. ISBN: 978-1-61761-483-5 (E-book)

International Aspects of Child Abuse and Neglect
Howard Dubowitz and Joav Merrick (Editors)
2010. ISBN: 978-1-60876-703-8

**Positive Youth Development: Evaluation and Future
Directions in a Chinese Context**
Daniel T.L. Shek, Hing Keung Ma and Joav Merrick (Editors)
2010. ISBN: 978-1-60876-830-1 (Hardcover)
2010. ISBN: 978-1-61668-376-4 (E-book)

**Positive Youth Development: Implementation of a Youth Program
in a Chinese Context**
Daniel T.L Shek, Hing Keung Ma and Joav Merrick (Editors)
2010. ISBN: 978-1-61668-230-9

**Pediatric and Adolescent Sexuality and Gynecology:
Principles for the Primary Care Clinician**
*Hatim A. Omar, Donald E. Greydanus, Artemis K. Tsitsika, Dilip R. Patel
and Joav Merrick (Editors)*
2010. ISBN: 978-1-60876-735-9

**Understanding Eating Disorders: Integrating Culture,
Psychology and Biology**
Yael Latzer, Joav Merrick and Daniel Stein (Editors)
2010. ISBN: 978-1-61728-298-0

Advanced Cancer Pain and Quality of Life
Edward Chow and Joav Merrick (Editors)
2010. ISBN: 978-1-61668-207-1

**Positive Youth Development: Implementation of a Youth Program
in a Chinese Context**
Daniel T.L Shek, Hing Keung Ma and Joav Merrick (Editors)
2010. ISBN: 978-1-61668-230-9

Bone and Brain Metastases: Advances in Research and Treatment
Arjun Sahgal, Edward Chow and Joav Merrick (Editors)
2010. ISBN: 978-1-61668-365-8 (Hardcover)
2010. ISBN: 978-1-61728-085-6 (E-book)

Environment, Mood Disorders and Suicide
Teodor T. Postolache and Joav Merrick (Editors)
2010. ISBN: 978-1-61668-505-8

Social and Cultural Psychiatry Experience from the Caribbean Region
Hari D. Maharajh and Joav Merrick (Editors)
2010. ISBN: 978-1-61668-506-5 (Hardcover)
2010. ISBN: 978-1-61728-088-7 (E-book)

Narratives and Meanings of Migration
Julia Mirsky
2010. ISBN: 978-1-61761-103-2 (Hardcover)
2010. ISBN: 978-1-61761-519-1 (E-book)

Self-Management and the Health Care Consumer
Peter William Harvey
2011. ISBN: 978-1-61761-796-6

Sexology from a Holistic Point of View
Soren Ventegodt and Joav Merrick
2011. ISBN: 978-1-61761-859-8

**Principles of Holistic Psychiatry: A Textbook on
Holistic Medicine for Mental Disorders**
Soren Ventegodt and Joav Merrick
2011. ISBN: 978-1-61761-940-3

HEALTH AND HUMAN DEVELOPMENT

SOCIAL AND CULTURAL PSYCHIATRY EXPERIENCE FROM THE CARIBBEAN REGION

HARI D. MAHARAJH
AND
JOAV MERRICK
EDITORS

Nova Science Publishers, Inc.
New York

Copyright © 2010 by Nova Science Publishers, Inc.

All rights reserved. No part of this book may be reproduced, stored in a retrieval system or transmitted in any form or by any means: electronic, electrostatic, magnetic, tape, mechanical photocopying, recording or otherwise without the written permission of the Publisher.

For permission to use material from this book please contact us:
Telephone 631-231-7269; Fax 631-231-8175
Web Site: http://www.novapublishers.com

NOTICE TO THE READER

The Publisher has taken reasonable care in the preparation of this book, but makes no expressed or implied warranty of any kind and assumes no responsibility for any errors or omissions. No liability is assumed for incidental or consequential damages in connection with or arising out of information contained in this book. The Publisher shall not be liable for any special, consequential, or exemplary damages resulting, in whole or in part, from the readers' use of, or reliance upon, this material. Any parts of this book based on government reports are so indicated and copyright is claimed for those parts to the extent applicable to compilations of such works.

Independent verification should be sought for any data, advice or recommendations contained in this book. In addition, no responsibility is assumed by the publisher for any injury and/or damage to persons or property arising from any methods, products, instructions, ideas or otherwise contained in this publication.

This publication is designed to provide accurate and authoritative information with regard to the subject matter covered herein. It is sold with the clear understanding that the Publisher is not engaged in rendering legal or any other professional services. If legal or any other expert assistance is required, the services of a competent person should be sought. FROM A DECLARATION OF PARTICIPANTS JOINTLY ADOPTED BY A COMMITTEE OF THE AMERICAN BAR ASSOCIATION AND A COMMITTEE OF PUBLISHERS.

Additional color graphics may be available in the e-book version of this book.

LIBRARY OF CONGRESS CATALOGING-IN-PUBLICATION DATA
Social and cultural psychiatry experience from the Caribbean region / editors, Hari D. Maharajh, Joav Merrick.
p. ; cm. -- (Health and human development series)
Includes bibliographical references and index.
ISBN 978-1-61668-506-5 (hardcover)
1. Cultural psychiatry--Caribbean Area. 2. Social psychiatry--Caribbean Area. I. Maharajh, Hari D. II. Merrick, Joav, 1950- III. Series: Health and human development series.
[DNLM: 1. Community Psychiatry--Caribbean Region. 2. Cultural Characteristics--Caribbean Region. 3. Mental Disorders--ethnology--Caribbean Region. WM 30.6]
RC455.4.E8S63 2010
362.196'89009729--dc22

2010034046

Published by Nova Science Publishers, Inc. + *New York*

CONTENTS

Foreword		**xiii**
Section One: Introduction		
	The Caribbean Region *Hari D. Maharajh and Joav Merrick*	**1**
Section Two: Medicine and the Caribbean Region		**5**
Chapter 1	History of Medicine in the Caribbean Region: A Medical Association Perspective (1938-2008) *Hari D. Maharajh*	**7**
Chapter 2	Defining "Caribbeing Psychiatry" *Hari D. Maharajh*	**17**
Chapter 3	Forging a New Dimension of Black Psychiatry in the Caribbean *Katija Khan and Hari D. Maharajh*	**29**
Chapter 4	Indentureship as a Contributory Factor to Mental and Physical Illnesses in the Indo-Caribbean Diaspora *Hari D. Maharajh*	**39**
Chapter 5	Dopamine, Demons Or Divination? The Dichotomy of Science and Religion in Traditional Societies *Hari D. Maharajh*	**51**
Section Three: Culture, Behavior and Mental Illness		**61**
Chapter 6	Recognizing Social and Cultural Behaviors in Trinidad and Tobago *Hari D. Maharajh and Akleema Ali*	**63**
Chapter 7	Race, Politics and Behavior in Trinidad and Tobago *Hari D. Maharajh*	**87**
Chapter 8	The Effects of Multiculturalism and Multi-ethnicity in Group Dynamics in a Caribbean Setting *Hari D. Maharajh*	**101**

Chapter 9	Do Trinidadians Have a Carnival Mentality? *Hari D. Maharajh*	**109**
Chapter 10	Dancing Frotteurism or Rubbing at the Carnival Celebrations in Trinidad *Hari D. Maharajh*	**117**
Chapter 11	Anorexia Nervosa and Religious Ambivalence in a Developing Country *Hari D. Maharajh*	**123**

Section Four: Suicidal Behavior and Suicide — **129**

Chapter 12	Culture and Suicide *Hari D. Maharajh and Petal S. Abdool*	**131**
Chapter 13	Adolescent Suicide in Trinidad and Tobago *Hari D. Maharajh and Akleema Ali*	**145**
Chapter 14	Patterns of Suicide and Suicidal Behaviors: Context and Causation *Hari D. Maharajh*	**155**
Chapter 15	Derma-abuse with Cutting in Young Adolescents *Hari D. Maharajh and Rainah Seepersad*	**165**
Chapter 16	Cybersuicide and the Adolescent Population: Challenges of the Future *Ria Birbal, Hari D. Maharajh, Risa Birbal, Maria Clapperton, Johnathan Jarvis, Anushka Ragoonath and Kali Uppalapati*	**183**
Chapter 17	Self-poisoning by Pesticide and Other Substances in a General Hospital *Hari D. Maharajh and Monique Konings*	**193**
Chapter 18	Consultation-liaison Psychiatry in Trinidad and Tobago with Reference to Suicidal Behavior *Hari D. Maharajh, Petal Abdool and Rehannah Mohammed*	**201**

Section Five: Alcohol and Substance Abuse — **211**

Chapter 19	Crime, Alcohol Use and Unemployment *Hari D. Maharajh and Akleema Ali*	**213**
Chapter 20	Aggressive Sexual Behavior of Alcohol-dependent Men in Trinidad *Hari D. Maharajh and Akleema Ali*	**223**
Chapter 21	Alcoholics Anonymous in Trinidad *Rainah Seepersad and Hari D. Maharajh*	**229**
Chapter 22	Cannabis Use: Context and Controversy *Hari D. Maharajh*	**245**

Chapter 23	Depression and Psychosis Associated with Cannabis Abuse in a Developing Country *Hari D. Maharajh and Monique Konings*	**257**
Chapter 24	Cocaine Use and Social Transformation *Hari D. Maharajh*	**269**

Section Six: General and Specialty Psychiatry — **000**

Chapter 25	Deinstitutionalization in the Caribbean *Hari D. Maharajh*	**277**
Chapter 26	Depression in Trinidad and Tobago: Incidence and Social Trends *Hari D. Maharajh and Akleema Ali*	**287**
Chapter 27	Schizophrenia Revisited: Consensus and Confusion *Hari D. Maharajh*	**297**
Chapter 28	Somatization Disorders among Indians in Jamaica and Trinidad and its Association with Social and Psychological Factors *Astra Kassiram and Hari D. Maharajh*	**309**
Chapter 29	Forensic Psychiatry in the Colonial and Post Colonial Eras *Hari D. Maharajh*	**329**
Chapter 30	Lunacy, Time of the Year and Absconding from a Psychiatric Hospital *Hari D. Maharajh and Akleema Ali*	**355**

Section Seven: Reflections — **363**

Chapter 31	The Way Forward *Hari D. Maharajh and Joav Merrick*	**365**

Section Eight: Acknowledgments — **367**

Chapter 32	About the Authors	**369**
Chapter 33	About the Department of Clinical Medicine at the University of the West Indies, Mount Hope, Trinidad	**373**
Chapter 34	About the National Institute of Child Health and Human Development in Israel	**375**
Chapter 35	About the Book Series "Health and Human Development"	**379**
Index		**381**

FOREWORD

The ability to express your thoughts is a precious one especially for psychiatrists. Hari Maharajh has always been dedicated to the practice of this expression. As a result, he is sometimes controversial, sometimes provocative, but always stimulating, always challenging. I began my own career in psychiatry working with him as my first consultant and can trace many of my current interests to those early encounters on the wards and in the clinics of St Ann's Hospital, Trinidad and Tobago's sole in-patient mental hospital.

We are now colleagues again in an academic environment and I can only admire and seek to emulate his example that is represented by his appetite for work, his dedication to his craft, commitment to his students and his ongoing desire and facility to express himself.

He has written a book in collaboration with many of his students and research associates that attempts to give meaning to the term Caribbeing Psychiatry. The colonial history of the region and the multiple origins of its people have created a fascinating cauldron of cultures and ideas. This most spectacularly applies to Trinidad and Tobago and Dr Maharajh has heroically attempted to describe the way in which this melting pot has informed the social dimensions of mental health in this complex and ever changing environment.

He is well prepared for this task, having practiced psychiatry in Trinidad for well over thirty years. He was trained at St Georges Hospital in South London and Institute of Neurology at Queen's Square and was there at a time when psychiatry was undergoing a revolution as it sought to prepare itself for the reality of a multicultural Britain and a globalized world. It was no surprise then that on his return he founded the Transcultural Society at St Ann's Hospital and facilitated the celebration and discussion of the many cultural and religious festivals that are recognized in Trinidad and Tobago. He eventually left that institution as the Medical Chief of Staff to join the University of the West Indies' Psychiatry Unit.

He has written extensively on the many sociocultural dimensions of life in Trinidad and Tobago and how these impact on societal norms and mental health and he has compiled these writings together with his most recent work into this very fascinating volume.

As Edward Kamau Brathwaite (1) wrote: "We who are born of oceans can never seek solace in rivers" and this volume that he has produced together with his collaborator and friend from Israel, professor Joav Merrick from the National Institute of Child Health and Human Development there, represents a landmark effort to document our struggle to make sense of our world, a landmark that also challenges us to interrogate our practice and so chart a meaningful future for professional mental health practice in Trinidad and Tobago and the Caribbean.

Gerard Hutchinson, DM
Professor of Psychiatry
Head of Department of Clinical Medicine
University of the West Indies
Mount Hope
Trinidad

REFERENCES

[1]   Brathwaite E. South from middle passages. London: Heinemann, 1992:50-2.

SECTION ONE: INTRODUCTION

In: Social and Cultural Psychiatry Experience from the...   ISBN: 978-1-61668-506-5
Editor: Hari D. Maharajh and Joav Merrick   © 2010 Nova Science Publishers, Inc.

THE CARIBBEAN REGION

Hari D Maharajh and Joav Merrick

To the newcomer, the Caribbean is often perceived as an exotic, easy going, homogenous region with a striking similarity of all the islands. On the surface, this mirage holds merit with the cross-over and linkages of behaviour, music, food, sports and landscape. However, within the Caribbean islands, there are major differences with a common bond of unity in diversity. Notwithstanding the absence of major unifying forces among the islands of the Caribbean, there is a strange and almost mystical connection to each other. Among the islands, there is pride and prejudice, unity and insularity, competition and cooperation and similarities and differences resulting in disparate and diverse lifestyles that render uniqueness to each island. The blend of people, races and cultures from across the globe has set a stage for a rainbow existence together but yet apart.

The geographical area of the Caribbean region has expanded over time. It comprised at one time six million people of the Anglophone Caribbean islands and was interchangeably equated as the West Indies. Today, the Caribbean consists of fourteen million inhabitants including the Dutch influenced islands of St Marten, Aruba, Bonaire, Curacao and Suriname, the Spanish speaking countries of Cuba and Puerto Rico, the French dependencies of Santo Domingo and Haiti together with the original Francophone islands of Martinique and Guadeloupe and Anglophone islands of the West indies including Bahamas in the northern Caribbean. Despite their differences, primordial historical antecedents have brought the people together. These are a history of servitude, slavery and indentureship, a belief in superstition, magic and supernaturalism and the differences of the colonizers and the colonized ever present in the minds of inhabitants. Colonizers, whether they were Dutch, English, French or Spanish had a profound effect on the development and establishment of post colonial societies.

Slavery and indentureship, the rejection of the traditional beliefs of the migrant groups in a new and hostile environment, the forced conversion to Christianity, the loss of masculinity of men folk in their inability to garner control over the women folk in a slave-master society and the political sanctions of divide and rule thereby turning people against themselves sowed the seeds of a major proportion of the social disorder and psychological pain experienced in modern day society. It is often argued that in the Caribbean, there is a superimposition of a slave-like mentality in people basically born free, a convenient all purpose excuse.

It is on this background of historical perspectives, definitions, dimensions and a Caribbean Diaspora, the interpretation of behaviours and mental disorders with contributions from witchcraft, priestcraft and science that this book was designed. The local interpretation of mental illness is challenged, by asking: "Is mental illness due to divinity, demons or dopamine." According to John Milton, this book truly represents 'the precious life blood of a master spirit embalmed and treasured up on purpose to a life beyond life.'". It is not synthetic, but syncretic attempting to capture the history, lifestyles and beliefs of Caribbean people relating them without impunity to the psychology of their emotion, thought and behaviour. To any group, behaviour is always meaningful and is a culmination of latent transgenerational and present day experiences unconsciously superimposed onto them. Structures, be it psychological or physical, internally or externally dictated determines behaviour. A false pluralism born out of economic needs and multiculturalism dictated by the colonizing forces provided the basis for divisiveness, hate, antagonism and abnormal psychic experiences. The Caribbean today is viewed by some as a melting pot, but on closer analysis remains a pepper pot of a bitter-sweet experience.

This book is divided into several sections with an introduction in nature, which reviews the history of medicine in the Caribbean region, as 2008 marked seventy years of the prolific Caribbean medical journal, a platform that has allowed the creative process of doctors and many alike in the publication of articles of a medical nature. Focal to the text is the introduction of the concept of Caribbeing Psychiatry, which is based on the transgenerational influences and treatment modalities formulated though archetypes, images and emotions unique to our culture that are necessary when entering the curative process. We also address the emergence of Black psychiatry in order to address the cultural diversity of the Caribbean people, which seems to be a Black dominated psychiatry myopic in its view to the other cultures that comprise the Caribbean. Slavery, indentureship and the concept of 'blackman rising' has been pivotal in the underdevelopment of the region. Similarly, the effects of 'coolie migration' in it's own right has contributed to a commonality of social, psychological and physical diseases in these migrant groups within the diaspora. Modern western scientific medicine is in this region meeting magic and supernaturalism. Religion used as a tool of control continues to be conveniently used to keep individuals in a state of religious servitude. The conflict of whether mental illness is caused by demons or dopamine have strengthened the various religious bodies resolve to propagate such noxious nuances in order to win souls.

The section on culture, behavior and mental illness explores the effect of race, culture, politics, sexual habits and lifestyle on behaviour in contemporary Trinidad. Some of the identified behaviours that are observed in Trinidad are presented perceived to be a part of the Trinidadian culture - liming, carnival mentality, player or playboy personality, Tabanca and obsessional lateness. Contentions and accusatons of racism stemming from political dominance within Trinidad and Tobago has been objectively reviewed with critical analyses of numerous cases. We also examine the behaviors that are displayed during our time of Carnival frolic and relaxation highlight the eclectic nature of Trinidadian culture with references to negative and positive outcomes with further investigation into the behavior at the carnival celebrations and its bordering on paraphilic behavior. Religious ambivalence as an etiological factor in anorexia nervosa in a developing country is also highlighted.

A common problem of suicide and suicidal behaviour endemic in Trinidad is presented in a section by itself. The interesting ethnic reversal patterns of suicidal behaviour in Indians and homicidal behaviour in Africans are reviewed with respect to the various cultural imperatives affecting their lives. Suicide has evolved from the agrarian use of pesticide to the new technological habit of cybersuicide, which has become as popular mode due to the proliferation of website activity worldwide. Self harm and the introduction of a new term 'derma-abuse' has been investigated in 2009 in Trinidad in terms of its prevalence and socio-demographic characteristics among adolescents. Among adolescents, self harm without intent such as cutting is utilised more so as a manipulative cry for help while actual suicide attempts are concentrated among adult populations.

The Caribbean as a region is in the big league with respect to alcohol and drug use, which is often associated with crime that is prevalent in our country. The relationship and role that unemployment and alcohol has contributed to the increase of criminal activity is investigated. Further alcohol and its relationship with sexuality, namely aggressive sexual behaviour in men is highlighted as a problem that Trinidadian women face. The socio-demographic features of alcohol dependent individuals that comprise Alcoholics Anonymous (AA) groups are also investigated showing great consistency with previous research surrounding the Indo-Trinidadian man and his relationship with alcohol. Concerns and controversies concerning the use of cannabis and cocaine are also explored; it reviews the clinical effects of marijuana use, its relationship with suicide, mood disorders, psychoses and other mental disorders and discusses controversies associated with its decriminalization and de-legalization. Mood disorders seem to be a common finding among adolescents using cannabis and we put forward guidelines for the implementation of public health strategies and legislation concerning the use of cannabis in youths. In this section the history, introduction, development, culture, methods of use and effects of the use of cocaine in Trinidad and Tobago and its worldwide implications is also discussed.

In a section on common topics in general and specialty psychiatry we present the local setting, that is, the status of community psychiatry and the concept of deinstitutionalization, the major problems of depression and schizophrenia with absence of consensus and propagation of confusion, forensic issues, somatization and absconding from psychiatric hospital.. We found that the admission to psychiatric hospitals in Trinidad and Jamaica seem to be less preferred with alternative treatment for patient care being more prevalent and such findings are useful in providing invaluable information for the development of community care programmes in developing countries. Social parameters of gender differences, age cohort, attendence to religious institutions, prayer with the family use of alcohol, type of school attended, ethnicity and family structures are also investigated. These variables were found to be significant contributory factors to adolescent depression in the Republic. Schizophrenia is investigated and there was no consensus on the rates of schizophrenia among ethnic groups at home in the Caribbean and abroad. Investigations of gender and ethnic differences on the rates of first contact outpatients with schizophrenia in two geographically different areas in Trinidad are reported with a preponderance of young African males. The prevalence of somatization disorder in an Indian Trinidadian and Indian Jamaican Population with comparison to Asian populations worldwide is also reviewed and the concepts of common and statute laws are reviewed with respect to their application and the duties of the psychiatrist. The history, development and practice of Forensic Psychiatry in the colonial period in Trinidad are explored and later following independence during the establishment of a Mental Health Act and the introduction of the Sectorization Plan in 1975. We have also looked at the relationship between time of the year and absconding among psychiatric patients in the psychiatric hospital.

The preparation of this book has been immersed in debate. A number of persons of different disciplines and religious backgrounds have been extremely instrumental in effecting a balanced view on many controversial issues in thought and practice. We wish to graciously thank Ms Rainah Seepersad for her patience, interest and assistance in the preparation of this manuscript. Ms Akleema Ali, a former research assistant on whose shoulders Rainah stood had previously put the wheels in motion for this book. To both of them we are greatly indebted. Dr. Monique Konings from the Netherlands spent a year in research and her unyielding enthusiasm was an inspiration to all. As an outsider she brought a new perspective to Caribbeing issues. These three women of different backgrounds provided useful information for most of the chapters, not only the ones that they co-authored. We wish to acknowledge with gratitude their support and input in this project and the many discussions around the topics discussed in this book.

The undergraduate and post graduate students under the tutelage at the University of the West Indies have been a continuous and pervasive source of knowledge, wisdom, and inspiration. Those listed as collaborators and others who have participated in lectures, seminars, discourses and discussions have all been mirrors that afforded a brighter expression and reflection of self.

Hari D Maharajh wishes to thank his colleagues both at San Fernando and St Anns Hospital for their paradoxical contribution in the compilation of this book. Their defiant approach to the University and its members provided a guiding light to success. The colleagues at Eric Williams Medical Sciences Complex, Professor Gerard Hutchinson who has always been extremely supportive and shares a common interest in many of the issues discussed. His collaborative efforts have been curtailed by other commitments. Dr. Sandra Reid, Dr. Nelleen Baboolal and Dr. Tony Bastick have shared interesting hypotheses, which may have filtered into this work. They have provided a wealth of knowledge emanating from their diverse backgrounds. Two friends, Pamela Hosein and Ali Khan are thanked for walking Hari through religious and cultural journeys that were unfamiliar. The secretarial staff, for their unending tolerance demonstrated over time. It would be unremitting of me (Hari) not to thank my wife Indra and children Anujh Viren and Ashti Sidhi for the opportunity of taking invaluable time away from the family for the purpose of academic involvement. Last but not least, special thanks must be bestowed upon my co-author Professor Joav Merrick who has guided this process from its inception to the end. Without Joav, this book would not have been put together. He has been responsible for the editorial process, announcement and technical knowledge of production. It has been a pleasurable experience in working together with such an energetic, structured, resourceful and experienced person, who prevents floundering.

This project has also crossed borders, created friendships and incentive that we hope the reader will find useful. We both hope that can serve as a good model for international collaboration and academic inspiration.

SECTION TWO: MEDICINE AND THE CARIBBEAN REGION

In: Social and Cultural Psychiatry Experience from the...
Editor: Hari D. Maharajh and Joav Merrick

ISBN: 978-1-61668-506-5
© 2010 Nova Science Publishers, Inc.

Chapter 1

HISTORY OF MEDICINE IN THE CARIBBEAN REGION: A MEDICAL ASSOCIATION PERSPECTIVE (1938-2008)

Hari D. Maharajh

Two thousand and eight (2008) remains a landmark in the history of the Medical Association. We celebrate seventy years (70) of publication of the Caribbean Medical Journal (CMJ), first published in 1938 by the Government printery under the editorship of the indefatigable Dr James Waterman. It was indeed an arduous task in sifting through the pages of 70 years of publications, but this was sustained and motivated by the genius, enthusiasm, eloquence and debates of 'the medical men of the West Indies who in the early years outshined their colonial counterparts in every possible way. Post independence we have witnessed a fall out in medical interests as we became more insular in our practice. More recently, there has been a resurgence of interests in medical matters as we battle a vindictive government in a failing health system promulgating draconian legislations in health care to cover their inefficiencies. A review of our history indicates that doctors have survived the wrath of the imposing British Empire and no government present or future will have the ability to superimpose their will on learned men of multimodal distinctions. A limitation of this review is that many volumes of the journals are lost or packed away in boxes in some obscure, darkened, termite ridden room at Xavier Street. This is indeed a loss of the most valuable treasure of the Association. This may have resulted in the omission of important historical occurrences in the Association's history. It is hoped that this review will serve as a landmark for the Association to further build upon, as we continue to document our trials and tribulations, hopes and aspirations in an ever changing environment.

INTRODUCTION

This year marks the 70th year of publication of the Caribbean Medical Journal which was founded in 1938. Among others, the aims of the journal was 'the exchange of ideas among the medical men of the West Indies' and the publication of a 'correspondence page to invite criticism' [1].

The composition of the British Medical Association at that time comprised the Council of the Caribbean Branches of the BMA. The Council was formed from the elected representatives of the following territories, Barbados, British Guiana, British Honduras, Jamaica, Leeward Islands, Trinidad and Tobago and the Windward Islands. Early interests included, malaria, tuberculosis, venereal diseases, maternity and infant welfare, filariasis, paralytic rabies, ankylostomaisis, nutrition, diahorrea, drainage and other public health problems. Among the contents of the journal was a section entitled 'notes of interest.' This provided an update of the medical activities of members of the profession. The following are excerpts from a 1939 publication.

"We must take this opportunity to congratulate Dr P.A. Rostant for the splendid production of the well known play" The wind and the Rain' put on at a San Fernando theatre quite recently; also Dr S Littlepage for his fine acting in the role of 'leading man' [2]

"Dr EP Mason of the Trinidad Government Medical Service is at present studying psychological medicine." As a former director of the Psychiatric hospital, there is today a ward named after him

"Dr H Pierre of the Trinidad Government Medical Service is at present in England studying surgery. We hope to hear that he has obtained the coveted F.R.C.S." He received it the next year. After yeoman service to this country, he died in England in 1986. The Caribbean Medical Journal has dedicated an Issue to this noble gentleman with dedications from E.L.S. Robertson and George Wattley [3]

"Doctors V Lawyers – On the 26th March 1939 an interesting cricket match took place at the Queen's Park Oval, Port of Spain between members of the medical and legal fraternities. The lawyers under the veteran international Andre Cipriani, and including Clifford Roach, another international player, Peterkin of Grenada and Clark of St Vincent batting first made 169. The doctors under the captaincy of AG Francis of the Colonial hospital, Port of Spain replied with a snappy 170 for seven wickets" Cricket at one time was a major uniting force in the Caribbean

As we look back through the annals of medical history nothing much has changed. The issues remain the same along a time line of developmental changes. In an invited editorial of 1939 QB De Freitas wrote,

"The trend of Medical Practice has undergone considerable change; modern agencies such as the radio, cinema, recent works of fiction and the press have contributed to a new conception of medicine and medical men. The public appears to think that the scale on which operating theatres and laboratories are represented on the films with the latest gadgets are to be found in all hospitals and when disillusioned, it is apt to conclude that the profession in these latitudes is backward and out-of –date" [4]

And again, Sir John Boyd Orr, one of the highly esteemed members of the profession in Great Britain wrote:

"The profession would lose its influence if it allowed itself to become the battleground for conflicting political and economic theories. While members of the profession as citizens should be free to hold any political views they think right, the profession as a profession should be apart from and above politics"[5]

These opinions are relevant to the Medical Association today, as it was seventy years ago. It is well known that many doctors with enduring personalities feel they have the right of passage to hold office. Their self-indulgent aim albeit personal, religious or political should be set aside putting the business of the Association on the front burner. Those who seek office for personalized and social power should do the right thing and recuse themselves from such positions. This is a contemporary dilemma and while doctors shall never be slaves to anyone, it has resulted in a 'same old, same old situation' wherein the same people hold office year after year more invested in ego protection that medical advancement. This is a major reason why the Medical Association has not been able to attract medical men of substance or if they have they are temporary or operate more effectively in absentia.

In 1944, six years after the initiation of the C.M.J, there was widespread support from all Caribbean countries. These included editorial board constituted from Antigua, Bahamas, Barbados, British Guiana, British Honduras, Dominica, Grenada, Jamaica, St Lucia, St Vincent and Trinidad and Tobago. James A Waterman, editor, writes in 1944 about the justifiable pride of those colonies which have been unflaggering in their support [6].

Dr. Esau J Sankeralli was the first Trinidadian to be appointed Director of Medical Services in Trinidad [7]. He was born of humble parentage in the county of St Patrick. Educated at Queen's Royal College, he obtained his Senior Cambridge Certificate, Grade 1 with honors in 1913. He worked with the Agricultural Department until 1919, and then thereafter proceeded to Belfast, Ireland to pursue a very successful academic career graduating in 1924. On return, he joined the Medical Department at the San Fernando General Hospital. He was fond of surgery but ran into conflicts with the Surgeon General and was compelled to join the Public Health Section in 1930. He blazed the trail and through hard work reached to the top position. He was indeed a gifted son of the soil who died prematurely at his own hand on 22nd June 1948 at the age of 52.

An article written by Phillip M Sherlock in the CMJ reads: 'University College of the West Indies inaugurated':

In October 1948, the first group of undergraduates entered the University College. It has been necessary to begin the hard way and to start with the teaching of medicine, but every effort is being made to begin the teaching of art and of science quickly. Only medical students can be accepted this year, and every care has been taken in their selection. There were 130 applicants for admission, 29 of them being women. They came from many parts of the West Indies, and a method of selection had to be found which gave the preference to intellectual capability. It was clearly the best to make this the chief test rather than to allocate a certain number of places to each contributing Colony, since the enterprise was West Indian and not local, and since the aim was to give opportunities for training to the best who applied [8]

Two icons of medicine, actively participating in various aspects of medicine today and who attended the October Update and Research Conference this year (2008) are Dr David Picou and Dr Premchan Ratan. These noble gentlemen were in the first class of medicine in October 1948 and today remain unsung heroes of the Caribbean. Their lifetime performance gives credence to a meritocratic system of admission to medical school. It is worrying that this system to which most doctors have been selected has given way to another system that is politically driven to favor affirmative action to a particular ethnic grouping.

In January 1951, the First Caribbean Conference of the British Medical Association Branches was held at Port of Spain, Trinidad [9]. The major point of discussion was the desire among delegates to obtain an improved medical service for the Caribbean area through the establishment of Unification of the Medical Services. The resolution recommended the appointment of a Unified Medical Services Commission consisting of seven (7) full time salaried officers and the Chairman of the Caribbean Council of Branches of the British Medical Associations. The assumption is that the pooling of medical knowledge will be beneficial to the Caribbean peoples with a federation of the Caribbean colonies. The conference was addressed by His Excellency the Governor, Sir Hubert Rance and the Honorable Minister of Health, Mr. Norman Tang. It should be noted that this proposal of a Unified Medical and Health Service for the British West Indies was adopted from Sir Alexander Russell's report which was carried in the editorial of the CMJ in 1944 [10]. These recommendations were not realized due to non agreement by the various governments.

In 1959, the twenty first anniversary of the publication of the Caribbean Medical Journal was celebrated. To mark this occasion, a special issue devoted to "Paralytic Rabies" in Trinidad and the valuable researches of Dr. J. L Pawan were produced. In 1925 animals began dying of a disease which was erroneously diagnosed as Botulism, or Bulbar Palsy. In 1929, twelve cases of "Acute Ascending Myelitis" were diagnosed in humans. The diagnoses were changed to Anterior Poliomyelitis. In September 1931, Negri bodies were demonstrated by Dr Pawan in the brains of bat and those infected with the disease. Dr Pawan moved from the tentative hypothesis to conclusive proof that the Desmodus bat was the vector of rabies in Trinidad. This is fully recorded in 1959 issue of the Caribbean Medical Journal [11]. Altogether 72 patients were affected and all died, 20 of which were admitted to the San Fernando General Hospital. This was the first record in medical history of the bat Desmodus Rufus causing disease but no one has been able to trace where and when was the bat infected with rabies.

Joseph Lennox Pawan was born in Trinidad in 1887. He attended St Mary's College where he won the Island Scholarship in 1907. He graduated from Edinburgh University in 1912 and returned to Trinidad where he rose to the position of Government Bacteriologist and Senior Pathologist at the Colonial Hospital in Port of Spain. He died in 1959. In 1961, the Second Annual Lennox Pawan Memorial Lecture was delivered at the Nurses' training School, General Hospital, Port of Spain by Dr David B.E. Quamina entitled, The Borderland of Dermatology and other specialties .It is an excellent paper that is worth reading [12]. Again in 1964, the 4th Pawan memorial Lecture was delivered by Dr Percival Harnarayan entitled Clinical Manifestations of Endometrial Pathology [13]. In 1987, one hundred years after the birth of Lennox Pawan, a state of the art lecture was delivered in honor of the latter during the 10th Annual Medical Update by Dr D Carleton Gadjusek who discovered the Kuru virus [14]. It is interesting to note that the Present editor of the CMJ Dr Rasheed Adams knew Dr Pawan and as a child, rode in his car.

With the attainment of Independence In 1962, there was a slow but predictable demise of the structure of the Caribbean Branches of the British Medical Association. The attempts to have a West Indian Federation of Islands previously a brain child of the Medical Association failed. The vision for a West Indian Federation arose from the Association previous attempt to establish a Medical Federation with Unification of Services. This was spear headed by Dr Patrick Solomon, now Deputy Prime Minister and former President of the Medical Association. This, like the Specialists Unification proposal was a miserable failure. Thus, with the passage of time, the Journal increasingly became more insular with little input from other Caribbean territories.

The seventies witnessed a turn in medical education in Trinidad and other Caribbean countries. The fall out from Canada and the USA in inducing medical practitioners to make meetings a means of continuing medical education benefited the Association. Thus, the first International Medical Convention was hosted by The Trinidad and Tobago Medical Association from 17th -19th October 1975 of which abstracts of the proceedings were carried in the CMJ [15].

Members of the medical fraternity have been concerned with social and political issues. Historians have pointed out cyclical racial groupings in Trinidad with the African man seeking supremacy. Examples are the 1937 Butler Riots, Organization of the PNM in 1956, Black Power Movement of 1970 and the Muslimeen Insurrection in 1990. Dr. Pierre Rostant writes: [16].

"A general strike was organized involving the whole colony and the rabble took over spearheaded by a man called Uriah Butler. There developed the worst riots ever seen in Trinidad. A general strike was organized involving the whole colony. It started at Fyzabad where Butler was holding a large meeting on a Saturday night. The mob got out of control and there was shooting on both sides, the people and the police. An English Inspector was killed, a Corporal King of the police were captured and after being severely beaten gasoline was thrown on him and he was burnt to death. The Governor meanwhile had cabled for the HMS Ajax to come to our aid but only after shootings took place in San Fernando, Penal, Waterloo, Rio Claro and Port of Spain. We in San Fernando had a very terrifying time. Several people were shot and after that they dispersed and rushed to the Hospital with their wounded. Andrew Krogh and I had a very tough time on account of our color. That night all the residents of the Pasture gathered in the Assistant Matron's two room house protected by Sgt Belfon. There was not much sleep for anyone. A strange sense of distressing tranquility pervaded the town and also in our isolated hideout…….. As a result of the strike, Trade Union movement was started but deep down below there was the enmity and hate of the people against the so called 'European whites' and other foreigners. It took a long time before relationships became normal and a return to the so called peaceful racial harmony which to my mind was coated with just a very thin veneer and will always be so"[16]

The Medical Updates coordinated by Courtney Bartholomew is yet another milestone in the medical history of Trinidad and Tobago. In an article entitled 'Ten Years of Medical Updates-An Appraisal' penned by the then Professor of Medicine at UWI [17], gives credence to these meetings being 'recognized as one of the more famous international conferences'. During this period five Nobel prize winners and several who were knocking on the door of Stockholm had graced the Updates. At the Trinidad conferences, there were 75 presentations by foreign lecturers and 92 by local lecturers and it had been an opportunity of a lifetime for local lecturers to share the same podium with these international men of science and medicine. Many lasting contacts, opportunities and friendships were established. These Updates, many of which I attended as a student and young doctor are fixed in my mind as the best I have ever attended home and abroad. There existed a fanfare and culture that united the three hundred doctors that attended annually who put their hands together to honor the best brains in the medical world at that time, each capturing that moment. These conferences brought out the best in Dr Bartholomew and have endeared him to many notwithstanding his present day hostility to many colleagues and acrimonious approach to the medical profession. It is a sad day that he has lost favor with the medical profession supported only by a few Afro-centric personalities.

The nineties were dominated by concerns in the changes associated with Health Care Reform in Trinidad and Tobago. In 1993 Parliament approved the 1993 Regional Health Authorities Bill which administratively divided the country into five (5) Health Regions, four in Trinidad, namely, The Northwest Health Region ,the Central Health Region, the Southwest Health Region and the Eastern Health Region and one in Tobago, the Tobago Health Region. The Trinidad and Tobago Medical Association supported a decentralization process but remained wary in the way it was being done. The Association was concerned about the quality of health care that the state will provide for patients. The fear of patrimony, nepotism, political interference, corruption and increased cost were serious concerns with patients receiving the centre of the ringed doughnut. Fifteen years later, it seems as though the words of the Association were indeed prophetic as stated by Austin Trinidade, 'this bill will change the practice of medicine for the worst' [18]. Today, the health service lies in shambles with poor services at every institution. Details on Health Reform are also found in other issues of the CMJ [19,20].

Nineteen ninety eight (1998) marked the 60th Anniversary of the CMJ. It was also the year that this author accepted the chain of office as President of the Medical Association. With an able secretary, Dr Omar Ali, much was accomplished. After several journeys and meetings with doctors from Tobago namely Dr D Quamina, Dr J Armstrong and Dr Sandeep Kumar, on Saturday 28th May 1998, the 4th Branch of the Trinidad and Tobago Medical Association was founded [21]. Dr Armstrong died at the age of 80 years in 1992.

The Medical Association paid homage to a great medical visionary Dr Maxwell Phillip Awon who as a Minister of Health introduced health planning into Trinidad and Tobago, started the Caribbean Health Minister's conference, served as President of the Medical Association in 1978 and was one of Trinidad and Tobago most illustrious, medium size carnival band leader. He was an artist extraordinaire and I recall being invited to his home with Dr Anthony Changkit a man without an artistic flair to be taught how to tie a bowtie!

It is noteworthy that in the March issue of 1998 there were three eulogies of prominent doctors who rendered sterling services of an unusually high quality to the nation. Tribute was paid to Dr Percival Harnaryan (1923-1996) [22], Dr Russell William Barrow (1925-1997) [23] and Dr Elizabeth Quamina (1929-1997) [24].

The turn of the century (Y2K) witnessed a change in the medical profession. The RHA's with its many deficiencies attempted to superimpose their will onto doctors providing them with 'scab-like contracts' under unacceptable terms and conditions without any opportunities for advancement. In a most high handed manner, doctors were told with what bargaining body they should seek affiliation. Many were in a quandary and questioned to whom their responsibility laid since they were both accountable to the Ministry of Health and the Regional Health Authorities. This undermined the determination and dedication of doctors who had labored for decades in the desert-like vineyards. Groups of doctors bandied together at the various hospitals forming hospital doctor's association, later formalizing themselves as a powerful bargaining body - the Medical Professional Association of Trinidad and Tobago (MPATT).They withdrew en masse from the Public Service Association despite Government's insistence that that body was their rightful bargaining union. To date, they have failed to gain recognition under a vindictive government that continues to use doctors as scapegoats for a failed health system when the real problems are nepotism, square pegs in round holes and poor management. They are continuing the struggle and must be commended for being the watchdog of the Medical Fraternity.

Osler in 1932 emphasized that the practice of medicine is not a business and can never be one. Today, medicine is viewed as a health care industry, where physicians are viewed as providers of health and patients as consumers. Medicine is about compassion, judgement, character and intellectual honesty. It cannot be viewed as a business [25]. Another change in the Medical Profession has been the dictatorial Government's decision to found a parallel Medical Board since they could not have their own way in introducing differently trained non-English speaking Cuban doctors. This move allowed them to register medical practitioners hitherto not qualified for registration in the Republic. Since that time, there has been legislation passed and the formulation of a new Medical Board Act including non-medical components and politically motivated doctors of the sitting government.

The Trinidad and Tobago Medical Association according to an outgoing President, Dr Colin Furlonge, viewed by many as a maverick, seemed to have lost its way. He wrote:

"here was an organization that seemed to be in perpetual non-motion. Nothing that implied change was acceptable. Stay isolated, be non-committal, be politically correct at all times, massage the egos of a few and all will be well. If you look through the Council minutes of the last five years you see the same 15-20 or so names reappearing and reappearing.....The T&TMA, if it is to serve and not self – serve and be self indulgent, must open itself to elections where there is open elections and true democracy" [26]

Over the past five years, the Association has been riddled with poor management, the lay secretary calling the shots and skillfully manipulating the committee heads playing off each one against the other. With the exception of 2005 and 2008, where there were changes in the conference chairperson, the Association has suffered massive losses in hosting conferences for more than a decade. The House Committee has no accountability with cheques written willy-nilly by four signatories 'who cannot recall that they have done so'. The present President Dr Boysie Mahabir vows to clean up the mess, with little knowledge that his term is coming to an end like all previous misdemeanors all will be forgiven by the same old, same old executive and their friends. Those who have erred most will be elected to higher positions in the coming year without any investigations into procedural impropriety. There is no prudent financial management of the Association funds with fixed deposits being the major investment over the last decade. The selling of the Medico Dental House on Abercromby Street for a paltry sum and the purchasing of a house in Xavier Street Chaguanas has not been astute financial management. Nineteen ninety three (1993) was dubbed the year of change, not only the Medical Board Act was changed to accommodate Cuban and other doctors but the Association moved its headquarters from Port of Spain to Chaguanas. [27, 28]. Other plans of the Association never materialized. '..we will seek to purchase properties for South, North and Tobago Branches' [29].

Continuing Medical Education (CME) has been on the Association's agenda since 1995. First introduced by Rasheed Adams, little progress has been made in this area for more than thirteen years. It is still not mandatory for doctors to have CME for continued registration and practice. In an editorial by Dr Rasheed Adams, he wrote:

The time has come to take CME seriously and to lay down rules and regulations for MOC (Maintenance of Certification). This must be done with some urgency or it will be yet another area where Trinidad and Tobago would be left behind [30].

A shinning light of the Association has been the Caribbean Medical Journal. A perusal over 70 years of the journals' publication reveals that there are no organized archives at the Xavier Street Medical House. Many issues are lost or missing. The journals are the lifeblood of the Association and carry its history that is so important to future generations. More information should be recorded in the journal of decisions by the Executive Council of the Association, as was done in the early years. As was the case with former editors, the presence of a surgeon as editor has realized a trust in the documentation of surgical activities. Over the last seven years, the proceedings of the Urological society, Opthalmological society, Development in Emergency Medicine, Traumatology, Reports on the Society of Surgeons of Trinidad and Tobago, Advances in wound care and Ambulance Services and proceedings of the American Fracture Association have been highlighted. In fact, the Society of Surgeons of Trinidad and Tobago have written to the Association seeking permission to adopt the CMJ as the official organ of that society. This is indeed not acceptable and will be a break in the 70 year tradition of the journal. There is a need more than ever now to establish the journal into a reputable indexed journal with a new look, moving away from the present form as an ego-enhancing pictorial magazine of oversized fonts. There is a need for balance in publication.

Nevertheless, over the years, the following have served well as Editors in Chief of the CMJ. These are Dr James A Waterman who served for 32 years, Dr Val Massiah who was editor for 18 years, Dr Percival Harnarayan, Dr John Chin, Dr Hari D Maharajh, Dr Anirudh Mahabir and the present editor Dr Rasheed Adams. These gentlemen must be applauded for their hard work noting that articles for journal publication are difficult to obtain and contents of the journal are often not by design but based on availability.

CONCLUSIONS

The Trinidad and Tobago Medical Association has had a long and glorious history with the involvement of the most eminent doctors of the day. This tradition should be maintained at all cost. Great men like Dr Waterman and Dr Messiah now deceased dedicated their soul and spirit to the Association with a common request in their final hour, that is, that the name of the Caribbean Medical Journal should not be changed. The baton, so often dropped must be carried by the younger doctors to the winning post. The Association needs to reinvent itself with younger doctors with new dispensations, The old guards should demit office.

I wish to end by referring to an editorial written by Dr V I Massiah [31] on the assumption of a politically motivated doctor, Dr Martin Sampath as President of the Medical Association. Dr Massiah noted that a great responsibility devolves on the shoulder of the President to do nothing that lessens the image of the T&TMA or divides it. He quoted from the essays on Democratic Parliamentarianism by the great Burke, who recalls - it is as mandatory for each, once elected, to realize their new role as taking precedence over the demands of the isolated groups of constituents whose votes may have put them into office- a simple extension of the axiom-the whole being greater than the part. Medicine is more difficult to administer when swallowed with politics. The Association should be mindful of those who seek to climb the medical ladder to enter into national politics and those who manifest a partisan approach in self-indulgence, promulgation of their religious belief and party affiliations. Dr Massiah, a quiet, unassuming gentleman has been prophetic in his utterances.

REFERENCES

[1] Francis AG. Correspondence to the Caribbean Medical Journal 25th January, 1939. Caribb Med J 1939;l(3):237.

[2] Waterman JA. Notes of interest. Caribb Med J 1939;1(3):254-5.

[3] Wattley G. The life and times of Sir Henry Pierre. Caribb Med J 1992;53(1):37-8.

[4] De Freitas QB. Editorial of 10th April 1939. Caribb Med J 1939;1(3):201-3.

[5] Waterman JA. Editorial. The profession and health problem in the West Indies. Caribb Med J 1941;3(2):59-60.

[6] Waterman JA. Editorial. Caribb Med J 1944;1(5).

[7] Waterman JA .Editorial on Dr Esau .J. Sankerali. Caribb Med J 1948;10(1-2):4-5.

[8] Sherlock MP. University College of the West Indies inaugurated Caribb Med J 1949;11(3):116-20

[9] Dain HG. Chairman, Caribbean conferences of British Medical Association held on January, 1951 a Port of Spain Trinidad. Caribb Med J 1951;13 (1-):6-50.

[10] Waterman JA. Sir A Russell Report, Editorial. The 'CMJ' in prospect. Caribb Med J 1944;6(5):315-6.

[11] Waterman JA. Paralytic Rabies transmitted by bats in Trinidad. CMJ 21st Anniversary Issue 1938-1959. Caribb Med J 1959;21(1-4):1-238.

[12] Quamina DBE. The borderland of dermatology and the other specialties. Paper presented at the 4th conference of the Caribbean branches of BMA. Caribb Med J 1961;23(1-4):24-45.

[13] Harnarayan P. Clinical manifestations of endometrial pathology. 4th Pawan Memorial Lecture. Caribb Med J 1964;26(1-4):9-12.

[14] Gadjusek DC. Island isolates: The contribution of high incidence foci of disease to elucidating cause and pathogenesis. Caribb Med J 1987;48(2):27-34.

[15] Massiah VI. Abstracts and papers. Caribb Med J 1975;36(4):35-43.

[16] Rostant P. San Fernando Hospital Part II. Caribb Med J 1981;41(4): 37-54.

[17] Bartholomew C. Ten years of medical updates. An appraisal. Caribb Med J 1987;48(1): 44-6.

[18] Trinidade A. The position of the Trinidad and Tobago Medical Association on the bill regionalization of the health services. 1994/1995;56(1-):10-3.

[19] Mahabir A. Editorial. Health sector reform. Caribb Med J 1996;57(1):2-3.

[20] Gopeesingh T. Annual memorial lecture. The future of the health sector in Trinidad and Tobago. Caribb Med J 1998;60(3-4):15-28.

[21] Maharajh HD. Inauguration address. The Tobago branch. Caribb Med J 1998;60(3-4):10-4.

[22] Indar R. Eulogy, Dr. Percival Harnarayan. Caribb Med J 1998;60(1):38-9.

[23] Ince WE. An appreciation of Dr. Russel William Barrow. Caribb Med J 1998;60(1):40-2.

[24] Bartholomew C. Tribute to Dr. Elizabeth Qaumina. Caribb Med J 1998;60(1):43-5.

[25] Osler W. On the educational value of the medical society. In Aequanimitas, with other addresses to medical students, nurses and practitioners of medicine. 3rd ed. Philadelphia, PAP, Blakiston's Sons, 1932:329-45. Caribb Med J 2001;63(2):3-5.

[26] Furlonge C. Inauguration address. Outgoing President's address. Caribb Med J 2002;64(1):8-12.

[27] Adam RU. Editorial. Changes. Caribb Med J 2003;65(2):3.

[28] T&TMA House. New Premises, Chaguanas. Caribb Med J 2003;65(2):27.

[29] Ramlackhansingh F. Inauguration address. Incoming President's address. Caribb Med J 2006;68(1):8-9.

[30] Adams R. Editorial. Continuing medical education. Caribb Med J 2006;68(1):5.

[31] Messiah VI. Editorial. Anniversary issue. Caribb Med J 1975;46(2):6.

In: Social and Cultural Psychiatry Experience from the...
Editor: Hari D. Maharajh and Joav Merrick

ISBN: 978-1-61668-506-5
© 2010 Nova Science Publishers, Inc.

Chapter 2

DEFINING "CARIBBEING PSYCHIATRY"

Hari D. Maharajh

Caribbeing psychiatry is a novel concept borrowed from the Caribbean film industry and applied here to Caribbean psychiatry. Caribbeing psychiatry is eclectic in nature, it is distinctly different to Western psychiatry and there is a need for psychiatrists and psychologists to analyse the pictures, styles, language and culture of Caribbean psychiatry. The emphasis on international classificatory systems of mental disorders does not represent the nature of Caribbeing psychopathology. Caribbeing psychiatry examines supernaturalism and magical realism and the trans-generational linkage of these life forces with reference to their influences on emotions, behavior and thought. The aim is to articulate a Caribbeing identity and self definition in a post colonial society devoid of references to Eurocentric and North American standards. Secondly, to apply culturally appropriate treatment modalities (Caribbeing therapy) not aligned to the irrelevance of western psychological theories. It is necessary to harness the uniqueness of the Caribbeing experience and environment, the multicultural, plural and syncretic elements and the aesthetic style of psychological hybridity. Three cases are presented here that captures the exotic salience of Caribbeing people closely knitted into a web of witchcraft, priestcraft and mental ilness.

INTRODUCTION

The term Caribbeing in juxtaposition to Caribbean is not new. It is a term coined by Robert Yao Ramesar in 1986 in relation to the representation of people and indigenous traditions in the Caribbean film industry. Ramesar, a film auteur (artist) introduced a new perspective in the region creating films with his own techniques of lighting, camera movement, shots, angles, sound, frames and styles of supernaturalism in the Caribbean [1]. His intention is to bring a new perspective to the region in response to the inordinate amount of western films in the Caribbean that reflected mainly foreign lifestyles and cultures Ramesar is bent on authenticating the images of the Caribbean by articulating a Caribbean identity of self-definition. He digresses from the influences of colonial cultural sovereignty and western hegemony and is dedicated in putting Caribbean reality into the world of cinema [2]. Life in the Caribbean should not represent visions of external observers.

HISTORICAL PERSPECTIVES

The history of the Caribbean is different from that of Europe and America. A number of factors have influenced its development. These are, the discovery of Caribbean islands mostly inhabited by the indigenous Amerindians by Christopher Columbus, a Portuguese sailing under a Spanish Flag, the influx of many colonizing forces, the French, Spanish, Dutch and English conquering and claiming sovereignty over the islands and inter-Caribbean migration due to rebellion and importation by the French Aristocrats of the plantation system. Later, under British rule the effects of slavery and indentureship were dehumanizing systems that have resulted in post-colonial societies of aggression, hate, divisiveness and mental illnesses. Western religions were later introduced in an attempt to control the masses. Today, Psychiatry in the Caribbean remains a unique blend of current scientific knowledge purporting a neurobiological basis of diseases and Third World Traditional practices based on superstition, religion and folk medicine [3]. This complex psychological mental apparatus is not fully understood by those unfamiliar with Caribbean peoples.

Caribbean islands are often seen as Tropical paradise for fun, rest and relaxation. According to Warner [4], films that represented life in the Caribbean are gazes from the outside, not unlike description of culture–bound syndromes by European island-hopping psychiatrists of the past. These glimpses into behavior without an understanding of cultural behaviors can result in cultural imperialism as exemplified in Dr Littlewood's [5] description of Tabanca in Trinidad: an indigenous conceptualization of depression, an affliction of working–class Afro-Caribbean males who aspire to white and middle class values. These misrepresentations created by Europeans are recorded and passed on to posterity.

WHAT IS CARIBBEING PSYCHIATRY?

Ramesar's displeasure in the preponderance of western influences and the absence of Caribbean reality in the world of cinema inspired him to redesign approaches to the Caribbean film industry. His theory is eclectic in nature; his ideological concerns intersect with western influences which are distinctly different. His approach is ethnographic in style and represents the cultural and spiritual landscape of the Caribbean [1]. Like Ramesar, a number of Caribbean psychiatrists have attempted to introduce Caribbean reality into the interpretation and diagnosis of Caribbean mental behaviors and disorders. Some have argued about the relevance of Freudian and neo-Freudian therapies that lack relevance to a society immersed in the supernaturalism of culture-forms of demon possession, magical realism, obeah, priestcraft and witchcraft. Supernaturalism and magical realism reflective of Caribbean societies are the controlling aesthetics of Caribbeing. This is dependent on popular memory through story-telling and folklore by persons in the community who relate expressions of peoples' experiences intermingled with the historical past. This mental surrealism now depicted as neo-realism relates with the collective unconscious thereby linking present memories to the past [1].

Caribbeing psychiatry is a study of these life forces and their trans-generational influences on the emotions, behavior and thoughts of individuals and groups and the effects on their lifestyles. Thus, Caribbeing is the introduction of a new term derived from a novel concept. Caribbeing psychiatry aims at focussing at the Caribbean reality into the world of treatment and therapy. Caribbean mental health professionals have been long concerned about therapies that reflect mainly foreign cultures and lifestyles. The philosophy of Caribbeing psychology is to understand ourselves, the symbols, mores and customs that define us, thereby capturing the very essence of our existence. The aim is firstly, to articulate a Caribbeing identity and self definition following colonialism, cultural sovereignty and imperialism and not measure our successful outcome as proximity to Eurocentric and North American standards. Secondly, to apply culturally appropriate treatment modalities (Caribbeing therapy) not aligned to the irrelevance of western psychological theories but drawing from our own symbols, images and archetypes. It is necessary to capture the uniqueness of the Caribbeing experience and environment, the multicultural, plural and syncretic elements, the aesthetic style of psychological hybridity and the mystical and spiritual landscape of the Caribbean.

THE NEED FOR CARIBBEING PSYCHIATRY

Classificatory systems such as the DSM IV and ICD-10 are often picture-fitting and menu-driven and fail to capture the essence of presentations of Caribbean peoples. Psychological treatment modalities are not tailored to third world countries that have struggled against cultural imperialism, slavery and indentureship, political, religious and cultural independence. Western psychotherapy is an anathema to the Caribbean since the theory critiques the negative representation of the regions' people. There is an attempt to introduce Caribbeing therapies that addresses the above and the effect of hybridization with an emphasis on what we were and what we have become [6-8]. Therapy must be culture-fitting and syncretic-driven. Therapy should not be a medium to re-colonize minds, to hold people into a western mode to prevent evolution of native cultures and customs. There is a need for Caribbeing therapy, that is, the indigenization of therapy with the inclusion and emphasis of the religio-magical-cultural dimensions that is so pervasive among Caribbean people.

Gazes from the outside [4], looking into a mirror and constantly seeing someone else's face [1] creates an invalidation of oneself and a denial of our cultural beliefs, psychological mindset and existence as we constantly press ourselves into a mould that does not fit. Forging and articulating a Caribbean identity with a renewed definition of self uncontaminated by Eurocentric and North American domination and description of Psychiatry is essential for our development. This can only be viewed as the continuation of a colonial mentality and marginalization of a people. The Caribbean is unique in its experience and environment with ethnic differences and cultural diversity among communities. It cannot be painted with a single stroke of a brush. Caribbeing psychiatry gives visibility to the plural nature of the Caribbean islands which is a product of a history of migration of many peoples of different race, religion and ethnic backgrounds. The narrating voices of Caribbeing psychiatry with a Caribbean consciousness are crucial to its development.

A number of cases are presented below that are of Caribbeing interest, and not highlighted in western psychiatry. These defy a European phenomenological approach, which according to Jaspers is to depict as clearly as possible the various psychological conditions as they are experienced by the patient [9].

CASE STORY 1

Khan is a 33 year old Muslim with a BSc in Marketing from York College, City University of New York. He returned to Trinidad with his wife Sharon and their three children, ages 7, 5, and 3 years, after 22 years of residing in New York. In his formative years, Khan was raised with the principles of Islam. He is an avid reader, a trivia and history buff, psychologically minded and shows an interest in psycho-social issues of the American society, since he was raised in the US from the age of 9 years. He has held many positions in the US, but none followed a professional career. He is multi-skilled and has an aptitude for electronics and construction.

Sharon, his wife, was raised in Trinidad until the age of 20 years and is of mixed Hindu and Muslim background. Her family did not practice Islam but claimed they were Muslims. Sharon's family is vested in witchcraft known locally as Obeah and believes in the power of the occult. She comes from an unstable family background; her mother committed suicide and her father, had children outside of the marriage. Her oldest sister got pregnant before marriage and her husband, had an affair with her youngest sister. He later committed suicide claiming to have slept with all three sisters, inclusive of Khan's wife, Sharon. Her younger sister, ran away and married, a man older than her father, had four children with him, then left him for an even older man. Their only brother is addicted to alcohol and various drugs, his 13-year-old daughter, has been involved in an incestuous relationship with her stepfather. Khan himself has suffered enormous psychological and financial distress due to the infidelity of his wife and dysfunction within the family, but he has always been supportive of his three children.

On return to Trinidad, the family of five had negotiated a temporary stay at the home of Sharon's father until their apartment was completed. At that time, he lived alone with his youngest unmarried daughter. This did not please Sharon's sister. In the midst of such acrimony, Khan moved into his in-laws home. The atmosphere was tense, tempers flared, expressed emotions and hostility pervasive. Sharon's older sister made several visits to Obeahmen returning with potions saturated with incantations from the witch doctor that was strategically concealed in prescribed areas of the house. These included liquids of various colors, animal parts, scented trinkets, food, body balms and guards, the latter for her own protection. During this time, Khan discovered that Sharon's brother in law was sleeping with another sister, the youngest of the lot. When he informed Sharon of what was going on, she dismissed it and called him a liar.

The apartment was completed and the Khans moved out on really bad terms with the in-laws. He did not want them at his home. Every time he traveled they came without his knowledge. Khan claimed he was not aware of Sharon's eldest sister activities and dismissed it as nonsense, until his 3 year old daughter told him. Sharon's oldest sister had taken her to a man in a pajama and sweat shirt to pray over her. Sharon did not believe her daughter. With time, arguments and tensions became greater. Their daughter began saying strange things such as to throw her in the drain and began crying uncontrollably. When verses of the Koran was read and blown over her, she calmed down. Sharon began to talk in her sleep saying she will kill the children and will sleep walk to do so. Khan being 235 pounds would sit on her to prevent her from getting up. There would be "possession states" that Khan witnessed with sexual eructations at night resulting in orgasms. The next morning Sharon would remember nothing. This continued for months and every week Sharon's oldest sister and husband would bring holy offerings for Khan and Sharon. The fights became worse as time passed.

A powerful group of Muslim businessmen brought a Sheik from India. One of them invited Khan to come and get a "check" by the Sheik. He did not believe in these things but still came along with Sharon. The sheik placed a 'taweeze' in each hand, sitting opposite to Khan with his eyes closed, began reciting verses of the Holy Koran, Khan had no reaction. The local English translator said Khan's lack of reaction was because he 'had nothing with him'. Next was Sharon's turn, she started to shake as the Sheik continued to recite verses from the Koran. They were told that Sharon had a jinn on her. Jinns in Islamic theology are beings that Allah created from fire, they cannot be seen by humans and cannot take human forms, and they can possess humans and animals. They are documented in various 'suras' of the Koran. The Sheik wrote down some verses on pieces of paper and told them to place it in a large jug of water. The water must be consumed in three days, putting a new sheet every three days for twenty-one days. They followed his instructions. He did not tell them who did this, because people seek revenge.

The Sheik had to go back to India before the 21 days and the English translator who lived here handled all the loose ends after he left. Khan accompanied one of the businessmen and the Sheik to NY for his return to India. They stayed with Khan's sister. One evening the Sheik told Khan he wanted to show him something, he taught Khan an exercise which involved sitting on the floor with legs outstretched, eyed closed, while repeating the phrase "Allah hoo", inhaling slowly with Allah, and exhaling slowly with 'hoo.' As Khan continued with the exercise he began to see a light which became brighter and brighter as he continued to chant "Allah hoo". The light became overwhelming and he started to twitch, and opened his eyes. He could not see and the Sheik told him to recite the "darood sahreef". Khan did not know it by name so they started to recite the darood sahreef aloud, recognizing it, Khan started to recite it, after approximately ten minutes his eyesight returned. The Sheik told Khan that he had some spiritual qualities since it's extremely rare for someone to see the lights on the first attempt and within a few minutes. He stated that others have tried for years and have not been able to see anything.

On returning to Trinidad, things were not getting better in the Khan's household. Sharon's behavior got worse, with her picking up knives to stab everyone. Khan called on the Sheik's consultant who lived here in Trinidad and told him he had enough and was leaving to go back to New York to live. He then finally described the people who did this, the description fitting Sharon's eldest sister and her husband. They did a hog puja (religious sacrifice of a hog) and realized what had possessed him wanted a life, that is, someone had to die to satisfy this entity. The consultant told him that he had a jinn that the Sheik was looking for and he could remove what was on Sharon.

He needed an innocent person to be the medium, and Khan's youngest son fitted the bill, he was ten years old, and naïve about sex. The consultant placed the young boy prone on his back, with his eyes closed recited the verses form the Koran. He began to see the lights of various colors and was told to give each one Salams (salutations). The jinn appeared to the boy and told him his name was Peer. This was the jinn the Sheik was looking for. Next, along with his wife they used the jinn to act on Sharon, who started to have convulsions and gyrations, her eyes rolling, it was no easy task, and this took a few hours. They held her until the consultant pulled the jinn from her abdomen to the tip of her hair, placing it in a glass bottle, twisting a cover on and them snipping the ends off. He tied around the cap with some string and hung the bottle from a rafter. All the windows were closed and Khan asked how he knew that there was a jinn in the bottle. He recited something and the bottle began to sway back and forth as if someone was swinging the bottle. Khan was told to bury the bottle or throw it in the river; if the bottle ever broke the jinn will escape and go in search of the person who incarcerated it. The bottle was thrown in the Couva River.

Things calmed down at Khan's home and the youngest daughter never said anything strange again. Khan went away on a business trip and got the news that his brother in law had drank poison, and died three days later. It was common prophecy that the jinn had escaped and that this force must again be contained, this time burying it in cement.

Case Story 2

Ms AB is a single, thirty-one year old, female. She was a former airline hostess and a born Presbyterian but has practiced the Pentecostal religion. She was referred to the psychiatrist for healing after complaints of experiencing what she described as a 'spiritual possession'. She showed physical manifestations of panic and paranoia: nervousness, sweating, palpitations, hyperventilation, as well as skin dryness, skin peeling, pins and needles throughout her body, muscle spasms and brain 'tightness' or 'loss of electricity'. She also complained of noticing changes in her personality, bodily image, became more isolated and antisocial and she reported not feeling like herself'.

Ms. AB was well until September 2007. She claimed she had an 'attack' which she described as a 'spiritual possession' by the evil forces of witchcraft. She linked this episode back to a relationship in her life which began four years prior, in 2003. She described this relationship as a 'soul tie' with an individual who was both a believer and practiced the art of witchcraft (Black magic) in her presence but without her knowledge at the time. She said that he cast a 'spell of love, money and personal gain' on her soul at the beginning of the relationship, 'opened a door' in her mind and made her entire being susceptible to the overwhelming spiritual, physical, mental and psychological trauma she began experiencing after her attack in 2007.

She recounted the attacks as follows. AB was at her home lying in her mother's bed when suddenly she heard a 'loud explosion' of voices in her mind and experienced a physical state of 'convulsive paralysis' which she stated was 'not epilepsy'. She recalled feeling paralyzed and unable to gain control of her body to make the slightest movement. She also lost control of her mind and her voice, and felt it was being controlled by an external force for she could not stop talking about her relationship with Mr J and how much she loved him. The patient did not understand what had become of her and as she insisted that she no longer had those feelings for him at the time of the attack. This episode of extreme and uncontrollable rambling lasted for about twenty (20) minutes.

The patient next described being bombarded by 'deadly chemical vapors of bleach and turpentine' which engulfed her entire house. She said her mother was at home at the time and witnessed the choking sensation of the deadly fumes and both of them tried to evacuate. Ms AB described trying to escape as a 'life or death experience' and she barely escaped alive because she felt herself being crippled trying to escape as her right leg began to give way. She stated it began to 'shorten on the inside' and subsequently limped away from her house. The attack finally ended when she was able to get into a car and drive away from home. Her mother also made it out alive.

At this point, Ms AB experienced a life-altering revelation. She realized that the voices during the loud explosion were repeating phrases and commands of her encounter with an Obeah Man, that she suddenly remembered once visiting sometime between 2004 and 2006. The voices made her relive the experience she never knew she had. She described it as a 'hypnotized experience' and 'not déjà vu' because it actually was an event of the past.

She explained that Mr J was never baptized but an 'Anglican' from a Spiritual Baptist family. She always thought he was Christian and thus never knew he was a witch, since she associated witchcraft with Anti-Christ behavior. She realized that she was blindfolded by her soul tie and only then realized that was why his spiritual mother tried to protect her in the past by performing a Spiritual Baptist ritual of protection called a 'guard' and a 'seal', some phrases of which she repeated in her mind at the time of the attack and still continue to do so everyday of her life. She said they were the voices of the 'good spirits she was bathed in'.

Ms AB also got into an accident during her relationship with Mr. J sometime between 2004 and 2005, which she attributed to him. She had a feeling that the accident was as a result of the 'psychic and spiritual influence' of her former soul tie, Mr J who said he put a curse on her, her home and her entire family. She stated, "Everything he did he only did once. He put a spell on her once. He visited her home once." According to the patient, her life at home was never the same since he stepped into her house one day. Her father's alcoholism worsened as well as her mother's ill health.

At the garage to which she took her vehicle for repairs, she met a mechanic who thought his uncle could have rid her of the negative energy she carried with her. This uncle was an Obeah Man of Islamic beliefs. Ms AB went to see him with her sister at a 'forested location near Chaguanas'. She did not know who this person was going to be or how he would help her. All he said to her was "There is a problem and I can fix it. I will try to help you." She stayed there from 6pm one evening to 6am the following morning, and played tarot cards with some young boys. He performed the séance in her absence, using only Mr J's name for lack of an actual photograph of him. He then 'erased her memory' of the encounter and never thought of it or spoke of it even once since. All she remembered at the time after the visit of the mechanic's uncle was 'waking up shocked' in front of a fire with camphor and a pentagon with a candle at each point lying on the ground before her. The memories of the events have only come back during the attack in 2007. She also recollected the Obeah Man requesting but not insisting on a payment of one thousand dollars for completing his work on her. She did not pay him. Her sister who apparently witnessed the entire incident never had any memory of it and still does not. When inquired about it she responds "What are you talking about!?" However, she claims the Obeah Man left a door to her subconscious realm open, a door that was supposed to be closed. She also said the Obeah Man had a religious influence in her life. He turned her against the Spiritual Baptist faith.

Ms AB continued speaking about Mr J and his current life. She spoke about their relationship and mentioned that he was always seeing someone else during their entire courtship, but blindfolded her to believe otherwise. Mr. J was serious about this other woman, who was apparently also a believer in witchcraft and was a practicing witch of White Magic (good magic), compared to Black Magic or bad magic that Mr J sometimes indulged in because he knew how to 'manipulate spirits to the dark'. These two witches eventually got married and migrated to New York and had a child. Ms AB believes that his wife put a spell of protection over her new family.

This is how Ms AB justifies the attack that she experienced. Everything finally added up in her mind. She realized that the Obeah Man was not one she could have trusted. He left a door open to her subconscious realm and the negative energy he tried to release from her to send to Mr. J ended up as a backlash that went right back to her. The Obeah Man made sure to protect himself. The law of Threefold Return in witchcraft holds that whatever benevolent or malevolent actions a witch performs will return to the source with triple force. This is a principle similar to the eastern idea of Karma. She believed if the Obeah Man had closed the door that had been opened in her mind, evil energy would not have been able to enter and instead be 'neutralized in the universe'.

She thinks she eventually had to pay the price for whatever séance was performed on Mr J by the Obeah Man, for Mr J sending Ms AB's spirit to the 'kingdom of darkness'. She believed that his intention was to send her 'mad'. Despite the attack being in 2007 Ms AB still experiences visual hallucinations of a white owl flying over her house every night that lands on a tree outside and stares straight at her. She still complains of incessantly hearing voices in her mind, which speak to her, refer to her by her name, and also speak amongst themselves about her. According to the patient, she hears voices both internally and externally and described it as "not schizophrenia but a symptom resembling it". Similarly she described her convulsion during the spiritual attack as 'resembling epilepsy, but not'. She constantly also reported hearing 'playbacks' of conversations she had with Mr J's spiritual Baptist mother, The Obeah Man as well as her new Pentecostal leader as though a 'recording device was placed in her mind'. She only recently sought the help of a Pentecostal leader in 2007 when she decided to convert for the spiritual aspect of healing from the possession she experienced. AB stated she thought this would be the best way for her soul to be 'delivered' but expressed disappointment in how long the healing process is taking. She explained that she chose the Pentecostal faith over Baptist due to their principle, being 'reversal of her mindset' compared with 'removal of witchcraft'.

CASE STORY 3

A 29 year old engineer, 5ft 7 inches tall with a weight of 85lbs was diagnosed as suffering from an eating disorder. She complained of constant pains in her body, burning in the abdomen and bouts of frequent vomiting; she was so weak that she could not walk. She stated that God had called her to suffer- "a suffering of souls". God had determined that she will die in November and like Sister Faustina she is one of God's special people. She cannot take communion but "sits under the adoration of the blessed sacrament" with the divine mercy chaplet. She describes her body as "beat up" and her predicament as suffering before death. She thinks "she is suffering for souls" and must pray and help poor people. As for the future she says "I don't want to be in this world for too long, I want to go with God. I will die in November. God is my spouse and my home is in the church-the Eucharist". Each day, away from work she would attend church for peace sitting under the adoration of the blessed sacrament and would distribute her money and food to the poor.

She comes from a religiously mixed- Christian middle class African family. Her parents hold good positions with the government and her other three siblings reside abroad. Her parents are concerned about her waste of money to the poor and her involvement with the working class, especially adolescent youths with whom she harbours unconscious sexual desires. She herself appears to be regressed and presents herself in language, thought and dress as someone ten years younger than her age. When seen, she was initially reluctant to speak about being mentally ill, but a cultural approach to her problems allowed her to develop a trusting therapeutic relationship with the psychiatrist. She later accepted treatment. She was less bothered about the religious instructions given to her, her connection with Sister Faustina broke; she began saving her money and spent little time sitting under the adoration of the blessed sacrament. The diagnoses of Holy Anorexia and Religious Mania were abandoned and she was thought to be suffering from schizophrenia.

DISCUSSION

The field of psychiatry faces many challenges in a country whose belief in supernaturalism is constantly reinforced by an inundation of cases that are of questionable origin. Mental health practitioners in Trinidad are bombarded with sessions of clients and patients convincing them of demon possessions and supernatural occurrences. The interplay of religion and schizophrenia raises a number of questions about the relationship between religion and mental illness. This is discussed in subsequent chapters.

In Case 1, in spite of his lack of belief in Islamic possessions of jinns, Khan eventually experienced an overwhelming experience of spirituality that he believed saved his family in offering his son as a vessel. The details of his story when read for the first time seem to be of a nature far beyond the realms of psychiatry. The interaction of psychiatry and religion has been a topic of much controversy especially in a country such as ours steeped in deep mystical and cultural practices that may be unheard of to many. Religious practices at times hinder the job of the psychiatrist or sometimes make it easier. On one hand strong beliefs in the power of the priest deters the reception or approval of psychiatric and psychological modalities of treatment. But on the other end allowing clients to seek advice from their religious leader or healers eases their mind, and they may return to the psychiatrist in a less agitated state for what they may believe to be "just a check up", a management plan rather then a cure. Culturally sanctioned events such as that experienced in the intensity of case 1 remains solely up to the continuation of religious and spiritual beliefs of people. As a big business in our culture, with the laying of hands, it seems the psychiatrist continues to experience context specific cases coupled with the stigma of seeking mental health treatment.

In Case 2, AB had experiences ranging from revelations to hypnotic states, her story ripe with vividness and suggestive of schizophrenia. The strong beliefs held by AB in a Caribbean context reinforce the stories of possession pervasive in our culture. AB who presently receives pharmacological treatment is still of the belief that she is in a state of possession, obsessed with the cleanliness of her house to ward off the evil that may be lurking in her home. The Caribbean psychiatrist seems to have to constantly appease the thoughts of individuals who hold strong to there cultural beliefs of spiritual possession and allow them to seek treatment in other ways that hold a cultural flavour, inclusive of psychiatric treatment modalities. In the Western, Eurocentric world, axes classification and matching treatment modalities are the jest of the psychiatric realm ignoring popular folklore of our past. In our society we cannot ignore that which adds to our caribbeing experience, and calls for caribbeing psychiatry. If the society is unique in this way, practitioners cannot ignore the atypical treatment that is necessary.

In Case 3, the well educated young woman has in a dissociative state adopted the personality of Maria Faustina Kowalska, a saint who has dedicated her life to her higher power who has appeared to her on numerous occasions. Saint Maria has experienced revelations, visions, hidden stigmata, the reading of human souls and prophecy. She has visited the Abysses of Hell so that she may tell souls about it and testify to its existence. She has spoken of tortures of indescribable sufferings suffered by all the damned souls in hell. The Chaplet of Divine Mercy is a devotion based on the visions and diary of Sister Faustina. It consists of a series of prayers said with the aid of the rosary beads. On February 22, 1931 Jesus appeared to her as the "King of Divine Mercy" wearing a white garment and said to her paint an image according to the pattern you see with the inscriptions "Jesus I trust in You" [10].

So too, case 3 has sacrificed her possessions as well as her body under the instruction of God himself, her beloved. Her acts of giving and "suffering" epitomized her doting relationship; a manifestation of her belief of being a "chosen one," an adoration of his gift to her. In this case the patient lost a tremendous amount of weight by refusing to consume anything preferring to give to the poor. In such a case the young woman met the criteria for a diagnosable disorder, anorexia nervosa as expressed in Western world today. But she believed she was acting in accordance with a higher being, God himself of which most individuals have worshipped themselves for centuries.

Unlike contemporary anorexia, Bell [11] has proposed that acts of starvation in adoration of a higher being be termed "holy anorexia", such as that experienced by Saints such as Catherine of Siena, Veronica Giuliani and Mary Magdalen de'Pazzi. Instead of the usual intention of starving oneself for the pursuit of thinness as it relates to social acceptance it is more of an act of their pureness, worship and mission of saintliness.

"Nothing so pleases God as a thin body; the more it is emaciated by sharp mortifications, the less will it be subject to corruption in the grave and it will thus be resurrected all the more gloriously" [12].

A Caribbeing approach to psychiatry presents choices to the healers and the afflicted individual. While in western medicine there has been a distinct separation of priest and the psychiatrist with clear cut therapeutic approaches, there is in the Caribbean a blurring of role definitions with the psychiatrist participating in cultural aspects of treatment and the priest and obeahman in the dispensing of talismans and potions.

The complexity of these cases interwoven with religion, mental illness and cultural beliefs are made more confusing by the incorporation of symbols, images and magic imported from other religions. Cases 1 and 2 are studded with inter-religious practices coupled with Caribbeing black magic or witchcraft. The disagreement of these practitioners in their fight for souls, power and wealth sets a stage for a quest of supernatural causes for their behavior. Case 1 is interpreted as an emeshed dysfunctional family with collective dissociation states of possession. Cases 2 and 3 were diagnosed as schizophrenia and so treated without reference to the contextual nature of their ailments. This approach of dealing with diseases and not their context or causation appeared to be a denial of the patients' belief and an inability to speak in the language of the people. The questions must be asked, do we trust a lifetime of belief in religion based on many unexplained phenomena which our nation is highly committed to, or psychiatry which has its strength in empirical data? A blending is hardly possible, hence the need for Caribbeing psychiatry. The caribbeing psychiatrist must adopt an eclectic approach utilizing his knowledge of western scientific medicine blended with an appreciation and sensitivity for Caribbean cultural imaginations and realities.

ACKNOWLEDGMENTS

I wish to thank Ms Pamela Hosein, BA, MA, Bed, a secondary school teacher at a local high school. She did both her undergraduate and postgraduate training at the University of the West Indies. She has studied cinematography but enjoys the teaching of English Literature. Her contribution review to this paper has been invaluable.

REFERENCES

[1]   Ramesar RY. Lecture "Caribbeing cultural imperatives and the technology of motion picture production.' CARIFESTA VI, 1995.
[2]   Hosein PH. The theory of Caribbeing and representation in nine short films of Robert Yao Ramesar. Dissertation. St. Augustine: Univ West Indies, 2006.
[3]   Maharajh HD, Parasram R. The practice of psychiatry in Trinidad and Tobago. Int Rev Psychiatr 1999;11:173-83.
[4]   Warner KQ. On location. London: Macmillan Educ, 2000.
[5]   Littlewood R. An indigenous conceptualization of reactive depression in Trinidad. Psychol Med 1985;15:275 81.
[6]   Hickling FW. Catalyzing creativity: Psychohistoriography, sociodrama and cultural therapy. In: Hickling F, Sorel E. Images of psychiatry. The Caribbean. Jamaica: Stephenson's Litho Press 2005:241-71.
[7]   Hickling FW, Hutchinson G. Roast breadfruit psychosis: disturbed racial identification in African-Caribbeans. Psychiatr Bull 1999;23(3):132.
[8]   Maharajh H. Afro-Saxon psychosis or cultural schizophrenia in African Caribbeans? Psychiatr Bull 2000;24:96-7.
[9]   9. Jaspers K. General psychopathology.Manchester: Manchester Univ Press, 1962:1-6.
[10] Wikipedia Free Encyclopedia. [Online] 2009 [cited 10 October 2009]. Available from: http://en.wikipedia.org/wiki/Mary_Faustina_Kowalska.
[11] Bell RM. Holy anorexia. Chicago, IL: Univ Chicago Press, 1985.
[12] De Montargan H. Dictionnaire Apostolique 3, article I. In: Delumeau J. Sin and fear: The emergence of a Western guilt culture, 13th to 18th centuries. New York: St Martin's Press, 1991 (original 1752).

In: Social and Cultural Psychiatry Experience from the...
Editor: Hari D. Maharajh and Joav Merrick

ISBN: 978-1-61668-506-5
© 2010 Nova Science Publishers, Inc.

Chapter 3

FORGING A NEW DIMENSION OF BLACK PSYCHIATRY IN THE CARIBBEAN

Katija Khan and Hari D. Maharajh

There is a concerted effort among many black politicians, academics and writers to paint the Caribbean with a black brush, unmindful of the presence and contribution of other ethnic groups within the Caribbean region. The recent upsurge of black consciousness among Afro-Caribbean people is necessary, but not at the detriment of other ethnic groups who have also contributed to the social, economic and cultural lifestyles of the Caribbean.

Attempts to foist a version of United States imported Black Psychiatry in Jamaica, with the introduction of a curriculum in black psychology have raised some concern among Trinidadian students studying there. In this chapter, A Trinidadian Psychologist who studied in the Jamaican system discusses the concept of Black Psychiatry and its relevance to the Caribbean.

INTRODUCTION

Caribbean psychiatry today is not clearly defined. Its practice has been shaped by colonizing forces, influx of cultures and the history of the islands. In one Caribbean island, psychiatry has been described as a unique blend of current scientific knowledge purporting a neurobiological basis of diseases and third world traditional practices based on superstition, religion and folk medicine [1]. Over the past decade, there has been a tendency among many foreign trained professionals on return to their homeland, to introduce concepts that are irrelevant to the indigenous landscape, misrepresenting determinants of illness and the health care needs of the communities. This practice, at times supported by foreign interests has proven useful in advancing the academic welfare of the collaborators but contributes little to the development of psychiatry in the third world setting. Hsu [2] has suggested that Western advances in psychiatry through research and practice cannot be applied directly to meet the needs of the non-Western world. The priority needs of non-Western countries are different. He identifies four needs: rehabilitation of the chronically mentally ill, treatment of major depression by primary care physicians, developing a more culturally acceptable form of psychotherapy and the stigma of mental illness. The Caribbean interest has been otherwise. The rise of ethnic psychiatry on either side of the Atlantic over the past decades has had a ripple effect in the Caribbean with a particular focus on the Afro-Caribbean population. In response, some Caribbean psychiatrists have embraced the North American concept of black psychiatry and have attempted to study psychopathology in terms of the legacies of African slavery and diaspora. The introduction of this new dimension warrants debate in light of its potentially parochial and divisive frame of reference as it fails to address the heterogeneous nature of the Caribbean people and the historical antecedents that have shaped the Caribbean landscape.

WHAT IS BLACK PSYCHIATRY?

In the biannual rotation of meetings of the Caribbean Psychiatrists' Association (CARPA) [3] among the islands, host country Jamaica has in the past and will continue to partner with the Black Psychiatrists of America in producing a Joint Annual Conference. This has prompted the authors to look at the concept of black psychiatry and to study its relevance to the Caribbean region. Black psychiatry in the Caribbean has been dismissed by many psychiatrists as a frivolous and reductionist approach that attempts to perceive the Caribbean as black and as such establish African domination. Whatever its criticism, however, its application in the Caribbean is a concept in evolution that is worthy of consideration.

The formation of the Black Psychiatrists of America in 1969 signalled the advent of black psychiatry in the United States. Black psychiatry was conceived as a mental health response to institutionalized racism of which blacks were being victimized. Racism was seen by blacks as a mental health disease, a delusion based on the "false belief of ideas of superiority as a function of skin color" [4]. White racism was seen as the major domestic issue affecting the United States and since it was a mental health problem, it should be addressed by the mental health sector. At the outset, Black psychiatrists in addressing the American Psychiatrists' Association, sought, among other things, a task force of black psychiatrists, desegregation of mental health facilities, increased hiring of black mental health professionals, training of blacks as black experts in the assessment and evaluation of black programmes and involvement of the APA in fighting racism in mental health [4]. The black psychiatry movement is fully established today and continues to seek the interests of the African American minority. The Association of Black Psychiatrists of Greater New York (2004) stated as its mission "the expansion of American psychiatry and Behavioural Health Sciences so that they are more responsive to the mental health needs of peoples of African descent" [5]. Black psychiatry denounces the emphasis of a genetic or biological explanation for the differences in ethnic psychopathology and proposes social, psychological, cultural and environmental factors for the disparity. For example, ethnicity and culture of non-black psychiatrists are seen as possible sources of clinician bias and stereotyping with respect to diagnosis and treatment [6]. In the design of training programmes in black psychiatry, an emphasis is laid on the legacy of African slavery. It has been suggested that the discrimination and injustices that were perpetuated by slavery infiltrated the mental health care system and the biases and prejudices that were present then, are still being manifested today.

ACROSS THE ATLANTIC

Notwithstanding major differences in the approach to ethnic psychiatry in the United States and the United Kingdom, the consistency of certain findings is striking. British researchers have a long history of interest in transcultural studies, first in distant and exotic lands and later, in-house investigations of ethnic groups domiciled in Britain. In the United States the advent of black psychiatry has focused attention on the African American minority. A major difference across the Atlantic is the view that European researchers have been more multiethnic while North American researchers have focused on black psychiatry which is intrinsically interwoven with issues of race and politics.

Reports and commentaries from both America and United Kingdom have been strikingly similar: People of African descent are over diagnosed with schizophrenia, [7] they are the ethnic group most likely to be diagnosed with schizophrenia [8-12] they have higher rates of involuntary admission, [13,14] and they are given higher drug doses than whites [15,16].

In the United Kingdom, recent interest in ethnic psychiatry was spawned by a rush of research findings on the high prevalence of schizophrenia in the African-Caribbean population [17]. Causative factors proposed included misdiagnosis [18-20], statistical inaccuracies [21] genetic predisposition [22-24] social disadvantage [25-28] racism [29-31] and migration [32,33]. There was an immediate knee jerk reflex in three Caribbean islands where research findings indicated that rates of schizophrenia in the Caribbean were in keeping with international rates [34-36]. No mention was made of the inaccuracies of the sampling and data collection, the interests and ethnic biases of the researchers and local research prior to these findings [37-38]. If the exponents of scientific research are vested in issues of ethnic defense then certainly research will lose its meaning and purpose and result in the group 'herofication' of the proposers. There are thin lines dividing ethnic defense, group protection and racism.

Cochrane and Sashidharan [39] have suggested that racism and correlates of prejudice and discrimination have been insufficient in explaining the high treated prevalence of schizophrenia in African Caribbeans. Other similar prejudicial experiences have not produced the same effect in other targeted groups such as South Asians in Britain. Depression and neuroses which may be a result of racism occurred in even lower rates in African Caribbeans than in Whites.

SERVITUDE IN THE CARIBBEAN

The existing sociocultural landscape of the Caribbean is a direct legacy of the region's economic history. Slavery and indentureship were major responses to the labour question of the plantation economies of the seventeenth to the early nineteenth centuries and the survivors and descendants constitute the majority of the population of the region. The movement of African slaves, trapped, abducted and transported through the middle passage, their brutal and dehumanizing treatment on the sugar plantations is well documented. It appears as though the legacy of slavery is still part of the identity of black youth today. Recently, in the United States, a psychiatric defense of Post Traumatic Slave Syndrome was unsuccessfully offered in the criminal trial of the accused charged for the abuse and murder of his two year old son [40]. Post Traumatic Slave Syndrome is described as "the persistent presence of racism, which has created a physiological risk for black people that is virtually unknown to white Americans" [41].

Caribbean historians have moved away from the portrayal of slaves as completely dehumanized, depersonalized and assimilated into a system of white dominance [42]. Africans managed to retain much of their sense of individuality and community spirit. African languages have also endured in the speech patterns and Caribbean dialects. African religion also influenced the brand of Christianity accepted from Europe. Slave resistance and rebellion which invited further cruelty were common occurrences on the plantations.

Williams [43] has pointed out that servitude and sugar were seemingly indelibly linked and the plantation relentlessly reduced its workers to a servile condition, whether they were imported as indentured servants from the British Isles or as slaves from Africa. Indentureship was just a new system of slavery. Between 1845 and 1917, over 400,000 indentured Indian labourers came to the Caribbean. "When the coolies arrived on the sugar estates, the world of slavery still existed" [44]. Many of the slave customs of the Caribbean survived and were extended to indentureship: these included arbitrary cuts in food quotas, exceptionally long work hours, delayed and frozen wages, absence from work punishable by fine or jail, confinement to the barracks unless given permission by planters, institution of punishable offences such as tardiness and insolence, instability of marriage unions due to shortage of women. Beating or flogging by cattle whip was routine and necessary for plantation discipline. This was often delivered by free African slaves who also possessed the power of arrest outside the estates.

There was no difference between the slave and the coolie, the slave was a coolie and the coolie had become the new slave who was used as an all purpose work animal, doing work which could be better performed by animals in order to earn their keep. The right of punishment derived from slavery was the prerogative of the planter.

Mental health-related terms such as 'vagrancy' were coined, describing the Indians' instinctive urge to wander. This justified penal legislation which was deemed necessary to restrain Indians from their 'antisocial' tendencies. Vagabondage or maroonage also described in slavery were conditions used to explain the poor worn out state of some Indians [44]. Indentureship in the Caribbean ended in 1917, some seventy nine years after the emancipation of slavery. Notwithstanding differences between slavery and indentureship, the latter has not been studied as a contributory factor to Indo-Caribbean psychopathology. The association among depression, suicidal behaviour and alcoholism commonly found among the Indo-Caribbean population is one area that warrants further investigation. If the legacy of slavery is psychopathological as stated by black psychiatrists, then indentureship of which there are still survivors in Caribbean countries would have been likewise unhealthy. To many, indentureship was painful, not because of its recency but because the coolies had to contend with both the rules and whims of the colonial masters and the supremacy of the freed African slaves who viewed themselves as the rightful inheritors of the British legacy. This was reinforced during indentureship when the free slaves were made policemen over the coolies returning them to the plantations for a shilling, if they were caught without their papers of release.

ESTABLISHING LIAISONS IN PSYCHIATRY

Historically, African slave descendents of the United States and the Caribbean islands share a common origin, experience and legacy of slavery. Great care however, must be taken in extrapolating the effect and significance of ethnic similarities in the light of distinct demographic, political, social and cultural differences between these countries. African Americans represent approximately 12% of the white dominated North American population. They lack social, political and economic power and suffer disproportionately from violence, unemployment and poverty. In Britain, African Caribbeans account for less than 1% of the population. In the Caribbean, people of African descent are the major and dominant ethnic group accounting for almost 90 % of the population. In the republics of Trinidad and Guyana, people of Indian origin are in the majority with some degree of economic power. There has been a long history of antagonism and discrimination between the Indians and Africans in these countries. In Trinidad and Tobago, affirmative action in education and employment is being advocated for Afro-Trinidadians. Kangal (2004) surmised that "Afro-Trinis must not enjoy a divine monopoly or sacred right or preference in the State sector. Their current over-representation can only result from a history of endemic discrimination, nepotism and political patronage" [45].

The shared historical, political, social, economic and cultural experiences of all Caribbean people should be the uniting force. This makes the region unique. To establish academic liaison on the basis of ethnicity is a contradiction in terms where there are shared experiences of slavery and indentureship. Afro-Caribbeans in Britain and American Africans are in the minority in their regions. Africans in the Caribbean are the dominant group and according to Mansingh (2004) look down on Indians, Hinduism and the Indian culture. Who then are the oppressors? The oppressed? [46].

Black psychiatry as advocated in North America is valid in a certain context and for a particular social setting that are not features of contemporary Caribbean society. Its import and application in the Caribbean will facilitate a tangential over identification and over prioritizing of 'blackness' as a factor in psychiatric care. This is at the expense of a collaborative development of Caribbean psychiatry. Mental health issues in the Caribbean should not surround a crux of African slavery; when there are other issues such as substance abuse, family structure, group behaviour and politically motivated violence. There is a crying need for regional collaboration and inter island liaison.

THE WAY FORWARD

There is another side to Caribbean psychiatry that is all encompassing. Phenomenological presentations and diagnostic classification follow international patterns as in the DSM IV-TR (APA, 2000) and the ICD-10 (WHO, 1992) [47].

Caribbean psychiatry is not black psychiatry. It cannot be imported from a developed country to a developing region, from a country with a minority, marginalized black population to a region perceived as being African with black domination. Black psychiatry is limited, myopic and fails to capture the cultural diversity of the Caribbean people.

The racial and cultural heterogeneity of the Caribbean make it more ideal as a centre for cultural psychiatry or ethnic studies. As Knight (2004) states, "there are probably no indigenous people in Jamaica… contemporary Jamaicans trace their ancestry to China, India, various parts of Africa and Europe as well as other parts of the Americas. In Jamaica to speak of a melting pot is not a hyperbole….it is not uncommon to see families reflecting a wide spectrum of colour, shades and phenotypes. 'Out of many, one people' is no empty slogan" [48].This is true of all Caribbean islands with varying degrees of fusion. History has determined that contemporary Caribbean society is pluralistic in nature. It is therefore necessary for each group to understand the historical nuances which have served to fashion the fortunes of the other. For those in positions of power, albeit political, academic or otherwise. It is evident that the concepts of authoritarian personalities, cultural imperialism, racial hegemony, ethnic superiority and triumphalism are not the best prescriptions for social harmony in the Caribbean. This behavior reflects a defense mechanism based on feelings of insecurity, inadequacy and inferiority. The Caribbean is a rainbow region of many races rich in its cultural diversity. The import of black psychiatry is a misfit and will only serve to widen the ethnic cleavages.

CONCLUSION

Attempts by politicians, academics and journalist to project the Caribbean region as being Black have been severely criticized. Ryan [49] on his reflection of Dr. David Owen's book "In Sickness and in Power" has described a Hubris syndrome among leaders, that is, a fetish obsession with power akin to madness among Caribbean leaders. Once they have entered the corridors of power, they do as they please without reference to those they serve. Among academics alike, the need for originality and difference may result in the importation and introduction of concepts that are not relevant to the region. Caribbean Blacks, the dominant group of the region are different to American Blacks who remain marginalized despite a black president. As previously mentioned Black psychiatry is limited, myopic and fails to capture the cultural diversity of the Caribbean people. It is an anathema to the practice of Caribbean psychiatry.

REFERENCES

[1] Maharajh HD, Parasram R. The practice of psychiatry in Trinidad and Tobago. Int Rev Psychiat 1999;11:173-83.
[2] Hsu LK. International Psychiatry- An agenda for the way forward. International Psychiatry– Royal College of Psychiatrists 2004;4:5-6.
[3] Caribbean Psychiatrists' Association. Proceedings from Meeting. N.d.

[4] Pierce CM. The formation of the Black psychiatrists of America in racism and mental health. In: Willie CV, Kramer BM, Brown BS, eds. Racism and mental health. Pittsburgh: Univ Pittsburgh Press, 1973.

[5] American Psychiatric Association. Diagnostic and statistical manual of the mental disorders, text rev. Washington, DC. Assoc Black Psychiatr Greater New York, 2000.

[6] Bender E. Curriculum aims to improve MH care of African Americans. Psychiatr News Am Psychiatr Assoc 2004;39(8):36.

[7] Koffman J, Fulop NJ, Pashley D, et al. Ethnicity and use of acute psychiatric beds: one-day survey in North and South Thames regions. Br J Psychiatr 1997;171:238-41.

[8] Hu TW, Snowden LR, Jerrell JM, et al. Ethnic populations in public mental health: Services choice and level of use. Am J Pub Health 1991;81:1429–34.

[9] Lawson WB, Hepler N, Holladay J, et al. Race as a factor in inpatient and outpatient admissions and diagnosis. Hosp Com Psychiatr 1994;45:72–4.

[10] Snowden LR, Cheung FK. Use of inpatient mental health services by members of ethnic minority groups. Am Psychol 1990;45: 347–55.

[11] Strakowski SM, Shelton RC, Kolbrener ML. The effects of race and comorbidity on clinical diagnosis in patients with psychosis. J Clin Psychiatry 1993;54:96-102.

[12] Strakowski SM, Lonczak HS, Sax KW, et al. The effects of race on diagnosis and disposition from a psychiatric emergency service. J Clin Psychiatry 1995; 56:101-7.

[13] Davies S, Thornicroft G, Leese M, et al. Ethnic differences in risk of compulsory psychiatric admission among representative cases of psychosis in London. BMJ 1996;312:533-7.

[14] Chung H, Mahler JC, Kakuna T. Racial differences in the treatment of psychiatric inpatients. Psychiatr Serv 1995;46:586-91.

[15] Kuno E, Rothbard AB. Racial disparities in antipsychotic prescription patterns for patients with schizophrenia. Am J Psychiatr 2002;159:567-72.

[16] Walkup JT, Me Alpine DD, Olfson M, et al. Patients with schizophrenia at risk for excessive antipsychotic dosing. J Clin Psychiatr 2000;61:344-8.

[17] Cox JL, ed. Transcultural psychiatry. London:: Croom Held, 1986.

[18] Hickling FW, McKenzie K, Mullen R., et al. A Jamaican psychiatrist evaluates diagnosis at a London psychiatric hospital. Br J Psychiatr 1999;175: 283-5.

[19] Littlewood R, Lipsedge M. Some social and phenomenological characteristics of psychotic immigrants. Psychol Med 1981;11:289-302.

[20] Sashidharan SP. Afro-Caribbeans and schizophrenia: the ethnic vulnerability hypothesis re-examined. Int Rev Psychiatr 1993;5: 129-44.

[21] Lewis G, Croft-Jeffreys C, David A. Are British psychiatrists racist? Br J Psychiatr 1990;157:410-5.

[22] Hutchinson J, Takei N, Fahy TA., et al. Morbid risk of schizophrenia in first-degree relatives of white and African—Caribbean patients with psychosis. Br J Psychiatr 1996;169:776-80.

[23] Ineichen B, Harrison G, Morgan HG. Psychiatric admissions in Bristol. I. Geographical and ethnic factors. Br J Psychiatr 1984; 145:600-4.

[24] Giggs JA, Cooper JE. Ecological structure and the distribution of schizophrenia and affective psychoses in Nottingham. Br J Psychiatr 1987;151:627-33.

[25] Bhugra D, Leff J, Mallet R., et al. Incidence and outcome of schizophrenia in whites, African—Caribbeans and Asians in London. Psychol Med 1997;27:791-8.

[26] Burnett R, Mallett R., Bhugra D, et al. The first contact of patients with schizophrenia with psychiatric services: social factors and pathways to care in a multi-ethnic population. Psychol Med 1999; 11:581-99.

[27] Cox JL. Aspects of transcultural psychiatry. Br J Psychiatr 1977; 130:211-21.

[28] Littlewood R, Lipsedge M. Aliens and alienists. London: Penguin, 1982.

[29] Nazroo J. Rethinking the relationship between ethnicity and mental health: the British Fourth National Survey of Ethnic Minorities. Soc Psychiatry Psychiatr Epidemiol 1998;33:145-8.

[30] Neighbours HW, Jackson JS, Broman C et al. Racism and the mental health of African Americans: the role of self and system blame. Ethnicity Dis 1996;6:167-75.

[31] Williams-Morris RS. Racism and children's health: issues in development. Ethnicity Dis 1996;6:69-81.

[32] Odegaard O. Emigration and insanity: a study of mental disease among Norwegian-born population in Minnesota. Acta Psychiatr Neurol Scand, 1932;7 (suppl 4):1-206.

[33] Thomas CS, Stone K, Osborn M, et al. Psychiatric morbidity and compulsory admission among UK-born Europeans, Afro-Caribbeans and Asians in central Manchester. Br J Psychiatr 1993;163:91-9.

[34] Bhugra D, Hilwig M, Hossein B., et al. First-contact incidence rates of schizophrenia in Trinidad and one-year follow-up. Br J Psychiatr 1996;169:587-92.

[35] Hickling FW, Rodgers-Johnson P. The incidence of first-contact schizophrenia in Jamaica. Br J Psychiatr 1995;167:193-6.

[36] Mahy GE, Mallett R, Leff J, et al. First-contact incidence-rate of schizophrenia in Barbados. Br J Psychiatr 1999;175:28-33.

[37] Lewis LFE. A seven year follow up of female schizophrenic patients treated in St Ann's Hospital, Trinidad. Archives, St Ann's Hospital, 1973.

[38] Neehall J. An analysis of psychiatric inpatient admissions from a defined geographic catchment area over a one-year period. WIMJ 1991;40:16-21.

[39] Cochrane and Sashidharan. Mental health and Ethnic Minorities: A review of the literature and implications for services. [Online] 1995 [cited 2009 Oct 21]. Available from: http://www.academicarmageddon.co.uk/library/ETHMENT.htm.

[40] Danks H. Judge rejects slave trauma as defense for killing. [Online] 2004 [cited 2009 Oct 21]. Available from: http://www.oregonlive.com/news/oregonian/index.ssf?/base/news/1086004710123410.xml

[41] Poussaint AF, Alexander A. Lay my burden down: unravelling suicide and the mental health crisis among African Americans. Boston, MA: Beacon Press, 2000.

[42] Goveia E. Slave society in the Bristish Leeward Islands at the end of the Eighteenth Century. New Haven, CT: Yael Uni Press, 1965.

[43] Williams E. Capitalism and slavery, 2nd ed. Oxford: Oxford Univ Press, 1964.

[44] Tinker H. A new system of slavery. The export of Indian labour overseas 1830 to 1920. London: Oxford Univ Press, 1974.

[45] Kangal S. Confusing fact with fiction. Trinidad Guardian 2004 Aug 27:27.

[46] Mansingh A. Expectations of Indians of indentureship origin and others in Jamaica from India. Presented GOPIO Conf New Delhi 2003 Jan 09. [Online] 2003 [cited 2009 October 21] Available from: www.gopio.net/jamaica.doc

[47] World Health Organisation. The ICD-10 classification of mental and behavioural disorders: clinical descriptions and diagnostic guidelines. Geneva, WHO: 1992.

[48] Knight, F. Jamaica the global village. Trinidad Express 2004 Aug 12:11.

[49] Ryan S. The hubris syndrome. Trinidad Express 2009 Jun 14. [Online] 2009 [cited 2009 Oct 23]. Available from: http://www.trinidadexpress.com/index.pl/article_opinion?id=161490666

In: Social and Cultural Psychiatry Experience from the... ISBN: 978-1-61668-506-5
Editor: Hari D. Maharajh and Joav Merrick © 2010 Nova Science Publishers, Inc.

Chapter 4

INDENTURESHIP AS A CONTRIBUTORY FACTOR TO MENTAL AND PHYSICAL ILLNESSES IN THE INDO-CARIBBEAN DIASPORA

Hari D. Maharajh

There is an ethnic pattern of mental and physical diseases associated with the export of Indian labor overseas between the period of 1830-1920. The establishment of Indian communities overseas emerged from the culture and civilization of the Indian sub-continent and was a direct consequence of mainly British exploitation of economic wealth overseas. This movement of Indians from their homeland with the maintenance of the practice of their religion, culture and lifestyle is referred to as the Indian diaspora. This chapter looks at the effects of 'coolie migration' particularly to Trinidad, but with reference to other Caribbean islands and at least a dozen countries across the seas. Information is gathered from published reports but more importantly, from dozens of immigrants and hundreds of first generation Indians with whom the author has been in contact during their treatment. There appear to be a commonality of social, psychological and physical diseases in these migrant groups within the diaspora. A possible explanation is the similarity of the genetic pool and environmental influences experienced by the early migrants overseas.

INTRODUCTION

During the period 1845-1919, 143,939 East Indians journeyed from Calcutta, India to Trinidad under the British indentureship programme, to work in the sugar cane plantations. Like other Caribbean countries, they brought with them their religion, culture, language and social behaviors which were the foundation for the establishment of new communities. There were some variations to the earlier African slave trade that was discontinued in 1834 following the emancipation of slavery. Arrivals from Africa were denied the practice of their religion and lifestyles and were recruited and treated in such a manner as to avoid integration. The arrival of Indians sowed the seed for an Indian Diaspora throughout the world in their exportation to various plantations for the cultivation of tea in Ceylon renamed Sri Lanka, rubber in Malaya renamed Malaysia and sugar cane in the Caribbean, Mauritius, Fiji, Africa and other countries. The early Indians brought with them their ingrained traditional beliefs, religion and culture, looking toward India as the mother country. In Trinidad, one of the furthest outposts from India, they were employed in contractual servitude in the sugar cane plantations.

The sugar cane plantations in the Caribbean cultivated by the English, French, Dutch and Spanish colonizers provided a flourishing economic trade. Sugar gave meaning to the Caribbean dictating the economic, political and social structure. The East Indians were brought for the sole purpose of working on the fields for low wages, and were characterized by their resilience and thrifty nature. They had difficult jobs, as work on sugar plantations involved cut wages and untiring days of long hours of hard work. Their difficult journey from India where many died from shipboard diseases, their placement into a new and hostile environment with inhumane working conditions and the perception of being brought to Trinidad under false promises set the stage for poor mental and physical health. After years of renewed contracts on the plantations and unfulfilled promises of return to India, the early Indians accepted land for their return passage establishing themselves in the Caribbean community.

HISTORY

Indian indentured laborers in the Caribbean

The end of the slave trade did not precipitate the end of slavery in 1838. The British Empire was unable to produce enough sugar to maximize its profits and searched for a new system of slavery. Lord John Russell of Britain disagreed with the indentureship system and commented that:

'I should be unwilling to adopt any measure to favour a new system of slavery' [1]

A former Prime Minister of Trinidad and Tobago in his book Capitalism and slavery noted that:

'the plantation relentlessly reduced its workers to a servile condition, whether they were imported as indentured Indians from the British Isles or slaves from Africa.' [2]

It is apparent that the slave system laid the foundation on which the coolie system, the popular term of reference, was later erected. Between 1845 and 1917 over 400,000 indentured Indian laborers came to the Caribbean. Both the sending and receiving countries were under British rule and administrative decisions were made solely on an economic basis to export Indian labor abroad. British Guiana renamed Guyana received the largest number of indentured laborers followed by Trinidad as shown in table 1 below [1].

Table 1. Immigrant arrivals during the indentureship period

COUNTRY	YEARS	NUMBERS
Guyana	1838-1917	238,909
Trinidad	1845-1917	143,939
Guadeloupe	1854-1885	42,326
Jamaica	1845-1885	36,412
Suriname	1872-1916	34,000
Martinique	1854-1889	25,509
St Lucia	1858-1895	4,354
Grenada	1856-1885	3,200
St Vincent	1861-1880	2,472
Belize	1860'S	382
St Kitts	1860'S	Small Number

In many Caribbean and South American countries with the exception of Trinidad, Guyana and Suriname, the Indian identity was absorbed into the local population with a recent resurgence in Martinique and Gaudeloupe. Cheap labour with the establishment of Indian culture was also exported to other countries where Indians are domiciled today such as Sri Lanka, South Africa, Uganda, Fiji, Mauritius, Malaysia and Indonesia.

On the plantations in Trinidad, conditions were harsh and cruel. Indentured laborers were housed in barracks one hundred feet long subdivided into rooms ten feet long for families and an extra ten feet was added for kitchen amenities [1]. Toilets were outhouses adjoining the cane fields. Their hours of toil in the fields were long as much as twelve hours a day. The early immigrants showed loyalty to their religion be it Hinduism, Islam or Christianity. They shared a common Indian culture they brought with them from India and found great solace and comfort in its practice. Their hope to return to India one day sustained their efforts.

Educational opportunities for East Indians came late and this was spearheaded by the Canadian Mission of the Presbyterian Church around 1860 [3]. Indian parents were reluctant to send their children to school out of fear of proselytization. In fact, their plans were to return to India and did not see the benefits of a western education.

RECRUITMENT AND THE JOURNEY

India in the 1830's and onwards was a country plagued by poverty, social and religious divisions. Intermarriages among different castes or religions were not acceptable. With poverty rampant and the promise of a better life and opportunities in Trinidad, many East Indians seized the opportunity to leave their poverty-stricken villages which was under control of the British Government. Many young men left because of marital and family problems. An indentured worker who came to Trinidad as a child with his father was stolen from the mother and brought here due to family disagreements in India. A first generation child of an immigrant in Trinidad reported that his father left out of fear of returning home after one of the cows he was tending died from a snake bite. And yet another, related that he ran away and enlisted to Trinidad, because he had ran afoul of the laws in India and was being sought by the British for murder. They signed their papers and travelled from the shores of Calcutta in many cases without knowledge of their loved ones, bringing along with them their religious books, the precious gems of their culture and untold secrets of their life in India.

The journey to the Caribbean across the 'kala pani' (the black waters) was fraught with difficulties of overcrowding, poor conditions and diseases. In this journey to the Caribbean, between 1837 and 1917, there were instances of "shipboard diseases" such as cholera, typhoid and dysentery. As much as one quarter of the human cargo died and their bodies were thrown overboard as food for the sharks. Their first stop was an island off Trinidad where they were 'deloused' and later distributed to the plantation owners on a 'as needed basis'. Later, there were epidemics of "plantation diseases" such as anemia and hook worms. Diseases of the body were rampant in such base conditions, and as time progressed issues of mental health emerged. When the immigrants arrived they were physically and psychologically starved as they continued to feel lost and betrayed:

> "....they spent their first year in Trinidad crying as they remembered their homes and realized how badly they had been tricked..." [4]

Social problems such as vagrancy, vagabondage or maroonage [1], post traumatic syndrome, racial hatred, family problems, alcoholism and drug use were common. The seeds of racism were sowed by the British rulers who adopted the policy of 'divide and rule' putting the freed African slaves as policemen over the indentured Indians. If an Indian was found wandering from his plantation, he would be arrested by a freed slave who demanded from the Indian a presentation of his papers- "Coolie, where's your papers?" If he did not have it in his person, he will be taken to the authorities and disciplined. Erstwhile the negro will be given one shilling for his good work. Later, crime, turning onto oneself, depression, abuse, suicidal behavior, revenge, anxiety, personality deviation, self esteem issues and malingering were some psychosocial vulnerabilities and consequences of the plantation workers. These conditions persist even today as we highlight in subsequent chapters.

In the Trinidad Immigration Report for 1871 there was a high mortality rate on the plantation with as much as 6.4 percent of those who arrived in 1867 and 1868. The Immigration Agent- General stated:

> "the work is hard, monotonous and in high canes may almost be called solitary; he loses heart, makes a task in double time in which an experienced hand would make a whole one, returns at a later hour, cold, wet and fatigued, to renew the struggle on the morrow with decreased vitality till at the end of his first year it is found that his work has not paid for his rations...he embarks on the second year of apprenticeship saddled with a considerable debt from his first year's ration." [1].

The above gives a disillusioned picture of the life of an indentured laborer even at the beginning of their work on the island of Trinidad. The experience left them feeling disenchanted for the further days of toil, with no promise of steady remuneration. These conditions weakened their souls, contributed to low self esteem, depression and personality deviation as the state of affairs worsened in the guises of contractual work.

Strict limitations were employed, the planters argued that "African and Creole were constitutionally prone to wander and stray and must be restrained." [1] Later on, Lord Harris, a British Governor in Trinidad provided little comfort for anyone on a Trinidad sugar estate and condemned the Indians also for their habits of wandering and vagrancy [5]. This label of vagrancy and vagabondage fueled many new restrictions, imposition of penal legislation and the planters reneging on promised returns to India were common practice. Those whose contracts expired were not given the opportunity to return home and such unexpected circumstances exacerbated the already diminished state of affairs and homesickness of the Indians. It was later recognized that the unwillingness of the East Indians to be baptized conjured the allegations of vagrancy, as many left the compounds as a means of avoidance of their situation. In 1861, the Bishop of Barbados in a letter to CS Fortes cue at the Colonial Office stated " the Indians were only interested in saving money to purchase land in his native country...he avoided expenditure,...so falling into the conditions of a miserable vagrant..." [1]

Alcoholism was of most interest to this population as "drink was the anodyne to which most of the coolies turned" [1]. Many of the East Indians had never tasted alcohol in their home country but suddenly consumption was their most enjoyable pastime. They worked the sugar plantations which produced the rum industry and the Indians reaped their benefits with eventual inebriation. The East Indians consumption of alcohol increased as their hard work went unnoticed and the work days grew longer. It was a quick remedy that was obtainable and provided the dissociative state necessary to survive the indentureship period. Muir McKenzie reporting on Reunion in 1893 noted that alcoholism was a serious problem among the East Indian Population. He averaged nine liters per annum as compared to Mauritius with three and a half liters per annum. Governor Phayre speculated that "the absence of restraints of village society, and the ease with which drink was obtained" was one of the main reasons for the addiction habit that grew among the East Indian population. The governor stated:

"At any time on a Saturday, a number of coolies will be found seated round a table in the verandahs of Portuguese or Chinaman's rum shop...it was a novel experience...to see coolies from the north west, who had never tasted liquor in their own country, boozing in the verandah of a rum shop and resisting with angry vehemence the entreaties of their children to come home." [1]

At the start of the emigration process, suicide was also prevalent. East Indians would throw themselves overboard as the journey became unbearable. This self punitive behavior continued into the indentureship period and was also a coping mechanism for terrible working conditions and maltreatment by plantation owners. In the Mauritius batch of immigrants, Lord Kimberly, Secretary for the Colonies remarked:

"the extraordinary frequency of suicide among the Indian immigrants in this colony...I myself believe that a very large proportion of the suicides are due to nostalgia or an intense desire to return to India which they have no means of gratifying" [1]

This explanation was attributed to many of the other colonies inclusive of Trinidad. Many who committed suicide was for the usual offence of illegal absence from work, of which they felt ashamed with suicide seeming to be the only inevitable conclusion to their problems. Another possible explanation was the shortage of women that was a result of separation during the recruitment phase. An estimate of suicide rates indicated 46 per million in Madras to 54 per million in the United Provinces. In Natal the rates were recorded at being ten times higher with 640 per million and 780 per million in Fiji in 1904. By 1910 the rates in Fiji grew to 831 per million. In 1904 the Governor of Fiji stated that "the coolies life was monotonous and unattractive" and often complained over the lack of women and this contributed to many murders and suicides, [1]. Suicide rates were greatly increased across the Indian diaspora.

The causes of the suicides though, were not fully investigated and the reasons based on mere speculations. In 1904 Dadhabai Naoroji, veteran Congress and Liberal leader, and Sir M Bhownaggree a Member of the House of Commons addressed the India Office on the abnormal suicide rate among the indentured coolies, but in 1912 reports of high rates of suicide still existed in the West Indies, specifically Demerara because of low wages and poor conditions. In 1921 in Fiji, soaring food prices did not match any increase in laborers wages and suicide prevailed as men refused to see their children going hungry [1].

Under these conditions of poverty, many sought refuge in the Asylums for comfort and treatment of their maladies. Many patients died there of plantation induced physical and mental diseases. During the indentureship period the St. Ann's Lunatic Asylum in Trinidad reported an estimated mortality rate of 48.5% as shown in Table 2. This data included all inhabitants of which recruits from India and their descendants were a substantial percentage, [6].

Table 2. Admissions/Deaths 1858-1919 St Ann's Lunatic Asylum

YEAR	ADMISSIONS	DIED
1858-1909	4866	2534
1910-1911	153	70
1911-1912	112	51
1912-1913	127	58
1913-1914	155	70
1914-1915	175	60
1915 apr-dec	115	45
1916	181	70
1917	141	53
1918	167	49
1919	169	27

Most of the inpatients were of Indian descent or East Indian themselves from India, see Table 3. They comprised of 87 males, 82 females [6].

Table 3. Number of immigrants of East Indian Descent at St. Ann's Lunatic Asylum

COUNTRY	TOTAL
Antigua	1
Barbados	5
China	2
Guadeloupe	1
India	24
Madeira	3
St Vincent	4
Trinidad and Tobago	116
Venezuela	1
Unknown	12
Total	169

Among the population the following table shows a diagnosis of admission and inmates to St Ann's Lunatic Asylum in 1919 [6].

Table 4. Diagnoses of admissions to St Ann's Lunatic Asylum. Total 790. Male to Female ratio 2:1

Congenital or Infantile Mental Deficiency	Numbers
With Epilepsy	11
Without Epilepsy	40
Epilepsy Acquired	43
Mania	5
Acute	171
Chronic	130
Recurrent Melancholia	33
Acute, Chronic, Recurrent, Senile, PP	64
Senile	3
Puerperal	6
Dementia(Primary, Secondary, Senile)	284

Family problems also existed among the laborers, as Hindu and Muslim marriages were not recognized and many marriages separated on the grounds of their 'illegality' according to the Christian marriage rites. The East Indians did not have the finances to re-register a marriage under this religion and hence marriage ties weakened. They realized that their wives could be taken away to become the partner of men of higher status, resulting in her 'freedom' from plantation responsibility. Charles Kingsley in his report on Trinidad revealed that 'no mere laws' protected the laborer from his employer when under 'bond' and was as he stated the 'weakest and meanest of bonds.' Consequently many Indians left their wives in India because of the risk of further loss.

Not until 1856, an Indian Marriage ordinance was introduced which encouraged men to bring their wives with them, but this did not give credence to previous marriages. In Trinidad it was not uncommon to sell their daughters for a 'bride price.' Girls in Trinidad were sold at the age of 13 inspite of laws prohibiting the practice [1]. The Heathen Marriages act of 1860 and 1888 increased the age of marriage from 12 to 14 in girls, but Trinidad continued with the median age. The lack of women was the reason for this practice and many murders was the result of eventual polyandry. It took more than 100 years after the Indian arrival in Trinidad for Hindu and Muslim marriages to be made legitimate, evidence of the deep hate and disdain that Christian-based administration held against Hindus and Muslims. In fact, great opportunities were afforded to these migrant groups if they converted to Christianity. Some did, the majority resisted.

Racial hatred which is still an issue among Blacks and Indians in Trinidad today had its foundation set after the introduction of the slavery and indentureship periods. Both races brought here for essentially the same reasons led to obvious comparisons and resentment to each other. Charles Kingsley's assessment of the relationship that existed between the two races was that the Indians saw the Blacks as 'savages…the Negro hates the coolie as a hard working interloper and despises him as a heathen" [7]. Today there has been speculation that the same reasons exist for cases of racial hatred as a punitive Black Government under an Afro-Trinidadian leader Patrick Manning systematically seeks to dismantle all the structures that have supported the Indian lifestyles including the closing down of the sugarcane industry that has sustained Indians since indentureship. On the other hand, he has instituted a policy of affirmative action for Afro-Trinidadians.

PHYSICAL ILLNESSES TO THE INDIAN DIASPORA

The physical illnesses of the journey to the West Indies and the indentureship period can be attributed to poor physical and health conditions. In Trinidad there was an average of 11.1 percent among the Indians in the 1870's [8]. Some of the recorded sicknesses were fevers, venereal diseases, dysentery, cerebrospinal meningitis, cholera, diarrhoea, fever, measles, small pox, pneumonia, bronchitis and other respiratory diseases, opthalmia, anaemia, hydrocele, jaundice, tuberculosis, typhoid fever and anklyostmiasis [9]. In 1908 at the Chaguanas Ward in Trinidad, 39% of the deaths were Indians while 64% of deaths in all the hospitals were Indians [10]. Many of which were caused by lack of medical support. In comparison, the Indian population today is afflicted with physical diseases mostly due to changes in lifestyle and diet choices, distinct to their group. Both have been attributed to the pervasion of the same diseases in subsequent generations. Health statistics for Trinidad and Tobago show increasing prevalence of obesity, hypertension, and diabetes mellitus. The main causes of death are cardiovascular disease and cerebrovascular accidents [11]. Some of the major physical diseases that are prevalent in the Indian Diaspora today with reference to Trinidad are discussed below.

Metabolic Syndrome

Metabolic Syndrome (MS) also known as metabolic syndrome X is a grouping of cardiac risk factors that result from insulin resistance. Insulin resistance is essentially when the body's tissues do not respond normally to insulin. A person with metabolic syndrome has a greatly increased risk of cardiovascular disease and premature death. A person who gets metabolic syndrome is one increasing in age, on a diet that's high in calories and saturated fat, lacks exercise and physical activity, has a family history of diabetes, has a history of gestational diabetes (diabetes during pregnancy), a history of polycystic ovary syndrome (a metabolic disorder that affects a woman's hormones and reproductive system) and being of Asian descent.

Worldwide it is estimated that 20-25% of South Asians have metabolic syndrome and may be prone to it because of poor lifestyle measures, adverse body fat patterning and genetics [12]. Globally, MS was identified in 77% of Indian patients who also had concurrent diabetes and clusters of four factors of hypertension, large waist circumference, hyper-triglyceridemia and Low HDL-C were also more common in Indians. Those with type 2 diabetes were at 5 fold higher risk for MS than the general population, [13]. In Trinidad metabolic syndrome is a common problem affecting 40% of Indian men. It is argued that, economic success, opulence and adherence to a western lifestyle are important contributory factors, since Indians are genetically constituted to work hard.

Diabetes Mellitus

Diabetes is a disease in which the body does not produce or properly use insulin. Insulin is a hormone that is needed to convert sugar, starches and other food into energy needed for daily life. The two major types of diabetes are: Type 1 Diabetes and Type 2 Diabetes. Type 1 Diabetes affects a young population, persons between the ages of 1 to 10. This is a condition where there is too much glucose in the blood and not enough in the cells of your body. High glucose levels in Type 1 are due to lack of insulin because the insulin producing cells have been destroyed. Type 2 Diabetes occurs at the onset of age 45 and occurs when the body's cells become resistant to insulin that is being produced.

There is a high prevalence of Type 2 diabetes in migrant Asian Indians. Asian Indians are more hyperinsulinemic than Caucasians and hyperinsulinemia may be important in the development of these diseases [14]. Results in other studies have indicated that the prevalence of insulin resistance is 3-to 4-fold higher in young, lean, healthy Asian-Indian men compared with men in other ethnic groups. The increased prevalence in insulin resistance in the Asian-Indian men was associated with increased liver triglyceride (HTG) content and plasma IL-6 concentrations [15].

In a UK sample, the prevalence of diabetes in South Asians is 22.5% higher than their Caucasian counterparts, [16]. In Trinidad there are approximately 39,000 individuals living with diabetes with an estimated increase to 86,000 by 2025 [17]. Thirty to 40 percent of the Indian population in Trinidad is diabetic. Some have attributed this to lifestyle, with the onset in indentureship that initiated diets of high carbohydrates and sugars, alcohol, and a stressful existence.

Hypertension

Blood pressure is determined by the amount of blood your heart pumps and the amount of resistance to blood flow in your arteries. The more blood your heart pumps, and the narrower your arteries, the higher your blood pressure. You can have high blood pressure (hypertension) for years without a single symptom. Uncontrolled high blood pressure increases your risk of serious health problems, including heart attack and stroke. It is postulated that, long hours of work in the blistering sunshine of the Caribbean without sufficient water intake has resulted in the retaining of body salt that increases blood pressure. This explanation has been attributed more so to Africans, who are more prone to hypertension.

Heart disease

Heart disease describes a variety of disorders and conditions that can affect the heart. The most common type of heart disease is coronary heart disease (CHD), also called coronary artery disease. Heart disease is the number one killer of both women and men today but can be prevented. One can reduce the risk of heart disease by making certain lifestyle changes. In 1989 a ten year community survey was conducted to investigate heart disease incidence

Obesity

The characteristics of obesity are body weight in excess of 120% of average for age, sex and height and increased risk of MI, CVA, high blood pressure, diabetes, cancer, arthritis, and accidents. The epidemic of obesity has already entered the childhood and adolescent age groups, with rates of overweight of up to 10% having been reported in the developing countries of the Americas, including Trinidad and Tobago [19]. It has been observed that the waist circumference of Indo Trinidadian males is much larger than their counterparts. The pejorative term of fat belly Indian (FBI) or dhal belly Indian is in local usage.

Other

Indo-Trinidadians are also prone to asthmatic attacks and respiratory disorders, snake and insect bites and accidental self and other inflicted cutlass wounds and gastrointestinal disorders. The use of pesticides for suicide is discussed later. Reasons are occupational hazards of involvement in agriculture, rural residency and heavy alcohol use. Psychosomatic diseases are common in Indo-Trinidadian population with higher neuroticism scores observed by the author.

DISCUSSION

The indentureship period was characterized by immense suffering and hardship. Poor conditions contributed to the enfeeblement of the East Indians through lack of medical care and poor living arrangements, and diet. The inability to cope with these circumstances contributed to many psychological and psychiatric vulnerabilities, that inevitably led to maladaptive coping mechanisms. Among these were alcoholism and suicide as escape routes.

In Trinidad high rates of alcoholism and suicide are peculiar to Indo Trinidadians, the descendants of the East Indian indentured laborers. In treatment facilities and support groups they comprise the majority of alcoholic and suicide cases within the country. At hospitals which cater to certain catchment areas that are heavily populated with Indians, weekly suicide attempts surrounding alcoholic stupors are the norm. Many of the explanations behind the alcoholic bouts and attempted suicides encircle family strife and transgenerational differences. With suicide and alcoholism most prevalent amongst the East Indian migrants who were here for contractual servitude, it seems the torment experienced through the introduction of indentureship has inevitably introduced two coping mechanisms associated with self harm either slowly through alcoholism or quickly through suicide that are most used among the Indian community.

Suicide has been linked to the agricultural regions of Trinidad which are populated mostly by Indo Trinidadians. The initial settlers their ancestors have populated these areas that were initially there areas of work. The industry has also influenced their drug of choice for suicide by ingestion through the use of insecticides. Many cases have also reported that they mistook the bottle for alcohol in their intoxicated state.

As with most mental illnesses heredity is a deciding factor in most cases. The ancestral history of the East Indian was filled with years of mental and psychological problems such as alcohol dependency, depression, malingering, adjustment disorders, vagrancy and personality deviations recorded in the indentureship period. With the occurrences of these psychiatric concerns still present one can speculate on the contribution that the indentureship period now has on present behavior, personality, culture, emotions, thoughts and diseases.

The physical diseases that were present 164 years ago were distinctive to meager conditions and meager bodies. Diseases such as dysentery, cholera, fevers and venereal diseases were prevalent at a time where crowded ships, filthy latrines and close quarters were the norm. Today, ship-bourne diseases and medical conditions of squalor seldom exist and worldwide lifestyle diseases have dominated the field of medicine. Obesity, diabetes, hypertension and cardiac disease are prevalent and characteristic of a western lifestyle. The Western diet is high in fats and with sedentary lifestyles the effects are multiplied. Generally, data has been shown to point in the direction of Asian emigrants. In Trinidad, the East Indian community has higher prevalence rates of such lifestyle diseases.

CONCLUSION

Since 1820, the onset of the British economic-induced Indian diaspora, Indians uprooted from their motherland have made tremendous progress in all areas worldwide, with the sole exception to that of their own health. Within the last three decades, clinical observations and mortality data indicate that, there is an escalating incidence of hypertension and coronary artery disease in Indians [20]. It was noted that Indians experience the first coronary event at an earlier age compared to western counterparts and studies conducted in the UK, US, Trinidad, and South Africa have confirmed a high rate of cardiovascular disease among expatriate Indians. Lifestyle diseases of suicide, depression, drugs (tobacco) and alcohol, eating disorders and psychosomatic illnesses are more commonly found among Indians in the diaspora. The irony exists that our ancestors have been afflicted with diseases of poverty and scarcity but the present generation seems to be affected by an overabundance. It seems the vulnerability for diseases existed but hard work, struggle and difference in lifestyle may have deterred the effects of genetic predisposition. Notwithstanding the experiences of indentureship, valuable lessons can be learnt in the study of lifestyles changes of Indians from the diaspora since the beginning of their exportation to the present time. Trans-generational Indians who have settled abroad need to take a closer look at themselves.

REFERENCES

[1]   Tinker H. A new system of Ssavery. London: Oxford Univ Press, 1974.
[2]   Williams E. Capitalism and slavery, 2nd ed. London: Oxford Univ Press 1964:16-9.

[3]   Ramesar M. The Impact of the Indian immigrants on Colonial Trinidad Society. Caribb Quart 1976;22(1):5-18.

[4]   Klass M. East Indians in Trinidad: a study of cultural persistence. New York: Columbia Univ Press, 1961.

[5]   Parliamentary Papers. 1847-8 XLVI: "Correspondence between the Secretary of State and the Governors of the Sugar Growing Colonies as to the Distress now existing in those Colonies..." Harris to Grey, 19 June 1848.

[6]   Archives. St. Ann's Lunatic Asylum. N.d.

[7]   Kingsley C. At last: a Christmas in the West Indies. London 1871; 1:187.

[8]   Colonial Emigration from no. 13- Form of Depot Sickness report. Proceedings of the Lieutenant-Governor of the Bengal, General Department, emigration, Calcutta, 1900:166.

[9]   Colonial Emigration Form No. 14- Form of weekly Hospital report. Proceedings, 1900:525.

[10]   CD, 5192, Report of the Committee on the emigration from India to the crown colonies and protectorates, Great Britain, June 1910:135.

[11]   Pan American Health Organization. Health conditions in the Americas. Washington DC: Pan Am Health Org 1994;1:91.

[12]   Eapan D, Kalra GL, Merchant N, Arora A, Khan BV. Metabolic syndrome and Cardiovascular disease in South Asians. Vasc Health Risk Manage 2009;5:731-43.

[13]   Foucan L, Deloumeaux J, Donnet JP, Bangou J, Larifla L, Messerchmitt C, Salmi LR and Kangambega P. Metabolic syndrome components in Indian migrants with type 2 diabetes: A matched comparative study. Diabetes Metabol 2006;32(4):337-42.

[14]   Banerji MA, Faridi N, Atluri R, Chaiken RL, Lebovitz HE. Body composition, visceral fat, leptin, and insulin resistance in Asian Indian men. J Clin Endocrinol Met 1999;84(1):137-44.

[15]   Assisi FC. Recent findings on diabetes among desis. [Online] 2009 [cited 19 Oct 2009] Available from:

[16]   http://www.indolink.com/displayArticleS.php?id=111806070206.

[17]   Patel JV, Lim HS, Gunarathne A, Tracey I, Durrington PN, Hughes EA, Lip GY. Ethnic differences in myocardial infarction in patients with hypertension: effects of diabetes mellitus. QJM 2008; 101(3):231-6.

[18]   Cockburn BN, Bermano G, Boodram LG, Teelucksingh S, Tsuchiya T, Mahabir D, et al. Insulin promoter factor-1 mutations and diabetes in Trinidad: Identification of a novel diabetes-associated mutation (E224K) in an Indo-Trinidadian family. J Clin Endocrinol Met 2004; 89(2):971-8.

[19]   Miller GJ, Beckles GLA, Maude GH, Carson DC, Alexis SD, Price SGL, Byam NTA. Ethnicity and other characteristics predictive of coronary heart disease in a developing community: Principal results of the St James Survey, Trinidad. Int J Epidemiol 1989;18(4):808-17.

[20]   Gulliford MC, Mahabir D, Rocke B, Chinn S, Rona R. Overweight, obesity and skinfold thickness of children of African or Indian descent in Trinidad and Tobago. Int J Epidemiol 2001;30(5):989-98.

[21]   Ram VS. Hypertension and other cardiac risk factors among Asian Indians. Am J Hypertens 1995;8:124–7.

In: Social and Cultural Psychiatry Experience from the...
Editor: Hari D. Maharajh and Joav Merrick

ISBN: 978-1-61668-506-5
© 2010 Nova Science Publishers, Inc.

Chapter 5

DOPAMINE, DEMONS OR DIVINATION? THE DICHOTOMY OF SCIENCE AND RELIGION IN TRADITIONAL SOCIETIES

Hari D. Maharajh

The presentation and interpretation of mental disorders is the Caribbean region is often considered to be the effect of divine intervention, demonical possession, drug abuse or defects in dopamine synthesis. Common occurrences are families, friends and priests advising the diseased person to seek help in one or all of these modalities. Thus, while increasing numbers of mentally ill persons seek treatment from western trained psychiatrists, they likewise cover all the other bases of traditional, folk, and spiritual treatments. This results in a medley of healing processes which are in conflict with each other since empirical scientific findings are not in keeping with religious-driven values, which purports an ontological claim to human existence. The dichotomous relationship between science (authoritative facts) and religion (ethics and values) has caused an epistemological divide, with the consequences of reductionism, in both areas. Disturbed persons, their families and caregivers are engaged in a prolonged and expensive journey with traditional healers, priests and doctors who complicate the curative process. These practices undermine the principle of western scientific medicine, while at the same time attributing credence to magic and supernaturalism, thereby reinforcing the behavior of the patient adding mysticism to the folk practitioner.

INTRODUCTION

Religion and psychiatry has had a long and familial relationship. Of Jesus many of them said: "He has a demon, he is mad, why listen to him?" [1]. There is no line drawn between religion and psychiatry in Trinidad and Tobago. Supernatural phenomena, divine apparitions, glossolalia, demon possession, weeping-stone virgins, miracle cures and psychic predictions are almost weekly occurrences. The Christian-based churches have embraced the opportunity, peddling a wide range of arcane supported by biblical quotations and spiritual injunctions. So lucrative is this business of laying of hands and exorcisms, that there has been a mushrooming of a multitude of small Pentecostal churches fighting to save the souls of Catholics, Muslims and Hindus alike. A Hindu leader has objected to a Christian sect denouncing Hinduism as pagan and claiming that their deity "Shiva to be immoral and a deranged vagrant" [2]. Despite the religious nature of Trinidadian society, like other Caribbean countries, the population is very superstitious at all social levels [3].

Demoniacal possession states are common findings in Trinidad and Tobago. Two-thirds of all patients presenting to a psychiatric clinic will interpret their symptoms as being caused by 'spiritual wickedness from high places', obeah or jadoo- a superstitious belief in the casting of spells on people, 'spirit lash' or evil influences. These beliefs are reinforced by priests and 'holy men' who on initial visits will vaguely suggest the complicity of malefactors in bewitchment. Thus, with the mystical sanction that 'someone is doing you bad', the possessed one of the family will be able to identify the evil one. That person is usually a family member, relative, divorced spouse, in-law, individual within the community or deceased one who is perceived as being a threat to the family's welfare. This is supported by families, various denominational groups and to some extent the state. Christian theologians on a daily basis cite biblical evidence for demoniacal presence and possession states and conduct a thriving business in 'casting out demons', exorcisms, and faith-healing. This is the foundation of new born-again miracle churches. So demanding are these facilities that the Catholic Church has established a deliverance ministry and has designated a priest to look after exorcisms. This practice is being now extended to other non-Christian religious groups.

Demonical presence or possession states are not only Christian-based phenomena. It is also a belief of Hindus who can be possessed with 'devi or devitas' and Muslims with 'jinns'. In Hinduism possession states have been associated with Mother Kali goddess of time and change [4]. In Islam the word jinn refers to something that is concealed or hidden, with varying beliefs of their source. Some have their roots in primitive culture and fear of natural forces, some are a reflection of human thoughts and hidden desires, some from myths and fables from witches, charlatans and soothsayers while others believe some jinns come from whispers of 'Shaytan' (a wicked jinn) [5].

Deliverance among all groups are effected through culturally relevant practices such as the laying of hands, commands or 'jahraj'- an indian custom of removing forces through prayer, touch, blowing on the patient and brushing with symbolic images and religious incantations and recitations.

REVIEW OF PAST FINDINGS [6]

In a questionnaire survey of 288 persons comprising of 100 secondary school students between the ages of 16-18, 50 non-medical hospital workers, 52 nurses and 86 chronic psychiatric patients, 71% of the sample believed in the existence of demons and 65% thought that demons could possess people; hospital workers and nurses were particularly strong in their beliefs of demoniacal existence [E] (81.8% and 82.6%) and possession [P] (76.0% and 75.3%) respectively. Females were significantly higher in their beliefs of demoniacal states than males (P <0.05) and this may explain their higher rate of possession states. Teenage students had a significantly lower score than adults (workers and nurses). Students E =59.4% P =56.3%, Adults E =82.2% P =75.7%. (P =0.01).

Indians as an ethnic group did not believe in demoniacal states as much as people of African or Mixed origin. (p<0.05). This may be explained by the finding that 74.4% of the Indians belonged to the Hindu or Islamic religions and were perhaps less exposed to Christian indoctrination of demoniacal manifestation and deliverance; in support there were no differences amongst Indian Christians and African or Mixed Christians. Due to cross-cultural influences and reinforcement by the church there is today a widespread belief by all ethnic groups of the interpretation of mental illness as evil. It is not strange that Trinidad and Tobago remains a religious but superstitious society with its beliefs in these phenomena undifferentiated.

A recent survey of fourth-year medical students by the author indicates that 65% believed in the existence of demons that were capable of possessing individuals. The majority were of the Christian belief.

DYNAMICS OF POSSESSION STATES

Possession is a dissociative state in which unconscious conflicts surface, bringing emotional tension within socially and psychologically acceptable limits, thereby minimizing ego disintegration. In possession states the patient's symptom is obscured from consciousness by the defense mechanism of dissociation and repression. The manifested symptoms are understood as symbolic expressions of the feelings aroused in some post-traumatic experience. These emotions are now being relived as strong discharges of the affect or displaced versions of the trauma.

In repression, there is the blocking of a wish or desire from expression so that it cannot be experienced consciously or expressed directly in behavior. The need for the frustrated emotions to seek expression in a state of resistance, results in the subconscious part of the ego projecting itself as an 'alter ego' embodying the normally inexpressible thoughts, feelings and behavior. In many cultures, the 'alter ego' takes the form of spirits, (discarnate entities), devils, gods and even the Devil [7].

Possession may also be viewed as an attempt to communicate distress to others. These individuals assume the sick role and attempt to gain attention and benefits. Women seem to become more frequently afflicted than men because in many societies they are under-represented in authority structures. Possession may satisfy their desires for a variety of material and emotional gains, [8]. In Trinidad and Tobago, spirit possession is culturally sanctioned and there is strong suggestion that this behavior is the expected response to work through one's problem. Such behavior has adaptive function, sanctioned by society, giving to the possessed one some power and prestige [9].

TREATMENT: DEMONS OR DOPAMINE

The majority of patients believed to be suffering from possession disorders are not initially seen by the psychiatrist. The first treatment contact is invariably the priest, pandit, imam or obeahman. A range of religio-magical procedures, authenticated by the use of known traditional and religious symbols, images and incantations or mantras are utilized. These are often tailored to meet the needs of the patient and include low magic, protective guards, laying of hands, religious commands and exorcisms. Frequently, after several visits without improvement to one or many healers and with great economic loss, the family is encouraged to take the 'possessed one to the psychiatrist with the assurance that the evil spirit has been released but not without some damage to the patients' nerves'.

The process of expelling demons is called deliverance. The religious and traditional healers claim that they can determine the existence of evil spirits by a process of discernment (spiritual intuition) and secondly, by detection, that is, observing the effect of the evil spirit on the behavior of the person. Criteria for deliverance are an absolute wish by the victim of wanting to be free, humility to and acceptance of the healer, repentance and renunciation of evil, prayer to God and warfare toward the enemy (Satan).

In Trinidad and Tobago, there is no clear cut prescription of exorcisms. Acts of deliverance appear to be personalized practices of over-dramatic individuals cloaked with the mystical mantles of Africa and India and exotic salience of Caribbean religious and superstitious beliefs.

The psychiatrist is faced with a serious dilemma. His attempt at times to interpret demoniacal possession as dopamine over-activity is met with resistance by the healers, patients and their relatives. Such explanations are seen as confrontational and against the doctrines of religious orders. This often results in resistance and splitting between the church and clinic which interferes with patients' treatment and outcome. While the psychiatrist may not wish to reinforce the superstitious beliefs of society, he has to work along with them in order to provide a cure. This is not always easy. Even though the psychiatrist is willing to cooperate with the priest or healer giving him undue recognition and importance, the door is one way. In addition, after failure of treatment by the healers, patients are referred in 'depossessed state' to the psychiatrist for 'rest and building up'! Following discharge to the community services the patient returns to social role enactment of behavior. He may be advised by the healers to stop his medication and join the fellowship at church since 'Jesus is the only answer.' The discontinuation of medication can in some circumstances results in 'repossession' due to relapse and creates a revolving-door situation.

It is not uncommon therefore to encounter on a daily basis many individuals in the Caribbean who are living in mental darkness. The first two highly publicized tragic events highlight the superstitious nature of the Trinidad society.

CASE STORY 1

A seventeen-year old ill student Candace, fell ill with a fever. She was taken by her father to her sister's home in South Trinidad, to be healed by the spirit of his late mother, a Baptist known as Mother Irene. She was taken to a humble, thatched roof Baptist church, situated in an abandoned train line now run by her aunt and other family members. A spiritual ceremony was performed for her there. The illness got worse and Candace died two days later on Sunday.

Her relatives did not accept that the teenage student had died and therefore kept the body at home for three days. Four days later on Thursday, her decomposing body was removed to the Forensic laboratory following police intervention. Neighbors had reported a foul stench coming from the house, and had noticed her aunt spraying aromatic substances around the house. The Head of the National Orisha Baptist movement condemned the resurrection ritual of Candace and her family while others in the faith felt the rituals were not done in the right way [10].

The autopsy finding has been inconclusive and samples of stomach content and body fluids have been sent for further testing.

CASE STORY 2

Mary, a sixteen-year old girl began exhibiting strange behavior approximately one month before. Her sister reported to the newspaper that she said "strange things" and wanted forgiveness because "she did a lot of bad things". She also said that "people had done things to her". Her brother reported a complete change in her personality. Her father stated that Mary 'started seeing spirits and claimed that her mother wanted to kill her' [11].

Mary lived with her father, a mason with four of her thirteen siblings in the mountainside in East Trinidad. The house is a patched-up wooden house with no electricity, few furniture and a battery-operated television. Her mother had separated from her father approximately one year ago, and was cohabiting with someone else. Mary had recently moved to her sister's place where her mother had joined her to help in her supervision in preparation for spiritual treatment. An exorcism was planned for later that week, at the Open Bible church in Laventille, near Port-of Spain.

She did not reach the church but following a "prayer session" at home, she became combative, uncontrollable and ran out of the house. Attempts by her mother to calm her resulted in Mary stabbing her mother to death. The police was summoned for help to restrain her. She died after being shot five times in her chest, abdomen, head and leg. It is believed that she was demon-possessed with evil spirits. The policemen claimed that they had no training in dealing with evil spirits.

CASE STORY 3

Young Ram, a 23 year old Hindu lived an epicurean life of 'eat, drink and be merry, when dead be buried'. He was a fourth generation Indo-Trinidadian whose forefathers had migrated from India approximately 165 years ago. They had brought with them the custom of animal sacrifice to the Goddess Kali which was done religiously every year.

Suddenly, Ram became seriously ill with many unexplainable symptoms. He lost 40 pounds, became weak with 'jaundice and rash'. His back itched forming hypergraphic markings of differently interpreted praedolia – some religious, others satanic and still others supernatural. All his body organs were affected despite normal medical findings. While preparing meals, so the story goes, the rice will turn into worms and the milk into blood. His older brother age 23 had died three years earlier from what doctors reported as a connective tissue disorder which was not substantiated by laboratory findings. Western science had no cure, no answers, no explanations but to pigeon-hole him into some American classificatory system of madness.

The family sought treatment from the Kali temple. They contacted a 'pujarie' a man of impeccable character who has made many sacrifices and has dedicated his life to the Lord. He with the power that comes over him (shakti) and 'in a dissociative state' is able to advise, counsel, predict and cure.

In dialogue, it was revealed by family members that since their arrival from India, they had for generations made animal sacrifices to Mother Kali to ward off evil and for financial prosperity. They had succeeded well in business. Over the last few years, the fourth generation had stopped the rituals due to influences from the Pentecostal churches. This, according to the elders has in the past 'wiped out whole generations'. Young Ram had brought upon himself a generational curse by not doing the sacrifice.

He joined a Kali temple, where after becoming a vegetarian, he was advised by the pujarie (priest) to do various sacrifices. He was advised not to do animal sacrifices since it is against the wishes of Kali whose dictate is 'those who cannot give life should not take it.' Miraculously, his illness of five years duration disappeared and today he is a successful businessman.

CASE STORY 4

The following is an excerpt extracted from a white Caucasian patient who was advised to discontinue his studies at the School of Philosophy. He was diagnosed as suffering from schizophrenia: complex partial seizures were ruled out.

"Being a senior member of the School of Philosophy and practicing the various exercises and techniques given to me, having been initiated some time earlier, a daunting experience, had to perform various duties. One of my duties was to read material to a class of new students and answer relevant questions. It was one such occasion we journeyed to a venue in Port of Spain to perform duties. The day in question there were energies operating in me that made it difficult to focus, so instead I was given the job of counting the Cash Box because one of my duties was doing the accounts of the school. As stated earlier, my mind was not able to focus and I had difficulty doing even mundane tasks."

"After the session ended, the headmaster of the school took me to the wash room and suggested that I wash my head. As if out of nowhere I could see my body on the floor of the room as if looking down from the ceiling with dim eyes, and thinking to myself 'where do I go from here?' What next, unaware that the headmaster was shouting 'come back' several times. Next thing I knew I was looking through my physical eyes unaware that the headmaster had given a jab to my midsection (solar plexus area) with his fist."

"I recovered, but my body particularly my head was heating up. So they decided to put ice on my head, what I found remarkable was that my awareness was very acute. My vision was not normal but encompassed my whole body. Aware too of a stillness in which I could hear with clarity the sounds around."

"The next few days, over a week I realized the energy of this experience was still there, I saw life and people in a different way. People were going about their lives unaware of the connectedness with other people, blinded by their own wants and desires not aware that this was not a destination but part of a journey, in a sense I was dead, not being in control, for want of a better term, my mind. Only aware of consciousness observing whatever ensued."

"It was in this state that my parents sought medical help. I always remember the headmaster's words that if you turn to medication you will need them lifelong. So it is on this note that I am not part of a group that I so endured, their ideals summed up by these words 'in the world but not of the world' a system called the 'forth way' laid down by Gurgdiff. My tenure with the school of philosophy I will always value."

DISCUSSION

Cases 1 and 2 presented here highlight a number of issues in the practice of psychiatry in Trinidad and Tobago. In a population of 1.3 million people, two thirds are Christians belonging to a variety of denominations and approximately one third subscribe to Hinduism and Islam. In all groups, the first line of contact for help is the priest or traditional healers regardless of their religious persuasion.

In the first case the attempts at the resurrection of a dead girl is linked to the Orisha Baptists' practice of the 'morning ground ceremony'. In this practice, those who are chosen are required to lie on concrete slabs in a darkened room, with earplugs and deprived of sensory stimulation. The ceremony lasts for 7-10 days and individuals are attended by a 'nurse' for food and toilet purposes. The process of sensory deprivation results in 'astral travel' where the individual's "spirit" leaves the body and travels to far and distant places engaging in different trying experiences.

Successful mourning is marked by the return of the 'spirit' to the body and a recantation of the traveler to an experienced member of the church. This is rewarded with ascendancy within the hierarchy of the group.

Over the year a number of individuals have been admitted to the psychiatric hospital with florid auditory and visual hallucinations following mourning. The belief that Candace's spirit had left her body to meet that of her grandmother gave the family hope that she would be resurrected when the spirit returned to her body, as it is the belief in the mourning ground ceremony.

The belief in demon possession is widespread at all levels in Trinidad and Tobago. As stated, a cross-sectional study of 288 persons reported that 71 per cent of the total sample believed in the existence of demons and 65 per cent thought that demons could possess people [6].

Mental illness is perceived by many to result from such possession states, thus the relationship between the priest and the psychiatrist is for the most part strained, ranging from the mutual agreement with grave suspicion to open hostility and confrontation. Despite the passage of 2000 years and increased scientific knowledge of the functioning of the brain, the "new age churches" continue to interpret mental illness as a product of evil spirits and demons. In well-rehearsed sermons with cleverly inserted relevant scriptural verses, religious leaders perpetuate superstition among the poor and less educated in their attempts to achieve spiritual slavery among their followers. This has become so lucrative a business that some of the practices are being currently adopted by non-Christian groups.

Case 3 is a disciple of the Kali temple whose life has been transformed because of his devotion to the Goddess. Lying outside the circle of mainline Hinduism in Trinidad, it is the fastest growing sect steeped in mysticism and animal sacrifices. Kali is a Hindu goddess associated with eternal energy. Despite negative connotations, Kali is considered today to be the goddess of time and change. She is often considered to be the kindest and most loving of all Hindu goddesses and is regarded by her devotes as mother of the whole Universe [4]. Kali represents a variety of symbols that disciples can choose from, symbols that they can identify and choose from to suit their own needs and taste. She is like a matrix that provides each and every need of an individual who worships her. She is also feared due to her multifaceted symbolic representations. Rams power of autosuggestion and his belief in Kali Mai (Kali the mother) may have been responsible for his cure. According to Fulford religion is an important part of the world of values and psychiatry must move closer to religion in its day to day values [12]. The tendency to ignore religion, and identify with science reflects a one-sided understanding of its own nature.

In case 4 Mr D's preoccupation with his study, in his pursuit of philosophy compelled him to interpret his mental disorder not in terms of religion or science, but in a third dimension of philosophy. He believed he had an out of body experience with a disruption of his consciousness. He described an experience of being detached and unbridled. "I was aware, I was seeing through my eyes, but not my eyes" He saw himself lying on the ground. Philosophy permits the stretching of our imaginations and by so doing can partner with psychiatric phenomenology. According to Fulford the very aims of its discipline is to challenge common sense, to show the insecurity of our assumptions, to stretch our imaginations. This rationale on a background of fact-value dualism of science and religion can blur the boundaries of health and disease [12].

Trinidad and Tobago has one of the best mental health programmes in the Caribbean. The country is divided into nine catchment areas, each with a multidisciplinary team of psychiatrists, social workers, mental health officers and auxiliary workers. The major problems that exist are the negative attitude that the population has towards mental health and as a consequence, reluctance of families to access psychiatric care. Of the four cases described, the first three cases described here failed to access medical care. Candace was denied medical attention in favor of prayers, and Mary, the disturbed teenage girl who killed her mother and was killed by the police, was about to be taken to church for exorcism, not to the health centre for treatment. In the third case, there was a perception that there was no cure in western medicine. The fourth case was found medically unfit to continue his trade as a refinery operator at an oil company.

At the present time, there is a need for structured educational programmes on mental illness in this country. This is not an easy task, since it will erode the foundation of many churches and will be resisted by their leaders. In addition, policemen are in need of training in handling mentally ill persons. There is no need to use unreasonable force, especially on a sixteen-year old mentally ill girl.

In January 1999, the Vatican issued its first updated for exorcism since 1614. In the 84-page Latin language text known as 'Roman Rituals', practical as well as spiritual guidance were given for exorcists. The Archbishop of the Roman Catholic Church in Trinidad and Tobago has noted that he has three appointed exorcists [13].

The Vatican's release will certainly reinforce the concept of demon possession and take us back to the dark ages. In my opinion, it is unlikely that the Royal College of Psychiatrists, in its infinite wisdom will comment on the Vatican's views on 'possession' and 'obsession' and their stated differences between these entities and psychiatric disorders.

According to a newspaper report [14] a large part of the blame must be carried by the media, which routinely refuse to distinguish facts from fiction. Generally, they pursue an economically viable form of sensational journalism. Until such time, when the church, the media and the population are willing to effect a paradigm shift, many more lives will be lost. To many psychiatrists, there is a view that some churches remain the worst demon, taking lives in their bid to save souls, and have a need to exorcise themselves.

The Government is unlikely to intervene since the present government has pandered to superstitious beliefs in order to gain popular support. In addition, freedom of choice and worship is enshrined in the constitution. It seems as though the population will continue to live in mental darkness and there is very little the psychiatrist can do.

CONCLUSION

The belief in demon possession is widespread in Trinidad and Tobago. Cultural, traditional and religious belief systems often delay contact with primary health-care providers and may have negative outcome. The cases of two teenage girls whose family sought religio-magical healing are presented. Both girls tragically died. The third case of 'religious cure' underline the need for incorporation of traditional treatment modalities in psychiatric treatment. While in this and other publications, it is the general understanding that the western trained psychiatrists cannot give credence to traditional beliefs, superstition and supernaturalism, it appears that there is a need for further collaboration with these agencies by the multidisciplinary treatment teams.

Negative attitudes to mental health and an unwillingness to access it remain major problems to mental health professionals, despite the establishment of well-structured programs. A paradigm shift of the population and church leaders is needed with grater collaboration among these groups. Attempts to work together with the various churches have failed since, local religious leaders, some versed in witchcraft (obeah) and other versed in priestcraft attribute mental illness to possession states, a view not supported by the medical model. This frequently results in conflicts between the priest and the psychiatrist with opposing views on demons and dopamine [6]. However, the priest, the pandit, the imam and the obeahman remain today the first contact for the majority of patients suffering from mental illnesses. The psychiatrists have replaced the priest, the obeahman, emerging as new priests, dealing with confessions in therapy and giving absolutions with medication.

REFERENCES

[1]   James K. The Holy Bible. John 10:20.National Publishing Company, 1978:1112.

[2]   Rostant R. Maha Sabha declares 'war'. Sunday Trinidad Guardian 1994 Jan 31.

[3]   Beaubrun MH. Mental health and the Interaction of cultures. Proceedings of Tenth Biennial Conference of the Caribbean Federation for Mental Health, Caracas 1975.

[4]   Wikipedia, Free Encyclopedia. Kali. [Online] 2009 [cited 2009 Oct 9] Available from: http://en.wikipedia.org/wiki/Kali.

[5]   Ibraaheem Ameen AK. The Jinn and human sickness- Remedies in the light of the Qur'aan and the Sunnah, 2005.

[6]   Maharajh HD, Parasram R. Mental illness: Demon or dopamine. WI Med J 1997;Suppl:46.

[7]   Ross RA. Multiple personality disorder diagnosis. Clinical features and treatment. New York: Wiley-Intescience, 1989.

[8]   Carstairs, GM, Kapur RL. The great universe of Kota. London. Hogart Press, 1976.

[9]   Wittkower ED. Trance and possession States. Int J Soc Psychiatr 1970;118:133-8.

[10]   Sookraj R, Alonzo R. We won't bury her- relatives still hope to resurrect dead girl. Trinidad Guardian 1999 Jan 23.

[11]   Henville M. Family says girl was demon possessed. Trinidad Express 1999 Jan 27:3.

[12]   Fulford KWM. Religion and psychiatry. Extending the limits of tolerance. In: Bhugra DKL. Psychiatry and religion: Contest, consensus and controversies. London: Routledge, 1996:5-22.

[13]   Pantin A. I exorcised demon from girl barking like a dog. Sunday Newsday 1999 Jan 31:6.

[14]   Editorial. Living in mental darkness. Our opinion. Daily Express 1999 Jan 28:3.

SECTION THREE: CULTURE, BEHAVIOR AND MENTAL ILLNESS

In: Social and Cultural Psychiatry Experience from the...
Editor: Hari D. Maharajh and Joav Merrick

ISBN: 978-1-61668-506-5
© 2010 Nova Science Publishers, Inc.

Chapter 6

RECOGNIZING SOCIAL AND CULTURAL BEHAVIORS IN TRINIDAD AND TOBAGO

Hari D. Maharajh and Akleema Ali

Trinidad and Tobago, not unlike many Caribbean countries is a plural society resplendent in its cultural diversity. It prides itself with an ethno-historical background of African slavery, Indian indentureship and European migration emerging into a post emancipation society of open expressions of social commentaries in song, dance and language. It remains today an easy going society with a style of picong communication which to the observer remains strange. This chapter underlines the relevance of the behaviour of migrant groups both from the sending and receiving countries since the relics of a culture persist despite cultural changes. A questionnaire survey on the culture of Trinidad and Tobago is undertaken to study the cultural behaviours existing in Trinidad and Tobago and to assess the population's awareness, perception and description of these behaviours. A questionnaire survey (n = 536) on the culture of Trinidad and Tobago was undertaken to study the cultural behaviours existing in Trinidad and Tobago and to assess the population's awareness, perception and description of these behaviours. Respondents were presented with nine identified behaviours and perceived five of them to be a part of the Trinidadian culture: Liming, carnival mentality, player or playboy personality, Tabanca and obsessional lateness were identified as existent cultural behaviours.

INTRODUCTION

In any established society, notwithstanding its level of development, there exist social and cultural behaviours that are unique to its inhabitants. These behaviours, if not understood as social and cultural manifestations of a complicated system of human interpretation and expression may be mistakenly interpreted as patterns of psychological disorders. Consequently, normal behaviour may be exaggerated in some societies but still falls within the rubric of the pathoplastic effect of culture.

The influences of culture and mental health have been an area of interest of early researchers [1-3]. Later, social scientists viewed psychiatric illness as a form of social deviancy where the individual was regarded as mentally ill because he had broken the local codes of social conduct [4]. This concept of psychiatric disorders as a deviation from social and cultural norms rather than a product of an underlying biological dysfunction has not been accepted by many psychiatrists [5]. Some are of the opinion that social impairment is insufficient and psychiatric diagnosis should be made only on the basis of mental status, not in terms of cultural behaviour. Today, the tangential progression from behaviour to rationalization of identity to syndrome and then to psychosis remains invariably enigmatic and untenable. However, attempts to bridge this divide have been made through the introduction of a multiaxial system that promotes the application of a biopsychosocial model [5].

Cultural behaviors can be defined as an adaptive response occurring in organized social groups whose lifestyles, sentiments and interactions have been transgenerationally transmitted. These behaviours are often associated with compensatory processes of rationalization and are sometimes conceptualized in the context of native humour.

Cultural behaviors are different from culture-bound syndromes. The latter is defined as recurrent locality-specific pattern of aberrant behaviour and troubling experiences that may or may not be linked to a particular DSM-IV-TR diagnostic category. These are indigenously considered to be illnesses or at least afflictions and most have local names [5]. Culture-bound syndromes are thus culturally determined abnormal behaviour patterns that are specific to a particular culture or geographical region. These express core cultural themes, and have a wide range of symbolic meanings – social, moral and psychological [6].

Genuine culture-bound syndromes are not exclusively linked to a particular culture but rather related to a prominent cultural emphasis or to a specific social stress situation [7,8]. Syndromes have been described with a cultural emphasis on a number of themes. Many are related to fertility and procreation such as koro in Malay-Indonesian language, Jiryan in India, Dhat syndrome [9-13] and suo-yang in Madarin-Chinese [9-11,13]. Others focus on physical appearance such as taijin-kuofu among the Japanese [14-16], learnt dissociation such as latah and amok in Malay-Indonesia language [17-25], and acculturative stress such as brain fag symptoms in African students [26-27].

Over the past two decades, Trinidad and Tobago resplendent in its cultural diversity has attracted a number of visiting researchers. Littlewood [28] has described Tabanca (lovesick behaviour) as an indigenous conceptualization of depression in rural Trinidad. This, he claims, is an affliction of working class Afro-Caribbean males who aspire to white and middle class values and lifestyles. His views are considered to be a misinterpretation of this cultural phenomenon. Local psychiatrists [29,30] have been critical of his findings stating that he did not take into account the cultural milieu that colours expression of the behaviour and that he was blinkered by his own unconscious cultural assumptions. Eriksen [31] has described liming in Trinidad as a dignified art of doing nothing, noting that one cannot be recognized as a real Trinidadian unless one masters the art of doing nothing. A British research team [32], in a socio-political motivated study investigated the incidence of psychosis in Trinidad in response to reports of high incidences amongst the Afro-Caribbean population in Britain. He noted that there was no excess in the incidence of psychosis in Trinidad as reported among the black Caribbean population in the United Kingdom.

There is concern for the misinterpretation and misrepresentation of indigenous cultural phenomenon and the utilization of findings and conclusions by foreign researchers. Their interpretations of cultural behaviours as culture-bound syndromes or progressing to chronic insanity [28] can be quite misleading and border on assumptions of cultural hegemony.

RECOGNIZING CULTURAL BEHAVIOURS

In an attempt to recognize cultural behavioural patterns in Trinidad and Tobago, a two-fold approach was implemented:

- To document cultural behaviours that exist in Trinidad and Tobago thereby minimizing interpretation and misrepresentation of these phenomena by those not exposed to the culture.
- To study the indigenous population's awareness, perception and description of these behaviours.

A questionnaire survey (n = 536) on the culture of Trinidad and Tobago was undertaken to study the cultural behaviours existing in Trinidad and Tobago and to assess the population's awareness, perception and description of these behaviours. In a pilot study, respondents were presented with nine identified behaviours and perceived five of them to be a part of the Trinidadian culture: Liming, carnival mentality, player or playboy personality, Tabanca and obsessional lateness were identified as existent cultural behaviours.

A PILOT PROJECT

Cultural behaviors were identified by a pre-study survey of a semi-structured interview designed to identify cultural behaviour patterns of Trinidad and Tobago (see appendix 1) a stratified random sample of 52 respondents were chosen. This sample was representative of the general population with respect to age, sex, ethnicity, social class, marital status and education [33].

Behavior was defined as "the whole way of life of people" and involved both traditional practices handed down from generation to generation and descriptions of contemporary social behaviours. Interestingly, more than half, 30 respondents (58%) considered religious or spiritual beliefs and practices as not being part of culture. A total of nine (9) behaviours were identified: Obsessional lateness, Smartman Syndrome, liming, Middle Age Indian Woman Syndrome, Tabanca, carnival mentality, demon possession, spiritual travel and playboy (player or macho) personality. A tenth behaviour, obeah, was excluded because 62% felt it was also widespread in other Caribbean regions.

DESCRIPTION OF BEHAVIOURS UNDER STUDY LIMING

Liming is a term commonly used in Trinidad for hanging out. Its origin is unclear with villagers' view that it originated from sailors afflicted with vitamin C deficiency sitting in the sun on the limestone covered areas. Another view is that it is a description of inhabitants sitting under the shaded citrus fruit trees socializing with alcoholic beverages, sometimes gambling, idling their time away.

CARNIVAL MENTALITY

Trinidadians have been dubbed as having a carnival mentality. This is a preoccupation with leisure, music, dance and a slack and laid back attitude to work. It is seen as a behavioral pattern that has emanated from the carnival celebrations. Carnival has its origin from the emancipation of slavery and is annually celebrated with two days of street dancing, revelry, debauchery and freeing up. This behaviour is considered to be pervasive throughout the year.

PLAYER OR PLAYBOY PERSONALITY

There is generally the loss of the courtship cycle among the male gender in Trinidad and Tobago.

The origin of the playboy has been fashioned by the early American influence at the war base in Chaguaramas and later by the influences of the electronic media and the country's oil wealth. The player is described as a well-dressed, slick, seemingly rich charmer with a fancy car who has many women with whom he is sexually but not emotionally involved. Such a person gains the admiration of the younger generation.

TABANCA

Tabanca is a form of "love sickness", derived from the French word to be thrown onto a bank. It is described as 'a state of depression' accompanied by withdrawal symptoms (can't eat, can't sleep, can't think) that occurs when one has been rejected by a loved one or experiences unrequited love. It is the loss of a love object.

OBSESSIONAL LATENESS

The people of Trinidad and Tobago show little concern for keeping time. They walk at a leisurely pace, stop to greet others with little regard for punctuality or lateness. Being fashionably late culturally confers respectability to the person underlining his importance or heavy work schedule.

SMARTMAN SYNDROME

Trinidadians are regionally referred to as 'Trickidadians' with a history of being dishonestly smart using techniques of lying, deceit, trickery and fraud. These individuals are well known con-artists or hagglers who are constantly attempting to make a fast dollar by ripping off someone else.

DEMON POSSESSION

Steeped in superstitious and religio-magical occurrences, the people of Trinidad and Tobago believe in the existence of jinns, demons and powers that can possess them. These spirits can take over or possess the body of a person and control their behaviour. Many mental disorders are interpreted as demon possession.

SPIRITUAL TRAVEL

Spiritual travel is practiced by members of the Spiritual Baptist religion. Through a process of sensory deprivation in the mourning ground ceremony, a person's spirit can travel out of the body to far off lands meeting people of all walks of life from whom prescriptions can be obtained for healing. It's a method of transcendence that unifies you with God.

MIDDLE AGE INDIAN WOMAN SYNDROME

A common finding among Indo-Trinidadian women in their fourth and fifth decades is the occurrence of somatic complaints of headaches, body aches and pains, cardiac and gastrointestinal symptoms. There is no physical disease on investigation with causation being attributed to social and psychological disorders. It is viewed as somatoform disorders that are more common in Indo-Caribbean women.

ANALYSIS OF CULTURAL BEHAVIOURS

Through quota sampling, a new sample of five hundred and thirty-six respondents (N=536) were administered a questionnaire that gathered self-report data on Trinidad culture (the nine behaviours identified). The sample population was similar to the population distribution of Trinidad and Tobago with respect to employment, religion, ethnicity, gender and social class (C.S.O., 1992). The questionnaire collected data on the following:

Demographic information

Data was gathered along the variables of age, sex, ethnicity (Afro-Trinidadians, Indo-Trinidadians, mixed and other), nationality and social class (low, middle and upper). Ethnicity or an individual's ethnic group was determined on the basis of the following criteria: 1) having at least three out of four grandparents belonging to the same ethnic group or if criteria 1) was not met, they were then categorized as mixed. The mixed ethnicity refers to individuals who are the resulting offspring of a union between two different ethnic groups and usually have distinctive physical traits that mark him from both parent ethnic groups, but may also possess some characteristics of manner, thought and speech, which are derived from both lines of ancestry. The ethnicity category of "other" included those individuals who cannot be placed in the ethnic categories of Afro-Trinidadians, Indo-Trinidadians and mixed. They also belong to ethnic groups that comprise a small percentage of the total population of Trinidad. e.g. Chinese, Syrian and Caucasian [34]. Social class was derived using both occupation and income brackets [35].

Awareness of behaviour

This variable was dichotomous and respondents were asked if they had ever heard of each of the nine behaviours. The response set was either "yes" or "no".

A description of the behaviour

If a respondent was aware of a particular behaviour, they were asked to give a brief description of the behaviour, state whether it is an entity or not, and if it is associated with any particular symptoms. The descriptions of the behaviours were then coded into several categories by two raters. It must be noted that the coding of the descriptions were done twice to ensure that there would be inter-rater reliability.

Perception of the behaviour as being part of Trinidad culture

The response set was again either "yes" or "no". Respondents were asked for each of the nine behaviours whether they perceived it to be part of the culture of Trinidad and Tobago.

Data was entered and analyzed by the use of SPSS (Statistical Package for the Social Sciences, Version 8.0). The statistical test chosen for awareness of behaviour and perception of the behaviour as being part of Trinidad culture was Chi-Square tests as data was collected along a nominal level. In order to distinguish behaviours that were strongly perceived as being part of Trinidad culture, percentiles that were within the upper quarter (75% cutoff point) were utilized [36]. Additional correlation analyses were also performed. The level of significance was set at a $p < 0.05$ level.

OUR FINDINGS

From the questionnaire survey of 536 participants, the nine behaviours (obsessional lateness, Smartman Syndrome, liming, Middle Age Indian Woman Syndrome, Tabanca, carnival mentality, demon possession, spiritual travel and playboy personality) were analysed in the following categories:

- Demographic data of sampled population
- Awareness of the behaviour
- Description of the behaviour
- Perception of the behaviour as part of culture

Demographic data of sampled population

Majority of the sample (98%) was Trinidadian with 2% non-Trinidadian. Indo-Trinidadians accounted for 39% of the sample, Afro-Trinidadians 35%, Mixed 24% and Other 2%. Ages of the respondents ranged from 14-56 with the mean age being 35. Sixty percent (60%) was in the 14-25 age group, 18% in the 26-35 age group, 12% in the 36-45 age group and 10% in the over 45 age group. With respect to social class, 52% was from the middle class, 27% from the lower class and 21% from the upper class.

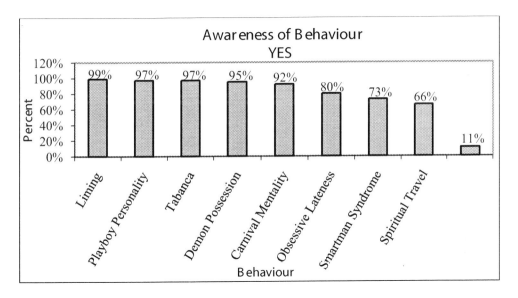

Awareness of behaviour

Overall, ninety-nine percent (99%) of the sample were aware or familiar with the behaviour of liming, 97% each for carnival mentality and playboy personality, 95% tabanca, obsessive lateness 92%, smartman syndrome 80%, demon possession 73%, spiritual travel 66% and middle age Indian woman syndrome 11% (see figure 1). A significantly greater percentage of Afro-Trinidadians were familiar with the behaviour of obsessional lateness than Indo-Trinidadians, Mixed persons and Others (Chi-square = 8.404, df = 3, $p < 0.05$). Indo-Trinidadians were also significantly more familiar with smartman syndrome than Afro-Trinidadians, Mixed and Other individuals (Chi-square = 11.590, df = 3, $p < 0.01$). Significant differences existed for the awareness of carnival mentality and smartman syndrome between social classes. Middle class individuals (55%) were more aware of the behaviour of carnival mentality than lower class (24%) and upper class (22%); and also were more aware of demon possession (53%) than lower class (25%) and upper class individuals

(21%). These differences were significant where Chi-square = 13.337, df = 2, p < 0.001 and Chi-square = 7.150, df = 2, p < 0.05, respectively.

The 14-25 age group was more aware of the term smartman syndrome and carnival mentality than other age groups, where Chi-square = 15.049, df = 3, p < 0.01 and Chi-square = 12.721, df = 3, p < 0.001. No other significant differences were found between this variable and other demographic data. In addition, awareness was not a determinant of cultural behaviour, but was strongly correlated with the perception that the behaviour was a part of culture (r = 0.894, p<0.001) and that there was a relationship between perception of the behaviour as part of culture and the number of descriptive levels constituting that behaviour (r = - 0.677, p< 0.05).

Description of behaviour

The following descriptions of different behaviour are summative characteristics based on answers given by respondents who were familiar with the culture.

Liming was described as a scheduled or non-scheduled event where a group of people (friends, family, acquaintances etc.) takes time to "hang out". The concept transcends ethnicity, class and religious barriers. It is an activity geared towards relaxation, stress relief through the means of talking, eating and drinking or just "doing nothing". As clearly put by one respondent, liming is a major cultural activity from river lime, after work lime or duck lime; and can also be seen as working in sync with our "poor work ethic" and "carnival mentality" (see table 1).

Table 1. Characteristics of liming

Characteristics	%
1. Major cultural activity / Scheduled or Non-scheduled episode where a group of people take time off to "hang out"/be idle/get together/do nothing	96
2. Activity geared towards stress relief	3
3. Mentality of liming causes laid back attitude / poor work ethic / carnival mentality	0.5
4. Turn any place into a liming spot	0.5

Carnival mentality was seen as having two dimensions: during carnival season and outside of carnival period. During the carnival season, carnival mentality has been viewed as a "time to free up", "time to break away and get on bad" or take part in every carnival activity or event and indulging in alcohol, immoral, vulgar, and promiscuous activities without thinking of the consequences. Outside of the carnival season, carnival mentality refers to the "non-stop party mentality" that is practiced throughout the year; where every event or occasion is treated as an excuse "to lime or party". Some respondents have regarded carnival mentality as "extreme liming" or "continuous fun in the sun". Carnival mentality was also seen as having filtered into the workplace where individuals have a very slack, laid back or "don't give a damn" attitude towards work. Carnival mentality was also referred to by a minority of respondents as mindlessness, when you hear music nothing could stop you from dancing, having too many parties in the calendar and events having attributes of carnival (see table 2).

Table 2. Characteristics of carnival mentality

Characteristics	%
1. Non-stop party mentality/ continuous fun in the sun/ "extreme liming"	51.4
2. Take part in every carnival activity or event/ time to break away and get on bad, immoral vulgar activities/ time to free up	21.0
3. Attitude to work very laid back, slack/ don't give a damn	19.0
4. Mindlessness, not thinking of consequences/ indulging in alcohol, promiscuity	3.0
5. Time to free up	3.2
6. When you hear soca, nothing could stop you from dancing	0.9
7. Having attributes of carnival e.g. cricket or football match	0.9
8. Too much parties in calendar	0.5

Playboy personality was described as Trinidadian men, who have multiple girlfriends, but only seek attention and sexual satisfaction from them. They dress sharp, have lots of money and drive expensive cars. They are sexually involved with all of their partners, but never emotionally involved. A player (one who has a playboy personality) was also identified as one who thinks he is God's gift to women, a real charmer and is said to tackle "anything in a skirt that pass". He is identified as a "sweetman", that is someone who knows all the right words to say (lyrics) and how to wine and dine the women he is currently seeing. Less than 1% of respondents viewed playboy personality as a person who commits adultery, behavior that is adopted from another culture or passed on by adults when a guy says he is in love but he is lying (see table 3).

Table 3. Characteristics of playboy personality

Characteristics	%
1. Trini men with multiple girlfriends who just crave attention, sexual interests/ sexually involved but not emotionally involved	74.5
2. One who thinks he is god's gift to women and plays the hearts of many women/ charmer / sweetman/ player / have to have "anything in a skirt that pass"	23.5
3. Commits adultery or cheats on partner	0.8
4. Player attitude passed on by adults	0.4
5. Adopted from a different culture	0.4
6. Guy says he is love but he is lying	0.4

Tabanca is a form of "love sickness". It was described as 'a state of depression' accompanied by withdrawal symptoms (can't eat, can't sleep) that occurs when one has been rejected by a loved one or experiences unrequited love. It is an adjustment disorder of losing a loved one. The term is also used to describe the feeling of being in love where one is constantly thinking, daydreaming and totally "head over heels" with someone, the mental anguish of getting "horn" and having girlfriend/boyfriend worries or "a case of Love Jones". Severe tabanca has been described as "tabantruck" (see table 4).

Table 4. Characteristics of Tabanca

Characteristics	%
1. Love sickness; person who gets dumped goes through a state of depression and withdrawal symptoms: can't eat, sleep/ adjustment disorder of losing a loved one / if symptoms severe known as tabantruck	71.2
2. Being in love, fall head over heels with someone, daydreaming etc.	17.9
3. Mental anguish of getting "horn"	6.1
4. Girlfriend/boyfriend worries/ "Love Jones"	3.1
5. Don't eat, don't sleep	1.3
6. When a male and female think they should be together	0.4

The respondents have clearly defined obsessional lateness as having no regard for punctuality and lateness as being a part of our nature. In short it is functioning with "trini time". It is arriving late for any event or occasion at least 15-45 minutes after the scheduled time. According to respondents, "any time is trini time" shows exactly how laid back individuals are in their behavior; and it has often been said that "a trini will be late for his own funeral". Arriving late was seen by some as being fashionably late and was due to being disorganized, waiting on the 11th hour to do something that leads to rushing and thus being late (see table 5),

Table 5. Characteristics of obsessional lateness

Characteristics	%
1. Reaching late for all events, may even reach late for own funeral / No regard for punctuality / Fashionably late, "just to show your face" / Operating on "trini time"	99
2. Watching too much TV at night	1

Individuals who have the ability to outsmart anyone or "hoodwink anyone" usually by means of lying, trickery, deceit and dishonesty display the Smartman syndrome. These individuals are con artists who seek to get things for little or no value. In local parlance, it refers to individuals who are trying to get "something for nothing" or "trying to pull a fast one." This behavior is also used to describe people who always have an answer for everything, a "smart retort" or "a bandage for every cut". Few respondents described a smartman as being one who fools and uses many women for their own benefit (similar to player), being a bully, being quiet and not talking too much and acting very stupid, that is, "playing dead to catch corbeaux alive" (see table 6).

Table 6. Characteristics of Smartman Syndrome

Characteristics	%
1. The ability to outsmart or "hoodwink" somebody, usually through dishonest means / conmen / trying to get "something for nothing" or "trying to pull a fast one"	65
2. Always a smart retort / "bandage for every cut"	19
3. People who act smart	5
4. Getting things for little or no value	4
5. Player who uses many women/ fooling them	3
6. Bully	2
7. Quiet, not talking much	1
8. Playing very stupid – "playing dead to catch corbeaux alive"	1

Demon possession was mostly viewed as when a spirit or demon took over the body and the person is unaware of what is happening. It was also seen to be attributed to an individual acting in a strange and unexplainable manner not consistent with his /her normal behavior pattern, or acting crazy. Some people referred to demon possession as similar to evil, obeah, witchcraft and bad things constantly happening to you. Few described demon possession as an anxiety attack, talking constantly, folklore and myths and as a manifestation of abnormal behavior usually schizophrenia. Table 7 describes the characteristics associated with demon possession (see table 7).

Table 7. Characteristics of demon possession

Characteristics	%
1. When spirits/demon take over body and person unaware of what is happening	55.5
2. Acting crazy/ acting similar to if a demon possessed a person/ strange unexplainable behavior	29.4
3. Obeah / evil/ witchcraft	11.3
4. Folklore and myths as part of culture	1.7
5. Manifestation of abnormal behavior, usually schizophrenia	0.8
6. Anxiety attack	0.8
7. Talks constantly/ overly energetic and frisky	0.4

Spiritual Travel was defined as the ability of a spirit to travel out of the body; more specifically, respondents identified the transcendental travel of the soul on the mourning ground as a practice of the Spiritual Baptist faith. It is also associated to other religious sects involved in the practices of "ketching power" and loud singing and clapping. Other views of spiritual travel were that it is an episode that occurs while praying and brings you closer to God, is obeah/voodoo or it is when you are given the word of God in order to practice religion properly. It occurs in a state close to death when the spirit gradually leaves the body and is a state when one can have visions or dreams. It was described as a mostly religious related activity (see table 8).

Table 8. Characteristics of spiritual travel

Characteristics	%
1. The ability to travel out of the body/ transcendental travel on mourning ground / practice of Spiritual Baptists.	65.0
2. Religious sect involved in practices like that/ "ketching power" and loud clapping and singing	17.2
3. Going through an episode that brings you closer to god/ holy trance evoked while praying	8.0
4. Obeah/Voodoo	4.3
5. After baptism, given information to practice religion/ behavior when speaking the word of god	3.1
6. Stage close to death and spirit gradually leaving body	0.6
7. Visions, dreams, or dazed while in that state	1.8

Middle age Indian woman syndrome was neither clearly nor consistently defined within one category. It was referred to as Indian women who stay at home, are extremely obsessional about their family and who neglect their physical appearance. In addition, the syndrome was seen as being associated with behavior directed to recapture a youthful past, being fat around the waist and complaining of pains in the joints, forever quarrelling with the children and husband and having extra marital affairs (see table 9).

Table 9. Characteristics of Middle Age Indian Woman Syndrome

Characteristics	%
1. Extremely obsessive about family, stays at home and neglects physical appearance	30
2. Types of behavior associated with youthful past	23
3. Behaving like an Indian woman at middle age	10
4. Fat around the waist and complaining of joints	10
5. Individual attracted to middle age Indian women	10
6. Looking old and tired but they are young	7
7. Forever quarrelling with children and husband	3.3
8. Extra marital affairs between 30-40	3.3
9. Menopause	3.3

Perception of behaviour as part of culture

The measurements of respondents' perception of behaviours seen as part of the culture of Trinidad and Tobago were as follows: Liming (96%), carnival mentality (93%) were perceived as being part of the culture of Trinidad and Tobago, followed by playboy personality 83%, tabanca 82%, obsessive lateness 77%, smartman syndrome 65%, demon possession 55%, spiritual travel 46% and middle age Indian woman syndrome 9% (see figure 2).

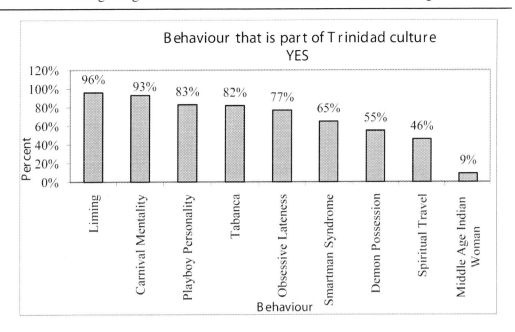

Significant differences existed between ethnic groups and their view of demon possession as a part of Trinidad culture. Indo-Trinidadians were more likely (50%) than Afro-Trinidadians (30%), Mixed (17%) and Other (3%) individuals to view demon possession as a part of Trinidad culture. This was significant where Chi-square = 16.369, df = 3, p < 0.001.

Middle class individuals (52%) and lower class individuals (32%) were more likely than upper class individuals (16%) to view demon possession as being a part of Trinidad culture. This difference was near significance where Chi-square = 5.3481, df = 2, p = 0.06.

The 14-25 age group was more likely than other age groups to view smartman syndrome and playboy personality as a part of culture, this was significant where Chi-square = 10.014, df = 3, p < 0.01 and Chi-square = 8.449, df = 3, p < 0.05 respectively. No other significant differences were found between this variable and other demographic data.

Link between awareness and perception of behaviour as part of culture

A strong correlational relationship existed between awareness and the perception that the behaviour is a part of culture. This was significant where r = 0.894, p < 0.001. However, it was discovered that high awareness is not a necessity for a determinant of culture. This is evident especially for demon possession where 95% of respondents were aware of culture but only 55% perceived it as being a part of culture.

Another significant correlational relationship existed between the perception of the behaviour as a culture and the number of levels constituting a behaviour where r = - 0.677, p < 0.05. Therefore as the number of levels in describing a behaviour increases the less likely it is to be considered a part of the culture. This however, did not pertain to demon possession and spiritual travel.

DISCUSSION

Nine behaviours namely, Liming, Carnival Mentality, Player or Playboy Personality, Tabanca, Obsessional Lateness, Smartman Syndrome, Demon Possession, Spiritual Travel and The Middle-Age Indian Woman Syndrome were identified as existent cultural behaviours. Attempts to validate whether a particular behaviour was part of the culture of Trinidad and Tobago were no easy task. Using a cut-off point of more than a 75 percent respondent rate [36] resulted in the rejection of four behaviours namely, Smartman Syndrome, Demon Possession, Spiritual Travel and the Middle-Age Indian Woman Syndrome which fell below the 75 percentile (see figure 2).

There were however a number of limitations. The use of an opportunity sample may have resulted in lower figures in awareness and perception of behaviour as part of culture due to the skewing of the age groupings to the younger working groups. This, in our opinion may have resulted in lower figures in awareness and perception of the behaviour as part of culture. The strong correlation between awareness and perception that behaviour was part of culture was not always robust. In the case of demon possession 95% of respondents were aware of the culture, but only 55% perceived it as part of culture. This substantiates the view that awareness of a phenomenon is not sufficient to categorize it as a cultural behaviour. In addition, it was found that the greater the number of levels used in describing a culture, the less likely it was found to be part of the culture ($r = -0.677$, $p < 0.05$). However, it must be noted that the correlation coefficient be interpreted with caution, as correlation does not equal causation and there is possibility of third variables that may have an impact on the investigated variables [37].

Another interesting finding was that while respondents viewed social and traditional practices as cultural behaviour, they were less likely to perceive religious related behaviour as part of culture. This may have resulted in the low response rates for Demon Possession and Spiritual Travel. The divide of religion and culture in Trinidad and Tobago is promulgated by the dichotomy of one culture (East Indian) with many religions and one religion (Christianity) with many cultures often in competition with each other. The post slavery emphasis of distancing religion from culture may have been an attempt to gain reputation and respectability for religious beliefs.

LIMING – 'THE ART OF DOING NOTHING'

Almost all the respondents (99%) were aware of liming and ninety-six percent described it as a scheduled or non-scheduled episode where a group of people take time off to hang out, be idle, get together or do nothing. The concept of liming as a social institution and cultural state of mind in Trinidad was reviewed by Eriksen [31]. He described it as a unique Trinidadian pastime of 'the art of doing nothing' and noted that whereas idling and inactivity are frequently perceived unequivocally as shameful and immoral in most societies, liming in Trinidad is an activity that one would not hesitate to indulge in proudly. Despite its occurrence elsewhere, in Trinidad it is different; it is a social situation acknowledged as a form of the performing art linked to the key symbols of carnival, calypso and steelband. In our study, liming was a feature of all groups, regardless of age, ethnicity, religion or class that utilized cultural archetypal mechanisms for the relief of stress.

CARNIVAL MENTALITY 'A HAPPY GO LUCKY PEOPLE WITH A NON-STOP PARTY MENTALITY'

Carnival is the Republic's best known festival ushering the season of Lent. The carnival season extends from Christmas to Lent, but outside this period 'a carnival mentality of having attributes to carnival' was described (see table 2). There is abandonment of the social structures of work, family life, education and law. One commentator, the Prime Minister of Singapore, a country well known for its industry has argued that the behaviour depicted at carnival is pervasive throughout the year and has referred to the population of Trinidad as having a carnival mentality [38]. In response, Liverpool [39], has pointed out that "in speaking of Trinidadians as having a carnival mentality, they seek to degrade our people, for they seek to say that to possess such a mentality is to live for today, to play 'mas', to have a good time and then to beg on Ash Wednesday morning. In other words, it is to live aimlessly." The urgency of carnival to many is well portrayed in Lovelace's novel – "The Dragon Can't Dance" in the characterization of Aldrick Prospect. He would get up at midday from sleep, not knowing where his next meal was coming from, 'his brain working in the same smooth, unhurried nonchalance with which he moved his feet, a slow cruising crawl which he quickened only at carnival" [40]. Thus, the enthusiasm and energy devoted to carnival is not displayed in everyday life. Trinidadians, especially those of African descent are often described as a 'happy go lucky people' with little commitment to hard work. According to Eriksen [31] "a common assumption, not least common in the urban working class itself is that black-working-class Trinidadians don't invest themselves in respectable activities such as wage work and family life. Life is too sweet".

In our study the carnival mentality was described as having a "non stop party mentality", a time to indulge in "bad or immoral activities" and having a "slack and laid back attitude to work" (see table 2). The invariable negative connotation of carnival mentality in our sample goes against the possibility of subgroup bias or stereotypy. A significant number, 97 percent of our respondents were aware of the carnival mentality behaviour and 92 percent identified it as being part of the islands' culture. A significant finding was that the middle social class was more aware of the carnival mentality (p < 0.001). A possible explanation is that members of this group are employed with the Civil Service and will be aware of the established work ethics. A common word of affirmation by mechanics after tuning up cars is "boss, your car idling like a civil servant".

THE MACHOMAN OR PLAYER PERSONALITY – 'GOD'S GIFT TO WOMEN'

It has been argued that this phenomenon is more Caribbean than Trinidadian. It is unique to the region since it is argued that the Caribbean man or the 'Carib-being man' is polygamous in nature but jealously guard fidelity in his woman. The courtship cycle from introduction to intimate relationship with women is foreshortened in the Caribbean with an emphasis on sexual conquest rather than a meaningful relationship.

The Trinidadian male and by extension the Caribbean man attain social ascendancy and status if they are perceived as 'macho'. Such behaviours of male individuals with multiple partners as "sexually involved but not emotionally involved" and "god's gift to woman" (see table 8) have been met with exaltation and reinforcement in many national songs such as the Mighty Sparrow calypso – "The Village Ram" [41]. The playboy personality or 'player' the term commonly used by teenagers is a 'woman charmer or sweetman' who is by nature is polygamous but will jealously guard fidelity in his partners. For him, there are no restrictions in making a 'play' on any woman. Contingencies of marital or social status, the feelings of others or moral issues are non-consequential. Within society there are social sanctions that undermine values of honesty, integrity and morality. The young age group of 14-25 years were more convinced that the playboy personality was a part of the culture of Trinidad and Tobago and more common among Afro-Trinidadians.

TABANCA – 'LOVESICKNESS-LOSS OF A LOVE OBJECT'

Eighty-two percent of the respondents felt that Tabanca was part of the Trinidad culture. In Trinidad and Tobago, Tabanca or the loss of a loved one with ruminations of the loss object has been described as an indigenous conceptualization of depression [28]. Local researchers have argued that this love-struck behaviour is the feeling one gets when rejected by a partner or love object and is circumscribed in the pathos of culturally-determined confrontational humor known as 'picong' [29]. This process allows the individual to work through his feelings of loss and rejection in a cognitive behavioural context of minimization, levity and social support. Although contemporarily considered to be a 'culture bound syndrome' this behaviour has been locally described as an adjustment disorder. It is culturally recognizable particularly when the loss is known to one's peers. The individual may experience a temporary decrease in worth, humour and esteem by way of the satirical and jocular treatment from his or her peers. This in itself is cathartic and leads to resolution. Trinidadians have popularized four stages of love sickness namely 'tabanca' -feeling down after the departure of a lover, 'fufooloo'-behaving in a foolish or dotish manner, 'kairkathay'-so dazed spinning like a top and 'tirangebanji'-when one gives up and is psychotic or suicidal.

OBSESSIONAL LATENESS – 'ANYTIME IS TRINIDAD TIME'

In Trinidad and Tobago, there is a pervasive cultural attitude of disrespect or unconcern for time. It is customary for individuals even in high office to arrive late for all events without any regard for protocol or punctuality. There is no feeling of shame since their lateness is culturally perceived as a commitment to duty and dedication to hard work that prevented them from being on time. In addition, this behaviour is reinforced since their late appearance is often announced with adequate excuses of 'circumstances beyond their control' and being late due to the latecomers 'busy schedule and commitment to hard work'. Due to the looseness of time, "just to show your face" is considered sufficient. Ninety-nine percent of the sampled population correctly described this behaviour.

Obsessional lateness or the inability to keep time is inherent in our population and is well tolerated. In this behaviour, appointments are made and never met and lateness is culturally accepted. Trinidadian sportsmen in the United Kingdom have been disciplined and heavily fined for lateness. In the recent World Trade Centre disaster, the Trinidad Guardian newspaper [42] carried the following story: "Many Trinidadians and Tobagonians are thanking God, and some because of their place of birth they were either late for work, still making their way to work or took a day off on Tuesday when two hijacked planes hit New York's World Trade Centre, killing an unknown number of people".

It is noteworthy that the cultural behaviours, liming, carnival mentality, playboy personality, tabanca and obsessional lateness are closely related. These behaviours have as their themes negative characteristics of doing nothing, sexual liaison and its sequaelae and a lack of respect for time. The latter can be interpreted as subsets of the carnival mentality, all interrelated to the basic instincts of primary process thinking.

From our analysis, Smartman Syndrome, Demon Possession, Spiritual Travel and Middle-Age Indian Woman Syndrome were rejected by the respondents as being part of the culture of Trinidad and Tobago. The summative characteristics for the most part were multidimensional with many levels of description. The Trinidadian 'smartman' is not unique in his ability to contrive, connive, scheme and out do other people when compared with other countries. Guyanese and Barbadians are similarly perceived as schemers and smartmen in the Caribbean region. Indo-Trinidadians were more familiar with the Smartman Syndrome. A possible explanation is their involvement in business.

Demonical Possession and Spiritual Travel were not considered to be culture-based behaviours. This may be due to the perception that they are established religious practices ordained by the Christian and Baptist churches respectively. Indo-Trinidadians however, were more likely to view demon possession as part of the Trinidadian culture while the majority of Afro-Christians attributed it to their religious beliefs. A cross-sectional study indicated that 71 percent of the total sample believed in the existence of demons and 65 percent thought that demons could possess people [43]. It is however, difficult to separate religion from culture since all religious groups have incorporated religio-magical thinking and exorcism as part of their theological practices and are engaged in faith-healing and the casting out of demons.

Many religious groups in Trinidad and Tobago believe in the concept of spiritual or astral travel. This is an out-of-body experience, induced by sensory deprivation whereby the soul of the pilgrim (mourner) leaves the body and travels to distant lands, meeting new people and becoming exposed to experiences that serve to strengthen one's faith and allow his/her ascendancy within the hierarchy of the church. This practice is not well known locally and commonly performed by followers of the Baptist religion in the mourning ground ceremony. It is not unique to Trinidad [44].

The Middle-Age Indian Woman Syndrome is a somatoform disorder of mostly female Indo-Trinidadians who present for treatment with multiple somatic complaints at clinics and hospitals. This was rejected by the respondents, as it was not clearly or consistently defined within one particular dimension. This in itself gave statistical credibility to the respondents' responses by incorporating an entity known in the medical circles and testing it within the general population.

The question must be asked as to whether these phenomena are unique to Trinidad and Tobago? The obvious response will be no. However, on a more detailed analysis, it will be evident that these are culturally determined behaviours that are specific to a mixed cultural heritage in a geographical region that has a uniqueness of its own. Similar syndromes may be present in other Caribbean countries but their presentations will be coloured by historical social, economic, political and cultural diversities. The phenomena will be the same but the emphasis and level of presentation will vary.

Trinidad and Tobago is a socially stratified society with a large middle class population. The latter being more educated tends to identify and popularize local customs giving it sanctions. The working class is rarely involved in self-analysis of their behaviour. The younger age groups are invested in behaviours in which their peer group is involved, such as liming, player and tabanca. Ethnicity is not a major determinant of behaviour in the younger age groups especially in urban areas. Among the over forty population, there is a tendency for ethnic sub-grouping with particular emphasis, for example alcohol use among Indo-Trinidadians with increased tabanca and polygamy among Afro-Trinidadians who are more invested in carnival.

In conclusion, using a 75% response rate, respondents were aware of six of the nine identified behaviours and perceived five of them to be part of the Trinidadian culture. Smartman syndrome and the middle age Indian woman syndrome were rejected as cultural phenomena both with respect to awareness and perception. The religious nature of the people of Trinidad and Tobago and their tolerance and respect for each other strengthened by elements of cultural fusion are plausible explanations for respondents' exclusion of religious-related activities as culture based. This would have resulted in the exclusion of Spiritual Travel and Demon Possession. Carnival Mentality, Liming, Obsessional Lateness, Tabanca and the Player Personality were accepted as cultural behaviours in Trinidad and Tobago The validity of these findings are supported by the triangulation of the results with previous reports and descriptions. In addition, inter-rater reliability (95%) demonstrated no differences in dimensions of behaviours of the people of Trinidad and Tobago.

Cultures are dynamic rather than static and while the wheel of culture can go around for centuries without notable disturbance [45], cultures can change when the value system of a society changes. Nevertheless, the relics of a culture can still remain around when the culture changes. According to Jones [46] many cultures see their future in terms of preserving the past. It is important therefore, that documentation be made of the cultural behaviours of immigrants from both the sending and receiving countries in order to understand their emotional, behavioural and thinking processes. For many, the old culture remains fixed on migration, despite changes in the country of origin.

GLOSSARY

Trinidad – term used in this study to mean the islands of Trinidad and Tobago
River lime – activity of liming that takes place near or on the bank of a river
After work lime - liming that takes place after working hours, usually on Fridays, at the end of the working week
Duck lime - liming that involves the cooking and eating of a duck

Time to free up & Time to get on bad – chorus from calypsoes urging the population to relax. Sometimes refers to indulgence in alcohol, vulgar and immoral activities without even thinking of the consequences of one's actions

Anything in a skirt that pass - refers to an attraction to all female individuals regardless of age, ethnic group or marital status

Macho – refers to an individual, usually a male who is domineering, assertive and polygamous. Taken from the advertisement, "Rum is macho".

Sweetman – someone who is considered to be very charming and doesn't hesitate to spend money entertaining a woman

Horn - refers to the act when the your partner is unfaithful to you in the relationship – infidelity

Tabantruck – symptoms of tabanca so severe they cannot figuratively, fit in a car but needs a truck ("taban-truck" as opposed to "taban-car")

Trini time - is the term coined by Trinidadians to refer to their own inherent nature of being late to any event

Just to show your face - the term used to describe when someone only makes an appearance at an event or occasion.

Picong – communication pattern of mild but humorous confrontation with persons

Something for nothing & Trying to pull a fast one – refers to when an individual tries to outsmart someone or tries to negotiate an offer where he is the only one gaining

Bandage for every cut – having an answer for every question or problem

Obeah – refers to an African tradition of sorcery

Mourning ground – refers to the place where a follower of the Spiritual Baptist faith goes in order to perform Spiritual travel

Ketching power - refers to acting in a state similar as if one were possessed by a spirit or demon (shaking and trembling of body, eyes rolling etc.)

Playing dead to catch corbeaux alive – corbeaux are vultures that feed on dead carcasses. 'The smartman' will pretend to be stupid to gain an advantage.

ACKNOWLEDGMENTS

We wish to thank Ms Astra Kassiram, Psychologist and Lecturer at the University of the Southern Caribbean in Maracas for reviewing this chapter. Her comments and validations were encouraging.

APPENDIX 1

Semi-structured interview for identifying cultural behaviour patterns of Trinidad and Tobago

Introduction: We are conducting a survey on people's behaviour in Trinidad and Tobago and we are requesting your participation in answering a few questions.

Demographics

1. Age _____

2. Sex:

Male [1]   Female [2]

3. Ethnic Group:

African [1] Indian [2] Mixed [3]   Other [4]
4. Marital Status:

Single [1]   Common-Law [2]   Married [3]
Separated [4]   Divorced [5]

5. Education Level:

Primary [1] Secondary [2]   Tertiary [3]

6. Occupation & Monthly Income _____

7. Social Class:

Lower [1]   Middle [2]   Upper [3]

Culture

8. What do you understand by the word behaviour?

9. Does behaviour include culture – lifestyle, food, music etc. of people?

10. If yes, to question 9, what are the cultural practices (handed down behaviour) that you are aware of in this country?

11. Are there any other social patterns i.e. how people generally behave that are unique to our people?
12. If hitherto not mentioned, do you consider religious or spiritual beliefs or practices as part of behaviour or culture?

If yes, can you describe them?
If no, how would you interpret these religious practices?

13. Are your descriptions only found in:

a) Trinidad and Tobago

b) Other regions

c) Don't know.

Thank You.

REFERENCES

[1] Kraeplin E. Psychiatrie, 8te Auflage, Leipzig : Barth, 1909. [German]

[2] Voss G. Die Aetiologie der Psychosen. In: Aschaffenburg G, ed. Handbuch der Psychiatrie. Leipzig: Deuticke; 1915. [German]

[3] 3. Durkheim E. Suicide: A study in Sociology.   Glencoe, IL: Free Press, 1951.

[4] Kiev A. Transcultural psychiatry. New York: Free Press, 1972.

[5] American Psychiatric Association. Diagnostic and statistical manual of mental disorders IV-TR. Washington DC: APA, 2000.

[6] Dein S. Mental health in a multiethnic society. BMJ 1997;106:473-7.

[7] Jilek WG. Culturally related syndromes. In: Gelder MG, Lopez-Ibor JJ, Andreasen N, eds. New Oxford textbook of psychiatry. Oxford: Oxford Univ Press, 2000:1061-6.

[8] Jilek WG, Jilek-Aall L. Kulturspezifische psychische storungen. In: Hemlchen H, Henn F, Lauter H, Sartorius N, eds. Psychiatrie der Gegenwart. Vol. 3: Psychiatrie spezieller Lebenssituationen. Berlin: Springer, 2000. [German]

[9] Paris J. Dhat: the semen loss anxiety syndrome. Transcult Psychiatry Res Rev 1992;29:109-18.

[10] Yap PM. Koro - a culture bound depersonalization syndrome. Br J Psychiatry 1965;3:43-50.

[11] Jilek WG. Epidemics of "genital shrinking" (koro). Curare (Heidelberg) 1986;9:269-82.

[12] Jilek WG, Jilek-Aall L. A koro epidemic in Thailand. Transcult Psychiatr Res Rev 1977;14:57-9.

[13] Tseng W-S, Mo KM, Hsu J, Li LS, Ou L-W, Chen G-Q, et al. A sociocultural study of Koro epidemics in Guangdong, China. Am J Psychiatry 1988;145:1538-43.

[14] Kirmayer LJ. The place of culture in psychiatric nosology: taijin kyofusho and DSM-III-R. J Nerv Ment Dis 1991;179:19-28.

[15] Kimura B. Zwischen Mensch and Mensch: Strakuren japanischer Subjaktivitat. Darmstadt: Wissenschaftliche Buchgesellschaft, 1995. [German]

[16] Lee SH, Shin YC, Oh KS. A clinical study of social phobia for 10 years. J Korean Neuropsychiatr Assoc 1994;33:305-12.

[17] Winzeler RL. Latah in Southeast Asia: The Ethnography and history of a culture bound syndrome. New York: Cambridge Univ Press, 1995.

[18] Simons R. Boo! Culture, experience and the startle reflex. Oxford: Oxford Univ Press, 1996.

[19] Van Wulfften Palthe PM. Amok. Nederlandsch Tijschrilfl voor Geneeskunde 1991;77:983-91. [Dutch]

[20] Burton-Bradley BG. The amok syndrome in Papua and New Guinea. Med J Aust 1968;1:252-6.

[21] Burton-Bradley BG. Stone age crisis: A psychiatric appraisal. Nashville: Vanderbilt Univ Press, 1975.

[22] Westermeyer J. A comparison of amok and other homicide in Laos. Am J Psychiatry 1972;129:703-9.

[23] Westermeyer J. On the epidemicity of amok violence. Arch Gen Psychiatry 1973;28:873-6.

[24] Murphy HBM. History and the striking evolution of syndromes: the striking case of latah and amok. In: Hammer M, Salzinger K, Sutton S, eds. Psychopathology. Contributions from the biological, behavioural and social sciences. New York: Wiley, 1973:33-5.

[25] Pfeiffer WM. Transkulturelle Psychiatrie, 2nd rev ed. Thieme: Stuttgart, 1994. [German]

[26] Prince R. The "brain-fag" syndrome in Nigerian students. J Ment Sci 1960;106:559-70.

[27] Prince R. The concept of culture - bound syndromes: anorexia nervosa and brain fag. Soc Sci Med 1985;21:197-203.

[28] Littlewood R. An indigenous conceptualization of reactive depression in Trinidad. Psychol Med 1985;15:275-81.

[29] Maharajh HD, Hutchinson G. Tabanca in Trinidad and Tobago: Myth, mirth or mood disorder. Caribb Med J 1999;61(1):21-4.

[30] Maharajh HD, Clarke TD, Hutchinson G. Transcultural Psychiatry. Psychiatr Bull 1989;10:574-5.

[31] Eriksen TH. Liming in Trinidad: The art of doing nothing. Folk 1990;32.

[32] Bhugra D, Hilwig M, Hossein B, Marceau H, Neehall J, Leff J, et al. Incidence rate and one year follow up of first contact schizophrenia in Trinidad. Br J Psychiatry 1996;169:587-92.

[33] Central Statistical Office. Statistics at a Glance. Port Spain: Republic Trinidad and Tobago, Office Prime Minister, 2001.

[34] Lewis LFE. Admission of schizophrenic patients at St Anns Hospital. Port of Spain, Trinidad: Archives St Anns Hospital, 1973.

[35] Meltzer H, Gill B, Petticrew M. The prevalence of psychiatric morbidity among adults aged 16-64 living in private households in Great Britain. OPCS Surveys of Psychiatric Morbidity in Great Britain. London: HMSO, 1995.

[36] Kurtz N. Statistical analysis for the social sciences. Boston, MA: Allyn Bacon,1999.

[37] Martin D. Doing psychology experiments, 5th ed. Belmont, CA: Wadsworth, 2000.

[38] Panday B. Speeches made by the political leader - the Expansion on the LNG operations. The United National Congress: Trinidad and Tobago, 2000.

[39] Liverpool H. Culture and education. Carnival in Trinidad and Tobago. Implications for education in secondary schools. London: Karia Press, 1990.

[40] Lovelace E. The Dragon Can't Dance. London: Andre Deutsh, 1979.

[41] Rohlehr G. Sparrow as poet. In: Anthony M, Carr A, eds. David Frost introduces Trinidad and Tobago. London: Andre Deutsch, 1975.

[42] Wanser D. Mad scramble for safety. Trinidad Guardian 2001 Sep 14:15.

[43] Maharajh HD, Parasram R. Mental Illness: Demons or dopamine. West Indian Med J 1997; Suppl 46:17.

[44] Griffith EEH, Mahy GE. Psychological benefits of spiritual Baptist "Mourning". Am J Psychiatry 1984;141:769-73.

[45] Toner B. An ethic for the third millennium. Working notes. Dublin, Ireland: Jesuit Centre Faith Justice, 2001.

[46] Jones D. Learning culture. Presented 2001 AERC Conf Proceed, 2001.

In: Social and Cultural Psychiatry Experience from the...
Editor: Hari D. Maharajh and Joav Merrick

ISBN: 978-1-61668-506-5
© 2010 Nova Science Publishers, Inc.

Chapter 7

RACE, POLITICS AND BEHAVIOR IN TRINIDAD AND TOBAGO

Hari D. Maharajh

Racism is a loaded word with too much surplus meaning. Its contemporary common usage encompasses every aspect of human and social sciences. It is an emotive word that is often avoided since it also defines the unconscious processes of the commentators whose creations are invariably within their own experiences rather than the spoken context. Regardless of which Government is in power, the stereotypes associated with whether the party is Indo or Afro-dominated add fuel to the phenomenon of racism, with each race fighting for eventual control. Whether this is a historical or evolutional instinct, the political parties employ means to get their supporters aroused and incensed, tugging at their emotions, a psychological display to secure party votes. This phenomenon sows the seed for human destructiveness and crime that is now rampant in the twin island states. The simple solution to this complex problem is power sharing, but the sociopathic leaders obsessed with power and control will have none of it.

INTRODUCTION

Racism is a loaded word with too much surplus meaning. Its contemporary common usage encompasses every aspect of human and social sciences. It is an emotive word that is often avoided since it also defines the unconscious processes of the commentators whose creations are invariably within their own experiences rather than the spoken context. It is not unusual therefore, to read in the newspaper of Trinidad and Tobago, nonsensical deliberations of Trinidadian academics utilizing the psychological defense mechanisms of sublimation, intellectualization and identification as they attempt to defend their stated positions. These commentators serve to rationalize hierarchical domination of one racial or ethnic group over other group(s), in an effort to maintain psychological, social, and material advantages on behalf of the dominant group [1]. They are known to be controversial, disruptive, divisive and contentious with an inner void, often seeking support and approval from their like-thinking peers.

Within recent times a number of nosological entities have been substituted for the description of racist behavior. Some are more civil and euphemistic while others are considered extreme. There is the use of the words race thinking, racialism, discrimination, apartheid, segregation, xenophobia, prejudice, oppression, persecution and more recently affirmative action and a new-style ethnic cleansing in Trinidad. The commonality lies however, in the dislike of one group by another due to historical, social, economic, geographical, political and anthropomorphic differences.

To hate is healthy, it strengthens the ethos of a group, it enhances consolidation of the group members flavoring it in a positive direction of socialized power against an identifiable threat. A fitting example though imprudent, is the decision of the Prime Minister of Trinidad and Tobago, the Honourable Patrick Manning, while addressing his Afro-Trinidadian followers at Harris Promenade on 20th July 2009 declared "make a commitment from deep within your hearts, people may be different from us (Africans), but nobody is better and nobody is worse"[2]. He strengthens his African base through segregation and also elevates them as being superior, since he is the Prime Minister. It is obvious that the Prime Minister is playing the race card to call his supporters together in an atmosphere livid with concepts of ethnic cleansing.

In the establishment of communities in multiracial societies, race-thinking is pervasive; there is however, less racism in societies with the predominance of one race and individuals in that community are often healthier. In Jamaica for example, ninety five (95) percent of the population is of African descent, there is no race differences and therefore no need to define inter-racial differences. In such a homogenous society, other social discriminants will be invented. Social dimensions of 'shadism' or 'colourism' is today well defined where bleaching creams are in common usage strangely even among men folk also, thereby paradoxically embracing the slave-hating concepts of "whiteness" and stratification by skin tone [3]. It is not uncommon to see a Jamaican woman with almost white face and arms and dark legs. In addition, racism is openly taught at schools where children are instructed that every White person is responsible for slavery and how they were treated. There seems to be no logic or rationale for racist behavior other than self or group-seeking dominance.

Hence, in Jamaica with a predominance of Afro-Jamaicans, the hostility and direction of hostility are towards the White population. On the other hand, in Trinidad, racism is often defined by the interaction of the two major ethnic groupings Indian 40.5% and Africans 39.5% population with each of the two major races, constituting more than 80% of the population. There is constant hostility among these two groups. This has resulted in those who belong to other groups being free and protected from racist imperatives. Thus, the Chinese, Syrians, Portuguese and Whites buffered by the Indo-African warring sections enjoy more opportunities and favors. A common example is the social, legal and economic privileges enjoyed by the Syrian, White and Chinese communities.

It has been argued that if there are perpetrators and victims of racism then the perpetrator is not in a position to tell the victim how to think, how to feel, how to behave and how to respond in the face of racism. This in itself is the super imposition of the beliefs of an authoritarian group unto another which also falls within the rubric of racism. When both groups claim that the other is racist, then it is imperative to analyze who holds the power, to whom the opportunities are given and which group sees itself as the natural inheritors of the colonial past.

A review of the contemporary Trinidad literature reveals that the Peoples' National Movement, a mostly African party has not been equitable in its distribution of housing, academic scholarship, high profile Government positions such as Permanent Secretaries in Government offices and State Boards. In fact there have been citations of Indo Trinidadians taking the Government to the Privy Council and winning cases after the Prime Minister vetoed the appointments.

In Third World countries like Trinidad and Tobago racism appears to be based on the anthropomorphic features of racial origin and issues of power and political control. Ethnic cleansing has been proffered as contemporary practice in Trinidad with affirmative action towards the Afro Trinidadians and lack of equal opportunities for even Indo-Trinidadian professionals by an African Government. This chapter reviews these occurrences and attempts to look at the race -related behaviors in Trinidad and Tobago.

DEFINING RACISM

Racism is the belief that there are characteristics, abilities, or qualities specific to each race, which fuels discrimination against or antagonism towards other races [4]. Race is the primary determinant of human traits and capacities, and those racial differences that exist produce an inherent superiority of a particular race [5]. The basic premise behind these definitions is a perception of a power differential between self proclaimed perpetrators and unwilling victims. Trinidad's well known mix of races, cultures and religions has been suggested to be the root cause of the conflict, that is part of life in Trinidad in the twenty-first century [6]. One can speculate that the phenomenon of racism may be inevitable in any multicultural society.

There are three levels of racism: institutionalized racism, personally mediated racism and internalized racism [3]. Institutionalized racism is defined as differential access to the goods, services, and opportunities of society by selected races. It is structural, having been codified in institutions of custom, practice and law, so there is not an identifiable perpetrator. This can be likened to accusations of discrimination against the Trinidad Government under the rule of the People's National Movement, an African party that provides the needs of mostly African people. Personally mediated racism is defined as prejudice and discrimination, where prejudice means differential assumptions about the abilities, motives and intentions of others according to their race, and discrimination refers to differential actions toward others according to their race. Internalized racism is defined as acceptance by members of the stigmatized races of negative messages about their own abilities and intrinsic worth. Four types of racism exist: historical racism, scientific racism, institutional racism and new racism [7]. Historical racism refers to countries which share a population that has common lineage and ancestry. Scientific racism categorizes individuals based on physical traits and believes that some races may possess superior qualities that put them in a position to civilize others. Institutional racism aims to widen the inequality between a perceived dominant and a subordinate group. New Racism is the development of new terms that tend to disguise the emotive factor behind previously controversial expressions, an attempt to be politically correct [7]. The latter is pervasive in Trinidad and Tobago.

LEGAL ASPECTS

The Constitution of the Government of Trinidad and Tobago provides for issues of racial and ethnic discrimination. Chapter I, section 4, of the Constitution addresses the rights and freedoms as recognized in the Universal Declaration of Human Rights. This declaration allows the citizens of Trinidad and Tobago all of the fundamental rights without discrimination "by reason of race, origin, color, religion or sex"[8].

An Equal Opportunities Act No 9 (2000) also exists which lobbies against the "fight against discrimination in education, employment, the provision of goods and services, and housing." These have not been enacted for almost a decade by the present government. Specific legislation to prevent racial discrimination in the leisure and entertainment field which covers a wide area, including access to discotheques and dance halls (Registration of Clubs Act as amended by Act No. 14 of 1997, Theatres and Dance Hall Act as amended by Act No. 15 of 1997) has also been put in place [8,9].

The Public Holidays and Festivals Act (chap. 19:05) recognizes festivals specific to the different religions in Trinidad and Tobago: Divali for the Hindus; Eid-ul-Fitr for the Muslims; and Good Friday, Easter, Christmas and Corpus Christi for the Christians. Public holidays also mark days with historical significance for particular ethnic and racial groups, such as Spiritual Baptist/Shouter Day, Liberation Day and Emancipation Day for the Afro-Trinidadians and Arrival Day for the Indo-Trinidadians [9].

CONTEMPORARY PRACTICES

In a search of the contemporary local literature, no social or legal procedures have been highlighted of offensive racial behaviors of Indo-Trinidadians other than the Hindus objection to cross-race fertilization and marriage especially to people of African origin. The latter is commonly referred to as 'douglarization'. Religious prescriptions in Hinduism forbid the intermixture of castes while in Islam some Indo-Trinidadians still interpret the Koranic injuction of 'marrying your own kind' concretely. The recent influx of Africans into Islam in Trinidad has resulted in increased douglarization and may be related to the destruction of Hindus religious symbols in mandirs and temples. Protection of dharma is a major tenet of Hinduism and many see their roles as protective against others who are destructive. A number of cases of contemporary occurrences are presented here to capture race relations and behaviors in Trinidad and Tobago.

Case 1: "Ethnic cleansing"

On July 17th, 2009 Dr Tim Gopeesingh, senior lecturer, UWI School of Medicine, medical practitioner for 35 years and a politician, has raised the issue of ethnic cleansing at the Port of Spain General Hospital where he believed senior East Indian doctors were forced to leave the hospital because of "perceived political bias". Dr Gopeesingh in talks with the 20 doctors who reportedly stated part of their frustrations was indeed racial discrimination, has also stated that he had within his possession letters that were written to the Medical Chief of

Staff and Administration airing their grievances over a period of time, which makes his claims evidence based. He also further claims to know of 150 senior East Indian doctors who he astoundingly states " have been forced out of the service" [10]. The Prime Minister of Trinidad and Tobago, members of Parliament of the Peoples' National Movement as well as members of the media has called on Dr Gopeesingh to withdraw his comments because of the strength of the term "ethnic cleansing" as well as their disagreement with his view. Dr Gopeesingh has acknowledged that his comment was probably inappropriate for Parliament, but he continues to stand by his claims and now questions why the Prime Minister, Mr Patrick Manning would suggest this issue is not viable for discussion in the Parliament chamber.

He reinforces his evidence with his definition of ethnic cleansing as it applies to the case in hand. He cites Mr Bell-Fialkoff in his book titled "Ethnic cleansing" as he quotes "Despite its recurrence, ethnic cleansing nonetheless defies easy definition. At one end it is virtually indistinguishable from forced emigration and population exchange while at the other it merges with deportation and genocide. At the most general level, however, ethnic cleansing can be understood as the expulsion of an "undesirable" population from a given territory due to religious or ethnic discrimination, political, strategic or ideological considerations, or a combination of these" [11,12]. This seems to support the idea that the racial discrimination in Trinidad is strongly tied to political control which may inevitably trickle into the rest of the population, their supporters. The PNM which maintains political power may serve as a catalyst in the rejection of ancestral culture and upward mobility of the Indo Trinidadian population.

In response to Dr Gopeesingh, leader of Government Business in Parliament, Colm Imbert has expressed that the member of Parliament has made "racist statements that could provoke racial hatred. He quotes "I can say without any fear of contradiction that the majority of doctors in every hospital in the public health service, with the possible exception of Tobago, are of East Indian descent" [10].

Notably though, the issues of ethnic cleansing has also emerged in Barbados concerning the naturalization and repatriation of Guyanese in Barbados [13].

Case 2: Rejection of radio license to Sanatan Dharma Maha Sabha

In 1999 Satnarayan Maharaj, Secretary General of the Sanatan Dharma Maha Sabha (SDMS) applied to the PNM Government under the leadership of Mr. Patrick Manning for a radio license to broadcast as Radio Jaagriti 102.7 F.M. While awaiting approval for the license the said Government awarded another body Citadel Limited owned by PNM member Louis Lee Sing a grant for their radio station i95.5F.M within 24 hours [14,15]. He alluded to the fact that their allegiance to the PNM party facilitated the approval of their license in favor over that of the Maha Sabha, thus fuelling a discrimination case against the PNM Government. In 2004 the Maha Sabha won its case against the Government of Trinidad and Tobago under the rule of San Fernando High Court Justice Carlton Best stating that the SDMS "was denied equality of treatment before the law by the State" [14, 16].

At the level of the Privy Council the SDMS further won its appeal against the Government of Trinidad and Tobago for the prolonged refusal to award SDMS the radio license. Lord Justice Mance stated in a 19 page judgment that "the exceptional circumstances" of the discrimination placed sole responsibility on then Attorney General of

Trinidad Tobago Justice John Jeremie to ensure that the granting of the license to SDMS, as well as an order to the State to cover all costs incurred by SDMS during the legal proceedings [16].

Case 3: Committees on race relations

The President's Committee for National Self Discovery was established on August 12th, 2003 to examine the race relations within Trinidad and Tobago. President Maxwell Richards felt the committee came at a time where racial tensions were at a high in Trinidad. Their main purpose was not to address racial discrimination directly but act as a vessel for increased knowledge about cultural and historical issues unique to the various ethnic groups, thus indirectly resolving racial tensions and discrimination. The committee hoped to get individuals of Trinidad and Tobago to view themselves more as "Trinbagonians" rather than African, Indians, Chinese, Syrians, Portuguese. The committee was disbanded due to financial and administrative constraints, until they receive proper allowances and an allocated budget.

The Chairman of the Committee Professor Kenneth Ramchand has stated that "The premise of our committee is that a lot of what is going wrong in the country in terms of the ethnic differences, appreciation of the culture, unequal development of the region... all of that were symptoms of the fact that the society did not know itself and what to value about itself...If there is an ethnic problem, we just can't talk ethnic. We have to talk about the whole history of scarcity and inequality in the country and then people would realize."

In an unsettled multicultural society such as ours which begs for equality, the disbandment of such a committee which has required pro bono work from its members and borrowed staff seems like a set back. If the country is willing as Professor Kenneth Ramchand has stated, why then does this not take priority when individuals of society such as Dr Ann Marie Bissessar have acknowledged "racial tension will never go away"[17].

The Prime Minister also heads a Race Relations Committee, but the Committee on the Elimination of Racial Discrimination has rejected the assertion by the government of Trinidad Tobago that there was no racial discrimination in Trinidad and Tobago. Even though the Prime Minister chairs the Ethnic Relations Commission the "political consensus in the process is still in question" [8].

Case 4: Rejection of national awards

Deokinanan Sharma, President of the National Council for Indian Culture (NCIC) is questioning the criteria for selection of recipients for national awards. Former Government Minister Kamaluddin Mohammed and Justice of the Peace Ackbar Khan were both nominees for National Awards 2009 and were both rejected.

Mr. Mohammed was one of the two nominees for the Order of Trinidad and Tobago, the country's highest award given for outstanding national achievement [18]. The recipient of the award was Jizelle Salandy (posthumous) for service in the boxing arena [19]. Mr. Sharma has put forward allegations of "racial discrimination in the selection of awardees" and has further highlighted his personal observation of the "racial imbalance in the list of awardees" over the years. He expressed disbelief at the fact that a man who has served as councilor, minister in several PNM governments, former deputy Prime Minister and President of the World Health Organization (WHO) could have been rejected for such an honor.

The Indo-Trinbago Equality Council (ITEC) has disclosed "documentary evidence" that has been obtained from the Office of the Prime Minister suggestive that Indo Trinbagonians have been continuously underrepresented as recipients of National awards. From an observation of the list of 20 awardees, only three (3) recipients were of East Indian descent representing a mere 15 percent. As ITEC noted "Indians constitute a statistical majority of the national population of over 43 per cent as compared to the 38 per cent for their African counterparts. It is inconceivable how and why Indians only receive a mere ten per cent of the national awards handed out annually. Interestingly, two of the three awards going to Indians were posthumous. It is as if the only good Indians are dead Indians" [20].

Previous to this Sanatan Dharma Maha Sabha (SDMS), Secretary General stated that the SDMS has withdrawn participation in the awards because of the racial imbalance noticed. Due to this year's decisions he has alluded to the fact that the National Award Ceremony should now be known as Patrick Manning's Awards [21]. ITEC has suggested that our Prime Minister by his actions is remaining a "tribal leader and not a true national leader" and has also sated that the awards should be called the "Prime Ministerial awards or the PNM awards" [20].

Present leader of the United National Congress (UNC), Mr. Basdeo Panday has referred to the method of selection of the National Awards Committee as one based on patronage and the need for an overhaul of the system [22]. So too has Deputy Political leader of the Opposition, UNC. Mr Jack Warner has criticized the present Government of Trinidad and Tobago under Prime Minister Patrick Manning in relation to the ethnic imbalance shown at the awards ceremony. He stated "The imbalance was a very unflattering and uncomplimentary recognition of the East Indian Diaspora ... the racial imbalance could have the effect of further marginalizing the Indo-Trinidadian community in a society that was already significantly polarized" [20].

Political leader of the Congress of the People (COP), Winston Dookeran has also stated his disappointment. He revealed "a new approach reflective of the multicultural and multi-ethnic properties of the national state of T&T to be installed for National Awards among other state systems"

Case 5: Absence at Indian Arrival Day Celebrations

The Indo-Trinbago Equality Council (ITEC) has again accused Mr Patrick Manning of racial and ethnic discrimination. This has been suggested in the light of Emancipation day celebrations on August 1, 2009. Mr Devant Maharaj, chairman of ITEC has publicly highlighted his observations from over the years. Mr Patrick Manning, Prime Minister of Trinidad and Tobago has been consistently attending Emancipation Day celebrations but avoiding Indian Arrival Day celebrations. He stated "Mr. Manning is very visible during Emancipation Day celebrations, dressed in appropriate African attire, and endorses Emancipation Day celebrations" he believes that "this sends a positive signal to corporate and state sponsors and redounds to the benefit of the Afro-Trini community....we are however, saddened by the converse absence of PM Manning at Indian Arrival Day celebrations."

Mr Maharaj has cited this instance due to previously expressed concern over the PM's absence from Indian Arrival day celebrations, which was he was made aware of by letter. The recommendation for his attendance was not acknowledged as well another "no show" by the PM at this year's Indian Arrival Day celebrations [23,24].

On July 27, 2009 Mr Maharaj met with the President of Trinidad and Tobago to discuss issues of race relations and "alleged inequality of treatment of Indo Trinidadians" in Trinidad. The topic of concern was complaints since 2008 of unequal hiring practices from the Indian community. Maharaj referred to CEPEP contracts that were granted to 80% Afro Trinidadians in comparison to the proportion granted to Indo Trinidadians. He also highlighted court cases which raised the issue of bypassing Indo Trinidadians for advancements in spite of relevant qualifications and experience in the public sector. He also highlighted to the President of Trinidad and Tobago that even the allocation of finances for cultural celebrations were in unequal proportions. The Government allocated $4.4 million for Emancipation Day celebrations and $800,000 for Indian Arrival Day celebrations.

Mr Maharaj was also adamant about the issue of race relations with the Prime Minister and the rejection of recommendations previously made. Mr. Maharaj felt that if allocations for jobs and finances were unequally distributed he questioned the President about the purpose of the Equal Opportunities Commission (EOC). The result of the meeting seemed to propose a functioning EOC within 90 days of the meeting [25,26].

Case 6: Devant Maharaj vetoed by Prime Minister Patrick Manning

In 2002 Prime Minister Patrick Manning vetoed the promotion of Mr. Devant Maharaj who was the most senior of officers for the position of Deputy Director of the National Lotteries Control Board. He was referred for this position by the independent Statutory Authorities Service Commission [SASC] who subsequently sought the concurrence of the Prime Minister. This act was deemed as very old fashioned and was out of practice for 35 years. As a result Maharaj took the Government of TT to court and the "Prime Ministerial veto was deemed illegal and put to an immediate end" [27].

Case 7: Privy Council rulings on discrimination

The Prime Minister is adamant in replacing the Privy Council by a Caribbean Court of Justice and in instituting a new constitution that will declare him Executive President. The majority of the population seems to be opposed to these views and a referendum has been rejected by the government. It is believed that he will have his own way through political machinations as he garners support from his tribal base.

A number of failed judgments in the local courts have been overturned by the Privy Council and many are indeed suspicious of the motives of replacing the Privy Council with a local Caribbean Court of Justice that will eventually favor the politicians [30].

Public servants Feroza Ramjohn and Ganga-Persad Kisoon have won appeals under the Appeals Court, when the ruling was made that they were both "unfairly treated" by Prime Minister Patrick Manning.

Feroza Ramjohn had been a public servant with the Foreign Affairs Ministry for 38 years and had served in the Permanent Mission to the United Nations, and the New York Consulate. She was deterred from taking up a foreign diplomatic position in London because she was declared a security risk by the Government. On May 27th, 2007 her appointment to leave Trinidad was approved initially, after which Ramjohn made necessary arrangements releasing her apartment, securing her possessions and even undergoing medical and psychological evaluations. Subsequently her appointment was vetoed by the Prime Minster without explanation. Due to allegations of drug trafficking between the London Commission and the Ministry Ramjohn was subsequently accused for 200 missing passports, which the court suggested as "purely circumstantial" [31,32].

On July 8th, 2009, the ruling under the Appeal Court was that the Prime Minister treated Ramjohn "unfairly by blocking her transfer to London, without informing her that she was considered a threat to National Security. The Court resolved that in spite of having "an unblemished record of performance for over 35 years," Ramjohn was never given an opportunity to address the matter.

The other public servant Ganga-Persad Kisoon was also "unfairly treated" when his promotion for Commission of State Lands was vetoed by Prime Minister Patrick Manning. Mr Kisoon had applied for the position on March 2001 being the most senior and qualified individual for the position. The person second in line subsequently got the job without giving reasons to Mr. Kisoon for his unsuitability. Chief Justice Ivor Archie, and Justices Margot Warner and Allan Mendonca, found "Persad-Kisson was treated unfairly when he was bypassed for promotion, and that the PM was wrong to veto his promotion without telling him why."

The main issue that arose out of these two cases was stated succinctly by Justices Margot Warner, Wendell Kangaloo and Alan Mendonca. They wondered whether "the power the Prime Minister has under Section 121(6) of the Constitution attracts the principles of natural justice." The terms natural justice and procedural justice have been used interchangeably, however in administrative law, the concept comprises two well known and fundamental rules of fair procedure- a man not be a judge in his own course and his deference must be heard." Lawyer Anand Ramlogan also stated that "if veto can be used to destroy lives of persons. Veto can be used like a 'carrot on a stick'" [32].

Other public servants such as prisons officers have also been subject to bypassed promotions. In the case of Dougnath Rajkumar, has acted for 14 years but never was appointed in the vacancy of Head of department which was available to him [33]. So too the case of Khimraj Bissessar against the State for discrimination when he tried to aim for the position of Commissioner of Prisons he was ridiculed and told "No Indian will ever see that position." ·

It has been documented that less Indians apply to the nation's protective services. In comparative research the London metropolitan Police service introduced ethnic monitoring programmes to remove divisiveness and guarantee ethnic diversification in the police service. From the research, the data suggested that all White interview panels that rarely targeted minorities with a history of few positions that were held by the minority, possessed traces of institutionalized racism. The researchers felt that "the signal sent to non-whites was that they were neither welcome nor wanted" [34]. So too a largely Afro dominated workforce in the protective services in Trinidad may send the message of "Indians not welcome." It seems as though the gusto by the few Indo Trinidadians who may be present in the system may be stagnated as there may be no room for promotion as presented by the above case. This emphasizes therefore that the reasons behind bypassed promotions and covert appointment without advertisements required by law may well be due to racial discrimination.

DISCUSSION

The seven vignettes presented here is only the tip of the iceberg. On a daily basis people of Indian descent huddled in a predominantly Indian community are denied the basic amenities of light, water, housing, smart cards for receiving groceries, proper roadways for doing their trade and scholastic opportunities at school. On a perennial basis, they are further burdened by flooding of their agricultural fields realizing heavy losses with inadequate compensation by the government. This pattern is not duplicated to the other races that members of the Government belong too. This is institutionalized racism where the entire system is set up to serve one group of people. There is de facto, the widening of the inequality of goods, services and other amenities between the dominant preferred group and the subordinate group.

A simple analysis will demonstrate that racism is practiced in all its form in Trinidad. Historical racism is seen where members of the Government, mostly African, share the national purse mostly to the sector of the population that has in common the same lineage and ancestry. In the near past, Indo-Trinidadians excelled in education and business. This has recently changed where top awards of excellence have curiously been attributed to young Afro-Trinidadian students. Many Afro-Trinidadians are made into contractors, some with little experience and knowledge. There is no doubt that people of African origin have prowess in sports, and excel. These individuals are over compensated and made into role models thereby attributing to them superior qualities to civilize others. A twenty one year old boxer who died under mysterious conditions while driving with another female athlete was awarded the highest award of the land. This process can be described as scientific racism at its best. It seems that the political and administrative power held by Afro dominated PNM Government is being used to their advantage even though Indo Trinidadians dominate positions of economic power [9].

New Racism is alive and well in Trinidad and Tobago. This is defined as the development of politically correct neologisms that serve to minimize the emotive factors while at the same time concealing the true meaning in intellectual jargon. An apt reference is an article written by Selwyn Ryan in the Sunday Express newspaper of August 16, 2009 entitled "A gaseous mixture of racial hyperconsciousness"

Dr. Ryan states that the racial imbalance in favor of Indo-Trinidadians in the medical profession created a lack of trust and discomfort of the Afro Caribbean community. He thinks it is inadvisable that in a society such as Trinidad and Tobago, there should be a health system in which 80-plus percent of the doctors are of one ethnicity. He makes no reference to the Government's Cabinet of Ministers that comprises of less than 10% Indo Trinidadians. Even though a percentage of them may be of 'other' races, the majority of cabinet members are Afro Trinidadians inclusive of the Prime Minister's wife.

On the Sunday Express Newspaper of August 23, 2009, Devant Maharaj, Chairman of ITEC made a call for Selwyn Ryan to defend other ethnic groups also. He pointed out inter alia, the following occurrences:

- The preponderance of Indian doctors is not limited to Trinidad and Tobago. A disproportionate number of Indian doctors are also found in North America and the United Kingdom and other Caribbean countries.
- There is merit in having a policy objective for racial diversity for doctors. Ryan noted that ethnic imbalance is reversed in the nursing profession, but made no call for an increase in the number of Indo-Trinidadian nurses.
- Dr Ryan supports the call by other Black professionals for entry requirements to be varied to allow Afro-Trinidadian students to study medicine, but remains silent about similar calls made by the Indo-Trinidadian community for inclusion in the army, police service, prison service, fire service, coast guard and the public service.
- Dr Ryan has turned a blind eye to the inequitable and biased distribution of state housing to Afro-Trinidadians to the virtual exclusion of Indo-Trinidadians. Such inequitable distribution violates the right to equality of treatment in our constitution.
- Dr Ryan failed to comment on the fact that Indian students' admission into medical school is not based on affirmative action or secret government's scholarship but on academic achievement [28].

Mr Devant Maharaj is of the opinion that a nation's security services ought to reflect the ethnic composition of the society it intends to protect and service. He is concerned about Dr Ryan's voice of reason and temptation to defend one side when at present the hierarchy of the security services and the entire public service is over 90 percent African, with successful legal cases of proven discrimination in favour of the removal, replacement and failed promotion of Indo-Trinidadians. In addition the CEO's and Chairman of all state enterprises and special multi-purpose companies are also 90 percent non-Indians.

It is indeed an interesting phenomenon where Black African professors, now retired, who spent their entire career shackled to the loin cloth of the whiteman now jump in defence of a group that they once loathe. This new racism seems to be immersed in the psychological defenses of denial, reaction formation and undoing. One therefore, cannot expect any degree of objectivity due to their race-related dissonance.

CONCLUSIONS

The views expressed in this chapter reflect contemporaneous behaviors in the Republic of Trinidad and Tobago. The author is aware of the usage of arbitrary inferences and selective abstractions in essays of this nature. To this end, the opinions of established groups and respected individuals were heavily relied upon. Opinions were sought from newspaper articles, semi-structured group discussions, interviews of clients and friends. Further, the author is in close association with family and friends who are strong supporters of the present government. In discussions with them, many who have benefited from the present Government, they seem to be in support of the latter against their own race perceiving it to be politics rather than race. Their identification with the aggressor is exemplified by an Indo-Trinidadian lawyer who has attempted to racially profile the legal profession with a majority of Indians as being racist and anti-government. In addition, past Indo-Trinidadian supporters of the African based government remain aloof, all-knowing and extremely critical and even abusive of their own kind. It could be a case of singing for their supper since they all have prestigious government contracts or positions. It appears as though Indo-Trinidadians are lacking in loyalty to their genus, when compared to Afro Trinidadians.

In 1995-2001 period, a mostly Indo Trinidadian run and supported party, the United National Congress was in power. Despite their drive for equity and accusations by their supporters that they favoured the African population, supporters of the Afro-dominated People's National Movement (PNM) claimed that "they were being sidelined as that government attempted to address the racial imbalance of employment practices. They suggested at that time, that the name of the state-owned oil company, Petrotrin should be changed to 'Petro-Singh' " [10]. Africans are paranoid about the 'Indianization before their very eyes' of the country [29].

Regardless of which Government is in power, the stereotypes associated with whether the party is Indo or Afro-dominated add fuel to the phenomenon of racism, with each race fighting for eventual control. Whether this is a historical or evolutional instinct, the political parties employ means to get their supporters aroused and incensed, tugging at their emotions, a psychological display to secure party votes.

This phenomenon sows the seed for human destructiveness and crime that is now rampant in the twin island states. The simple solution to this complex problem is power sharing, but the sociopathic leaders obsessed with power and control will have none of it.

REFERENCES

[1]   American Psychological Association. Psychological Causes and Consequences of Racism, Racial Discrimination, Xenophobia and Related Intolerances: Intervention of the American Psychological Association Delegation to the World Conference Against racism (WCAR)[Online].2001 [cited 2009 Sept1] Available from: http://www.apa.org/pi/oema/wcarplenary.html.

[2]   Prime Minister Public Address. Harris Promenade 2009 Jul 20.

[3]   Jones CP. Going public, levels of racism: A theoretic framework and a gardener's tale. Am J Public Health 2000;90(8):1212-5.

[4]   Oxford Online dictionary [Online]. 2009 [cited 2009 Sept 1]. Available from: http://www.askoxford.com/results/?view=dev_dict&field-12668446=racism&branch=13842570&textsearchtype=exact&sortorder=score %2Cname

[5]   Merriam-Webster online dictionary. [Online] 2009 [cited 2009 Sept 1]. Available from: http://www.merriam-webster.com/dictionary/racism

[6]   Agostini C. Racism in Trinidad: Using the approach of process oriented psychology. [Online] 2000 [cited 2009 Sept 1] Available from: http://www.processwork.org/Finalprojects/Agostini-RacisimTrinidad.pdf

[7] Social Work with People of Colour, Module 17. [Online] 2009 [cited 2009 Sept 1] Available from: http://www.socialpolicy.ca/52100/m17/m17-t2.stm.

[8] Mr Doudou Diène Racism, Racial Discrimination, Xenophobia and all forms of Racism. Report submitted by, Special Rapporteur on contemporary forms of racism, racial discrimination, xenophobia and related intolerance. Economic and Social Council Commission on Human Rights, 16th Session. [Online] 2004 [cited 2009 Sept 4] Available from:http:// daccessdds.un.org/doc/ UNDOC/GEN/ G04/101/24/ PDF/ G0410124.pdf?OpenElement

[9] Immigration and Refugees Board of Canada. Trinidad and Tobago: New Government policies regarding racial discrimination and tension between the Afro Trinidad and Indo Trinidadian communities; levels of ethnic or racial strife currently being experienced; whether protection is available in cases of racially motivated attacks (January 2003-November 2005), 14 December 2005, TTO100702.E [Online] 2005. [cited 2009, Sept 4]. Available from: http://www2.irb-cisr.gc.ca/en/research/rir/?action=record.viewrec& gotorec=449746

[10] Richards P. Ethnic cleansing, Trinidad Style. [Online] 2009 [cited 2009 Sept 4].Availablefrom:fromCaribbeanNationalWeekly.http://www.cnweeklynews.com/conte nt/view/4123/66/1/1/lang,en/

[11] The Trinidad Guardian. Gopeesingh defends his statements-My duty to speak out. [Online] 2009 [Cited 2009 Sept 2] Available from: http://guardian.co.tt/ taxonomy/term/5629/all.

[12] Cleansing Ethnicity. [Online] 2009 [cited 2009 Sept 2]. Available from: http:// www.wikio.com/themes/Tim+Gopeesingh

[13] Ethnic Cleansing Remark was in relation to editorial not Barbados – Sir Shridath. Stabroek News. [Online] 2009 [cited 2009 Sept 7]. Available from: http://www.stabroeknews.com/2009/stories/08/26/ethnic-cleansing-remark-was-in-relation-to-editorial-not-barbados-%E2%80%93sir-shridath/

[14] Lewis J. Universal Journal, The association of Young Journalists and Writers. Discrimination and Differential Treatment are not the same. [Online] 2009 [cited 2009 Sept 3. Available from: http://www.ayjw.org/articles.php?id=324531.

[15] Reasons to Fire the Prime Minister. [Online] 2009 [cited 2009 Sept 3] Available from:Facebookhttp://hiin.facebook.com/topic.php?uid=30232595092&topic=8957

[16] Human Rights Abuses under the watch of the Manning Administration. [Online] 2009 [cited 2009 Sept 3]. Available from: Trin, Surviving life in Trinidad and Tobago http://trin.typepad.com/main/diversity-awareness.html.

[17] Connelly C. Racial tensions will never go away. [Online] 2009 [cited Sept 3 2009]. Available from: Trinidad and Tobago Newsday http://www.newsday.co.tt/sunday_special_report/0,105212.html.

[18] Trinidad and Tobago hosts National Awards on August 31st, 2009. [Online] 2009 [cited 2009 Sept 3]. Available from: http://news.bn.gs/article.php?story=20090710113516924

[19] National Award Recipients. [Online] 2009 [cited 2009 Sept 3]. Available from: the Trinidad and Tobago Express, http://www.trinidadexpress.com/index.pl/ article_news?id=161525912

[20] Indians omitted again from National Awards. Commentary, Centre Stage. [Online] 2009 [cited 2009 Sept 3] Available from: the Trinidad Guardian.

[21] Lord R. NCIC questions Kamal's rejection. The Trinidad Guardian pA3. [Online] 2009 [cited 2009 Sept 4]. Available from:http://guardian.co.tt/commentary/letters/2009/09/02/indians-omitted-again-national-awards.

[22] Indian Diaspora upset over Trinidad and Tobago awards. [Online] 2009 [cited Sept 3 2009]. Available from: Thaindian News http://www.thaindian.com/newsportal/world-news/indian-diaspora-upset-over-trinidad-and-tobago-awards_100241128.html.

[23] Group Accuses Manning of Discrimination . [Online] 2009 [cited 2009 Sept 3]. Available from: i95.5 News. http://www.i955fm.com/News.aspx?id=7497

[24] Grant L. Waiting in vain for nompumelelo ntumi. [Online] 2009 [cited 2009 Sept 3]. Available from: The Trinidad Guardian http://guardian.co.tt/commentary/columnist/2009/08/09/waiting-vain-nompumelelo-ntumi.

[25] Dowlat R. President to meet Indo Equality Council. [Online] 2009 [cited 2009 Sept 3]. Available from: Trinidad Newsday http://www.newsday.co.tt/ news/ 0,104470.html

[26] Max talk race relations. [Online] 2009 [cited 2009 Sept 3]. Available from: Trinidad Newsday http://www.newsday.co.tt/politics/0,104526.html

[27] Maharaj D. [Online] 2009 [cited 2009 Sept 3]. Available from: Wikipedia http://en.wikipedia.org/wiki/Devant_Maharaj.

[28] Maharaj D. Defend other ethnic groups too, Letter of the day.Trinidad and Tobago Express 2009:13.

[29] Cudjoe S. The indianization of society. [Online] 2009 [cited 2009 Sept 4]. Available from:Trinicenter.com,http://www.trinicenter.com/Cudjoe/2004/2601.htm.

[30] Shah R. Executive President, yes…elected by the people. [Online] 2009 [cited2009Sept9].Available from: http:// www.trinidadexpress.com/ index.pl/ article_opinion?id=161521634.

[31] James O. Public Servants win their appeals after "unfairly treated" by PM. Trinidad Newsday. [Online] 2009 [cited 2009 Sept 9]. Available from: http://www.newsday.co.tt/news/0,103443.html

[32] Renne D. Double blow for PM- Public Servants win appeals. Trinidad Newsday [Online] 2009 [cited 2009 Sept 9]. Available from: http://www.trinidadexpress.com/index.pl/article?id=161502114

[33] Ramlogan A. Manipulating Promotions. The Freedom Chambers. [Online] 2009 [cited 2009 Sept 9]. Available from: http://www.anandramlogan.com/node/401

[34] Ramlogan A. Exposing Discrimination. The Freedom Chambers. [Online] 2009 [cited 2009 Sept 9]. Available from: http://www.anandramlogan.com/node/376

In: Social and Cultural Psychiatry Experience from the... ISBN: 978-1-61668-506-5
Editor: Hari D. Maharajh and Joav Merrick © 2010 Nova Science Publishers, Inc.

Chapter 8

THE EFFECTS OF MULTICULTURALISM AND MULTI-ETHNICITY IN GROUP DYNAMICS IN A CARIBBEAN SETTING

Hari D. Maharajh

The ethnic and racial composition of the Caribbean is a convergence of many cultures that were brought together through slavery and indentureship. The region holds similar characteristics among the islands because of similar history and subsequent settling of migrants. This heterogeneous lifestyle has produced new cultures distinct to the Caribbean which to some extent acts unifying forces among the migrant population. The reality is the social, economic and political structures are still realms which serve as opportunities for dominance and power, segregating rather than integrating. Stereotypical views of each race are used as a means to an end. Africans dominate the political arena and are seen as discriminating against the Indian race, and Indians with the financial advantage are easy targets for criminal attack. Women of the two main races are still characterized by stereotypical characteristics of their history. African women are seen as 'strong black women' and Indian women as 'passive and docile' independent of circumstance. These self appraisals and natural competitiveness among individuals of a country or group highlights the negative aspect of multicultural societies. The Caribbean today remains a hot pot of multiculturalism rather than a melting pot.

INTRODUCTION

Multiculturalism and multi-ethnicity clearly has an effect on the dynamics in Caribbean group settings due to the clashes in customs, norms, and practices among different races. In the Caribbean, the psychological effects of almost four hundred years of slavery and over one and a half century of East Indian indentureship have impacted on the self esteem and identity of both the African and East Indian groups. This in turn has manifested itself in a struggle for power, authority, respect and superiority. Culture is defined as the belief systems and value orientations that influence customs, norms, practices and social institutions, including psychological processes. Race is the category to which others assign individuals on the basis of physical characteristics, such as skin colour or hair type, and the stereotypes made as a result.

Ethnicity is the acceptance of group mores and practices of one's culture of origin and the concomitant sense of belonging. Multiculturalism includes a broad scope of dimensions of race, ethnicity, language, sexual orientation, gender, age, disability, class status, education, religious/spiritual orientation and other cultural dimensions. Historically, the African and East Indian immigrants who came to the Caribbean brought with them a gamut of disparate cultural properties, which today, still influence the varied differences in culture which dictate language, religion, social attitudes, dress, cuisine and musical preference.

Culture behaviors can be defined as an adaptive response occurring in organized social groups where lifestyles, sentiments and interactions have been transgenerationally transmitted. These behaviors are often associated with compensatory process of rationalization and are sometimes conceptionalised in the context of native humour [1].These cultural differences continue to influence the way in which Caribbean people relate to each other in their social environment. According to Hickling and Hutchinson, culture serves the sole purpose of defining a group identity, which in effect facilitates a sense of belonging and identity [2].

In a multiethnic group setting, personality conflicts often arise among members of different ethnic groups. This may be due to the need of individuals to assert themselves and identify with a particular group in their social setting. These factors ultimately create disharmony, conflict and racial tension among the various ethnic groups. Each culture brings with it, its own often disparate perception of power, authority, interpersonal boundaries and family dynamics [3].

Afro-Caribbean people have traditionally been taught to be strong, independent, assertive and outspoken, whereas their East Indian counterparts have been raised in contrast to be passive, respectful, obedient, and conscientious. This is explained in studies of the Caribbean family structure with regards to the descendants of African slaves refer to a matricentric African family based upon a mother and her daughters, one in which the women exhibit a high degree of independence [4,5]. Reddock argues however that Caribbean women are "reluctant matriarchs' and are strong and independent out of necessity [6].

Certain stereotypes still exist today among the races. African people are stereotyped as loud, aggressive, boisterous and confrontational. Some have described a "negro personality" which had "developed due to segregation and discrimination and was believed to be characterized by low self esteem, apathy, fears of relatedness, mistrust, problems with the control of aggression and orientation to pleasure in the moment [7-9]. East Indians, particularly women, are seen as docile, submissive, and clandestine. In many traditional East Indian families, women are expected to be subservient to their husbands. Indian men are typically characterized as being domineering, possessive and over-protective with their wives and children – particularly their daughters.

Phillips and McCaskill [10] asserted that all women of color were subjected to the same oppression and this transcends social background. The social context of women of both African and Indian decent in the region has not been vastly different. According to Green [11] both groups were subjected to enormous hardship and subjugation both during and after slavery and indentureship. In African families, the grandmother is seen as the head of the household, knitting together the extended family system. She plays the role of nurturer and protector. In Indian families, the father is seen as the authority figure. He usually plays the role of breadwinner, rule-maker, and discipliner. Members of the immediate family share a very close bond where family unity and loyalty are held sacred. Psychologically they perform with a collective unconscious approach. There is an unofficial code in East Indian families that family business must be kept private.

Research has demonstrated that "persons from some Asian cultures are likely to deal with problems by internalizing them to avoid loss of face" [12,13]. This is not altogether a negative factor since the shared unconsciousness of internalization leads to forced treatment of individuals in terms of illnesses. However, communication and authority in a patriarchal family flows from top to bottom [14]. Children in East Indian families grow up with paternal authority figures who remain a strong influence in their lives; they are rewarded for obedience and conformity [14]. On the other hand, according to the findings of Brice-Baker [15] persons of Caribbean-African ancestry, tend to prefer to seek help from family, friends and churches. They have no guilt in receiving handouts from non- governmental or governmental agencies. In Trinidad and Tobago, an African government has maintained power in investing into handouts to its mostly African supporters, thereby creating a dependency syndrome among this group. These attitudes will be reflected in communication patterns during engagement. These cultural differences play a critical role in how people interact with one another in their own ethnic group and how both races interact with each other.

Within Trinidad and Tobago, members from a variety of racial, social and cultural groups interact with each other on a daily basis. From an early age, children are exposed to people of different ethnic, cultural and religious backgrounds in their schools, neighborhoods and community. Children are less apt to categorize, judge or discriminate on the basis of race, religion or cultural differences. As they grow older though, and form themselves into social groups, their level of consciousness regarding these differences between themselves and others become more apparent. This too is shaped by the attitudes of our parents in respect to other races. Children are prone to adopt the same beliefs, attitudes and moral judgments of their parents. Engaging a person from a different culture requires considerable sensitivity, openness to difference, willingness to acquire knowledge of other cultures and understanding of self [16].

If children are taught to stigmatize and discriminate against people on the basis of race, skin color, socio-economic status, religion or gender, this will ultimately affect how they interact with others of different ethnic and cultural groups. These personal perspectives and ideals, which are shaped from an early age, filter into our schools, communities, work places and Ministries, which makes it more difficult to co-exist, understand and appreciate the unique differences in our cultures, respect the viewpoints of others and recognize the negative and positive attributions and contributions made by different ethnic and cultural groups. In chapter 9 on Carnival mentality, the early induction of children to calypso that breathes racist comments have had an effect on the formation of early attitudes and later personalities. As Jung [17] suggested, the individual is impacted by not only the content of their individual unconscious, that is their personal experiences stored in the unconscious, but also by the collective unconscious which stores information channeled through the home, television and wider society. The individual's social setting also plays an integral role in how they interact with people of other social, cultural and ethnic groups. Misconceptions and stereotypes about people are developed through negative personal experiences or lack of interaction with people of different cultures.

These unconscious factors impact on the way we relate to each other in everyday life. According to Salvendy [7] people are perceived as a representation of their ethnic group. But we must be carefully mindful about generalizing people of one ethnic group because each individual has a unique set of characteristics which shape his personality and dictate his behavior. Cultural norms are adopted at birth and passed on from one generation to the other. According to Anung San Suu Kyi [18], it is precisely because of the cultural diversity of the world that it is necessary for different nations and people to agree on those basic human values which will act as a unifying factor. The transition from 'pepper pot' to 'melting pot' in the Caribbean is incomplete as groups are stuck in perpetuity in the stage of storming, each tenaciously holding on to their views which are unshakeable.

While the Caribbean is inhabited by other ethnic groups such as the Spanish, British, Chinese, French, and Japanese, there seems to be a perpetual conflict between those of African and East Indian descent. In a cosmopolitan country like Trinidad and Tobago where these two races comprise the large majority in 'our melting pot of race', culture and ethnicity it appears that discrimination only exists among them, with the other groups enjoying all the benefits of society. The culture of Trinidad is unique from other cultures in the Caribbean region, with Trinidad comprising the most versatile composition of people. The cultural differences which exist between the different ethnic groups add color, flavor and diversity to our land. The differences extend from the way we dress to the foods we eat.

Both verbal and non-verbal patterns often reflect cultural norms related to racial and ethnic group membership [19].There are however many similarities among the ethnic groups, in the way we speak, the dialect we use, and the celebration of Carnival, which forms part of our heritage. According to 'Culture and Behavior' in chapter 6 'liming,' which is a behaviour we have in common in Trinidad, is an activity that one would not hesitate to indulge in proudly.

Lack of punctuality also seems to be a common trait in Trinidadians. We have also adopted the West Indian style of giving and receiving 'picong'. It is believed that this type of 'culturally- determined confrontational humour' can serve to aid others to become aware of emotions with a view to addressing such through cognitive-behavioral means [20]. Compared to other countries in the Caribbean, there is a high level of tolerance for the racial diversity which exists in Trinidad. This is evident by the quantity of holidays in the year with the observance of all religious celebrations, such as Easter, Divali, Eid, Baptist Liberation Day, and Christmas, and appreciation for various types of music such as Soca, Chutney and Parang – which all express our multi-cultural society. In the Caribbean mixed race persons and other 'off white people' enjoy a social status and economic status disproportionate to their numbers and national contribution. Many operate outside the rule of law. This is particularly true of light skinned mixed people with Caucasian, Spanish, French, Chinese or Japanese roots. Power and wealth are also factors which contribute to society's perception of superiority. There is a great disparity between the rich and the poor with the former commanding more respect based on social status rather than race.

There are also sub-cultures among our cultures, such as in the Hindu, Muslim and Christian societies. For instance, there are different "Castes" in the Hindu religion which is dictated by one's family tree and the family name they consequently bear. However, there seems to be constant struggle for political and socio-economic control between the African and Indian races with the Africans dominating the political arena and the Indians being at a financial advantage in owning their own homes and businesses. While there exists, a high level of racial tolerance in Trinidad, there are varying levels of ethnic or racial bias existing in our small population. For this reason, the topic of race and ethnicity remains taboo. Discussions on the topic may evoke more emotion in Africans. According to Salvendy [7] talk about race and ethnicity can arouse powerful feelings related to the problems of difference, wishes for recognition and desires for domination and control. The situation is further compounded by politicians who use race as propaganda to rally support and by individuals and groups who propagate race superiority.

Africans in Trinidad and Tobago seem to be more rooted in their African ancestry and more sensitive to the issue of race, quick to take offence whenever they feel their racial pride has been trampled on. It is paradoxical that when an African talks about race, it is viewed as black consciousness but when an Indian makes the same statement, it is viewed as racism. Their hypersensitivity in relation to this topic is perhaps rooted in slavery. The kinship or brotherhood that exists between people of African decent seems to transcend blood relations. When one individual in their ethnic group is verbally attacked, the entire race feels victimized. They will also band together and support one another in all endeavors, such as political gain, for the sake of that brotherhood. The multi-dimensional effects of slavery have left psychological scars in people of African descent. To some extent, it has created a syndrome of mental slavery, particularly in poverty stricken areas where crime seems to supersede the pursuit of an education. Those born into stigmatized and disadvantaged communities develop a poor sense of image and often use their circumstances or history as excuses for getting ahead. This has given rise to feelings of jealousy and resentment in some Africans who have been accused of victimizing the Indian community.

This hostility is fueled by the socio-economic disparity between both races. Some Africans in Trinidad believe that Indians were given an advantage with the acquisition of land following indentureship without the understanding that they sacrificed their return passage for land. Yet everyone is afforded with the same opportunity to receive a primary, secondary and tertiary education. Indians on the other hand feel politically disadvantaged, having only been able to secure office for one term following the country's Independence in 1962.

Even today, with a black Prime Minister being in power, Indians still complain of discrimination with regards to Government employment and housing. Indian indentureship, although it was ameliorated as compared to slavery, has also impacted on the Indian community. The restrictions placed on the laborers, such as the right to practice their religion, speak in their language, co-habit and congregate freely, were similar to that endured by the Africans during slavery. The humiliation suffered as a result of indentureship, has also impacted negatively on the identity of Indians in the Caribbean. This has perhaps created a greater level of competitiveness between Africans and Indians in this region. The self-perception theory addresses the issue of how individuals make self appraisals, that is, how people evaluate their behavior given the particular social context [21].

The Self-Perception theory states that people make appraisals of their behavior on the same basis as the appraisals they make of others' behavior. The early period of indentureship created a demographic imbalance in relation to gender with men outnumbering women and disrupting family life. Caribbean and North American authors of the African Diaspora have identified the multi-dimensional effects of slavery referred to a dual consciousness or identity which can be observed in post-emancipated individuals of African decent [22]. The basic assumption of post-emancipated Africans was the belief that to be civilized was equivalent to being European [23].

This loss of African cultural identity can best be illustrated from the continued sale of skin bleaching creams in the Caribbean. It has been illustrated that there is still a negative perception of Blackness among black people and also, that it is believed that acceptance can result from the attainment of Whiteness [23]. Historians have documented the strained relationship between Africans and Indians during the colonial period [24]. Some of the factors which have been attributed to this phenomenon are suspiciousness, social segregation, misconceptions and stereotypes. Both races, however, have suffered similar hardships and have been the objects of oppression, segregation, and discrimination. Both the Indians and Africans have struggled to preserve their religion, culture and heritage. The various religious groups have fought for the right to set up their own schools and places of worship i.e. churches, mosques and temples. The certification of marriages under the Hindu and Muslim faiths took decades to be recognized. The Baptist religion was also condemned and criticized by the larger society. The Caribbean has come a long way with the tolerance of all religions and races. For instance, inter-racial marriages have now become customary with a large portion of the population falling into the "mixed category".

In a paper entitled, "Alice in wonderland: The multiracial small group in clinical practice" by the present author [25], he depicts multiculturalism as a tea party with Alice in Wonderland. As one remembers in the childhood story, Alice went to a tea party with the March hare, the Mad Hatter and the Door Mouse, on returning, she commented, 'this is the stupidest tea party I have ever been to, I shall never go there again!' Multiculturalism is no different.

CONCLUSION

Multiculturalism as it relates to all levels of society from the individual, the family, the school, the religious institutions, and the community gives credence to the sensitivity and acceptance of Caribbean people to integrate many cultures into their life. But dominancy and competiveness seem to be pervasive, and an underlying silent accomplishment that is inherent among the members of a multicultural society. A blending of cultures seem to be a distant dream. Societies must first learn to appreciate and accept the values, beliefs and practices of each other without prejudice, before attempts are made for fusion and cross over.

REFERENCES

[1] Maharajh HD, Ali A. Recognition of cultural behaviors in Trinidad and Tobago. Internet J Third World Med 2004;3:1.

[2] Hickling FW, Hutchinson G. Post-colonialism and mental health. Understanding the roast breadfruit. Psychiatr Bull 2000;24:94-5.

[3] Tsui P, Schultz G. Ethnic factors in group process : Cultural dynamics in multi-ethnic groups. Am J Othopsychiatry 1988;58:1142.

[4] Herskovits MJ, Herskovits FS. The myth of the Negro past. New York: Harper Brothers, 1947.

[5]   Smith MG. Pluralism ands social stratification. In: Ryan S, ed. Social and occupational stratification in contemporary Trinidad and Tobago. Trinidad: Inst Soc Econ Res, Univ West Indies, 1991:3-35.

[6]   Reddock R. Caribbean sociology: Introductory readings. Jamaica: Ian Randle, 2001.

[7]   Salvendy J. Ethnocultural considerations in group psychotherapy. Int J Group Psychother 1999;49(4):429-64.

[8]   Kardiner A, Oversy L. The mark of oppression. New York: World, 1951.

[9]   9. Karon AB. The negro personality: A rigorous investigation of the effects of culture. New York: Springer, 1958.

[10]   Phillips L, McCaskill B. Who's schooling who? Black women and the bringing of everyday into academe, or why we started the womanist. Signs 1995;20:1007-18.

[11]   Green W. British slave emancipation: The sugar colonies and the great experiment 1830–1865. Oxford: Oxford Univ Press, 1991.

[12]   LeResche D. Comparison of the American mediation process with a Korean-American harmony restoration process [Special issue]. Mediation Quart 1992;9:323–339.

[13]   Tamura T, Lau A. Connectedness versus separateness: Applicability of family therapy to Japanese families. Fam Process 1992;31(4): 319-40.

[14]   Sharpe J. Mental health issues and family socialization in the Caribbean. In: Roopnarine JL, Brown J, eds. Caribbean families: Diversity among ethnic groups. Greenwich, CT: Ablex Publ, 1997: 259–74.

[15]   Brice-Baker J. Jamaican families. In: Giordano J, McGoldrick M, Pearce JK, eds. Ethnicity and family therapy, 2nd ed. New York: Guilford Press, 1996:85-96.

[16]   Dungee-Anderson D, Beckett JO. A process model for multicultural social work practice: Families in society. J Contemp Hum Serv 1995;76:459-68.

[17]   Jung CG. Psyche and symbol. Princeton, NJ: Princeton Univ Press, 1991.

[18]   Kyi ASS. Nobel Peace Prize Winner Speech, 1991.

[19]   Carter R. Language and creativity: The art of common talk. London: Routledge, 2004.

[20]   Maharajh HD, Hutchinson G. Tabanca in Trinidad and Tobago: Myth, mirth or mood disorder. Caribb Med J 1999;61(1):21-4.

[21]   Bem, DJ. Self-perception theory. In: Berkowitz L, ed. Advances in experimental social psychology. New York: Acad Press, 1972:1-62.

[22]   Gilroy P. The Black Atlantic: Modernity and double-consciousness. London: Verso, 1993

[23]   Hickling FW, Hutchinson G. Post-colonialism and mental health: Understanding the roast breadfruit. Psychiatr Bull 2000;24:94-5.

[24]   Brereton, B. Race relations in colonial Trinidad 1870-1900. Cambridge: Cambridge Univ Press, 1979.

[25]   Maharajh HD. Alice in Wonderland: The multiracial small group in clinical practice. Int J Soc Psychiatry 1984;30(1-2):84-8.

In: Social and Cultural Psychiatry Experience from the... ISBN: 978-1-61668-506-5
Editor: Hari D. Maharajh and Joav Merrick © 2010 Nova Science Publishers, Inc.

Chapter 9

DO TRINIDADIANS HAVE A CARNIVAL MENTALITY?

Hari D. Maharajh

Stereotyping characteristics of island people are well known throughout the Caribbean region. These labels often narrated in everyday humor have some hidden truths. In Jamaica, for example there is the belief that the population is homophobic. In Barbados, there is a perception that the native population is xenophobic, with a dislike for everyone not Bajan, with an exception for those with a lighter shade of black. In Trinidad, the population has been dubbed as having a carnival mentality where individuals have a very slack, laid back or "don't give a damn" attitude towards work. It is thought that this non-stop party mentality is continuous throughout the year with little commitment to hard work or industry.

INTRODUCTION

"It is black Trinidadians who expound most readily upon the theme of how their 'carnival mentality' is a barrier to the progress of their race, and how the other races are doing well because they are not given to spreading joy, etc...But the attitude of the Afro-Trinidadian to the life-styles of the other groups is ambivalent: it wavers between admiration and mild scorn for those who seem to spend so much time working and saving up that they miss out on living" [1].

According to Merle Hodge, the Carnival mentality seems to pertain more to the African population in Trinidad who sees it more as a barrier to their own personal progress and a source of ambivalence towards the contending Indians. There is much debate on the carnival mentality both at home and abroad where Trinidadians are caricatured as a happy go-lucky people, drinking rum and sleeping under coconut trees on the tropical beaches. To some, having a carnival mentality is laudable, since it is the basis of generating creativity, while to others it is derogatory since it depicts the population as being lazy, non-thinking and non-progressive (see table 1).

Table 1. Characteristics of carnival mentality

Characteristics	%
1. Non-stop party mentality/ continuous fun in the sun/ "extreme liming"	51.4
2. Take part in every carnival activity or event/ time to break away and get on bad, immoral vulgar activities	21.0
3. Attitude to work very laid back, slack	19.0
4. Mindlessness, not thinking of consequences/ indulging in alcohol, Promiscuity	3.0
5. Time to free up	3.2
6. When you hear soca, nothing could stop you from dancing	0.9
7. Having attributes of carnival e.g. cricket or football match	0.9
8. Too much parties in calendar	0.5

It is now accepted in many quarters, that the people of Trinidad and Tobago are stigmatized as having a carnival mentality. This alludes to a non-stop party mentality that is practiced throughout the year with little commitment to hard work or industry. This label extends throughout the year, outside the carnival season, and appears to be pervasive in the population's everyday lifestyle.

The Carnival mentality is seen to have filtered into the workplace where individuals have a very slack, laid back or "don't give a damn" attitude towards work. The energy and vitality seen towards carnival is not displayed in the workplace. Carnival is viewed as "a time to free up, a time to break away and get on bad." It is associated with a mentality of gay abandonment of the social structures of work, family life, education and law. It is a time where people behave in ways that they would consider immoral and wrong outside the season, like indulging in alcohol, getting involved in promiscuous activities without thinking of the consequences. In Trinidad and Tobago there is a local need of conduct for the celebration of carnival with stricter enforcement of the law.

CARNIVAL BEHAVIOR

Wining, a dance form with suggestive sexual movements, is most prominent at the carnival season, but is also found at other times of the year. This contemporary rhythmic gyration of the waist is dominated by women who have the prerogative to choose the man she wants to wine with. Frotteurism and other paraphilias are common occurrences during carnival but are generally ignored. It is culturally accepted for someone to rub against another person while wining (dancing) to the tempo of the rhythmic and lyrically suggestive calypso or 'soca' music. Touching and holding are commonplace and during these two days of street festivity the law turns a blind eye to minor offences and minor crimes. Non-consenting persons do not complain, since there is no redress. The celebration is perceived as being cathartic and the stipulated behavior as part of the process of "freeing up".

Alcohol abuse is also co-morbid with paraphilias [2] and is related to a wide variety of crimes. The acceptance of sexual behaviors within a given culture varies. It is culturally accepted that the wining behavior during carnival season and possibly preferential rapes are associated with the use of excessive alcohol during this celebrations. Close quarter dancing is a national pastime and that induces eroticism and sets the basis for paraphilias.

Frotteurism is not unique to Trinidad and Tobago; it exists in crowded buses, trains, pubs and festivals in other parts of the world as well. It differs, however, in that in Trinidad and Tobago it is linked to the country's most popular national celebration where there is a disruption of normal human male courtship behaviors. These sexual behaviors during carnival celebrations are unique to groups and communities and are influenced by historical, cultural, biological, individual and interpersonal factors.

In Jamaica, sociologist Blossom White, also cited that Carnival contributes to moral decline in Jamaica. She does not subscribe to the view that Carnival is an influential factor in social integration and an escape from tension and the negative impact of social prejudices [3].

Culture-bound syndromes have been described as culturally determined abnormal behavior patterns that are specific to a particular culture or geographical region. The behaviors express core cultural themes and have a wide range of symbolic meanings – social, moral and psychological [4]. Culture-bound syndromes are not exclusively linked to a particular culture but are rather related to a prominent cultural emphasis or to a specific social stress situation [5,6].

ORIGIN OF CARNIVAL

Carnival in Trinidad and Tobago is celebrated with a special cultural emphasis. It is not observed in the European tradition or the pagan cultural patterns adopted by the early Christian churches. The latter copied the Roman tradition of celebrating the onset of spring and ancient Germanic fertility rites as a way to usher in the Easter fast. Similarly, carnival in Trinidad was adopted by the French Creole aristocrats and colonial masters and welcomed by the Roman Catholic Church as a pre-lenten festival of a disguise ball for the ruling class. Later, the 'cannes brulees' (cane burning) festival of the freed slaves with stick-fighting, drinking and street-dancing normally held in August was merged with the pre-lent festival.

Following the emancipation of slavery in 1838, the Africans now free from bondage began mimicking and adopting the attitude of the French aristocrats and colonial masters at carnival time by means of a crude form of street theatre. They dressed in extravagant costumes, reminiscent of their masters and spoke an incomprehensible, broken french (Patois) with songs 'chantuelles' parodying the social issues of the day in a critical manner. The modern day calypso, an integral part of carnival has replaced the chantuelles and is retained as a bigoted source of social and political commentary directed to specific groups.

CONTEMPORARY PRACTICE

Today, carnival in Trinidad is a season that spans from Christmas to Ash Wednesday, all-inclusive with steelband yards and calypso tents, mas camps, live music and fetes, calypso and soca. On Sunday night there is the Dimanche Gras show where a calypso monarch, king and queen of carnival are crowned. On carnival Monday morning starting at 2:00 am there is early 'mas' known as 'J'ouvert' a corruption of the French 'jouvert' meaning 'open day'. The crowning glory of Carnival in Trinidad and Tobago is the two days before lent which ushers in the fasting period before Easter. During this period, there is 'pretty mas' with a riot of colours, sounds and lewd dancing.

The cultural emphasis is partly obscene, offensive and degrading to many, but this pales into insignificance on a background of the creativity of mask- makers, the imagination and skills of revelers, calypsonians and musicians and the catharsis of two days of revelry on the streets. Carnival has grown to the most popular national celebration, all inclusive with some objections from religious groups.

Commentators have argued that the behavior depicted at carnival is pervasive throughout the year and have referred to the population of Trinidad and Tobago as having a carnival mentality. According to Liverpool [7] " in speaking of Trinidadians as having a carnival mentality, they seek to degrade our people, for they seek to say that to possess such a mentality is to live for today, to play 'mas', to have a good time, and then to beg on Ash Wednesday morning. In other words, it is to live aimlessly."

The urgency of carnival to many is well portrayed in Lovelace's novel "The dragon can't dance" in the characterization of Aldrick Prospect. He would get up at midday from sleep, not knowing where his next meal was coming from, "his brain working in the same smooth unhurried nonchalance with which he moved his feet, a slow cruising crawl which he quickened only at carnival." [8].

Individuals have commented on the benefits of a carnival mentality, Ferraz [9] urges that he wants his children to have a carnival mentality since it will expose them to the brotherhood of men. This will enable them to exhibit their expressions by the fusion of culture and technology. They will learn about human resourcefulness – the art of street theatre, mas, dance and music and will learn to act humanly, appreciate and respect each other.

CRIME AND CARNIVAL

This is a far cry from the reality of carnival, which in 2002 was riddled with lawlessness and terrorism, with participants jumping on people's car for the sole purpose of destruction. This was mostly directed against women [10]. Over 50 people were arrested in one day in Port of Spain for having in their possession a variety of prohibited weapons including cutlasses and three murders were directly related to carnival activities [11].

Over the last few years, there has been an upsurge in criminal activity in Trinidad and Tobago including youth gang violence. Year after year, the Carnival season is marred with rape, brutality and murder. In 2007, the US Department of State issued travel advisories for its citizens on its Website, advising them to take special precautions when visiting Trinidad, following a spate of crime in the country. It was noted that the criminal activity in Trinidad and Tobago sees a major peak during Holiday periods, especially Christmas and Carnival. Incidents of violent crime were said to have been steadily on the rise on both islands. Violent crimes, including assault, kidnapping for ransom, sexual assault and murder, have involved foreign residents and tourists, including US citizens.

American citizens traveling to or residing in Trinidad and Tobago were urged to take responsibility for their own personal security, while on the island. Visitors were advised to exercise caution and good judgment particularly in areas such as Laventille, Morvant, Sea Lots, South Belmont, scenic rest stops and the Queen's Park Savannah [12].

"While non-violent demonstrations occur on occasion, widespread civil disorder is not typical. The downtown area of Port of Spain experienced four bombings in 2005. While no similar incidents have occurred since that time, the perpetrator(s) have not been arrested and their identities and motive remain unknown. Americans living or visiting Port of Spain are advised to exercise caution, especially in crowded urban areas". Visitors to Trinidad and Tobago were also advised to be cautious when visiting isolated beaches or scenic overlooks, where robberies can occur. In particular, they were advised against visiting the Ft George scenic overlook in Port of Spain because of lack of security and a number of recent armed robberies at that site. "In some cases, robberies of Americans have turned violent and resulted in injuries after the victim resisted handing over valuables. Tourists at La Brea Pitch Lake in South Trinidad were targets of criminals in 2004 and 2005. In Tobago, the media have reported an increase in the incidence of violent crimes and in 2009, there has been a significant increase of murders in Crusoe's tranquil Tobago. There have been reports of home invasions in the Mt. Irvine area, and robberies occurring on isolated beaches in Tobago" [12].

Carnival 2008 was also marred with violence, with five men including the brother of attorney Wayne Sturge, being killed in separate incidents during the Soca Monarch Competition and j'ouvert morning. Several others were stabbed and robbed during the Carnival celebrations. For the first time, the Government and security forces used closed circuit television to monitor Carnival activities during the two-day celebrations [13]. Presently, only nine months into the 2009 year, there are 402 murders and commentators predict that it would surpass the 545 of 2008 in a population of only 1.3 million people.

NEGATIVE ASPECTS OF CARNIVAL

Despite its status as the foremost national festival and a spectacle to the world, more than half the population does not participate, some on account of their Christian beliefs and others because of the nature of the festival. Notwithstanding, Carnival in Trinidad and Tobago is incorrigible, the culture is pervasive whether there is active or passive participation. It is the event that enhances the mind of the population for the most of the year, insomuch that a former Prime Minister of Singapore, a country well known for its industry referred to the population as having a carnival mentality [14]. This is even made more pronounced with the present Government's choice of a President for the Republic who has a reputation of "feting to the Max."

The Carnival mentality is conditioned in early life. Carnival shapes the mind of the population. The young are specially affected. There is an increase in crime and violence in schools [15]. Many take the fertility element seriously with carnival seen as an opportunity for flirtation and extramarital affairs. Following carnival there is an increase in the cases of AIDS and nine months later, there is an increase in birth rates. Parents become poor role models with nudity and skimpy costumes gyrating suggestively in public, participating in crude jokes, bad behavior and 'jumping and waving' in an inebriated and mindless state.

Yet there is a dictum that children should not participate in 'wining' - lewd, sexually suggestive dancing. Calypsoes sow the seeds of hate, racism and divisiveness as African children at school respond to racist sentiments depicted in the lyrics sung by their icons. The venom and hate of the slave masters depicted by the chantuelles or early calypsonians have today been redirected to other groups. As Lovelace points out, "Fight the people who keeping down black people. Fight the government" [8]. Today, the calypsonians have emerged as crude political canvassers espousing the cause of their tribes. Their songs are often derogatory, racist and anti-Indian causing divisions within the society. The inherent anger and hate of the slave masters have been directed onto the non-African elements in society. Notwithstanding, the emphasis that Black youths place on Carnival which remove them from the more serious aspects of life, affirmative actions are now being recommended for their development. In a newspaper report of the Daily Express [16], Lee Sing, advises that a two year program for national service should be first initiated in the East West corridor, La Brea to Point Fortin, since these Black youths are in need of very special attention. Sat Maharaj disagrees and claims that these youths come out to prey on the rest of the nation imprisoning it in fear and now these organizers have a solution to make the entire nation pay. He stressed that law abiding youths should not be saddled with compulsory national service when they are focused on academics. There seem to be a strong correlation between involvement in crime, academic performance and carnival.

Carnival in Trinidad and Tobago is embraced by the Afro-Trinidadian population who jealously guard it with a sense of propriety. People of non-African descent or persuasion are not welcomed, degraded and excluded from major events and are later criticized for their non-participation in this overvalued national festival. A fitting example is the 'boos' received by non-African calypsonians who have been greeted with rolls of toilet paper. Writers have attempted to establish a cultural base for the Afro-Trinidadian population by alleging that carnival was brought to Trinidad by African slaves [7]. A more acceptable view is that carnival is a ritual rooted in the experience of slavery and is a celebration of freedom from slavery. It is therefore an anniversary celebration of deliverance from the most hateful form of human bondage [17]. In the early days following emancipation, these cane burning fetes known as 'canboulay' got out of hand due to their profanity, smut, ridicule and mimicry of the more privileged groups. They were therefore moved from August to the pre-lent French Catholic disguise ball before the Easter fast in order to engender better spiritual and moral values.

After Emancipation, the over compensation for slavery resulted in the establishment of a culture of excessive behavior. This was made manifest by over indulgence in carnal desires of an immoral and promiscuous nature linked to an authoritarian behavior of protest and rebellion to "mash up the place". These behavioral characteristics crystallized in the celebration of carnival which provided the ideal vehicle of expression. One hundred and seventy one years later, the carnival mentality has persisted —'it is we time, time to get on bad' is touted by revelers during the carnival season.

A fitting example is the carnival of 2002 which was described as a carnival of lawlessness – 'firstly they seemed to prefer the surfaces of parked cars to the road, jumping on people's vehicles for the sole purpose of destruction [10]. Unprovoked attacks on women, sitting in cars were widespread, jumping on the cars, rocking the vehicles and banging on the windows and windscreens. One person unzipped his crutch and pressed his penis on the windscreen. As previously mentioned, in one day in Port of Spain 50 people were arrested for having in their possession a variety of prohibited weapons including cutlasses. There were at least three murders directly related to carnival activities, that year [11].

There is little doubt that Carnival in Trinidad and Tobago is celebrated with a special cultural emphasis, highlighting the primitive drives of man. It is an event set in the country's historical past that enhances the mind of the population for most of the year.

There are major benefits derived from carnival. These are economic gains, development of the creative and performing art forms, facilitating avenues for art and craft, increased socialization both nationally and internationally, the establishment of carnival-related industries and providing an escape from the boredom and stresses of daily activities. These factors are unfortunately not defined in the carnival mentality.

The carnival mentality is well recognized locally. In a sample of 536 participants interviewed on the awareness, perception and description of this phenomenon 97% of Trinidadians were aware of the existence of the carnival mentality behavior. The characteristics were outlined as described in table 1.

In the study Carnival mentality was seen as having two dimensions: during carnival season and outside of carnival period. During the carnival season, carnival mentality has been viewed as a "time to free up", "time to break away and get on bad" or take part in every carnival activity or event and indulging in alcohol, immoral, vulgar, and promiscuous activities without thinking of the consequences. Outside of the carnival season, carnival mentality refers to the "non-stop party mentality" that is practiced throughout the year; where every event or occasion is treated as an excuse "to lime or party". Some respondents have regarded carnival mentality as "extreme liming" or "continuous fun in the sun". Carnival mentality was also seen as having filtered into the workplace where individuals have a very slack, laid back or "don't give a damn" attitude towards work. Carnival mentality was also referred to by a minority of respondents as mindlessness, when you hear music nothing could stop you from dancing, having too many parties in the calendar and events having attributes of carnival.

CONCLUSION

Carnival mentality the so called 'joie de vivre' expressed by Afro Trinidadians has been reinforced by embracing the creativity of Carnival. The permeating effect throughout the year lends itself to instant gratification among a nations people who cannot seem to wait until the next years festivities. Those not involved are chastised as not revelling in what has been given to us to enjoy on our own volition. It seems that our country is defining itself as a 'knows no bounds' society that is all too pleased to 'thank god its Friday,' on a daily basis. Partying is no longer a weekend activity, and alcohol use is rampant. Our so called carnival mentality continuously reinforced by numerous public holidays, excuses for abridged work days and school days, coupled with an impulsive nature gives way for an extremely laid back and 'doh care' lifestyle. We seem to be ruled by our id impulses as a nation, a child without a parent, in Freudian terms. This is tenable as a fitting expression and description for the stereotypical lives of Caribbean People. While million and perhaps billion of dollars are invested by governments each year to boost 'the greatest show on earth', there has been no proper auditing on the benefits accrued. While the emphasis has been on creativity and the pleasure principle, the cost of carnival has become too burdensome serving as a divisive tool in national integration, disintegration in social and moral values with the wrong signals sent to youths and the embellishment of a nation with a carnival mentality. The long term cost of the Trinidad carnival is too high and there is a need to restructure this celebration rather than utilize it as a tool for political patronization.

REFERENCES

[1]   Hodge M. People. In: Saft E, ed. Insight guides: Trinidad and Tobago. London: APA Publ, 1996.

[2]   Allnutt SH, Bradford JM, Greenberg DM, et al. Co-morbidity of alcoholism and the paraphilias. J Forensic Sci 1996;41(2):234-9.

[3]   Mills C. Irony of Carnival in Jamaica. Yard Flex 2006 Apr 25.

[4]   Dein S. Mental health in a multiethnic society. BMJ 1997;106: 473-7.

[5]   Jilek WG. Culturally related syndromes. In: Gelder MG, Lopez-Ibor JJ, Andreasen N, eds. New Oxford textbook of psychiatry. Oxford: Oxford Univ Press, 2000:1061-6.

[6]   Jilek, WG, Jilek-Aall, L. Kulturspezifische psychishe storungen. In: Hemlchen, H, Henn, F, Lauter, H, Sartorius, N, eds. Psychiatrie der Gegenwart: Psychiatrie spezieller lebenssituationen. Berlin: Springer, 2000:3. [German]

[7]   Liverpool H. Culture and education. Carnival in Trinidad and Tobago Implications for education in secondary schools. London: Karia Press, 1990.

[8]   Lovelace E. The dragon can't dance. London: Andre Deutsh, 1979.

[9]   Ferraz M. The Carnival Mentality. Trinidad Guardian 2002 Feb 12:5.

[10]   George E. Carnival of lawlessness. Sunday Express 2002 Feb 17:10.

[11]   Seetahal D. Zero tolerance for crime. Sunday Guardian 2002 Feb 17: 12.

[12]   Bureau of Consular Affairs Traveling tips for American citizens visiting Trinidad and Tobago. Washington, DC: US Dept State, 2007.

[13]   Yard Flex. Trinidad Carnival 2008: Violence leaves five dead. [Online]. 2008 [cited2009Sept29].Availablefromhttp://www.yardflex.com/archives/002198.html.

[14]   Panday B. Speeches made by the political leader. The expansion on the LNG operations. Trinidad and Tobago: United Natl Congr, 2000.

[15]   Morgan J. Too much UNC, PNM racism. The Bomb 2002 Feb 15:7.

[16]   Neaves J. Lee Sing pushes for compulsory service... Sat slams 'fascist' idea.' Daily Express 2009 Sept 29:7.

[17]   Hill E. The Trinidad carnival. Austin, TX: Univ Texas Press, 1972.

In: Social and Cultural Psychiatry Experience from the... ISBN: 978-1-61668-506-5
Editor: Hari D. Maharajh and Joav Merrick © 2010 Nova Science Publishers, Inc.

Chapter 10

DANCING FROTTEURISM OR RUBBING AT THE CARNIVAL CELEBRATIONS IN TRINIDAD

Hari D. Maharajh

Paraphilias are sexual disorders characterized by sexual impulses, urges, fantasies or practices that are strange, deviant or bizarre. It is more common in men and attributed to fixation at one of the psychosexual phases of development, learning theory, child abuse or culture. Trinidad and Tobago has been influenced by a medley of cultures which find its greatest expression during the carnival season. During this time a local dance form of wining with suggestible sexual movements is pervasive. It is associated with distortions of normal courtship behavior with paraphilic disturbances. In a case presentation, a young male is presented showing paraphilic disturbances of touching, holding, rubbing and coercive sex. This behaviour of frotteurism and other paraphilias are common occurrences at carnival in Trinidad and Tobago and are considered to be cultural normative practices. This case-report therefore, identifies a number of paraphilic behaviors such as toucherism, frotteurism and preferential rape during the carnival celebration and examines their relationship with the law. Professionals abroad ought to be aware of the local culture due to the recent export of carnival to metropolitan countries.

INTRODUCTION

Obscenity in art form is as old as humankind itself has been pervasive throughout the ages with social acceptance. Among the performing art, dance is a representation of rhythmic movements shaped by music and visual images. It is an expression of the philosophy of a people, their lives and country. Dance may be communal, that is, vested in religious, ceremonial, folk or social practices or theatrical, which is performed by specially trained members and intrinsically interwoven with creativity and abstraction.

The people of Trinidad and Tobago comprise a medley of dancing cultures. It is a multicultural society with exposure to African and Indian rhythms, Spanish and Latin American and European influences, cross-over and Jamaican art forms, and the locally developed calypso, rapso, soca and fusion music. People dance to rhythm and Trinidadians are well known for their "wining and jamming" to the calypso beat, especially at carnival time. Wining is a term used to describe sensuous gyrations of the hip in a manner and form suggestive of sexual movements, while "jamming" refers to the closeness of physical encounter or the crowdedness of the setting. Wining is most prominent at the carnival season, but is also found at other times of the year especially at local Indo-Trinidadian folk festivals known as chutney. Locally, this contemporary dance form is dominated by women across all cultures.

Trinidadians have been described as having a "carnival mentality" that is a pervasive cultural behavior of 'liming and partying' both during and outside the carnival season which is not translated at the work place [1]. Carnival is viewed as "a time to free up, a time to break away and get on bad." It is a time where people behave in ways that one would consider immoral and unlawful outside the season. Dance therefore, finds the most creative, spontaneous and rhythmic expressions during this period in the form of wining dictated by the local music.

Sexual behavior finds its expression in the mores and social customs of a society. The utopian definition of sexuality as mere sexual desire and will to identify is too limited. Ethnographically, sexual behavior is more rooted in the context of relations [2]. Furthermore, human male courtship behaviour can be differentiated into four phases: that is, finding and choosing a partner; pre-tactile interaction of smiling, talking and posturing; tactile interaction of embracing, petting and kissing and lastly, genital union [3,4]. Distortion of this normal courtship behaviour motivated by erotic interests results in a courtship disorder of voyeurism, exhibitionism, toucheurism, frotteurism and preferential rape. These are expressions of a common underlying disturbance and are often interrelated [5-7]. These are supported by research as possible development risk factors of child abuse or family dysfunction [8,9]. These sexual disorders are classified as paraphilias and are characterized by sexual fantasies and intense sexual urges with personal distress. This behavior is often compulsive and individuals are unable to control their impulses. Men in particular, have made physiological claims that during the sexual cycle of desire, arousal, penetration, orgasm and resolution, they cannot stop since a man lights up like a match and a woman like an oven. This view is not supported in law.

Frotteurism or rubbing for sexual gratification is defined as recurrent, intensive sexually arousing fantasies, sexual urges or behaviour involving rubbing against a non-consenting person resulting in distress or interpersonal difficulties [10]. Preferential rape is a paraphilic preference for coercive sex. These together with exhibitionism or indecent exposure and voyeurism or peeping are all common expressions of a common underlying disturbance [5].

Miller [11] has researched the dancing form of wining in relation to sexuality. Rival et al [2] have researched sexuality and desire in different societies throughout the world and Trinidad was one of the described countries with wining described as an expression of sexuality. Sexuality in Trinidad was described as "a highly overt and a constantly foregrounded mode of social relationships". Sex was said to be seen in Trinidad as a comparative performance, both for men and women. Activities like dancing, wining and jamming can be seen as a form of "virtual sex" or as an expression of this sexuality. Sexuality and its expressions can be seen as a large idiom in Trinidad, it plays a central role in Trinidad "despite" the islands diverse populations. Wining can also be seen as an expression of sociality itself with wining reflecting 'absolute freedom', finding its roots in the history of slavery and comparable to philosophical projections found worldwide [11].

Emanating from a history of slavery, the Caribbean man today is polygamous in nature, yet he jealously guards fidelity in his women. His social interaction with his female partner is invariably sexual in nature and he will not give up until he lays her in bed. He then loses interest. There is a fast-tracking for sex without the establishment of normal courtship behaviour. This results in the absence of attachment to the female partner resulting in polygamous relationships for sexual recreation and the loss of respect for women. This deviant courtship behaviour has contributed to unstable family structures and dysfunctional families. It is not uncommon within the African population to find one woman with a dozen children all for different partners.

We wish to present a case of frotteurism with preferential rape in the context of a courtship disorder, during Carnival in Trinidad. The aim of this case report is to emphasize the importance of cultural elements in psychiatric diagnosis of sexual disorders and to examine the effects of cultural behaviour on the legislative framework.

CASE REPORT

A 26 year old male Trinidadian was referred for psychiatric evaluation through the court system for a sexual offence which involved touching, holding, fondling, rubbing and alleged rape. This outrage of modesty or molestation occurred during a 'carnival jump up', while dancing with an unknown female.

He was single, a musician by trade, part time gym instructor and an excellent dancer who chose to attend parties alone, where according to him, "he played the field". Due to his skill and artistry in movement on the dance floor, he was a spectacle to behold and had no difficulties in approaching new female acquaintances as dancing partners at the various venues he attended.

On this occasion, he approached a skimpily dressed female previously unknown to him, who willingly agreed to dance with him. After a few minutes of footwork and body spins, he began dancing at close quarters to his partner rubbing his torso in a rhythmic manner against his dancing partner. On the background of the soca-calypso music, their limbs were gracefully interlocked and with their pelvic region in close contact, they simultaneously gyrated, wining in a form and manner reminiscent of a sexual act. The rubbing, touching, holding and fondling continued until they walked off the dance floor together to the outside.

While standing on the outside under a dark hedge, he began kissing and cuddling her and attempted to lower her skimpy pants for sexual penetration. According to his report, she was a willing partner at first, but then changed her mind and raised an alarm. Her husband, who was in search of her, arrived on the scene and, in a fit of rage, uprooted an iron pole from a nearby fence, maliciously wounding him. A charge of rape was preferred against the dancer, who was brought before the courts.

The accused gave a history of interpersonal difficulties experienced while dancing with partners in the past. On numerous occasions women would walk off the floor in the middle of a set due to their discomfort with his body parts pressing against theirs at close quarters. On one occasion a year ago, he was involved in dance hall skirmish and was asked by the manager to leave the party.

On examination, he was a well dressed, athletic man with good muscular tone and development. He was well mannered, polite and friendly. He viewed the incident as "jealousy by the husband who was drunk at the time". He did not think that he had crossed the line and stated that "this is what normally happens at carnival fetes". He was not anxious, depressed or homicidal and had no previous abnormal experiences of hallucinations or delusions. There was no cognitive impairment. He did not use alcohol or other substances since it interfered with his routine workout as a dance instructor at the gym.

His birth and development were normal. He attained puberty at the age of 12. He was raised by both parents who were civil servants. He had two girl friends in his adolescent period and showed no aberrations in his interpersonal skills or sexual behaviour. He had no history of substance abuse.

Baseline laboratory testing of full blood count, urea and electrolytes, liver function tests, random sugar, thyroid function tests and urine screen for alcohol and drugs were all within normal range. His EEG showed no abnormality. On psychological testing, he scored high on the neuroticism-extroversion score, but did not meet the criteria required for Cluster B Personality Disorders [12].

The court report of the psychiatrist noted that although the behaviour of the accused was exaggerated, it was still in keeping within the normal practices of the carnival celebrations. There was no formal psychiatric disorder or evidence of a personality disorder. On the basis of this report and also with the view that there was a contributory negligence in part of his partner, the judge in court decided that the accused person was not guilty of rape and he was put on a bond for two years for good behaviour.

DISCUSSION

The predominance of wining at the Trinidad carnival is an expression of sexuality embedded in the social and cultural dimensions of the country's history. From an etic point of view, there is a culture of frotteurism incorporating other paraphilic interests of exhibitionism, voyeurism and preferential rape.

These sexual behaviors during carnival celebrations are unique to groups and communities and are influenced by historical, cultural, biological, individual and interpersonal factors. Carnival in Trinidad and Tobago and other Caribbean islands has its origin in the freedom from slavery, with an exhibition based on a paradox of the rejection and acceptance of the customs, behaviour and lifestyles of the colonial masters. Consequently, the post emancipation development of sexual attitudes and behaviour cannot be measured on the merit of British Laws or classified through American or European diagnostic criteria. These practices, evidently paraphilic by western standards, cannot be deemed to be so but must be seen as culturally based sexual behaviours. The law has no jurisdiction on a man's culture, however abnormal it may appear to the outsider.

During the carnival season in Trinidad and Tobago, that is, from Christmas to Lent, there is an absence of the normal courtship behaviour with fast tracking from dancing to sexual union. During the two days preceeding the Lenten season, there is street dancing (notably wining) of participants dressed in costumes with differential degrees of body exposure ranging from almost nude to fully clothed. Individuals have the free choice to join parading bands and those with skimpy costumes are the most popular. The latter attracts a high viewing audience both locally and internationally and has been deemed as avenues for exhibitionism and even voyeurism.

Knowing the countries history of slavery and the existence of the English law, it is difficult to determine where to draw the line between cultural behaviours and sexual deviancy. The accused stated that "this is what normally happens at carnival fetes", indicating that it was normative practice to behave in the form and manner as he did. He did not think that he had acted wrongly but blames the plaintiff husband for being jealous. The magistrate, knowledgeable of the culture appeared to have had difficulties in determining innocence or guilt and therefore requested a psychiatric assessment. The fact that there was some element of contributory negligence on the part of the plaintiff complicated matters even more.

Frotteurism and other paraphilias are common occurrences during carnival but are generally ignored. It is culturally acceptable for someone to rub another person while "wining" (dancing) to the tempo of the rhythmic and lyrically suggestive calypso music. Touching and holding are commonplace and during these two days of street festivity the law turns a blind eye to minor offences and minor crimes. Non-consenting persons do not complain, since there is no redress. The celebration is perceived as being cathartic and the stipulated behaviour as part of the process of "freeing up".

Alcohol is related to a wide variety of crimes. The use and abuse of alcohol beverages are also comorbid with paraphilias [13]. In this case-report, there was no evidence of alcohol abuse or alcohol dependence or excessive alcohol use during the incident. It is culturally accepted that the wining behaviour during carnival season and possibly preferential rapes are associated with the use of excessive alcohol during this celebrations. Close quarter dancing is a national pastime and that induces eroticism and sets the basis for paraphilias.

CONCLUSION

This case study of frotteurism and other paraphilias demonstrates the difficulty in the interpretation of native, cultural sexual behaviors as pathological despite their deviant and bizarre presentations to those from foreign lands. This acceptance of sexual behaviours within a given culture varies and is difficult to legally control. Lawmakers however, must be consistent in their legislations.

Frotteurism is not unique to Trinidad and Tobago; it exists in crowded buses, trains, pubs and festivals in other parts of the world as well. It differs, however, in that in Trinidad and Tobago it is linked to the country's most popular national celebration where there is a disruption of normal human male courtship behaviours. There is also, the provision of an avenue for the expression of common underlying paraphilic disturbances. The export of the Trinidad carnival to Brooklyn, Toronto, London and other metropolitan cities will in effect transfer indigenous behaviours to foreign lands where there may be less tolerance to sexual deviancy. The social differences in behaviour should be of interest to the criminal justice system and health care professionals abroad in the management of these patients. In addition, in Trinidad and Tobago there is a need for the introduction of a code of conduct for the celebration of carnival with stricter enforcement of the law. A misunderstanding of these phenomena can lead to stereotyping.

REFERENCES

[1] Maharajh HD, Ali A. Recognition of cultural behaviors in Trinidad and Tobago. Internet J Third World Med 2004;3(1):1.

[2] Rival L, Slater D, Miller D. Sex and sociality. Comparative etnographies of sexual objectivation. Theory Culture Soc 1998;15(3):295-321.

[3] Freund K, Blanchard R. The concept of courtship disorder. J Sex Marital Ther 1986;12(2):79-92.

[4] Money J. Paraphilias: Phenomenology and classification. Am J Psychother 1984;38(2):164-79.

[5] Freund K, Seto MC. Preferential rape in the theory of courtship disorder. Arch Sex Behav 1998;27(5):433-43.

[6] Freund K, Scher H, Hucker S .The courtship disorders: A further investigation. Arch Sex Behav 1984;13(2):133-9.

[7] Freund K, Scher H, Racansky IG, Campbell K, Heasman G. Males disposed to commit rape. Arch Sex Behav 1986;15(1):23-35.

[8] Lee JK, Jackson HJ, Pattison P, Ward T. Developmental risk factors for sexual offending. Child Abuse Negl 2002;26(1):73-92.

[9] Saunders E, Awad GA, White G. Male adolescent sexual offenders: The offender and the offense. Can J Psychiatry 1986;31(6):542-9.

[10] American Psychiatric Association. Sexual and gender identity disorders. In: Diagnostic criteria from DSM-IV-TR. Washington DC: APA, 2000:255-9.

[11] Miller D. Absolute freedom in Trinidad man. New Series 1991;26(2): 323-41.

[12] American Psychiatric Association. Diagnostic criteria from DSM-IV-TR. Washington DC: APA, 2000:255-259.

[13] Allnutt SH, Bradford JM, Greenberg DM, Curry S. Co-morbidity of alcoholism and the paraphilias. J Forensic Sci 1996;41(2),234-9.

In: Social and Cultural Psychiatry Experience from the... ISBN: 978-1-61668-506-5
Editor: Hari D. Maharajh and Joav Merrick © 2010 Nova Science Publishers, Inc.

Chapter 11

ANOREXIA NERVOSA AND RELIGIOUS AMBIVALENCE IN A DEVELOPING COUNTRY

Hari D. Maharajh

The aim of this study is to report the first case of the primary nuclear form of anorexia nervosa in Trinidad and the West Indies in an 18-year-old female Islamic student attending a Roman Catholic Convent. Ambivalent values due to her early development in a strict Muslim home with Catholic influence and contemporaneous exposure to a Western society are explored. The dynamics of family interaction in a dual religious home are investigated. Similarities are noted from reports from western countries that link ritualistic fasting to the month of Ramadan. The influence of the Roman Catholic period of fast, Lent, and the dynamics of family interaction are discussed. We wish to propose religious ambivalence as an etiological factor in anorexia nervosa in a developing country.

INTRODUCTION

Anorexia nervosa is an eating disorder characterized by self induced weight loss of at least 15% below that which is expected, avoidance of fattening food, body image distortion and amenorrhoea [1]. Crisp [2] has suggested that the primary nuclear form of anorexia nervosa is characterized by a central symptom of phobia of normal adolescent weight following the growth changes of puberty. Two types have been identified: the Restraining Type without regular engagement in binge eating or purging; and the Binge Eating- Purging Type in the DSM-IV [3]. Among a host of etiological factors, anorexia nervosa has been described as a culture bound syndrome, rare in non-western people [4].

Attempts have been made to link anorexia nervosa to religion. Huline-Dickens has examined the religious and ascetic features of anorexia nervosa [5]. It is argued that there exists many connections between the religious ascetic and the anorexic, and that there are many psychopathological features common to both. Whilst empirical evidence for religious themes in anorexia is not strong, in the family therapy literature there are indications of ethical codes of sacrifice, loyalty and sexual denial. Anorexia and asceticism are considered to be connected conceptually in the process of idealization. Clinicians working with women with anorexia have pointed out their abstinence from worldly comfort and pleasures through the process of self-denial, heightened morality, asexuality and immortality [6].

Other researchers have attempted to link anorexia nervosa to socio-cultural factors [7,8]. Khandelwal et al. [9], took an Indian perspective in describing five cases of young women who presented with anorexia nervosa in India; and discussed sociocultural reasons for its atypical presentation. Case reports of anorexia nervosa in subjects of Asian (Indian subcontinental) have been rare. Bhadrinath discussed three cases of Asian adolescents, two of which describes the impact of the Muslim festival of Ramadan [10].

The Republic of Trinidad and Tobago comprises a non-secular population of 1.3 million people with a ratio of approximately two Africans to two Indians to one mixed and others. Two-thirds of the population belongs to Christian-based religions, the majority being Roman Catholics while others belong to a variety of denominations. One third subscribes to Hinduism and Islam, the latter though only ten percent exerts tremendous socio-religious and political force. Over the last decade Islam has been on the rise with a return to traditional dress and koranic injunctions.

The religion of Islam encompasses religious duties such as Salah (prayer), Hajj (pilgrimage), Sawm (fasting) and Zakat (charity). Fasting takes place every lunar year from the first of Ramadan to the first of Shawwal (the following month) and entails restraining from food, drink, smoking and sexual pleasure from dawn until sunset. Fasting is a religious obligation on every Muslim who has attained the age of puberty and who is sane and able.

Fasting is also a long procedure of obedience and for every day for that prescribed month, the individual has to get up before dawn, stop all eating and drinking precisely at the breaking of dawn, do work during the day, break fast at the time of sunset and then hurry up for Taravih (night prayers). According to A'la Maudoodi [11] every year for one month, the dutiful Muslim from dawn to dusk is kept continuously tied up with rules and regulations like a soldier in the army and then he is released for eleven (11) months so that the training he has received during that one month may show its effects. If any deficiency is found it may be made up in the training of the next year.

Fasting occurs in other religions besides Islam, such as Judaism and Christianity. The most common motives for fasting are religious ones. In a religious fast, there are three primary purposes: self control over the body and appetites, focusing the mind on God or prayer and making sacrifice to God for offences committed. The religions of Islam and Christianity have from their inception, set aside certain times in the year for regular fasting observances. Early Christianity developed a number of fasting periods: food was not eaten on Fridays in commemoration of the death of Jesus. Later a period of forty days before Easter, called Lent, was set aside to allow Christians to meditate on the sufferings of Jesus.

The season of Lent is the time of preparation for Holy week. It is a sacred and spiritual time for every Christian. No matter how far removed an individual might be from their studies of Lent, most Catholics know that the 40 days of Lent remind them of giving up something that is a sacrifice, acts of self denial, acts that are geared to remind them of Christ. During the Lenten season, dietary restrictions are implemented with abstinence from meat. Many people also perform acts of penance or mortification, such as giving up sweets, or it may be a time for some to attend Mass more frequently.

Fasting regulates the desires of the lower physical self and trains the higher moral self to control them; it has a direct effect on a person's psychological, social and physical being by changing his/her habits and emotional attitude toward exercising patience in virtually every aspect of life.

The aim of this study is to report the first case of the primary nuclear form of anorexia nervosa in Trinidad and the West Indies in an 18-year-old Islamic student attending a Roman Catholic Convent. Ambivalent values due to development in a strict Muslim home with Catholic influence and contemporaneous exposure to a Western society are explored. The dynamics of family interaction in a dual religious home are investigated.

CASE REPORT

Dija, an eighteen-year-old post pubertal Muslim girl, was referred to a psychiatrist after completing Advanced level exams. The patient had previously been treated by a psychologist through counseling sessions including programmes in weight gain and mantras to repeat to develop her self esteem.

The last of four female siblings of a middle class, Indo-Trinidadian family, Dija has never been away or been exposed to Western culture. The family structure is rigid along the lines of Islam (mother) and Roman Catholicism (father). Due to the home being dual-religious, two periods of fasting takes place for the year: for Ramadan (30 days) and for Lent (40 days). During these periods of fasting, meals are centered and planned around the fasting person. For example, during Ramadan chick peas and chutney are often prepared while during Lent, meals are centered around fish.

Dija has a three-year history of body image disturbance, morbid fear of fatness and an abnormal attitude to food and periods of amenorrhoea. At the age of 15, her height was 5' and weight 118 lbs. The patient decided to lose 5-10 lbs., but later decided to lose more and lost 30lbs within a 4-month period falling to 88 lbs. The month of Ramadan coincided with this 4-month period. She began exercising heavily with a strict routine of one hour daily.

At school, even though she was a model student, her weight continued sliding and caused concern among her classmates, as they were aware that she used to throw away her food. They reported it to a teacher who called in her father at school. Within the family, the patient's body weight misperception caused family conflict especially with her mother. Her mother is described as controlling, overpowering, dominant and intrusive while father is passive.

During the months of Ramadan, between the ages of 15-17, the patient started to fast but was stopped by her mother, as her mother did not see her fit enough to do so. She however performed 3 of the 5 daily salats required by the religion. During the next year, she manipulated her weight and was in constant conflict with her mother who insisted that she should eat. Her exercise routine also became more vigorous as, she now exercised for two hours every day and joined a Tai-Chi class which had interested her greatly. Her mother continued to blame her for causing her immense stress.

At the age of eighteen, she zealously fasted for 10 days before being stopped by her mother. Also, she now performs all of the five daily prayers, not missing any. She suffers from feelings of sadness, hopelessness and unhappiness. In therapy for six months with the psychiatrist, she was treated with a combination therapy involving antidepressants, journal recording of daily calorie intake and weekly weight and psychotherapeutic sessions with a

DISCUSSION

Reports from Western countries [10,12] seem to support our view that ritualistic fasting during the month of Ramadan sensitizes young Muslim girls to weight manipulation through fasting and binging and provides a religious sanctioned substrate for eating disorders. It is interesting that this Muslim girl's problems began at Ramadan and worsened over subsequent Ramadans where she was forcibly exempted from fasting. It appears therefore, that this religiously motivated behaviour is linked to ascetic components of control, self-denial, sacrifice and loyalty, rather than the secular western concept of physical beauty and the pursuit of thinness which is frowned upon in Islam.

Notwithstanding her Islamic lifestyle, there have been extraordinary influences from Roman Catholicism both at home and at school. At the age of 10 years, the patient's father rejected Islam and embraced Catholicism. Her father's decision was triggered by constant criticisms from his wife's extended family who viewed him as a Kafir (i.e. a non-believer). Her schooling at a Roman Catholic Convent between the ages of 11-18 years must have subconsciously reinforced her identification with her father. She had described her father as passive and avoiding conflicts while her mother was dominant, overpowering and intrusive. She has therefore incorporated cultural symbols both from her mother, a devout and zealous Muslim and her father, a religious convert to Catholicism. Her religious ambivalence is manifested by her preoccupation with fasting. The atmosphere of fasting is very prominent in this family as it occurs twice for the year: at Ramadan and at Lent. This culture reinforces indulgence in food intake, or abstinence by the patient as she fasts with both her mother for Ramadan and her father for Lent. The eating patterns of the family have influenced her choice to abstain from meat, as she is mostly vegetarian using fish as her only intake of animal protein.

The patient utilizes symbols from both religions that are highly ritualistic in their attitude to food. Selective symbols are transformed to express her anxiety, pain and schisms with the family. She ritualizes her behaviour through starvation, a form of self-inflicted penance to cope with her religious ambivalence. This view is supported by psychological anthropologists who are of the opinion that culture and religion as symbolic systems, have underpinnings in deep motivation [6].

Of particular interest, this 18 year-old Muslim student has lived a very sheltered life adhering steadfastly to the pillars of Islam. She has never lived away from home or visited relatives abroad and has not been actively exposed to western customs. She perceives herself as a devout, practicing Muslim, traditional in belief and dress with no confusion of identity. Significant findings of the family dynamics along the lines of the McMaster model of family functioning [13,14] revealed dysfunctions in resolving problem, communication, roles, clarity of rules and concern for each other. Like many West Indian families, flight into religion provided a coping mechanism for members of the family. It is known that dysfunctional family interaction is linked to anorexia nervosa [15-17]. In our case study, family disagreement arose from non-adherence or over indulgence in selective religious mores. Food became the common acceptable form of communication.

Religion is an important factor in the daily lives of Caribbean people. Trinidad and Tobago like other West Indian islands is influenced by diverse religious and cultural practices. Inter-religious practices are common and religion has become a thriving business peddling a wide range of arcane supported by religious quotations and spiritual injunctions with an elaborate system of ritualization. It is possible that religious based behaviour with clear cut injunctions masks a number of psychiatric disorders including anorexia nervosa. As in the case of our Muslim student these disorders can be treated by a religio-cultural based therapy. Not only the ambivalence of religious or inter-religious practices will generate family based disorders, but in any society where there is a high rate of teenage pregnancy, it is expected that the incidence of anorexia nervosa will be low.

In the Trinidadian society, food is commensurate with religious practices. Among many religious groups, there are lavish spreads of high carbohydrate foods that are often served late in the evening and at nights. Among the Islamic group, there is a pattern of binge eating before sunrise in preparation for a long day of fasting followed by the breaking of fast and later a heavy meal to celebrate the day's event. It is not uncommon for some Muslims to complain of weight gain during the fasting period. In addition, the Muslim garb designed to conceal sexuality does not favor the western notion of the pursuit of thinness as a prerequisite to beauty. A contributory factor may be the avoidance of exercise and hard work during this period which in the tropical setting induces thirst. Within the Caribbean, food and religion provide important avenues for communication. It is conceivable therefore, that the dynamics associated with religion and anorexia is different from those of western countries.

Despite the similarity in clinical presentation, the pathogenesis of anorexia nervosa in developing countries appears to be different to those in western countries. Needless to say, the interplay of Third World traditional practices based on religion, superstition and folk medicine and the influences of Western culture will result in a borderline cultural state. Individuals may therefore have difficulties in conceptualizing the culture or religion they belong to interphasing between the traditional or home culture and the modernizing or host culture.

CONCLUSION

In this case report, there is greater amplification of the problem since there is the further splitting within the home culture resulting in a confusion of archetypal references. Within the West Indian community, each family appears to be a medley of religious and cultural diversity. Attitudes to religion and food are major determinants of sociability and adaptability. Ambivalence to these will result in psychosocial stress and disease.

Anorexia nervosa is rare in Trinidad and Tobago and other Caribbean countries. While the core symptoms of the disease remain constant; etiological and psychodynamic factors are variable. The non-secular nature of Trinidad and Tobago with religio-cultural fusion has resulted in a form of holy anorexia or religious ambivalence. The emphasis is different from the West obsessed with the pursuit of thinness. It appears as though those in developing countries place more emphasis on their religious practices than their perceived physical attractiveness.

REFERENCES

[1] World Health Organization. The ICD-10 Classification of mental and behavioural disorders. Geneva: WHO, 1992.

[2] Crisp AH. Anorexia nervosa. Hosp Med 1967;1:713-8.

[3] American Psychiatric Association. Diagnostic and statistical manual of mental disorders IV. Washington DC: APA, 1994.

[4] Dolan B. Why women? Gender issues and eating disorders: Introduction. In: Dolan B, Gitzinget I, eds. Gender issues and eating disorders. London: Athlone Press, 1994.

[5] Huline-Dickens S. Anorexia nervosa: some connections with the religious attitude. Br J Med Psychol 2000;73(1): 67-76.

[6] Banks CG. The imaginative use of religious symbols in subjective experiences of anorexia nervosa. Psychoanalytic Rev 1997;84(2): 227-36.

[7] Mumford DB, Whitehouse AM, Platts M. Sociocultural correlates of eating disorders among Asian schoolgirls in Bradford. Br J Psychiatry 1991;158:222-8.

[8] Iancu I, Spivak B, Ratzoni G, Apter A, Weizman A. The sociocultural theory in the development of anorexia nervosa. Psychopathology 1994;27(1-2):29-36.

[9] Khandelwal SK, Sharan P, Saxena S. Eating disorders: an Indian perspective. Int J Soc Psychiatry 1995;41(2):132-46.

[10] Bhadrinath BR. Anorexia nervosa in adolescents of Asian extraction. Br J Psychiatry 1990;156:565-8.

[11] A'la Maudoodi SA. Fundamentals of Islam. Delhi: JK Offset Printers, 1985.

[12] Lacey JH, Dolan BN. Bulimia in British Blacks and Asians: A catchment area study. Br J Psychiatry 1988;152:73-9.

[13] Epstein NB, Bishop DS, Levin S. The McMaster model of family functioning. J Marriage Fam Couns 1978;4:19-31.

[14] Epstein NB, Bishop DS, Levin S. The McMaster family assessment device. J Marital Fam Ther 1983;9:171-80.

[15] Waller G, Slade P, Calam R. Who knows best? Family interaction and eating disorders. Br J Psychiatry 1990;156:546-50.

[16] Kog E, Vandereycken W. Family characteristics of anorexia nervosa and bulimia: a review of the research literature. Clin Psychol Rev 1985;5:159-80.

[17] Kagan DM, Squires RL. Family cohesion, family adaptability, and eating behaviours among college students. Int J Eat Disord 1995;4: 269-79.

SECTION FOUR: SUICIDAL BEHAVIOR AND SUICIDE

In: Social and Cultural Psychiatry Experience from the... ISBN: 978-1-61668-506-5
Editor: Hari D. Maharajh and Joav Merrick © 2010 Nova Science Publishers, Inc.

Chapter 12

CULTURE AND SUICIDE

Hari D. Maharajh and Petal S. Abdool

Undefined cultural factors cannot be dismissed and significantly contribute to the worldwide incidence of death by suicide. Culture is an all embracing term and defines the relationship of an individual to his environment. This chapter seeks to investigate the effect of culture on suicide both regionally and internationally. Culture-bound syndrome with suicidal behaviours specific to a particular culture or geographical region are discussed. Opinions are divided as to the status of religious martyrs. The law itself is silent on many aspects of suicidal behaviour and despite decriminalization of suicide as self-murder, the latter remains on the statutes of many developing countries. The Caribbean region is of concern due to its steady rise in mean suicide rate, especially in Trinidad and Tobago where socio-cultural factors are instrumental in influencing suicidal behaviour. These include transgenerational cultural conflicts, psycho-social problems, media exposure, unemployment, social distress, religion and family structure. The methods used are attributed to accessibility and lethality. Ingestion of poisonous substances is most popular followed by hanging and most recently shooting. The gender differences seen with regard to suicidality can also be attributed to gender related psychopathology and psychosocial differences in help-seeking behaviour. These are influenced by the cultural environment to which the individual is exposed. Culture provides coping strategies to individuals; as civilization advances many of these coping mechanisms are lost unclothing the genetic predisposition of vulnerable groups. In the management of suicidal behaviour, a system of therapeutic re-culturation is needed with an emphasis on relevant culture- based therapies

INTRODUCTION

The effect of culture on human behaviour is equivocal with opposing views of both protective and destructive tendencies. Culture may provide a support system to an individual's vulnerability and defences related to ego-functioning, or, on the other hand, may perpetuate an ecologically unhealthy environment. Often, the transgenerational loss of the old culture will result in conflicts between the mores of the traditional culture and the expectations of the modernizing society. Thus, renunciation of the old culture without assimilation of the new predisposes individuals to behavioural disturbances such as suicide.

Suicidal behaviour with completed suicide is one of the leading causes of premature death [1]. This high prevalence has resulted in a growing desire to elucidate the underlying or associated factors. This chapter seeks to review suicidal behaviours across cultures with special reference to ethnicity, religion, lifestyles, legislation and methods used in Trinidad and Tobago. Within the Caribbean region, the issue of suicidal behaviour is a growing problem. According to the World Health Organization, Trinidad and Tobago have the second highest rate of suicide in all the West Indian islands [2]. Very few of these islands have conducted community surveys with an emphasis on causation and prevention.

Currently, there exist few cross-national comparisons of the rates of suicidal ideation and attempts across diverse culture and countries. Interestingly, one US publication involving nine independently conducted epidemiological surveys that utilized similar diagnostic assessment and criteria provided an opportunity to obtain that data. This was possible since it was performed on over 40,000 subjects drawn from the US, Canada, Puerto Rico, France, West Germany, Lebanon, Taiwan, Korea and New Zealand. Females when compared to males had only marginally higher rates of suicidal ideations in most countries but this reached a two-fold increase in Taiwan. The rates of suicidal ideation varied widely in each country and attempts to explain these variations led to the conclusion that cultural factors which are not yet clearly defined may be partly responsible [3].

Therefore, the impact of culture on suicide is one which cannot be dismissed and this relationship needs further evaluation if we hope to decrease the escalating numbers of suicides and attempted suicides across the globe.

CULTURE AND MENTAL HEALTH

The influences of cultural behaviours on mental well-being have been an area of long and intensive investigations [4-6] and remain an enigma even today. In the past, social scientists have interpreted disorders of the mind as a form of social deviancy where the individual was regarded as mentally ill because he had broken the local codes of social conduct [7]. These concepts of psychiatric disorders as a deviation from social and cultural norms rather than a product of an underlying biological dysfunction have not been accepted by many psychiatrists. Many are of the opinion that social impairment is insufficient and psychiatric diagnosis should be made only on the basis of mental status, not in terms of cultural behaviour.

Cultural behaviours can be defined as an adaptive response occurring in organized social groups whose lifestyles, sentiments and interactions have been transgenerationally transmitted. These cultural factors determine behaviour and through a system of ego-protective defense mechanisms seek to explain an individual's relationship with his environment. These behaviours are often associated with compensatory defenses which are sometimes conceptualized and socially contrived in the context of native humour [8].

CULTURE BOUND SYNDROMES

Culture-bound syndromes are current locality-specific patterns of aberrant behaviour and troubling experiences that may or may not be linked to a particular DSM-IV-TR diagnostic category. Many of these patterns are indigenously considered to be illnesses or at least afflictions and most have local names [9]. Culture-bound syndromes are thus culturally determined abnormal behaviour patterns that are specific to a particular culture or geographical region. These behaviours express core cultural themes and have a wide range of symbolic meanings – social, moral and psychological [10].

Genuine culture-bound syndromes are not exclusively linked to a particular culture, but rather related to a prominent cultural emphasis or to a specific social stress situation [11,12]. Syndromes have been described with a cultural emphasis on a number of themes. Some are related to suicidal behaviour such as amok in south east Asia and Malaysia [13-15], tabanca in Trinidad [16] and Hi-Wa-itck in Mohave American Indian [17].

Over the past two decades, Trinidad and Tobago resplendent in its cultural diversity has attracted a number of visiting researchers. Littlewood [16] has described Tabanca (lovesick behaviour) as an indigenous conceptualization of depression in rural Trinidad that leads to suicide. This, he claims is an affliction of working class Afro-Caribbean males who aspire to white and middle class values and lifestyles. His views are considered to be a misinterpretation of this cultural phenomenon. Local psychiatrists [18,19] have been critical of his findings stating that he did not take into account the cultural milieu that colours expression of the behaviour and that he was blinkered by his own unconscious cultural assumptions. Similarly, Eriksen [20] has described liming in Trinidad as a dignified art of doing nothing, noting that one cannot be recognized as a real Trinidadian unless one masters the art of doing nothing. This descriptive transcendence into anomie of an entire population underlines the need for local input in the interpretation of socio-cultural phenomena.

LAW, CULTURE AND SUICIDE

Culture is an all-embracing term and incorporates input from both ethnicity and race. Ethnicity refers to selected cultural and physical features of groups varying in language, religion, tradition, food, dress, skin colour and body morphology. Race refers to a biological subspecies with distinct phenotypes but racism has moved to the social domain and appears to be based on issues of power and political control rather than biological superiority.

Mention has already been made of culture-bound syndromes with suicidal behaviour, which are unconscious acts resulting in death. These acts in the true meaning of the word suicide cannot be classified as deliberate acts of self-annihilation. Suicidal behaviour is an illegal act and this criminal offence must have the elements of actus reus which denotes a guilty act and mens rea which denotes a guilty mind. Suicide remains a criminal act in the Caribbean region but has been decriminalized in many countries. Suicide is no longer considered to be self-murder or an offence. Legally, a person's life belongs to the state and not to himself and he is therefore, forbidden from bodily harming himself as he cannot others. Suicide attempters are not charged but deemed to be of unsound mind and must be assessed by a psychiatrist. In complete suicide, the coroner's verdict is based on the following [21]:

- The death must be deemed as unnatural
- The perpetrator of the course of action that resulted in death has to be determined as the deceased himself
- Motive for self-destruction has to be established.

In the defence of a survivor of a suicidal pact, since he caused the death of another deliberately and is prima facie guilty of murdering him, he must prove that there was an agreement that they should both die and when he committed the act, he himself was under the settled expectation of dying.

The strict legal approach does not take into consideration the diverse cultural beliefs of populations and results in census inaccuracies. It is well known that there are culturally sanctioned forms of self-annihilation, for example, it is acceptable in the Japanese culture to commit suicide if you have lost face. This however is not coded as suicide. Another contemporary problem is that of suicide bombers and altruistic suicides. Research suggests that they may not be different from other suicides [22]. If this is indeed the case then more evidence is needed to elucidate the psychological aspects behind these acts.

SUICIDE ACROSS CULTURES

While culture remains an important determinant in the patterns of suicide worldwide, loss of cultural emphasis due to the superimposition of western values, a reactive cultural revolution back to fundamentalist principles, social and political upheavals and road maps of geographical possession have all influenced suicide rates. These rapidly changing variables over time make it difficult to compare rates across cultures since they are often contextual. Instead, suicidal patterns across various cultures will be reviewed here with references to ethnic variations and religious practices.

The close relationship between culture and ethnicity makes discussion of one without the other almost impossible. A study from the United States in Fulton County examined ethnic difference in patterns of suicide across the life cycle and found that African Americans commit suicide at rates much lower than those for whites. The former group does so at a younger age group and have a narrow, age-defined window of vulnerability which has been ascribed to certain unidentified protective factors and age-specific psychopathological processes [23].

In many Muslim countries, low rates of suicide are reported. This may be the result of strict legal and religious sanctions against suicidal behaviour. In Pakistan, very low rates of suicide are reported and this may be misleading due to underreporting [24]. Culture therefore, may sometimes affect the reporting rather than the suicidal act. Suicide is reportedly low in the Jewish population, however, Lubin et al [25] have reported higher suicide rates in Israeli Jewish males and females than Arab males and females. The effect of lifestyles, immigration, military service, absence of peace and media exposure to violence and contagion need further study in that country.

Latinos or Latin Americans appear to be relatively protected against suicidal behaviour and some of these protective factors are thought to be related to cultural constructs that provide a buffer against suicidal behaviour [26]. One study used the Reasons for Living

Inventory (RFLI) in order to capture protective factors against suicidal behaviour in Latinos and non-Latinos. The results showed that being Latino was independently associated with less suicidal ideations while the decrease in other suicidal behaviours was attributed to a stronger relationship to moral objections to suicide and coping skills [26].

During the period 1830-1920, there was the export of Indian labour overseas to Fiji, Malaysia, Ceylon, Mauritius, Burma, Uganda, South Africa and the Caribbean [27]. High rates of suicide have been reported for immigrant groups of East Indians for all generations throughout the world. These rates are in comparison to the indigenous populations in the new environment rather than that of the sending country.

In Fiji, higher rates among East Indians were associated with rurality, biocides, religious and cultural factors [28]. Although the incidence of suicide in Malaysia was relatively low, forty nine percent of all suicides were ethnic Indians who constituted only eight percent of the Malaysian population, 38 percent suicide rates among Chinese who formed 26 percent of the population and 3.6 percent Malay that represented 59 percent of the population [29]. Similarly in Singapore, Indians had the highest suicide rates (19.3 per 100,000) compared to the other ethnic groups of Chinese 16.2 per 100,000 and Malays (2.3 per 100,000) [30].

Some studies from Hong Kong have reported lower rates of suicide among adolescents aged 10-24 years than the adult population [31,32], while others have revealed a significant increase in the suicide rates among adolescents aged 15-24 years in the 1980s [33]. These authors have postulated protective cultural factors that inhibit suicidal behaviour, since killing or hurting oneself is regarded as an unfilial act in Confucian teaching and suicidal behaviour itself discouraged in the Buddhist and Taoist philosophies. Suicidality has been related to inwardly directed aggression. Aubert et al [34] looked at the prevalence of suicidal ideations and behaviours in Canadian students of Chinese and non-Chinese origin. While the Chinese Canadians had higher levels of suicidality and hostility, the actual incidence of aggressive behaviours directed toward self or others was less frequent. These results were attributed to the influence of Chinese culture on emotional restraint especially with regards to aggressiveness [34].

Suicidal behaviour has been reported as being high in East Indian women. Young Fijian Indian women [28] and young South African Indian women have high rates of suicidal behaviour [35]. In these multi-ethnic societies, not unlike Trinidad, women are caught between the western modernizing culture and their own traditional home culture and often have difficulties in conceptualizing to which culture they belong. Adoption of western values with a shifting of traditional role definitions results in a borderline cultural state which serves as a precursor for marital dysfunction, emotional disorders and suicidal behaviour. Culture and religion are protective factors in suicidal behaviour [1].

In Saudi Arabia, despite its economic prosperity and development, suicide rates are low in the native population. In one study, immigrants accounted for 77% of all cases with East Indians accounting for 43% [36]. High suicide rates were also found among young Asian women, 20% of which were by burning [37]. Suicide ratios were significantly low in Bangladeshi, Sri Lankan and Pakistani born men at all ages but raised in young Indian and East African men [37].

SUICIDE RATES IN THE CARIBBEAN REGION

Suicide rates among Caribbean countries are variable with a clear cut trend of male predominance and higher incidences in those islands with a multiethnic population. The WHO rates listed below are ten years or more old and it is expected that over this period rates have changed (see table 1).

In a more recent study in Trinidad and Tobago, the overall mean suicide rate calculated for the eight year period 1990-1997 was found to be 20.6/100,000 male population and 5.4/100,000 female population. For males, two peaks were found at the 25-34 and 55 to 64 age groups and also for females at the 15-24 and over 65 age groups [38]. In Trinidad and Tobago, adolescent suicide rate was 2.3 times more common in males than females in the 15-24 age groups and overall rates were approximately 3.5 to 4 times more common in males than females.

Table 1. Suicide rates per 100,000 in the Caribbean Islands (WHO 2002)

Country	Year	Total Suicide	Male Suicide	Female Suicide
Bahamas	1995	1.1	2.2	0
Barbados	1995	6.5	9.5	3.7
Cuba	1995	18.3	24.5	12.0
Guyana	1994	10.5	14.6	6.5
Jamaica	1985	0.3	0.5	0.2
St. Lucia	1988	7.5	9.3	5.8
Trinidadand Tobago	1994	11.6	17.9	5.0

In an analysis of 1,845 respondents aged 14-20 years from 24 schools across Trinidad and Tobago a number of predictors of suicidal behaviours were identified. These were attendance to a religious institution which lowered suicidal ideation while prayer with the family altered both suicidal ideations and attempts. Other factors identified were gender, family structure and alcohol abuse [1]. The Indian family system was perceived as being suicide prone with the dynamics of its family structure being a contributory factor. Individuals with alcohol abuse present in the family had a two fold increase in suicidal behaviour. Research in Trinidad has reported alcoholism being highest among the East Indian population [39,40]. Indian adolescents were more likely to report alcohol abuse in the family than the other races. In Trinidad and Tobago, ethnic differences were evident in current suicidal ideation with Indian adolescents having higher mean scores than African adolescents [1].

A number of reasons have been proffered for the high suicide rates amongst Indo-Trinidadians:

TRANSGENERATIONAL CULTURAL CONFLICTS WITH FAMILY CULPABILITY [41,42]

The following case history highlights a common occurrence of dying with dignity. A 20 year old Indo-Trinidadian University student from an Orthodox Hindu background was seen in consultation following the ingestion of a few teaspoonfuls of a poisonous substance. Clinical observations of the blistering of her lips, mouth and throat, laboratory and family investigations revealed that she had drank gramoxone (paraquat), a deadly biocide. According to her room-mates, during her first year at University she began 'hanging out with the wrong crowd and was shunned'. Unknown to her parents, she had established a relationship with an Afro-Caribbean male student, neglected her work, allegedly drank heavily and failed her first year. Her father, on receiving news of her behaviour was furious and verbally abused her for bringing shame and disgrace to his family. In a fit of temper, he implied that her death may return some dignity to the family's name and that 'she was better off dead since she had shamed the family.' That evening she took the fatal weedicide. Findings on psychological autopsy revealed that the father felt little guilt and had poor insight into his culpability. He justified his actions by acting in accordance with the Hindu religious text that denounces the intermixture of caste. Purity, avoidance of shame and contamination and codes of behaviour are entrenched in the teachings of the holy Hindu texts.

PSYCHO-SOCIAL PROBLEMS

Lover's quarrels, interpersonal problems, religious beliefs cultural rigidity, marginalization, ethnic disadvantage, poverty, family problems and depression have been stated as precipitating causes of suicidal behaviour among Indo-Trinidadians [43]. In addition, when compared to Afro-Trinidadians, Indians suffered more from physical abuse and unwanted pregnancy [1]. The two major races in Trinidad and Tobago are Indo-Trinidadians (40.3%) and Afro-Trinidadians (39.6%). The government is African based and Indo-Trinidadians are faced with discrimination in position and promotion, housing, unequal educational opportunities, for example in obtaining government scholarships or placement in training programmes. Crime directed against the Indo-Trinidadian community is on the increase with young Indo-Trinidadian businessmen being kidnapped for ransom. The Principle of Fairness Committee founded in 2004 recently held a meeting at the University of the West Indies and warned that Trinidad and Tobago was nearing collapse, because of racial division, crime and improper governance by political leaders. They called for constitutional reform [44].

Here is another example of stress on the job: 49 year old civil servant in a Government's Ministry complained of a lack of satisfaction at the workplace and his inability to cope with the administration at the office. He was an extremely diligent worker who spent extra hours every evening 'in clearing his desk'. Despite his seniority in the public service and periods of acting as head of his division, he was always denied the permanent position as director. On two previous occasions, people junior to him were promoted as his supervisors and he was asked to train them for their positions. According to him, he did all the work, while they held the senior positions and did nothing. He was denied vacation leave when he applied, received bad reports from his supervisors and felt marginalized in the office, since he belonged to a different ethnic grouping than other workers who openly made references 'about his kind of people'. A few weeks after he was denied promotion for the third time, he began drinking heavily. He hardly turned up for work and his physical health deteriorated. He was admitted to an Alcohol Rehabilitation Centre, where he spent six weeks. He improved well, but relapsed on returning to work two months later. He continued missing work and sliding downhill refusing further treatment. One year later he was found dead in bed with an empty bottle of a toxic substance on the carpet. On psychological autopsy, his family blamed the lack of equal opportunity, marginalization and ethnic disadvantage as the cause of his death.

MEDIA REPORTING OF SUICIDES

There are no guidelines for the reporting of suicides in Trindad and other Caribbean countries. These are often sensationalized with graphic descriptions in headline coverage. There is the depiction of live televised suicides and homicides. This is contributory to the high suicidal rates [41]. Another contributory factor may be the viewing of popular Hindi films that often depict maladaptive methods of handling personal, family and stressful situations. There seems to be a need for control.

UNEMPLOYMENT AND SOCIAL DISTRESS

Researchers in Trinidad have identified unemployment as possible factors of increase rates of suicide. An association has been established between social distress and suicidal behaviour [45]. Preliminary findings in an ongoing study have shown no relationship between suicide and employment in Trinidad and Tobago for the period 1998-2002.

RELIGION AND SUICIDE

In 1879 Morselli reported decreased rates of suicide among Catholics when compared to Protestants and Jews [46]. Subsequently, religious persuasions have been associated with suicidal behaviour with higher rates being found among Hindus in Trinidad [1] and in Suriname [47]. Islam has strong religious sanctions against suicide and it is therefore expected that suicide rates will be low. In Judaism, Islam and Christianity to take one's life is considered a transgression against God's law. The Judeo-Christian teachings disapproved of the burial of suicide victims according to the Talmud (Mishnah). Death by suicide prevented the individual from eternal happiness. Hinduism is more tolerant of suicide, but has prescriptions for the wandering of the soul in disruptions of the cycles of birth and death in reincarnation. Ritualistic suicide of suttee now illegal, allowed the wife to throw herself into her husband's funeral pyre. The early Christian voluntary martyrdom is now being adopted by followers of Islam. It seems as though religion has a meaningful part to play in the lives of individuals and is associated with socially acceptable behaviour.

FAMILY STRUCTURE

Most Indo-Trinidadians live in extended families or nuclear families that are in close contact to the extended families. The family structure is patriarchal with the father being the provider of the basic needs of culture, education, religion and discipline. The African family is patterned in a matriarchal model, unstable with multiple relationships and absent fathers. Indo-Trinidadian families with extended collective supervision of adolescents and young adults result in more family quarrels, conflicts and acting out behaviour. Depression and alcohol abuse that had its origin during the indentureship period in the sugar plantations are common findings in the Indian family. These are well known precursors of suicidal behaviour.

METHODS USED IN SUICIDE

The methods used in suicidal acts are closely equated to the mores, occupation, educational and economic development and accessibility of lethal substances or weapons in that society. Suicidal victims are not usually creative and have a tendency to use tested methods in everyday use.

In Trinidad and Tobago, the commonest method of death by suicide is self-poisoning caused by the ingestion of a deadly weedicide known as paraquat or gramoxone, a member of the organophosphate group of compounds. It is popularly used by farmers in the rural agricultural regions and can be purchased by anyone. There is no legislation with respect to purchasing the compound or storage at home.

Forty years ago death by hanging was the most used method of suicide followed by drowning. Again in rural areas, those associated with farming strangled themselves with rope that was utilized for tethering animals. The rope was first smoothened with candle wax to facilitate easy movement and tied to branches of trees or the beams and ceilings of dwelling houses. The other end was made into a noose and placed around the neck. Death was quick due to strangulation or in some cases through broken necks due to jumping. This method was more common among males, while females preferred drowning. Hanging is still the second most popular form of suicide.

Over the last five years, there has been an increase of suicide by gunshot wounds. This is due to the high level of crime within the country and the inability of the authorities to control the distribution and possession of illegal firearms within society. Jumping is uncommon and may be due to the absence of high rise buildings. Asphyxiation through carbon monoxide poisoning is about 1-2 per million and when reported often involves suicidal pacts of lovers in motor vehicles. Rare cases of auto-erotic asphyxiation have been reported as well as locking oneself into a deep-freeze refrigerator. Self immolation by fire is unknown. Suspected suicidal death through motor vehicular accidents, voluntary drowning or fire-setting to self occupied buildings are difficult to establish.

Among adolescents the commonest form of suicidal attempts is through prescription drugs overdose. Within recent times parasuicidal attempts of substance intoxication are becoming more common. Self–mutilation with wrists cutting and body carvings are on the rise. In this group daring drug induced behaviour can result in fatal outcomes such as drowning, jumping or accidents.

DISCUSSION

Culture is dynamic, it is ever changing. Contemporary human behaviour is influenced by political, economic, social, technological and cultural factors. These influences have affected the most primitive societies and are not always beneficial. Lambo [48] noted that in many parts of Africa social and cultural changes led to altered social habits, to economic pressures and the relaxation of the traditional authority. The changes in the structure and function of the traditional African family have resulted in higher incidences of behaviour disturbances such as drug addiction, abnormal sexuality delinquency and other antisocial behaviour.

Valid distinctions are made between culture and culture bound-syndromes. The most significant is that the latter involved aberrant behaviours that are specific to particular regions or group of people.

The role of the law in defining suicide and the inherent short-comings in such a definition is a prime example of the need for further consideration of the impact of culture on suicidal behaviour. Once this is firmly established it may dispel any misconceptions and census inaccuracies. It may also lead to new legislation with regard to suicide bombers and altruistic suicides.

Recent studies have classified suicide bombers within the same group as conventional suicides. This however may be an instance where strongly held cultural and religious beliefs help motivate their decision to commit suicide. In the Islamic faith, the suicide bomber is upheld as a hero (Shahid or martyr) by those who support the cause. 'Hamas' or rewards of the afterlife may serve as additional impetus [49]. Coercion and deception may be other factors that are not relevant in other cases.

The above findings indicate that suicidal ideation and behaviour vary from nation to nation and across cultures. The latter statement assumes that ethnicity and religion can be used as a means of assessing various cultures. It is therefore evident from the research that some cultures appear to be more suicide prone than others. Religious beliefs, cultural norms endorsed by certain groups and the family structure can act as buffers for suicidal behaviour [26]. A good example of this is the explanation given for the lower rates of suicide among adolescents in Hong Kong when compared to Western nations [31]. In other cases however, ethnicity and religion as seen in the Hindu (East Indian) population may inculcate maladaptive coping styles that serve as a foundation for suicidal behaviour. A genetic predisposition to alcoholism and a turbulent family structure are considered to be risk factors for suicidality [1]. An essential consideration when reviewing suicide patterns across cultures is the propensity for under-reporting that is indigenous to cultures that do not sanction suicidal behaviour.

The gender differences seen with regard to suicidality can also be attributed to gender related psychopathology and psychosocial differences in help-seeking behaviour [50,51]. The latter are all influenced by the cultural environment to which the individual is exposed. One common factor that is evident cross culturally is the clear cut trend of male predominance.

The Caribbean region is an area that is cause for growing concern due to its steady rise in overall mean suicide rate. Trinidad and Tobago was particularly highlighted, since studies showed many socio-cultural factors were instrumental in influencing suicidal behaviour. These factors included transgenerational cultural conflicts, psycho-social problems, media exposure, unemployment, social distress, religion and family structure.

Analysis of the methods used revealed a common trend across some cultures. This was attributed to accessibility and lethality. Ingestion of poisonous substances was most popular followed by hanging.

CONCLUSION

A great deal of research needs to be performed on a global scale to ascertain the degree to which culture impacts on suicidality and this in turn can be used to address the rising rates of these self-destructive behaviours. Culture provides coping strategies to individuals, as civilization advances many of these coping mechanisms are lost unclothing the genetic predisposition of vulnerable groups. In the management of suicidal behaviour a system of therapeutic re-culturation is needed with an emphasis on ethnohistiography, psycho-spiritual and culture therapy.

REFERENCES

[1]   Ali A, Maharajh HD. Social predictors of suicidal behaviour in adolescents in Trinidad and Tobago. Soc Psychiatry Psychiatr Epidemiol 2005;40(3):186-91.

[2]   World Health Oragnisation. World Health Report, October 2001.Geneva: WHO, 2001.

[3]   Weissman MM, Bland RC, Canino GJ, Greenwald S, Hwu HG, Joyce PR, et al. Prevalence of suicide ideation and suicide attempts in nine countries. Psychol Med 1991;29(1):9-17.

[4]   Kraeplin E. Psychiatrie, 8te Auflage, Leeipzig: Barth, 1909. [German]

[5]   Voss G. Die Aetiologie der Psychosen. In: Aschaffenburg G, ed. Handbuch der Psychiatrie. Leipzig: Deuticke, 1915. [German]

[6]   Durkheim E. Suicide: A study in sociology. Glencoe, IL: Free Press, 1951.

[7]   Kiev Λ. Transcultural psychiatry. New York: Free Press, 1972.

[8]   Maharajh HD, Ali A. Recognition of cultural behaviours in Trinidad and Tobago. Internet J Third World Med 2004;3(1):2.

[9]   American Psychiatric Association. Diagnostic and statistical manual of mental disorders IV-TR. Washington, DC: APA, 2000.

[10]   Dein S. Mental health in a multiethnic society. BMJ 1997;106:473-7

[11]   Jilek WG. Culturally related syndromes. In: Gelder MG, Lopez-Ibor JJ, Andreasen N, eds. New Oxford textbook of psychiatry. Oxford: Oxford Univ Press, 2000;1:1061-6.

[12]   Jilek WG, Jilek-Aall L. Kulturspezifische psychische storungen. In: Hemlchen H, Henn F, Lauter H, Sartorius N, editors. Psychiatrie der Gegenwart. Vol. 3: Psychiatrie spezieller Lebenssituationen. Berlin: Springer, 2000. [German]

[13]   Van Wulfften Palthe PM. Amok. Nederlands Tijdschrift voor Geneeskunde 1991;77:983-91. [Dutch]

[14]   14.. Burton-Bradley BG. The amok syndrome in Papua and New Guinea. Med J Aust 1968;1:252-6.

[15]   Westermeyer J. On the epidemicity of amok violence. Arch Gen Psychiatry 1973;28:873-6.

[16] Littlewood R. An indigenous conceptualization of reactive depression in Trinidad. Psychol Med 1985;15:275-81.

[17] Kaplan HI, Sadock BJ. Pocket handbook of clinical psychiatry,3nd ed. Philadelphia, Lippincott Williams Wilkins:2001:126.

[18] Maharajh HD, Hutchinson G. Tabanca in Trinidad and Tobago: Myth, mirth or mood disorder. Caribb Med J 1999;61(1):21-4.

[19] Maharajh HD, Clarke TD, Hutchinson G. Transcultural psychiatry. Psychiatr Bull 1989;10:574-5.

[20] Eriksen TH. Liming in Trinidad: the art of doing nothing. Folk (Sweden), 1990;32. [Online] 1990 [cited 2009 Oct 28]. Availble from: http://www.skettel.com.

[21] Farmer RDT. Assessing the epidemiology of suicide and parasuicide. Br J Psychiatr 1989;153:16-20.

[22] Leenaars AA, Wenckstern S. Altruistic suicides: are they the same or different from other suicides? Arch Suicide Res 2004;8(1):131-6.

[23] Garlow SJ, Purselle D, Heninger M. Ethnic differences in patterns of suicide across the life cycle. Am J Psychiatry 2005;162(2):319-23.

[24] Khan MM. Suicide and attempted suicide in Pakistan. Crisis 1998;19(4):172-6.

[25] Lubin G, Glasser S, Boyko V, Barell V. Epidemiology of suicide in Israel: a nationwide population study. Soc Psychiatry Psychiatr Epidemiol 2001;36(3):123-7.

[26] Oquendo MA, Dragatsi D, Harkavy-Friedman J, Dervic K, Currier D, Burke AK, Grunebaum MF, Mann JJ. Protective factors against suicidal behaviour in Latinos. J Nerv Ment Disord 2005;193(7):438-43.

[27] Tinker H. A new system of slavery. The export of Indian labour overseas 1830-1920. London: Oxford Univ Press, 1974.

[28] Morris P, Maniam T. Suicide in Fiji: a review of the literature. Asia Pac J Public Health 2000;12(1):46-9.

[29] Nadesan K. Pattern of suicide: a review of autopsies conducted at the University Hospital, Kuala Lumpur. Malays J Pathol 1999; 21(2):95-9.

[30] Ko SM, Kua EH. Ethnicity and elderly suicide in Singapore. Int Psychogeriatr 1995;7(2):309-17.

[31] Shek DTL, Lee BM, Chow J. Adolescent suicide and Hong Kong. ScientificWorld Journal 2005;5:702-23.

[32] Shek DTL. Sex differences in the psychological well-being of Chinese adolescents. J Psychol 1989;123:405-12.

[33] Yip PS. Suicides in Hong Kong, Taiwan and Beijing. Br J Psychiatry 1996;169(4):495-500.

[34] Aubert P, Daigle MS, Daigle JG. Cultural traits and immigration: hostility and suicidality in Chinese Canadian students. Transcult Psychiatry 2004;41(4):514- 32.

[35] Wassenaar DR, van der Veen MB, Pillay AL. Women in cultural transition: suicidal behavior in South African Indian women. Suicide Life Threat Behav 1998 28(1):82-93.

[36] Elfawal MA. Cultural influence on the incidence and choice of method of suicide in Saudi Arabia. Am J Forensic Med Pathol 1999;20(2):163-8

[37] Raleigh VS. Suicide patterns and trends in people of Indian subcontinent and Caribbean origin in England and Wales. Ethn Health 1996;1(1):55-63.

[38] Ameerali D. Suicide in Trinidad and Tobago. An ecological study. [Thesis]. St Augustine, West Indies: Faculty Med Sci, Univ West Indies, 2002.

[39] Beaubrun MH. Treatment of alcoholism in Trinidad and Tobago,1956-65. Br J Psychiatry 1976;113(499):643-58.

[40] Parasram R Ethnic differences in reported rates of alcoholism in Trinidad and Tobago. Paper presented Int Congr Alcohol Drug Depend. Alberta, 4-10 August, 1995.

[41] Maharajh HD. Assisted or culpable suicide: is there a difference. Psychiatr Bull 1993;17; 348-9 .

[42] Maharajh HD. Transgenerational cultural conflicts and suicide among Hindu girls. Caribbean Med.J 1998;60(1);16-8

[43] Parasram R, Maharajh HD. Suicide and attempted suicide in Trinidad and Tobago. Caribb Med J 1993;54(1):17-9:

[44] Mohammed S. T&T at the brink of collapse. Sunday Guardian 2005 Jul 31:5.

[45] Hutchinson GA, Simeon DT. Suicide in Trinidad and Tobago: associations with measures of social distress. Int J Soc Psychiatry 1997;43(4):269-75.

[46] Morselli E. Il Suicidio: Saggio di Statistica Morale Comparata. Milan, Italy: Fratelli Dumolard, 1879. [Italian]

[47] Perriens J, Van der Stuyft P, Chee H, Benimadho S. The epidemiology of paraquat intoxications in Surinam. Trop Geogr Med 1989;41(3):266-9.

[48] Lambo, TA. Malignant anxiety: A syndrome associated with criminal conduct in Africans. J Ment Sci 1964;108: 256-64.

[49] Pape R. Dying to win: The strategic logic of suicide terrorism. London: Random House, 2005.

[50] Fergusson DM, Horwood LJ. Male and female offending trajectories. Dev Psychopathol 2002;14(1):159-77.

[51] Fergusson DM, Horwood LJ, Woodward LJ. Risk factors and life processes associated with the onset of suicidal behaviour during adolescence and early adulthood. Psychol Med 2000;30:23-9.

In: Social and Cultural Psychiatry Experience from the... ISBN: 978-1-61668-506-5
Editor: Hari D. Maharajh and Joav Merrick © 2010 Nova Science Publishers, Inc.

Chapter 13

ADOLESCENT SUICIDE IN TRINIDAD AND TOBAGO

Hari D. Maharajh and Akleema Ali

Previous research in Trinidad and Tobago has been limited in examining suicidal behavior through psychological autopsy, secondary data and psychiatric populations. To date there has been no community survey with an emphasis on causation and prevention. A total of 1,845 respondents age 14-20 were selected in 24 schools across the country. Data were collected on socio-demographic variables and suicidal behavior. Gender differences existed for both suicidal ideation and attempts ($p< 0.001$). Respondents from reconstituted families had higher suicidal ideation compared to other family structures ($p<0.001$), while intact families had the lowest rate of suicide attempts ($p<0.01$). Attendance to religious institutions lowered only suicide ideation ($p< 0.05$), while prayer with the family lowered both suicidal ideation ($p< 0.01$) and suicide attempts ($p< 0.001$). Individuals with alcohol abuse in the family had a higher suicidal ideation ($p<0.001$) and attempts ($p<0.001$). Significant social predictors of suicidal behavior in Trinidad and Tobago are gender, attendance to religious institution, prayer with family, family structure and alcohol abuse in the family. It is essential to consider these predictors in planning public health policies.

INTRODUCTION

Suicidal behavior with completed suicide is one of the leading causes of premature death in the adolescent age group. The 1997 US Youth Risk Behavior Survey showed that 20.5% had considered suicide in the past [1] and in Hong Kong as much as 49.6% of the sample had thought about committing suicide [2]. General trends have been identified with respect to the different types of suicidal behavior. Males have a higher suicide rate than females, largely due to the fact that they employ more violent means (e.g. hanging) but the gender difference appears to be greater for adolescents than the general population [3]. Generally males are more successful in committing suicide because they use more irreversible means [4].

In a worldwide review of suicide attempts ranges have spanned from 2.8% in Dutch adolescents to 13.2% in British adolescents [5,6]. American adolescents seemed to hold the middle range with a 7.3% -7.7% rates [1, 7], followed by Norwegian adolescents (8.2%) [8],

South Brazilian and Chinese adolescents (9%) [9,10] and then Slovenian adolescents (10.4%) [5].

There are significant gender differences that have been reported regarding suicidal behavior. In Britain, France, the United States and Slovenia female adolescents report higher levels of suicidal ideation and suicide attempts. In France female adolescents showed significantly higher rates of suicidal ideation when compared to males (12% vs. 5%) [11]. American females also had more thoughts of suicide more than males (27.1% vs. 15.1%) [1] and in female adolescents in Britain [6] suicidal ideation among females were more prevalent than among males, (22.4% vs. 8.5%). Higher percentages were also reported in Slovenia, [5] with large proportions of female adolescents indicating suicidal ideation (55.2% vs. 31.2%).

Major precipitants for self harm or attempted suicide include fights with a girlfriend/boyfriend [12,13] high rates of depression and psychiatric disorders [14,15] truancy, abuse and behavioral problems [16], family dysfunction [13,14] and previous exposure to suicidal behavior [14,17]. In a comparison of adult and adolescent populations measuring suicidal behavior, role of religion and spirituality have been associated with higher rates of suicidal behavior in adult samples with less religiosity [18]. The research in this area is limited regarding adolescent populations, but data from a Longitudinal Study of Adolescent Health, Nonnemaker et al [19] studied the association of both public and private domains of religiosity and health related outcomes. It was found that only private religiosity was associated with a lower probability of having suicidal thoughts or having suicide attempts.

Adolescent's use of alcohol has also been linked to suicidal behavior [20-22]. So too, the association between parents alcohol abuse has been known to have permeating effects on their children. Christofferson and Soothill [23] investigated the long term consequences of parental abuse of alcohol on individuals aged 15-27 years. Their findings revealed that the children of the alcohol abusing parents have increased mortality with a tendency for destructive behaviors such as drug addiction and attempted suicide.

In the Caribbean region, according to the World Health Organization [24], Trinidad and Tobago has the second highest rate of suicide in all West Indian islands, with males having a rate of 17.5/100,000 and females a rate of 5.1/100,000. The estimates of suicide attempts range from 67-95/100,000 and most common in females between the ages of 15-29 years [25].

Previous research in Trinidad and Tobago has been limited in examining suicidal behaviors either through psychological autopsy [26, 28] secondary data [29], psychiatric populations [13,30-32] or social factors of culpability and culture [33,34]. To date there has been no community survey with an emphasis on causation and prevention.

This study attempts to identify social predictors of suicidal behavior in adolescents in Trinidad and Tobago and to examine the role of age, gender, ethnicity, religious practices, family structure, alcohol abuse in the family and type of school in the presentation of such behavior.

OUR STUDY

Trinidad and Tobago has eight counties and a stratified random sample was organized according to these counties. The random sample drawn was an attempt to match the population ratio of each county according to Central Statistical Office reports [35]. A total sample of 1,845 respondents between the ages of 14 and 20 (Form 4-Upper 6) was selected within the various schools in each county. Overall, there were 24 schools, of which 21 were from Trinidad (n= 1642) and 3 from Tobago (n= 203).

- The Suicidal Ideation Questionnaire (SIQ) was used to examine current suicidal ideation. The SIQ is a 30 item questionnaire designed specifically to assess suicide ideation. It is an efficient and economical method of screening for suicidal thoughts and intent in adolescents. It has been tested on grades 10-12 with Cronbach's coefficient alpha of 0.969 and 0.974 respectively and with a total sample reliability coefficient of 0.971. The SIQ is valid through the congruence of item content with specified suicidal cognitions and item total scale correlation (item consistency). In testing the validity, the majority of the item totals ranged from 0.70 to 0.90 [36].
- To measure the demographic variables a questionnaire was developed. The data collected was about age, gender, ethnicity, family structure, religious practices (religious attendance and frequency of prayer with family), suicide attempts, alcohol abuse in the family and type of school. Gender was defined as being either male or female. Age and ethnicity was self reported using one of the given response categories. Ethnicity was coded into four main ethnic groups: Indian, African, Mixed and Other. Family Structure was coded into one of the following categories: living with an intact family (both mother and father), one parent family (either mother or father), single step-parent family (either stepmother or stepfather) and living with relatives. Religious attendance was and frequency of prayer with family was self reported for the period of the past 6 months. The response sets for each variable were 'more than 7 times', '4-6 times', '1-3 times' and 'no time.' Suicide attempts were assessed by the following question: "Have you ever attempted suicide?'. Schools were coded into 'prestige' and 'non prestige' for the variable 'Type of school'. The government assisted secondary schools, which are managed by denominational boards, are generally considered to be prestige schools, while the others are generally considered non-prestige schools. Presence of alcohol use in the family was self reported by the respondent using the response set of either 'yes' or 'no'.

The project required the use of the school population in Trinidad and Tobago. Due to its sensitive nature of the research ethical approval was sought and granted from the Guidance Unit, Ministry of Education. Permission was also granted from the District supervisor of each county as well as the Principals of each school before data was collected. In Tobago permission had to be additionally requested from the Tobago House of Assembly, the governing body for all Tobago affairs.

Data was subsequently collected from the schools in the form of an administered questionnaire. To ensure confidentiality, questionnaires were placed in manila envelopes. Verbal consent was also sought and students were allowed to withdraw from the study at any point in time and questionnaires were returned upon completion in the sealed manila envelopes. All students participated and took 25 minutes to complete the questionnaire.

Data was analyzed using the Statistical Package of Social Science (SPSS version 11). To determine significant differences in suicidal ideation and the respective groups of the variables Analysis of Variance (ANOVA) and independent sample t-tests were used. Pearson chi Square analyses were utilized due to the level of measurement for 'suicide attempts'. The level of significance was set at p<0.05.

OUR FINDINGS

A total of 145 students were sampled across Trinidad and Tobago. For this research 35 questionnaires were excluded due to its incompletion. Therefore, 1810 questionnaires were used for the analysis. The age of the sample ranged from 14 to 20 with a mean age of 16.03 and a standard deviation of 1.13. Sixty percent (60%) of the sample (n = 1078) were females and 40% (n= 730) were males. The ethnic composition was dominated by Indians (40%, n= 722) followed by Africans 34% (n = 609), Mixed 24% (n = 431) and Other 2% (n= 34).

Significant gender differences existed in suicidal ideation, F [1,807] = 24.312, p < 0.001 and suicide attempts, Chi square = 17.309, d.f. = 1, p < 0.001. Females had higher rates for both behaviors (see figure 1).

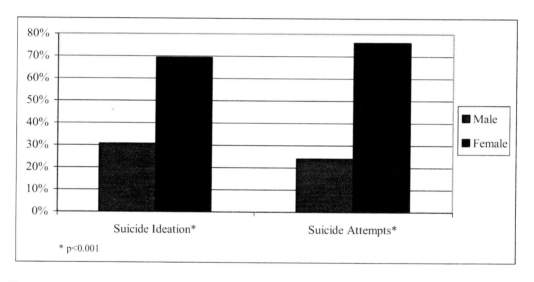

Figure 1. Gender differences in suicidal behaviour

Ethnicity

An ANOVA revealed no significant differences existed between ethnic groups and current suicidal ideation, F (1809) = 2.178, p = 0.069. However Tukey HSD revealed that a significant trend existed between African and Indian individuals, with Indian individuals having higher mean SIQ scores than Africans p< (0.05). Indians and Africans had mean SIQ scores of 28.81 and 23.51 respectively. No significant differences between suicide attempts and ethnic groups existed, Chi-square = 2.163, df = 3, p < 0.539. Suicide attempts according to ethnic groups were as follows: Africans 7.1%, Indians 7.3%, Mixed 8.9% and Other 11.8%.

Religious practices

There were no significant differences (p = 0.64) in suicide attempts between those individuals who attended a religious institution more than seven times within the last 6 months and those who had not attended a religious institution over the same time period. But those who had attended a religious institution more than seven times within the last 6 months had significantly lower suicidal ideation (mean 25.76) compared to those who had not attended a religious institution over the same time period (mean 30.52), t = 2.065, df = 560.96, p < 0.05.

In terms of the levels of suicide ideation, individuals who prayed with their family more than seven times had significantly lower suicide ideation (mean 22.99), compared to other students who had never prayed with their families over the 6 month period (mean 32.33), t = 4.487, df = 1098..62, p< 0.01.

There was also a significant difference with respect to suicide attempts, Chi-square = 14.991, d.f. = 1, p < 0.001 reported by the students who had never prayed with their family, and had higher rates of suicide attempts (11%) compared to those who prayed with their family (4.5%).

Family structure

There was a significant difference between family structure and suicidal ideation. Individuals from reconstituted families had the greatest suicidal ideation, F (1801) = 9.319, p< 0.001. Tukey HSD highlighted that individuals from reconstituted families had a significantly higher mean compared to intact families (p < 0.001) and one parent families (p< 0.01). Significant differences were also found between suicide attempts and family structure, Chi sqaure = 16.394, d.f. = 4, p< 0.01. Intact families had suicide rates of 6.1%, those living with relatives 8.3% rate, one parent families 9.6%, reconstituted families 14.6% and single parent families 16.7%.

Alcohol abuse

There were significant differences between alcohol abuse and suicidal ideation, F (1809) = 49.522, p < 0.001 and alcohol abuse and suicide attempts, Pearson Chi-square =27.466, d.f. = 1, p< 0.001 (see figure 2).

Type of school

There was no significant difference between type of school and suicidal ideation (p = 0.704) or type of school and suicide attempts (p= -0.959).

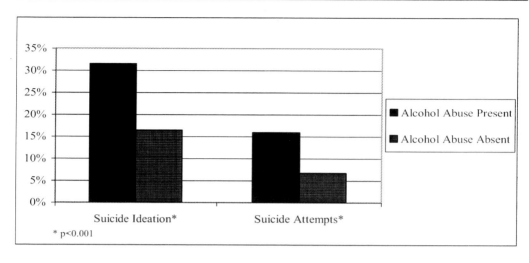

Figure 2. Differences in suicidal behavior and the presence of alcohol abuse in the family

DISCUSSION

Significant gender differences existed in the presentation of suicidal ideation and attempts in Trinidad and Tobago. Females had higher mean SIQ scores compared to male students (29.64 vs. 21.74, p < 0.001) as well as higher rates of suicide attempts compared to males (9.8% vs. 4.5%, p< 0.001). As evidence in the literature, researchers' have found similar findings among American and British adolescents. Velting [37] found that American adolescents females had significantly higher mean adult SIQ scores compared to males (11.73 vs. 9.32). In Europe, Hawton et al [6] found that in British adolescents females also had higher rates of suicidal ideation (22.4% vs. 8.5%) and deliberate self harm (11.2% vs. 3.2%) compared to males.

Suicide attempts were also found to be higher among males compared to females (9.8% vs. 4.5%) with females attempting twice as often as males. In American and Canadian adolescents similar findings were evident. Among American adolescents females had higher rates (11% vs. 4.5%) almost on par with Canadian adolescents (11% vs. 4.6%) [1,38]. In Trinidad the present findings showed that in suicidal behaviour females harbored suicidal ideation 2.3 times more than male students.

Many studies have noted gender differences among suicidal ideation and attempts. These significant differences have been ascribed to gender related psychopathology, intent of the suicidal act and psychosocial differences in help seeking behaviour. Among females, rates of internalizing disorders such as depression and anxiety are approximately twice as much as those of males. In comparison to females, males have higher rates of externalizing behaviors namely antisocial and violent behaviors, substance abuse and school-related and behavioral disorders [39,40]. Of interest though is that females use less lethal methods when they exhibit suicidal behaviour with intent which gives the assumption of lower risk [41]. Females were also more likely to exhibit help seeking behaviour, by visiting doctors, and have further help offered to them [42].

The findings of the present study have revealed that religious practices and suicidal behavior has an inverse relationship. Attendance to a religious institution and prayer with

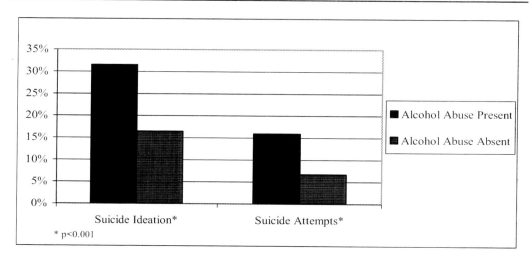

family produced individuals with lower suicidal ideation. Of significant interest is that individuals who prayed with their family had significantly lower rates of suicide attempts in comparison to individuals who never prayed with their family (4.5% vs. 11%). While attendance and prayer with family lowered the risk of suicidal ideation, the family worship seemed to provide an added protection from the risk for suicidal behaviour. In the Caribbean setting, a multicultural society permits various religions and cultures; hence it may be difficult for the protective factor to be present in families where members of one family may belong to different religions.

Our findings indicated that adolescents from reconstituted families had the highest risk for suicidal ideation (mean SIQ 40.45) compared to other family structures. The lowest risk of suicidal behaviour was found in intact family structures compared to other family structures as evidenced by Garnesfski and Diekstra [43]. Those belonging to single step parenting families (n = 6) showed a low SIQ score, but this can be attributed to the small number of step parenting families, rather than it being peculiar to the family dynamics. It is however important to note that the family structure of any home has permeating effects on the identity formation of an adolescents' development.

Of interest to a multicultural society are the ethnic differences that were noted. Between the two major races in Trinidad and Tobago, Indian adolescents had higher mean suicidal ideation scores compared to African adolescents. Analysis of the results showed a trend of significantly more family and social upheavals present within Indo Trinidadian families. Among the Indians when compared to African students they reported significantly more general family problems (p<0.01), quarrels at home (p < 0.05), boyfriend/girlfriend problems (p < 0.05), physical abuse (p < 0.01) and pregnancy (p < 0/01). These occurrences may make the risk of suicidal behaviour more prevalent as a means of a coping mechanism.

In Trinidad the family structure of the Indian family is traditionally of the extended and nuclear type. It holds strong roots in the patriarchal model of family structure, with the father being the main provider and 'head of the household.' The male figure typically provides the home with their basic needs, reinforcer of cultural practices, provider of means for education and disciplinarian This somewhat stable environment still was the bearer of more quarrels at home and more family problems compared to African adolescents in the study. In the African home, the family system is usually characterized by instability, multiple relationships and absent fathers and reported less of the above family problems.

As described by Maharajh [34], transgenerational conflicts are present in the Hindu population in Trinidad and can be a deciding factor in many family squabbles. It has been noted though that in Indian families the kinship ties is very strong in an already extended type family system leading to collective supervision of adolescents. This constant monitoring seems to create dysfunction in the Indian family relationships. A report on suicide in Trinidad and Tobago has perceived the Indian family system as suicidogenic [44].

Adolescents with alcohol abuse present in their family were twice as likely to have high suicidal ideation and also 2.5 times more likely to attempt suicide compared to those who did not have alcohol present in their family. As reported by Lease [45] drinking behaviors disrupts family functioning and directly influence family processes. Alcohol abuse is usually accompanied by disruptive styles of behaviour and may hinder the formation of healthy relationships. Our findings suggest that Indian adolescents reported higher rates of alcohol abuse present in the family (42.4%) compared to the other major race of the island, African who reported much less (29.2%), Mixed (26.4%) and Other (2%). Demographic reports on alcohol use in Trinidad has documented Indians within the island as having higher rates of alcoholism [46, 47] confirming an association between alcohol abuse in the family system and suicidal ideation and suicidal attempts among the Indian adolescent population.

The present study has represented the school enrolled adolescent population and cannot be generalized to adolescents not enrolled in the school system. Another limitation of the research is the use of one clinical instrument to measure current suicidal ideation. This left the result without confirmation that could have been reinforced by the use of another instrument the Beck Scale for Suicidal Ideation [48]. The study also used bivariate associations rather than multivariate models; this is a suggestion for future research.

CONCLUSION

The identification of social predictors for at risk adolescents is important when planning for reformulation of treatment modalities and interventions. The present study has documented that variables such as gender, ethnicity, attendance to a religious institution, prayer with the family, family structure and alcohol abuse in the family may be significant social predictors for adolescent suicide in Trinidad and Tobago.

REFERENCES

[1]   Brener ND, Kruh EG, Simon TR. Trends in suicidal ideation and suicidal behaviors among high school students in the United States 1991-1997. Suicide Life Threat Behav 2000;30(4):304-12.

[2]   Lai KW, Mc Bride-Chang C. Suicidal ideation, parenting style and family climate among Hong Kong adolescents. Int J Psychol 2001; 36(2):81-7.

[3]   National Centre for Health Statistics, 1993.

[4]   Disley B. Suicide prevention initiatives: Youth suicide. The world and New Zealand wide picture. Comm Ment Health NZ1994;8(4): 5-11.

[5]   Tomori M, Keinhorst CWM, de WILDE EJ, van der Bout J. Suicidal Behaviour and family factors among Dutch and Slovenian high school students: a comparison. Acta Psychitr Scand 2001;104: 198-340

[6]   Hawton K, Rodham K, Evans E, Weatherall R. Deliberate self harm in adolescents: self report survey in schools in England. BMJ 2002;235:1207-11.

[7]   Gutierezz PM, Rodriguez PJ, Garcia P. Suicide risks factors for young adults: testing a model across ethnicities. Death Stud 2001;25:319-40

[8]   Wichstrom, L.Predictors of adloscent suicide attempts: anatioanlly representative longitudinal study of Norwegian adolescents. J Am Acad Child Adolesc Psychiatry 2000;39(5):603-10.

[9]   Feijo RB, Saueressig M, Salazar C, Chaves MLF. Menatl health screening by self report questionnaire among community adolescents in Southern Brazil. J Adolesc Health 1997;20:232-7.

[10] Hesketh T, Ding QJ, Jenkins R. Suicide ideation in Chinese adolescents. Soc Psychiatry Psychiatr Epidemiol 2002;37:230-5.

[11] Choquest M, Kovess V. Suicidal thoughts in adolescents: an intercultural approach. Adolescence 1993;28(111):649-60.

[12] Hurry J, Storey P. Deliberate self-harm in young people: the hospital response. Final report to the Department of Health. London: HMSO, 1998.

[13] Neehall J, Beharry N. Demographic and clinical features of adolescent parasuicide. West Indian Med J 1994;43(4):123-6.

[14] Joyce P. Suicide and self harm. In: Mc Dowell H, Ziginskas D, eds. Feelings stink: A resource on young people's mental health – issues for those who work with them. Wellington: Min Health, 1994:26-8.

[15] Drummond WJ. Adolescents at risk: causes of youth suicide in New Zealand. Adolescence 1997;32(128):925-35.

[16] Incidence Survey of At-Risk in New Zealand Secondary Schools. Survey commissioned by Porirua College as a follow up to the "Successful programmes for At-Risk students" conference. Wellington, Apr 1993.

[17] Mercy JA, Kresnow M-J, O'Carroll PW, Lee RK, Powell KE, Potter LB, et al. Is suicide contagious? A study of the relation between exposure to the suicidal behaviour of others and nearly lethal suicide attempts. Am J Epidemiol 2001;154(2):120-7.

[18] Kaslow NJ, Prce AW, Wyckoff S, Bender Grall M, Sherry A, Young S, et al, Person factors assicted with suicida l behaviour in African American women and men. Cult Divers Ethnic Minor Psychol 2004; 10(1):5-22.

[19] Nonnemaker JM, Mc Neely CA, Blum RW. Public and private domains of religiousity and adolescent health risk behaviours: evidence from the National Longitudinal Study of Adlscennt Health. Soc Sci Med 2003;57(11):2049-54.

[20] Kelly TM, Cornelius JR, Clark DB. Psychiatric disorders and attempted suicide among adolescents with substance use disorders. Drug Alcohol Depend 2004;73(1):87-97.

[21] Licanan I, Music E, Laslo E, Berg-Kelly K, Masic I, Redzic A, et al. Suicidal thoughts related to psychoactive substance abuse among adolescents. Med Arh 2003;54(4):237-40.

[22] Markowitz S, Chatterji P, Kaestner R. Estimating the impact of alchol policies on youth suicides. J Ment Health Policy 2003;6(1):37-46.

[23] Christofferson MN, Soothill K. The long term consequences of parental alcohol abuse: a cohort study of children in Denmark. J Subst Abuse Treat 2003;25(2):107-16.

[24] World Health Organization. World Health Report, October 2001. Geneva: WHO, 2001.

[25] Parasaram R, Maharajh HD. Suicide and attempted suicide In Trinidad and Tobago. Caribb Med J 1993;54(1):17-9.

[26] Hutchinson G, Daisley H, Simmons V, Gordon A. Suicide by poisoning. West Indian Med J 1991;40:69-73.

[27] Hutchinson GA, Daisley H, Simeon D, Simmonds V, Shetty M, Lynn D. High rates of paraquat-induced suicide in southern Trinidad. Suicide Life Threat Behav 1999;29(2):186-91.

[28] Daisley H Jr, Simmons V. Forensic analysis of acute fatal poisonings in the southern districts of Trinidad. Vet Hum Toxicol 1999;41(1): 23-5.

[29] Hutchinson GA, Simeon DT. Suicide in Trinidad and Tobago: associations with measures of social distress. Int J Soc Psychiatry 1997;43(4):269-75.

[30] Burke AW. Clinical aspects of attempted suicide among women in Trinidad and Tobago. Br J Psychiatry 1974;125(0):175-6.

[31] Burke AW. Socio-cultural aspects of attempted suicide among women in Trinidad and Tobago. Br J Psychiatry 1974;125(0):374-7.

[32] Burke AW. Attempted suicide in Trinidad and Tobago. West Indian Med J 1974;23(4):250-5.

[33] Maharajh HD. Assisted suicide or culpable suicide: is there a difference. Psychiatr Bull 1993;17:348-9.

[34] Maharajh HD. Transgenerational cultural conflicts and suicide among Hindu girls. Caribb Med J 1998;60(1):16-8.

[35] Central Statistical Office. Annual Reports, Port Spain, Trinidad: Office Prime Min, 2001.

[36] Reynolds WM. Suicidal ideation questionnaire: Professional manual. Odessa, FL: Psychol Assess Resources, 1988.

[37] Velting DM. Suicidal ideation and the five factor model of personality. Pers Individ Dif 1999;27:943-52.

[38] Edwards MJ, Holden RR. Coping, meaning in life and suicidal manifestations: examining gender differences. J Clin Psychol 1998; 57(12):1517-34.

[39] Fergusson DM, Horwood LJ. Male and female offending trajectories. Dev Psychopathol 2002;14(1):159-77.

[40] Fergusson DM, Woodward LJ, Horwood LJ. Risk factors and life processes associated with the onset of suicidal behaviour during adolescence and early adulthood. Psychol Med 2000;30:23-9.

[41] Beautrais A.L. Gender issues in youth suicidal behaviour. Emerg Med 2002;14:35-42.

[42] Hawton K, Fagg J, Simkins S, Bale E, Bond A. Deliberate self-harm in Oxford 1985-1995. J Adolescence 2000;23(1):47-55.

[43] Garneski N, Diekstra RF. Adolescents from one parent, stepparent and intact families: emotional problems and suicide attempts. J Adolescence 1997;20:201-8.

[44] Ameerali D. Suicide in Trinidad and Tobago. An ecological study. DM Psychiatry [Thesis]. St Augustine: Faculty Med Sci, Univ West Indies, 2002.

[45] Lease SH. A model of depression in adult children of alcoholics and non alcoholics. J Couns Dev 2002;80(4):441-52.

[46] Beaubrun MH. Treatment of alcoholism in Trinidad and Tobago, 1956-65. Br J Psychiatry 1976;113(499):643-58.

[47] Parasram R. Ethnic differences in reported rates of alcoholism in Trinidad and Tobago. Paper Int Congr Alcohol Drug Depend. Alberta, 1995 Aug 4-10.

[48] Beck A, Steer R. Beck Scale for suicide ideation. San Antonio, TX: Psychol Corp, 1993.

In: Social and Cultural Psychiatry Experience from the...　　ISBN: 978-1-61668-506-5
Editor: Hari D. Maharajh and Joav Merrick　　© 2010 Nova Science Publishers, Inc.

Chapter 14

PATTERNS OF SUICIDE AND SUICIDAL BEHAVIORS: CONTEXT AND CAUSATION

Hari D. Maharajh

The context and causation of suicidal behavior and suicide in many developing countries may vary from most developed societies. In this chapter, four local areas of interest are highlighted with respect to common but less reported precipitating factors in suicide and suicidal behavior. These are family culpability with reference to the present trend of assisted suicide, transgenerational family conflicts resulting in family dysfunction, imitation or copy-cat suicide in a child and suicidal behavior in a psychotic patient. The manifestations of these behaviors are often interwoven into a tangled net of social, religious, cultural, traditional and superstitious beliefs that prevent intervention. Even among children, excessive punishment viewed by some as abuse is acceptable. In Trinidad with a rainbow of modern and traditional influences, special training of cultural therapists are recommended for psychological and psychiatric intervention into this sensitive area.

INTRODUCTION

Within the Caribbean region, the issue of suicidal behavior is a growing problem. According to the World Health Organization [1], Trinidad and Tobago has the second highest rate of suicide in all West Indian islands, with males having a rate of 17.5/100,000 and females a rate of 5.1/100,000. A definite rate for attempted suicide is not known but estimates range from 67-95/100,000 with attempts most common in females between the ages of 15-29 [2]. Ethnically, the Indian population has dominated the suicide cases in Trinidad. Among the reasons identified for this occurrence are marginalization and ethnic disadvantage [3], psychiatric illness, lover's quarrel and family dispute [4] and substance abuse, unemployment and imitation suicidal behavior [5].

Attempted suicide is thought to be at least eight times as frequent at all ages as completed suicide and considerable more so in children and adolescents. Attempted suicide is a potentially disastrous and lethal event; and can be considered a risk factor for completed suicide and a potential indicator of other problems such as substance abuse, depression or adjustment and stress reactions [6]. As many as 6-11% of all high school students can be expected to have made at least one suicidal attempt. Attempted suicide is a serious problem as it reflects a considerable amount of psychological suffering and desperation for the attempters, and suicide attempters are at risk later for completed suicide [7]. Females are believed to attempt suicide three to four times as often as males and to rely upon less lethal methods in attempts than males [8,9].

General trends have been identified with respect to the different types of suicidal behavior. Males have a higher suicide rate than females, largely due to the fact that they employ more violent and irreversible means (e.g. hanging). This distinction allows them to be more successful in committing suicide [10]. This gender difference appears to be greater for adolescents than the general population [11].

An analysis of various papers originating from Trinidad has highlighted research on suicidal behaviors has been limited through psychological autopsy [12-14], secondary data [15], and psychiatric populations [16-19].

The chapter seeks to highlight some of the behavioral patterns and suicidal behavior that have been documented in Trinidad. Among these have been cases of culpable or assisted suicide, transgenerational conflicts leading to suicide and imitation or copycat suicidal behavior in children.

ASSISTED OR CULPABLE SUICIDE

In 1991, Derek Humphrey published "Final exit. The practicalities of self deliverance and assisted suicide for the dying" [20]. The book was written for mature adults who were suffering from terminal illnesses and required guidance in committing suicide, but it has encouraged suggestive and susceptible people to attempt suicide [21]. There appears to be a thin line between assisted suicide and culpable suicide. 'Culpable suicide' is used here to describe contributory negligence attributed to persons who unknowingly assist another person's suicide.

Trinidad and Tobago has a population of 1.3 million, of whom 40% are Indians [22]. Most Indians are Hindus, comprising approximately 30% of the total population. The suicide rate is highest among Indians, and paraquat poisoning is the main cause of death. Legislation to restrict the availability of paraqaut (an herbicide) has never been implemented. This substance, therefore, is readily available in the agricultural regions, where most Indians live.

Theories put forward for the high rate of suicide among Indians in Trinidad include marginalization and ethnic disadvantage [3], stress, the high rate of unemployment, family discord, and an increase in reporting of suicides by the media [5]. Religion and culture appear also to contribute. The following is a case of culturally determined culpable suicide.

CASE STUDY 1

An 18 year old female student from an Orthodox Hindu family was admitted to the medical ward of the General Hospital following the ingestion of a poisonous substance, gramoxone. Despite acute emergency procedures, she died two weeks later. An interview with her prior to her death revealed that, following a dispute with her father, she ingested the poisonous substance. Her father had arranged a marriage for her of which she had disapproved. On the evening of the ingestion, she attempted to leave home to visit her boyfriend of another religious persuasion; her father insisted that the only way she was going to leave his house that day was in a box. That night she drank the weedicide.

TRANS GENERATIONAL CONFLICTS

The majority of adolescents and young adults admitted to hospitals in Trinidad and Tobago for attempted or completed suicide are Indo Trinidadians. Among the precipitation factors identified, little attention has been directed to transgenerational cultural conflict over dress, food, music, social attitudes and religious beliefs. The changing patterns of the Trinidadian society have aroused ambivalent feelings towards subculture traditional beliefs and seem to have alienated individuals from their families and communities. This has resulted in a social situation of anomie wherein the normative values of Indo Trinidadian beliefs have lost their force. Thus, to members of this group in the absence of standards of guidance in times of stress may explain the high rate of suicide. The following is a case of Transgenerational cultural conflicts precipitating to suicide.

CASE STUDY 2

A 22 year old Indo-Trinidadian, recently employed as a bank clerk developed a relationship with an Afro Trinidadian worker unknown to her family. A few months later, news reached the family that their daughter was having a relationship with a socio-culturally unacceptable person. Her mother, a devout Hindu pleaded with her daughter on many occasions to terminate her relationship. Without success, she proceeded to a restaurant where she found her daughter having lunch with her boyfriend. She became very angry and said to her daughter, "You have disgraced the family, it is better for you to die with dignity than to let us live in this disgrace." That evening her daughter ingested two teaspoonfuls of paraquat and subsequently died.

IMITATION SUICIDE

Internationally, a number of studies have investigated the effect of media influence on aggressive and homicidal behaviour in children without definitive conclusions. These investigations are limited by defining and measuring the influence of the media and determining whether the association is causal. A recent review states that there is consistent evidence for violent imagery in television, film and video causing changes in arousal, emotions and behaviour which may result in aggressive or fearful behaviour in younger children with inconsistent evidence for the older children and adolescents [23]. The kind of imitation behaviour has been referred to as 'copycat suicide' and is "a duplication or copycat of another suicide that the person attempting suicide knows about, either from local knowledge or due to accounts or depictions of the original suicide on television and in other media." This type of behavior or idea contagion is known as the Werther effect, following Goethe's writing of the "The sorrows of Young Werther" that resulted in a spate of suicides [24].

Suicide behaviour among primary school children is uncommon with the mean annual world wide rate for suicide between the ages of 5 and 14 years reported to be as 0.5 /100,000 for females and 0.9 /100,000 for males [25]. Most suicides in children occur after the age of 12 years and suicidal behaviour in younger children is rare. Few studies are available on suicidal behaviour in preschool children below the age of 5 years. These are often associated with depression, family instability including child abuse and parental psychopathology [26-28]. In 1984 sixteen suicidal preschoolers were studied and these preschoolers showed significantly more aggression, loss of interest, depression, impulsivity, hyperactivity and running away behavior when compared to non suicidal preschoolers[29]. Pfeffer et al [30] assessed distinct types of suicidal children with the intensity of aggression, family instability and depression predicting the degree of assault behavioral problems and suicidal behaviour. There seems to be a gender difference in suicidal behaviour where psychotic disorders are reported to increase suicidality in boys of 7 years of age with higher incidence of personality disorders in girls associated with suicidal behaviour [31].

There is no information available about the incidence and prevalence of suicide and suicidal behaviour among preschool and primary school children in Trinidad and Tobago. A recent study in schoolchildren aged 14-20 years showed that females had higher rates of suicidal ideations and attempts with a number of social predictors of suicidal behaviour in these youths. Attendance to a religious institution, prayer with the family, gender, family structure and alcohol abuse were seen as factors influencing the risk for suicidal behaviour [32]. The following is a case of a six (6) year old girl in Trinidad, suggestive of imitation or copycat suicide.

CASE STUDY 3

A 6-year-old child and her mother were seen in the Psychiatry Clinic in a Health Centre after being referred by a General Practitioner. She had attempted to strangle herself with a rope on a tree. On examination, he found bruises in the neck caused by the strangulation with the rope and there were also bruises on her upper arms and back. The child was seen by the examiner in a separate room without the mother and she wrote down her story and spoke about it. She reported that another child hit her that day in her belly and she fell. She went home and took the rope and hung it in the tree. She had seen this in a movie ("Passion of Christ") the night before and wanted to try it because she was angry and sad at what she had seen. She was caught in the act by her grandmother who informed her mother and together they scolded her and gave her 'some good licks' a common practice of excessive physical punishment by care takers in the Caribbean region

The child describes herself as being happy, having plenty of friends and likes to play and write down things. She is living with her mother, stepfather and her 15-year-old brother in one house, in the same yard with her grandmother and other family members. They look after her when she comes from school, since her mother is still at work. She says that she gets along well with her stepfather describing him as 'nice' and also her mother who she "likes but she gets easily angry". She fights a lot with her brother 'who gives her licks sometimes'.

During pregnancy with her daughter, her mother was involved in a motor vehicle accident in which she lost her second son. She became tearful and depressed and after childbirth was treated with antidepressants. The child's development is normal and she is a happy well adjusted person who has many friends at school and excels at her work. There has been no family history of mental disorders in the family.

On Mental Status Examination, this six year old female Afro-Trinidadian girl appeared older than her age. She was assertive but playful, friendly and cooperative. She was talkative and asked a lot of questions. She had good attachment to her mother involving her in the things she was doing. On agreement to speak to the examiner alone she related a story of being punched in the stomach (belly). She appeared restless and easily distracted and wanted to play with the computer on the desk. She was not hyperactive, her mood was normal and she had no abnormal perceptions. She was not cognitively impaired. With respect to the attempted hanging, she had no concept of suicide or death and was simply imitating what she saw portrayed in the film.

CASE STUDY 4

Mr JC is a 34 year old Afro-Trinidadian male of the Spiritual Baptist faith. He is employed as a Police Constable, and resides in Chaguanas. He was referred from the Eric Williams Medical Sciences Complex (EWMSC) to a psychiatric clinic after attempting to hang himself, three (3) months ago. Mr. C had not planned the incident which occurred at about midday of his off-day which is usually on a Monday.

JC described the scenario as follows. He was watching television at home while his wife was in the kitchen. J.C proceeded upstairs, wrapped a rope around the rafter of the roof and used it to hang himself but stated he had no intention of dying. Of interest is that he reported having several spiritual encounters with a male figure that he was familiar with. He was quite guarded in his response as he refused to divulge how long he has been having these encounters. He claimed the male figure has previously given him revelations that proved to be true and had most recently directed him to hang himself while assuring him no harm.

JC reported that he saw this incident as a test of faith and drew reference to the story of Abraham, who was asked to sacrifice his son. Though he did not believe he was Abraham, he emphatically stated that he would be willing to perform any act or task the being asked of him even if he was asked to repeat the most recent episode, the hanging.

At the time of Mr JC's visit to the psychiatric clinic there was no depressive or anxiety symptoms elicited or current suicidal ideation. He denied any substance abuse, however third party information from a co-worker and friend indicated heavy alcohol consumption by JC. He has no concurrent medical conditions, no past psychiatric history and no family history of psychiatric illness.

The Mental Sate Examination revealed an alert, well dressed, coherent man with auditory and visual hallucinations. He showed poor insight into his condition, but no cognitive impairment. JC seems to be in denial of his condition and refuses to understand the seriousness of the incident. He strongly believes that the incident is a spiritual one that can only be understood by him.

Overall JC has a strained marital and family relationship. He has a tense relationship with his father and presently has a limited relationship with his three children who live with their mothers, due to a past history of "playing the field" (infidelity). He also has difficulties with his present wife as he gambles, and she suspects infidelity. He presently lives with his in laws, experiences economic difficulty, has a stressful job and in the process of finding a new house, his wife refuses to live where he attempted to hang himself.

DISCUSSION

In cases 1 and 2, the parents acted in accordance with their orthodox religious instructions that denounces the "intermixture of castes" as stated in the Bhagwad Gita [33]. After 164 years of arrival from India, Indo Trinidadians still hold strong to their religious and cultural beliefs. There is much resistance to change, and cross-cultural fertilization is unacceptable to most Indians. Marriages are still arranged on the basis of caste, and adherence to religion is a source of hope in this subculture that perceives itself to be alienated.

With this background, older members of families feel justified in pronouncing death sentences on offspring who deviate from the cultural norms. They appear to experience little guilt and seem to have poor insight in their culpability. They are assisted by an existing religious cultural framework that has prescribed a certain amount of defensive aggression. Undoubtedly, the parents perceived a threat to their families and that which they hold as sacred. Fromm in 1974 supported this view when he wrote "The individual or the group reacts to attack against the 'sacred' with the same rage and aggressiveness to an attack against life" [34]. Their behaviour is therefore understandable.

Such occurrences, however, have generated much debate among 'traditionalists', who are intent in preserving their beliefs at any cost, and the 'modernists' who perceive parental adherence to religiosity and culturally sanctioned behaviour as being too rigid. Attempts to introduce change are challenged by a belief in Karma, cycles of births and deaths, reincarnation and other Hindu philosophies. Similarly, assisted suicide is justifiable to some on the basis of the avoidance of pain and suffering of patients with terminal illnesses. Guidance on committing suicide is a Western notion, where the preservation of life is weighed against economic cost, physical burden and absence of emotional attachment.

In case 2, social causation seems to be an important determinant in her suicide. The changing patterns of Trinidadian society have resulted in increased social pressures to those belonging to orthodox religions. The changing female role of increased assertiveness, more independence and more liberation both inside and outside the home have eroded the foundation of orthodox stability. This has resulted in ambivalent values within family systems with skewing and schism of family members. Thus on a cultural background of an extended family system, quarrels, disputes and discord with collusions and coalition amongst family members are pervasive. Suicide can be seen here as a means of conflict resolution. In addition, the absence or denial of socialized power, prestige and position to members of the Indian subculture in Trinidad and Tobago have been cited as contributory factors to suicide [3].

There is no doubt that cultural factors play an important role in the lifestyles of Indian Trinidadians. The latter being the last migrants to this country, have for many years been denied the rights to their beliefs. Following movement to a new environment, their traditional beliefs were challenged and devalued, first by the British colonist and later by the Christian indoctrination. Still later, political mechanisms were introduced that were adverse to the religious and cultural development of this group, while simultaneously propagating the culture of African Trinidadians as the national norm. The attempt to force social and cultural change among Indo Trinidadians has resulted in a stressful situation, since attempting to change the structure and function of a traditional family, members having renounced that their old culture, have failed to assimilate the new. Such splitting will result in that group becoming more prone to suicide and other anti social behaviour.

The third scenario describes suicidal behaviour in the form of attempted hanging in a 6-year-old girl. While it is difficult to determine causation, it is noteworthy that this child is immersed in a culture of violence namely aggression at school from another child, a brother who 'gives her licks' and possibly punitive parents and grandparents as evidenced by the bruises found on her back and arms. In addition, to her caretakers it matters little that she was exposed to a movie that depicted violence, bloody scenes and hanging. A child learns what she sees, and exposure to such cruelty and violence seem to be the norm in this family. At the present time, the entire society in Trinidad is riddled with uncontrollable violence and murder.

Notwithstanding inconclusive evidence on the relationship between the media and violent behaviour among children, recent findings indicate clear evidence of aggression in media resulting in increased aggressive behaviour in young children [23]. Some studies have cautioned parents on the effects of the media and also violent video games on the behaviour of their children [35-37].

Suicidal behaviour among psychotic patients are considered to be less common when compared to patients with depression and substance abuse. It is estimated that among all suicides in Trinidad 5-10% are completed with those with psychotic disorders. This excludes patients with bipolar diseases. As in Case 4 above, the majority of these patients are diagnosed as suffering from schizophrenia coloured by religious supernaturalism that they consider beyond the understanding of medical doctors. Two groups are identified in practice, those with command hallucinations of voices or forces urging or commanding them to behave in a certain manner and a second cluster of suicide following recovery, that is, post psychotic suicide. Religious based command hallucinations associated with scriptural injunctions are compelling and this patient emphasized that he would be willing to perform any act or task that is being asked of him, even if he was asked to repeat the most recent episode, the hanging. Post psychotic suicide is the practice of suicide after recovery from a psychotic illness. These patients, on regaining insight of the course and nature of their illness, make a rational decision to end their life. The traditional view that the risk of suicide is highest during the early recovery period is not without merit, but it is equally important to carefully walk the patient through personal and social adjustment after recovery. This is particularly true of patients of middle and upper social classes who previously interacted with others.

CONCLUSION

It is important to differentiate between the end of one's suffering and the end of one's life, as in cases 1 and 2 presented both patients sought forgiveness for their actions and wanted to live after their suicidal act. It is unacceptable to resolve such conflict through the publication of guides to suicide. In such deaths, responsibility must lie somewhere. If there is assistance there is culpability. The culpability therefore of culturally determined suicide may not only rest with the individuals or families in crises, but in myopic governmental strategy of nation building. The solution to the high suicide rate amongst Indians highlights the need for mental health professionals who are experienced in working with Indian families, and who have an understanding of relevant cultural issues.

Case 3 illustrates the possible dramatic effect media, in combination with other psychosocial stressors, can have on behaviour in young children resulting in a dangerous strangulation attempt in the case of this 6-year-old girl. It can also be that her aggressive behaviour with her brother is influenced by violence on television and other media sources. The influence of media, including violent video games, computer games and internet, should not be underestimated in this time where very young children spend increasing time with these forms of media. There is a responsibility for parents to be aware of this situation and limit the amount of aggressive images for their children. Also the government has an important role in this with legislating types and amounts of violence in video games and making warnings for movies. In third world countries like Trinidad and Tobago, there is an absence of available facilities to monitor the exclusion of children from exposure to violence. In fact children are often used by parents to protest with placards poor conditions in schools and communities. There is a need for proper legislation.

Less attention has been given to the study of psychosis and suicide as reported in Case 4. This is a complex area as in the case reported here, that needs some investigation of the patient's religious philosophy and practices. This is a sensitive area that many psychiatrists are unwilling to tread. In a country like Trinidad with a multitude of ethnic groups, religions and culture intermingled with a callaloo of obeah, superstition and magic, there is need for the training and introduction of cultural therapists in mental health.

REFERENCES

[1] World Health Organization. World Health Report, October 2001. Geneva: WHO, 2001.
[2] Parasaram R, Maharajh HD. Suicide and attempted suicide In Trinidad and Tobago. Caribb Med J 1993;54(1):17-9.
[3] Parasram R. Suicide and ethnic disadvantage. Paper presented Conf Suicide Fam Life, Trinidad, 1992 Sept 20.
[4] Hutchinson G, Daisley H, Simmons V, Gordon A. Suicide by poisoning. West Indian Med J 1991;40:69-73.
[5] Maharajh HD. Imitation suicidal behaviour in Trinidad and Tobago. Paper Conference Suicide Fam Life, Trinidad 1992 Sept 20.
[6] Centers for Disease control. Attempted suicide among high school students-United States. MMWR 1991;40:633-5.

[7]   Meehan PJ, Lamb JA, Saltzman LE, O'Carroll PW. Attempted suicide among young adults: progress towards a meaningful estimate of prevalence. Am J Psychiatry 1992;149:41-4.

[8]   Garland AF, Ziglar E. Adolescent suicide prevention: current research and social policy implications. Am Psychol 1993:48:169-82.

[9]   Gelman D. The mystery of suicide. Newsweek 1994 Apr 18:44-9

[10] Disley B. Suicide prevention initiatives: Youth suicide. The world and New Zealand wide picture. Comm Ment Health NZ 1994;8(4):5-11.

[11] National Centre for Health Statistics, 1993.

[12] Hutchinson G, Daisley H, Simmons V, Gordon A. Suicide by poisoning. West Indian Med J 1991;40:69-73.

[13] Hutchinson GA, Daisley H, Simeon D, Simmonds V, Shetty M, Lynn D. High rates of paraquat-induced suicide in southern Trinidad. Suicide Life Threat Behav 1999;29(2):186-91.

[14] Daisley H Jr, Simmons V. Forensic analysis of acute fatal poisonings in the southern districts of Trinidad. Vet Hum Toxicol 1999;41(1): 23-5.

[15] Hutchinson GA, Simeon DT. Suicide in Trinidad and Tobago: associations with measures of social distress. Int J Soc Psychiatry 1997;43(4):269-75.

[16] Neehall J, Beharry N. Demographic and clinical features of adolescent parasuicide. West Indian Med J 1994;43(4):123-26.

[17] Burke AW. Clinical aspects of attempted suicide among women in Trinidad and Tobago. Br J Psychiatry 1974;125:175-6.

[18] Burke AW. Socio-cultural aspects of attempted suicide among women in Trinidad and Tobago. Br J Psychiatry 1974;125(0);374-7.

[19] Burke AW. Attempted suicide in Trinidad and Tobago. West Indian Med J 1974;23(4):250-5.

[20] Humphrey D. Final exit. The practicalities of self deliverance and assisted suicide for the dying. Eugene, OR: Hemlock Society, 1991.

[21] Lavin M, Martin G, Roy A. Suicidality and final exit. Am Psychiatr Assoc, 145th Ann Meet, Washington DC, 1992.

[22] Central Intelligence Agency. The World Fact Book, Trinidad and Tobago. [Online] 2007 [cited 2009 Aug 20]. Available from: http://www.ece.gov.nt.ca/Maps/World%20and%20Canada%20Maps%20Publish/factbo ok/print/td.html

[23] Browne KD, Hamilton-Giachritsis C. The influence of violent media on children and adolescents: a public-health approach. Lancet 2005;365(9460):702-10.

[24] Wikepedia free encyolpedia. Werther Effect. [Online] 2009 [cited 2009 Oct 07]. Available from: http://en.wikipedia.org/wiki/Werther_effect.

[25] Pelkonen M, Marttunen M. Child and adolescent suicide: epidemiology, risk factors, and approaches to prevention. Paediatr Drugs 2003;5(4):243-65.

[26] Pfeffer CR, Normandin L, Kakuma T. Suicidal children grow up: suicidal behavior and psychiatric disorders among relatives. J Am Acad Child Adolesc Psychiatry 1994;33(8):1087-97.

[27] Pfeffer CR, Trad PV. Sadness and suicidal tendencies in preschool children. J Dev Behav Pediatr 1988;9(2):86-8.

[28] Rosenthal PA, Rosenthal S, Doherty MB, Santora D. Suicidal thoughts and behaviors in depressed hospitalized preschoolers. Am J Psychother 1986;40(2):201-12.

[29] Rosenthal PA, Rosenthal S. Suicidal behavior by preschool children. Am J Psychiatry 1984;141(4):520-5.

[30] Pfeffer CR, Plutchik R, Mizruchi MS. Suicidal and assaultive behavior in children: classification, measurement, and interrelations. Am J Psychiatry 1983;140(2):154-7.

[31] Hog V, Isager T, Skovgaard AM. Suicidal behavior in children--a descriptive study. Ugeskr Laeger 2002;164(49):5790-4. [Danish]

[32] Ali A, Maharajh HD. Social predictors of suicidal behaviour in adolescents in Trinidad and Tobago. Soc Psychiatry Psychiatr Epidemiol 2005;40(3):186-91.

[33] Swarupananda S, Gita SB. Indian Press Pvt Ltd Calcutta 700013, 1982.

[34] Fromm E. The anatomy of human destructiveness. London: Penguin, 1974.

[35] Muscari M. Media violence: advice for parents. Pediatr Nurs 2002;28(6):585-91.

[36] Villani S. Impact of media on children and adolescents: a 10-year review of the research. J Am Acad Child Adolesc Psychiatry 2001;40(4):392-401.

[37] Vessey JA, Lee JE. Violent video games affecting our children. Pediatr Nurs 2000;26(6):607-9,632.

In: Social and Cultural Psychiatry Experience from the... ISBN: 978-1-61668-506-5
Editor: Hari D. Maharajh and Joav Merrick © 2010 Nova Science Publishers, Inc.

Chapter 15

DERMA-ABUSE WITH CUTTING IN YOUNG ADOLESCENTS

Hari D. Maharajh and Rainah Seepersad

Derma-abuse or self-inflicted epidermal damage is introduced here for the first time to describe a number of blood-letting behaviours among adolescents. Formerly classified under the umbrella of suicidal behaviours, it is associated with low lethality and the absence of suicidal attempts. Derma-abuse encompasses a number of behaviours replete with synonyms and acronyms. Researchers for the most part have described a medley of behaviours that have been categorized as life threatening and equated with suicidal intent. The purpose of this study was therefore two-fold: First, to present and discuss vignettes of four young adolescents and second to study the dynamics and characteristics of six derma-abusers who have attended Dual Group Therapy (DGT) concurrently with their parents for a six month period with an emphasis on the dynamics of behaviour and treatment. Our findings suggest that patients involved in derma-abuse are generally non suicidal but engage in comfort cutting for the psychological release of pain, tension reduction and anger management. There is a preponderance of females (80%) with an over-representation of mixed origin and borderline cultural states. In this small group, males amounted to 20% and were more bizarre, gruesome and brutal in their self-abuse. Of the total sample, 10% were of African origin, 60% were of Indian descent and 30% were of mixed ancestry. Psychodynamic factors explored in Dual Group Therapy (DGT) are the emphasis on non-suicidal intent, association with tension reduction, reclaiming power and mastery over self and others, life and death instincts, the significance of bloodletting in a socio-cultural context, trans-generational, dysfunctional family dynamics frequently with parental separation and sexual abuse and early sexual induction. A novel form of DGT is introduced for the treatment of these patients. The changing attitudes of adolescents in today's culture as they freely engage in risky behaviors present a major mental health crisis to service providers both in developing and developed countries.

INTRODUCTION

Self-inflicted epidermal damage, referred to as derma-abrasion and derma-contusion are common practices among young adolescents. This preoccupation of 'seeing blood flow', especially among school children generates a tremendous amount of concern, emotion and help-seeking behaviour for families and institutions alike. It conjures up medieval tales of vampires and witches, superstition and obeah in the Caribbean setting and new age, electronic induced cultures of satanic cults of self sacrifice, blood drinking and unholy music. School authorities are often harsh on students with such behaviours out of fear of contagion, the perceived risks of death and its association with demonical possession.

There is much confusion in the classification of suicidal behaviours with the general view that self-inflicted human blood release is equated to suicidal behaviour. The literature is replete with descriptive terminologies: Suicide and parasuicide [1] suicide and deliberate self poisoning/injury [2], and non-fatal deliberate self-harm [3]. Other synonyms are "self injury" (SI), "self-harm" (SH) "self-mutilation," "deliberate self-harm", (DSH) "self injurious behaviour" (SIB), and "self inflicted violence" (SIV) which are used interchangeably to explain a common pattern of behaviour where demonstrable injury is self inflicted [4-9].

Self-mutilation has its origin in many cultures around the world. In ancient Mayan civilizations, Sadhus or Hindus ascetics and early Catholic and Jewish Canaanite rituals, all involved some form of bloodletting or self flagellation that are associated with great religious and spiritual sacrifice or rites of passage [10]. In the 1880's, this form of behaviour was the norm among cultures and was not distinguished from other behavioural problems. In 1935 and 1938, an important distinction was made with a modification of the term self-mutilation that was initially introduced by LE Emerson [10]. This differentiation considered the view that suicidal behaviour and self-mutilation were two separate entities. As Menninger stated in his book, "self-mutilation was a non-fatal expression of an attenuated death wish" [10].

Early definitions of self-harm behaviour was characterized by the low lethality associated with the practice, noting that the deliberate behaviour associated with self-harm is not to be confused with suicidal and parasuicidal behaviour, [11-14]. This distinction was emphasized as levels of lethality and conscious intent to die are indeterminable in cases of drug overdose. This definition holds commonality in later conceptualizations. Favazza, has also defined self-mutilation as the direct destruction of body tissue without conscious suicidal intent. He categorizes mutilation into pathological and culturally sanctioned self-mutilation. Further, he divides pathological self-mutilation into major, stereotypic, and superficial-moderate self-mutilation. Superficial–moderate pathological self-mutilation was further subdivided into three subtypes: compulsive, episodic and repetitive. He excluded the swallowing of objects and chemicals since he opined that these methods did not affect body tissue directly [12].

Self-harm has been on a steady rise over the past decade. A conservative estimate of the incidence rate of students referred to a psychiatric clinic is about 0.5% percent of secondary school students in Trinidad. Approximately four cases per month are reported at the Eric Williams Medical Sciences Complex at Mt Hope with an emphasis on derma-abuse or skin cutting. In comparison to larger countries such as in England 6.9% of students' ages 15 and 16 in a cross sectional study of 41 schools reported acts of deliberate self-harm [15].

Internationally, the most common form of clinically determined self-harm is skin cutting. This occurs in 70% of the individuals that harm themselves, followed by the act of banging or hitting oneself (21% to 44%) and lastly 15% to 35% of persons who engage in acts of burning themselves [16,17]. In non-clinical populations such as college samples, the most common form of self-injurious behaviour was severe forms of scratching and pinching which results in bleeding and scarring (51.6%). This was followed by acts of banging and punching objects to the point of blood release (37.6%), then cutting (33.7%) followed by acts of punching and banging with blood release (24.5%). Body surface areas targeted by self-harmers are the areas that are of easiest access such as arms, hands, wrists, thighs and abdomen [18-20].

Deliberate self-harm (DSH) is not listed as a disorder but is listed in the criterion of Borderline Personality disorder [21] and have also been documented as occurring in other diagnosable disorders such as eating disorders, mood disorders, and anxiety disorders [22]. Deliberate self-harm can be found in both clinical and non clinical populations. Worldwide a large proportion of hospital admissions in countries such as the United States, Europe, Asia, Australia and Africa report deliberate self-harm in the categories of self-poisoning and self-mutilation [23-26]. Reports from a United Kingdom sample have quantified deliberate self-harm as one of the top five causes of acute and medical admissions for males and females with 140,000 cases each year in England and Wales [27]. In the United States, 21% of the adult clinical population has been engaged in such behaviour. In studies of adolescent psychiatric inpatients, the prevalence rates were higher (40% to 80%) [28-30], when compared to community samples (6.2%- 37.2%) [31, 32]. In the United States 37.2% had indicated to self-harm behaviour within the past 12 months [32].

However, there seems to be no agreement on findings of deliberate self-harm since similar rates have been reported in both institutional and community populations. In non-clinical populations, 4% of the adult population had engaged in deliberate self-harm with a similar finding of 4% in military recruits, [33]. College populations as a rule have reported higher rates of DSH, ranging from 14% - 38%, [4,17,34,35]. In Europe, for persons over the age of fifteen (15), there is an average rate of 0.14% for males and 0.19% for females [36].

In the local setting, in 2007, a newspaper report on 'cutting' among girls in Trinidad sparked the issue of a mental health crisis [37]. Further, two recent surveys conducted on non-clinical populations have revealed high rates of self-harmers. In a sample of 215 students at the University of the West Indies, the overall prevalence of self-harmers was found to be 24.2 percent with 9.3 percent notated as recent self-harmers and 14.9 percent engaged in self-harming behaviour over the past year [38]. Among the students reporting recent (within the past twelve months) self-harm, the most frequently utilized methods were cutting (70%), sticking oneself with sharp objects (50%), and scratching oneself (45%). Analysis of self-harmers over a one year period revealed that those who reported recent self-harm behaviour had an average of seven times as many (M = 35.6 s.d = 54) incidents than those with a past history of self-harm behaviour. In another study of 174 students, [39] there was an overall prevalence rate of 31.6 percent with a history of self-harm. In terms of recent self-harm 11.5 percent indicated this in comparison to 20.1 percent who engaged in self-harm behaviour more than a year ago. Within this sample 8.6 percent reported cutting, 8.6 percent indicated severe scratching and 6.9 percent, needle sticking. Of interest, 9.2 percent admitted to consuming pills, consumption of excessive amounts of alcohol, hair pulling (trichotillomania) and food refusal, [39]. An interesting finding is that although these studies were conducted at the same University in Trinidad during the same year, differential rates of 31.6% [39] and 24.2% [38] were recorded for self-harm behaviours. A possible explanation is that population samples used were from different faculties. It appears that students enrolled in psychology programs are more prone to self-harm than those in natural sciences and engineering.

It is evident that many researchers have described a medley of behaviours that have been categorized as life threatening and equated with suicidal intent. While some authorities [12,14,15] have commented on the low lethality of derma-abusers, the boundaries appear to be blurred. The purpose of this study therefore is two- fold: Firstly, to present and discuss vignettes of four young adolescents and secondly to study the dynamics and characteristics of six derma-abusers who have attended group psychotherapy for a six-month period with emphasis on their suicidality and treatment.

THEORIES OF SELF HARM

There are many explanatory models of self-harm that encompass various theories in psychology. Self-harm has been described through Behavioral and Systems theories, Psychodynamic and Psychoanalytical models as well as Interpersonal and Object relations approaches [40, 41].

Behavioral and Environmental models theorized that self-mutilation creates internal or environmental responses that are reinforcing to the individual. The Drive models purport a psychoanalytical understanding of the self-harm behavior, specifically with the Anti-suicide and Sexual model. The Anti-Suicide model claims that self-mutilation is a suicide replacement, an attempt to avoid suicide, a compromise between life and death drives, a sort of 'microsuicide.' The Sexual model states that self-mutilation stems from conflicts over sexuality, sexual development, masturbation, menarche and menstruation, [40,41].

The Affect Regulation Models offer a psychodynamic explanation through the Affect regulation model and the Dissociation model. The Affect Regulation model claims self-mutilation stems from the need to express or control anger, anxiety, or pain that cannot be expressed verbally or through other means whereas the dissociation model states that self-mutilation is a way to end or cope with the effects of dissociation that results from the intensity of affect. Many self-harmers report that they want to feel alive again and acts such as skin cutting removes their feelings of numbness, [40, 41].

The Boundaries Model which builds it explanatory power on Interpersonal and Object Relations theories state that self-mutilation is an attempt to create a distinction between self and others. Its use is a way to create boundaries or an identity to protect against feelings of being engulfed, on other hand a fear of loss of identity. It reinforces self-mutilation as evidence of familial or environmental dysfunction, [40, 41].

OUR STUDY

In this clinical study, prefaced with a comprehensive review of the local and international literature, four vignettes and six patients and their families in Dual Group Therapy (DGT) are studied over a six month period. The purpose is to define socio-demographics characteristics and to understand the dynamics of derma-abusers in the context of interpersonal, trans-generational and environmental factors. An appropriate management strategy is devised.

CASE STORY 1

IS is a 13 year old female student, of Caucasian descent, who resides in Singapore. She was born in Florida, of mixed origin and Roman Catholic faith. She came to Trinidad for treatment since she could not be contained in Singapore. She has Trinidadian roots as most of her family is originally from the island. The patient has been reportedly skin-cutting since 2007 when she was eleven years old. She reported that she had accidentally cut herself with a broken tea cup during one of the many arguments of her parents. She further stated that her 'accidental injury' had alleviated her emotional confusion and made her feel relaxed. In 2008, she was hospitalized for a two (2) week period after a cutting incident while in Singapore. On her release, it was discovered that she smuggled a piece of glass into the hospital by concealing it in her clothing and had continued cutting herself on her thighs and was further warded at the facility. In July, in Trinidad, she became so distraught and tense, she begged her Aunt who was visiting from Florida to allow her 'to make just a little nick on her wrist to alleviate her confusion'. Her most recent episode was in September 2009. She presented for cutting her left wrist at the Health Facility and subsequently taken to the University Hospital and warded at the Paediatric Ward. The patient with a history of skin cutting and burning indicated her most recent cutting was not a suicidal attempt but was used to eliminate stressors in her life, inclusive of a strained relationship with her cousins. In a review of her developmental, personal and family history she has had somewhat of a tumultuous past from an early age. As a toddler, she exhibited temper tantrums at age 3, her parents divorced when she was age five (5), and she reported that her mother has been in abusive relationships, not only with her father, resulting in her having to move between Malaysia and Singapore.

Her developmental milestones were normal but early visits to her Paediatrician had shown evidence of precocious development. At a routine pediatric checkup at age 6, the patient was noted to have a unilateral breast bud and pubic hair. The pediatrician referred her to an Endocrinologist where FSH, LF and other hormonal levels testing were done. They were all within normal range. A bone age scan was also done which showed that the age of her bones were consistent with her chronological age. Subsequently, a unilateral ovarian cyst was discovered via ultrasound. This was monitored for six months and at the second ultrasound no cysts were found. The endocrinologist has since disconfirmed precocious development despite her advanced sexual development. In Trinidad, brain scans CT and MRI were found to be normal as well as Electroencephalographic (EEG) studies.

In her personal history, she has shied away from her usual extracurricular activities such as netball, football and swimming when she started cutting. Her attempts to conceal the scars have resulted in her lack of interest in other activities but she still continued in the school choir. I.S. described herself as always being below average, and always had difficulty concentrating since very young expressing that she has always been taken long periods to complete assignments. She has never got into any physical fights at school or otherwise. Her history of friendships has been mixed with some "bad" friendships, but presently she has trustworthy friends. She lives with her mother, her mother's fiancée and his children and will be returning to Singapore soon. Her maternal aunts and mother are being treated for depression.

CASE STUDY 2

MA is a 16 year old female student of East Indian descent who resides in Trinidad. She is the youngest of three children. She presented on this occasion with ingestion of six (6) Painol tablets and two (2) painkillers. The incident occurred in August 2009 and was precipitated by an argument with her current boyfriend who is eight years older and a friend of her brother. She described herself as feeling depressed, hopeless and frustrated, with loss of interest in activities. She normally enjoyed listening to music and watching television, but did not have any intent to die. After this incident, she reported feelings of sadness for long periods over the next two days. M.A has a prior history of skin cutting which had started two years ago.

Her first incidence of skin cutting was in early Form 3 (age 13). She described feeling angry but cannot remember the details of the incident. She also stated that she engaged in banging her fists against the walls in her bedroom when she felt upset and frustrated due to arguments with her parents surrounding incidents with her boyfriend.

Her second and most recent incidence of skin cutting by a sharp instrument (razorblade) occurred in 2009 after leaving school without the permission of her parents or school officials. She left school with her boyfriend, a 25 year old taxi driver after being dropped off by her father in the morning. Two days later, she cut herself because she felt that her boyfriend's parents were turning him against her. She has also been involved in other methods of self-harm. Four months ago, she reportedly tried to choke herself with a belt after an argument with her boyfriend. M.A described her cutting behavior as first slashing and then pressing the razorblade into the wounds.

Her developmental history was insignificant as developmental milestones were reported in congruence with her age. She began puberty at around age twelve (12). She has had no major accidents or illnesses that required hospitalization. She has visited a psychologist for a few sessions after she broke school on the first occasion. Her relationship with her parents and brother has been somewhat average since the incidents occurred but presently the family ties are improving.

In terms of her personal history, MA has reported to having two previous relationships from the age of 12 which lasted two (2) months, and then at age 13 with a twenty one (21) year old man, which lasted one (1) year and eight (8) months. MA's current boyfriend is twenty five (25) and this relationship developed as she enjoyed conversing with him, he is a family friend. She expressed that she enjoys school very much and gets along with everyone including her friends. She has no history of aggressive behavior. Her performance in school is fair, and her grades have been falling due to her involvement with her boyfriend.

Both her parents' family have a history of depression. Her father's two cousins have depression and her mother's family also has a history of depression. One of her mother's brother has been committed to a mental institution following a nervous breakdown and one has committed suicide. The patient herself has also been treated for depression on her initial visits to the psychiatrist.

CASE STORY 3

SM is a fourteen year old Secondary School student who was referred to the Psychiatric Services for self-harm, following a self inflicted tattoo which he carved on his left arm with a symbol of his initial S. He did this without the permission of his parents because "he wanted to feel pain". He mutilated his forearm with a razor blade and covered it with ink in order to make a tattoo.

In addition, the school guard found letters in his possession written in blood and ink which were messages of hate. He stuck a fountain pen into the vain of his forearm thereby withdrawing blood and wrote a letter to his alleged girlfriend.

In his past history, at the age of five years on a school excursion he was separated from the class and claimed that people stamped on his chest. He was found by two strangers who carried him back to school. At the age of nine years, he received electric shocks from open wires with no serious injuries. It is not known whether these were accidental.

Both his parents are alive and he will drink with them on special occasions and will even smoke cigarettes. He has no sexual relationship but claims that he has many girlfriends, defining a girlfriend as "someone to be with when feeling down." At the age of fourteen, he suffered a fracture of the radius due to a fight at school. He was close to his grandfather who recently died.

On interview, he was properly groomed adequately clothed with a relaxed behavior. His affect was appropriate and speech fluent. He said he did not believe in God. He gave no reasons for his behavior and appeared to be smug about it.

CASE STORY 4

AP is a thirteen (13) year old male, Form 3 secondary school student of Indo-Guyanese descent. He was referred by the school guidance officer with a two month history of carving a tattoo on his left forearm with the inscription 'Sasha' his girlfriend. He painted it with ink creating a self- made tattoo. His mother reported that he is aggressive at home, stealing jewelry and money allegedly giving it to his girlfriend. He spends a considerably amount of time at night speaking to the girl on the phone which his mother attributes to his poor performance at school.

He was born in Guyana and was kept at the hospital for an extra week due to an infection. His developmental milestones were normal but his mother noted that he is extremely short tempered and responds with rage at the slightest provocation. He is the last of three (3) siblings with an older sister and brother. He does not get along with his brother and recently pulled a knife at him.

He came to Trinidad six (6) years ago with his mother, who has been separated from his father for nine (9) years. Presently he lives with his grandmother, grandfather and brother aged seventeen (17). His mother is now in a second relationship with a new husband for the past eight (8) years. A.P does not get along with his stepfather and accuses him of stealing the lost money and jewels. All members of his family except his stepfather are of Guyanese origin. He denies the use of tobacco, alcohol and drugs. He was diagnosed as having an impulse control disorder in his first contact with the psychiatric services on the island.

With respect to his derma-abuse, he feels no pain on carving and is supported by his girlfriend who is extremely thrilled at his show of love. His mother has contacted her on this issue and she has denied receiving money and stolen rings from him but is adamant that no one can stop him from seeing her.

ANALYSIS OF STUDIED GROUP

In Figure 1 below, a classification based on a small sample of ten (10) derma-abusers is presented. Patients involved in derma-abuse are generally non suicidal but engage in comfort cutting for the psychological release of pain, tension reduction and anger management. In this small group, males amounted to 20% and were more bizarre, gruesome and brutal in their self-abuse. Females accounted for the majority of the sample (80%) and among these; approximately 38% were of mixed origin. Of the total sample 10% were of African origin, 60% were of Indian descent and 30% were of mixed ancestry. The high percentage of abusers of mixed origin was unexpected and a plausible explanation is that these adolescents find themselves in a borderline cultural state. These are individuals who are unable to conceptualize which culture they belong to and consequently develop identity issues in their attempts to please both parents. The value assigned to each parent is often based on stereotyped racial pecking order and the environmental influences of parental dominance and autonomy.

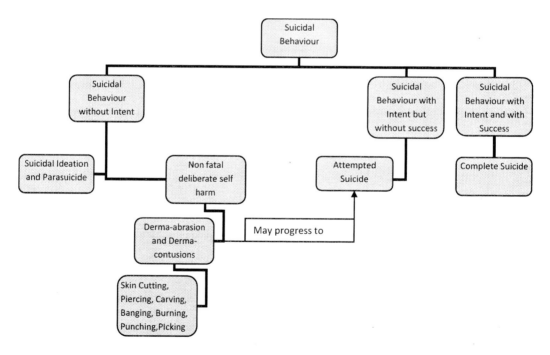

Figure 1. General classification of derma abusers

In this small sample of ten derma-abusers, patients were categorized into three groups: those without suicidal intent, those with suicide in mind and a third category of delayed onset, secondary suicidal thoughts. It is noteworthy that in more than 80% of the sample, suicide or thoughts of death was not the initial intent and apparently developed following intervention, after the patient's discovery of its importance as a powerful manipulative tool, (see table 1).

Table 1. Categorization of derma abusers in Trinidad

Derma- Abusers		
Without Suicidal Intent	With Suicidal Intent	Mixed Group with later suicidal onset
• Chronic Harmers • High Predictability • Low lethality • Intense family Pathology • Low impulse • control	• Harmer usually fits the criteria below: Plan- distinct Lethality- High Intent- HighMethod Timing • Intense personal Pathology	• Chronic attempters • Any available method • Family pathology • Personal Pathology

In table 2, a number of characteristics of derma-abusers are outlined. These are observations taken from group psychotherapy and concurrence with the group therapist following the sessions.

Table 2. Characteristics of derma-abusers as recorded in group psychotherapy

Psychodynamics of adolescent Derma-abusers in Trinidad
1. Emphasis on non-suicidal intent
2. Associated with tension reduction
3. Spontaneous overflow of emotion with low impulse control
4. Rejuvenation of loss of emotional resonance
5. Life and Death instincts- Eros and Thanatos considered
6. Reclaiming power and mastery over self and others
7. Significance of bloodletting in a socio-cultural context
8. Transgenerational dysfunctional family dynamics frequently with parental separation and sexual abuse
9. Physical and developmental disorders in early childhood
10. Morbid relationship with creativity with respect to body carving and architectural designs
11. Contemporaneous influences of youth culture
12. Reinforcement by family and help-seeking services.

In table 3 the socio-demographic characteristics of adolescents in group psychotherapy were tabularized to highlight commonalities among derma-abusers

Table 3. Socio-demographic Characteristics of the four (4) patients presented in the vignettes and six (6) in group psychotherapy

Demographics	Vignettes* and Group Psychotherapy Cases									
	I.S*	M.A*	S.M*	A.P*	R.A	K.E	A.M	O.M	A.T	T.S
Sex	F	F	M	M	F	F	F	F	F	F
Ethnicity	Mixed	East Indian	East Indian	East Indian	Mixed	East Indian	Mixed	East Indian	African	East Indian
Religion	Roman Catholic	Roman Catholic	Hindu	Hindu	Roman Catholic	Hindu	Roman Catholic	Roman Catholic	Christian (Pentecostal)	Pentecostal
Educational Level	Secondary (Junior)	Secondary (Senior)	Secondary (Junior)	Secondary (Junior)	Tertiary (University)	Tertiary (University)	Secondary (Senior)	Tertiary (University)	Secondary (Senior)	Secondary (Junior)
Family Structure	Single Parent	Nuclear	Nuclear	Single Parent	Nuclear	Single Parent	Single Parent (father died)	Adopted blended	Single Parent	Nuclear dysfunctional
School Performance	Borderline	Fair	Fair	Poor	Borderline	Good	Poor	Poor	Poor	Poor
Intermarriage by race/ religion/ nationality	Caucasian white & Indian	Hindu & Muslim	Presbyterian & Hindu	Guyanese & Trinidadian	Indian & African	Guyanese & Trinidadian	Indian &African	Muslim & Roman Catholic	No	No
Method	Skin Cutting	Banging & Cutting	Carving	Carving	Skin Cutting	Skin Cutting	Skin Cutting	Skin Cutting	Wrist /Skin Cutting	Skin cutting
Onset of self harm	11	13	13	15	20	16	13	18	16	13
Co morbidity	Depression	Depression	Non	Family Dysfunction	Depression	Depression	Childhood Epilepsy &Conduct Disorder	Borderline Personality Disorder	Conduct Disorder & Hyper-sexuality	Conduct Disorder; early sexual induction & Somatic complaints
Family history of Psychopathology	Bipolar disorder	Depression	Non	Non	Depression & Alcohol Dependence	Alcohol Dependence	Non	Personality Disorder (mother) Psychopath (brother)	Non	Nervous disorder (mother)

PROFILE OF ADOLESCENT DERMA-ABUSERS

From the sample investigated, a general profile was deduced to represent the description of a typical derma-abusing Trinidadian adolescent. Eighty percent (80%) of the cases in Trinidad appear to be adolescent girls, ranging from ages 11 to 16 years with onset of self harm in early teenage years. They appear to be of East Indian or mixed descent of both the Roman Catholic or Hindu faith and attending Secondary School. The derma-abusing adolescent seems to have an equal chance of coming from either a nuclear or single parent family (absence of father figure), though, within the nuclear family there is usually a dominant parent, the mother. Their family background seems to be of mixed origin, either by religion, race or nationality and there is a history of family dysfunction and instability. Their performance at school spans the extremely low/poor to borderline ranges and the individual is usually diagnosed with a depressive disorder due to relational conflicts. In some cases there is a history of Conduct Disorder in childhood.

Associated psychosocial factors are low self-esteem, body image and identity disturbances and early courtship and sexual induction. This is on a background of Trinidad and Tobago having the second highest rate of suicide in the Caribbean region and may be a precursor for such behaviour in adulthood. Different forms of derma-abrasion and derma contusion observed among the sample were skin cutting, banging, scraping, carving, burning and branding, picking at the skin and removal of blood with instruments (pen and needles). Skin cutting was more prevalent amongst the female sample and carving with tattooing was present in all the the male derma- contusion cases. It seems the intensity of the latter paints a more bravado picture of sacrifice to a loved object when compared to skin cutting by the females. Sexual drives are a major operative factor in both male and female derma- abusers.

DISCUSSION

An examination of the four (4) vignettes and six (6) cases treated in Dual Group Therapy (DGT) highlights significant commonalities in the life histories and presenting concerns of all patients. The case stories and group psychotherapy cases presented are of adolescent individuals who began self-harm between the ages of 11 to 20, with a mean of 14.8 years and 80% between the 11-16 age group. According to the literature, studies have reinforced that individuals aged 11-25 have been known to self-injure [42]. Eighty percent (80%) of the cases discussed here were children of intermarriages by race, religion or nationality. It raises the issue of identity confusion and misunderstanding of culture and practice as it starts at the family level. The authors are of the opinion that these individuals suffer from a borderline cultural state which results in their poor conceptualization of which culture they belong to. This cultural confusion in ethnicity, religion and nationality is often stratified by the environment in which one lives and can result in identity splitting and confusion. In psychodynamic terms, blood- letting can be viewed as an individual attempt to remove the bad blood or bile of their mixtures in a purging process. Durkheim's theories of anomie, egoistic and altruistic behaviors and Erikson's stages of development are applicable here.

On closer inspection, the precipitating cause of self-harm is strongly associated with the establishment of early relationships with sexual induction as evidenced by 70% of the cases.

This holds commonalities as those purported by the Sexual Model of self-mutilation. Among the teenage population, sexual experimentation and risk taking behavior is a common aspect of this age group. With numerous coping strategies to aid in the tension reduction needed, caused by volatile partnerships, derma -contusions seemed to be prevalent. Within the present sample of self-harmers skin cutting was observed in all of the females and carving, being the derma-contusion of choice among the male cases. It seems the intensity of the latter paints a more bravado picture matching the male image, in comparison to 'skin cutting' portraying a slightly less gruesome, 'romantic' sacrifice. Though two different forms, both make the assumption of the ultimate sacrifice, bloodshed.

The cases presented underlie the occurrence of trans-generational dysfunctional family dynamics as shown in table 3. Approximately sixty percent of cases report family separation, divorce, transcultural differences and family psychopathology. In the nuclear family there was invariably the presence of a dominant parent which served as a major stressor in the individuals' life. In addition, there were high rates of psychiatric disturbances (80%) and psychosocial difficulties (100%), especially the prominence of mood disorders (40%) in individuals who self-harm within the present sample, as reported by previous studies [43]. Aggressive tendencies, emotional disorders, temper tantrums, conduct disorders and teenage angst were prevalent. The aggregate of emotions that are expected of this age group coupled by intense family psychopathology as expressed by 60% of the sample and personal psychopathology as indicated by 90% of the cases seem to be antecedents of self-harming behavior. Most of the individuals in the vignettes and group therapy cases have stated that they use these behaviors as a way of expressing anger and frustration when emotions are at a high and the overflow is unbearable, whereas some individuals self-harm to prevent suicide, or escape unwanted feelings, as indicated by the Anti Suicide Model.

As expressed by case story 2, she was unable to explain the situations surrounding her first skin cutting episode but was certain of the fact that she was extremely overwhelmed by anger. Since banging her fists on the wall ceased to work anymore, she upped the ante to a more punitive method that she felt helped at stressful times. In a recent interview with MA she stated that she was faced with a situation concerning an assignment, in which she had to redo a portion that she assumed was finished. She reported that for a brief moment she thought of cutting but reconsidered her actions. MA's behavior seemed to hold commonalities to the Affect Regulation Model of self-mutilation as she was overwhelmed by emotion. The extent of the behaviors and meaning of their acts are unknown to them and are often given interpretative credence in treatment. Also, their behavior is significantly different from suicidal behavior with intent as the individuals in these cases have made their scars public. As suggested by Hawton [44] self harm behavior is distinctly suicidal if the act is "planned for, carried out and followed through in such a way as to keep it from the notice of others." Even though derma-abusers may try to hide their wounds the target areas are easily noticeable despite concealment with hand bands or clothing.

The new found control that has been indicated by some of the above cases and vignettes has been the main function of the deliberate derma-contusions that are self-inflicted. It may be apparent that the manifestation of family psychopathology and family strife is showing itself in adolescence as creative forms of 'bloodletting' as it parallels Hippocrates early assumptions of 'purging of bad humors' [45]. Seventy five percent of the cases report their bloodletting as an addiction that they desperately need to engage in with the likes of alcohol and drugs. It seems that a derma-contusion returns it users to an equilibrium state that is required for their existence. This supports the underlying commonality among the cases with the lack of suicidal intent. They perceive their self-harming behavior as a form of rejuvenation by letting the bad blood out rather than as a destruction of body tissue.

An important observation is the predictability and chronicity of the self-harming behavior without suicidal intent. In most of the vignettes derma-abusers repeated these behaviors as certain events presented in their lives, indicative of maladaptive coping mechanisms as well as a need to remedy the situation at the moment, suggestive of perhaps a hopeful future. An emphasis here can be placed on a compromise being made between life and death instincts of psychoanalytical theory, specifically the Anti Suicide Model. They derive pleasure not from stereotypical pleasurable behaviors but rather from aggressive, self punitive behaviors that widens the power differential between themselves and others. In an effort to heal, they set themselves apart from normal methods of remedy, lending resemblance to the Boundaries model of self-mutilation. In case story 4, AP felt that he was showing his commitment to his cause when he carved the name of his girlfriend along his forearm. He seemed to be giving of himself wholly in a way he probably could not express in words as proffered by the Affect Regulation Model of self-mutilation.

The excessive compulsion and obsessive psychological dependence of derma-abusers seems to be cognizant of its chronicity among the individuals inflicted with the addiction. Fifty percent of them seem to experiment with different methods of self-harm before the addiction of the tool of choice develops. It seems though, when in desperation the tool of choice may best be substituted with an available option. As illustrated by vignette 1, I.S went to great lengths to conceal a piece of glass within her clothing, and thought nothing of it as she continued to deliberately harm herself at the hospital, even though she found comfort using razorblades. Prior evidence of this kind of dependent behaviour can also be seen where she begged a relative to allow her to cut her wrist in an attempt to equilibrate herself again.

In this study, derma-abusers were not generally involved in acts with suicidal intent (see figure 1, table 1). The ten patients were categorized into three groups, those without suicidal intent, those with suicide in mind and a third category of delayed onset, secondary suicidal thoughts. It is noteworthy that in more than 80% of the sample, suicide or thoughts of death was not the initial intent. These thoughts apparently developed following intervention, on discovery that their behaviors were enmeshed with the feelings of power and mastery over self and others, effects on tension reduction and as a form of revenge and hostility directed against family members. The act itself became the most powerful manipulative tool reinforced in a Caribbean setting with a history of aggression, violence and more recently high murder rates in Trinidad (see table 2).

The treatment of derma-abusers is difficult and presents a major challenge. After failure of individual therapy designed along the lines of Linehan's Dialectical Behaviour Therapy model (DBT) [46] another method was employed. DBT states, and failed for the following reasons: Patients were too young and disturbed to acquire what Linehan calls 'wisemind'. With respect to the 'what' and 'how' skills, they could not focus on mindfulness. They could not develop interpersonal effectiveness to say no, or resist their urges of cutting and had little distress tolerance and emotional regulation.

A novel system of Dual Group Therapy (DGT) was devised. This is the simultaneous occurrence of two group sessions of one and a half hours held concurrently in two adjoining sound proof rooms of the same building once per week. The following screening process was instituted. First the initial interview with the patient and the attendants in the presentation of the problem (30 minutes). In the local setting, it is customary for the entire extended family, caretakers and friends to accompany the patient. In the second stage, the patient was interviewed individually (45 minutes) being allowed to tell their story and assessing significant others in her life. In the third stage, two significant others, determined by the patient and therapist were asked to be seen together with the patient. In a client centered approach, the dynamics of interaction of family members and patients were observed. The therapist had to be cautious in not ascribing blame to anyone person, attempting to avoid confrontation and acting-out behavior commonly found in our setting. Information on ethno-historiography, that is, the characteristics of origin, race, culture, religion and lifestyle were sought. This socio-cultural academic exercise presented little threat to those involved. In the final stage, an agreement (non-signed contract) was reached by the parents (caretakers) and the patient to attend two concurrently run groups namely 'The Adolescent Group' and 'The Parent Support Group'. They were asked to attend for a twenty four sessions (six months) period. The third and fourth stages lasted approximately one hour with a total assessment time of two hours. Parents were given the charge of bringing the patients to the groups. Two trained psychologists conducted the groups and met together with two co-therapists who also were in the group and the psychiatrist for weekly reviews following the meetings. With shared information and emotions from both groups, a tailored management approach was devised for each patient introduced within the dynamics of group therapy.

The cases presented are individuals who have used maladaptive coping in an attempt to remove dysfunctional events in their life. The adolescents have challenged the status quo of 'normal behavior' in the hope of normalizing their own lives. Their commonalities are striking and lend itself to distinct characterization of the phenomena of derma-abusing in Trinidad.

CONCLUSION

This is a preliminary study that highlights a growing problem among secondary school children in Trinidad. The author works closely with the School Supervision Unit of the Ministry of Education in Trinidad where a number of students are referred by the Guidance Officers who are not equipped to deal with the intensity of problems encountered. The behavior of these students are devastating to both fellow students and staff members alike and can undermine the spiritual and moral values of the schools' discipline. The fact that there is an element of contagion or copy cat behavior has led many school authorities, especially those of the denominational Christian schools to perceive the problem to be one of demonical possession and it is not unusual to have these students ostracized and referred for exorcism and spiritual healing.

In the presentation of this small sample of ten patients, the intention is to demonstrate the similarities of behavior, personal and family psychopathology and dynamics. The psychopathology of the individuals and their families must be emphasized as these may be major precursors to their condition. While there is room in any institution for pastoral care and counseling, the presentation of four (4) case stories and study of the dynamics of six (6) students in group therapy provide a better understanding of these patients and provide a psychological framework for treatment. While this paper does not address their outcome in treatment, it is necessary to recognize that in group therapy, the inclusion of non-derma abusers in groups can lead to the recruitment of deviants. Family involvement is mandatory since disturbed kids invariably come from disturbed families.

Notwithstanding the limitations of it being a small, descriptive observational study, it is however the first clinical study of this nature coming out of the Caribbean region. As highlighted in a daily newspaper two years ago as 'a mental health crisis' [37], it is understandable that this will be a major public health issue of adolescents in the future, especially in Trinidad and Tobago now on the threshold of first world status.

The increased attention to derma-abusing cases may be an indication of additional adolescents engaging in the behavior. So too, it can be attributed to the changing attitudes of adolescents in today's culture as they freely engage in risky behavior. As previously stated [47], service providers may now have a more keen ability to recognize and report derma-abusing behavior with a better understanding of the dynamics involved.

ACKNOWLEDGMENTS

We wish to thank Dayna Mohammed of the Psychology Department of the University of the West Indies and Katija Khan, Psychologist of University of Hull in England for their useful comments and contribution to this paper.

REFERENCES

[1]   Kreitman, N. Can suicide and parasuicide be prevented? J Royal Soc Med 1989;82:648-52.

[2]   Kessel N, McCulloch W. Repeated acts of self harm and self injury. J Royal Soc Med 1966;59:89-92.

[3]   Morgan HD, Burns-Cox CJ, Pocock H, Pottle S. Deliberate self-harm: Clinical and socio-economic characteristics of 368 patients. Br J Psychiatry 1975;127:564-74.

[4]   Gratz KL. Measurement of deliberate elf harm: Preliminary data on the deliberate self harm inventory. J Psychopathol Behav Assess 2001;23:253-63.

[5]   Platt S, Bille-Brahe U, Kerkhof A, et al. Parasuicide in Europe: The WHO/EURO Multicentre Study on Parasuicide I. Introduction and preliminary analysis for 1989. Acta Psychiatr Scan 1992;85:97-104.

[6]   Clarke L, Whitaker M. Self mutilation: Culture, contexts and nursing responses. J Clin Nurs 1998;7:129-37.

[7]   Nock MK, Prinstein MJ. Contextual features and behavioural functions of self mutilation among adolescents. J Abnorm Psychol 2005;114(1):140-6.

[8]   Baral I, Kora K, Yuksel S, Sezgin U. Self mutilating behaviour of sexually abused female adults in Turkey. J Interpers Violence 1998; 13:427-37.

[9]   Brodsky BS, Cloitre M, Dulit RA. Relationship of dissociation to self mutilation and childhood abuse in borderline personality disorder. Am J Psychiatr 1995;152:1788-92.

[10] Wikipedia. Self injury. [Online] 2009 [cited 2009 Sept 20] Available from: http://en.wikipedia.org/wiki/Self-injury.

[11] Pattison EM, Kahan J. The deliberate self harm syndrome. Am J Psychiatr 1983;140:867-72.

[12] Favazza AR. The coming of age of self mutilation. J Nerv Ment Dis 1998;186:259-68.

[13] Hawton K, James A. Suicide and deliberate self harm in young people. Br J Psychiatr 2005;330:891-4.

[14] Suyemoto KL. The functions of self mutilation. Clin Psychol Rev 1998;18:531-54.

[15] Hawton K, Rodham K, Evans E, Weatherall R. Deliberate self harm in adolescents: self report survey in schools in England. BMJ 2002; 325:1207-11.

[16] Briere J, Gil E. Self mutilation in a clinical and general population samples: Prevalence, correlates and functions. Am J Orthopsychiatry 1998;68:609-20.

[17] Favazza AR, Conterio K. Female habitual self mutilators. Acta Psychiatr Scand 1989;79:283-9.

[18] Muehlenkamp JJ. Self injurious behaviour as a separate clinical syndrome. Am J Orthopsychiatry 2005;75:324-33.

[19] Favazza AR. Bodies under siege: Self mutilation and body modification in culture and psychiatry, 2nd ed. Baltimore, MD: John Hopkins Univ Press, 1996.

[20] Whitlock J, Eckenrode J, Silverman D. Self injurious behaviours in a college population. Pediatrics 2006;117:1939-48.

[21] Linehan MN. Cognitive-behavioural treatment of borderline personality disorder. New York: Guilford, 1993.

[22] Mangnall J, Yurkovich E. A literature review of deliberate self harm. Persp Psychiatric Care 2008;44:175-84.

[23] Spandler H. Who's hurting who? Young people, self harm and suicide, 2nd ed. Gloucester: Handsell Publ, 2001.

[24] Eddleston M, Gunnell D, Karunaratne A, De Silva D, Sheriff MHR, Buckley NA. Epidemiology of intentional self poisoning in rural Sri Lanka. Br J Psychiatr 2005;187:583-4.

[25] Kinyanda E, Hjelmeland H, Musisi S. Negative life events associated with deliberate self harm in an African Population in Uganda. Crisis 2005;26(1):4-11.

[26] Penrose-Wall J, Farris Z, Berkery P. Coping without self harm: Treatment guide for young people. The Royal Australian and New Zealand College of Psychiatrists. [Online] 2003 [cited 2009 September 20] Available from : http://www.ranzcp.org/pdffiles/cpgs/Coping%20without%20Self%20Harm%20Consu mer%20CPG%20Youth%20Pocket%20Size.pdf

[27] Bennewith O, Stocks N, Gunnell D, Peters TJ, Evans MO, Sharp DJ. General Practice based intervention to prevent repeat episodes of deliberate self harm: Cluster randomized controlled trial. BMJ 2002; 324:1-8.

[28] Darche MA. Psychological factors differentiating self mutilating and non-self-mutilating adolescent inpatient females. Psychiatr Hosp 1990;21:31-5.

[29] DiClemente RJ, Ponton LE, Hartley D. Prevalence and correlates of cutting behaviours: Risk for HIV transmission. J Am Acad Child Adolesc Psychiatr 1991;151:1305-11.

[30] Nock MK, Prinstein MJ. A functional approach to the assessment of self-mutilative behaviour. J Consult Clin Psychol 2004;72:885-90.

[31] Hilt LM, Cha CC, Nolen-Hoeksema S. Nonsuicidal self-injury in young adolescent girls: Moderators of the distress-function relationship. J Consult Clin Psychol 2008;76:63-71.

[32] Yates TM, Tracy AJ, Luthar SS. Nonsuicidal self injury among "priveleged" youths: Longitudinal and cross-sectional approaches to developmental process. J Consult Clin Psychol 2008;76:52-62.

[33] Klonsky ED, Oltmanns TF, Turkheimer E. Deliberate self-harm in a non-clinical population: Prevalence and psychological correlates. Am J Psychiatr 2003;160:1501-8.

[34] Favazza AR. Repetitive self mutilation. Psychiatr Ann 1992; 22:60-3.

[35] Gratz KL. Risk factors for deliberate self harm among female college-students: The role and interaction of childhood maltreatment, emotional inexpressivity, and affect intensity/reactivity. Am J Orthopsychiatry 2006;76:238-50.

[36] WHO, Euro Multicentre Study of Suicide. [Online] 2004 [cited 2009 Sept 22] Available from: http:// cebmh.warne.ox.ac.uk/csr/monitoring.html.

[37] Castillo K. Mental health crisis looms, expert says: Girls cutting themselves. Trinidad Express 2007 Oct 4. [Online] 2007 [cited 2009 Sept 22] Available from: http://www.trinidadexpress.com.

[38] Mohammed R. Deliberate self-harm in a non-clinical population: Emotion and coping strategies. Dissertation. St Augustine: Univ West Indies, 2008.

[39] Allum S. Risk factors associated with deliberate self-harm. Dissertation. St Augustine: Univ West Indies, 2008.

[40] Suyemoto KL, Macdonald ML. Self cutting in female adolescents. Psychotherapy 1995;32:162-71.

[41] Messer JM, Fremouw WJ. A critical review of explanatory models for self-mutilating behaviors in adolescents. Clin Psychol Rev 2008;28(1):162-78.

[42] Young people and self harm: A national inquiry. What do we already know? Prevalence, risk factors & models of intervention. [Online] 2004 [cited 2009 Sept 22] Available from http://selfharmuk.org.

[43] Harrington R, Dyer E. Suicide and attempted suicide in adolescence. Curr Opin Psychiatry 1993;6:467-9.

[44] Hawton K. Suicide and attempted suicide among children and adolescents. London: Sage, 1986.

[45] Wikipedia. Bloodletting. [Online] 2009 [cited 2009 Sept 20] Available from http://en.wikipedia.org/wiki/Bloodletting.

[46] Linehan MM. Understanding borderline personality disorder: The dialectic approach manual. New York: Guilford, 1995.

[47] Cornell research program on self injurious behaviour in adolescents and young adults. What do we know about self-injury? [Online] 2009 [cited 2009 Sept 22] Available from http://www.crpsib.com/whatissi.asp.

In: Social and Cultural Psychiatry Experience from the...
Editor: Hari D. Maharajh and Joav Merrick

ISBN: 978-1-61668-506-5
© 2010 Nova Science Publishers, Inc.

Chapter 16

CYBERSUICIDE AND THE ADOLESCENT POPULATION: CHALLENGES OF THE FUTURE

Ria Birbal, Hari D. Maharajh, Risa Birbal, Maria Clapperton, Johnathan Jarvis, Anushka Ragoonath and Kali Uppalapati

Cybersuicide is a term used in reference to suicide and its ideations on the internet. It is associated with web sites which lure vulnerable members of society and empower them with various methods and approaches to deliberate self-harm. Ease of accessibility to the internet and the rate at which information is dispersed; contribute to the promotion of 'offing' one's self which is particularly appealing to adolescents. This study aims to explore this phenomenon which seems to be spreading across generations, cultures and races. Information and articles regarding internet suicide and other terminology as well as sub classifications concerning this new form of suicide were reviewed. Through search engines such as google, yahoo and wikipedia differentiations between 'web cam' suicide, 'net suicide packs', sites which merely offer advice on how to commit suicide and sites which are essential in providing the means of performing the act were investigated. Also, materials published in scientific journals and data published by the Public Health Services, Centers for Disease Control, and materials from private media agencies were reviewed. Resources were also sourced from The Faculty of Medical Sciences Library, UWI at Mt. Hope. Cybersuicide is a worldwide problem among adolescents and is a challenge of the future.

INTRODUCTION

In this information oriented age, the internet is an indispensable tool with little differences between industrialized and developing countries Twenty-two out of every 100 persons in Trinidad and Tobago use the internet [1]. Alexa reported that many persons in Trinidad and Tobago use the internet as a way of making friends and sharing life experiences with sites such as Facebook, Hi5, YouTube and Tagged being in the top 10 most viewed websites [2]. The use of these sites in Trinidad and Tobago is comparable with other first world countries [3]. However, for some persons, similar web casting sites are used as a means of finding companions in death. This resulted in a new culture of suicide which is now commonly referred to as Internet Suicide or Cybersuicide [4-10].

Internet suicide refers to the process of recruiting, staging and committing suicide using the internet [8]. There are three main types of internet suicide: suicide pacts, deathcasting and fake suicide [8,11]. A suicide pact is an agreement between two or more persons to commit suicide together at a designated place and time, arranged over the internet [8]. Deathcasting refers to the live broadcasting of one's death using an online broadcasting service [12]. Fake suicide refers to the false simulation of taking your life.

Of the three types mentioned above, suicide pacts are by far the most common [8,11]. Since the first reported case occurred in Japan in October 2000 there have been more than 400 similar deaths worldwide [8,13-18]. The increased publicity and success of pact suicides has led to the development of chain suicides; where vulnerable individuals sought refuge [8,19-21]. The 2007 Global School based Student Health Survey in Trinidad reported that 18.1 percent of students between the ages 13-15 years considered attempting suicide within the past twelve months [22].

Deathcasting is less prevalent than suicide pacts with only a few cases attracting public attention. The most recent and widely publicized case was that of a Florida teenager Abraham Biggs, on November 2008, which was subsequently highlighted in the Trinidad Express Newspaper [23]. It is inferred that this publicity has increased the awareness of webcam suicide locally and may indirectly promote this method of suicide to vulnerable individuals.

The purpose of this study was two-fold: firstly, to sensitize the local and international communities on the popularity of internet suicide and its rapid growth and secondly, to recommend measures to prevent the occurrence of chain suicides (the Werther Effect) and other modalities of internet suicide.

OUR STUDY

A number of internet suicide case reports were reviewed from electronic news articles, journals and databases along with reports from library databases and local newspapers. A systematic review of selected cases was done in keeping with the following guidelines: 1) Method of suicide, 2) Psychosocial reasons for committing suicide and 3) The influence of these acts on others i.e chain suicides (Werther Effect). A table was then constructed comparing the above factors with the selected cases. These were then compared to suicides in Trinidad and Tobago to identify any associations or tendencies towards adopting the phenomenon of internet suicide. Trinidad and Tobago has the second highest rate of suicide in the Caribbean region with an incidence of 13/100,000. It is expected that the adolescent population with increasing technological knowledge will participate in novel and creative methods of imitation suicide.

OUR FINDINGS

Case study 1: November 2008 in Florida

One of the most recent and also most publicized internet suicidal events was that of a 19 year old male of Florida, on November 19th 2008 [24,25]. While using an internet forum, he stated his suicidal intentions to other bloggers but was not taken seriously due to his previous suicidal ideations which all proved to be uneventful. Agitated by this rejection, he subsequently engaged in a live webcam, posting a link to this site while encouraging members of the forum to view his webcam posting. He then overdosed on pills while members of the site looked on, some encouraging him, others attempting to dissuade him and some debating whether the pills were enough to be lethal. Twelve hours later, the site's moderator was informed as well as the police, but by that time he had already succumb to the lethal mixture of pills. The teenager had a long history of depression and previous attempts of suicide. A suicide note was found on his MySpace profile [26].

Case study 2: March 2007 in Britain

The first reported internet webcam suicide in Britain was that of a 42 year old male on March 25th 2007 [27]. The British male had just been separated from his wife and 2 children, who were under his wife's custody. Reports stated that a previous vehicular injury, the breakdown of his marriage and the death of his father lead to him developing depression [13,27,28]. While on an internet chat room, he threatened to commit suicide via online webcam. After tying a rope to his ceiling, he stood on a chair and tied the rope around his neck. Bloggers who did not believe he would hang himself continuously taunted and encouraged him and were equally shocked when he stepped of the chair and became strangulated.

Table 1. Comparison of the selected cases by type, method and reasons for suicide, and the influence of these cases on chain suicide

SUICIDE	CASE 1	CASE 2	CASE 3
Type	Deathcasting	Deathcasting	Suicide Pacts
Method	Medication Overdose (tablets)	Asphyxiation via tying a rope around his neck	Carbon Monoxide Poisoning
Reasons	History of depression, urged on by online viewers	Depression due to death of father, marital problems, injury from vehicular accident, encouraged by many viewers	Dispute with girlfriends, frustrated and tired of life
Werther Effect	Possibly	No	Yes
Previous Suicide Attempts	Yes	No	Yes

Case study 3: February 2005 in Japan

Six bodies were found dead in an estate car on February 5th 2005, in Tokyo. The vehicle also contained four sets of portable clay cooking stoves with charcoal and three of the victims had left suicide notes. All the victims had gotten to know each other over the internet. One of the victims stated in his note that a dispute among two of his girlfriends was the reason for his suicide, whilst another stated that she was tired of life and wanted to die. Three of the victims had a history of previous suicide attempts [8, 11, 17].

DISCUSSION

Eight cases of cybersuicide are presented in three case reports. Case 2 is not an adolescent but is included to underline that internet suicide is not only found in adolescents, but also in older individuals where the psychodynamics of completed suicide is different to the adolescent and young adult group. Older individuals appear to be emotionally immature, regressed and attention-seeking with increased loading of life events and psychiatric disorders (see table 1)

People with suicidal ideations seek encouragement via the internet. Those with suicidal obsessions are influenced by internet resources on suicide. The importance of copycat suicide, ambivalence, suicide pacts and suicide notes are important factors with respect to assisting vulnerable individuals [29].

The internet has now revolutionized the way suicide pacts are organized. A suicide pact employs certain factors: first, it provides an escape from painful emotional problems arising from individual and social anguish, secondly, it gives the individual a sense of control in instances where they think that their rights have been infringed. A third and noteworthy factor is that many internet users may be mentally ill. The act of suicide may be due to alien beliefs that may originate from an untreated psychiatric illness (usually one or more persons in the pact have a mental illness) [30]. This is seldom highlighted in the public domain.

Individuals enduring emotional disarray and depression feel a strong sense of despair and are highly vulnerable. Such people find solace in other people like themselves and can appreciate the misery of others because it makes them feel better [30]. This may initially resemble some form of internet group therapy. Feelings and thoughts, which may be suicidal, are shared and common activities that appear to be mutually supportive are attempted. However, it fails to qualify as a form of group therapy because there is no true moderator to help them when they cannot help each other. The essential reasoning behind a suicide pact is that the fear of living is worse than dying. They support their suicidal behavior and the dread of dying alone, is eliminated.

A suicide planned to include a public display, stems from a desire to give death a sense of purpose. Public suicide is an attention seeking act meant to inflict harm and psychologically punish others. Lifecasting is a continual broadcast of events in a person's life through digital media, typically via the internet [31]. Deathcasting may be thought of as the grand finalé in which the act of suicide is glorified. In many instances, the person may simulate suicide to preempt a response i.e to determine the impact their actions may have on their audience by merely exhibiting parasuicidal behavior. Users are often left baffled and indecisive as to whether or not to believe what they are seeing. Under such circumstances, the bystander effect is easily set in motion. It is a social and psychological phenomenon in which individuals are less likely to offer help or do not know how to help in an emergency situation when other people are present. The probability of help on these situations is inversely proportional to the number of bystanders [32].

Since the first known internet based suicide pact occurred in Japan in October 2000, it is reasonable to select Japan as the model country in which to gauge the effect of this phenomenon and assess its possible impact on mental health in Trinidad and Tobago [8,33]. In 2006, Japan's suicide rate of 23.7/100,000 was the ninth highest worldwide [34].

Japan, one of the most technologically savvy nations, had an estimated total of 94,000,000 internet users as of March, 2008 73.8% of the population, according to the International Telecommunications Union (ITU) [35]. Also according to the ITU, the total number of internet users for Trinidad and Tobago as of September 2006, was 160,000, 12.1% of the population [36]. Suicide is a multifaceted problem encompassing cultural, social, religious and economic dimensions [8]. The suicide rate in Trinidad and Tobago in 2000 was 13/100,000 [36]. Therefore, in an attempt to predict the likelihood of cybersuicide contagion in Trinidad and Tobago, this paper will compare and contrast popular methods of suicide, age ranges and cultural perspectives between Trinidad and Tobago and Japan along with the role and influence of the media.

Common suicide methods in Japan are jumping in front of trains, leaping off high places, hanging, or overdosing on medication. A newer method, gaining popularity partly due to publicity from Internet suicide websites, is the use of household products to make hydrogen sulfide, a poisonous gas. In 2007, only 29 suicides used this gas, but from January to September 2008, 867 suicides resulted from this gas poisoning [8,37]. Charcoal burning is becoming the most popular method for internet suicide in Japan. It has become popularized for a number of reasons. Death by Carbon Monoxide poisoning resulting from charcoal burning in a small sealed space has been considered to be more convenient than other previously mentioned methods. It is more conducive to pact deaths and is appealing for those who prefer not to die alone. It is also portrayed on some websites as being non-disfiguring and a painless method [8].

Trinidad and Tobago is a multi-ethnic country comprising: Indian (South Asian) 40%, African 37.5%, mixed 20.5%, other 1.2%, unspecified 0.8%, [38]. In Trinidad and Tobago, the suicide rate is highest among East Indians, and paraquat poisoning is the main cause of death. This substance is readily available in the agricultural regions, where most Indians live (39). During the period 1991-2000 suicide methods in Trinidad and Tobago included: Poisoning 64.2%; Hanging 30.3%, other – including jumping from heights, self-wounding, firearms 4.5%. [40]

Trinidad and Tobago is often acclaimed for its professional input abroad. Many students seek a foreign education in the finest institutions in United Kingdom, Europe, United States, Canada and Australia. The senior author (HDM) is aware of the death of a young brilliant Trinidadian law student in United Kingdom. The mystery surrounding his death is unknown except that a small charcoal pot was found in his flat. He was a computer whiz and the family is waiting in hope for a time release computerized message from him in the future!

The Japanese once viewed suicide as an honorable means of escape in the face of failure. Hara-kiri also known as seppuku in feudal periods is translated as an act of killing oneself by cutting open ones stomach with a sword, performed especially by Samurai in the past to avoid losing honour [8]. The current suicide trend in Japan is largely not about a noble exit, but about an escape from isolation and pain. The careful planning behind the Internet pacts suggests to some, the depths of that isolation and pain [41]. In Trinidad and Tobago, suicide is still considered to be a criminal offence. Religious persuasions in Trinidad and Tobago are as follows: Roman Catholic 26%, Hindu 22.5%, Anglican 7.8%, Baptist 7.2%, Pentecostal 6.8%, Muslim 5.8%, Seventh Day Adventist 4%, other Christian 5.8%, other 10.8%, unspecified 1.4%, none 1.9% (38). In keeping with their religious beliefs, most perceive suicide to be sinful and an offence against the Supreme Being.

In all countries, suicide is now one of the three leading causes of death among people aged 15-34 years; until recently, suicide was predominating among the elderly, but now suicide predominates in younger people in both absolute and relative terms, in a third of all countries [42].

Younger people seem to be most vulnerable to the influence of the media, although limited evidence also shows an impact on elderly people. Another factor is similarity between the media stimulus or model and the observer in terms of age, sex, and nationality. An important aspect of the presentation of suicide in the media is that it usually oversimplifies the causes, attributing the act to single factors such as financial disasters, broken relationships, or failure in examinations. The most common factor leading to suicide, mental illness, is often overlooked [43].

What is evident in the comparison of these two countries with high suicidal rates, is the method, socio-cultural and economic differences proffered for the high suicide rates. It is expected that cybersuicide with a common technological culture of its own will eliminate these factors in all countries world wide, thereby adopting a new internet culture of suicidal behavior.

The media plays a significant role in any society. Whether it is by radio, television or print, the nature of the information and the manner in which it is reported can influence the thoughts, perceptions and behaviour of its recipients. It also plays a crucial role in the social, economic and political structure of a society. Past studies conducted to assess the impact of the media have likened the media's role in this issue of suicide to that of a double- edged sword since it can either promote or prevent its occurrence. The majority of people who consider suicide are ambivalent. They are not sure that they want to die. One of the many factors that may lead a vulnerable individual to suicide could be suicide publicity in the media. How the media report on suicide cases can influence other suicides [44].

There have been known incidents in which books had been banned because their portrayal of suicide and suicidal ideation had led to an increase in the number of cases of suicides committed in the same manner as that depicted in the text. One known example is Goethe's 1774 novel "The Sorrows of Young Werther" from which the term "Werther Effect" was coined. The depiction of Werther's fictional death reportedly led to a series of copycat suicides among young European romantics of the time. Other books were, "Final Exit" by Derek Humphrey which took effect in the United States and "Suicide, Mode D'emploi" which impacted in France. According to Phillips and colleagues, the degree of publicity given to a suicide story is directly correlated to the number of subsequent suicides in a particular geographical location [45,46]. The highly publicized deaths of celebrities had the greatest impact. More recently, the Internet has introduced a number of new issues.

With the advent and increasing popularity of cybersuicide, suicide pacts and deathcasting, one must seriously consider the possibility of contagion. Gould, Wallenstein and Kleinman found supporting evidence of the contagion hypothesis, which suggests that an adolescent suicide may trigger a cluster of subsequent suicides among peers [47]. With incidents being reported in Japan, the United Kingdom and the United States -the most recent being the case of Abraham Biggs which had made it's way into local newspapers in Trinidad and Tobago, one must assume that the seed has been planted and it will only be a matter of time before the first reported locally based internet related suicide comes to fruition. Hence, this paper also aims to prevent the importation of this scourge to the shores of Trinidad and Tobago, a country with the highest suicide rate per capita in the English speaking Caribbean, and by extension the Caribbean region [40].

Studies support the hypothesis, that the quality of reporting could trigger short-term increases of suicides in certain population subgroups. In Austria, "Media Guidelines for Reporting on Suicides" were issued. After the introduction of the media guidelines, the number of subway suicides and suicide attempts dropped more than 80% within 6 months [48].

CONCLUSION

In 2000, the World Health Organisation (WHO) acknowledged the impact of careless media reporting of suicide cases on its prevalence and issued guidelines for media professionals. It is thus recommended that these guidelines be adopted along with other measures to monitor these websites and their users.

With respect to internet suicide, sites managers and moderators must be held liable. Internet legislation is needed to curb suicidal behavior. Systems for mandatory reporting of suicidal behavior should be legally implemented with notification to the public health services. Encouragers or cyber-bullying should be prosecuted as participants in assisted suicide due to their culpability.

Cybersuicide is here to stay. As adolescents devise more creative and novel ways of dying, it is imperative that we study the process in order to develop cyber-based intervention techniques. Cybersuicide remains a serious public health concern and a major challenge for the future.

REFERENCES

[1] United Nations: Internet users per 100 population. [Online]. 2006 [cited 2009 Jan 13];[2 screens]. Available from: http://data.un.org/Data.aspx?q=internet&d=MDG&f=series RowID%3a605

[2] Orelind G. Top Sites in Trinidad and Tobago. [Online]. 2008 [cited 2008 Dec 12];[2 screens]. Available from: http://www.alexa.com/site/ds/top_sites?cc=TT&ts_mode= country&lang=none

[3] Alexa. Top Sites by Country. [Online]. 2008 [cited 2008 Dec 15];[3 screens]. Available from: http://www.alexa.com/site/ds/top_500

[4] Alao A, Adekola O, Soderberg S, Maureen A, Elyssa L, Lola A. Cybersuicide: review of the role of the internet on suicide. Cyberpsychol Behav 2006;9(4):489-93.

[5]   Alao AO, Yolles JC, Armenta W. Cybersuicide: the internet and suicide. Am J Psychiatry 1999;156:1836-7.

[6]   Baker D, Fortune S. Understanding self-harm and suicide websites: a qualitative interview study of young adult websites. Crisis 2008;29(3):118-22.

[7]   Biddle L, Donovan J, Hawton K, Kapur N, Gunnell D. Suicide and the Internet. BMJ 2008;336:800-2.

[8]   Naito A. Internet suicide in Japan: Implications for child and adolescent mental health. J Child Psychol Psychiatry 2007;12(4):583-97.

[9]   Rajagopal S. Suicide pacts and the internet. BMJ 2004;329:1298-9.

[10] de Silva CO. Too lonely to die alone: internet suicide pacts and existential suffering in Japan. Cult Med Psychiatry 2008;32(4):516-51.

[11] Arnold B. Caslon analytics cybersuicide notes. [Online]. 2008 [cited 2009 Jan 13];[9 screens]. Available from: http://www.caslon.com.au/cybersuicidenote3.htm

[12] Mahalo. Deathcasting. [Online]. 2008 [cited 2008 Dec 2];[1 screen]. Available from: http://www.mahalo.com/Deathcasting

[13] British man commits suicide online. [Online]. 2008 [cited 2008 Nov 6];[1 screen]. Available from: http://www.wayodd.com/british-man-commits-suicide-online/v/6881/

[14] Brookes N. Suicide on the internet. [Online]. 2003 [cited 2009 Jan 10];[2 screens]. Available from: http://www.churchofeuthanasia.org/press/bathchronicle.html

[15] Cathcart R. Woman pleads not guilty in internet suicide. [Online]. 2008 [cited 2008 Nov 15];[2 screens]. Available from: http://www.nytimes.com/2008/06/17/us/17plea.html

[16] Gutierrez T, McCabe K. Parents: Online newsgroup helped daughter commit suicide. [CNN Online]. 2005 [cited 2008 Nov 25];[1 screen]. Available from: http://www.cnn.com/2005/US/11/04/suicide.internet/index.html

[17] McCurry J. Seven die in online suicide pact in Japan. [Newspaper Article Online]. 2005 [cited 2008 Dec 9];[2 screens]. Available from: http://www.guardian.co.uk/technology/2005/mar/02/japan.internationalnews

[18] Tasker F. Teen's webcam suicide raises red flags for copycats, experts say. [Online]. 2007 [cited 2008 Nov 25];[1 screen]. Available from: http://www.miamiherald.com/news/nation/story/782905.html

[19] Frei A, Schenker T, Finzen A, Dittmann V, Kraeuchi K, Hoffmann-Richter U. The werther effect and assisted suicide. Suicide Life Threat Behav 2003;33:192-200.

[20] Marsden P. The 'Werther effect': Fact or fantasy? Dissertation. Sussex: Univ Sussex, 2000.

[21] Siebers T. The Werther effect: The esthetics of suicide. Mosaic (Winnipeg) 1993;26.

[22] WHO. Global school-based student health survey: Trinidad and Tobago 2007 Fact sheet. [Online]. 2007 [cited 2008 Dec 5];[2 screens]. Available from: http://www.who.int/chp/gshs/Trinidad_and_Tobago_fact_sheet.pdf

[23] Teen Commits suicide in front online audience. Trinidad Express 2008 Nov 22;

[24] BBC. Florida boy's suicide live on web. [Online]. 2008 [cited 2009 Jan 15];[2 screens]. Available from: http://news.bbc.co.uk/2/hi/americas/7743214.stm

[25] Suicide note of Abraham Biggs, teen whose death was broadcast via webcam. [Online]. 2008 [cited 2009 Jan 15];[3 screens]. Available from: http://www.nydailynews.com/news/us_world/2008/11/21/2008-11-21_suicide_note_of_abraham_biggs_teen_whose.html

Cybersuicide and the Adolescent Population: Challenges of the Future   191

[26] Chatroom users 'egged on father to kill himself live on webcam'. [Online]. 2008 [cited 2008 Dec 15];[5 screens]. Available from: http://www.thisislondon.co.uk/news/article-23390052-details/British+man+commits+suicide+on+live+webcam/article.do

[27] Kevin Whitrick. [Online]. 2008 [cited 2008 Dec 5];[3 screens]. Available from: http://www.mahalo.com/Kevin_Whitrick

[28] BBC. Net grief for online 'suicide'. [Online Article]. 2008 [cited 2009 Jan 14];[3 screens]. Available from: http://news.bbc.co.uk/2/hi/technology/2724819.stm

[29] Baume P, Rolfe A, Clinton M. Suicide on the internet: a focus for nursing intervention? Aust NZ J Ment Health Nurs 1998;7(4):134-41.

[30] Conner MG. Understanding and dealing with violence and suicide pacts By. [Online]. 2008 [cited 2009 Jan 3];[3 screens]. Available from: www.OregonCounseling.Org

[31] Lifecasting (video stream). [Online]. 2008 [cited 2009 Jan 5];[4 screens]. Available from: http://en.wikipedia.org/wiki/Lifecasting_(video_stream)#cite_note-0

[32] Darley JM, Latane B. Bystander intervention in emergencies: Diffusion of responsibility. J Pers Soc Psychol 1968;8:377-83.

[33] Ueno U. Suicide as Japan's major export? A note on Japanese Suicide Culture. [Online]. 2005 [cited 2009 Jan 15];[4 screens]. Available from: http://www.espacoacademico.com.br/044/44eueno_ing.htm

[34] WHO. Mental Health. [Online]. 2008 [cited 2008 Dec 5];[6 screens]. Available from: http://www.who.int/mental_health/prevention/suicide/country_reports/en/index.html

[35] ITU. Japan Internet usage, broadband and telecommunications reports. [Online]. 2008 [cited 2008 Dec 12];[2 screens]. Available from: http://www.internetworldstats.com/asia/jp.htm

[36] ITU. Internet World Stats Usage and Population Statistics Trinidad. [Online]. 2008 [cited 2008 Dec 3];[2 screens]. Available from: http://www.internetworldstats.com/car/tt.htm

[37] Chung WSD, Leung CM. Carbon monoxide poisoning as a new method of suicide in Hong Kong. Psychiatr Serv 2001;52(6):836-7.

[38] CIA. CIA : the world factbook. [Online]. 2008 [cited 2009 Jan 15];[13 screens]. Available from: https://www.cia.gov/library/publications/the-world-factbook/geos/td.html

[39] Maharajh HD. Assisted suicide or culpable suicide: is there a difference? Psychiatr Bull 1993;17:348-9.

[40] Hutchinson G. Variation of homicidal and suicidal behaviour within Trinidad and Tobago and the associated ecological risk factors. West Indian Med J 2005;54(5):319-24.

[41] Huus K. Japan's chilling Internet suicide pacts: New trend highlights social problems, mental health crisis. [Online Article]. 2003 [cited 2009 Jan 4];[5 screens]. Available from: http://www.msnbc.msn.com/id/3340456/

[42] WHO. Introduction: Suicide. [Online]. 1999 [cited 2009 Jan 12];[2 screens]. Available from: http://www.who.int/mental_health/media/en/382.pdf

[43] Hawton K, Williams K. Influences of the media on suicide. BMJ 2002;325:1374-5.

[44] WHO. Preventing Suicide: a resource for media professionals. [Online]. 2000 [cited 2009 Jan 15];[9 screens]. Available from: http://www.who.int/mental_health/media/en/426.pdf

[45] Maris RW, Berman AL, Maltsberger JT. Assessment and prediction of suicide. New York: Guilford, 1992:499-519.

[46] Philips DP. The impact of fictional television stories on US adult fatalities: new evidence on the effect of the mass media on violence. Am J Sociol 1982;87:1340-59.

[47] Gould MS, Wallenstein S, Kleinman M. Time space clusterng of teenage suicide. Am J Epidemiol 1990;131(1):71-8.

[48] T.Niederkrotenthaler, Herberth A, Sonneck G. The "Werther-effect": legend or reality?. Neuropsychiatry 2007;21(4):284-90.

In: Social and Cultural Psychiatry Experience from the... ISBN: 978-1-61668-506-5
Editor: Hari D. Maharajh and Joav Merrick © 2010 Nova Science Publishers, Inc.

Chapter 17

SELF-POISONING BY PESTICIDE AND OTHER SUBSTANCES IN A GENERAL HOSPITAL

Hari D. Maharajh and Monique Konings

Self-poisoning by pesticides is a major public health problem, especially in agricultural communities. The purpose of this study is to investigate the pattern of poisoning of all patients admitted to an emergency care at a general hospital in Trinidad for the period 2003-2004. In a two-year retrospective study, data on self-poisoning from hospital archives were analyzed for demographic and other patterns. A total of 765 cases of self-poisoning were identified. The most common source of poisoning was ingestion of pesticides (n = 275, 35.9 % of all cases). Differences in age and gender were found; patients with pesticide ingestion were younger (mean age 25.8 years) and more frequently female. The majority of patients with pesticide poisoning were admitted to wards, and one death was reported. Poisoning by pesticides is prevalent in South Trinidad. The high incidence indicates an urgent need for implementing public health strategies for prevention in keeping with the recommendations of the World Health Organization

INTRODUCTION

Self-harm by intentional ingestion of pesticides is the most frequent type of poisoning worldwide, with self-poisoning by pesticides accounting for about a third of all suicides [1]. Estimates suggest that deliberate self-poisoning with pesticides leads to several hundred thousand deaths each year, with some 700,000 people having died in 1999 [2].

The use of pesticides for self-harm seem to be particularly prevalent in the developing world. More than two decades ago it was estimated that there were approximately 2.9 million cases of acute pesticide poisoning, resulting in about 220,000 deaths each year in the developing world [3]. In a more recent study, Gunnell and Eddleston [4] estimated that there were as many as 300,000 deaths each year from poisoning by pesticide in the rural areas of China and South East Asia. A conservative estimate is that ingestion of pesticides accounts for approximately half a million deaths each year in developing countries.

Little attention has been given to pesticide poisoning, despite the global scope of the problem and a proactive initiative by the World Health Organization [5]. The widespread availability and use of pesticides without restrictions has resulted in high suicide rates via this method in developing countries [6,7]. An earlier study in Trinidad found that over 80% of suicides in a rural area were by pesticide poisoning [8], and a similar figure was found in Malawi [9]. In Suriname, a recent report indicated that 55% of fatal poisonings involved ingestion of pesticides and in the Tobacco growing area of Campinas, Brazil, 25% of patients who were admitted to the hospital for self harm had ingested pesticides [10]. A study in Zimbabwe found increased admissions for self-poisoning with organophosphate compounds, which account for approximately three-quarters of hospital admissions [11]. These findings reveal the enormity of the problem of pesticide poisoning in developing countries.

The term pesticide includes weedicides, herbicides, insecticides, and fungicides and generically describes all substances or products that are utilized to exterminate unwanted or harmful animal or plant pests. Ingestion of pesticides can have damaging effects on health and can result in death. Within the Caribbean region, the most popular pesticides used are the organophosphates, particularly gramoxone, or its constituent paraquat, which is a highly toxic and effective biocide that is used mainly as a herbicide. Malathione is the most commonly used insecticide.

These biocides are commonly used for self-poisoning. Paraquat is the most used method of self poisoning in developing countries and can be described as a major suicide agent [5], because of its acute toxicity, the nonexistence of an antidote, its easy availability, and its cheapness. The rates of paraquat poisoning are directly related to the availability of this pesticide, with less availability resulting in a decrease in paraquat suicides [12]. Paraquat poisoning results in a very high fatality rate, with reports ranging from 27 % in Tokyo [13], to 65% in South Mexico [14].

Deaths due to pesticide poisoning are also reported in Europe, but seem relatively uncommon. Pesticides were responsible for 1.1% of all the deaths due to poisoning in England in 1990-1991 [15]. Only 0.11 % of all the hospitalizations due to poisoning in Finland were due to pesticides [16]. In developed countries, mortality rates are reduced due to adherence to legislative requirements on safety procedures, better education of the population on following instructions for use, and ready availability of basic commodities such as water for washing. In addition, purchase of safety equipment recommended by WHO and other organizations is often unpractical and expensive for developing countries. A major stumbling block is the lack of commitment and investment by governments in developing countries [2,4,5]. This results in an increase of both intentional and non-intentional deaths.

Paraquat poisoning is common in the rural, agricultural regions of the Caribbean. In Jamaica a country with low rates of suicide, 41% of poisoning cases involved paraquat poisoning [17]. Suicide rates in Trinidad and Tobago are high [8], with the majority due to paraquat ingestion. Poisoning by paraquat ingestion accounted for 76% of the deaths due to poisoning in south Trinidad [8]. Regional data from Trinidad and Tobago in the years 1986 to 1990 showed paraquat as the most popular poison used in 63% of suicide attempts, while other agrochemicals were used in 20% of the cases [18]. In 1996, 48 cases of suicides were reported with 81.3% due to paraquat ingestion.

Herbicide ingestion is not only common in adults but also appears in children. In a general hospital study over a three-year period in Trinidad ,169 children under the age of 16 were seen with acute poisoning, with 84.6% being accidental ingestion, 11.2% due to suicidal ideation, and 4.1 % due to forced poisoning. Pesticides were used in 15.9 % of the cases, and 5.3% involved paraquat [19]. It is evident that despite problems in estimating the regional and global burden of pesticide poisoning, the latter remains a major public health issue in developing countries that results in the loss of hundred of thousands of lives in their most productive years.

OUR STUDY

The purpose of our study was to investigate poisoning data from the period 2003-2004 from an emergency department in a general hospital in South Trinidad and to compare the findings with the rates and results from studies in other developing and more developed countries. Demographic factors, as well as methods of self-harm, are described and analyzed.

Trinidad and Tobago are twin islands located in the southern Caribbean Sea just off the coast of Venezuela. The country has a population of 1.3 million people. The sex ratio is 1.07 male to 1.0 female: in 2006 (49.9% female; 50.1% male) [20]. The ethnic composition is 40.3 % Indo-Trinidadian, 39.6 % Afro-Trinidadian, 18.4 % mixed, and 1.7 % others. About 20 % of the inhabitants of Trinidad and Tobago are under 14 years of age; the majority (71.3 %) is between 15 and 64 years of age; and 8.6 % are over the age of 65.

The Southern and Central Region of Trinidad, where the study was conducted, is a less urbanized region. It is situated in the agricultural belt and comprises approximately half the population of the twin state republic. The population is mostly of Indian origin (55 %), about 30% is of Afro-Trinidadian origin, and the rest is of mixed and other origin. The San Fernando General Hospital is the major hospital servicing the Southern Region and covers a catchment area of 600,000 population.

Data from hospital archives on poisoning were analyzed. Variables which were retrospectively collected from the emergency care service of the hospital included date of admission, age, gender, ethnicity, causes of ingestion, type of substance ingested and first contact dispensation for discharge at home or admission to the ward. Data were obtained from computerized files for the two most recent calendar years that were available, which were 2003 and 2004. The cases analyzed included all people presenting themselves to the emergency service with any form of poisoning. Those who were pronounced "dead on arrival" were not included in this study, and mortality rates were not analyzed for those who were admitted to hospital wards. No information was available on the intent of suicidal behaviors.

Patients admitted for emergency care service were categorized according to the type of poisonous substance they used. The different substances were divided into the following categories: liquid chemicals (e.g., acid, bleach, disinfectant); oral medications (e.g., antibiotics, psychotropic medications, liquid preparations); substances of abuse (e.g., alcohol, cocaine, cannabis); contamination (of food or water); and mixed substances. In the cases of mixed poisoning, patients were assigned to the category of the more toxic substance ingested; for example, those who used pesticides and alcohol were categorized as pesticide poisoning. Contaminants of potable water or food were also present and were mostly accidental poisoning. Data was analyzed using the Statistical Package for Social Scientists (SPSS version 11). Frequencies, t-tests and chi squares were utilized to identify significant differences.

OUR FINDINGS

During the 2-year period of 2003 and 2004, 765 cases of poisoning were treated at the emergency care service. The data for type of substance ingested are presented in table 1. Of the total number of poisoning cases, the most common category was ingestion of pesticides (n = 275, 35.9 %). Ingestion of medications was second, with 230 cases (30.1 %). Ingestion of various kinds of chemical agents accounted for 143 cases (18.7 %), substances of abuse accounted for 8 cases (1.1 %), contamination of food or water accounted for 17 cases (2.2 %), and the miscellaneous category accounted for 80 cases (10.5 %). The latter included substances such as paint, petrol, inhaled gases, and other substances. There were 12 cases with no indication of the type of substance ingested.

In an analysis of the group defined as pesticides, which constituted approximately 36% of the cases of poisoning, 51% were documented in the patient files as "pesticides" without further classification. "Herbicides ingestion" accounted for 24.0% (66 patients) while 5.8% (16 patients) had taken "insecticides" and 13.1 % (36 patients) had ingested a "weedicide." There was no clear cut classification system for pesticides.

Table 1. Types of poisonous substances ingested (N = 765)

Category	n (%)	Specific Substances (n)
Pesticides	275 (35.9%)	Herbicides (66); weedicides (36); insecticides (16); not specified (157)
Medications	230 (30.1%)	Benzodiazepines (30); analgesics (19); antibiotics (18); hypoglycaemics (5); anticonvulsants (4); antidepressants (4); antipsychotics (2); bronchodilators (3); vitamins (6); unknown (97); others (42)
Liquid Chemicals	143 (18.7%)	Acid (8); bleach (13); detergent (2); chlorox (77); disinfectant (25); ammonia (1); antiseptic (17).
Contamination	17 (2.2%)	Water (1); food (16)
Substances of Abuse	8 (1.1%)	Alcohol (2); cocaine (2); cannabis (3)
Other	80 (10.5%)	Paint (7); petrol (39); toxic inhalation (24); others (10)
No Report	12 (1.6%)	--

In 2003, 340 cases of poisoning were reported, while in the following year 425 cases presented for treatment. This is an increase of 25% between these years. In 2003, the number of cases of poisoning per month ranged from 18 (April) to 42 (February). In 2004 there was also a similar range, but there was a very high peak in October with 148 cases. This was not found in 2003, with only 19 reported patients seeking treatment in that month.

The mean age of the total sample is 23.4 years, with a standard deviation of 15.9 years (range 0 – 89 years; see Table 2). People who used intoxicants such as drugs or alcohol were the oldest age group, with a mean age of 32.6 years. The mean age of patients seeking treatment for pesticide ingestion at the emergency service was 25.8 years. The youngest groups were those who experienced food or water contamination (mean age 16.2 years) and those who ingested liquid chemicals (mean age 19.7 years).

Table 2. Age and type of substance

Type of Substance	Mean Age	SD	Range (years)
Pesticides	25.8	15.3	0-83
Medications	23.6	14.5	0-84
Liquid chemicals	19.7	17.4	0-89
Contamination	16.2	9.6	10-41
Substances of abuse	32.6	13.5	16-52
Other	22.1	19.8	0-85
No reort	23.8	5.0	18-34
Total sample	23.8	13.6	0-89

The individuals who ingested substances of abuse were significantly older than all of the other groups except those who ingested pesticides. The individuals who ingested pesticides were also significantly older than those who ingested contaminated food or water and those who ingested liquid chemicals.

Table 3 presents the data by gender for each type of substance ingested. Numerically, more women presented with poisoning in all categories except for substances of abuse and liquid chemical agents. The gender differences for each type of substance were analyzed using the chi-square test. Significant gender differences were found for the total sample, with 437 females and 328 males seeking treatment at the emergency service ($X2 = 15.53$, p< 0.001). There was also a significant difference for ingestion of pesticides, with a predominance of women ($X2 = 4.46$, p < 0.05).

Table 3. Gender and type of substance ingested

Type of Substance	Males (n)	Females (n)	Total
Pesticides	120	155	275
Medications	81	149	230
Liquid chemicals	73	70	143
Contamination	7	10	17
Substances of abuse	6	2	8
Other	17	43	80
Total	328	437	753

Table 4 presents the data for outcome of the emergency room visit for poisoning. An analysis of outcome revealed that the majority of patients, except those with exposures to contaminated food or water, were admitted to a ward. Of the 753 patients for whom data were available, 65.7% were admitted to the wards, 30.7% were discharged and 3.3% absconded. These included poisoning with chemicals, medications, pesticides substances of abuse, food/water contaminants, and other substances. Two deaths were recorded (0.3%), one from poisoning with pesticides and the other from an overdose of medication. Although the highest percentage of patients sought treatment for pesticide poisoning (35.9%), only 46.2% of these patients were admitted to the hospital, while of the 29.2% that were treated for overdosing with medication, 87.4% were admitted for further treatment.

Table 4. Outcome of poisoning by substance ingested

Substance Ingested	Discharged n (%)	Admitted n (%)	Died n (%)	Absconded n (%)
Pesticides	143 (52.0)	127 (46.2)	1 (0.4)	4 (1.5)
Medications	19 (8.3)	201 (87.4)	1 (0.4)	9 (3.9)
Liquid chemicals	27 (18.9)	107 (74.8)	0	9 (6.3)
Contamination	15 (88.2)	2 (11.8)	0	0
Substances of Abuse	0	8 (100)	0	0
Other	27 (33.8)	50 (62.4)	0	3 (3.8)

DISCUSSION

There have been many attempts to make pesticides safer and less available. In the late 1980's blue pigment and an emetic were added to paraquat. In 1991 the Global Safe Use Project was launched to train pesticides users in developing countries and to make them aware of the health danger. In 2002 a code of conduct was set up to rationalize the use of pesticides and to reduce the risk to environmental well being and the danger to health. Pesticides were also classified by the World Health Organization (WHO) in classes ranging from Class I (extremely hazardous) to Class III (slightly hazardous). Use of Class I pesticides was banned or strictly forbidden in the industrialized world, but not in developing countries.

The data presented here indicate that poisoning with pesticides is still very prominent, accounting for 35.9% of all cases of poisoning. It is not known whether these poisoning were intentional or non-intentional, but it is likely to be a mix of these two. Despite efforts to provide clear rules for use as mentioned above, pesticides poisoning is still common in Trinidad and Tobago. These findings are similar to those found in other studies in developing countries, where poisoning with pesticides, together with ingestion of prescription drugs, continue to be quite prevalent [21].

The pesticide poisonings occur in young people, (mean age 25.8 years) and in this study differed statistically from many other groups, like intake of chemicals and contaminated food and water, indicating that this group is a more mature group. There were no statistical differences in ages of the group with ingestion of prescription drugs and ingestion of pesticides. These people are in a phase of there lives with being active, working in agricultural areas therefore increasing the risk of being in contact (intentional or non-intentional) with all kind of pesticides. This study was done in the emergency ward in a hospital in the southern region, a rural and agricultural region, which may be a limitation in the study showing higher rates of pesticides intoxication in this country.

Gender differences were also found in this patient population where on the whole, more women visited the emergency ward during the two year period. The group of patients who had intoxication with tablets and pesticides were predominantly women (p values < 0.05). It is known from the literature that intoxication with medication are mainly done by women, so these findings of this study confirm the literature [12,13,22].

It can be thought that in the southern part of Trinidad, more men work in the agricultural areas but pesticides are easily available. This increases the risk of intake as a suicidal gesture with women.

The outcome with intake of pesticides showed that many patients were discharged well, but also many patients were admitted to a ward (46.2%). Even one of the patients died. It is not known what the severity of intoxication is in the patients admitted to a ward. Intoxication with tablets was also a major group of patients on the emergency ward with the majority (87.4%) being admitted to a ward in a hospital. The tablets intoxication (antipsychotics) was fatal for one person. Many different tablets were found to have been taken, as well somatic medication as more psychiatric medication, like benzodiazepines, who accounted for 29 cases (10.9%) of the known taken (n=266). Also ingestion of chemicals was associated with high rates of ward admission, just like intake of solely drugs.

There was also an increase in people attending the emergency ward for intoxication from 2003 to 2004; with 25% more reported cases in 2004.

We can conclude from these analyses of data that intake of pesticides is still a major problem in Trinidad despite international limitations and rules of use. It is a major burden to health care since the majority of patients were admitted to a ward and death can occur. Intoxications with pesticides occur mainly in young people and in women. It is very important that the government pays attention to this and it proves that rules should be made here as well.

REFERENCES

[1] Bertolote JM, Fleischmann A, Eddleston M. Gunnell D. Deaths from pesticide poisoning: a global response. Br J Psychiatry 2006:189:201-3.

[2] Murray CJL, Lopez AD. The global burden of disease – a comprehensive assessment of morality and disability from diseases, injuries and risk factors in 1990 and projected to 2020. In: Murray CJL, Lopez AD, eds. Harvard School of Public Health: Global burden of disease and injury series, vol 1. Cambridge, MA: Harvard Univ Press, 1996.

[3] Jevarathnam J. Health problems of pesticide usage in the Third World. Br J Ind Med 1985:42(8):505-6.

[4] Gunnell D, Eddlestone M. Suicide by intentional ingestion of pesticides; a continuing tragedy in developing countries. Int J Epidemiol 2003:32(6):902-9.

[5] Eddlestone M, Karalliedde L, Buckley N, Fernando R, Hutchinson G, Isbister G, et al. Pesticide poisoning in the developing world – a minimum pesticide list. Lancet 2002;360(9340):1163-7.

[6] Van der Hoek W, Konradsen F, Athuhorala K, Wanigadewa T. Pesticide poisoning: a major health problem in Sri Lanka. Soc Sci Med 1998;46(4-5):495-504.

[7] Lin JJ, Lu TH. Association between the accessibility to lethal methods and method-specific suicide rates: An ecological study in Taiwan. J Clin Psychiatry 2006;67(7):1074-9.

[8] Hutchinson G, Daisley H, Simeon D, Simmonds V, Shetty M, Lynn D. High rates of paraquat-induced suicide in southern Trinidad. Suicide Life Threat Behav 1999;29(2):186-91.

[9] Dzamalala CP. Suicide in Blantyte, Malawi (2000-2003). J Clin Forensic Med 2006;13(2):65-9.

[10] Graafsma T, Kerkhof A, Gibson D, Badloe R, van de Beek LM. High rates of suicide and attempted suicide using pesticides in Nickerie, Suriname, South America. Crisis 2006;27(2):77-81.

[11] Dong X, Simon MA. The epidemiology of organophosphate poisoning in urban Zimbabwe from 1955 to 2000. Int J Occup Environ Health 2001;7(4):333-8.

[12] Perriens J, Van der Stuyft P, Chee H, Benimadho S. The epidemiology of paraquat intoxication in Surinam. Trop Geogr Med 1989;41(3):266-9.

[13] Yamashita M, Matsua H, Tanaka J, Yamashita M. Analysis of 1,000 consecutive cases of acute poisoning in the suburb of Tokyo leading to hospitalization. Vet Hum Toxicol 1996;38(1):34-5.

[14] Tinoco R, Tinoco R, Parsonnet J, Halperin D. Paraquat poisoning in southern Mexico: a report of 25 cases. Arch Environ Health 1993;48(2):78-80.

[15] Thompson JP, Casev PB, Vale JA. Deaths from pesticide poisoning in England and Wales 1990-1991. Hum Exp Toxicol 1995;14(5):437-45.

[16] Lamminpää A, Riihimaki V. Pesticide-related incidents treated in Finnish hospitals – a review of cases registered over a 5-year period. Hum Exp Toxicol 1992;11(6)473-9.

[17] Escoffery CT, Shirley SE. Fatal poisoning in Jamaica : a cornor's autopsy study from the University Hospital of the West Indies. Med Sci Law 2004;44(2):116-20.

[18] Hutchinson G, Daisley H, Simmons V, Gordon AN. Suicide by poisoning. West Indian Med J 1991;40(2):69-73.

[19] Pillai GK, Boland K, Jadgeo S, Persad K. Acute poisoning in children. Cases hospitalized during a three-year period in Trinidad. West Indian Med J 2004;53(1):50-4.

[20] Central Statistical Office. Republic of Trinidad and Tobago. [Online] 2006 [cited 2006 May 21]. Available from: http://WWW.cso.gov.tt/.

[21] Werneck Gl, Hasselmann MH, Phebo LB, Vieira DE, Gomes VL. Suicide attempts recorded at a general hospital in Rio de Janeiro, Brazil. Cad Saude Publica 2006;22(10):2201-6.

[22] Hwang KY, Lee EY, Hong SY. Paraquat intoxication in Korea. Arch Environ Health 2002;57(2):162-6.

In: Social and Cultural Psychiatry Experience from the...
Editor: Hari D. Maharajh and Joav Merrick

ISBN: 978-1-61668-506-5
© 2010 Nova Science Publishers, Inc.

Chapter 18

CONSULTATION-LIAISON PSYCHIATRY IN TRINIDAD AND TOBAGO WITH REFERENCE TO SUICIDAL BEHAVIOR

Hari D. Maharajh, Petal S. Abdool and Rehannah Mohammed

Consultation-Liason Psychiatry (C-LP) has been defined as the area of clinical psychiatry that encompasses clinical, teaching and research activities of psychiatrist and allied mental health professionals in the non psychiatric divisions of a general hospital. Over the years, consultation-liason services have expanded to provide care in health care facilities other than the general hospital, such as community health clinics, rehabilitation centers, convalescent hospitals, nursing homes and doctors' private offices. The term "Consultation – Liaison" reflects two interrelated roles of the consultant. "Consultation" refers to the provision of expert diagnostic opinion and advice on management regarding a patient's mental state and behavior at the request of another health professional. "Liaison" refers to a linking up of groups for the purpose of effective collaboration. The present chapter reviews how these roles are addressed in Trinidad and Tobago.

INTRODUCTION

Consultation - Liaison Psychiatry (C-L Psychiatry) is not well established in Trinidad and Tobago. Notwithstanding the endorsement of the General Medical Council of United Kingdom of liaison psychiatry as a sub-specialty within general psychiatry and the approval of psychosomatic medicine, the preferred terminology, as a sub-specialty field of psychiatry by the American Board of Medical Specialties in 2003 [1], little attention has been given to this area of practice and research in our setting. At St Anns Hospital in Trinidad, a 1000-bed psychiatric hospital, there is no training or service in C-L Psychiatry despite previous attempts to establish a consultation service with Port of Spain General Hospital [2]. At the San Fernando General and Scarborough Hospitals, there are routine services in C-L Psychiatry, but unfortunately these services are managed by junior doctors with inadequate training, thereby defying the basic principles that consultations are made and done by consultants. C-L Psychiatry is defined as the area of clinical psychiatry that encompasses clinical, teaching and research activities of psychiatrists and allied mental health professionals in the non-psychiatric divisions of a general hospital. Over the years, consultation - liaison services have expanded to provide care in health care facilities other than the general hospital, such as community health clinics, rehabilitation centers, convalescent hospitals, nursing homes and doctors' private offices. Within hospitals, C-L services may be established with a mono-disciplinary or medical model or multidisciplinary or mental health model team [3].

C-L Psychiatry started in the United States in the 1930's as an outgrowth of general hospital psychiatric units. The first viable general hospital psychiatric unit in the United States was opened in the Albany Hospital in 1902. Following that, the Rockefeller Foundation funded the establishment of 5 psychiatric liaison departments in 1934 [4,5]. The development of C-L Psychiatry was aided by the emergence in the 1920's of psychosomatic medicine. Before 1950 Alexander's concept of psychosomatic medicine dominated, proposing a casual link between a specific constellation of unconscious conflicts, of psychological methods of coping with them and the development of one of several organic diseases. Between 1951 and 1965, the Chicago Institute of Psychoanalysis postulated a 'psychosomatic specificity hypothesis' for a number of physical diseases [6]

The field of C-L Psychiatry has grown from a trickle to a flood at the present time. The extension of C-L Services to the community and other medical facilities and the de-emphasis on institutionalization has relegated psychiatric units in general hospitals as a relic of the past. The role of C-L Psychiatry is defined by the American Hospital Association (1970) as follows:

'The development of liaison psychiatric services is based on the acknowledged fact that psychiatry applied in general or specialty medicine contributes to the quality of care provided, affects hospital utilization, and results in a savings of the physician's time...the liaison psychiatrist often serves the unserved, by helping to ensure the identification and appropriate management of mental and emotional aspects of illness throughout the hospital.'

Today, there is overwhelming evidence to show that psychological factors are major determinants of the presentation and consequences of physical illness and medically unexplained symptoms. There is also a high prevalence of diagnosable psychiatric disorder in in-patient and out-patient populations, which is associated with significant disability and increased use of resources. Hence, the critical role of C-L Psychiatry cannot be overemphasized.

The term "Consultation – Liaison" reflects two interrelated roles of the consultant. "Consultation" refers to the provision of expert diagnostic opinion and advice on management regarding a patient's mental state and behavior at the request of another health professional. "Liaison" refers to a linking up of groups for the purpose of effective collaboration.

THE ROLE AND FUNCTION OF THE C-L PSYCHIATRIST IS THREE-FOLD. IT INVOLVES CLINICAL WORK, RESEARCH AND TEACHING:CLINICAL WORK

C-L psychiatrists are involved in the following:

- The diagnosis, prevention and management of mental illness in physically ill patients. Common C-L problems encountered include suicide attempts or threats, depression, agitation, hallucinations, sleep disorder, disorientation (usually secondary to delirium or dementia) or patients presenting with somatic complaints for which there is no organic basis (somatoform disorders).
- The assessment and management of atypical presentations of psychiatric disorders due to medical, neurological and surgical illnesses and their treatments.
- Assessment of capacity of patients to give informed consent for medical and surgical procedures.
- Providing non-pharmacological interventions to patients experiencing the emotional effects of their medical conditions.
- Providing mediation between patients and members of the clinical team and allaying conflicts between them.
- Acting as mediators and bridge-builders between non-psychiatric and psychiatric professionals.

Table 1. Essential steps in the consultation process (Herzog et al 2000)

Before the interview	Interview with the patient	After the interview
• Use structured referral forms • Review medical records/charts thoroughly • Talk with referring doctor, nursing staff or other medical staff • Identify the reason for referral	• Introduce yourself or be introduced by referring physician • Inform patient about the purpose and procedure of consultation • Assess and consider the patient's anxieties and expectation about the consultation; obtain agreement from patient • Perform psychiatric assessment	• Make short notes in the medical records • Inform referring doctor/staff comprehensively about the consultation and your final opinion (diagnosis and formulation) • Discuss your treatment recommendations thoroughly
• Formulate objective of psychiatric consultation • Check whether patient is informed about consultation	• If appropriate, interview relatives and friends • Inform the patient about your impressions, diagnoses and recommended treatment • Inform the patient about follow-up visits and/or your availability	• Clarify responsibilities for carrying out your recommendations • Ensure feasibility of your recommendations • Make appointment for next follow-up visit • Write a concise consultation note.

RESEARCH

Liaison psychiatrists have made numerous research contributions related to the psychiatric aspects of AIDS, cancer, transplantation, cardiology, neurology, pulmonary, renal and GI diseases and obstetrics and gynaecology. Their research has extended our knowledge about genetic, neurochemical and behavioral factors contributing to the development of psychiatric disorders among complex medically ill patients.

TEACHING

C-L psychiatrists are involved in teaching medical students, physicians, nurses, social workers, psychiatric residents and non-psychiatric residents in internal medicine, family practice, paediatrics, obstetrics & gynaecology and neurology. Crucial skills taught include interviewing techniques, approach to comprehensive diagnosis and management, personality assessment, proper use of drugs and brief psychotherapy. Included is staff education in psychological aspects of illness. The Psychiatry Unit at Mt Hope is dedicated to this vision (see table 1).

SETTING UP A CONSULTATION – LIAISON UNIT

A Consultation-Liaison service should be an administrative unit treated as an integral component of every psychiatric service, be it a psychiatric unit of a general hospital, a community health clinic or forensic service. In the multidisciplinary team model, a C-L service should be staffed by psychiatrists, liaison nurses, social workers and psychologists. The number of people involved will depend upon the size of the hospital or population served and the availability of staff and funds. The person in charge should be a senior psychiatrist who is experienced in C-L Psychiatry, able to coordinate the activities of the service and able to negotiate with other physicians on an equal footing. Their duties are full time liaising with physicians, families, NGO's, community groups and members of the multidisciplinary team. Consultations are a priority and ought not to be fitted in as time out from the consultants' lucrative private practices. On the other hand, physicians should descend from their exalted state and not perceive the psychiatrist to be of less value. The consultant should define what patients have to be seen and what services are to be delivered. The direct and indirect functions of the unit should be defined with predetermined responsibilities for medico-legal issues. Liaison Psychiatry should be funded and managed alongside other medical specialties with equity in funding for all services. Ideally, the psychiatrist should be a formal member of the medical organization of the hospital.

OUR STUDY

The purpose of this study was twofold: First, to review the present status of C-L Psychiatry locally and regionally with respect to its development as a sub-specialty, to define its role, to walk health professionals through the essential steps in the consultation process and to advise on the establishment of a Consultation-Liaison Unit. The second objective is to investigate some socio-demographic factors on consultations of suicidal behavior at a general hospital. Referral for suicidal behavior is the commonest cause for consultation in the general hospital and psychiatric clinics in Trinidad and Tobago.

A one year (January-December 2005) retrospective analysis was done on all patients referred to the psychiatric unit at the San Fernando General Hospital in the Consultation-Liaison (C-L) service. An analysis was done on patients with suicidal behavior since this constitutes almost half of the patients seen in C-L Psychiatry. An analysis was conducted on the method, type of substances used and demographic data of age, gender and ethnicity using the SPSS (Statistical Package for the Social Sciences, Version 11.0).

WHAT DID WE FIND?

During the period of January to December 2005, a total of 708 patients were referred for psychiatric consultation. Among this population, 291 or 41% were referred for suicidal behavior. Sixty six percent (192) or twice as many women attempted suicide than men (34%). Indo-Trinidadians were over-represented in the referrals for suicidal behavior with 195 of 291 (67%) requests for consultation being for people of Indian origin. Indo-Trinidadian males and females outnumbered Africans in all areas.

Twenty six percent (26%) of all cases of suicidal behavior were diagnosed with clinical depression and 3% were thought to be suffering from a psychotic illness (schizophrenia). Eight percent (8%) (24/291) of all suicidal attempts were carried out under the influence of alcohol and these were all older Indo-Trinidadian males from rural areas. Adjustment disorders due to stressors were common among adolescents but no figures were available.

Analysis according to age groupings revealed that the most vulnerable group was the 25 to 35 years age group accounting for 27% (78/291) of attempters. This age group also had the largest number of female attempters. The 36 to 55 year old males were most likely to attempt suicide (35/99). Fifteen percent (15%) of all cases occurred in the less than 20 years age group with the expected female predominance. Only 4% of cases were older than 55 years (see table 2).

Table 2. Parasuicides in S.F.G.H for 2005 according to age group and gender

	<20 years	20 -24 years	25-35 years	36-55 years	>55 years
MALE	13	23	31	35	2
FEMALE	32	29	47	33	9
TOTAL	45	52	78	68	11

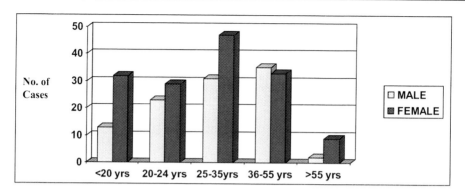

Figure 1. Bar chart illustrating data from table 2

There were only four cases of attempted hanging for the entire year and two cases of self-immolation (burns). Ingestion of a toxic substance was the most popular method among all races, gender and age groups. The 4 most popular substances ingested were weedicide/gramoxone 34%, bleach or household cleaner 9%, prescription drugs 52% and kerosene/diesel oil/battery acid. (4%) weedicide/gramoxone was the most popular method among males, the majority of whom were of East Indian descent. Among the females ingestion of tablets accounted for 55% of this population with East Indians again showing the highest prevalence rates (see table 3).

Table 3. Toxic substances ingested according to sex and race in percentages

	Household cleaner	Insecticide or gramoxone	Kerosene or diesel oil	Prescription drugs
African male	4 (1%)	10 (3.6%)	2 (0.7%)	4 (1%)
African female	4 (1%)	10 (3.6%)	2 (0.7%)	20 (7.2%)
E. Indian male	6 (2%)	40 (14.5%)	3 (1%)	28 (10.1%)
E. Indian female	16 (6%)	30 (10.8%)	3 (1%)	94 (34%)

Percentages were obtained by dividing by total number of ingestion cases

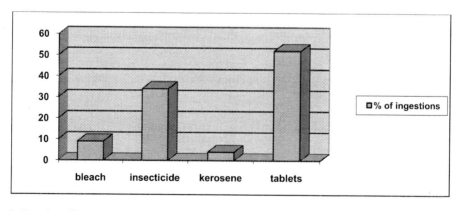

Figure 2. Bar chart illustrating substances ingested as a percentage of total cases of ingestion

More than 95% of all referrals originated from the medical wards of this General Hospital for 2005. The most common reason cited for attempted suicide was depressed mood secondary to a domestic dispute with a family member or significant other.

DISCUSSION

Trinidad and Tobago are twin islands located in the southern Caribbean sea just off the coast of Venezuela. Formerly a British colony, the islands attained Independence in 1962 and Republican status in 1975 and covers a land area of 1,932 square miles; it has a total population of approximately 1.3 million with 40.3% of the population being of East Indian descent, 39.6% of African origin, 18.4% mixed and 1.7% belonging to other ethic groups (13). The country is classified as a more developed country (MDC) with an economy based principally on oil and gas and a per capita gross domestic product (GDP) of US $8948 and total health expenditure of 5.2% of the GDP [7].

Trinidad and Tobago has the second highest rate of suicide in the Caribbean. According to WHO World Health Report [8] the twin island republic has a suicide rate of 11.6/100,000 and is only exceeded by Cuba. A more recent study has reported the overall mean suicide rate calculated for the period of 1990-1997 to be 20.6/100,000 for the male population and 5.4/100,000 for the female [9]. Organophosphate poisoning with paraquat ingestion is the commonest form of self-poisoning. Mortality rates due to self-poisoning by paraquat ingestion accounted for more than 80% of the deaths in South Trinidad [10]. Regional data from Trinidad and Tobago for the years 1986 to 1990 indicated that paraquat was the most popular poison used in 63% of suicidal attempts and other biocides were used in 20% of the cases [10]. In 1996, 48 cases of suicide were reported with 81.3% due to paraquat poisoning [11].

The Southern and Central regions of Trinidad are less urbanized areas situated in the agricultural belt and comprise approximately half the population of the twin state Republic. The San Fernando General Hospital is the major hospital servicing the southern region and serves a population of approximately 600,000 people with a 60 percent Indo-Trinidadian residency. On this background, it is not surprising that of the 708 patients seen for C-L psychiatry at the San Fernando General Hospital in 2005, 41 percent of the consultations were for suicidal behavior and of the 810 in-patient referrals made in 2006, a similar percentage (43%) were for suicidal behavior. A detailed analysis of 2005 revealed a predominance of females with 66% female referred for post admission psychiatric consultation. With respect to the nature of poisonous substances used, 34% of those seen in C-L Psychiatry on the wards used pesticides, 52% oral medication, 9% cleaning agents and 5% kerosene. Approximately 8% of the C-L population carried out their acts under the influence of alcohol. These were mostly older males of East Indian origin.

In Trinidad and Tobago, suicidal behavior is a common finding among the Indo-Trinidadian population. More than 95% of all referrals originated from the medical wards of the General Hospital. Sixty seven percent (67%) of all requests were for people of Indian origin. The mean age of all attempters was 23.4 years underlying a need to address the problems of substance abuse and poisoning among adolescents in structured community C-L services. Despite the global burden of pesticide poisoning and a proactive initiative by the

WHO [12], little attention has been given to pesticide poisoning in Trinidad and Tobago. This is in part due to lack of government's investment in the agro-industries and its pursuit of policies of political expediency rather than human suffering. The widespread use and availability of pesticides with poor restriction and control has resulted in high suicide rates in developing countries [13] This is evident in Trinidad and Tobago. This further underlines the need to invest in C-L community psychiatry.

The European Consultation-Liaison Workshop for General Hospital Psychiatry and Psychosomatics [14] has identified two groups of patients namely attempted suicide and substance abuse that make up between a quarter to a third of those referred for C-L service. In this study, 41% were referred for attempted suicide of which 8% were under the influence of alcohol. and 26 % found to be depressed. Since these disorders are common in Trinidad and Tobago [15,16], C-L Psychiatrists have a major role to play in the delivery of service to these groups, facilitating the transition of care from admission in the emergency room to discharge and follow up in the community.

There is a changing culture within general hospitals both in the developing and developed world. There is a change in functions of the hospital with a shift to a client–oriented service, new technologies requiring specialized skills, implementation of organizational structures and the need to put effective economic measures in place. This changing trend on a background of the closure or downsizing of large mental institutions has placed greater demands on the general hospitals [17]. There is now an influx of more patients for treatment, reduced length of stay in the hospital, increase in the proportion of severely disordered patient and consequently an increase in suicidal behavior within the hospital setting. While education and extensive screening programs are mandatory at all levels in the community, the time has come for the establishment of a C-L rolling programme for the early and vigorous treatment of patients both at the community and hospital levels.

Given the importance of C-L Psychiatry and the vast advances that have been made in this field in recent times, it is regrettable that formal training in this area is lacking and/or inadequate in Trinidad and Tobago. This matter is currently under review at the University of the West Indies Psychiatry Unit at Mt Hope in Trinidad.

ACKNOWLEDGMENTS

We wish to thank Dr Shivanand Gopeesingh, consultant in ER trauma at the San Fernando General Hospital for the provision of data for this study.

REFERENCES

[1] Giltin D, Levenson J, Lyketsos C. Psychosomatic medicine: A new psychiatric subspecialty. Acad Psychiatry 2004;28:4-11.

[2] Maharajh HD. A proposal for registrars and specialist medical officers to be on call at the Port of Spain General Hospital following closure of Ward 8. Policy statement submitted to the NWRHA from the Medical Chief of Staff Office, St. Anns Hospital, 1999.

[3] Huyse FJ. The organization of psychiatric services for general hospital departments. In: Gelder MG, Lopez-Ibor JJ, Andreasen N, eds. New Oxford textbook of psychiatry. Oxford: Oxford Univ Press, 2000:1237-42.

[4] Lipowski ZJ. Consultation-liaison psychiatry: An overview. Am J Psychiatry 1974;131:623-9.

[5] Lloyd G, Mayou R. Liaison psychiatry or psychological medicine? Br J Psychiatry 2003;183:5-7.

[6] Buckley P, Bird J, Harrison G. Examination notes in Psychiatry. A post graduate text, 3rd ed. London: Arnold, 1996:222-33.

[7] World Health Organization. Project atlas: Country profile-Trinidad and Tobago. Geneva: 2002. [Online] 2002 [cited 2009 Oct 27]. Available from www.cvdinfobase.ca?mhatlas/

[8] World Health Organization. World Health Report, October 2001, Geneva: WHO, 2001.

[9] Ameerali D. Suicide in Trinidad and Tobago: An ecological study. Dissertation. St Augustine: Univ West Indies, 2002.

[10] Hutchinson G, Daisley H, Simmons V, Gordon AN. Suicide by poisoning. West Indian Med J 1991;40(2):69-73.

[11] Hutchinson G, Daisley H, Simeon D, Simmonds V, Shetty M, Lynn D. High rates of paraquat-induced suicide in southern Trinidad. Suicide Life Threat Behav 1999;29(2):186-91.

[12] World Health Organization. The prevention of mental disorders: Effective interventions and policy options. Geneva: WHO, 2004.

[13] Bertolote JM, Fleischmann A, Eddleston M, Gunnell D. Deaths from pesticide poisoning: a global response. Br J Psychiatry 2006; 189:201-3.

[14] Bassett D, Tsourtos G. Inpatient suicide in a general hospital psychiatric unit: A consequence of inadequate resources? Gen Hosp Psychiatry 1993;15(5):301-6.

[15] Maharajh HD, Ali A. Adolescent depression in Trinidad and Tobago. Eur Child Adolesc Psychiatry 2006;15:30-7.

[16] Maharajh HD, Konings M. Suicidal behavior and cannabis-related dosorders among adolescents. In: Merrick J, Zalsman G, eds. Suicidal behaviour in adolescence. An international perspective. London: Freund Publ House, 2005:119-29..

[17] Murray CJL, Lopez AD. The global burden of disease – a comprehensive assessment of morality and disability from diseases, injuries and risk factors in 1990 and projected to 2020. In: Murray CJL, Lopez AD, eds. Harvard School of Public Health: Global burden of disease and injury series, vol 1. Cambridge, MA: Harvard Univ Press, 1996.

SECTION FIVE: ALCOHOL AND SUBSTANCE ABUSE

In: Social and Cultural Psychiatry Experience from the...   ISBN: 978-1-61668-506-5
Editor: Hari D. Maharajh and Joav Merrick   © 2010 Nova Science Publishers, Inc.

Chapter 19

CRIME, ALCOHOL USE AND UNEMPLOYMENT

Hari D. Maharajh and Akleema Ali

Criminal activity is a major social problem faced by governments and there is consensus that different types of crime will have different causes. Two major predictors of crime include alcohol and unemployment. In Trinidad and Tobago, minor crimes are the most prevalent when compared to serious crimes and minor offences. The purpose of this study was to examine the types of crime in Trinidad and Tobago and to identify the role of unemployment and alcohol. This study utilised the use of secondary data from the Central Statistical Office (CSO) for the period 1990-1997. Statistical analyses took the form of Pearson Product Moment correlations and stepwise multiple regression analysis to identify significant predictors. Stepwise regression models revealed unemployment accounted for 69.2% of the variance for serious crimes, beer consumption 64% of the variance of minor offences and both unemployment and beer consumption accounted for 92.2% of the variance of minor crimes. Beer consumption and unemployment play a significant role in criminal activities in Trinidad and Tobago. However, it is recommended that a further examination of the unemployment-crime (U-C) relationship needs to be done where the unemployment measure accounts for age, gender and county differences. Reductions in beer consumption would significantly reduce the occurrences of minor offences in the country.

INTRODUCTION

Increasing criminal activity is a major social problem faced by governments. This growing menace has resulted in widespread research to identify predictors of crime so that they can be recognised. Many designs and methods have been used in an attempt to examine crime and its predictors. Research in identifying alcohol as a predictor of crime has mainly used two approaches: individual-level studies and analysis of aggregate-level data. In individual-level studies, occurrence of crimes committed is related to individual intoxication; while aggregate-level studies, demonstrates that an increase in one predictor (e.g. alcohol) is followed by an increase rate of violence within that population [1]. In addition, it has been noted that for the purposes of cross-cultural comparisons, aggregate-level data is very useful. The possible existence of a relationship between unemployment and crime (U-C) has been examined extensively through econometric analyses, both time series and cross-sectional analysis [2-7]; and in a review of the empirical evidence.Chiricos [8] argued that the direction of the U-C relationship is conditional on factors such as types of crime, the measure of employment used and the time period studied.

Major predictors of crime identified have been alcohol [1,9-13], unemployment [14-16], spatial dynamics of neighbourhood structure [17], handgun sales [18] and the economy [19,20]. Even though an attempt has been made to identify predictors of crime, there is general agreement that crimes will differ from country to country and that different types of crime will have different causes [21-25].

Within the Caribbean, previous studies have examined the region as a whole and have focused on suicide and homicide [26] and also unemployment and crime [14]. However, an examination of aggregate level data of Trinidad and Tobago needs to be done to identify specific predictors of crime, so that these can be directed towards policy making in dealing specifically with crime within Trinidad and Tobago. General trends in crime rates have been identified over the period 1990-1997 (see figure 1).

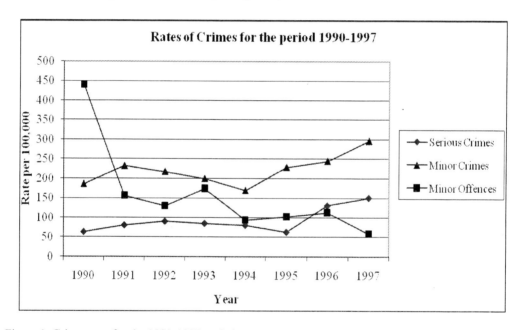

Figure 1. Crime rates for the 1990-1997 period

Minor offences have sharply decreased from 440.5 in 1990 to 59.3 in 1997, with the sharpest decrease occurring between 1990 and 1991. The trend lines for serious crimes and minor offences had similar and almost parallel patterns. Rates began to decrease from 1991 to 1994 for minor crimes (from 232.5 to 169.5) and to 1995 for serious crimes (from 80.1 to 62.4). However, after these points, rates began to steadily increase to a rate of 296.5 for minor crimes and 150 for serious crimes in 1997. Of all three types of crime, minor crimes were the most prevalent having the highest rate throughout the period 1991-1997. The purpose of this study was to examine the types of crime in Trinidad and Tobago and to investigate the role of two major predictors- alcohol use and unemployment for each type of crime.

A Review of Alcohol, Unemployment and Crime

This study seeks to investigate the relationship between the use of the alcoholic beverages beer, stout and rum and unemployment on various types of crimes in Trinidad and Tobago

This study utilised the use of secondary data from the Central Statistical Office (CSO). The CSO is the sole institution in the Republic of Trinidad and Tobago that is responsible for the collection and dissemination of data related to Trinidad and Tobago. Data available for the public ranges from 1990-1997. Prior to 1990, data is not available in printed form. At the time of this study no data was available after 1997.

The following statistics were gathered for the period 1990-1997 to examine the relationship between alcohol, unemployment and crime: serious crime, minor crime, minor offences, litres of alcohol consumed (for beer, rum and stout) and unemployment rates. Serious crimes included all crimes carrying a penalty of five years and over for which prosecutions have been instituted in the High Court. Minor crimes included all crimes carrying a penalty of five years and under for which prosecutions have been instituted in the High Court. Minor offences include all offences for which prosecutions have been summarily instituted in the Magistrates' Court. Litres of alcohol consumed referred to litres of beer, rum and stout that were available for home consumption.

SPSS version 11 was used to conduct all statistical analysis. The p value was set at $p < 0.05$. Pearson Product Moment correlations were used to examine the overall direction and strength of the relationships between the variables before analysing the variables with stepwise multiple regressions. Stepwise multiple regression analyses were used to identify significant predictors of the dependent variable and because the independent variables are ordered according to the proportion of their contributions to the variances in the dependent variables. Only those independent variables that produce a "significant" increment in the coefficient of determination (R^2) are introduced one by one into the regression equation. It is said that this procedure produces the best-fitting multiple regression model [27]. The regression analyses were performed with the dependent variables being defined as the types of crime (serious crime, minor crime and minor offences) and predictor variables being unemployment, litres of beer consumed, litres of rum consumed and litres of stout consumed. Predictor variables were lagged one year to explain variation in crimes. These statistical procedures have been widely used in similar lines of research [18,28,29].

What did we find?

Between 1990 and 1993, the mean unemployment rate was 19.48%. This rate decreased steadily from 1993 to 1997. Overall the eight-year period, unemployment decreased by 5.8% from 20% in 1990 to 14.2% in 1997 (see figure 2).

The trend lines for alcohol consumption (see figure 3) showed that total litres of alcohol available for home consumption is highly dependent on beer consumption ($r = 0.960$, $p < 0.001$). Stout was the second most popular with rum consumption being third and all their respective quantities being under 500 litres between 1990-1997.

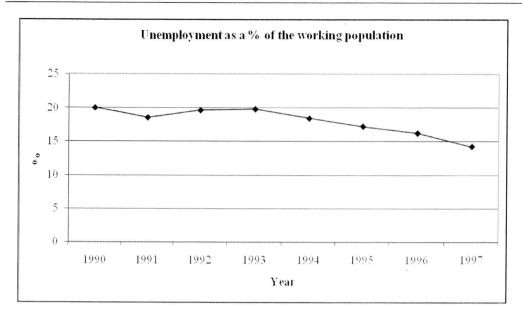

Figure 2. Unemployment for the 1990-1997 period

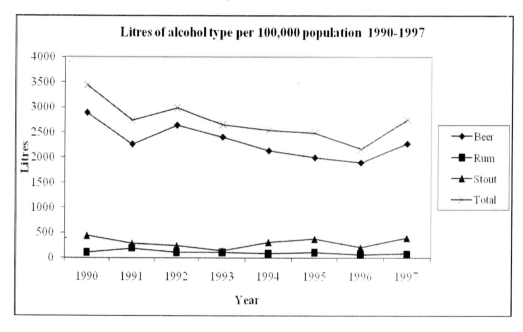

Figure 3. Alcohol consumption for the 1990-1997 period

Correlation relationships revealed that unemployment was significantly and negatively correlated with serious crimes ($r = -0.832$, $p < 0.05$) and minor crimes ($r = -0.833$, $p < 0.05$). Minor offences were positively correlated with unemployment ($r = 0.693$, $p < 0.05$) and beer consumption ($r = 0.800$, $p < 0.05$). The correlation relationships are summed in table 1.

Crime, Alcohol Use and Unemployment

Table 1. Correlations between types of crime, unemployment and alcohol consumption

	Unemployment	Beer	Rum	Stout
Serious crimes	-0.832*	-0.622	-0.308	-0.82
Minor crimes	-0.833**	-0.548	-0.431	0.284
Minor offences	0.693	0.800*	0.439	0.448

* $p < 0.05$, ** $p < 0.01$

The stepwise regression models revealed three significant models to account for crime. Table 2 summarises all regression models. In the first model to predict serious crime, unemployment was the only predictor accounting for 69.2% (R = 0.832, R 2 = 0.692) of the variance. All other variables were excluded.

Table 2. Stepwise regression models in predicting crime

Model		R	R^2	Unstandardized Coefficients B	Unstandardized Coefficients Std. Error	Standardized Coefficients Beta	t	Significance
Serious Crimes	Constant	-	-	436.435	101.543	-	4.298	.008
	Unemployment	.832	.692	-.832	-.832	-.832	-3.352	.020*
Minor Offences	Constant	-	-	-84.540	68.759		-1.230	.274
	Beer	.800	.640	8.758E-02	.029	.800	2.982	.031*
Minor Crimes (i)	Constant	-	-	654.958	127.347	-	5.143	.004
	Unemployment	.833	.694	-23.091	6.856	-.833	-3.368	.020*

In the second model to predict minor offences, beer consumption was the only predictor and accounted for 64% (R = 0.800, R 2 = 0.640) of the variance. Other predictor variables were excluded in this model.

The third model which predicted minor crimes revealed two predictors, unemployment and beer consumption with both accounted for 92.2% (R = 0.960, R 2 = 0.922) of the variance. This model illustrated that unemployment alone accounted for 69.4% of the variance while beer consumption contributed for an additional 22.8% of the variance. Other predictors were excluded.

DISCUSSION

This study attempted to identify predictors of various types of crime within Trinidad and Tobago. Overall, it can be said that both unemployment and beer consumption have significant impact on the crime situation in Trinidad and Tobago. Unemployment accounted for 69.2% of the variance in serious crimes and 69.4% of the variance in minor crimes. Beer consumption was the sole predictor of minor offences accounting for 64% of the variance and contributed to minor crimes with 22.8% of the variance.

The Beta values of the stepwise multiple regression models (see table 2) confirmed that the role of unemployment could be used as a predictor in both serious and minor crimes but that the directional effect is a negative one i.e. falling unemployment rates result in higher crime rates. Previous research [2] and economic theory [30] has supported the negative U-C relationship on the basis that as unemployment decreases there are more economic goods or crime targets that are in circulation. Thus as unemployment falls, opportunities increase for criminal activities and the successful accomplishment of these activities.

Of all alcoholic beverages, beer was the only one that contributed significantly to crime and can be attributed to two factors: the beverage-specific effects of alcohol and the drinking culture or pattern of Trinidad and Tobago. The literature has noted the possible differential beverage-specific effects of alcohol on various behavioural outcomes [31]. Trends identified in Europe have focused on the "Mellanby Effect" which occurs when the blood alcohol concentration (BAC) rises more rapidly and to higher levels when spirits are consumed compared to when beer is consumed. In addition the differential effects of alcoholic beverages will be directly linked to the drinking culture of the country. Stronger associations have been established between violent behaviour and the 'explosive' drinking patterns of Finland, Sweden and Norway when compared to the 'moderate' drinking patterns of France [9]. In Sweden, spirit consumption was strongly associated with crime but no associations were found with beer or wine consumption. Parker & Cartmill [32] in an analysis of US data found that spirits consumption was positively related to white homicides, while beer consumption was linked to non-white homicides.

The drinking culture of Trinidad and Tobago incorporates the beverages of beer, stout and rum. However, beer was the most popular of all three beverages from 1990-1997 and in 1997 was available for home consumption 28.32 times more than rum and 5.68 times more than stout (see Chart 3). Due to the fact that beer is dominant in the drinking context of Trinidad and Tobago, it is likely that this would be a predictor of crime, more specifically to minor crimes and minor offences.

Our findings support the Forst and Bennett Caribbean study [14] where there was no evidence to support the hypothesis that increases in unemployment are related to increases in crimes. However, our study is limited by the fact that the measure of unemployment represents rates at a national level and thus, does not account for influences of age and gender. Rates of unemployment should be differentiated between young males and older males and male unemployment from female unemployment. Research has shown that the direction of the U-C relationship varies when these differences are accounted for [6,8].

Other factors that could additionally be studied and possibly add to the variance in serious crimes would be poverty (factors such as malnutrition, unsanitary dwellings, congested living) and the role of inequality (the manner of distribution of wealth) and minimum wages. Previous researchers have noted that the factors of poverty and inequality should not be neglected in attempting to explain crime [34,35].

This study has shown that beer consumption and unemployment play a significant role in the crime situation of Trinidad and Tobago though it is recommended that a further examination of the U-C relationship needs to be done where the unemployment measure accounts for age, gender and county differences. The U-C relationship should also be examined across the counties or administrative areas of Trinidad and Tobago to establish whether the direction of the U-C relationship remains the same, so that policies targeting to deal with the various types of crime would be addressed specifically to the needs of each country. Additionally, measures should be taken to reduce the amount of litres of beer made available for home consumption, as this was the sole predictor of minor offences (64%) and a predictor of minor crime. Reductions in beer consumption would significantly reduce the occurrences of minor offences in the country.

CONCLUSION

At present, in 2009 with 1.6 billion dollars earned on tobacco and alcohol tax revenue over the last three years, the Government of Trinidad and Tobago has taken extreme measures to curb the inevitable decline in health of the country by an increase in the alcohol taxes, as presented in the last National Budget of 2009. Surprisingly though as our present murder rates are increasing there seems to be an inverse relationship with our unemployment rate. With an astonishing 3.9% rate at present in comparison to other countries of the Caribbean estimating 15-25%, [35,36] and reported crimes also increasing over the years, one may assume that the criminals are already seasoned in their game. Career criminals as they are so rightly called, may not rely anymore on the effects of employment and alcohol consumption to fuel their gains.

Murder is now the leading cause of death for young black men in Trinidad. A newspaper report states that in the last eight years 73% of the 2,500 murders were Afro-Trinidadians [37] with a steady increase of annual murders from 151 in 2001 to 544 in 2008. It is expected that the 2009 rates will be higher. In Trinidad, crime is a complex phenomenon interrelated with perception of political freedom, low detection rates, hierarchical gang promotion with pips, the drug trade and the low value placed on human life.

REFERENCES

[1]   Rossow I. Alcohol and homicide: a cross-cultural comparison of the

[2]   relationship in 14 European countries. Addiction 2001;96(1): S77-S92.

[3]   Elliott C, Ellingworth D. Exploring the relationship between unemployment and property crime. App Econ Lett 1998;5:527-30.

[4]   Gould ED, Weinburg BA, David B. Crime rates and local labour market opportunities in the United States: 1970-1997. Rev Econ Stat 2002;84(1):45.

[5]   Witt R, Clarke A, Fielding N. Crime, earnings inequality and unemployment in England and Wales. App Econ Lett 1998;5: 265-7.

[6]   Kleck G, Chiricos T. Unemployment and property crime: a target-specific assessment of opportunity and motivation as mediating factors. Criminology 2002;40(3):649-79.

[7]   Carmichael F, Ward R. Youth unemployment and crime in the English regions and Wales. App Econ 2000;32:559-71.

[8]   Lester BY. Property crime and unemployment: a new perspective. App Econ Lett 1995;2:159-62.

[9]   Chiricos TG. Rates of crime and unemployment: an analysis of aggregate research evidence. Soc Probl 1987;32(2):189-212.

[10]   Lenke L. Alcohol and criminal violence: time series analyses in a comparative perspective. Stockholm: Almquist Wiksell, 1990.

[11]   Pernanen K. Alcohol in human violence. New York: Guildford, 1991.

[12]   Gustaffson R. Is it possible to link alcohol intoxication causally to aggression and violence? A summary of the Swedish experimental approach. Stud Crime Crime Prev 1995;4:22-42.

[13] Bushman BJ. Effects of alcohol on human aggression: validity of proposed explanations. In: Galanter M, ed. Recent developments in alcoholism: Alcohol and violence. New York: Plenum, 1997: 227-43.

[14] Stevenson RJ, Lind B, Weatherburn D. The relationship between alcohol sales and assault in New South Wales, Australia. Addiction 1999;94(3):397-410.

[15] Forst B, Bennett RR. Unemployment and crime: Implications for the Caribbean. Caribb J Criminol Soc Psychol 1999;3(1-2):1-29.

[16] Britt CL. Reconsidering the unemployment and crime relationship: variation by age group and historical period. J Quant Criminol 1997; 13(4):405-28.

[17] Hale C, Sabbagh D. Testing the relationship between unemployment and crime: a methodological comment and empirical analysis using time series data from England and Wales. J Res Crime Delinquency 1991;28(4):400-17.

[18] Gorman DM, Speer PW, Gruenewald PJ, Labouvie EW. Spatial dynamics of alcohol availability, neighbourhood structure and violent crime. J Stud Alcohol 2001;62(5):628-36.

[19] Sorenson SB, Berk RA. Handgun sales, beer sales and youth homicide, California, 1972-1993. J Public Health Policy 2001;22(2): 182-97.

[20] Lester D, Motohashi Y, Yang B. The impact of the economy on suicide and homicide rates in Japan and the United States. Int J Soc Psychiatry 1992;38(4):314-7.

[21] Reinfurt DW, Stewart JR, Weaver NL. The economy as a factor in motor vehicle fatalities, suicides, and homicides. Accid Anal Prev 1991;23(5):453-62.

[22] Wolpin KI. An economic analysis of crime and punishment in England and Wales, 1984-1967. J Political Econ 1978;86(5): 815-40.

[23] Wolpin KI. A time series – cross section analysis of international variation in crime and punishment. Rev Econ Stat 1980;62(3): 417-23.

[24] Cameron S. The economics of crime deterrence: a survey of theory and evidence. Kyklos 1988;41(2):301-23.

[25] Cornwell C, Trumbull WN. Estimating the economic model of crime with panel data. Rev Econ Stat 1994;76(2):360-6.

[26] Marselli R, Vannini M. Estimating a crime equation in the presence of organised crime: evidence from Italy. Int Rev Law Econ 1997;17(1):89-113.

[27] Lester D. The suicide and homicide rates of 14 Caribbean islands in the 1970's were predicted in part by the proportion of the population of African descent. Percept Mot Skills 1999;88(3Pt2):1350.

[28] Fox J. Regression diagnostics. Newbury Park, CA: Sage, 1991.

[29] Preti A, Miotti P. Some social correlates of homicide rates in Italy. Psychol Rep 1999;85(3:1):770.

[30] Hutchinson G, Simeon DT. Suicide In Trinidad and Tobago: associations with measures of social distress. Int J Soc Psychiatry 1997;43(4):269-75.

[31] Cantor D, Land KC. Unemployment and crime rates in post-world War II United States; a theorectical and empirical analysis. Am Soc Rev 1985;50:317-32.

[32] Smart RG. Behavioural and social consequences related to the consumption of different beverage types. J Stud Alcohol 1996;57: 77-84.

[33] Parker RN, Cartmill RS. Alcohol and homicide in the United States 1934-1995 – or one reason why US rates of violence may be going down. J Crim Law Criminology 1998;88:1369-98.

[34] Tsushima M. Economic structure and crime: The case of Japan. J Socio-Econ 1996;25(4):497-515.

[35] Hojman DE. Explaining crime in Buenos Aires: the roles of inequality, unemployment and structural change. Bull Latin Am Res 2002;21(1):121-8.

[36] Browne J. Downside to historic 3.9%, Nunez Tesheira on unemployment. Trinidad Express 2009. [Online] 2009 [cited 2009 Oct 24]. Available from: http://www.trinidadexpress.com/index.pl/article?id=161499953.

[37] Crime in Trinidad and Tobago. 1999-2009 crime statistics. [Online] 2009 [cited 2009 Oct 24]. Available from: http://www.ttcrime.com/stats.php

[38] Baldeosingh, K. Murder-leading cause of death among young black men. Sunday Express 2009 Oct 25:5.

In: Social and Cultural Psychiatry Experience from the... ISBN: 978-1-61668-506-5
Editor: Hari D. Maharajh and Joav Merrick © 2010 Nova Science Publishers, Inc.

Chapter 20

AGGRESSIVE SEXUAL BEHAVIOR OF ALCOHOL-DEPENDENT MEN IN TRINIDAD

Hari D. Maharajh and Akleema Ali

The purpose of this study is to report the aggressive sexual behaviour of alcohol-dependent men and its implications in clinical practice. A total of thirty women of male alcohol-dependent partners were taken from a psychiatric clinic and matched with a control group of spouses of healthy non-drinking men for the variables of age, gender, ethnicity and social class. These groups were tested for sexually induced marks over a one month period, areas of the body that were marked, duration of body marks and love-making experiences. Our findings indicate that the spouses of alcohol-dependent men are subjected to more aggressive and painful sexual experiences, more body marks in more regions that lasted an average of 7 days and more biting of body surfaces than wives of non-alcohol-dependent men. These behaviours are interpreted as subtle signs of domestic violence which should not be ignored in clinical practice.

INTRODUCTION

Wife beating or battering, even though it is not a recent phenomenon, does not always present clearly recognisable symptoms to primary caregivers [1]. Battered women present with many psychosomatic complaints such as headaches, backaches, choking and gastrointestinal disorders of nervousness. In addition, injuries may range from bruises to fractures, with the explanation of these injuries usually being inappropriate [1].

Wife beating has been associated with many factors such as being young, having an early age at marriage, low-income [2,3] conflict with families [2,4] and alcohol consumption by the batterer [3,5-8]. Alcohol as identified by the research above is one of the major factors linked to wife battering and sexual aggression. In a recent review of the link between alcohol consumption and perpetration of sexual aggression [9] both epidemiological and experimental literature were examined. It was reported that both associational and experimental studies have suggested a moderate link between alcohol consumption and sexual aggression. Women with alcoholic husbands are between 6-11 times at risk for violence compared to women without alcoholic husbands [10,11]. In Trinidad and Tobago associations exist between alcoholism, sexual abuse and wife battering. Singh [12] found that forty three percent of abusive partners used alcohol or marijuana at the time of wife battering. In another study, domestic violence was documented as being the highest in the homes of alcoholics in Trinidad [13]. In a six year analysis (1988-1994) of 423 cases of domestic violence at a home for battered women in Port of Spain, Trinidad, eighty percent of women were assessed to be victims of sexual abuse [12].

Biting and sucking during sex is not an uncommon practice among young adults. Although not stated as a paraphilia, women partners of alcohol-dependent men have complained of excessive aggression of their partners in lovemaking. Some have attempted to conceal their body marks by the use of heavy cosmetics, while others have invented explanations of trauma and insect bites. The research focusing on the aggressive sexual behaviour of alcoholic men has been limited with studies focusing within the context of marital dysfunction [14] and through event-based analyses in newlyweds [6]. The purpose of this study is to report the aggressive sexual behaviour of alcohol-dependent men and its implications in clinical practice.

OUR STUDY

A quasi-experimental case-control design was chosen. The sample was taken from a private psychiatric clinic in Central Trinidad. A total of thirty women of male alcohol-dependent partners, comprising the experimental group, were interviewed by means of a questionnaire about the sexual behaviour of their spouses. This group was matched against a control group of the spouses of thirty male, non-drinking, healthy security officers for the variables of age, gender, ethnicity and social class. All women had been in the current relationship for at least five years. Alcohol abuse was determined by use of the CAGE questionnaire [15] and meeting the criteria for alcohol-dependency according to DSM-IV-TR [16]. The CAGE questionnaire is used as a screening instrument for identifying subjects with alcohol abuse. Respondents needed to fulfill two or more criteria on the CAGE questionnaire to meet the criteria of alcohol abuse. The groups were compared along the following: having at least one sexually induced mark over a one month period, areas of the body that were marked, duration of body marks and love making experiences. All analyses were done on SPSS Version 11. The significance was set at $p < 0.05$.

OUR FINDINGS

The mean age of the tested group was 42 years (range 30 to 51 years) and 38 years for the control group (range 25 to 48 years). The spouses of both the tested and control groups were of the same ethnicity as their sexual partners. The household in each group earned less than 30,000 dollars per annum categorizing them as belonging to the lower social class.

Significant differences were found with sexually induced body marks between the two groups, Chi-square = 6.417, df = 1, $p < 0.01$, with 70% (n = 21) of the alcohol-dependent group having sexually induced body marks when compared to 26.7% (n = 8) of the control group. When odds estimates were assessed wives in the alcoholic group were 2.5 times more likely to sustain at least one sexually induced body mark when compared to controls over the one month period (OR = 2.49, 95% CI 1.376 – 4.520).

Bodies of the women in the alcohol-dependent group were marked in more areas when compared to controls. Main areas of the body that were marked in that group were the left neck and shoulder (71.43%), right neck (28.57%), breasts (47.62%) and abdomen and leg regions (28.57%). There were three subjects who sustained body marks in all regions. Of the eight controls that sustained body marks, six (75%) were in the neck and shoulder regions. The body marks in both groups also varied in time of disappearance and number. Spouses of alcohol-dependent men received more body marks in more regions that lasted an average of seven days compared to four days for the control group.

The groups also significantly differed in their love-making experiences, with 56.7% (n = 17) of the alcoholic group having unpleasant and painful lovemaking compared to 10% (n = 3) of controls, Chi-square = 14.7, df = 1, p < 0.001. The alcohol-dependent group were 2.6 times more likely to rate their love-making experiences as unpleasant and painful when compared to controls (OR = 2.62, 95% CI 1.613 – 4.240). All alcohol-dependent husbands had initiated sexual behaviour over the past month but only 16 (53.33%) had completed sex (penetration and ejaculation). In comparison, 24 (80%) of the control group had completed sex.

DISCUSSION

Our findings indicate that the spouses of alcoholic-dependent men are subjected to more aggressive and painful sexual experiences than wives of non-alcoholics (p < 0.001). Similar results were found by O'Farrell et al [14] where wives of male alcoholics experienced less sexual satisfaction, more sexual dysfunction and painful intercourse than the control group. Sucking and biting of body surfaces were also more common in the spouses of alcoholics (p < 0.01) compared to non-alcoholics. Alcoholic spouses received more body marks in more regions that lasted an average of 7 days compared to 4 days for the control.

Alcohol is indeed a potent antecedent of aggressive behaviour [17]. Gustafson [18] revealed that male aggression was a function of alcohol, frustration and subjective mood, the latter being a pervasive and sustained feeling tone that is experienced internally and which influences a person's behaviour. In his study that compared alcohol-drinking subjects against placebo-drinking subjects, the alcohol-drinking subjects were move aggressive than the placebo group. In addition, intoxicated subjects increased their aggression when frustrated.

Alcoholism has also been associated with reduced brain serotonin concentrations [19]. Serotonin helps regulate many chemical processes in the brain and helps regulate functions such as sexual behaviour and response to pain [20]. In addition, alcohol reduces the protective control of anxiety, so that alcohol-intoxicated individuals may be more likely to engage in aggressive behaviour. The finding that the partners of the alcohol-dependent men experienced more sexually induced body marks can be attributed to reduced serotonin levels which will induce aggressiveness. In addition, the numbing of sensations due to alcohol use and failing sexual ability may result in excessive aggression necessary for sexual responsiveness. Pathological jealousy common among alcohol-dependent men may result in intentionally inflicted body surface marks both as a manifestation of their machismo and as a paranoid indicator of territorial occupancy.

The findings of this study should not be dismissed, as it is possible that these behaviours may be subtle signs of domestic violence. It has been suggested that domestically violent men are more likely to be heavy drinkers than non-violent men [6]. Our clinical experiences indicate an increase of aggressive behaviour in alcohol-dependent men due to failing sexual potency. Women are often silent suffers who are unwilling to volunteer information on sexual aggressive behaviour, partly due to the fear of shame on exposure, but more so, due to culturally sanctioned notions of marriage. It is recommended that clinicians who notice these behaviours pay specific attention to these individuals and family behavioural patterns that are displayed. It appears as though deviant sexual behaviour precedes domestic violence and can be utilised as a marker of subsequent violence.

REFERENCES

[1]   Blair KA. The battered women: is she a silent victim. Nurse Pract 1986;11(6):38:40-4.

[2]   Subramaniam P, Sivayogan S. The prevalence and pattern of wife beating in the Trincomalee district in eastern Sri Lanka. Southeast Asian J Trop Med Public Health 2001;32:186-95.

[3]   Pan HS, Neidig PH, O'Leary KD. Predicting mild and severe husband-to-wife physical aggression. J Consult Clin Psychol 1994;62(5):975-81.

[4]   Keenan CK, el-Hadad A, Balian S.A. Factors associated with domestic violence in low-income Lebanese families. Image J Nurs Sch 1998;30(4):357-62.

[5]   Maffli E, Zumbrunn A. Alcohol and domestic violence in a sample of incidents reported to the police of Zurich City. Subst Use Misuse 2003;38(7):881-93.

[6]   Leonard KE, Quigley BM. Drinking and marital aggression in newlyweds: an event-based analysis of drinking and the occurrence of husband marital aggression. J Stud Alcohol 1999;60(4):537-45.

[7]   Rao V. Wife-beating in rural south India: a qualitative and econometric analysis. Soc Sci Med 1997;44(8):1169-80.

[8]   Bergman B, Larsson G, Brismar B, Klang, M. Aetiological and precipitating factors in wife battering. A psychosocial study of battered wives. Acta Psychiatr Scand 1988;77(3):338-45.

[9]   Testa, M. The impact of men's alcohol consumption on perpetration of aggression. Clin Psychol Rev 2002;22(8):1239-63.

[10]   Fals-Stewart W. The occurrence of partner physical aggression on days of alcohol consumption: a longitudinal diary study. J Consult Clin Psychol 2003;71(1):41-52.

[11]   Rodgers K. Wife assault: the findings of a national survey. Juristat 1994;14(9):1-21.

[12]   Singh CC. Mental Disorders in female victims of intimate partner violence in Trinidad. A project report. Dissertation. St Augustine: Univ West Indies, 2002.

[13]   Gopaul R, Morgan P, Reddock R. Women, family and family violence in the Caribbean: The historical and contemporary experience with special reference to Trinidad and Tobago. Prepared for CARICOM Secretariat, 1994:65.

[14]   O'Farrell TJ, Choquette KA, Cutter HS, Birchler GR. Sexual satisfaction and dysfunction in marriages of male alcoholics: comparison with nonalcoholic maritally conflicted and non-conflicted couples. J Stud Alcohol 1997;58(1):91-9.

[15]   Ewing JA. Detecting alcoholism: The CAGE questionnaire. JAMA 1984;252:1905-7.

[16]   American Psychiatric Association. Diagnostic and statistical manual IV-TR. Washington, DC: APA, 2000.

[17]   Taylor SP, Chermack ST. Alcohol, drugs and human physical aggression. J Stud Alcohol 1993;11(Suppl):78-88.

[18] Gustafon R. Male physical aggression as a function of alcohol, frustration and subjective mood. Int J Addition 1991;26(3):255-66.

[19] Whitaker-Azmitia P, Peroutka SJ, eds. The neuropharmacology of serotonin. New York: NY Acad Sci, 1990.

[20] Pihl RO, Peterson J, Lau M. A biosocial model of the alcohol-aggression relationship. Stud Alcohol 1993;11(Suppl):128-39.

In: Social and Cultural Psychiatry Experience from the...   ISBN: 978-1-61668-506-5
Editor: Hari D. Maharajh and Joav Merrick   © 2010 Nova Science Publishers, Inc.

Chapter 21

ALCOHOLICS ANONYMOUS IN TRINIDAD

Rainah Seepersad and Hari D. Maharajh

Alcoholics Anonymous is well established in Trinidad and serves as an indispensable modality in the rehabilitation of alcoholics.This study seeks to investigate socio-demographic characteristics and gender differences of members attending AA groups in Trinidad. Data was collected along the following variables: age, gender, ethnicity, religion, age of onset of alcohol use, psychiatric diagnoses and intentions for seeking treatment. A descriptive study of 107 members attending AA groups in Trinidad was studied and analyzed utilizing a demographic questionnaire and the Michigan Alcohol Screening Test (MAST). The Statistical Package for the Social Sciences (SPSS, Version 16) was used to conduct all statistical analyses. The age of the sample ranged from 22 to 78 with a mean age of 48.01. Males dominated the sample, accounting for 68% (n = 73), while females were 32% (n = 34). In terms of Ethnicity, East Indians accounted for 62% (n = 65) of the sample, Africans 14% (n = 15), Mixed 16% (n = 17) and Other 7% (n = 7). Religious constitution was dominated by Hindus 36% (n = 38), Roman Catholics 21% (n = 22), Other 14% (n = 15), Presbyterian 10% (n = 11), Pentecostal 9% (n =10), Muslim 5% (n = 6) and Anglican 4% (n = 5). Results utilizing the t-test showed that mean scores for males versus females differed significantly from each other (t (1, 105) = 2.11, p = 0.036) with males having a higher score on the MAST compared to females. Overall 14% of individuals indicated to having a co-morbid psychiatric disorder of which 10.5% were depression. There was no significant difference between genders. The composition and structure of AA groups in Trinidad is fashioned on a male gender bias. There is a need to address specific gender issues in the treatment of female alcoholics.

INTRODUCTION

There is no better definition of Alcoholics Anonymous (AA) than the preamble that is internationally recited at the commencement of every AA meeting:

'Alcoholics Anonymous is a fellowship of men and women who share their experience, strength, and hope with each other that they may solve their common problem and help others to recover from alcoholism. The only requirement for membership is a desire to stop drinking....our primary purpose is to stay sober and help other alcoholics to achieve sobriety'

AA today is repository of success based on understanding, wisdom, humility and honest self disclosure sometimes with humor. It stands on three pillars - the patient, the doctor and the priest and remains today one of the most important treatment intervention where other modalities have failed.

AA has been established in Trinidad and Tobago for fifty three years and has been a near miracle in the rehabilitation of alcoholics for whom there was no hope. Despite its effectiveness in its goal of maintaining both sobriety and serenity, a number of criticisms have been leveled at its meeting. Some of these are that they substitute alcohol addiction with caffeine addiction, gambling and confessions based on pathological liars; that they do not appeal to younger alcoholics who having heard the life histories and experiences of older members conclude that they have not done enough yet to be in that group; women often feel alienated and insulted in mixed groups. Despite AA ideology not to be associated with any religious group, their dictum 'to improve our conscious contact with God as we understand him' and 'a spiritual wakening' in steps 3, 11 and 12, is often viewed by many as being too religious [1].

Notwithstanding its long and effective history of patients' recovery in Trinidad and Tobago, there are no comprehensive studies of this group other than its establishment by Michael Beaubrun in 1956 [2]. The objective of this study is to review some socio-demographic factors of AA members attending meetings in Trinidad.

HISTORY OF ALCOHOLICS ANONYMOUS

The beginnings of Alcoholics Anonymous (AA) have been influenced by the Swiss Psychiatrist Carl Gustav Jung from an encounter with one of his patients Roland Hazard (III) who was diagnosed with chronic alcoholism [3]. During treatment Jung noticed that Mr Hazard had reached a point of near hopelessness and was unable to achieve any significant progress with his patient. He felt the only other available option was treatment through a spiritual experience, which had been documented at the time as a last resort reformation option for alcoholics.

When Rowland returned home to the United States he joined a Christian Evangelical Re-Armament movement known as the Oxford Group and shared his message of the importance of a spiritual experience in treatment of his condition with fellow alcoholics. He shared his message with Ebby Thacher, who was actually a close friend and drinking buddy of Bill Wilson, who would later be co-founder of AA. In discussing Jung's idea of treatment by spiritual experience Bill revealed he was having great difficulty maintaining sobriety. From Jung's initial idea of healing alcoholism through spirituality, the original foundation for the twelve step program was developed.

Bill, as he preferred to be called was the co founder of AA. Alcoholics Anonymous has as its main goal through support groups around the world, a fellowship that fosters sobriety among alcoholics. Bill maintained sobriety by helping other alcoholics achieve sobriety. But after a failed business trip in Akron, Ohio, he needed the help of another alcoholic to avoid the temptation to drink alcohol. He was subsequently introduced to Dr Robert Holbrook

Smith who belonged to the same Oxford alcoholic group. After his discussion with Bill, Dr Bob as he preferred being referred to "began to pursue the spiritual remedy for his malady with a willingness that he had never before been able to muster. He sobered, never to drink again up to the moment of his death in 1950". It was on this day of June 10, 1935 that AA was unofficially discovered.

Dr Bob and his wife Anne Smith played a large part in the development of the twelve steps of the program which is used along with the twelve traditions of AA written by Bill Wilson for use in the recovery process. The principle of AA can be summarized by the tenets of the Fifth Tradition on 'AA's Singleness of Purpose.' This tradition emphasizes that "Each group has but one primary purpose—to carry its message to the alcoholic who still suffers" The society remained nameless until 1939, when the book Alcoholics Anonymous recorded the recovery experience of about one hundred (100) members. Alcoholism, according to AA is defined as "an illness which prevents the alcoholic from controlling his drinking because they are ill in their bodies and in their minds (emotions) and if they persist, their alcoholism almost always gets worse." They believe the only requirement for membership is a desire to stop drinking and their primary purpose is to stay sober and help other alcoholics' to achieve sobriety [3].

AA offers the same help to anyone who has a drinking problem and would like to change their habit. Since they are all alcoholics themselves, they have a special understanding of each other, they know what illness feels like and they have learned how to recover from it in AA. Through the example and friendship of the recovered alcoholics in AA, new members are encouraged to stay away from a drink "one day at a time." They do not believe in swearing off forever but rather concentrate on not drinking right now – today.

An important fact about AA is that members say that they are alcoholics today- even when they have not had a drink for many years. They introduce themselves as "alcoholics" as they believe that once individuals have lost the ability to control their drinking, they can never again be sure of drinking safely, in other words they can never become "former alcoholics" or "ex-alcoholics" They hold the view, once an alcoholic always an alcoholic.

The AA members usually get together daily at different groups and share their experience with alcoholism, how they discovered AA and how the program has helped them thus far. Some meetings are open which will allow family members, supporters and researchers while other meetings are closed, solely for AA members to discuss personal matters as it may relate to their addiction. AA meetings are all guided by the 'Twelve steps' and 'Twelve Traditions' which are the basic principles by which each member lives by in their quest for sobriety [1].

ALCOHOLICS ANONYMOUS IN TRINIDAD

Trinidad, and its sister isle of Tobago are the most southerly of all the Caribbean islands. It is located between the Caribbean Sea and North Atlantic Ocean, northeast of Venezuela. Its population is approximately 1.3 million, with 40% of its population being of East Indian descent 37.5% of African descent, 20.5% Mixed, 1.2% Other and 0.8% unspecified [4]. Trinidad is divided into eight counties but for the purposes of this study the sample was chosen according to the Alcoholics' Anonymous (AA) division of groups within Trinidad (North, South and Central) as classified in the AA meeting list for Trinidad.

Less than two decades after the establishment of AA in the USA, attempts were made to obtain treatment for patients in Trinidad. The reason for this is that at the end of contractual servitude on the sugar plantations, the post-indentured society was in a state of readiness for reconstruction and rehabilitation. At the end of indentureship in 1919, drinking rates were high among East Indian immigrants as they are today among Indo-Trinidadians [4]. Alcohol was considered to be the solution for relaxation, socialization and all other maladies.

In the East Indian attempts at restructuring their communities along traditional lines, each village developed a 'panchayat' system where five (5) elders in each community were nominated to deal with the problems within the community [6]. A person with a problem be it alcoholism or sociopathic behaviour was labelled a 'kojhat' (undesirable) and was asked to leave the village. Later counselling and group discussions emerged giving birth to the village councils. This provided a ready stage for the development of AA in Trinidad.

The first acknowledgement of AA in Trinidad was in 1952, when a Gasparillo School Master wrote to the General Service Office (GSO) of AA in New York, seeking help for his alcoholic son. He received information about the philosophy of AA which he read and passed on to his son. The latter took no heed and went about on his merry way [7].

In March 1956, so too Stanley S, an alcoholic, in Trinidad, wrote to the General Service Office of Alcoholic Anonymous in New York for help for his drinking. He was asked to get in touch with Reggie G, a lone AA member in Trinidad. These two members approached Dr Michael Beaubrun, a psychiatrist and with the help of Father Brett of St Mary's College in Port of Spain, the first AA meeting was held at the College library on 20th April 1956. This was augmented by the introduction of an Alcohol Treatment Centre at St Anns Mental Asylum in 1956, the source of new members. In March 1957, the Roman Catholic Board made a decision to disband the AA members from meeting at the College; they sought refuge at the Greyfriars Presbyterian Church founding the first AA group in Trinidad. George E an alcoholic was instrumental in this process and Sammy who worked alongside Dr Michael Beaubrun was the first Alcoholic Rehabilitation Officer of the island involved in inpatient treatment. [8]. Today AA in Trinidad has moved from a trickle to a flood with more than 107 groups spread throughout the country.

RESEARCH FINDINGS ON ALCOHOLICS ANONYMOUS

A review of the international literature has documented some of the key factors that have been expressed by AA members which has aided in their recovery. They have cited the sponsorship system, abstinence model, anonymity, slogans such as "easy does it," and "one day at a time," the service structure and "hope and relief from guilt in discovering that one is sick, not bad" are among the list of benefits offered by AA [9]. The efficacy of AA has been questioned in the past. But, AA's no comment policy has made them an easy target over the years [10]. A group of Italian researchers have stated that "no experimental studies unequivocally demonstrated the effectiveness of AA or (professional 12-step therapy) for reducing alcohol dependence or problems," The conclusion of the study claimed that AA and AA-based therapies were no more or less effective than the alternatives of professional treatment or other types of alcohol therapies and interventions. But, according to Helliker a multitude of studies has also shown that AA attendance is associated with "reduced drinking and higher social functioning."

Helliker also cited an article which was published in the Journal for Studies on Alcohol which reflected that better outcomes are associated with recovery when professional therapy of any sort, is followed by AA attendance [10]. The study reported that of "466 problem drinkers who attended AA following professional treatment, the three-year abstinence rate doubled, to more than 50%." Further research also suggests that "addiction recovery programs like Alcoholics Anonymous help people stay away from alcohol even if they are skeptical of spirituality or suffer from mental illness." One study also suggested that men and women were benefiting equally from AA, especially with the most severe alcoholism [11]. Essentially the more meetings attended the better the results and likelihood of recovery without relapse. In Trinidad groups of alcoholics in treatment from St. Ann's, who had emetine aversion therapy and who religiously attended A.A. after discharge, also showed significantly better results than individuals who ended treatment on discharge. [2]

OUR STUDY

This study seeks to investigate socio-demographic characteristics of members attending AA groups in Trinidad. Data was collected along the following variables: age, gender, ethnicity, religion, age of onset of alcohol use, psychiatric diagnoses and intentions for seeking treatment. In addition, gender differences of symptoms of male and female alcoholics determined by the Michigan Alcohol Screening Test (MAST) were analysed.

The data was collected from men and women attending Alcoholics Anonymous (AA) meetings throughout Trinidad. Groups were visited in the North, South, and Central regions of the country. Interviews were conducted mostly in Schools and Health Centres and also from specialized treatment centres with AA Groups such as New Life Ministries Rehabilitation Centre, Piparo Empowerment Rehabilitation Centre, Families in Action, Serenity Place Women's Treatment Centre and the Caura Substance Abuse Prevention and Treatment Centre. A total of one hundred and sixteen (116) respondents participated in this study. From this a sample seventy three (73) men and thirty four (34) women were selected who met the criteria for alcohol dependency according to the Michigan Alcohol Screening Test (MAST- 22 item).

Prior to data collection, approval was obtained from the Ethics Committee of the Faculty of Medical Sciences, University of the West Indies, at the Eric Williams Medical Sciences Complex and the Ethics Committee of the North West Regional Health Authority, Port of Spain. Alcoholics Anonymous (AA) meetings were randomly selected from a listing of the locations and times obtained at an AA meeting (see figure 9). Participants were informed that it was a strictly private and confidential study (an anonymous study) on alcoholism. Sealed envelopes were distributed containing the questionnaire which was asked to be returned by the next two meeting sessions, approximately six (6) days later. Participants were given the choice upfront to participate voluntarily, decline or withdraw from the research [12].

RESEARCH INSTRUMENTS

The Michigan Alcohol Screening Test (MAST): The MAST was developed by Selzer in 1971 and is useful for detecting dependent drinkers. The original tool has twenty five (25) questions but has been shortened to a twenty two (22) item and further brief ten (10) and thirteen (13) item versions. The questions relate to respondents' self appraisal of drinking habits and to social, vocational and familial problems frequently associated with excessive drinking. The sensitivity of the MAST is 86-98% and the specificity 81-95%. The MAST (22-item) is useful as a case finder, to detect people who have serious alcohol problems, as it focuses on lifetime versus current drinking habits [13]. A total score of six (6) or more indicates hazardous drinking or alcohol dependence.

Data was collected along the following variables: age, gender, ethnicity, and religion. Gender was defined as being either male or female. Age, ethnicity and religion were self reported. Age was an open category. Ethnicity was reported using one of the given response categories of the four main ethnic groups: East Indian, African, Mixed, and Other. Religion was reported using one of the response categories given based on the major religions in Trinidad and Tobago: Roman Catholic, Presbyterian, Anglican, Pentecostal, Seventh Days Adventist, Methodist, Hindu, Muslim, and Other [4].

Questionnaire (structured from literature): Onset of use of alcohol was reported using the categories "younger than 12", "12-15," "16-19," "20-23," "24-27," "28-31," and "32 or older." Respondents intentions or reasons for seeking treatment was left open ended and further coded based on responses into the categories of : "self/life became unmanageable/point of no return," "family," "work related reasons," "health reasons," "intervention," "spiritual reasons," and "Don't know." Respondents' history of a diagnosis with a psychiatric disorder was assessed by self report for any of the following psychiatric disorders: Depressive disorder, Bipolar disorder, Post Traumatic disorder, Generalized Anxiety disorder, Antisocial Personality disorder and Other (other was left open ended).The above variables were designed in such a way to resemble a clinical interview which would document a basic history of the participants life.

The Statistical Package for the Social Sciences (SPSS, Version 16) was used to conduct all statistical analyses. Differences were considered significant at $p < 0.05$ level. Frequencies were utilized to describe the sample characteristics. The gender difference among the variables examined, were measured using Pearson Chi Square test for independence. A t-test was used to determine if the mean scores on the MAST were significantly different between genders.

OUR FINDINGS

A total of one hundred and sixteen (116) respondents were sampled across Trinidad for this study. Due to the fact that some of the research instruments were incomplete or the respondent did not meet the criteria for alcohol dependency (6 or more on the MAST), nine respondents (9) were excluded. Thus, one hundred and seven (107) members were used for the analysis.

The age of the sample ranged from 22 to 78 with a mean age of 48.01 and a standard deviation of 11.61 (see figure 1).

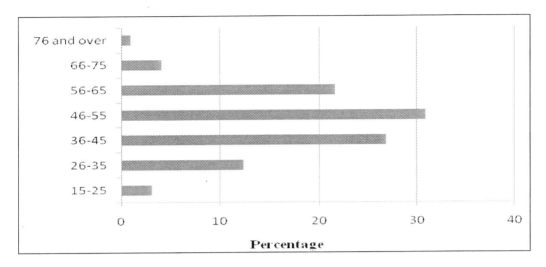

Figure 1. Percentage distribution of age range of alcohol dependents.

It was found that males dominated the sample, accounting for 68% (n = 73), while females were 32% (n = 34) as shown in figure 2.

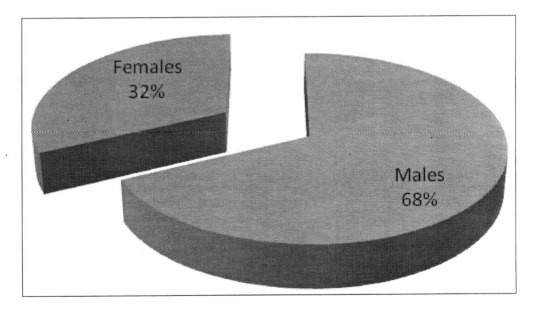

Figure 2. Percentage distribution of male to female alcohol dependents

In terms of ethnicity, East Indians accounted for 62% (n = 65) of the sample, Africans 14% (n = 15), Mixed 16% (n = 17) and Other 7% (n = 7), (see figure 3).

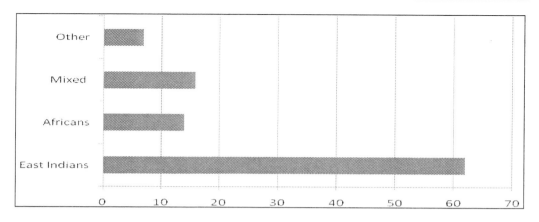

Figure 3. Percentage distribution of ethnic composition of alcohol dependents

Religious constitution was dominated by Hindus 36% (n = 38), Roman Catholics 21% (n = 22), Other 14% (n = 15), Presbyterian 10% (n = 11), Pentecostal 9% (n =10), Muslim 5% (n = 6) and Anglican 4% (n = 5).

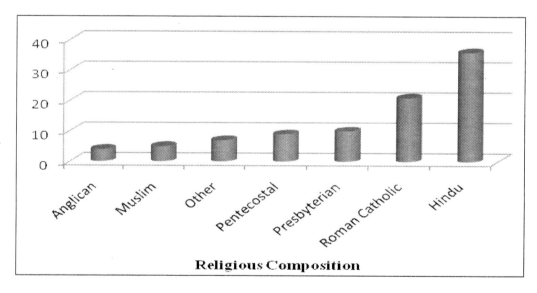

Figure 4. Percentage distribution of religious composition of alcohol dependents

In this population, scores on the MAST-22 item ranged from 6 to 21. Females had a mean score of 12.35, standard deviation 3.49 and males a mean score of 13.92, standard deviation 3.61. Results of the t-test showed that mean scores for males versus females differed significantly from each other (t (1, 105) = 2.11, p = 0.036) with males having a higher score on the MAST compared to females as illustrated in figure 5.

Significant gender differences existed among six (6) questions on the MAST-22 item questionnaire (items 1, 3, 7, 9, 11 and 22) with respect to the phenomenology of alcohol dependency in men and women. A significantly higher percentage of women 59% (n = 20) than 36% of men (n = 26) [Chi-square = 5.097, df = 1, p < 0.05] felt that they were a 'normal' drinker ('normal' defined as drinking as much or less than most other people). Ninety nine percent (99%) of males (n = 72) in comparison to 88% females (n = 30) [Chi-square = 5.627, df = 1, p < 0.05] indicated that a near relative or close friend worried or complained about their drinking.

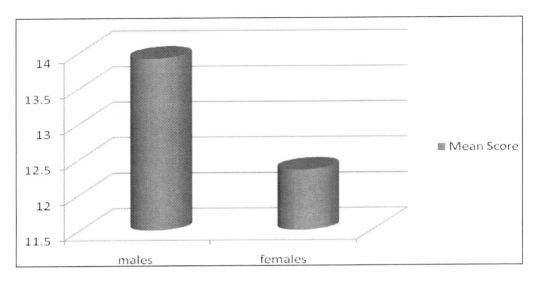

Figure 5. Differences in mean scores according to gender on the Michigan alcohol screening test

Significantly more men 75% (n = 55) than women 41% (n =14) [Chi-square = 11.823, df = 1, p < 0.05] indicated that they have gotten into physical fights when drinking. The majority of males 84% (n = 61) reported that a family member or close friend has gone to someone for help about their drinking in comparison to 56% of women (n =19) [Chi-square = 9.420, df = 1, p < 0.05].

Table 1. Significant differences in behaviour of alcohol dependence in males and females

Items on the MAST[a]	Males (n)	Yes %	Females (n)	Yes %	X^2	p
1. Did you feel you were a normal drinker? (normal is defined as drinking as much or as less than most people)	(26)	36	(20)	59	5.097	.024
3. Did any near relative or close friend ever worry or complain about your drinking	(72)	99	(30)	88	5.627	.018
7. Have you ever gotten into physical fights when drinking?	(55)	75	(14)	41	11.823	.001
9. Has any family member or close friend gone to anyone for help about your drinking	(61)	84	(19)	56	9.420	.002
11. Have you ever gotten into trouble at work because of drinking	(56)	77	(18)	53	6.145	.013
22. Have you ever been arrested, or detained by an official for a few hours, because of other behavior while drinking?	(25)	34	(2)	6	9.892	.002

Note .Chi square significant at the 0.05 level, d.f=1. [a]The items on the Michigan Alcohol Screening Test showing significant differences between male and female alcohol related problems (items 1, 3, 7, 9, 11, 22 respectively)

Seventy seven percent (77%, n = 56) of males in comparison to 53% (n = 18) of women reported that they have gotten in trouble at work because of drinking, indicative of a significant difference [Chi-square = 6.145, df = 1, p < 0.05]. A significantly higher percentage of males 34% (n = 25) than females 6% (n = 2) indicated to have been arrested or detained by an official for a few hours, because of other behaviour while drinking (see table 1).

Among the respondents four major reasons were stated as to why treatment was sought. Fifty one percent (51%) of individuals stated that their life had become unmanageable; most responses indicated a point of no return as they reported all aspects of their life were out of control. These individuals decided that treatment was the only way to save their life. Others respondents indicated that they sought treatment for main reasons such as family (15%), intervention (12%) and 11% indicated they sought treatment because of health reasons.

There were no significant gender differences with respect to the reasons for seeking treatment [Chi-square = 6.078, d.f. = 7, p < 0.05]. The majority of both males 49% (n = 36) and females 56% (n = 19) indicated that they sought treatment because they felt their life had become unmanageable and felt they reached a point of no return (see figure 6).

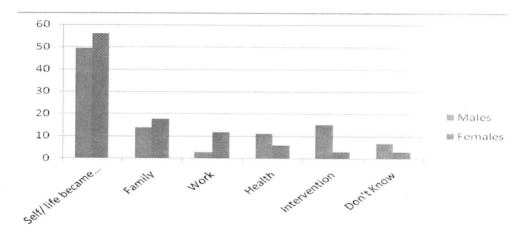

Figure 6. Percentage distribution of reasons for seeking treatment by gender

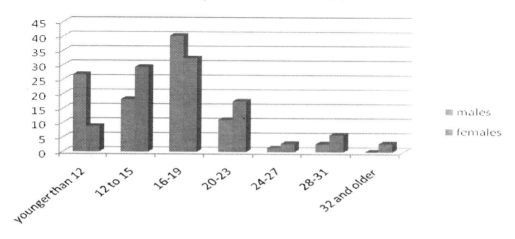

Figure 7. Percentage distribution of age of onset of alcohol use by gender

With respect to gender differences and the onset of alcohol consumption, 27% of males (n = 19) indicated that they began alcohol consumption before the age of 12 in comparison to 9% (n = 3) of females who indicated the same presenting a significant difference in age of onset of alcohol consumption, [Chi-square = 4.47, df = 1, p < 0.05]. Overall 37.7% of the sample indicated to having started consuming alcohol at the 16-19 age group as illustrated in figure 7.

Overall 14% of individuals indicated to having a co-morbid psychiatric disorder, and there was no significant difference between genders with respect to the presence of a co-morbid psychiatric disorder [Chi-square = .544, df = 1, p < 0.05], (see figure 8).

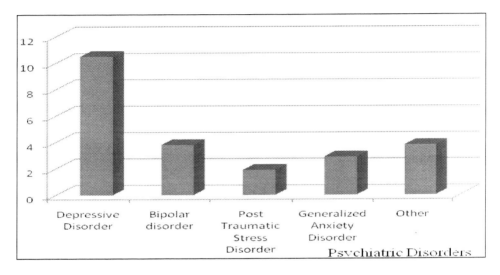

Figure 8. Percentage distribution of psychiatric disorders present in the alcohol dependent population

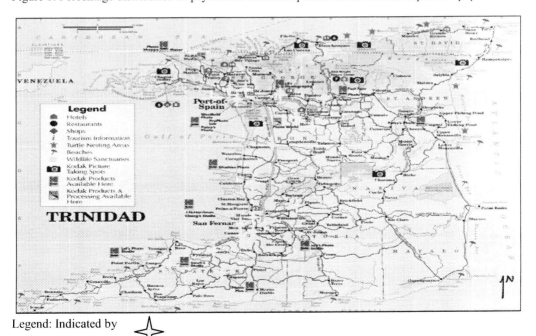

Figure 9. Geographical representation of Alcoholics Anonymous meetings visited.

DISCUSSION

In Trinidad, the presentation of alcohol dependency was dominated by males (68.2% vs. 31.8%) in the present research. Many Government surveys in most countries usually report about three times as many male as female alcoholics [14] with the male gender being a strong predictor for alcohol dependence [15]. The present study narrows the gap suggesting almost as twice as many males with alcohol dependency compared to female alcohol dependent women. In spite of this, a major factor that accounts for the small number of women is that treatment centres are notably underutilized by women [14]. The present sample was sourced from AA meetings and treatment centres throughout Trinidad with men still maintaining more than twice the presence. A possible explanation for this is that women experience more difficulties when entering alcoholism treatment settings. Barriers for women seem to be the social stigma and the fear to lose the right to care for their children, once an alcoholic problem is identified [14]. Women in Trinidad have reported that they do not attend meetings out of fear of being sexually harassed by men from past experiences [16].

The utilization of the MAST in this study enabled the researchers to confirm a diagnosis of Alcohol dependency among AA members and also served to differentiate behavioral characteristics of differences in the male and female alcohol dependent persons. Males in the sample had higher mean MAST scores compared to females (13.92 vs. 12.35, p < 0.05). Previous studies have also indicated that significant differences exist between males and females with respect to scores on the MAST. Males scoring higher on the MAST than females have suggested that males have a greater dependency for alcohol than females [17]. These results are supported by several other studies that found alcohol frequency to be higher among males than females [17]. Generalization of these results is difficult as many studies are usually testing the MAST on specific populations such as solely men or college populations. This is due to the fact that the MAST was originally designed for a male population [18].

The majority of the present sample was ethnically saturated with individuals of East Indian descent (62.5%) in comparison to those of African descent (14.4%). The prevalence of alcohol dependence in Trinidad and Tobago is higher than in the United States and also among individuals of East Indian ancestry when compared with those of African ancestry [5]. Research in Trinidad has reported alcoholism as being the highest among the Indian group [19]. A recent assessment survey reported alcohol dependence prevalence rates of 47% and 33% in persons of East Indian and African ancestry, respectively [5]. Notably though, the population of Trinidad being multi-ethnic and mainly composed of people of East Indian (40%) and African ancestry (37.5%) may account for ethnic differences in prevalence rates [4]. Similar findings with respect to the ethnic population consuming alcohol can also be identified among high school students, in Trinidad and Tobago [19]. However, the majority of the population sampled was sourced from South and Central Trinidad where larger AA groups are located, but also notably denser East Indian populated areas. The authors have noted that there is an ethnic reversal of alcohol and drug use in Trinidad and Tobago with Indo-Trinidadians having a tendency to favor the use of licit drugs such as alcohol and tobacco while Afro-Trinidadians favor illicit drugs such as marijuana and cocaine. This is associated with the high level of crime among the latter group.

It is also noteworthy that due to the family structures in the Caribbean, there is an immense pressure among Indo- Trinidadian families, especially extended families, to seek help for their loved ones because of strong kinship ties [19]. This has been linked to ethno-cultural traditional values and issues from the post-indentureship reconstitution of the Indo-Trinidadian society. East Indians resisted Christian indoctrination and organized themselves into small communities under the "panchayat system" led by Brahmin pundits [6]. This enabled easy resolution of social and psychological problems of the community. Hence, one can speculate that Indo-Trinidadians will be naturally attracted to such "satsang" (group discussions), like AA meetings.

There were also significant differences in the symtomatology of the profile of scores measured on the MAST. The MAST's results have been noted to be sensitive to demographic variables in the past. Previous researchers have demonstrated that men and women experience alcohol dependence and the concomitant symptoms and consequences differently. The MAST's original standardization sample was composed primarily of males convicted of driving under the influence [18]. As such, the MAST may be measuring different traits in men than it does in women. This is supported by the present study in which more males indicated to having been involved in negative legal behaviour, specifically "being arrested or detained by an official for a few hours, because of other behaviour while drinking" compared to women (34% vs. 6% respectively).

More males (75%) also indicated "to have been in physical fights when drinking" compared to women (41%). Findings were found in a United States population between men and women (40.2% vs. 32.7% respectively), [21] indicating more males than females express this form of aggressive behaviour. Interestingly though, it was found that more men had family members who complained or worried about them, or even went for help about their drinking. This interesting finding has been noted in previous research that women are less likely to receive support from family members or friends to enter treatment [22]. Within the Indo-Trinidadian population, there is less tolerance to female deviancy than that of the male gender. The male offspring is traditionally the favored child and carries more prestige than the female. This pattern is now changing as female offsprings are now actively involved in the care of both their maternal and marital families.

In addition, diversity of educational history and age has been known to affect MAST results. For instance, education has been linked to awareness and ability to identify the signs and symptoms of alcohol dependence [18]. The present population having been sourced at AA meetings where education about alcoholism inclusive of signs and symptoms are regularly reviewed may have influenced the sample to more readily disclose information about their alcohol dependency because of their awareness. The authors have recognized the influences of AA on the members. Their language, thought and behavior is modulated by the philosophy of AA; their responses are posited in language of AA, for example on questioning why they sought help for their problems, the majority of men and women stated that their lives had become unmanageable downplaying initial forced family treatment.

Alcohol-dependence symptom development may be a function of age [18], but according to the present study this was not supported indicating that in the Trinidad population, age and increased scores on the MAST were not significantly correlated in a positive direction ($r = -1.18$, $p < 0.05$). Thus, the MAST's usefulness with young and undereducated clients may not apply to alcohol dependents in Trinidad. This finding may be due to the fact that the population studied were not presently chronic drinkers, hence older individuals was the majority of the sample as respondents were sober for many years.

In terms of the age of onset reported, the findings suggested that higher rates of males start using alcohol at an earlier age than women (26.8% vs. 8.8%) respectively. Historically, men have reported an earlier age of onset of alcohol use initiation than women [23,24]. In the present research the findings indicated that more men began drinking at an earlier age at the 'younger than 12' age group.

With respect to similar age of onset most men and women started using alcohol around 16-19 age group in this research as it pertains to Trinidad. Likewise, other researchers have found remarkable similarity, with no significant differences in age of onset of male and female alcohol use leading to alcohol dependence. Interestingly, among persons who began drinking before age 14 years, 45% developed Diagnostic and Statistical Manual of Mental Disorders, Fourth Edition (DSM-IV) diagnosable dependence compared with 10% of persons who waited until they were 21 years or older [25]. In this research more males began consumption of alcohol before females which may also account to the saturation of males in the study.

Individuals with Alcohol use disorders such as alcohol dependence frequently meet criteria for other psychiatric disorders as well. Recent data from the National Epidemiologic Survey on Alcohol and Related Conditions (NESARC) reveal that among individuals with alcohol dependence, 15.15% met the criteria for a depressive disorder [24], of which similar findings were found in the present research (10.5%). It was also noted that in AA the camaraderie of the programme invokes overzealous behaviour among its members that may influence the usual depressive symptoms associated with alcohol dependency. A local psychiatrist who has worked closely with AA has observed that AA seems to be a self perpetuating group with an overzealous and enthusiastic approach. One of his patient's introduction into AA resulted in a Bipolar disorder. He has noted a 'high' amongst many AA members triggered by the new culture of the group process, personal disclosures, and storytelling combined with the historical development of Alcoholics Anonymous. Subsequently members are apt to be less negative in their outlook of life because of the new control they now have over their life [26].

With respect to treatment formulation women seeking pathways to recovery in institutionalized settings may be more likely to be screened for psychiatric disorders, but the reality of their condition becoming worse before they seek treatment may be more likely, since women tend to hide their drinking behaviour. This prevents friends, family and physicians from detecting alcohol dependency in many females [27]. This may account for the absence of diagnoses of co-morbid disorders in this present study.

Recent findings though may reflect a change in women's access to substance abuse care, which may be caused by reductions in stigma, increased awareness of alcohol problems and greater availability of women- focused treatment programs [22]. In Trinidad today, there is one AA group and one treatment centre that accommodates only women and both have provided an avenue for women to seek help without stigmatization. This points to the vital role of alcohol treatment services in non addiction settings in spite of the provision of mental health care by general medical providers or primary care physicians [22].

CONCLUSION

There is little doubt that AA in Trinidad has helped thousands of alcoholics and their families and would continue to do so in the future. Socio-demographic factors obtained from this study, profile the AA member in Trinidad as being a middle age (48 years), male Indo-Trinidadian of the Hindu religion who began abusing alcohol in their adolescent period. They invariably have good family support, that results in forced treatment. The commonest psychiatric disorder associated with alcohol dependency is a Depressive disorder. This in itself facilitates the group process of AA that provides a cognitive-behavioral approach to the treatment of both addiction and depression as members work through the structured twelve steps and traditions. Traditional values and culture seem to have an important part to play in the treatment process but is often underplayed due to the philosophy of AA.

The differences observed here in the female alcoholic raises a number of pertinent issues. Over the years the male and female alcoholics were painted with the same brush. It is evident that the female alcoholic has special needs and the onset, course, presentation and treatment modalities of women may be different to those of men. It was also noted that the entertainment quotient and sexual innuendos delivered at discourses at AA meetings ridicule women. These findings suggest that women have special and separate needs in treatment and future investments should be tailored to female only Treatment Centers.

The findings of this research cannot be generalized to individuals in the general population who have abused alcohol but have not met the criteria for Alcohol Dependence. Nor can it be applied to individuals who have not sought treatment for their alcohol dependence.

REFERENCES

[1] Alcoholics Anonymous Grapevine. A brief Guide to Alcoholics Anonymous. (Brochure). New York: Author, 1972.

[2] Beaubrun M. Treatment of alcoholism in Trinidad and Tobago, 1956-65. Br J Psychiatr 1967;113:643-58.

[3] Wikipedia [Online]. 2009 [cited 2009 Sept 8]. Available from http://en.wikipedia.org/wiki/Carl_Jung

[4] Central Intelligence Agency. The World Fact Book, Trinidad and Tobago. [Online] 2007. [cited 2009 Aug 20]. Available from
http://www.ece.gov.nt.ca/Maps/World%20and%20Canada%20Maps%20Publish/factbook/print/td.html

[5] Moore S. Association of ALDH1 promoter polymorphisms with alcohol-related phenotypes in Trinidad and Tobago. J Stud Alcohol 2007;68(2):192-6.

[6] Maharajh HD, Parasram R. The practice of psychiatry in Trinidad and Tobago. Int Rev Psychiatry 1999;11:173-83.

[7] Charlie AA member. Bonne Venture Group, Gasparillo. AA meeting. Personal communication, 1980.

[8] Edwards G. The authentic account on the birth of AA in Trinidad and Tobago. NCA Bull Trinidad and Tobago Natl Council Alcohol Other Addict, 1988.

[9] Anonymous Issue. The Twelve Steps. [Online] 2006 [cited 2009 Sept 8] Available from http://proquest.umi.com.ezproxygateway.sastudents.uwi.tt:2048/pqdweb?index=14&did=1022888391 &SrchMode=1&sid=3&Fmt=6&VInst=PROD&VType=PQD&RQT=309&VName=PQD&TS=12523 33648&clientId=45987

[10] Helliker K. The case for Alcoholics Anonymous: It works even if the science is Lacking. Wall Street Journal (Eastern Edition), p. D.1. [Online] 2006 [cited 2009 Sept 7] Available from ABI/INFORM Global. (Document ID: 1146446481).
http://proquest.umi.com.ezproxygateway.sastudents.uwi.tt:2048/pqdweb?index=5&did=1146446481&SrchMode=1&sid=2&Fmt=3&VInst=PROD&VType=PQD&RQT=309&VName=PQD&TS=1252336597&clientId=45987

[11] Health Behavior News Service; Addiction recovery programs help people stay away from alcohol. Lab Business Week. In: Academic Research Library [Online] 2006 [cited 2009 Sep 7]. Available from: http://www.proquest.com/; Document ID: 1092160511.

[12] American Psychological Association. The publication manual of the American Psychological Association, 5th ed.. Washington, DC: Author, 2001

[13] Alcohol Concern Primary Care Alcohol Information Service, Factsheet. Screening Tools for Healthcare settings. (Brochure) London: Waterbridge House, Author, nd

[14] Walter H, Gutierrez K, Ramsklogler K, Hertling I, Dvorak A, Leasch OM. Gender-specific differences in alcoholism: Implications for treatment. Arch Women's Ment Health 2003;6:253-8.

[15] Scholten A. Risk Factors for Alcohol Abuse and Alcoholism. [Online] 2007 [cited 2009 Apr 24]Availablefrom:http://www.aurorahealthcare.org/yourhealth/healthgate/getcontent.asp?URLhealthgate=%2219041.html%22

[16] AA member. Personal communication, 2009 Jun 27.

[17] Moulton M. Generic alcoholism: Are college athletes at risk? Sport J 2000;3(2).

[18] Laux JM, Newman I, Brown R. The Michigan Alcoholism Screening Test (MAST): A statistical validation analysis. Measurement Evaluat Couns Dev 2004;36(4):209.

[19] Maharajh HD, Ali A. Social predictors of suicidal behavior in adolescents in Trinidad and Tobago. Soc Psychiatr Epidemiol 2005; 40:186-91.

[20] World Health Organization. Trinidad and Tobago.Country profile. Geneva: WHO, Global Status Report Alcohol, 2004.

[21] Burnam A. Prevalence of alcohol abuse and dependence among Mexican Americans and Non-Hispanic Whites in the community. In: Spiegler D. Alcohol use among US ethnic minorities. Rockville, MD: Natl Inst Drug Abuse, NIDA Res Mongr, 1993.

[22] Wu L, Ringwalt CL. Alcohol dependence and use of treatment services among women in the community. Am J Psychiatry 2004;161(10):1790-7.

[23] McCreary DR, Newcomb MD, Sadava SW. The male role, alcohol use, and alcohol problems: A structural modeling examination in adult women and men. J Couns Psychol 1999;46(1):109-24.

[24] Gilbertson R, Prather R, Nixon SJ. The role of selected factors in the development and consequences of alcohol dependence. Alcohol Res Health 2008;31(4):389-99.

[25] Hingson RW, Heeren T, Winter MR. Age at drinking onset and alcohol dependence: Age at onset, duration, and severity. Arch Pediatr Adolesc Med 2006;160:739-46.

[26] Maharajh HD. Personal communication, 2009 Aug 25.

[27] Blume LN, Nielson NH, Riggs JA. Alcoholism and alcohol abuse among women: report of the council on scientific affairs. J Women's Health 2008;7:861-70.

In: Social and Cultural Psychiatry Experience from the... ISBN: 978-1-61668-506-5
Editor: Hari D. Maharajh and Joav Merrick © 2010 Nova Science Publishers, Inc.

Chapter 22

CANNABIS USE: CONTEXT AND CONTROVERSY

Hari D. Maharajh

Cannabis and its most active ingredient delta-9 tetrahdrocannabinol (THC) are derived from the plants cannabis indica and cannabis sativa which were transported to Trinidad during the indentureship period. Locally referred to as marijuana, ganja, hashish, pot and weed, the substance was originally intended for medicinal purposes but due to its hallucinatory and euphoric effects has found a place in creativity, religion and as a street drug of abuse. The lethality of this drug is increased when the smoke is inhaled directly, facilitating easy entry into the blood stream and quick absorption into the brain. Commercial cannabis is compressed, soaked in embalming oil and spices for removal of the scent in order to facilitate smuggling and these 'preservatives' in themselves may have adverse effects. Despite reports of its use as a drug associated with artistic creativity in the 1970's, cannabis remains today a serious drug of abuse both by adolescents and adults and a major problem in the educational system. This chapter reviews the clinical effects of marijuana use, its relationship with suicide, mood disorders, psychoses and other mental disorders and discusses controversies associated with its decriminalization and de-legalization. Those who support the latter have not looked far enough.

INTRODUCTION

Substance abuse is a worldwide problem with increasing use of tobacco, alcohol and cannabis among children and adolescents in the school systems. Internationally, the patterns of use are changing among youths, with an increasing use of cannabis [1] and alcohol [2,3]. Lifestyle changes associated with the use of these drugs have resulted in more social problems [4] and criminal violence [5].

Alcohol and cannabis use are common problems in Trinidad with high prevalence rates in both genders. Over a period of 15 years, a threefold increase from 8% in the rates of cannabis use has been observed in Trinidad [6,7] and substance use has been directly related to crime and suicidal behavior [8]. The sudden increases in crime rates [9] with a rise of murders from 151 in 2001 to 386 in 2005 and 544 in 2008 and gang-related murders moving from 54 in 2001 to 73 in 2005 and 270 in 2008 [10] suggest a culture of youth, drugs and crime. Thus, murder the leading cause of death in Black men in Trinidad and Tobago is drug and gang-related, resulting in a high availability of drugs like marijuana at low prices resulting in control of turfs and assassinations. This results in a higher rate of adolescent cannabis use, resulting in psychiatric and behavioral problems. Studies have shown that the use of drugs in Trinidad is related to traditional values, low self-esteem and low educational expectations [11]. Other well known factors are the ease of availability, untouchable upper class political networking and absence or failure of legislative enactment.

Recent international reports have linked cannabis use with poor performance at school and the risk of using other illicit drugs. In addition, alcohol and cannabis use have been implicated as trigger factors in precipitating anxiety states, mood disorders and suicidal behavior [12-14].Worldwide, the age of initial use has decreased to a mean of 12 years with the rates of cannabis use among adolescents who have used the substance at least once in their lifetime ranging from 32.5% to 43.0%. The lifetime incidence ranges from 3.5% to 8% cannabis use to 2.2% to 7% cannabis dependency. The incidence rates of alcohol, tobacco and cannabis use was even higher in youths with disabilities who reported significantly more exposure to risk factors and fewer protective factors. Studies in developing countries have also reported high rates of cannabis and alcohol use.

CANNABIS IN THE CARIBBEAN

The advent of indentured workers from India to the Caribbean following the emancipation of slavery in 1838 resulted in the introduction of the plant Cannabis indica. Cannabis referred to as marijuana, weed, ganja, herb, hashish, bhang or pot has many ingredients, the most well known being delta-9-tetra hydrocannabinol. It is prepared from flowers, leaves, stems and seeds of the plant, can be smoked, liquefied into teas and tonics or grounded and baked in cookies and cakes. Its earliest use was intended for adjustment of East Indians into a new and hostile environment, separated from their loved ones thousand of miles away, oppressed by the colonial masters and socially rejected by the freed slaves who perceived them to be strange and illiterate. It was used as a balm for solitude and quiet reflection and medicinally for stress related disorders, asthma, pain relief, arthritis, malnutrition and other ailments.

During the post indentureship restructuring of the Indian community in 1919, cannabis was adopted as a holy weed in the religio-cultural practices of the Hindus. It found a place in Guyana and Trinidad among some seeking spiritual enlightenment and others creativity in vocal and instrumental proficiency. Later in 1930, it was incorporated into the religious practices of the newly found Rastafarian movement in Jamaica that borrowed heavily from the habits of the indentured coolies from India.

Historically, cannabis use in the Caribbean was endemic with good social adjustment to its consumption. Until 1950, it was a legal drug that could be bought in shops and parlors. This was changed for economic and social reasons. The early pattern of collective use for recreation, enlightenment and socialization gave way to individual high quantity use for the sole purpose of "building a head". This changing pattern of use also created a lucrative market for the drug trade.

Positioned between the bio-psychosocial effects of alcohol and criminal culture of cocaine, cannabis is often viewed as a harmless drug. This perception may have emerged because of it presence for more than a century and a half with the establishment of a socially sanctioned discontinuation practice. The elders within the societies have over time determined how and by whom the drug should be used. Clear-cut prescriptions of abstinence for those with adverse effects are no longer tenable. Despite these in-built socially protective mechanisms, cannabis use among adolescents is on the rise with increasing adverse effects. Over the past 15 years, rates in Trinidad and Tobago have doubled from 8% to 16% according to some investigators [15,16] and tripled according to others [6,7].

Contributory factors associated with cannabis use in the Caribbean have been identified as peer pressure, negative family atmosphere, school difficulties, co-morbid psychopathology, and male gender [17,18]. Increasing rates of recreational drug use among adolescents have been reported in several Caribbean countries. A survey of secondary school students between the ages of 12 to 18 years in Jamaica revealed that 60.7% of 394 students tested admitted to the use of one or more drugs [19]. Alcohol was the most commonly used drug, with 50.2% of females having tried a psychoactive drug compared to 63% of the males. In Trinidad, alcohol and cannabis use is becoming more prevalent in the vocational school system with excessive usage of cannabis. Important contributory factors are family dysfunction, gender, age and peer pressure.

CANNABIS IN THE EDUCATIONAL SYSTEM

A study conducted in 2007 [20] in two contrasting school systems in Trinidad, Government Secondary Schools and Servol Vocational Schools, investigated the lifetime and current use of cannabis and alcohol. A questionnaire was administered to 468 students (age 12 to 23 years) at three grammar-styled schools and two vocational schools in North, Central and South Trinidad. Demographic data was collected on age, gender, family structure, religion and peer-group effect. Twenty-eight percent reported lifetime cannabis use and sixty-one percent lifetime exposure to alcohol. Current rates of cannabis use were almost four and half times more common among vocational school students. There was no significant difference in current alcohol use between the students of vocational schools or government schools. Both alcohol and cannabis were more commonly used by males in both school systems. The age of onset of cannabis and alcohol use was statistically lower in government-assisted school students. This may be attributed to the higher age of the school students in the vocational schools. One hypothesis for the later age of onset of cannabis use among vocational school students and still higher prevalence of cannabis use could be that the vocational students start to use cannabis at an older age and use it more and longer than do the other students. Cannabis use was positively correlated with peer group usage, increased with age, and positively correlated with a non-intact family. Another difference on demographic data was ethnicity; most students in the vocational schools were of African-Trinidadian descent in contrast with the Government schools in which the majority was of Indian-Trinidadian descent.

Most students of the vocational schools were living in a non-intact family, whereas most government assigned students were living with an intact family. Cannabis use in non-intact families, with parenting by single parents and family members, was significantly higher. This relationship between growing up in a single parent family and more common usage of cannabis is supported in another study [21], which found that cannabis use increased rapidly with age and was more common in adolescents living with a sole parent.

The influence of the peer group on drug use among adolescents was significant. Response on the questionnaire to "how many of our friends were using drugs" indicated that cannabis use was seen with more frequent use by friends. Students who did not use any drugs also had many friends who did not use at all. The students in the vocational schools who were non-users were confronted with many friends using cannabis. Students in vocational schools who were using cannabis were shown to have less contact with students who were not using cannabis.

This situation was also found in Government Assisted schools. This difference was statistically significant with 94% of students in Government schools who reported having more than one friend using cannabis compared with 58.3% of students in vocational schools. In government schools, 76.3% of students who used cannabis said they had at least one friend who used cannabis. Of the 104 governmental students who never used cannabis, 30.8% said they had friends using cannabis.

A previous study utilizing a questionnaire survey, in 1603 secondary school students, aged 14-18 years was conducted in Trinidad and Tobago in 1988. Prevalence of alcohol use was 84%, tobacco 35%, marijuana 8% and cocaine 2%. Significantly more Indo-Trinidadians reported using alcohol frequently. Conversely more Afro-Trinidadian students than Indo-Trinidadians reported using marijuana. For many years, people have argued that cannabis is non-addicting and virtually harmless schools and the one that parents objected to leasts. Observations in Trinidad reveal that alcohol is the most commonly used substance in secondary schools and the one that parents objected to least. This pattern is now changing where cannabis seem to be the choice of drug in secondary schools, especially those populated with Afro-Caribbean males.

Early exposure to Cannabis is reportedly a risk for psychosis [22]. In a well designed cross-sectional study, 472 pupils ages 12-23 years randomly selected from different schools in Trinidad were asked to participate in a study. The use of cannabis and other drugs were assessed using a self-report questionnaire. The Community Assessment of Psychic Experiences (CAPE), a self report instrument was used to assess positive psychotic experiences. In this first report in a non-Western country, the results indicated that the use of cannabis before the age of 14 years was significantly associated with higher levels of psychotic symptoms [Beta (CAPE scores) = 0.39, 95% CI:0.04;0.74, P = 0.029]. No such association was observed for the individuals who started their use of cannabis after the age of 14 years [Beta = 0.01, 95% CI: -0.32; 0.34, P = 0.95]. This finding may provide an explanation for the high incidence of psychosis found among Afro-Caribbeans and their offsprings at home and abroad.

METHOD OF USE

The use of cannabis in Trinidad and Tobago is a locally contrived system of buying pieces of 'bamboo paper' from the local shops and wrapping locally grown and dried marijuana leaves, seeds and stems into a cigarette. One end of the sticky bamboo paper is attached to a normal cigarette and then smoked. The active ingredients of marijuana can also be prepared as a tea known as 'ganja tea' in Jamaica, which is considered to be the elixir of life. In Trinidad, a custom among Indians brought from India was the use of a milky drink known as 'bhang' that is served during social and religious ceremonies. In addition, during local musical sessions, it was customary 'to pass the chylum' a tobacco pipe-like contraption filled with dried marijuana leaves, covered with a red cloth and passed from person to person for deep inhalation. Another method of use is to roll the dried marijuana leaves into a cigarette known as a 'spliff' (Bob Marley style) or 'post' or 'fatman'. It is not uncommon to see Jamaicans with crocus bags filled with marijuana at cricket matches. Duration of use and regular use are important factors for increased risk for later dependency and also mood disorders like depression. Toxicity of the preparations and the use of additives often unknown to the consumer may have extremely adverse effects on the well-being of individuals.

EFFECTS OF CANNABIS USE

Cannabis is not an innocuous drug as often purported by non-clinical observers who have not seen or studied its effects on the human body or those who attempt to justify their use or worship at the Rastafarian or Hindu shrines. The effects of cannabis include euphoria or dysphoria, social withdrawal, impaired judgment, increased appetite, conjuctival injection, low sperm count, dry mouth, tacycardia, bronchitis, amotivational syndrome, delusions and hallucinations and gynocomastia. Recreational use of the drug contributes to a number of mental conditions, including cannabis-induced psychosis paranoid psychosis or delusional disorder, schizophrenia, cannabis intoxication, cannabis delirium, cannabis-induced anxiety disorders and cannabis-induced sleep disorders. Cannabis also accounts for many mental disorders, including panic attacks, flashbacks, delusions, depersonalization, depression and uncontrollable hostility. The similarities of some of the abnormalities found in schizophrenics at an old age are strikingly the same as those who smoke cannabis. The risk of developing psychosis later on in life is dependent on certain variables, such as quantity of use and duration of use. Those who use marijuana at a younger age are more likely to develop psychosis because the brain is still at its developmental stage.

CANNABIS USE AND MENTAL DISORDERS

Studies conducted by various groups, including the Netherlands Institute of Mental Health and Addiction, have concluded that cannabis approximately doubles the risk of developing psychiatric illnesses, such as schizophrenia, later on in life. Drug induced psychosis, which is characterized by delusions and hallucinations, is brought on by sustained and/or excessive use of psychoactive drugs. Most at risk are people with existing personality disorders, pre-psychotic personalities, an unstable ego balance, or a great deal of anxiety. If the condition is left untreated, there is a possibility of self-harm or harm to others. In Trinidad, the most common drug-related psychosis seen in psychiatric clinics is induced by cannabis [22]. Over the decades, more patients have been admitted for treatment of cannabis use than any other drug. The male to female ratio is higher for schizophrenia in T&T, especially among males between 15-29 years. Females are more affected by the effects of cannabis due to differences in their body mass, metabolism and estrogen level.

Early and regular use of cannabis is associated with mood disorders and psychosis. There is growing evidence that early onset use of cannabis can lead to an increased risk for later onset of depression, suicidal behavior [21, 24-27] and psychosis with even schizophrenia [28,29]. Cannabis users in Trinidad and Tobago are commonly diagnosed with mood disorders. Patients who use cannabis show more symptoms of hypomania with euphoric mood and agitation compared to non-cannabis users [30, 31]. Grinspoon et al [32] presented case histories showing that some patients use cannabis as a mood stabilizer in bipolar disorder. The association between bipolar disorder and cannabis is an important public health concern, since co-morbidity of drugs and bipolar disorder are associated with impaired outcome of bipolar illness. The use of cannabis during the adolescent period may result in anxiety states, mood disorders and psychoses. The phenomenological presentations are determined by genetic factors, environmental factors and personal factors.

In 2006, a study was conducted in Trinidad to determine the psychiatric outcome of youths using marijuana in the local culture [33]. The study revealed that light or controlled use of cannabis seldom resulted in diagnostic problems. Long term, low dose of cannabis may result in mild euphoria and is related to increased artistic ability [34]. Heavy use of marijuana, which is defined as more than six joints or cigarettes per week over a short period of time, with a duration of less than a three-month period, may result in bipolar disease with continuous or episodic use, the study further revealed. This finding is supported by Rottanburg et al [31], who compared two groups of non-cannabis users and cannabis users in which the latter group showed more hypomanic symptoms and agitation compared to the group who did not use cannabis. The use of cannabis mixed with other stimulants and hallucinogens may cause visual hallucinations and identifiable paranoid symptoms, such as peeping or looking out for the police in the case of cocaine use. In such cases, drug use begins in early age with the use of gateway licit drugs such as nicotine and alcohol, graduating later to illicit drugs such as cannabis and cocaine. In 2005, 56 students (mean age 18 years) from a vocational school were asked to fill in a questionnaire about cannabis use, showing that almost 50 % of the students were using cannabis in combination with cigarettes.

CANNABIS AND SUICIDAL BEHAVIOR

There is compelling results about the increased risk of suicide with the use of cannabis. Four models are stated here to explain a possible association of cannabis and suicide. The first is that cannabis itself directly increases risk for suicidal behavior. A second model is that the increased suicidal risk due to cannabis use is related to already existing psychiatric disorders, therefore increasing suicidal risk factors. This is based on the premise that those who use cannabis are perhaps in the prodromal phase of a mental illness. A third model is causative that is, cannabis use can cause certain psychiatric disorders. The last model looks at social factors associated with drug use, that is, there are common etiological factors of housing, unemployment, poverty, deprivation and other social parameters related to cannabis use and psychiatric disorders that increases suicidal risk.

There is an increase in suicidal behavior with cannabis use and these results can be found across different cultures [35]. Studies in Sarajevo and New Zealand suggests much of the association between cannabis abuse/dependence and suicide attempt risk tend to come from disadvantaged socio-demographic and childhood backgrounds which, independently of cannabis abuse, are associated with higher risk of suicide attempts. Cannabis abuse/dependence is co-morbid with other mental disorders which are independently associated with suicidal behavior [36]. This includes the direct effect of cannabis on suicidal ideation.

A twin study [24] showed that the co-morbidity between cannabis and depression and suicidal attempts was more likely to arise from shared genetic and environmental vulnerability, but the results could not be explained entirely by that implicating that early onset of cannabis use may directly have an effect on suicidal attempts. Age of onset of cannabis use is an important factor with earlier onset of cannabis use resulting in a higher risk of becoming a regular user or developing dependency [37]. Teenagers, who smoke cannabis on a very regular basis (at least 3 times a week) or during a longer period of time, are three times more likely to have suicidal thoughts than non-users [35,38].

Cannabis use may also act as a cumulative risk factor by increasing stress and exacerbating co-occurring psychopathology [39]. Kelly [37] showed in his study that adolescents, both males and females were more likely to attempt suicide when there was co-occurrence with mood disorders. They started to use cannabis at 11 years and males at 12 1/2 years of age. Also the co-occurrence of conduct disorders was increased at adolescent suicides.

The theory of cannabis as a causal factor in psychiatric disorders and suicidal behavior is well documented [40]. When female adolescents used cannabis, there was a five more times likelihood for depression and anxiety. There was a two- fold increase in males with cannabis use. Depression and anxiety did not predict later cannabis use on the other hand. Cannabis use during at least one year, gave social withdrawal, anxiety and depression with suicidal thoughts among teenagers [35].

The last theory of co-morbid factors involved in cannabis use or abuse and suicidal behavior is also supported by several studies. Cannabis use seems to be associated with other factors like parental functioning, personality, factors within the peer group [41]. In conclusion the use of cannabis can cause a host of psychiatric disorders contingent on genetic factors, environmental factors and personal factors. The age of onset of cannabis use leads to an increased risk for mental health. Early use predicates greater effects.

JAMAICAN RASTAFARIANNISM AND CANNABIS USE

In Jamaica cannabis became popular though the Rastafarian religion. This was established in the 1920's, by the father of the Rastafarian movement Marcus Garvey who denounced the treatment of Blacks in Jamaica and the US. He was known to his deluded followers as a prophet who believed his play entitled the "Coronation of the King and the Queen of Africa' was a premonition that a black king was about to be crowned. Subsequently Prince (Ras in Aramaic) Tafari was crowed in Ethiopia and claimed to be a direct descendant of King Solomon. This led to the term "rastafaris" and their belief in Haile Selassie. The teachings of Haile Selassie paired the use of the herb with ritualistic purposes and were believed to aid in meditation and religious sanctity. Deeply inbred in the Jamaican culture, the herb became popular through the free expression of the Jamaican art form of reggae music and the romanticization of Jamaican reggae artist Bob Marley. With reference to their beliefs of scriptures in the Bible, they hold that ganga is the holy herb in the bible [42].

The belief in its curative properties is so strong that cannabis is used in the treatment of malnutrition, diarrhea and teething discomfort among children in Jamaica. This popular 'ganja tea' which is made from the young green plant and not from the mature plants used for smoking, is believed to alleviate many medical problems such as asthma, respiratory tract infections, glaucoma, gonorrhea, skin burns and abrasions and ultimately contributes to a stronger body free of illness [43]. An estimate of 60-70 percent of the Jamaican population has used marijuana in some form whether it is for a 'high' or a tonic on mornings [44].

CANNABIS AND THE AMSTERDAM EXPERIMENT

In Amsterdam drugs are categorized into two groups: hard drugs and soft drugs [45]. The categories are based on the effects that the drug may have on human consumption. The hard drugs which are prohibited in the Netherlands are cocaine, LSD, morphine, heroin and as of November 2008 the sale of 'magic mushrooms' has been forbidden as many cases were reported leading to serious accidents. Over 100 cases have been recorded that needed medical help, one of them being the tragic death of a 17-year old French girl [45].

In 1976, the Netherlands decriminalized possession of 'soft drugs' such as cannabis. Establishments known as 'coffee shops' with menus presented for a variety of cannabis preparations were displayed even for reduced prices with specials for the day. The soft drugs are cannabis in all its forms (marijuana, hashish, hash oil) and previously magic mushrooms. These drugs are deemed legal under the condition of "personal use". It is not rare to see cannabis being smoked by individuals in public, but it remains illegal to sell the drugs on the street under the Opium Act of 1919 of which cannabis was added as a drug in 1950. In the Netherlands it is believed once the soft drugs are consumed and sold in controlled amounts such as in the 'coffee shops' in 5 grams maximum transactions, it is permissible providing it is not sold to minors.

Today, (2009) Amsterdam is now on the path to reduce the number of 'coffee shops' from 75 to 35 in an effort to clean up the city. It seems as though the experiment has not been a success due to an increased number of criminal activities, prostitution, drug addiction and brothels. Also being targeted, are businesses the city sees as related to the "decay" of the area including peep shows, sex shows, sex shops, mini supermarkets, massage parlors and souvenir shops [46]. Although it worked fine for decades, the authorities in Amsterdam has said enough is enough. It has announced it will close half of the brothels and coffee shops that openly sell marijuana to clean the city of organized crime. To many, this experiment has been a failure.

DECRIMINALIZATION AND DE-LEGALIZATION

The island of Trinidad is a well known transshipment point for South American drugs destined for the US and European shores. It is also a producer of cannabis with an estimated 24 million marijuana plants found in the forested areas of north, east and south of Trinidad [47]. Penalties for drug offences are severe and possession of even small quantities of illegal drugs, including marijuana, may lead to imprisonment. When departing, visitors are thoroughly screened for drug possession. There are no laws guaranteeing freedom from persecution for the possession, use or pedaling of marijuana, although it is customary for police officers to turn a blind eye to street users of marijuana.

As early as the 1970's, attempts for decriminalization of cannabis in the United States were introduced. The proposals included the reduction of penalties for cannabis-related offenses by removing all penalties related to cannabis, including sale and cultivation. Those in favor of the decriminalization of cannabis argued that a substantial amount of law-enforcement resources would be freed, contributing to the prevention of more serious crimes [48]. In the United States, opponents to this view suggested that cannabis decriminalization will lead to increased crime, increased cannabis usage, and subsequent abuse of other illicit drugs. While the effort for decriminalization has been successful, with the use of cannabis for non medical purposes, being allowed in several jurisdictions since 1978 it is debatable whether positive outcome to mental health has been achieved.

A National Ganja Commission was founded in Jamaica in 2001 to concentrate on issues of illicit marketing of illegal drugs. Recommendations for reduction in drug demand and supply have been made. The Commission has also called for decriminalization of marijuana for personal and private use by adults as well as a sacrament for religious purposes, which has been an ongoing topic of controversy [49].

In Jamaica, a debate was sparked as to whether the decriminalization of marijuana would exacerbate the already inundated atmosphere of social ills experienced by that country. Dr Winston de la Haye, a psychiatrist from the University of the West Indies, Jamaica has suggested that cannabis use was linked to an increase in crime in the Jamaican society. An opponent to this, Dr Frederick Hickling a sympathizer of the Rastafarian culture has responded that in Jamaica, the crime problem has been a culmination of many other societal evils such as poverty and despair, and cannabis may not be the sole contributor [50]. It is interesting that these two lecturers from the University of the West Indies, Jamaica, sit on either side of the fence with respect to the decriminalization of marijuana. In a similar vein, Peter Hanoomansingh a PhD student in Trinidad has also questioned the use of cannabis as a causative effect in the presentation of psychosis [51]. The author of this chapter considers the latter view to be banal and ephemeral and limited by emotionalism and absence of scientific data. Decriminalization and de-legalization are not legislative models that should be introduced in the Caribbean. The reasons for this are the loose structure of families, the arbitrariness in the rule of law, a further burden to the justice system due to a predictable increase in crime that will be associated with this new legislation and the 'lazy' lifestyles of Caribbean people. With the emphasis of some Caribbean islands on sex and drug tourism, the authorization of the decriminalization of marijuana will lead to the recruitment of deviants locally and internationally resulting in further moral and economic decay. It could be a pyrrhic victory where the candles cost more than funeral.

Why marijuana should not be made a legalized drug:

- The legalization of marijuana is inevitably the addition of another legal scourge of mankind. It shifts the emphais to 'forbidden fruits' – cocaine and ecstacy.
- Legalization does not eradicate problems associated with abuse and also sends the wrong message of double standards to our population.
- There are no safe drugs: medicinal marijuana is more of an opinion that a fact. It is not only a delusion but a constructive snare.
- Legalization is not in keeping with the regional and international drug interaction policies.
- Legalization shifts the burden from medicine to law
- Moderation is drug use is non-specific and many vary

CONCLUSIONS

The Caribbean today is a major area of cannabis consumption and trade. There are problems of control despite assistance for drug interdiction by the United States Government. Cushioned between the vivid bio-psychosocial effects of alcohol abuse and criminal culture of cocaine, cannabis is often viewed as a harmless drug. This perception may have emerged because of its presence for more than century and a half with clear cut social sanctions of its use. These sanctions of consumption are no longer tenable since the pervasive youth culture has devised rules of its own. Consequently, cannabis use among adolescents is on the rise with increasing adverse effects. Cannabis remains the drug of choice for the modern day Caribbean youth merging without suspicion into educational, creative and sporting activities without the burden of bulk. Decriminalization of this drug will lead to criminalization of youths. Those who support the free use of cannabis have not looked far enough.

REFERENCES

[1] Rossow I, Groholt, Wichstrom L. Intoxicants and suicidal behaviour among adolescents: changes in levels and associations from 1992 to 2002. Addiction 2005;100(1):79-88.

[2] Berggren F, Nystedt P. Changes in alcohol consumption. An analysis of self-reported use of alcohol in a Swedish national sample 1988/89 and 1996/97. Scand J Public Health 2006;34(3):304-11.

[3] Poelen FA, Scholte RH, Engels RC, Boomsma DI, Willemsen G. Prevalence and trends of alcohol use and misuse among adolescents and young adults in the Netherlands from 1993 to 2000. Drug Alcohol Depend 2005;79(3):413-21.

[4] Javier Alvarez F, Fierro I, Carmen del Rio M. Alcohol-related social consequences in Castille and Leon, Spain. Alcohol Clin Exp Res 2006;30(4):656-64.

[5] Haggard-Grann U, Hallqvist J, Langstrom N, Moller J. The role of alcohol and drugs in triggering criminal violence: a case-crossover study. Addiction 2006;101:100-8.

[6] Singh H, Maharajh HD, Shipp M. Pattern of substance abuse among secondary school students in Trinidad and Tobago. Public Health 1991;105:435-41.

[7] Maharajh, HD, Koning, M. Suicidal behavior and cannabis-related disorders among adolescents. In: Merrick J, Zalsman G, eds. Suicidal behavior in adolescence. An international perspective. Tel Aviv: Freund Publ, 2005:119-29.

[8]	Ali A, Maharajh HD. Social predictors of suicidal behavior in adolescents in Trinidad and Tobago. Soc Psychiatry Psychiatr Epidemiol 2005;40:186-91.
[9]	Balroop P. Killers on the loose! Frightening senario for '05 260 murder toll in '04. Sunday Guardian 2005 Jan:2.
[10]	Baldeosingh K. Murder: Leading cause of death among young black men. Sunday Express 2009 Oct 25:5.
[11]	Singh H, Mustapha N. Some factors associated with substance abuse among secondary school students in Trinidad and Tobago. J Drug Educ 1994;24(1):83-93.
[12]	Nishimura ST, Goebert DA, Ramisetty-Mikler S, Caetano R. Adolescent alcohol use and suicide indicators among adolescents in Hawaii. Culture Divers Ethnic Minor Psychol 2005;11(4)309-20.
[13]	Ferdinand RF, Sondeijker F, van der Ende J, Selten JP, Huizink A, Verhulst FC. Cannabis use predicts future psychotic symptoms, and vice versa. Addiction 2005;100(5):612-8.
[14]	Fergusson DM, Horwood LJ, Ridder EM. Tests of causal linkages between cannabis use and psychotic symptoms. Addiction 2005;100(3):354-66.
[15]	Fornari V, Kaplan M, Sandberg D, Mathews M, Katz J. The relationship between depression and anxiety disorders in anorexia nervosa and bulimia nervosa. Int J Eating Dis 1992;12 (1):21-9.
[16]	Douzanis N, Fornari V, Goodman B, Sitnick T, Packman L. Eating disorders and abuse. Child Adolesc Psychiatr Clin North Am Philadelphia: Saunders, 1994.
[17]	Douzanis N, Fornari V, Goodman B, Sitnick T, Packman L. Eating disorders and abuse. In: Kaplan S, Pelcovitz D, eds. Child Adolesc Psychiatr Clin North Am, 1994.
[18]	Rumpold G, Klingseis M, Dornauer K, Kopp M, Doering S, Hofer S, Mumelter B, Schussler G. Psychotropic substance abuse among adolescents: A structural equation model on risk and protective factors. Subst Use Misuse 2006;41(8):1155-69.
[19]	Ljubotina D, Galic J, Jukic V. Prevalence and risk factors of substance use among urban adolescents: questionnaire study. Croat Med J 2004;45:88–98.
[20]	Chung PK. Drug abuse in Jamaican urban secondary educational institutions: A survey in four schools. Dissertation. St Augustine: Univ West Indies, 1986.
[21]	Koning M, Maharajh HD. Substance abuse in different school systems in Trinidad and Tobago: A controlled study of children with disabilities and their drug use. Int J Disabil Hum Dev 2007:6(1); 29-37.
[22]	Rey JM. Martin A. Krabman P. Is the party over? Cannabis and juvenile psychiatric disorder: the past 10 years. Am Acad Child Adolesc Psychiatry 2004;43(10):1194-205.
[23]	Konings M, Henquet C, Maharajh HD, Hutchinson G, Van Os J. Early exposure to cannabis and risk for psychosis in young adolescents in Trinidad. Acta Psychiatr Scand 2008;118:209-13.
[24]	Maharajh HD. Cannabis-head cause of psychosis. Trinidad Guardian 2005 Febr 21:25.
[25]	Lynskey MT, Glowinski AL, Todorov AA, Bucholz KK, Madden PA, Nelson EC, et al. Major depressive disorder, suicidal ideation, and suicide attempt in twins discordant for cannabis dependence and early onset cannabis use. Arch Gen Psychiatry 2004;61(10):1026-32.
[26]	Chen CY, Wagner FA, Anthony JC. Marijuana use and the risk of major depressive episode. Epidemiological evidence from the United States National Comorbidity Survey. Soc Psychiatry Psychiatr Epidemiol 2002;37(5):199-206
[27]	Degenhardt L, Hall W, Lynskey M. The relationship between cannabis use, depression and anxiety among Australian adults: findings from the National Survey of Mental Health and Well Being. Soc Psychiatry Psychiatr Epidemiol 2001;36(5):219-27.
[28]	Bovasso GB. Cannabis abuse as a risk factor for depressive symptoms. Am J Psychiatry 2001;158(12):2033-7.
[29]	Henquet C, Krabbendam L, Spauwen J, Kaplan C, Lieb R, Wittchen H, van Os J. Prospective cohort study of cannabis use, predisposition for psychosis, and psychotic symptoms in young people. BMJ 2005; 330:11-3.
[30]	Van Os J, Bak M, Hanssen M, Van Bijl R, De Graaf R, Verdoux H. Cannabis Use and psychosis: a longitudinal population-based study. Am J Epidemiol 2002;156(4):319-27.
[31]	Kohn L, Kittel F, Piette D. Peer, family integration and other determinants of cannabis use among teenagers. Int J Adolesc Med Health 2004;16(4):359-70.

[32] Rottanburg D, Robins AH, BenArie O, Teggin A, Elk R. Cannabis associated psychosis with hypomanic features. Lancet 1982;2(8312):13646.

[33] Grinspoon L, Bakalar JB. The use of cannabis as a mood stabilizer in bipolar disorder: anecdotal evidence and the need for clinical research. J Psychoactive Drugs 1998;30(2):171-7.

[34] Konings M, Maharajh HD. Cannabis use and mood disorders: patterns of clinical presentations among adolescents in a developing country. Int J Adolesc Med Health 2006;18(2):221-33.

[35] Kirk JM, Doty P, De Wit, H. Effects of expectancies on subjective responses to oral delta9-tetrahydrocannabinol. Pharmacol Biochem Behav 1998;59(2):287-93.

[36] Brook JS, et al. The effect of early marijuana use on later anxiety and depressive symptoms. NYS Psychol 2001;35-40.

[37] Beautrais AL, Joyce PR, Mulder RI. Cannabis abuse and serious suicide attempts. Addiction 1994;8:1155-64.

[38] Kelly TM, Cornelius JR, Lynch KG. Psychiatric and substance use disorders as risk factors for attempted suicide among adolescents: A case control study. Suicide Life Threat Behav 2002; 32(3):301-312.

[39] Greenblatt J. Adolscent self reported behaviours and their association with marijuana use. SAMSHA, 1998.

[40] Espito-Smythers C, Spirito A. Adolescent substance use and suicidal behavior: a review with implications for treatment research. Alcohol Clin Exp Res 2004;28(5 Suppl):77-88.

[41] Patton GC, et al. Cannabis use and mental health in young people: cohort study. BMJ 2002;325:1195-8.

[42] Morojele NK, Brook JS. Adolescent precursors of intensity of marijuana and other illicit drug use among adult initiators. J Genet Psychol 2001;162(4):430-50.

[43] Boekhout van Solinge T. Ganja in Jamaica. Amsterdams Drug Tijdschrift 1996;2:11-4.

[44] Dreher MC. Cannabis and pregnancy. In: Mathre ML, ed. Cannabis in medical practice. North Carolina: Mc Farland Publ, 1997:162.

[45] Rubin VD, Comitas L. Ganja in Jamaica: a medical anthropological study of chronic marijuana use. Hague: Mouton, 1975.

[46] Amsterdam drug laws. [Online] 2009 [cited 2009 October 27]. Available from: http://www.thesite.org/travelandfreetime/travel/beingthere/amsterdamdruglaws

[47] Coffee shops in Amsterdam. [Online] 2009 [cited 2009 October 28]. Available from: http://www.pubclub.com/amsterdam/coffeehouses.htm

[48] Crime and society a comparative criminology tour of the world, Trinidad and Tobago. [Online] 2009 [Online 2009 October 27]. Available from: http://www-rohan.sdsu.edu/faculty/rwinslow/namerica/trinadadtobago.html.

[49] Clifford ER. Clean living movements: American cycles of health reform. Westport, CT: Praeger, 2000:218.

[50] Reid SD. Substance abuse. In: Hickling FW, Sorel E, eds. Images of psychiatry. Jamaica: Stephenson's Litho Press, 2005:198-231.

[51] Jamaica Ganja and crime: shocking new suggestion that pot may be related to crime in some way. Ganja and Crime. The Jamaican Gleaner 2005. Nov 27. [Online] 2005 [cited 2009 Oct 28]. Available from: http://www.freerepublic.com/focus/f-news/1529584/posts

[52] Mokool M. Ganja and colonial power. Trinidad Guardian 2007. [Online] 2007 [cited 2009 October 27]. Available from: http://legacy.guardian.co.tt/archives/2007-08-13/features1.html

In: Social and Cultural Psychiatry Experience from the... ISBN: 978-1-61668-506-5
Editor: Hari D. Maharajh and Joav Merrick © 2010 Nova Science Publishers, Inc.

Chapter 23

DEPRESSION AND PSYCHOSIS ASSOCIATED WITH CANNABIS ABUSE IN A DEVELOPING COUNTRY

Hari D. Maharajh and Monique Konings

Notwithstanding the increase use of cannabis among adolescents in both developing and developed countries, few studies have looked at cannabis use and mood disorders. In a series of case studies, this research project seeks to investigate patterns of clinical presentations seen among cannabis users in psychiatric outpatients in Trinidad. Five clinical patterns of presentations are identified among cannabis users and abusers based on variables of dosing, age of initial use, duration of use, tolerance and reverse tolerance and poly-drug abuse. All patients in these case studies were standardized for method of use and potency of cannabis used. Patients were screened by urine tests to determine co-morbid use of other substances. Other variables such as environmental factors and genetic vulnerability were reviewed as far as possible from historical accounts of family members. The five patterns described are low, controlled use with mild euphoria and heightened awareness, moderate use with mixed depressive symptoms and suicidal behavior, heavy, short term use with manic symptoms, long term incremental use with psychotic symptoms due to the trumping of depressive symptoms and cannabis mixed with other substances resulting in florid psychosis. Mood disorders appear to be a common finding among adolescents using cannabis. Sensitization to symptomatic presentation and early detection of cannabis use in young adolescents are necessary. Further research is needed on the effect of cannabinoids on emotions, behavior and thinking and its relationship to mental disorders. This study is useful as a guideline for the implementation of public health strategies and legislation concerning the use of cannabis in youths.

INTRODUCTION

The association of cannabis use and psychiatric disorders is an area of nosological uncertainty. DSM-IV-TR classification system [1] does not include mood disorders as an effect of cannabis use or induced disorders as is categorized for alcohol (291.84), cocaine (292.84), amphetamines (292.84), opioids (292.84) and hallucinogens (292.84). This omission of cannabis induced mood disorder is rather puzzling since cannabis is also classified as a hallucinogen which according to the DSM-IV can induce mood disorders. Similarly, few studies have looked at cannabis use and its relation to bipolar and other mood disorders.

A strong association between cannabis use and schizophrenia is described in numerous studies [2,3]. The co-occurrence of cannabis use and major depressive disorders or depressive symptoms has been reported in some studies [4-7]. Cannabis use in patients with bipolar disorder has been less extensively investigated. Bipolar patients are prone to abuse substances and in one study [8] 25 % of a cohort with bipolar disorder was found to be substance abusers, mostly alcohol, cocaine or cannabis. In Jamaica 27 percent of patients who were known cannabis users, were diagnosed as having hypomania [9].

Another study from Jamaica reported no statistical differences in abnormalities in affective symptomatology between cannabis users and non cannabis users [10]. Clinical observations have indicated that patients who use cannabis show more symptoms of hypomania with euphoric mood and agitation when compared to a group of non-cannabis users [11-12]. Grinspoon and Bakalar [13] presented case histories showing that some patients use cannabis as a mood stabilizer in bipolar disorder. The research literature on cannabis use and mood disorder appears to be inconclusive and there is a need for further investigations.

Cannabis use in adolescents is common and has been associated with a world wide increase and a changing pattern of consumption. [14].The frequency of use has increased [15] and the age of initial use has dropped considerably to a mean of 12 years [16]. In Belgium, a recent study has reported that the prevalence rate of weekly cannabis use increased from 1.2% in 1990 to 9.2% in 1994 and was still increasing in 1998 [11]. In two well-designed cross sectional school surveys among Norwegian students in 1992 and 2002, cannabis use increased from 5.1% to 13.5% among boys and 3.9 to 9.3% among girls. In addition, there was a significant increase of the mean scale on the depression score in both genders [14].

Two thirds of all adolescents and young adults have had at least a single lifetime exposure to cannabis [15,17,18]. Life time incidence of cannabis abuse ranges from 3.5% to 8%, with cannabis dependence ranging from 2.2% to 7% [11,16,18]. In the Caribbean region, no comprehensive study of cannabis use among adolescents has been conducted. In 1991 the use of cannabis among secondary school students in Trinidad and Tobago was reported as 8% [19]. This has increased over the last 15 years to 20% [20].

The association between bipolar disorder and cannabis is an important public health concern since the co-morbidity of drugs and bipolar disorder is associated with impaired outcome of the bipolar illness [21]. The length of a manic episode seems to be related to the duration of use of cannabis with a longer duration of the manic period. Cannabis use is also associated with an increase in non-compliance to medication and an earlier onset of affective symptoms resulting in more hospitalizations [21,22]. This results in spiraling cost and burden to the health care system.

OUR STUDY

Five patients representing different patterns of cannabis use were selected from the out-patients clinics in Trinidad. Patients were assigned to different categories based on clinical presentations, age of first use, duration of use and toxicity. Duration of use and toxicity were determined by self-reports which were later confirmed by interviews with the family members.

Toxicity or degree of cannabis use/abuse was determined as follows: Each patient was interviewed on three occasions individually and together with a family member to determine the quantity of cannabis used. During these interviews clinical assessments were recorded and random urine screens for cannabis were done.

The method of use was standard. It is a locally contrived system of buying pieces of 'bamboo paper' from the shops at the cost of 50 cents (Trinidad and Tobago (TT) currency - one US dollar is approximately six TT dollars) and wrapping locally grown and dried marijuana leaves, seeds and stems into a cigarette. They are prepared in two sizes namely "a five piece or joint" and "a ten piece or post". A "joint" is the diameter of a standard cigarette and measures two and a half inches and is sold at five dollars on the streets and a "post" is twice the length and sold at ten dollars. One end of the sticky bamboo paper is attached to a normal cigarette and lighted from the cannabis end drawing through the tobacco end. It should be noted that one 'post' is equivalent to two' joints'.

The first category is the light, controlled use of cannabis, meaning one to two cigarettes (joints) per week, for more than a year. The second pattern is moderate, long term use of one year or more of two to six cigarettes per week. The third pattern seen is one of heavy use of cannabis of more than 6 cigarettes per week over a short period of time of less than three months. The fourth pattern is one of light use followed by increasing use over time. The last category is a combination of cannabis use with other psychotropic substances mostly alcohol, cocaine and other stimulants. All patients were screened for poly-substance abuse through urine testing. Tobacco use was common in all categories due to the method of cannabis use.

AxSYM system utilizing Fluorescence Polarization Immunoassay technology was used to analyze the presence of cannabinoids in the urine. AxSYM system was used to detect alcohol, cocaine or other drugs in urine and the immulite analyzer was used to detect nicotine in urine.

OUR FINDINGS

Table 1. Screening for substances isolated in patient's urine during first visit

cases	cannabis	alcohol	cocaine	nicotine	other
1	+	-	-	+	-
2	+	-	-	+	-
3	+	-	-	+	-
4	+	-	-	+	-
5	+	-	+	+	-

Five cases representing different patterns of cannabis use are described (see tables 1-3). Clinical presentations of psychiatric symptoms appear to be determined by dosages, frequency, duration and poly-drug use. All cases were interviewed by a senior consultant (HDM) and the files and notes were reviewed by both authors. Informed consent was

260 Hari D. Maharajh and Monique Konings

obtained from all patients over eighteen and the parents of those under eighteen. Permission was obtained from the head of the sector to do this study.

Table 2. Described cases in relation to different factors in adolescent cannabis use

Case	Age of onset of use	Duration	Frequency	Toxicity*	Symptoms	Family history
1	16	4 years	regularly	light	increased artistic ability	None
2	14	1 year	regularly	moderate	increased energy level, increased speech, grandiose ideas	alcohol dependence
3	19	10 days	regularly	heavy	decreased need for sleep, disruptive, increased energy	None
4	14	3 years	infrequent	heavy	paranoid, agitated, hallucinations, overvalued ideas	not known
5	17	7 years	regularly	moderate with		
Other drugs	hallucinations, formal thought disorders, delusions	none				

* light toxicity is defined as smoking 1 to 2 cigarettes of cannabis a week
moderate is defined by smoking 2-6 cigarettes use a week
heavy use is defined by smoking more than 6 cigarettes a week

Table 3. Different factors influencing the outcome of adolescent cannabis use

Environmental factors	Genetic factors	Personal factors	Cannabis factors
Peer or group pressure	Familial predisposition	Personality traits	Frequency
Parental drug use	Polygenic effect	Depressive symptoms	Age of initial use
Cultural beliefs	Dominant / recessive	Suicidal thoughts	Dosage
Social acceptance	inheritance	Comorbidity	Duration
Family problems		Constitution	Availability
Delinquent peers			

CASE STORY 1

A 20 year old foreign female medical student sought treatment for cannabis use at the University psychiatric service following advice from her boyfriend. She stated that she smoked two rolled cannabis cigarettes per week during midweek and on weekends, which 'increased her interpersonal skills allowing her to socialize better.' Her boyfriend had become concerned about her over friendliness, talkativeness and interactions with complete strangers. She has been using marijuana since the age of 16 years, while at Boarding school in the United States. At that time she smoked with other students, mostly at weekend parties and claimed she had no problems except on one occasion, when she was caught and her father was informed. She was born and raised in London, England and later was sent to school in America. Her father was a specialist medical doctor in London and mother a housewife. Her relationship with her father was strained and she described him as an alcoholic and distant and rarely communicated with him; she however spoke to her mother on a regular basis. Her pattern of drug use was two cannabis cigarettes per week for the past five years; she used no other drug but also smoked ten cigarettes of tobacco daily.

Clinically, she was not depressed, anxious, agitated or deluded. She had never experienced suicidal thoughts or abnormal perceptions and cognitive testing were normal. Her speech was normal flow, spontaneous, not circumstantial without evidence of formal thought disorder. She was advised to do the normal baseline laboratory tests of full blood count, urea and electrolytes, thyroid function tests, liver and renal functions and urine analysis. All findings were normal except the urine analysis that tested positive for tobacco and marijuana.

The sessions were aimed at the relationship with her father and bad experiences in the past. She stopped her cannabis use and her relationship with her father significantly improved. She started to use cannabis again stating that the use of marijuana made her more creative and easier for her to do exams.

CASE STORY 2

A 15 year old form four secondary school student was brought to an outpatient clinic by his mother and aunt who became extremely concerned about his recent and abrupt change of personality. Approximately one year ago, following his promotion from junior to senior secondary school his mother noticed that he began behaving strangely with social withdrawal and unpredictable emotional changes ranging from aggression to inappropriate happiness. On investigation from neighbours and friends, they found out that he was hanging out 'with the wrong kind of people' and smoking marijuana.

His mother and aunt related that he is more talkative than usual with inflated self esteem and expansive ideas. His teachers have complained that he is distractible and disruptive at school: he is unable to sit still, not concentrating or following instructions. He has a decreased need for sleep, feeling rested with a maximum of five hours of sleep at night. He has now become sexually active and in addition, over the past few weeks he has been stealing money. When confronted by his relatives about his antisocial behaviour, he became extremely irritable and aggressive threatening to commit suicide. He developed suicidal thoughts after quarrels with his parents about his behaviour, substance abuse and sexual indiscretions.

In his premorbid personality, the relatives described him as a nice, friendly and obedient child of a quiet disposition who got along well with everyone. His recent behaviour was puzzling and they did not know what to do about their only child.

On interview, he was tall, lanky and euphoric and admitted that he was using marijuana (cannabis) since he started at this new school. He said that he had succumbed to peer-pressure in order to gain acceptance into the new environment. He used approximately four locally made marijuana joints (cigarettes) per week and on occasions will consume two glasses of beer. When asked about his change of behaviour, he noted that his use of marijuana gave him increased energy. He has the feeling that he can do everything when he is smoking. The tempo of his speech was increased with no flight of ideas or evidence of thought disorder. He had little insight into his problem smiling fatously while his relatives related their troubles. There is a strong family history of alcohol dependency, both with the father and mother. There was no history of physical diseases and examination was normal. He was treated with low doses of an atypical antipsychotic and referred to an adolescent group for further psychological treatment. Further family sessions were arranged.

CASE STORY 3

A 19 year old cash crop farmer was forcefully brought to the psychiatric clinic by his father and brother. The father stated that he was no longer controllable at home, did not sleep all night, pacing and playing music loudly, being disruptive to the household and neighbourhood and talking nonsense. His family requested his admission to the psychiatric hospital through the Mental Health Act on the grounds that he was a danger to himself and others.

His father stand that over the last ten days, after selling his garden products, he utilized all this money to buy marijuana. He had not gone to work but has been continuously smoking 'the fatman', that is a giant size cigarette (three times the size of a cigar). He smoked on the street corners with friends and in his room at home and had not being eating or taking care of his personal hygiene. He played music and sang all night long, disturbing the neighborhood. He was an educated and well spoken young man who had attained seven passes at the Ordinary Level of the Caribbean Examination Council. He came from a religious background with no history of substance abuse or mental illness. After leaving school at the age of seventeen years, he worked for one year as a salesman in a manufacturing company and was successful. After one year he became tardy, did not meet his quota and was warned for frequent absenteeism. This coincided with the onset of his use of marijuana. He later abandoned his job and went into gardening which facilitated a ready source of 'herbs' (marijuana).

On examination he was tatty in dress, unshaven and unkempt with an elevated and expansive mood for more than eight days. His speech was spontaneous, pressured and circumstantial breaking into extempo calypsoes about the psychiatrist. He showed distractability with his attention drawn to the medical charts on the wall, where in a grandiose manner he demonstrated his knowledge of biology. He had a decreased need for sleep and requested that 'doc hurry up with your ting', since he had important business to attend. He had no insight in his behavior and denied heavy use of drugs stating that he used 'a little herb to cool the head'. There was no family history for psychiatric illnesses. His relatives were given a letter of urgent admission to the hospital.

CASE STORY 4

A 14 year old male secondary school student began using marijuana with friends during school hours. He would leave home in the morning and not attend school but will join older friends in an abandoned house where they smoked cannabis cigarettes. He lived with his grandmother who had no idea that he was absconding from school until she was informed by the school authority. His mother had migrated to the United States and supported him by sending him 'barrels of items' which he sold to maintain his habits.

After being away from school for one term he was expelled and the school guidance officer sought psychiatric help. He was detoxified and treated with individual therapy for six months. Through the school authorities, arrangements were made to reinstate him into the school system. After one month he again joined the street users and continued his previous habits. On this occasion he had doubled his previous use of marijuana from one to three cigarettes per week to two to six per week. He again defaulted from school and was asked to leave because of his influence on other students. On this occasion, he was admitted to a psychiatric unit where after three days he broke out and returned to the streets. He continued his use of marijuana. The following year having abandoned his schooling at the age of 17, he was held in a police raid after he was involved with other cannabis users in allegations of house breaking. He was sentenced for one year imprisonment at the Youth Prison.

Following his release he continued using marijuana on a daily basis and according to him he smoked "as much as I can lay my hands on". He continued smoking in large amounts for the next two years until his mother returned on a holiday from the United States with the intent of returning with him.

When brought to the psychiatrist he was found to be paranoid, agitated and quoting fluently from the bible. He paced the examination room looking at the ceilings and smiling fatuously. He spoke of the "plight of the black man"and was interested in their welfare. He spoke philosophically of the universe and of man's purpose in it. He held overvalued ideas of himself and felt that he was placed on earth to help the poor and suffering. On this occasion he had used at least four to six marijuana cigarettes on a daily basis. Despite his psychotic state the psychiatrist noted "that he was not aggressive, pleasantly amusing, voluble and incoherently intelligent". Family history was not known since his parents moved away and his grandmother could not give much information about it.

CASE STORY 5

A 24 year old unemployed man was referred to a psychiatrist from the Magistrate Court following charges of possession and use of illicit drugs, marijuana and cocaine. He was concurrently referred to a forensic detoxification and rehabilitation center on a court order for a period of two years with three-monthly follow up by a psychiatrist.

In his family history his father died when he was 17 years of age and he was looked after by an older brother and his wife. There was no personal or family history of substance abuse or mental diseases. In his drug history he began using tobacco while at secondary school at the age of 15, with occasional binges of alcohol. This was followed by cannabis use two years later. He graduated to cocaine use at the age of 19. Over the last four years he has used combinations of all four drugs, with marijuana and cocaine being his drugs of choice. He used three 'black cigarettes' that is a combination of marijuana and cocaine cigarettes five times per week. This involved removing the tobacco from a normal cigarette, adding marijuana and chips of rough cocaine and heating it over a flame until the cocaine melted and blended with the marijuana, resulting in a 'black cigarette.'

On mental status examination he was illogical and incoherent, not oriented in time and place. His speech was plentiful, ascetic, tangential and circumstantial with poverty of ideation. He experienced visual hallucinations where he saw objects coming out of the ground. He was not aggressive and suspicious to the interviewer and at times he left the examination room, peeping through the window in search of policemen. His affect was blunt with little changes in his emotional state. He was diagnosed as suffering from a drug induced psychosis. He was treated with a high dose of a typical antipsychotic which has cleared his mental state. Urine testing for drugs one month ago tested positive for cannabis only. The patient denied the use of drugs in prison.

DISCUSSION

The use of cannabis during the adolescent period may result in anxiety states, mood disorders and psychoses. The phenomenological presentations are determined by genetic factors, environmental factors and personal factors (table 3). The latter includes age of first use, toxicity of preparations, duration of use and drug-combination usage.

In this study five patterns of cannabis use/abuse are presented which represent the psychiatric outcome of youths using marijuana in the local culture. These patterns are not inclusive of all clinical presentations but focuses on expressions of mood disorders associated with cannabis use (see figure 1).

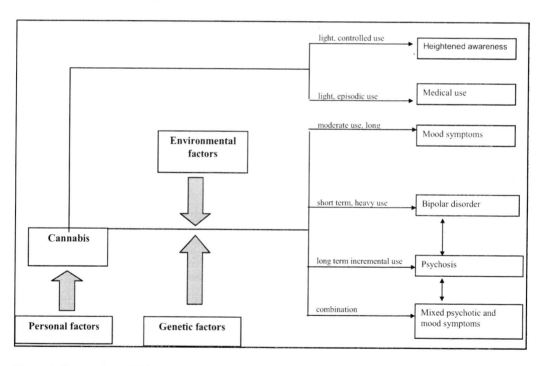

Figure 1. Proposed model for adolescent cannabis use in a developing country

There is no consensus on the association between cannabis use and depression. In a twin study, a modest association between early onset adolescent cannabis use (<17 years) and suicidal attempts, but not for major depressive disorders was reported [4]. However, other studies have reported an association with heavy cannabis use and depressive disorders [5,6]. Case 2 in our study, with moderate use of cannabis presented with mixed symptoms of both dysthymia and hypomania [23] with suicidal behavior. Suicidal behavior in this case may not be a direct effect of the use of cannabis, but seems to be a maladaptive response to the dysfunction within the family following disclosure of his drug related behavior.

As is demonstrated in Case 1, light or controlled use of cannabis seldom results in diagnostic problems. Long term, low dose of cannabis may result in a mild euphoria and is related to increased artistic ability [24]. Among adolescents, medicinal marijuana is more a defense in the magistrate's court rather than a therapeutic agent. In more than two decades of clinical practice, one of the authors (HDM) has never seen a genuine case of the medicinal use of marijuana among adolescents though it's a common defense in the magistrate's court (figure1).

The third pattern of cannabis use described (Case 3) is characterized by heavy use defined as more than six joints or cigarettes per week over a short period of time that is, with a duration of less than a three- month period. This may be continuous or episodic and results in bipolar disease. This finding is supported by Rottanburg et al [12] who compared study two groups of non cannabis users and cannabis users in which the latter group showed more hypomanic symptoms and agitation compared to the group who did not use cannabis. Acute intoxication or increased use of cannabis with an accumulation of cannabinoids will result in psychotic reactions not unlike schizophrenia. This must be differentiated from drug induced delirium.

A rapidly resolving psychosis with marked hypomanic features was reported when patients with psychosis continued using the cannabis [12]. The clinical presentation of Case 3 underlines the difficulty in differentiating the nosological differences between schizophrenia and mania especially in Caribbean patients where we have observed an excess of affective symptoms among patients diagnosed with psychoses.

Case 4 depicts the long term or incremental use of cannabis use with a clinical presentation of a conduct disorder, anxiety symptoms, paranoid delusions and psychosis. There is an absence of affective symptoms. A number of hypotheses may be proffered: firstly, that the progressive use of cannabis trumps depression, thereby delaying the onset of clinically diagnosable psychiatric disorders in patients without a genetic predisposition to mental disorders. This theory finds support in studies by Grinspoon and Bakalar [13] who reported the use of marijuana for the stabilization of bipolar disorder. Secondly, that the evolution and manifestation of psychiatric symptoms is supportive of the theory of a continuum in which psychiatric symptoms like psychotic symptoms are present in the general population as a continuum rather than as an all or non phenomenon. [25,26] . This continuum does not have to be limited to psychotic features but through the broad range of DSM syndromes. The expressions and experiences of individuals thought, emotions and behaviour during the adolescent period is determined by different patterns of cannabis use. An individual can therefore move interchangeably from one stage to another [12].

The use of cannabis mixed with other stimulants and hallucinogens provides a useful model for the study of drug co-morbidity. As is described in Case 5, drug use begins in early age with the use of gateway licit drugs such as nicotine and alcohol graduating later to illicit drugs such as cannabis and cocaine. Clinical presentations are generally of a florid psychotic nature of mixed symptoms. Visual hallucinations are common with identifiable paranoid symptoms such as 'peeping' or looking out for the police in the case of cocaine use (Case 5). The psychoses seen in cannabis abusers are for the most part non-florid. Many patients are a motivated and without an adequate history can be diagnosed as schizophrenia with negative symptoms. Phenomenological differences are differences in the possession, form and content of their speech. There is a preoccupation with philosophical, religious and social issues. As in Case 4, despite his psychotic state, the psychiatrist noted "that he was not aggressive, pleasantly amusing, voluble and incoherently intelligent".

The active ingredient of cannabis is a psychoactive substance identified as delta-9-tetrahydrocannabinol (delta-9-THC). More than 60 other cannabinoids have been identified [13,27].These metabolites may contribute directly or indirectly to psychiatric symptoms. Cannabis is known to increase cerebral dopamine an excess of which is found in mania and schizophrenia. This association is more complex and certainly not dose-related. Other personal variables other than social and genetic are storage, release, tolerance and reverse tolerance.

In the mild use of cannabis (once or twice a week) THC will accumulate in the body and slowly released affecting overall functioning to some degree resulting in a pleasant feeling of well-being [27]. In more frequent users, there is the development of reverse tolerance, in which there is over time more sensitiveness or responses to identical doses. This effect can occur only after one month of cannabis use [28,29]. This reverse tolerance is one of the mechanisms that may explain the increased and potential effect of cannabis use over a longer period of time. These findings are supportive of our own unpublished results that show no relationship between clinical presentations of cannabis users and percentage concentration of cannabinoids isolated in the blood and urine.

The world wide pattern of cannabis use and abuse among adolescents has changed over the decades with an increase use at a lower age and among girls [14]. The social pattern of use in the 1950's and 60's at large public gatherings such as concerts and festivals has given way to an almost ritualistic, solitary style of consumption at higher doses. This is not only applicable to developed countries but to developing countries in the Caribbean region where the rates of cannabis use among secondary school students has changed over a decade from 8% in Trinidad and Tobago in 1993 to 20% in 2005 [19, 20]. Substance use has been directly related to crime [30] and suicidal behavior [31].

There is a sudden increase in crime rates [32] in Trinidad and Tobago which is drug related, resulting in a high availability of drugs like marijuana at low prices. This causes a higher rate of adolescent cannabis use which affects their emotional and behavioral states.

The pattern of cannabis use among adolescents is a very complex problem with multi factorial etiologies and presentations. In this study emphasis were not placed on the important confounding variables of environmental factors and genetic predispositions. These are indeed important factors and only passing references (see figure 1) is indeed a limitation. This study investigates patterns of clinical presentation of cannabis users among the adolescent age group in a developing country with an emphasis on personal factors such as the age of first use, frequency of use, dose of use, duration of use, co-morbidity with other drugs and constant use. Genetic influence or vulnerability was determined as far as possible from family history. A family history of schizophrenia may induce a risk factor of developing psychosis when using cannabis, but the phenotype may not express itself in the most extreme form such as schizophrenia, but may also express itself as a single phenotype symptom in the form of psychotic experiences [3]. Psychotic experiences are not necessarily a diseased state.

This study has many strengths. It addresses patterns of clinical presentation of adolescents in a developing country. Most studies are from developed countries where the consumption of cannabis is from imported stock. Commercial cannabis is compressed, soaked in embalming oil and spices for removal of the scent in order to facilitate smuggling. These 'preservatives' in themselves may have adverse effects. In this study locally grown and dried marijuana without compression and treatment was used. There was no uncertainty of variations in strength or preparation since all the marijuana joints were made by the consumer himself and used in a standard manner. Only male adolescents were included in the case histories to eliminate gender differences.

CONCLUSION

Our findings suggest that affective or mood disorders and psychotic disorders are common findings in cannabis users in Trinidad and Tobago. These findings may differ from findings in developed countries because of the mode and local preparation of the cannabis used. Clinical presentations are determined by social, genetic and local factors. Further research is needed. The findings of this study are important to all developing countries for the future provision of health services, the planning and implementation of treatment strategies and the creation and enactment of new legislation concerning marijuana possession and use must consider the effect of cannabis on the young age group and its effect on school children.

REFERENCES

[1]   American Psychiatric Association, Cannabis related disorders. In: Desk reference to the diagnostic criteria from DSM-IV-TR, 4th ed. Washington DC, APA, 2000:127-9.

[2]   Henquet C, Krabbendam L, Spauwen J, Kaplan C, Lieb R, Wittchen H, van Os J. Prospective cohort study of cannabis use, predisposition for psychosis, and psychotic symptoms in young people. BMJ 2005; 330:11-3.

[3]   Van Os J, Bak M, Hanssen M, Van Bijl R, De Graaf R, Verdoux H. Cannabis use and psychosis: A longitudinal population-based study. Am J Epidemiol 2002;156(4):319-27.

[4]   Lynskey MT, Glowinski AL, Todorov AA, Bucholz KK, Madden PA, Nelson EC, et al. Major depressive disorder, suicidal ideation, and suicide attempt in twins discordant for cannabis dependence and earlyonset cannabis use. Arch Gen Psychiatry 2004;61(10):1026 32.

[5]   Chen CY, Wagner FA, Anthony JC. Marijuana use and the risk of major depressive episode. Epidemiological evidence from the United States National Comorbidity Survey. Soc Psychiatry Psychiatr Epidemiol 2002;37(5):199-206.

[6]   Degenhardt L, Hall W, Lynskey M. The relationship between cannabis use, depression and anxiety among Australian adults: Findings from the National Survey of Mental Health and Well Being. Soc Psychiatry Psychiatr Epidemiol 2001;36(5):219-27.

[7]   Bovasso GB. Cannabis abuse as a risk factor for depressive symptoms. Am J Psychiatry 2001;158(12):2033-7.

[8]   Miller FT, Busch F, Tanenbaum JH. Drug abuse in schizophrenia and bipolar disorder. Am J Drug Alcohol Abuse 1989;15(3):291-5.

[9]   Knight F. Role of cannabis in psychiatric disturbance. Ann N Y Acad Sci 1976;282:64-71.

[10]   Beaubrun MH, Knight F. Psychiatric assessment of 30 chronic users of cannabis and 30 matched controls. Am J Psychiatry 1973; 130(3):309-11.

[11]   Kohn L, Kittel F, Piette D. Peer, family integretion and other determinants of cannabis use among teenagers. Int J Adolesc Med Health 2004;16(4):359-70.

[12]   Rottanburg D, Robins AH, BenArie O, Teggin A, Elk R. Cannabis associated psychosis with hypomanic features. Lancet 1982;;2(8312):13646.

[13]   Grinspoon L, Bakalar JB. The use of cannabis as a mood stabilizer in bipolar disorder: anecdotal evidence and the need for clinical research. J Psychoactive Drugs 1998;30(2):171-7.

[14]   Rossow I, Groholt, Wichstrom L. Intoxicants and suicidal behaviour among adolescents: changes in levels and associations from 1992 to 2002. Addiction 2005;100:79-88.

[15]   Perkonigg A, Lieb R, Hofler M, Schuster P, Sonntag H, Wittchen HU. Patterns of cannabis use, abuse and dependence over time: incidence, progression and stability in a sample of 1228 adolescents. Addiction 1999;;94(11):1663-78.

[16]   Von Sydow K, Lieb R, Pfister H, Hofler M, Sonntag H, Wittchen HU. The natural course of cannabis use, abuse and dependence over four years: a longitudinal community study of adolescents and young adults. Drug Alcohol Depend 2001;;64(3):347-61.

[17]   Nyari TA, Heredi K, Parker L. Addictive behaviour of adolescents in secondary schools in Hungary. Eur Addict Res 2005;11(1):38-43.

[18]   Coffey C, Carlin JB, Degenhardt L, Lynskey M, Sanci L, Patton GC. Cannabis dependence in young adults: an Australian population study. Addiction 2002;;97(2):187-94

[19]   Singh H, Maharajh HD, Shipp M. Pattern of substance abuse among secondary school students in Trinidad and Tobago. Public Health 1991;105:435-41.

[20]   Maharajh HD. Cannabis-head cause of psychosis. Trinidad Guardian 2005 Febr 21.

[21]   Strakowski SM, DelBello MP, Fleck DE, Arndt S. The impact of substance abuse on the course of bipolar disorder. Biol Psychiatry 2000;48(6):477-85.

[22]   Sherwood BE, Suppes T, Adinoff B, Rajan TN. Drug abuse and bipolar disorder: co-morbidity or misdiagnosis? J Affect Disord 2001; 65(2):105-15.

[23]   American Psychiatric Association. Mood disorders. In: Desk reference to the diagnostic criteria from DSM-IV-TR, 4th ed. Washington DC, APA, 2000:167-208.

[24]   Kirk JM, Doty P, De Wit H. Effects of expectancies on subjective responses to oral delta9-tetrahydrocannabinol. Pharmacol Biochem Behav 1998;;59(2):287-93.

[25]   Van Os J, Hanssen M, van Bijl R, Vollebergh W. Prevalence of psychotic disorder and community level of psychotic symptoms. Arch Gen Psychiatry 2001;58:663-8.

[26]   Johns LC, van Os J. The continuity of psychotic experiences in the general population. Clin Psychol Rev 2001;21(8):1125-41.

[27]   McKim WA. Cannabis. In: McKim Wa. Drugs and behavior. An introduction to behavioral pharmacology, Fourth ed. Upper Saddle River, NJ: Prentice-Hall, 2000:298-321.

[28]   Breivogel CS, Scates SM, Beletskaya IO, Lowery OB, Aceto MD, Martin BR. The effects of delta9-tetrahydrocannabinol physical dependence on brain cannabinoid receptors. Eur J Pharmacol 2003;;459(2-3):139-50.

[29]   Wikler A. Aspects of tolerance to and dependence on cannabis. Ann NY Acad Sci 1976;282:126-47.

[30]   Maharajh HD, Akleema A. Crime in Trinidad and Tobago: The effect of alcohol use and unemployment. Rev Pan Am J Public Health 2004;15(6):417-23.

[31]   Akleema A, Maharajh HD. Social predictors of suicidal behavior in adolescents in Trinidad and Tobago. Soc Psychiatry Psychiatr Epidemiol 2005;40:186-91.

[32]   Balroop P Killers on the loose! Frightening senario for '05 260 murder toll in '04. Sunday Guardian 2005 Jan 02.

In: Social and Cultural Psychiatry Experience from the...
Editor: Hari D. Maharajh and Joav Merrick

ISBN: 978-1-61668-506-5
© 2010 Nova Science Publishers, Inc.

Chapter 24

COCAINE USE AND SOCIAL TRANSFORMATION

Hari D. Maharajh

There is little disagreement that the drug cocaine extracted from the plant Erythroxylon coca has had an extraordinary effect in the transformation of economies, lifestyles and governance. Those at the higher levels who are active in the trade, often with the consent of governments are untouchable and accumulate vast amounts of wealth and prestige, while the working class, those to whom it is peddled is further pushed downwards into the poverty line and death through drug-seeking behaviour. Not only has cocaine use resulted in social transformation but has had deleterious effects on the mental and physical health of nations. This chapter traces the history, introduction, development, culture, methods of use and effects of the use of cocaine in Trinidad and Tobago and its worldwide implications. Cocaine remains a scourge to mankind.

INTRODUCTION

Cocaine chemically formulated as benzoylmethylecgonine is a crystalline tropane alkaloid that is obtained from the leaves of the coca plant Erythroxylon coca [1]. It is an extremely addictive drug and a central nervous system stimulant which suppresses appetite. It inhibits the uptake of serotonin, norepineprine and dopamine.

The leaves of the coca plant have been chewed by South American native Indians for more than 1000 years. The indigenous people claimed that the leaves gave them strength and energy and allowed them to work for long hours without food. This finding was later exploited by the Spanish conquerors. The leaves of the coca plant are still used in religious ceremonies and the alkaloid is used in medicine, drugs and as a poison. In 1609, Padre Blas Valere wrote:

Coca protects the body from many ailments, and our doctors use it in powdered form to reduce swellings of wounds, to strengthen broken bones, to expel cold from the body or to prevent it from entering, and to cure rotten wounds or sores that are full of maggots. And if it does so much for outward ailments, will not its singular virtue have even greater effect in the entrails of those who eat it? [2]

Today cocaine has limited medical use and is even replaced as an anaesthetic as suggested by Sigmund Freud. Among the four substances of common abuse in Trinidad and Tobago, that is alcohol, marijuana, tobacco and cocaine, the latter is the most devastating to families and destructive to society. Cocaine was first introduced into the Republic in the early nineteen eighties. The Republic's strategic geographic location off the mainland of South America with established drug cartels enabled it to become an immediate transhipment port from South American countries and Colombia via Trinidad to Europe, America and other Caribbean islands.

COCAINE AND SOCIAL TRANFORMATION IN TRINIDAD AND TOBAGO

With the advent of cocaine, almost overnight the legal and penal systems were put to the test as assassinations and homicides increased followed by gang warfare, kidnapping and murder [3]. Crime and violence continued unabated as the cocaine trade flourished establishing itself as a permanent fixture in society. It trickled into big businesses with money laundering, the civil service, the police force, the private sector and even into the school systems. The government seemed incompetent in handling the situation, as they dished out to the population a plethora of crime plans designed by foreign experts that have to date been colossal failures.

On the streets, youths previously impoverished, donned expensive costumes with designer labels, bearing modern electronic equipments of multiple beepers and mobile phones. They drove around in a menacing manner in expensive or rented vehicles they could not afford and at the slightest provocation will sometimes brandish the most modern uzis and semi-automatic rifles. In their search for rank or pips they shot at anyone they did not like resulting in revenge killings by gang members. The cycle continues even now with murder rates expected to exceed the 546 mark of 2008. Overnight many became rich, while others became vagrants adding to the increasing number of street dwellers in their search for the 'white lady', the third scourge of mankind, cocaine. A new generation of street children previously unknown in the land was born. Shootouts, gang warfare, symbolic deaths by assassination, resulted in the now common occurrence of mangled bodies, headless corpses and disembowelled humans in dumps, swamps, ravines, forests and beaches. Tracing and detection of crime is low as the population live in fear with the understanding that there is no reprieve due to the entrenchment of the protective forces and perhaps the government themselves in crime. The latter is now before the court as a Muslim leader presents a sworn affidavit that he has helped the present government win the elections in return for favours [4].

The population grew tense. They invested in defensive aggression in arming themselves, protecting their homes with cameras, security alarms, and killer-guard dogs. The design and architecture of homes changed with buildings becoming more fortress-like equipped with fabricated burglar bars that prevented criminals from entering but also resulting in the death of entire families in preventing them from escape in the wake of a fire. Before their very eyes, the population witnessed the erosion of family values as social systems collapsed. They doubted the ability of the law to protect them as the protectors became illegal persecutors. Caring individuals saw loved ones of friends and families getting involved in drugs and drug-related criminal activities and helplessly predicted their demise, accepting the inability of the medical or legal institutions to help them. Involvement in drugs meant death and no place was safe; trust dwindled as the nation's insecurity grew. The law for many was only a word and money laundering a thriving business. In addition, the passing out of foreign traffickers was heralded in international headlines that damned the good name of the peoples' easy going nature. The islands of paradise were now dubbed 'an at risk tourist destination' as foreign governments released warnings after warnings. Over the years nothing has changed, as society plunges further into social and moral decay. Today cocaine is big business managed by organized urban street gangs on designated turfs, with implications of corrupt law enforcement officials. On the average 590 kilograms of cocaine pass through the Caribbean daily according to the UN Office on Drug and Crime 2001-2002 [5].

THE COCAINE INDUSTRY

The enigma of the Caribbean islands being depicted as a destination for drug and sex tourism has attracted a number of foreign deviants who have contributed to the drug industry. Not only are they involved in the local use of the drug, but they also participate in the transportation of these products as couriers to the United States and Europe where lucrative markets abound. Couriers are known as 'drug mules' who will stash their concealed drugs in creative spaces in their luggage, food or beverage. Recent innovations are 'swallowers' who will ingest the drug and hopefully excrete it at their destination. Many have died. 'Stuffers' are those who will conceal the drugs in body cavities and this method is popular among women. In December 2002, 23 passengers on an Air Jamaica flight to Heathrow were arrested and charged for allegedly swallowing cocaine with a street value of one million pounds. Such measures have resulted in the implementation of anti-drug trafficking strategies. A local newspaper in Trinidad has reported in 2004, success in these innovations which resulted in the arrest of 30 people between April and September who swallowed more than 13 kilograms of cocaine valued at TT 10 million dollars (1.6 million USD) [5].

Following the introduction of cocaine in the nineteen eighties, there has been the local development of refined methods of drug use. Pure cocaine is a white pearly powder and is seldom imported in this form. Cocaine is imported or 'cooked' into many forms. It can be precipitated into many salts such as cocaine hydrochloride which is water soluble. Freebase is the base form of cocaine which when smoked is more toxic to the heart and lungs. Crack cocaine has more contaminants than free base especially sodium bicarbonate which when smoked makes a crackling sound hence the name.

Common methods of cocaine use are insufflation in the form of snorting, sniffing or blowing, inhalation and injection. In Trinidad and Tobago the earlier method of 'getting high' was snorting. This is a method of placing the powdered cocaine on the palm of the hand or a flat surface such as a table or book and then sniffing it through each nostril. Other innovations are 'running a line' where the drug will be places in a linear manner on a flat surface or in two lines, 'railing' and inhaled through each nostril in tandem either with a straw, gold spoon, open pen barrel or folded dollar bill. This method though successful, was later plagued by nasal ulcerations and respiratory diseases as 'pushers', those who sell the drugs and 'runners', those who transport the drug decided to increase their profits by increasing the volume of the 'white lady' that is, the cocaine powder, by intermixing it with chalk, white bleaches, soda powder and other compounds. This soon gave way to a method of purification known as 'free-basing' that utilised the simple chemistry of acid plus base forms a salt and water. The impure cocaine powder was now 'cooked' with sodium bicarbonate to produce a 'rock' or crystallized salt of crack cocaine. This was then chipped into portions of 5, 10, 25, or 50 dollar rock pieces and sold to consumers.

A local innovative method of free basing has been the invention of the 'zooch bottle'. 'Zooch' is the local term used for 'speed'. It is not unusual for Trinidadians standing on the street to report 'that car just pass me zooch'. The 'zooch bottle' is a one or two ounces brandy bottle that has been emptied and prepared as a contraption for drug use. A hole is made at the bottom through which the cocaine is inhaled. At the mouth of the bottle a piece of wire gauze used for scrubbing dishes is cut and fastened to the top. The cocaine rock is placed here and lighted with matches or a flame. The fumes enter the bottle and are inhaled through the mouth at the bottom. This, according to users is effective and goes 'straight to the heart' producing an instant high. Sometimes, the crack cocaine is chipped into fine pieces and mixed with tobacco. This is now heated over a flame resulting in the absorption of the melted cocaine into the tobacco. This is known as a 'black cigarette' and is smoked as a normal cigarette. It is not unusual for addicts to add marijuana also into the concoction. Injections in the Caribbean settings are feared and seldom utilized among cocaine users.

REVIEW OF LOCAL STUDIES

Very few studies have addressed the issues of cocaine abuse in Trinidad and Tobago [6,7]. The findings indicate that cocaine use is more prevalent among the Afro-Trinidadian population. The gender ratio is approximately five males to one female. Those admitted to the public hospitals were mostly of the lower and middle social classes with at least 50 percent employed prior to their drug use. Cocaine use was associated with criminal activities. Two percent of cocaine users were found to be HIV positive [8].

In secondary school surveys, ages 11-19, a lifetime prevalence of 1.1% was reported in 1985 for cocaine use [9]. In the same year, another survey reported 3.3% [10]. The difference was that the second study included unemployed youths and an older age of 14-20. A lifetime prevalence rate of 2% was found in a study conducted in 1988 among 1,603 secondary school children aged 14-18 years [11]. Recent findings [12] have reported an increase of cannabis use in secondary school from 8.2% in 1988 to 31.7 % in vocational schools and 26.2% in grammar schools in 2007. While students are generally reluctant to disclose their cocaine-using practices, it is estimated that the 2% cocaine use reported in secondary schools in 1988 has increased to 7% in 2007.

EFFECTS OF COCAINE USE

The social effects of cocaine use are highlighted above with its use directly linked to increased criminal activities, murders and death. The methods of insufflation and inhalation reach an absorption rate of 30-60% absorption efficiency within 15 to 30 minutes. This is useful for the industry since the user is always in need of a 'quick fix'.

Common medical problems reported by patients are slowing or racing of the heart, dilatation of the pupils with agitation and walking as though there are springs in the shoes, a condition referred to as being 'sprang'. Chronic cocaine users are referred to as 'sprangers'. Cocaine addicts lose weight due to the effect of the drug on their appetite. In addition, there can be changes in their blood pressure due to the constriction of blood vessels, perspiration, chills, nausea and vomiting. In chronic heavy users, there are complaints of muscular weakness, breathing difficulties, chest pain and arrhythmias. Some of these patients proceed to seizures, confusion and death.

Withdrawal effects are seen in the hospital setting for patients admitted for detoxification. These are sadness, misery and dysphoria, weakness, vivid, frightening dreams often associated with the cocaine culture, poor sleep, increased blood pressure and an increased appetite [6]. The commonest psychiatric symptoms reported by cocaine addicts in clinical practice are paranoid-related disorders. These are described as 'peeping and laughing' and 'crawling, searching and digging'. During the active use of cocaine, often in broken-down abandoned houses, 'sprangers' will be constantly looking through holes, creases or louvers of the building. This habit known as 'peeping' is deemed to be paranoid behaviour in search of the police. They would often look at each other and laugh. Another habit is 'searching', where the addict will be on all four limbs searching for white specks of cocaine or rocks that may have fallen on the floor. This heightened sensitivity or obsession may result in removing the carpet or flooring, digging and upsetting the entire foundation. They search for white specks that they greedily consume. An addict once removed an entire staircase with a jackhammer in trying to find a fallen 5-piece rock!

The examination of a cocaine addict can escape one's attention if the examiner is not sensitized to the culture. The dishevelled and dilapidated state of the addict will be obvious. However, there must be careful examination of the fingers hands and lips. Burns will be seen on the hands due to the constant use of matches or toilet paper to burn the cocaine at the end of the zooch bottle. The bottle can become hot and the lips themselves become chapped, dry, glazed and parched. Recent use is manifested by bright, open eyes, a paced walk of urgency but going nowhere.

DISCUSSION

Drug trafficking is a major problem in the Caribbean region. The smuggling of cocaine is done through maritime vessels, fishing boats, yachts, light air planes and even international maritime and air services. International smuggling is destination bound whereas private aircrafts use pre-determined drop off areas that are perfectly coordinated with waiting vessels or vehicles. The sophistication of traffickers is so developed that the dropped cocaine sinks to the bottom of the ocean and emerges at whatever time is determined. This facilitates easy and synchronized retrieval. Maritime vessels sometimes tow the drug cargo underwater so that a search will be negative and there is also ease of dislodging if necessary. There are also rich drug loads with speedy vessels and off-mainland residences that stack the drop off for cooling time. They are often above the law. The Caribbean therefore, with its lengthy coastline, unmanned borders and inadequate customs and coastguard surveillance resources have led to these islands playing major roles in the transfer of cocaine to USA and Europe [5].

Mention has been made of human internal and external body trafficking of drugs. A small percentage of these have been found to be suffering from mental illnesses, noticeably paranoid schizophrenia. While their ego strength is maintained, they do have diminished insight and poor judgment. Others work as mules or detractors to the drug lord and are guaranteed compensation notwithstanding the outcome. In the drug-trafficking business deals can go sour and drug couriers can be set up if previous transactions have gone bad. This serves to get them out of the system.

The medical aspects of cocaine use are often down played. It is said that the first use of the drug provides a rush that the person is forever trying to recapitulate. This is often termed, 'chasing the dragon'. Cocaine is a dangerous drug in that one can become an addict only after a single exposure to the drug. While euphoria, hyper-alertness, excitability and obsession to hard work have been depicted as outcome of use, it is often forgotten that this is the effect of small doses of 0.05 gm as pointed out by Freud [13]. Other disastrous effects of this drug are confusion, paranoid psychosis, formication with 'cocaine bugs' on the skin, dilation of the pupils, perforated nasal septum, fever, cardiac dysfunctions, seizure and death. Sudden death among cocaine addicts is not an uncommon finding. The cocaine crash after cessation is a crucial time where depression, suicide and even aggression may be prominent. This is followed by a craving for the drug which leads to relapse.

Cocaine from its earliest introduction was shrouded with mystery and controversy. In 1887, Erlenmeyer a leading addiction specialist accused Freud of 'unleashing the third scourge of humanity' after alcohol and morphine. Freud treated his good friend Fleischl for morphine addiction by using cocaine as a withdrawal drug. Fleischl began using one gram a day and became the first cocaine addict in Europe [14]. In that year Freud published his last paper on cocaine 'Fear for and craving for cocaine'. He concluded that 'cocaine has claimed no victims of its own' and if a patient is not a morphine addict, he will not become a cocaine addict. He then withdrew cocaine as a cure for morphine addiction [15].

In this era of cocaine's widespread popularity, cocaine was seen as the intellectual beverage. John Styth Pemberton, a chemist from Atlanta in Georgia introduced coca-cola. An advertisement of the day stated, 'this intellectual beverage and temperance drink contains the valuable tonic and nerve stimulant of the coca plant and cola (or kola) nuts, and makes a delicious, exhilarating, refreshing and invigorating beverage' [16].

Sir Arthur Conan Doyle himself a cocaine user, created the famous detective Sherlock Holmes who was portrayed as someone using cocaine [14]. Schultz made a case that Robert Louis Stevenson wrote 'The strange case of Dr Jekyll and Mr Hyde' while under the influence of cocaine [17]. With the passage of time and the death of 50 patients reported by Watson-Williams in 1923 due to idiosyncratic toxic effects with cocaine used as an anaesthetic [18], regulations were enacted for the medical use of this substance. It is interesting to note that more deaths are recorded in the use of this substance as an anaesthetic than in its abuse as a recreational drug on the street. The reasons are not fully understood.

Young black youths, mostly Afro-Trinidadians and of mixed origin seem to be more attracted to the cocaine drug culture which lead them to crime and mental illness. Less than two decades after the popularisation of cocaine in 1884, negroes in some parts of the Southern United States were reported as being addicted to a new form of vice, that of cocaine sniffing or the coke habit [16]. Colonel JW Watson asserted that many of the horrible crimes committed in the southern states by the coloured people can be traced directly to the cocaine habit [16]. This is the contemporary picture in the Caribbean region in the absence of oppression and disenfranchisement of this group suggesting that other variables may be responsible for the predilection to a life of crime and drugs. It is proposed that slavery where white plantation owners, like the Spanish conquistadores 300 years earlier dispensed cocaine to black labourers to keep them working is a possible explanation. A similar pattern has been observed among indentured Indians in Trinidad who were given alcoholic beverages by the colonial British during the same period. Alcohol use and dependency is today a major problem among this group. It is interesting that each ethnic group has continued with the introduced substance as their preferred drug of choice which centuries ago was imposed upon them by their masters.

The establishment of the cocaine culture has also resulted in a new literary culture at the street level. This transformation of the language has changed it from a medium of comprehensive expressions to a version studded with new forms of dialect, various inventions of slangs and street neologisms. These verbal influences have filtered into everyday usage, hardly decipherable by someone unexposed to the culture. It is difficult to escape from this new found drug- related vernacular which the author captures in his poem entitled 'Cocaine Paranoia':

Two voices pongin meh head
Oh God, is better ah dead
On black and crack, a zooch spranger
'Till now I denied de danger

Two voices jumbie-ing meh system
Fighting up meh brains for mental decision
Using cocaine in nightmare and dream
'Ah clean man' ah wake up and scream

Two voices jus' like a cricket game
Running commentary dat ah man insane
Seeing t'ings in all Shapes and sizes
On radio and TV, dey plotting disguises

Two voices laughin at me
Peeping and searching on meh knee
Thru key holes and creases on the wall
Is de police and dem wid deh gun and all

Two voices controlling meh movement
Sprang-a-lang widout a black cent
Meh mother jewel pusher, for a ten rock
Ah use to cut for de boss on de block

Two voices arguing ah cyar duss de beat
Is de white lady dat have he so on de street
It look like dis man really gone thru
Take 'im to de mad house for a review

CONCLUSION

As depicted in this chapter, cocaine and its industry have transformed civilization, cultures countries, communities and governments. It has influenced creativity in art, language, drama, prose and poetry. Yet today, cocaine remains a permanent scourge to mankind. The inevitable introduction for medicinal purposes has done more harm than good, noting that the road to hell is sometimes paved with good intentions.

REFERENCES

[1]   Aggrawal A. Narcotic drugs. India: National Book Trust 1995:52-3.
[2]   2. Wikipedia Free Encyclopaedia. Cocaine. [Online] 2009 [cited 2009 Oct 12]. Available from: http://en.wikipedia.org/wiki/Cocaine.
[3]   Maharajh H. Cocaine and social transformation in Trinidad and Tobago. Letter from Trinidad. Psychiatr Bull 1997;21:184-5.
[4]   Renne D. Judge send Bakr affidavit to DPP. [Online] 2009 [cited 2009 Oct 12]. Available from: Trinidad Express http://www.trinidadexpress.com/index.pl/article_news?id=161530414.
[5]   Reid S. Substance abuse. In: Hickling F, Sorel E. Images of psychiatry. The Caribbean. Jamaica: Stephenson's Litho Press, 2005:197-231.
[6]   Maharajh HD, Dutta A, Gopeesingh SR. Cocaine addiction in Trinidad and Tobago. West Indian Med J 1987;36(Suppl):13.
[7]   Hutchinson G, Greenidge C, Lewis P. Socio-demographic features of cocaine dependence. West Indian Med J 1992; 46(Suppl):67.
[8]   Lewis PD, Hospedales CJ. HIV study of cocaine dependent persons. West Indian Med J 1991;40:25.
[9]   Remy F. Summary report of survey on drug use among secondary school students in Trinidad and Tobago. Port of Spain: General Hospital, Psychiatr Unit, 1985.
[10]   Bernard L. Drug use survey among young people (age 14-20) in Trinidad and Tobago. St Augustine: Univ West Indies, 1985.
[11]   Singh H, Maharaj HD, Shipp M. Pattern of substance abuse among secondary school students in Trinidad and Tobago. Public Health 1991;105(6):435-41.
[12]   Konings M, Maharajh HD. Substance abuse in different school systems in Trinidad and Tobago: A controlled study of children with disabilities and their drug Use. Int J Dis Hum Dev 2007;6(1):3-10.
[13]   Jones E. The life and work of Sigmund Freud. New York: Basic Books 1961.
[14]   Ahsley R. Cocaine: Its history uses and effects. New York: St Martin's Press, 1975.
[15]   Musto DF. A study in cocaine: Sherlock Holmes and Sigmund Freud. JAMA 1968;204(1):27-32.
[16]   Anonymous. The cocaine habit. JAMA 1900;34:1967
[17]   Schultz MG. The strange case of Robert Louis Stevenson. JAMA 1971;216(1):90-4.
[18]   Watson-Williams E. Cocaine and its substitutes. BMJ 1923; 2:1018-21.

In: Social and Cultural Psychiatry Experience from the... ISBN: 978-1-61668-506-5
Editor: Hari D. Maharajh and Joav Merrick © 2010 Nova Science Publishers, Inc.

Chapter 25

DEINSTITUTIONALIZATION IN THE CARIBBEAN

Hari D. Maharajh

Deinstitutionalization, the process of moving patients from large mental hospitals into the community is new to the Caribbean region. In keeping with trends of the more developed countries, World Banks' conditionality have requested the downsizing of psychiatry hospitals in order to qualify for monetary aid. Unfortunately, in the Caribbean region, there is an absence of extramural services for patient care and this has been a major handicap.

This study seeks to investigate the pattern of admission of patients to the psychiatric hospital in Trinidad and to make comparison with Jamaica, a country with a more robust community care programme. Data was collected from hospital records on gender and total admissions over a sixteen - year period (1985-2000) and mode of admission over a three-year period (1998-2000) in Trinidad and Tobago. For Jamaica, secondary data of total admissions and gender rates were extracted from published works for the years 1960 –1990. Data was analysed using SPSS Version 11. One-sample t-tests were used to test the significance of reduction in admission rates.

Trinidad and Tobago experienced a 46% significant decrease in admissions from 3,076 in 1985 to 1,659 in 2000 (p< 0.001), while Jamaica admissions were reduced by 58% from 3,094 in 1960 to 1,296 in 1990. Over these periods, there has been a reduction in both male and female admissions. In Trinidad, male admissions have decreased by 49% and female by 39% while in Jamaica male admissions have decreased by 52.8% and female 43.9%. In Trinidad voluntary admissions accounted for 50.6%, urgent 29.8%, court orders 16.6% and medically recommended and mental health order 1.5% each. Pearson Product Moment correlation revealed that a positive correlation existed between voluntary admission and court order (p<0.05) and negative relationship between mental health order and urgent admission (p<0.05)

Notwithstanding a greater investment in community psychiatry in Jamaica, the patterns of admission and deinstitutionalisation are similar in Jamaica and Trinidad. It seems that deinstitutionalization in these countries are an unforced process with less admission to psychiatric hospitals and alternative treatment for patient care These findings are useful in providing invaluable information for the development of community care programmes in developing countries.

INTRODUCTION

The implementation of social models of community psychiatric care in developing countries has closely followed those of industrialized societies. De-institutionalization has been the basic implementation strategy aimed at the movement of patients from the institution into the community. This involved the reduction of the hospital population or closure of mental hospitals with the concomitant establishment of extramural decentralized services. The focus therefore, has been the rehabilitation and integration of the mentally ill into the community instead of the institution.

De-institutionalization in itself has been critically reviewed; it has been dubbed as the largest failed social experiment of the twentieth century with inadequate after care, with the prisons and jails replacing mental hospitals as providers of care [1]. Birmingham [2] has reported that the closure of mental hospitals has resulted in the revolving door psychiatric patient of the nineties, rotated between the community and the prisons. The major problem of de-institutionalization does not lie with the conceptual core but with inadequate implementation [3]. According to Jorgensen [4], instead of organizing decentralized services and then gradually reducing the capacity of hospital treatment, things happen in many places the other way around.

In the English-speaking Caribbean, de-institutionalization takes a different meaning. Only in the larger islands of Jamaica, Trinidad and Barbados asylum-like mental hospitals were built by the British Colonizers. The issue of chronic hospitalization of mental patients does not arise in many smaller islands that utilize general hospitals and community clinics. The absence of psychiatric hospitals has resulted in a natural emphasis on community care. In this region, culturally based community treatment modalities based on traditional practices of superstition, religion and folk medicine are pervasive. Family support, volition for hospitalization and stigmatization are different to industrialized societies. Obviously, the implementation of decentralized community services should be the focus in developing countries.

Many developing countries have utilized model programmes in their implementation strategies [5-7] without considering that community care for people with mental illness in the developing world are complex and differ from those in industrialized societies [8]. Trinidad and Tobago is no exception. In 2000, a new mental plan [9] was approved based on the letter and spirit of the declaration of Caracas [10] and the World Health Organization vision for Mental Health [11]. The plan emphasized the development of primary care and among other provisions recommended the phase reduction of inpatient beds at St. Ann's hospital from 1026 to 600. In addition, the plan proposed an expansion of rehabilitation services.

The Sectorization Plan (1975) of Trinidad and Tobago [12] divided the country into five sectors aimed at providing community care in each catchment area. Two years later, interests waned as it became evident that the major objective of the program, which was the decongestion of St. Anns Hospital and the treatment of patients in the community, was not being achieved [13]. Since 1975, there have been no major changes in community mental health in the Republic. De-institutionalisation in Jamaica began in the sixties and three decades later there has been significant transformation in mental health. The mental hospital population has been reduced by 58 percent and the majority of chronic mental health patients are being treated in the community. A significant reason for the success has been the investment in community psychiatric facilities [14]. Unlike Jamaica, in Trinidad and Tobago there has been no investment in community facilities for a quarter of a century. In 1975 the Mental Health Act was introduced in Trinidad and Tobago which clearly defined modes of admission of patients into the psychiatric hospital. There was strict adherence to the legislative requirements by all mental health caregivers. However in Jamaica, the 1974 legislative amendments did not constitute compelling legislative reform leaving the procedures for admission and civil liberties open-ended.

The purpose of this study is to investigate the patterns of patient's admission to the St. Anns Hospital in Trinidad over a sixteen-year period 1985-2000. In addition a three-year analysis (1998-2000) of classes of admission [15] is undertaken. These findings in a country without a comprehensive community psychiatric service are compared with Jamaica, a country that has a program of investment in community psychiatry. A study of the patterns of admission, deinstitutionalization and community services in these countries will provide invaluable information for the planning and implementation of social models of community care in the Caribbean and other developing countries.

OUR STUDY

Data collection was conducted for Trinidad, Tobago and Jamaica and all data entered and analysed using SPSS (Statistical Package for the Social Sciences) Version 11. One-sample t-tests were used to test the significance of reduction in admission rates for each country over various time periods. The level of significance was set at a $p < 0.05$ level.

Trinidad and Tobago

St. Anns Hospital built in 1900 is a large 900-bedded Georgian style psychiatric hospital that serves the entire population of 1.3 million of Trinidad and Tobago. It is situated on five acres of land on the foothills of the scenic Northern Range, with twenty-seven wards in old and new structures. These wards house all categories of patients. Approximately 70 percent of the hospital population is male and 60 percent chronic patients.

The admission of patients is status determined, that is voluntary admissions, urgent admissions, order of courts or national security, medically recommended and mental health officers admissions. Except for the high security ward for Forensic patients, all patients are assigned wards according to their mental status rather than their admission status.

Analysis took the form of archival research where records from the hospital were used. The records contained data such as male, female and total admission rates over a sixteen-year period (1985-2000). Data on classes of admission were also extracted for a three-year period (1998-2000).

Jamaica

Bellevue Hospital was established in 1862 by the British Colonial Government and by 1971 was the major referral hospital for psychiatry in the island [16]. Today, the hospital houses 1,500 patients in 23 wards [17].

The research design for Jamaica utilized secondary data that was extracted from reputable journals of published work on community psychiatry and de-institutionalization in Jamaica [18, 16, 14]. Data was available for total admissions and male and female admission rates for the years of 1960, 1971, 1988 and 1990.

OUR FINDINGS

Trinidad and Tobago

In 1985 the total admission was 3076, with male admissions comprising of 2170 and female 906. Sixteen years later, in 2000, the total admission was 1659, a decrease by 46 percent. A one-sample t-test proved that this 46% decrease was statistically significant, $t(15) = 5.507$, $p < 0.001$. The test value for the one-sample t-test was set at the admission figure for the base year (3076). Figure 1 shows the trend line for admission rates (male, female and total) for 1985 to 2000 and table 1 shows admission rates for the same period.

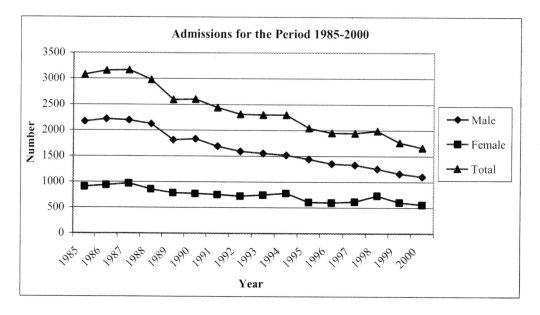

Figure 1. Trend line for admission rates (male, female and total) for 1985 to 2000

Deinstitutionalization in the Caribbean

Table 1. Admissions for the Period 1985-2000

Year	Male Admissions	Female Admissions	Total Admissions	Male % of Total	Female % of Total
1985	2170	906	3076	71	29
1986	2218	936	3154	70	30
1987	2195	969	3164	69	31
1988	2121	856	2977	71	29
1989	1809	783	2592	70	30
1990	1829	770	2599	70	30
1991	1688	752	2440	69	31
1992	1590	722	2312	69	31
1993	1554	745	2299	68	32
1994	1518	780	2298	66	34
1995	1437	603	2040	70	30
1996	1350	596	1946	69	31
1997	1328	614	1942	68	32
1998	1254	732	1986	63	37
1999	1160	601	1761	66	34
2000	1103	556	1659	66	34

On average, over the sixteen-year period (1985-2000), male admissions have accounted for 70 percent of total admissions while female only 30 percent. Male admissions have steadily declined by 49% from 2170 in 1985 to 1103 in 2000. Female admissions have fluctuated during the years, and have decreased by 39% from 906 in 1985 to 556 in 2000 (see figure 1). Due to the decreases in both male and female admissions, the percentage difference between the two groups has decreased from 41% in 1985 to 33% in 2000.

Table 2. Classes of admission 1998-2000

Mode of Admission	1998	1999	2000
Voluntary	1036	793	905
	(52.2%)	(45.0%)	(54.5%)
Urgent	567	651	393
	(28.5%)	(37.0%)	(23.7%)
Court Order	326	269	300
	(16.4%)	(15.3%)	(18.1%)
Medically Recommended	30	23	31
	(1.5%)	(1.3%)	(1.9%)
Mental Health Order	27	25	30
	(1.4%)	(1.4%)	(1.8%)
Total Admissions	1986	1761	1659
	(100%)	(100%)	(100%)

Voluntary admissions on average have accounted for half (50.6%) of total admissions over the three-year period from 1998-2000. Urgent admissions accounted for 29.8%, court order 16.6%, medically recommended 1.5% and mental health order 1.5%. Table 2 shows figures for classes of admissions, the mean difference and respective 95% confidence intervals. Pearson Product Moment correlation revealed that a significant positive relationship existed between voluntary admission and court order, r = 0.995, p < 0.05, and a significant negative relationship between mental health order and urgent admissions, r = -0.996, p < 0.05.

Jamaica

The resident population of Bellevue Hospital was 3,094 in 1960, with an admission rate of 67 per 100,000. In general, males accounted for the majority of total admissions but have experienced a decrease in admission rates over the years. From 1971, males had an admission rate of 174 and by 1988 had decreased by 52.82% to 82. Female admission rates have also decreased by 43.88% from 98 in 1971 to 55 in 1988. Overall Bellevue Hospital has seen a 58% reduction in admissions from 3,094 in 1960 to 1,296 in 1990. Chart 2 shows the steady decrease of admissions in Jamaica from 1960 to 1990.

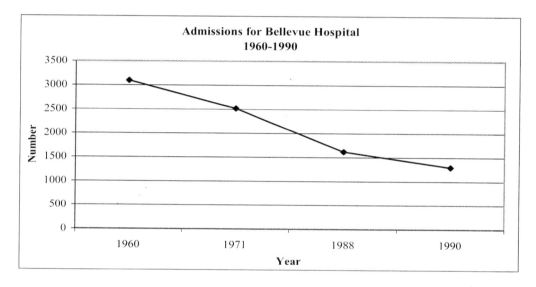

Figure 2. Admissions in Jamaica from 1960 to 1990

COMPARISON BETWEEN THE DIFERENT SITES

Trinidad and Tobago experienced a 46% significant decrease (p < 0.001) in admissions from 3,076 in 1985 to 1,659 in 2000 while Jamaica admissions were reduced by 58% from 3,094 in 1960 to 1,296 in 1990. Male admissions for Trinidad and Tobago have decreased by 49% over this sixteen-year period, while male admission rates in Jamaica experienced a decrease by 52.82%. Female admissions were also reduced in both countries, with Trinidad and Tobago having a 39% reduction in admissions and Jamaica a 43.88% reduction in admission rates. Table 3 shows the comparisons of community care and de-institutionalization between Trinidad and Tobago and Jamaica.

Table 3. Comparison of Community Care and De-institutionalization between Trinidad and Tobago and Jamaica

Variable	Jamaica	Trinidad and Tobago
Investigations	Hickling (1994) Bellevue 58% reduction in population over 31 years 1960-1990	St. Anns 46% reduction in population over 16 years 1985-2000
First Colonial Psychiatric Hospital	Sole Mental Hospital established in 1862	Belmont Lunatic Asylum established 1858, moved to St. Anns in 1985
Independence	Became independent in 1962	Became independent in 1962, Republican Status 1976
Legal Reformation	1974 – empowered MHO's No detailed legislative reform	1975 MHA empowered MHO's with clear legislative requirement
Community Psychiatric Service	14 Parishes Polyclinics 2.5 million population	5 sectors, 74 out patient psychiatric clinics held monthly
Community Case Load	1990 14,149 patients/year	52,000 old cases and 3,400 new cases yearly
Role of Extended Family	75% discharged patient Supported by extended family	Good family support but not studied
Reasons for Hospital Reduction	Investment in Community Psychiatry, role of MHO's acceptance of mental illness	Increased sophistication of psychiatry. NGO's reduction of indigents increased numbers of private psychiatrists
Political Context	Westminister two party political system	Westminister two party political system

DISCUSSION

There is a striking similarity in the development and practice of hospital and community psychiatry in Trinidad and Tobago and Jamaica (see table 3). These two countries of the English-speaking Caribbean have been influenced in a like manner by the colonisers, the British Government, consultants from the Pan American Health Organisation (PAHO) and the University of the West Indies. In addition PAHO's broad-brush approach of restructuring psychiatric care in Latin America and the Caribbean has been endorsed by all member states [10]. Not surprisingly, the implementation of models of psychiatric community care among Caribbean countries will not significantly vary.

In the islands of Trinidad and Tobago and Jamaica, there has been a steady decline of hospital admissions over the last decades. Over a sixteen- year period 1985-2000, there has been a 46% decrease in the population at the St. Anns hospital in Trinidad. (t (15) =5.507, p<0.001). At Bellevue Hospital in Jamaica, there has been a 58% reduction in hospital admissions over a 31- year period 1960–1990. In both countries males account for the majority of hospital admissions, being as much as 70% over the sixteen year period in Trinidad. In the latter, male admissions have steadily declined by 49% from 2170 in 1985 to 1103 in 2000. In Jamaica, over a seventeen-year period 1971 –1988 male admission rates have decreased by 53 percent. Over the same two time periods female admissions have decreased by 39% in Trinidad and 43.9% in Jamaica .In Trinidad, female admissions have fluctuated over the years. A possible explanation may be the socio-cultural differences in these countries.

Notwithstanding the similarities in deinstitutionalization patterns in these countries, analyses of the findings are disparate. The reasons proffered for hospital reduction in Jamaica are a reorientation of services from mental-hospital-based custodial care to rehabilitative, community based care, an investment in community psychiatry, the assignment of Mental Health Officers in the parishes, the public acceptance of mental illness and the role of the extended families. In Trinidad and Tobago, there appears to have been a natural reduction of hospital numbers without the implementation of decentralised community services. The decrease of hospital admissions is multifactorial. There is today an increased sophistication in the practice of psychiatry with documented international diagnoses. This has resulted in the cessation of the dumping of unwanted patients into a psychiatric hospital. In addition, there are at least fifteen psychiatrists in private practice and nursing homes admitting psychiatric patients. Various Non-Governmental Organisations (NGO's) and denominational churches have invested heavily in mental health care. At St Anns hospital, there has been a reduction of indigents due to decreased migration from other West Indian islands.

It is common knowledge that the conditions in large psychiatric hospitals such as St. Anns and Bellevue are not ideal. Absconding, not necessarily an index of hospital conditions is endemic at St Anns hospital. There is overcrowding, acute shortage of staff, long stay of patients, abandonment, rejection and absence of visits by relatives, unsatisfactory treatment of patients and absence of basic amenities [19]. Enduring themes such as institutional aimlessness, poor staff-patients relations, a narrow approach to mental health and a lack of attention to civil and human rights have been characteristic of psychiatric care [20]. Increased patients' awareness coupled with a negative media have resulted in alternative treatment rather than admission.

The mode of admission into a psychiatric hospital in Trinidad and Tobago follows the letter of the law (Sec 6) [15]. Over the three-year period 1998–2000, half the patients (50.6%) were admitted on a voluntary status and 30 percent as an urgent admission recommended by a medical practitioner. Approximately 17% of all annual admissions come from the forensic service (see table 2). An increase in compulsory admissions did not result in a decrease in court orders. Unlike Trinidad, in Jamaica the Forensic services are not at Bellevue Hospital and admissions of patients follow the 'common law' rather than the Mental Health Act (1996) [21]. The hospital population at St. Anns hospital can be reduced another 20 percent if the Forensic services are relocated. Patients who are sent by the courts and those sentenced on the President's Pleasure at the hospital constitute a major part of the languished service.

The population of Jamaica is twice that of Trinidad and Tobago. Jamaica with a population of 2.5 million is divided into 14 parishes or well-defined geographical areas. There are 335 clinics in primary care that are conducted by general practitioners and visited by mental health officers who together treat approximately 14,149 patients yearly. Trinidad and Tobago is divided into nine catchment areas with 74 outpatient clinics held monthly. Fifty two thousand returning patients and 3400 new cases are seen each year. A multidisciplinary team is attached to each sector and looks after the patient both at the hospital and in the community. Every mentally ill patient is assessed by a psychiatrist. In Trinidad and Tobago four times more patients are treated in the community than in Jamaica. This may in part reflect the absence or failure of rehabilitative programmes but can also be explained by the ease of access to these walk- in clinics, the nature of a doctor-seeking population and the fact that the social welfare system is linked to registration in the clinic hence reinforcing non-discharge.

Notwithstanding differences in mental health legislation, socio-political and cultural behaviours and emphasis on community–based care, the patterns of deinstitutionalization in Trinidad and Jamaica are comparable. Trinidad and Tobago experienced a 46% decrease in admissions from 1985 to 2000 while Jamaica admissions were decreased by 58 percent. In both countries there was a reduction of male admissions. However, a decline in hospital admission rates cannot be used as an index of deinstitutionalization. The fall out from hospital services may have sought treatment elsewhere or may have become part of the prison population. Surmising from the published literature, it appears that Jamaica with a greater commitment to community care may have a more effective and integrated primary care psychiatry programme. This is supported by the finding that the out-patient psychiatric population in Trinidad and Tobago is approximately 55,000 [22] compared to 14,000 in Jamaica.

This study has provided invaluable information on hospital admissions and patterns of community care in two developing Caribbean countries. The similarities and differences, the advantages and disadvantages and the outcome can be utilised in developing a rational model in community psychiatry for developing countries. A limitation of this study is that Jamaica and Trinidad and Tobago were not compared over the same time period. This however is not a central one and does not affect general trends in reductions and the comparisons identified. Another limitation is the use of secondary data from journal articles for Jamaica. The information gathered from the papers was not comprehensive and restricted comparisons and statistical applications.

REFERENCES

[1]   Torrey E. Jails and prisons. America's new mental health hospitals. Am J Public Health 1995;85:1611-3.

[2]   Birmingham L Between prison and the community. The 'revolving door psychiatric patient' of the nineties. Br J Psychiatry 1999; 174:378-9.

[3]   Garcia J, V'azquez-Barquero JL. Deinstitutionalization and psychiatric reform in Spain. Actas Esp Psiquiatr 1999;27(5): 281-91.

[4]   Munk-Jorgensen P. Has deinstitutionalization gone too far? Euro Arch Psychiatr Clin Neurol 1999;249(3):136-43.

[5]   Harding TW, d'Arrigo Busnello E, Climent CE, Diop M, El-Hakim A, Giel R, et al. The WHO collaborative study on strategies for extending mental health care, Ill: Evaluative design and illustrative results. Am J Psychiatry 1983;140(11):1481-5.

[6]   World Health Organization. Mental Health care in developing countries: a critical appraisal of research findings. Geneva: WHO Tech Rep Series, 1984;698.

[7]   Wig NN. The future of mental health in developing countries. Comm Ment Health News 1989;13:1-4.

[8]   Jacob KS. Community care for people with mental disorders in developing countries. Problems and possible solutions. Br J Psychiatry 2001;178:296-8.

[9]   Ministry of Health. New mental health plan. Port of Spain: Gov Trinidad Tobago, 2000.

[10]   Declaration of Caracas Annex A. Psychiatric care and mental health legislation in the English speaking Caribbean countries. Regional conference on restructuring psychiatric care in Latin America. Caracas: PAHO/WHO Regional Office, 1990.

[11] PAHO/WHO mental health 43rd directing council, 53rd session of the regional committee. Washington DC: PAHO/WHO, 2001.

[12] Ministry of Health. Sectorization plan for Trinidad and Tobago. Port of Spain: Gov Trinidad Tobago, 1975.

[13] James V. A review of psychiatry in Trinidad and Tobago over the decade 1970-1980. Archives, St Anns Hospital Trinidad, 1984.

[14] Hickling FW. Community psychiatry and deinstitutionalization in Jamaica. Hosp Comm Psychiatry 1994;45(11):1122-6.

[15] Mental Health Act No 30. Laws of the Republic of Trinidad and Tobago. Chapter 28:02; 1975.

[16] Hickling FW. Psychiatry in Jamaica-growth and development. Int Rev Psychiatry 1993;5:193-203.

[17] Wilson M. Planning your elective. The Caribbean. BMJ 2002;10: 332-3.

[18] Hickling FW. Psychiatric hospital admission rates in Jamaica, 1971 and 1988. Br J Psychiatry 1991;159:817-21.

[19] Maharajh HD, Ali A. Escapes from a West Indian psychiatric hospital. A two year retrospective analysis. West Indian Med J 2002; 52 (Supp 2):43.

[20] Walton P. Psychiatric hospital care. A case of the more things change, the more they remain the same. J Ment Health 2000;9(1):77.

[21] Hickling FW. A comparison of the Jamaican and the UK models of deinstitutionalization and community health mental services. Lecture Int Psychiatr Conf, Crowne Plaza Hotel, Port of Spain, Trinidad, 2002.

[22] Maharajh HD, Parasram R . Psychiatry in Trinidad and Tobago. Int Rev Psychiatry 1999;11:173-83.

In: Social and Cultural Psychiatry Experience from the...
Editor: Hari D. Maharajh and Joav Merrick

ISBN: 978-1-61668-506-5
© 2010 Nova Science Publishers, Inc.

Chapter 26

DEPRESSION IN TRINIDAD AND TOBAGO: INCIDENCE AND SOCIAL TRENDS

Hari D. Maharajh and Akleema Ali

Depression is a major problem worldwide and ranks within the first five common burden of disease affecting mankind. Rising rates of depression among youths and its association with the use of intoxicants present a major challenge to health care policy planners and governments alike. This chapter reviews major trends in adolescent depression in secondary schools in the Republic of Trinidad and Tobago and independently in the sister isle of Tobago. Incidence rates of 14% were found in Trinidad and Tobago and 10.1% in Tobago indicative of differences in population composition and social trends in both islands. Social parameters of gender differences, age cohort, attendence to religious institutions, prayer with the family, family use of alcohol, type of school attended, ethnicity and family structures were investigated. These variables were found to be significant contributory factors to adolescent depression in the Republic. An understanding of early depression in diverse communities will be helpful in reducing the global burden of common diseases.

INTRODUCTION

Adolescence is a critical period of development and represents a period of high risk for depression [1,2]. The presence of adolescent depression predicts a continued risk for recurrences of depressive episodes, negative consequences and suicidal risk into adulthood [3]. Depression can be described as a mood state, characterized by feelings of sadness, inferiority, inadequacy, hopelessness, dejection, guilt or blame [4]. Most investigators consider reports of sadness, helplessness, eating disturbances, social withdrawal, loss of ability to concentrate, ideas of inadequacy or worthlessness, tension, lack of energy and anxiety to be symptoms of depression [5,6].

Internationally, overall rates of adolescent depression have varied across countries and cultures. Low rates were reported in Western Europe, Asia and Australia. In a Swedish study of high school students aged 16-17 years, a depression score of 12.3% was found [7]. Lower rates were reported from Italy with rates of depression in adolescents as low as 3.8%, [8].

Stavrakaki et al. [9] reported rates of 10% in Canadian adolescents with a similar rate found in British adolescents (10%) [10]. Separate studies of Chinese adolescents have reported rates of 13% [11] and 11% [12] as being depressed while Boyd et al. [13] have reported rates of 14.2% in Australia. In Guatemala, a neighbouring Caribbean country, a high rate of adolescent depression (35.1%) was found [14].

In Trinidad and Tobago, few studies have focused on the measurement of depression in the community. Maharajh & Montane-Jaime have found that the incidence of major depression was 4.86 per 10,000 in a well-defined geographical sector [15].

INCIDENCE

Two studies were conducted on adolescent depression in secondary schools in Tobago and the other in Trinidad and Tobago [16,17]. These studies measured the incidence of depression among adolescents in both islands and attempted to identify any significant trends associated with its occurrence. A sample of 1,845 respondents between the ages of 14-20 (Form 4 – Upper 6) were administered the Reynolds' Adolescent Depression Scale (RADS) which is a 30-item self-report instrument designed specifically for adolescents and measures depressive symptomatology. In order to judge the severity of depressive symptomatology a cutoff score of 77 and above was used. Fourteen percent (14%) of the sample indicated symptoms of depression.

In the Tobago study 198 adolescents were selected from three schools from the sister isle and the subjects were also administered the RADS to assess depressive symptomatology. The result indicated that 10.1% suffered from a depressive disorder of which 6.06% was dysthymia and 4.04% major depression [17]. The larger study which sampled both islands showed fourteen percent (14%) of the subjects experiencing depressive symptomatology, which coincides with findings of the range reported in Australia (14.2%) and worldwide data of 3.5 to 35.7% [13].

SOCIAL TENDS

Significant gender differences were also found between female and male adolescents F $(1,807) = 103.148$, p< 0.001, with females accounting for 76.3% of all depressed respondents and males 23.7% (see figure 1). The rate of depression in females was 17.9% and 8.2% for males and depression was 2.18 times more likely to occur in females than males. In the Tobago study females were also more likely to have depression than males F (197) = 6.083, p< 0.01 and they had significantly higher mean RADS score (64.39) than males (57.37).

In a critical review, the following factors were identified as being likely to account for the gender difference in depression: adverse childhood experiences, sociocultural factors, psychological attributes related to vulnerability to adverse life events and coping skills [18]. Genetic and biological factors and poor social support were cited as having little or no effect in explaining the emergence of the gender difference. Gender differences have also been attributed to gender related psychopathology with females having higher rates of internalizing disorders (anxiety, depression) when compared to males [19] and the effect of recall [20]. It is noteworthy that in Trinidad and Tobago, the socio-cultural differences are protected by the ethos of school cultures.

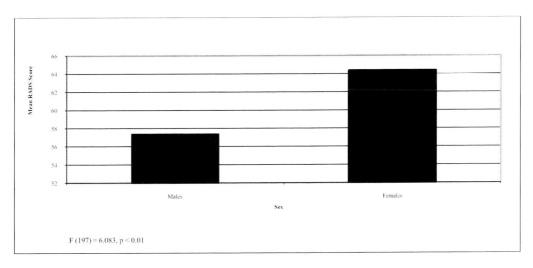

Figure 1. Sex difference in depression in Tobago adolescents

In the larger study, a significant trend was identified between depression and age with adolescents at age 16 having a higher mean RADS score than adolescents at age 14 years. Figure 2 highlights that adolescents at age 16 had the highest rate of depression (15.9%) of all age groups, Those at age 14 had a rate of 12.2%. This increase in both the rate of depression and the mean depression score at age 16 compared to earlier ages, is consistent with the literature, which states that there is not only higher depression scores but an excess of symptoms in adolescents aged 16-20 [21-23]. They have concluded that major depressive disorders which occur in less than 3% of school age children almost doubles in adolescence (6%).

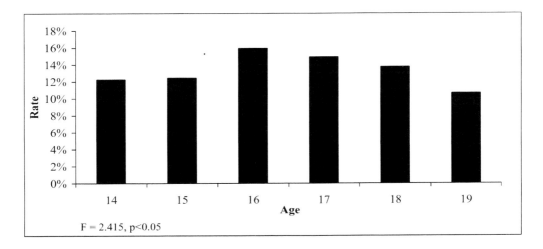

Figure 2. Rates of depression in age cohorts

Family structure, family alcohol abuse and prayer time with the family was also investigated to ascertain its link to depression in the Trinidad and Tobago 2006 study. The reconstituted family structure resulted in significantly higher mean depression scores than the intact and one-parent family structure. This supports research findings where children from step-parent families reported more depressed mood than children from intact families [24]. Adolescents from a reconstituted family structure also reported the highest rate of depression (25.7%) followed by adolescents living with their relatives (22.6%). Intact families reported the lowest rate (11.7%). Parental disharmony and quality of family relationships have been identified as a potential contributory factor for depression among young people [25] and family conflict has been identified as a major risk factor for internalizing behavior in adolescents [26]. The intact family structure represents a stable and important support for adolescents and communication with parents remain an element of protection against distress, problem behavior and poor psychosocial health.

Family stress, which is inevitable in any family structure, is likely to increase in family structures where both parents are not present and where the adolescent has to adjust to a 'new' reconstituted family structure. It has been suggested that family stress and parent-child conflict could lead to adolescents' lower sense of control and higher levels of emotional distress and depression [22]. In Trinidad and Tobago, family structures are varied and complex with a multiplicity of social unions. These are nuclear family, extended families, one parent family, visiting relationships, communal family and reconstituted family. Other hybrids of loose family structures are present mostly based on biological fathering of children with and without economic support.

The relationship between depression and the presence of alcohol abuse in the family revealed significant findings. Alcohol abuse in the family is a significant factor on the rate of depression (23.1%) and the mean depression score (66.57) for adolescents who had alcohol abuse present in their families when compared to their peers without abuse. In addition, individuals with alcohol abuse present in the family are 1.8 times more likely to be depressed than those without abuse present. Lease [27] reports that drinking behaviors disrupt family functioning and directly influence family processes, resulting in difficulties in forming healthy relationships. This disruptive style of behavior not only applies to the individual who engages in the drinking behavior but to other family members who are affected by the behavior. Alcohol exposure in adolescents and family abuse were previously investigated in Trinidad and Tobago [28]. Researchers have reported an association between adolescents and adult use and depression appears to be a contributory factor.

Adolescents who attended a religious institution or prayed with their family more than seven times over a 6-month period had lower mean depression scores and lower rates of depression than their counterparts who never engaged in these activities. Although attendance to a religious institution resulted in a depression rate of 2% less than those who never attended it seems as though prayer with the family has a stronger effect on the rate of depression in adolescents, with the depression rate being 7.6% lower than those who never prayed with their family.

There were significant gender differences for adolescents who never attended a religious institution. Females had significantly higher mean depression scores compared to males (88.79 vs. 83.54). Attendance to church was useful to females who by so doing lowered their mean depression scores. Griffith and Bility have pointed out that identification with a religious group leads to higher levels of psychological and social integration and thus acts as a buffer to stress [29]. It seems that attendance to a religious institution can act as a protective factor against depression in adolescent girls. This is again supported in the study, where it was found that girls from prestige schools which are denominational and religion-centered are less depressed than boys but are more depressed in non-prestige, non-religious schools. The importance and meaning of prayer locally, was pointed out by Singh et al. who demonstrated a significance decrease in substance abuse among secondary school children who participated in religious worship [28].

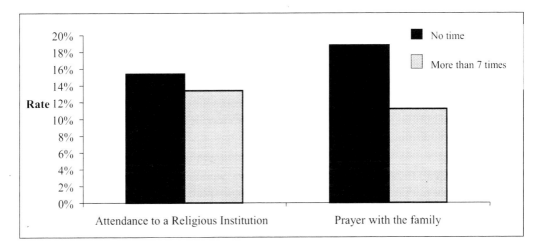

Figure 3. Depression and religious behavior

Type of school was also shown to significantly affect adolescent depression, with adolescents in non-prestige schools having a higher rate of depression than those from prestige schools (15.3% v. 11.5%) as shown in table 1. The composition of prestige schools in Trinidad and Tobago consist of students who are in the upper percentile group of academic achievers. Additionally, prestige schools in Trinidad and Tobago are mostly denominational in nature and smaller in size compared to non-prestige schools. Students in non-prestige schools face the additional stress of overcrowding, poor ventilation in classrooms and an increase in school violence which may add to their personal distress.

No differences were found between gender and ethnic groupings among Africans, Indians, Mixed and Others suffering from depression. Findings of ethnic differences with higher rates among Indo-Trinidadians in the adult population in Trinidad and Tobago are not seen in the adolescent population [30]. The adolescent school population remains a homogeneous group with decreased ethnic polarization or race thinking. Adolescent depression in Trinidad and Tobago appears to be unrelated to ethnicity. A consistent finding in the psychiatric epidemiology of adult depressive disorders is the gender differences. Varying rates however, have been reported for adolescents. In children, some studies report major depressive disorders occurring at almost the same rate in girls and boys, whereas in adolescents the female to male ratio mimics the adult figure of approximately 2:1 [23,31,32]. However, the literature on gender differences in the adolescent period remains confusing. Earlier studies have reported no differences between adolescent males and females [33-37]. This has been attributed to the differences in scale measurements [38] and inconsistencies due to the use of broad age categories [39].

Table 1. Trends in adolescent depression in Trinidad and Tobago

		Depression Rate (%)	Mean RADS	P
Age [a]	14	12.2	57.32	<0.05
	15	12.4	60.88	
	16	15.9	62.24	
	17	14.9	62.12	
	18	13.7	59.60	
	19	10.6	29.32	
	20	-	55.00	
Attendance to a religious institution [b]	No time	15.4	62.43	<0.05
	More than 7 times	13.4	60.67	
Alcohol abuse present in family [b]	Yes	23.1	66.57	<0.001
	No	12.6	60.39	
Ethnicity [a]	African	12.6	60.96	NS
	Indian	13.2	60.97	
	Mixed	17.4	62.05	
	Other	11.8	60.21	
Family Structure [a]	Intact	11.7	59.79	<0.001
	One Parent	13.5	62.28	
	Single Stepparent	16.7	62.83	
	Reconstituted	25.7	67.00	
	With relatives	22.6	64.79	
Gender [a]	Male	8.2	57.31	<0.001
	Female	17.9	63.88	
Prayer with family [b]	No time	18.8	63.74	<0.001
	More than 7 times	11.2	58.68	
Type of School [b]	Prestige	11.5	60.02	<0.01
	Non-prestige	15.3	61.88	

[a] ANOVA; [b] t-test; NS not significant

Studies on preadolescent school children consistently report that depression is higher among boys than girls [40-42]. A study of elementary school children up to the age of 12 identified higher levels of depressive symptomatology among boys than girls of the same age [43]. In a well-designed longitudinal study, Hankin et al. [44] followed a complete birth cohort from preadolescence to early adulthood. They found that the differences in the male-female ratio in major depressive disorders begin to emerge between the ages of 13-15 with maximum gender differences occurring between the ages of 15 and 18. Angold et al. have likewise identified the gender gap at about 13 years [41]. In a Swedish study of 2,300 high school students aged 16-17 years screened for depression, girls suffered two times more than boys for dysthymia and four times more from major depression [25]. The gender gap for depression that is the switch from high rates of depression from boys to girls in the adolescent period was found to be 15 years of age.

A number of factors have been attributed to gender differences in depression among adolescents. These are an inherited predisposition, an increase of anxiety disorders in females, pubertal changes, cognitive predisposition, socio-cultural factors and family environment [45-48]. The female preponderance of depression has been attributed to the social roles of marriage, unpaid employment, economic discrimination at the work place and the cultural

Depression in Trinidad and Tobago: Incidence and Social Trends 293

determinants of role definitions, role strain and value in society [18]. These factors however, are not important in the adolescent period where risky and problematic behaviors, family dysfunction, sexual indiscretion and pregnancy, eating disorders, alcohol and drug use, defiance and rebellion and poor self-esteem with problems of identity are pervasive.

In comparing depression rates for the Trinidadian adolescents (14.6%) to those found in Tobagonian adolescents (10.1%) the rates of depression were significantly different, with adolescents in Tobago being 1.5 times more likely not to be depressed compared to Trinidadian adolescents [17]. These rates are directly comparable to the Tobago study as the Reynolds Adolescent Depression Scale (RADS) was utilized as the depression instrument. The depression rate for Trinidad is higher due to the fact that in comparison to Tobago, it is multicultural, has a much larger population, is more industrialized and has a more hectic and demanding lifestyle with race thinking and crime pervasive. Tobago has a low average rate for depression when compared to other developing countries and cultures. A possible explanation for the low rates could be the presence of a well-integrated Christian-based society devoid of multiculturalism. Culture, however, does not seem to play a part in adolescent depression in Tobago. Table 1 summarise the major trends found in adolescent depression in Trinidad and Tobago.

CONCLUSION

This compilation of two studies on adolescent depression in Trinidad and Tobago provides important findings which should be considered invaluable in terms of both the treatment and the prevention of depression among adolescents in these countries. The following contributory factors have been identified as having an effect on depression in adolescents in Trinidad and Tobago: female gender, middle adolescence (age 16 years), being either in a reconstituted family or living with relatives, having alcohol abuse present in the family, no attendance to a religious institution or praying with the family and attending a non-prestige school. The significant difference in depression between Trinidad and Tobago sets the stage for further investigation of socio-cultural factors in adolescent depression. It is also suggested that future research should be directed towards any possible interactional effects between variables that may contribute towards the presentation of depression in adolescents. Since the management of adolescent depression affects the outcome in adulthood, an understanding of early depression in diverse communities will be helpful in reducing the global burden of common diseases.

REFERENCES

[1]   Kazdin A. Conduct disorders in childhood and adolescence. Beverly Hills, CA: Sage, 1987.

[2]   Rutter M. The developmental psychopathology of depression: issues and perspectives. In: Rutter M, Izard CE, Read PB, eds. Depression in young people: Developmental and clinical perspectives. New York: Guilford, 1986.

[3]   Weissman MM, Wolk S, Goldstein RB, Moreau D, Adams P, Greenwald S, Klier CM, Ryan ND, Dahl RE, Wickramaratne P. Depressed adolescents grow up. JAMA 1999;281(18):1707-13.

[4]   Reber AS. The Penguin dictionary of psychology. Toronto, ON: Penguin, 1995.

[5] Beck AT, Ward CH, Mendelsohn M, Mack J, Erbaugh J. An inventory for measuring depression. Arch Gen Psychitr 1961; 4:561-71.

[6] McGrath E, Keita GP, Strickland BR, Russo NF. Women and depression. Washington DC: Am Psychol Assoc, 1990.

[7] Olsson G, von Knorring AL. Depression among Swedish adolescents measured by the Self-rating Scale Center for Epidemiologic Studies - Depression Child (CES-DC). Europ Child Adol Psychiatry 1997;6(2): 81-7.

[8] Canton G, Gallimberti L, Gentille N, Ferrara SD. L'ideazione di suicidio nell'adolescenza: prevalenza in un campione di studenti e relazione con i sintomi psichiatrici [Suicidal ideation during adolescence: Prevalence in a student sample and its relationship with psychiatric symptoms]. Rivista di Psichiatria 1989;24:102-7. [Italian]

[9] Stavrakaki C, Caplan-Williams E, Walker S, Roberts N, Kotsopoulos S. Pilot study of anxiety and depression in pubertal children. Can J Psychiatry 1991;36:332-8.

[10] Ollendick TH, Yule W. Depression in British and American children and its relation to anxiety and fear. J Consult Clin Psychology 1990; 58:126-9.

[11] Dong Q, Yang B, Ollendick TH. Fears in Chinese children and adolescents and their relations to anxiety and depression. J Child Psychology Psychiatry 1994;35:351-63.

[12] Shek DTL. Depressive symptoms in a sample of Chinese adolescents: An empirical study using the Chinese version of the Beck Depression Inventory. Int J Adol Med Health 1991;5:1-16.

[13] Boyd CP, Gullone E, Kostanski M, Ollendick TH, Shek DTL. Prevalence of anxiety and depression in Australian adolescents: comparison with world wide data. J Gen Psychology 2000;161(4): 479-92.

[14] Berganza CE, Aguilar G. Depression in Guatemalan adolescents. Adolescence 1992;27(108):771-83.

[15] Maharajh HD, Montane-Jaime LK. The Caroni County study, Trinidad. Incidence and socio-demographic characteristics of mental illness. WIMJ 1998;47(Suppl: 26.

[16] Maharajh HD, Ali A Adolescent depression in Trinidad and Tobago. Eur Child Adolesc Psychiatry 2006;15(1):30-7.

[17] Maharajh HD, Ali A. Adolescent depression in Tobago. Int J Adolesc Med Health 2004;16(4):337-42.

[18] Piccinelli M, Wilkinson G. Gender differences in depression. Br J Psychiatry 2000;177:486-92.

[19] Fergusson DM, Woodward LJ, Horwood LJ. Risk factors and life processes associated with the onset of suicidal behavior during adolescence and early adulthood. Psychol Medicine 2000;30:23-9.

[20] Wilheim K, Parker G, Hadzi-Pavlovic D. Fifteen years on: evolving ideas in researching sex differences in depression. Psychol Med 1997; 27: 875-83.

[21] Cichetti D, Toth SL. The development of depression in children and adolescents. Am Psychologist 1998;53:221-41.

[22] Piko BF, Fitzpatrick KM. Depressive symptomatology among Hungarian youth: a risk and protective factors approach. Am J Orthopsychiatry 2003;73(1):44-54.

[23] Fleming JE, Offord DR. Epidemiology of childhood depressive disorders: a critical review. J Am Acad Child Adolesc Psychiatry 1990;29:571-80.

[24] Garnefski N, Diekstra RF. Adolescents from one parent, step-parent and intact families: emotional problems and suicide attempts. J Adolesc 1997;20:201-8.

[25] Olsson GI, von Knorring AL. Adolescent depression: prevalence in Swedish high-school students. Acta Psychiatr Scand 1999;99(5): 324-31.

[26] Formoso D, Gonzales NA, Aiken LS. Family conflict and children's internalizing and externalizing behaviour: protective factors. Am J Comm Psychol 2000;28:175-99.

[27] Lease SH. A model of depression in adult children of alcoholics and non-alcoholics. J Counsel Dev 2000;80(4):441-52.

[28] Singh H, Maharajh HD, Shipp H. Pattern of substance abuse among secondary school students in Trinidad and Tobago. Public Health 1991;105(6):435-41.

[29] Griffith EEH, Bility KM. Psychosocial factors and the genesis of new African-American religious groups. In: Bhugra D, ed. Psychiatry and religion. Context, consensus and controversies. London: Routledge, 1996.

[30] Maharajh HD, Parasram R. The practice of psychiatry in Trinidad and Tobago. Int Rev Psychiatry 1999;11:173-83.

Depression in Trinidad and Tobago: Incidence and Social Trends

[31] Kessler RC, McGonagle KA, Nelson CB, Hughes M, Swartz M, Blazer DG. Sex and depression in the national co-morbidity survey: II. Cohort effects. J Affect Disord 1994;30:15-26.

[32] Lewinsohn PM, Clarke GN, Seeley JR, Rohde P. Major depression in community adolescents: age at onset, episode duration, and time to recurrence. J Am Acad Child Adolesc Psychiatry 1994;33: 809-18.

[33] Baron P, Joly E. Sex differences in the expression of depression in adolescents. Sex Roles 1988;18:1-7.

[34] Friedrich WN, Reams R, Jacobs JH. Depression and suicidal ideation in early adolescents. J Youth Adolesc 1982;11:403-7.

[35] Jacobson R, Benjamin BL, Strauss CC. Correlates of depressed mood in normal children. J Abnorm Child Psychol 1983;11:29-40.

[36] Mitchell J, McCauley E, Burke P, Calderon R, Schloerdt K. Psychopathology in parents of depressed children and adolescents. J Am Acad Child Adolesc Psychiatry 1989;28:352-7.

[37] Kaplan SL, Hong GK, Weenhold C. Epidemiology of depressive symptoms in adolescents. J Am Acad Child Adolesc Psychiatry 1984;23:91-8.

[38] Roberts RE, Chen Y-W. Depressive symptoms and suicidal ideation among Mexican-origin and Anglo adolescents. J Am Acad Child Adolesc Psychiatry 1995;34:81-90.

[39] Wade TJ, Cairney J, Pevalin DJ. Emergence of gender differences in depression during adolescence: national panel results from three countries. J Am Acad Child Adolesc Psychiatry 2002;41(2): 190-205.

[40] Anderson JC, Williams S, McGee R, Silva PA. DSM-III disorders in preadolescent children: prevalence in a large sample from the general population. Arch Gen Psychiatry 1987;44:69-76.

[41] Angold A, Costello EJ, Worthman CM. Puberty and depression: the roles of age, pubertal status and pubertal timing. Psychol Med 1998; 28:51-61.

[42] Nolen-Hoeksema S, Girgus JS, Seligman ME. Sex differences in depression and explanatory style in children. J Youth Adolesc 1991;20:233-45.

[43] Nolen-Hoeksema S, Girgus JS, Seligman MEP. Predictors and consequences of childhood depressive symptoms: A 5 –year longitudinal study. J Abnorm Psychol 1992;101:405-22.

[44] Hankin BL, Abramson LY, Moffitt TE, Silva PA, McGee R, Angell KE. Development of depression from preadolescence to young adulthood: emerging gender differences in a 10-year longitudinal study. J Abnorm Psychol 1998;107:128-40.

[45] Breslau N, Schultz L, Peterson E. Sex differences in depression: a role for preexisting anxiety. Psychiatry Res 1995;58:1-12.

[46] Reinherz HZ, Giaconia RM, Lefkowitz ES, Pakiz B, Frost AK. Prevalence of psychiatric disorders in a community population of older adolescents. J Am Acad Child Adolesc Psychiatry 1993;32: 369-77.

[47] Rutter M. Age changes in depressive disorders: some developmental considerations. In: Garber J, Dodge KA, eds. The development of emotion regulation and dysregulation. New York: Cambridge Univ Press, 1991.

[48] Birmaher B, Ryan ND, Williamson DE, Brent DA, Kaufman J, Dahl RE, et al. Childhood and adolescent depression: A review of the past 10 years. J Am Acad Child Adolesc Psychiatry 1996;35(11): 1427-39.

In: Social and Cultural Psychiatry Experience from the...
Editor: Hari D. Maharajh and Joav Merrick

ISBN: 978-1-61668-506-5
© 2010 Nova Science Publishers, Inc.

Chapter 27

SCHIZOPHRENIA REVISITED: CONSENSUS AND CONFUSION

Hari D. Maharajh

There is no consensus on the rates of schizophrenia among ethnic groups at home in the Caribbean and abroad. Investigations of gender and ethnic differences on the rates of first contact outpatients with schizophrenia in two geographically different areas in Trinidad are reported. In a prospective study, 134 first contact patients with a diagnosis of schizophrenia were selected from two catchment areas in East and Central Trinidad. Almost fifty seven percent (56.7%) of the tested population was of African origin, 32.1% of Indian descent. Gender differences were significant with males accounting for 66.4 % (n= 89) of patients with schizophrenia (Chi-square = 14.448, df = 1, p = 0.0001). Further analysis by age categories revealed significant male predominance at the 20-24 (p = 0.0001) and 25-29 (p= 0.002) age groups. There was a predominance of young African males.(15-19 years, p = 0.049) in the East compared to Central. The findings revealed an excess of Afro-Trinidadian men in both outpatient clinics (p< 0.05).

INTRODUCTION

Within the Caribbean, the majority of studies conducted have reported that significantly more males present with schizophrenia than females. In Trinidad and Tobago, in a cohort of first admissions to an outpatient psychiatric clinic, schizophrenia was reported to be twice as common in males when compared to females (16.2% vs 8.2%, p<0.01) [1]. A similar trend of male preponderance in schizophrenia in Trinidad (75%) was reported by a British researcher [2].

In Jamaica, a study of the incidence of first-contact schizophrenia reported a significant gender difference with more men presenting with schizophrenia compared to women in the age group 20-29 years (p< 0.000001) [3]. Mahy's study in Barbados [4] was the only Caribbean study that reported no significant gender differences in schizophrenia with males accounting for 58% of all cases. There seem to be no consensus on gender differences in age-related onset of schizophrenia in the Caribbean region. This may not be surprising when the ethnic compositions of the islands are taken into consideration.

Internationally, The World Health Organization (WHO) ten-country study on schizophrenia has reported that the cumulated risk for males and females up to age 54 years were approximately equal [5]. Population studies of the older age groups have consistently reported higher cumulative lifetime risk in women than in men [6,7]. Recent findings have suggested that gender differences in schizophrenia vary in rates, age of onset, symptoms and course of illness [8-12]. A systematic review has confirmed that most studies show higher rates among males in the first onset of schizophrenia with a median male: female ratio of 1.4 : 1.0 [8]. Similarly, in a meta-analysis, Aleman et al. (2003) found that the mean risk ratio was 1.32 for males with no sex differences reported in studies from developing countries. These reports suggest that the gender ratio in schizophrenia is not equal with an age specific incidence higher in men until 35 years, an inversion of the male-female ratio over forty and increasing even more after the age of sixty [13]. The increase male rates of younger age groups together with the increase female rates of the over forty age group presents a nicely parceled summative male female ratio of 1:1

In schizophrenic outpatients, reports of gender differences with a male: female ratio of 2:1 has been reported [14,15]. In Saudi Arabia, males were more frequently admitted from outpatient clinics for schizophrenia [16] In India, no differences between ages of onset were found between the sexes, with a survival analysis of subjects having a documented date of birth revealing a female preponderance at younger ages [17]. The latter is not surprising, since within the Caribbean, young black men present with paranoid schizophrenia often associated with drug use resulting in skewing of this population while Indo-Trinidadians of both genders tend to present with disorganized schizophrenia.

Studies in the Caribbean region have not reported high rates of schizophrenia among ethnic groups within the islands [2-4]. Higher rates among Afro-Caribbean have been reported in the Netherlands [18] and United Kingdom [19]. In the latter population, schizophrenia is present more than 8 to 13 times higher in the black when compared to the white British population.

The purpose of this chapter is to investigate the gender and ethnic differences in age categorized rates of schizophrenia in two catchment areas in Trinidad These findings are interpreted within the local setting and are compared to regional and international findings.

OUR STUDY

The data were collected from two well-defined catchment areas geographically located in north east and central Trinidad. The north eastern region is a more urbanized region situated in the county of St George's East and has a population of approximately 220,000 people mostly of African descent (Africans 55 %, Indians 30 %, mixed and others 15 %). St George's East represents 18 % of the country's population with the inhabitants employed in the civil service, government projects and manufacturing industries. In this area the population density is 324 persons per km².

The central sector lies in County Caroni and during the time of this study was the base of the sugarcane industry. It is a less urbanized region situated in the agricultural belt, with a population of 193.500 people, mostly of Indian origin (Indian 70 %, African 20 % and mixed and others 10 %). This comprises approximately 13 % of the country's population. Recently there has been some progress in industrialization and business. The population density in this region is 264 persons per km².

Trinidad and Tobago has a population of 1.3 million people with a female: male ratio of 1.01:1.00. The ethnic composition is 40.3 % Indo-Trinidadian, 39.6 % Afro-Trinidadian, 18.4% mixed and 1.7 % others [20]. The Afro-Trinidadian group is the socially dominant group, while the Indo-Trinidadian population is involved in agriculture, agro-based industries and business.

The data were collected from the two out-patient clinics over a period of four calendar years from January 2000 till December 2003. All first contact patients attending the two sector clinics were screened and interviewed. The inclusion criteria were a modification of those used in the Determinance of Outcome study [21] and included at least 6 months residence in the catchment area, first lifetime contact with any helping agency, and a diagnosis determined by psychiatric symptoms that fulfill a DSM-IV-R diagnosis [22]. The exclusion criteria included those who had previous contact with the psychiatric services, those with a current or past history of substance abuse and those with an onset of illness more than one year. Only patients between the ages of 15-54 were selected for this study, based on the finding that 90% of the patients in treatment for schizophrenia are between 15 and 55 years old [12].

Each patient who attended the outpatient clinic was seen by a psychiatrist and registered into the database for first contacts for that year. Epidemiological data of age, gender and ethnicity were rated for each patient. Ethnicity was assigned to patients on the basis of three or more grandparents belonging to the same race.

Two consultant psychiatrists were responsible for the interviewing and the diagnosing of the patients. Diagnoses were made using the criteria of the DSM-IV-R classification for schizophrenia. Both psychiatrists are attached to the clinics, and made repeated visits to verify the reliability of diagnoses. All diagnoses from the first contact database were validated by both psychiatrists through the case notes before being accepted for this study.

All data were entered and analyzed by the use of SPSS (Statistical Package for the Social Sciences, Version 11.0). The data of the Eastern and Central regions were cumulatively and independently analyzed. Six categories of age groupings were utilized namely 15-19, 20-24, 25-29, 30-34, 35-49 and 50-54 years. Analyses were done for each of the age group at the two different out patient clinics and the total population.

OUR FINDINGS

During a four-year period, a total of 134 new patients were identified as meeting the inclusion criteria of which 56.7 % were of African origin, 32.1 % of Indian origin and 11.2 % of mixed or other origins. The mean age of patients was 30.65 with a standard deviation of 9.98 in the range of 17 years to 54 years. The median was 29 years.

In the studied population, significant gender differences in patients with schizophrenia were found with males accounting for 66.4% (n = 89), Chi-square = 14.448, df = 1, p=0.0001 of the total population. These significant gender differences were maintained for schizophrenia at the ages of 20-24 years (Chi-square = 12.448, df = 1, p=0.0001) and 25-29 years (Chi-square = 9.783, df = 1, p=0.002). No other age categories had significant gender differences (see figure 1). There was a tendency of decreased numbers of males at the later ages, without a statistically significant predominance of females. Between the ages of 35 to 44 more females presented with schizophrenia with equal gender rates at 50 to 54 years.

Table 1. Demographics on both outpatient clinics

Demographics	North eastern clinic	Central clinic
Males (%)	69.0	62.0
Females (%)	31.0	38.0
Age, mean	29.29	32.98
African	63.1	46.0
Indian	26.2	42.0
Mixed and other	10.7	12.0

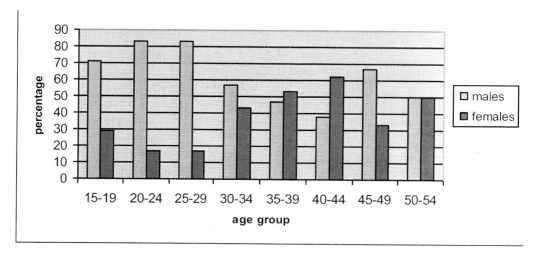

Age group 20–24: p = 0.000; Age group 25–29: p = 0.002

Figure 1. Gender and age groups in total population

Clinic- North Eastern Trinidad

The patients of this clinic in north eastern Trinidad comprised of 63.1 % of African origin, 26.2 % of Indian descent, 9.5 % mixed and 1.2 % other (Table 1). The mean age of this group was 29.29 with a range of 17 to 54 (SD 9.83) and median of 27 years. Males accounted for 69.0 % (n=58) and females 31.0% (n=26) of the total population, reflecting a gender difference of a statistically significant male predominance (Chi-square=12.190, df = 1, p= 0.0001). In an analysis of age categories, significant male gender differences were found at the age groups of 15 to 19 (Chi-square = 4.000, df = 1, p = 0.046), 20 to 24 (Chi-square = 9.800, df = 1, p = 0.002) and 25 to 29 (Chi-square = 5.400, df=1, p= 0.020). There was no significant predominance of females at later ages, (Chi-square = 0.667, df = 1, p = 0.414), though there was a trend of more females presenting with schizophrenia at the age category of 50-54 years (see figure 2).

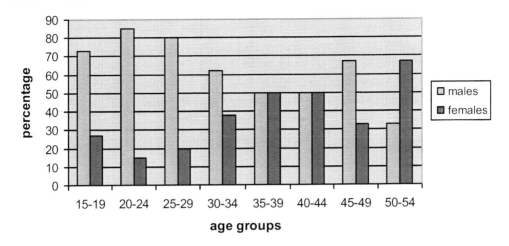

Age group 15-19: p = 0.046; Age group 20-24: p = 0.002; Age group 25-29: p= 0.020

Figure 2. Gender and age groups in North Eastern Trinidad

Clinic-Central region

The ethnic composition of patients at the Central clinic was 46.0 % of African descent, 42.0% of Indian origin, 8.0 % of mixed and 4.0 % other races. (see table 1). The mean age of this group was 32.98 with a range of 17 to 53 (SD 9.90) and the median of 32 years of age. There were gender differences with males accounting for 62 % (n=31) and females 38 % (n=19) of the population. The overall predominance of males was not statistically significant (Chi-square =2.880, df= 1, p= 0.090). In an analysis of different age categories, significant male gender predominance was found at the age group of 25 to 29 years (Chi-square = 4.5000, df = 1, p= 0.034). There was no predominance of females at the later age groups (see figure 3).

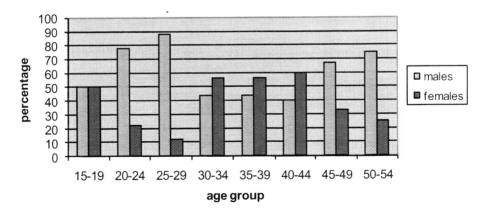

Age group 25-29: p = 0.020

Figure 3. Gender and age groups in Central Trinidad

DISCUSSION

Over a four–year period of 2000 to 2003, a total of 134 patients who met the inclusion criteria for schizophrenia were seen in two geographical regions in Trinidad. In the more urbanized north eastern region, 84 patients sought treatment while in the less urbanized central region 50 patients presented themselves for treatment for schizophrenia. Those seeking treatment were mostly of African (58.6%) and Indian origins (34.5%).

There was a cumulative predominance of the male gender. Males accounted for 60.7% of all patients with schizophrenia (Chi-square = 6.628, df=1, p= 0.01). These findings are supported by previous research in the Caribbean region that have reported higher rates of schizophrenia in men than in women [1-3,23] Amongst women, there was no significant peak of female predominance after the age of 40 years, as reported by Sajatovic et al [6].However, there was a non-significant trend of more women presenting with schizophrenia at later ages.

In both catchment areas, first contact of male patients with schizophrenia was maximal between the age groups of 20-24 and 25-29 years (p<0.01 and p=0.002 respectively). This significant overrepresentation at these specific age categories was also found in Jamaica [3], but differed from North American findings that have reported a predominance of males between the ages of 15 to 25 years [24]. A statistically significant difference of first contact male schizophrenic patients was found in the age categories of 15-19 and 20-24 years in the African population suggesting an earlier presentation in this ethnic grouping.

There are a number of explanations for the higher risk of schizophrenia in this young age group living in a more urbanized area. These are: place of upbringing [25], unemployment, social isolation and exposure to viral infections [26] level of urbanicity [18,27] noise pollution, safety factors, divorce and crime in the urban environment [28] neighbourhood socioeconomic deprivation [29] and cannabis use [30-34]. In addition, changes in neighbourhood ecology due to the building of housing estates in established communities will have an adverse effect on mental health.

In the population of both regions, more males between the ages of 20 and 29 presented with schizophrenia. The percentages of males in both groups are about equal, 69% in the North east compared to 62 % in the Central region. The county of Caroni (Central region) has a population of mostly Indian origin (70%) and 20% of African descent. The North-eastern sector located in the county of St George's East has a population of approximately 55% of African descent and 30% of Indian origin. In the Central Region 46% of the patient population is of African origin and 42% of Indian descent. Similarly, in the East these percentages were 63 % African and 26 % Indo-Trinidadian respectively. In both these regions this difference was significantly more than expected (Central: t = 13.3, df = 49, p= < 0.05; East: t = 0.77, df = 83, p < 0.05). These findings suggest that there is a high rate of Afro-Trinidadian males presenting with schizophrenia in the outpatient clinics regardless of the ethnic composition of the base population. Many researchers have shown an elevated rate of psychosis among the Afro-Caribbean in London and have concluded that the elevated risk may be due to environmental factors [2, 19, 34, 35].

Our findings are keeping with that of Selten et al [18] in Suriname, who have reported lower rates of schizophrenia among people of East Indian origin. This interesting finding of the low rates of Indo-Trinidadians who sought treatment in both the East and Central notwithstanding the ethnic composition of these regions finds less favour with environmental factors. It is unlikely that they sought treatment privately since a similar trend is observed in private practice in these regions.

Another contribution to the higher prevalence of males can be the factor of crime. There has been an increase in serious crime in Trinidad and Tobago over the past few years. The numbers of murders in Trinidad and Tobago at the time of this study (2004) were increased by almost 15% compared with the previous year. The perpetrators are reportedly youths between the ages of 16 and 22 years and the majority of victims are also from that same age group [36]. In an analysis of murder rates by counties for 2004, there were twice as many murders in the northeastern region (15%) when compared to the central region (8%). Kidnapping and the fear of crime is more pervasive in the central region. Perceptions of safety and vulnerability are therefore present in both populations with a preponderance of predictable drug-related gang violence in the north and random kidnapping with non-ransom murder in the central region. Crime in these regions are unrelated to urbanization but to the endemic cultural pattern of substance use, that is, marijuana and cocaine being the drug of choice of Afro-Trinidadians while alcohol use is high among Indo-Trinidadians.

Lifestyle, family structure and cultural norms are important variables. The predominance of Afro-Trinidadian patients in this study may be due to differential cultural and familial practices. Children of African families are exposed at an earlier age to the social environment than children of Indian origin; the Indian family being culturally more protective and goal oriented. The implication is therefore, that children of African origin living in any area are more likely to be exposed at a younger age to negative environmental factors which can increase their risk of developing psychosis or schizophrenia. Our findings in Trinidad, suggest that Afro-Trinidadians with schizophrenia are overrepresented in both catchment areas. These findings are difficult to interpret on the basis of environmental causation since differential rates were found for female gender and ethnic groupings. These findings may be best interpreted by the presence of neuro-protective factors of a genetic or physiological nature. The protective nature of estrogen in females could be responsible for their low rates of schizophrenia and the ability of female to adapt more readily to change. Neuronal plasticity in response to exposure to a new environment and its effects on the disease process is another area of interest that may help in solving this conundrum.

The finding in the central region of no gender differences is interesting and invites discussion on genetic predisposition, a mostly avoided and controversial issue. A meta-analysis of twin studies demonstrated a genetic effect in 88% of all patients with schizophrenia with only 12% attributed to environmental factors [37].

As mentioned above, both regions showed an over representation of Afro-Trinidadians. An analysis of rates among Indo-Trinidadians in both catchment areas, cumulatively and independently did not substantiate an excess of females presenting for the first admission. This finding differs from the results presented [17] in India that reported no differences between age of onset between the sexes and a female preponderance at younger ages. A possible explanation may be differences in presentation of the group of schizophrenic illnesses. Males of African origin seem to present at a younger age with paranoid schizophrenia while females of Indian descent present in later life with disorganized schizophrenia.

It is apparent that there is no international consensus on the socio-demographic factors of schizophrenia with a reign of confusion. There are many explanations: Schizophrenia, as is diagnosed today, is not a homogenous disease but a group of illnesses subdivided into five major categories as indicated in the DSM-TR [38]. It appears as though social and cultural factors may play a role in the presentation of the type of schizophrenia, for example in Trinidad and Tobago with an equal distribution of African and Indian descendents, paranoid schizophrenia is more common among the African population. The author has argued that paranoid schizophrenia does not fit into the other DSM subtypes and should be removed as a classification, noting its association with drugs and chronic stress factors. This will remove the over arching representation of Africans with schizophrenia thereby sanitizing the classification.

Cultural concepts enshrined in Caribbean humor, pathos and literary works have captured the confusion surrounding schizophrenia. Caribbean papers have been published on 'Roast Breadfruit Psychosis' [39] and 'Afro-Saxon Psychosis or Cultural Schizophrenia in African-Caribbeans' [40]. Following the 'windrush' of 300,000 West Indians who migrated to Britain between 1951-1961, little consideration was given to the negative factors of acculturation and assimilation into a new society, but emphasis was placed on the processes of social ascendancy, prestige and respectability. The new 'Afro-Saxons' adopted, absorbed and internalized the values of the White colonial masters. This was a natural phenomenon, since post colonization, the black ruling elites of the Caribbean who perceived them to be the natural inheritors of the British Empire pursued the norms of respectability and honor of the White man and aspired for acceptance.

The effects of colonization and emigration have been captured by authors, poets, writers, calypsonians and politicians. Nobel prize recipient Vidya Naipaul writes on the stilted schizophasic speech of Trinidadians who have never left the island:

"Everybody on Miguel Street said that Man-man was mad, and so they left him alone, but I am not sure that now that he was mad and I can think of many people much madder than Man-man was...That again was another mystery about Man-man. His accent, if you shut your eyes while he spoke, you will believe an Englishman- a good class Englishman who wasn't particular about grammar-was talking to you' [41].

Similarly, Samuels Selvon's 1956 novel "The lonely Londoners," captured the feelings and aspirations of West Indian immigrants in Britain [42]. He portrayed psychological conflicts of a rootless community, having given up the comfort and security of the past, struggling for acceptance and recognition in a new, exciting and hostile environment. Selvon's Harris with his bowler hat and copy of The Times cannot be diagnosed as suffering from cultural schizophrenia.

From experiences in Britain, the author of this chapter has proposed a theory of Borderline Cultural State as a prodrome to psychosis. In a comparison of two groups of patients attending outpatient clinics in London, he observed an excess of psychosis in the West Indian population compared to the Asian population. He noted the drive of those of West Indian descent for social assimilation into the greater society, while people of Asian origin were for the most part contented to have association for economic reasons. The West Indian had given up his history, identity and culture and attempted to adopt that of the Englishman and faced rejection. This practice resulted in a Borderline Cultural State where individuals had difficulties in the conceptualization of the culture they belonged to, living in two worlds at the same time hating one and rejected by the other.

The concept of urban lethality in disease causation is a complex one. Van Os [43] proposes that the urban environment with a set of environmental factors acting between birth and the onset of illness is a risk factor in the causation of psychotic illness. Lethality in any environment, albeit urban or rural will be determined by the stability of the social framework that governs the lives of individuals and the opportunities available. There are less opportunities for individuals in rural areas. In the Caribbean, social parameters of disadvantage are racism, alienation, political discrimination, unemployment, lack of opportunity, crime and fear of crime and substance abuse. These factors are present both in urban and rural areas and there is no rural beneficence in societies so possessed and many from country areas opt to escape through migration to foreign lands. It is also difficult to resolve why there is a lower incidence of schizophrenia in Indo-Trinidadian men who are considered to be more socially disadvantaged by the superimposition and paramount of an Afro-Caribbean lifestyle. Social disadvantage must be interpreted in the dynamics of stress, resistance and ego structure. It seems as though Indo-Trinidadians operate better with conflicts.

CONCLUSION

In this chapter, an analysis of the variables of gender and ethnicity in two ecologically contrasting regions has provided some insight into gene-environmental interaction and the lethality of urban or beneficence of rural factors. The question whether genetically-determined personal characteristics or social and environmental factors are responsible for disease causation remains unanswered and undetermined. With respect to schizophrenia, Trinidad, with almost equal numbers of people of African origin and Indian descent provided an ideal opportunity to study the ethnic and gender presentation of this illness. Indians appear to be less constitutional prone to schizophrenia than their African brothers. The input of genetic or environmental influences needs further investigation. What is quite certain is that there is little consensus with an abundance of confusion both regionally and internationally. The problems may well lie in the sub-typing of schizophrenia with too much emphasis on paranoid behaviour and its confusion with personality types and drug abuse among young people in developing countries.

REFERENCES

[1]   Hilwig MM, Maharajh HD. Patterns of first admissions in a psychiatric outpatient clinic in Trinidad. West Indian Med J 1992; 41(Suppl 1):65-6.

[2]   Bhugra D, Hilwig M, Hossein B, et al. Incidence of Schizophrenia in Trinidad. Br J Psychiatry 1996;169(15):587-92.

[3]   Hickling F, Rodgers-Johnson P. The incidence of first contact schizophrenia in Jamaica. Br J Psychiatry 1995;167:193-6.

[4]   Mahy G, Mallett R, Leff J, Bhugra D. Schizophrenia in Barbados. Br J Psychiatry 1999;175:28-33.

[5]   World Health Organization. International pilot study of schizophrenia. Vol. 1. Geneva: WHO, 1973.

[6]   Sajatovic M, Sultana D, Bingham CR, Buckley P, Donenwirth K. Gender related differences in clinical characteristics and hospital based resource utilization among older adults with schizophrenia. Int J Geriatr Psychiatry 2002;17(6):542-8.

[7]   Helgason T, Magnusson H. The First 80 years of life. A psychiatric epidemiological study. Acta Psychiatr Scand 1989;348(Suppl):85-94.

[8] McGrath J, Saha S, Welham, J, El Saadi O, MacCauley C, Chant D. A systematic review of the incidence of schizophrenia: the distribution of rates and the influence of sex, urbanicity, migrant status and methodology. BMC Medicine 2004;2:13.

[9] Aleman A, Kahn RS, Sultan JP. Sex differences in the risk of schizophrenia: evidence from meta-analysis. Arch Gen Psychiatry 2003;60:565-71.

[10] Halbreich U, Kahn LS. Hormonal aspects of schizophrenias: an overview. Psychoneuroendocrinol 2003;28(Suppl 2):1-16.

[11] Moriatry PJ, Lieber D, Bennett A, White L, Parella M, Harvey PD, et al. Gender differences in poor outcome patients with lifelong schizophrenia. Schizophr Bull 2001;27:103-13.

[12] Kaplan HI, Saddock BJ. Concise textbook of clinical psychiatry. Philadelphia, PA: Lippincott Williams Wilkins, 1996; 121-38.

[13] Jablensky A. Epidemiology of schizophrenia. In: Gelder MG, López-Ibor JJ, Andreasen N, eds. New Oxford textbook of psychiatry. Oxford: Oxford Univ Press, 2000:590-1.

[14] Usall J, Araya S, Ochoa S, Busquets E, Gost A, Marquez M, Assessment Research Group in Schizophrenia (NEDES). Gender differences in a sample of schizophrenic outpatients. Comprehen Psychiatry 2001;42(4):301-5.

[15] Usall J, Ochoa S, Araya S, Gost A, Busquets E, Assessment Research Group in Schizophrenia (NEDES). Symptomatology and gender in schizophrenia. Actas Espanol Psiquiatrica 2000;28(4):219-23. [Spanish]

[16] AbuMadini MS, Rahim SI. Psychiatric admission in a general hospital. Patients profile and patterns of service utilization over a decade. Saudi Med J 2002;23(1):44-50.

[17] Murthy GV, Janakiramaiah N, Gangadhar BN, Subbakrishna DK. Sex difference in age at onset of schizophrenia: discrepant findings from India. Acta Psychiatr Scand 1998;97(5):321-5.

[18] Selten JP, Zeyl C, Dwarkasing R, Lumsden V, Kahn RS, van Harten PN. First-contact incidence of schizophrenia in Surinam. Br J Psychiatry 2005;186:74-5.

[19] Sharpley M, Hutchinson G, McKenzie K, Murray RM. Understanding the excess of psychosis among the African-Caribbean population in England. Review of current hypotheses. Br J Psychiatry 2001;40: 60-8.

[20] Central Statistical Office. Trinidad and Tobago. [Online] 2009 [cited 2009 October 27]. Available from: htt://www.cso.gov.tt.

[21] Jablensky A, Sartorius N, Ernberg G, Anker M, Korten A, Cooper JE, et al. Schizophrenia: manifestations, incidence and course in different cultures. A World Health Organization ten country study. Psychol Med Monogr 1992; 20(Suppl):1-97.

[22] American Psychiatric Association. Cannabis related disorders. In: Quick reference to the diagnostic criteria for the DSM-IV-TR, text rev, Fourth ed. Washington DC: APA, 2000:127-9.

[23] Hutchinson G, Ramcharan C, Ghany K. Gender and ethnicity in first admissions to a psychiatric unit in Trinidad. West Indian Med J 2003; 52(4):300-3.

[24] Kaplan HI, Saddock J. Pocket Handbook of Clinical Psychiatry, 2001;

[25] Pederson CB, Agerlo E. National Centre for Register-Based Research. Aarhus, DK: Univ Aarhus.

[26] Marcelis M, Takei N, van Os J. Urbanization and risk for schizophrenia : does the effects operate before or around the time of illness onset? Psychol Med 1999;29:1197-1203.

[27] van Os J, Pederson CB, Mortenson PB. Confirmation of synergy between urbanicity and familial liability in the causation of psychosis. Am J Psychiatry 2004;161:2312-4.

[28] Bijl R, Van Zessen G, Ravelli A. Psychiatrische morbiditeit onder volwassenen in Nederland : het NEMESIS-onderzoek. II Prevalentie van Psychiatrische stoornissen. Nederlands tijdschrift van Geneeskunde 1997;166:2453-60. [Dutch]

[29] Drukker M, van Os J. Mediators of neighbourhood socioeconomic deprivation and quality of life. Soc Psychiatry Psychiatr Epidemiol 2003;38:698-706.

[30] Van Os J, Hanssen M, de Graf R, Vollebergh W. Does the urban environment independently increase the risk for both negative and positive features of psychosis? Soc Psychiatry Psychiatr Epidemiol 2002;37:460-4.

[31] Veen ND, Selten JP, van der Tweel I, Feller WG, Hoek HW Kahn RS. Cannabis use and age at onset of schizophrenia. Am J Psychiatry 2004;161:501-6.

[32] Stefanis NC, Delespaul P. Henquet C, Bakoula C, Stefanis CN, Van Os J. Early adolescent cannabis exposure and positive and negative dimensions of psychosis. Addiction 2004;99:1333-41.

[33] Smit F, Bolier L Cuijpers P.Cannabis use and the risk of later schizophrenia: A review. Addcition 2004;99:425-30.

[34] Bhugra D, Hilwig M, Mallett R, et al. Factors in the onset of schizophrenia : a comparison between London and Trinidad samples. Acta Psychiatr Scand 2000;101:135-41.

[35] Hutchinson G, Takei N, Fahy TA, et al. Morbid Risk of Schizophrenia in First/Degree Relatives of White and African-Caribbean Patients with Psychosis. Br J Psychiatry 1996;169:776-80.

[36] Balroop P. Killers on the loose! Frightening scenario for '05, 260 Murder Toll in '04 in: Sunday Guardian 2005 Jan 2.

[37] Van os J, Mc Guffin P. Can the social environment cause schizophrenia ? Br J Psychiatry 2003;182:291-2.

[38] American Psychiatric Association. Schizophrenia and other psychotic diorders. In: Quick reference to the diagnostic criteria for the DSM-IV-TR, text rev, Fourth ed. Washington DC: APA, 2000:153-65.

[39] Hickling FW, Hutchinson G. Roast breadfruit psychosis: Disturbed racial identification in African-Caribbeans. Psychiatr Bull 1999;23: 132-4.

[40] Maharajh HD. Afro-Saxon Psychosis or cultural schizophrenia in African Caribbeans? Psychiatr Bull 2000;24:96-7.

[41] Naipaul VS. Miguel street. London: Andre Deutsch, 1959.

[42] Selvon S. The lonely Londoners. Harlow: Longman, 1956.

[43] Van os J. Does the urban environment cause psychosis? Br J Psychiatry 2004;184:287-8.

In: Social and Cultural Psychiatry Experience from the... ISBN: 978-1-61668-506-5
Editor: Hari D. Maharajh and Joav Merrick © 2010 Nova Science Publishers, Inc.

Chapter 28

SOMATIZATION DISORDERS AMONG INDIANS IN JAMAICA AND TRINIDAD AND ITS ASSOCIATION WITH SOCIAL AND PSYCHOLOGICAL FACTORS

Astra Kassiram and Hari D. Maharajh

Data on presence of somatization disorder, depression, anxiety, distress, stigma associated with having somatic symptoms, having a female somatizing relative, a history of domestic violence, sexual abuse and the presence of an alcoholic spouse was collected from Indo Trinidadians and Indo Jamaicans. Within the entire sample elevated somatization was reported by 27.5% of the sample. Thirty percent (30%) had elevated scores for distress, 26% for depression, 10.5% for anxiety, and 15.5% gave a history of domestic violence, 7.5% reported stigma and 9% had a history of sexual abuse. Chi-square analyses revealed a significant moderate relationship exists between depression and somatization, there was a P value of .000 (Chi-square (1) = 45.580, p<0.05). There was also a significant relationship between somatization disorder and anxiety for the entire sample (Chi-square (1) = 22.710, p<0.00). A moderate relationship existed between somatization disorder and distress (Chi-square (1) = 28.691, p<0.00). A statistically significant relationship was found between somatization disorder and having a female relative with somatic symptoms, (Chi-square (1) = 9.391, p<0.002 and a significant relationship was found between persons feeling that they are weak or worth less than others if they have somatic symptoms and the presence of somatization disorder (Chi-square (1) = 8.591, p=0.03).

INTRODUCTION

Somatization has been variably defined as an unwillingness or inability to express emotional distress [1] the presentation of somatic complaints to medical providers in the presence of hidden anxiety and depression [2] and somatic symptoms with no clear medical explanation [3]. Mai [4] describes somatization as a condition in which "mental states and experiences are expressed as bodily symptoms."

Historical precedents of the term somatization include hysteria and Briquet's Syndrome [5] and after the inclusion of somatization disorder in the DSM-III R [6] in the 1980s, its use and study became more widespread. The ICD-10 and DSM-IV TR [7,8] classification systems define somatization disorder as a chronic condition characterized by the reporting of numerous unexplained pain, gastrointestinal, sexual and pseudoneurological symptoms, which started before age 30, persists for years, cannot be explained by a medical condition and have not been feigned. Somatization tends to have a long chronic course and results in the person seeking treatment for significant impairments in social, occupational, or other important areas of life [7,9,10].

Prevalence of somatization disorder ranges from 0.2 to 2% in females and 0.2% in males [7]. Kerry [10] stated that there are twenty females to every one male and the average age of onset is fifteen and the condition generally becomes full blown by the early twenties and then slowly and gradually improves, such that after the age of forty it has settled down, to perhaps less than 50% of what it was in the early twenties. The disorder can still flare up after the fifties and sixties, hence it is considered to be chronic in nature. Smith [11] estimates that 1% of all women in the United States possess symptoms of the disorder, and the estimated male-to-female ratio ranges between 5:1 and 20:1. Some psychiatrists think that the higher female-to-male ratio in this disorder reflects the cultural pressures on women in North American society and the social "permission" given to women to be physically weak and sickly. Somatization disorder rarely occurs in men in the United States of America, but the higher reported frequency in Greek and Puerto Rican men suggest that cultural factors may influence the sex ratio [7].

SOMATIZATION

This chapter investigates the prevalence of somatization disorder in an Indian Trinidadian and Indian Jamaican Population. It studies the relationship of somatization disorder with antecedents of depression, anxiety, distress, a female somatizing relative, a history of domestic violence, sexual abuse and the presence of an alcoholic spouse. The stigma associated with having somatic symptoms will also be investigated among the Indian population in both countries.

Cultural factors play an important part in somatization. Indeed Kirmayer and Young [12] noted that while somatization is present in all ethnic groups and societies studied, significant differences exist across groups. A cross national study of 14 countries revealed an overall of prevalence rate for somatization disorder of 0.9% which varied from 0% to 3.8%. Frequency of somatization averaged 19.7% but varied broadly from 7.6 to 36.8% [13].

Somatic symptoms have been variously described as "communicative acts" and "coded messages" which are conveyed in bodily terms by the individual who is having troubles in various areas of life [14, 15]. Somatic symptoms may be interpreted in many ways: as an index of disease, manifestation of intra-psychic conflict, cultural expression of distress or as an expression of social or personal discontent [12]. Thus it is the particular cultural stigma associated with expressing emotional distress that will determine how that distress will be expressed [15].

Western biomedical practice emphasizes a mind-body dualism which distinguishes between objective measures of disease and subjective reports of distress [12]. However the traditional theory and practice of Ayurvedic medicine in India is unitary and does not contain the same distinction between illness and disease as Western biomedicine. The concept of somatization as an illness unrelated to or different from disease does not exist since all distress (physical or mental) is considered significant [16].

It is assumed that Asian Americans somatize instead of "psychologize" or they tend to express psychological symptoms less than European Americans. Medical problems are thought to be less stigmatized than psychological problems and expression of an individual's feelings overtly is regarded as an admission of weakness, and therefore, socially undesirable. Thus, Asian Americans will manifest physical symptoms to avoid shame and maintain family honour because somatic complaints do not have the same social consequences as psychological complaints [17-19].

In an Indian population, researchers have reported that a significant number of all patients attending psychiatric clinics in developing countries have predominant somatic complaints [20]. The most frequent somatic complaint were pains in the head, abdomen, back, leg, neck, chest and shoulder. Other symptoms that were common were appetite and sleep disturbances, giddiness, distention in the abdomen, palpitations, constipation, weakness, a choking sensation and a sensation of heat in the body. But the most frequent complaints that were psychological in nature were feelings of sadness, feeling of nervousness and tension and lack of interest [20].

At the National Institute of Mental Health and Neurosciences in Bangalore, India, consultants felt that most of the Muslim population and in particular Muslim females, were presenting with peculiar somatic complaints such as; headaches, pain in all extremities and palpitation. Hence the term "somatic neurosis" was coined [18].According to Fernando [21] an Indian or Pakistani woman will more than likely complain of pain and weakness. The pain maybe diffused throughout the body and is described as "body ache". The discomfort in her chest and abdomen may be described as gas. The British-born woman will primarily describe her symptoms in terms of mood. The Asian patient does not attend a doctor unless they have something physical to mention, since in their view this is the reason the doctor is there.

Bhui [22] investigated common mental disorders among Indian and Pakistani peoples. He found that Asian patients have their problems identified less often; hence they are not treated, whereas Caucasians tend to verbalize their complaints and seek formal treatment. The findings that Asians rarely present with depression in primary care and that they are thought to present with somatic manifestations of distress more often have led to conclude that somatic symptoms are manifestations of masked depression. Indeed, Jabinsky, Satorius and Gulbinat et al [23] note that the somatization of depression in especially common in non-Western countries. Beiser and Fleming [24] too note that somatic symptoms may be especially common among some depressed patients who view physical symptoms as more legitimate reason than depressive feelings for seeing a doctor. These findings have led to the refutation of commonly held beliefs in the 1960s that the prevalence of depression in Asia and Africa was low [25].

Holloway et al [26] reported that somatization disorder is often co morbid with other psychiatric disorders such as, major depression (55% of patients), anxiety disorders (34%), personality disorders (61%), and panic disorders (26%). The authors also found that even some specialists have difficulty distinguishing between somatization and an anxiety or a mood disorder.

Farooq, Gayir, Okyere et al [27] found significant correlations between somatization and depression (0.72) and somatization and anxiety (0.53) among Asian patients attending general practice surgeries. Sexena et al [20] findings also support this reporting that among Indian patients presenting with somatic and psychological complaints at a psychiatric clinic, the most common diagnoses were dysthymic disorder and generalized anxiety disorder.

SOCIO-CULTURAL FACTORS

Chaturvedi et al [18] reported on a group of neurotic patients from distinct socio-cultural backgrounds in psychiatric clinics in India that presented predominately with multiple somatic symptoms. They are usually characterized by some consistent clinical features: a mixture of depression and anxiety, chronicity, and an ill-sustained response to treatment that is usually against a background of poorly verbalized long-standing life stresses. Such a presentation was mostly seen in the Muslim women who were from lower socio-economic groups and who were in their thirties and forties.

Domestic violence is a form of abuse and it has been theorized that individuals with a background of domestic violence are more likely to somatize. McCauley, Kern and Kolodner et al [28] found that women who had recently experienced domestic violence had higher scores on measures of somatization than women who had not.

Having a relative with somatization disorder, especially a mother predisposes an individual to eventually develop somatization disorder. The DSM IV-TR reports that 10-20% of female relatives also have somatization disorder [7]. A study comparing adolescents with functional abdominal pain and organic abdominal pain revealed that those with functional pain had higher scores on measures of somatization and were more likely to have a female relative with somatization disorder [29].

SOMATIZATION IN THE CARIBBEAN

In the Caribbean population, somatic symptoms are more commonly observed in the Indo-Caribbean population. In Trinidad, unlike findings in other countries, there seem to be an excess of somatic symptoms among women between the ages of 35 and 50 years. This finding has resulted in the coining of the descriptive term 'the Middle age Indian woman syndrome'. This is a syndrome characterized by masked depression in pre-menopausal and menopausal women who are forever quarrelling with their children and husbands who have neglected them through drug use or extra-marital affairs. Without the support of their children, now away from home due to marriage, work or education, these women have become lonely and isolated with numerous somatic complaints, often presenting with the complaints of physical diseases [30]. There were no differences between Hindu, Muslim or Christian Indian women of the Caribbean Diaspora.

Trinidad and Tobago

Trinidad and Tobago is the most southerly of all Caribbean islands and has a population of approximately 1.3 million, with 40.3% of the population being of East Indian descent,

39.6% of African descent, 18.4% of mixed descent and 1.7% belonging to other ethnic groups. The Republic of Trinidad and Tobago is a twin island state with Trinidad measuring 37 miles (60km) by 50 miles (80km), totaling 1864 square miles. The capital city is Port-of-Spain. Tobago has an area of 132 square miles.

The culture of Trinidad can be defined by the ethnic and religious composition of the country. In 1797, Trinidad was captured by the British and the ongoing slave trade then brought many Africans to the island to work on the plantation. When this slavery system was abolished in 1834 Portuguese labourers were introduced but the cultural diversity was broadened when in 1845 the first indentured (contract) workers were brought from India to work on these plantations. From 1845 to 1917 approximately 143,000 immigrant workers were brought to Trinidad, approximately 110,000 Hindus and 30,000 Muslims. They brought with them such festivals as Divali (Hindu) and Hosay (Muslim). Resplendent in its cultural diversity, there exist many religions: Roman Catholics 30%, Hindus 25%, Anglican 11%, Muslim 6%, and a small percentage of Presbyterians, Moravians and Seventh - day Adventist. Trinidad has a total of 13 public holidays: seven are considered to be religious, two ethnic (Indian Arrival Day and Emancipation Day) and four others. As one can notice the religious calendar reflects the ethnic composition of the country, which suggest that Indian immigrants have indeed maintained a lot of the culture they brought with them over 160 years ago [31].

Jamaica

Jamaica is an island nation of the West Indies. It is the third largest island in the Caribbean sea, after Cuba and Hispaniola. Jamaica is approximately 146 miles in length and between 22 to 51 miles wide and is situated 100 miles west of Haiti and 90 miles south of Cuba. The capital is Kingston [32] and the country has a population of 2,665,636 (July 2001 est.), its ethnic composition is as follows; Black 90.0%, East Indian 1.3%, White 0.2%, Chinese 0,2%, Mixed 7.3% and Other 0.1%. The religions of Jamaica fall in three main categories, these are Protestant 61.3%, Roman Catholic 4% and Spiritual Cults 34.7% Comprising the Protestant faith are: Church of God 21.2%, Baptist 8.8%, Anglican 5.5%, Seventh-Day Adventist 9%, Pentecostal 7.6%, Methodist 2.7%, United Church 2.7%, Brethren 1.1%, Jehovah's Witness 1.6%, and Moravian 1.1% [33].

Although the numerical preponderance of Blacks is dominating it cannot subsume the presence of other races. The Black identity had been well established by the time the Asians were introduced into Jamaica. After emancipation Blacks moved away from the plantations and in search for an alternative cheap source of labor the colonial government set its sight on India and China. Between 1845 and 1914 approximately 36,400 East Indians were brought to Jamaica under the indentureship program in which the Indians were to work under contract for the government. Although the both governments had agreed to fair treatment of workers this did not play out. Indian families had to work under exploitative conditions but despite this they managed to form permanent communities in Jamaica. They brought with them alien religions such as Hinduism (80%) and Islam (20%), as well as their inability to understand the English language. The colonial government pursued deliberate policies to segregate the Indian from the Africans in an attempt to forestall any Indian-African resistance.

OUR STUDY

A total of two hundred (200) respondents, one hundred (100) from Trinidad and one hundred (100) from Jamaica participated in this study. Criteria for selection were females eighteen years and over, of East Indian origin, descendents of the third and fourth generation. The sample consisted of females from the Port-of-Spain area in Trinidad while the Jamaican sample consisted of females living in the Kingston area in Jamaica. Participants were selected through purposive sampling.

Table 1. Socio-demographic factors

Socio-Demographic Factors	Trinidad (%)	Jamaica (%)	Overall (%)
Age			
18 – 30	27.0	42.0	34.5
31 – 50	50.0	38.0	44.0
51 – 60 +	23.0	20.0	21.5
Marital Status			
Married	60.0	44.0	52.0
Single	28.0	39.0	33.5
Divorced	1.0	6.0	3.5
Widowed	9.0	9.0	9.0
Common-law	2.0	2.0	2.0
Level of Education			
Primary	12.0	7.0	9.5
Secondary	39.0	34.0	36.5
Tertiary	48.0	59.0	53.5
None	1.0	0.0	0.5

The questionnaire consisted of three sections in a self report format. The first section documented demographic characteristics. This was followed by the Four Dimensional Symptom Questionnaire (4DSQ) [34]. This questionnaire was used to assess symptoms in the areas of distress, anxiety, depression and somatization. The 4DSQ contains 50 items distributed across four scales. Participants rate their presence or absence of symptoms over the last week using a Likert scale. Examples of items include: During the past week, "Did you feel easily irritated?" (Distress), "Did you feel that you can't enjoy anything anymore?" (Depression), "Did you suffer from panic or anxiety attacks" (Anxiety) and "Did you suffer from palpitations?" (Somatization). Elevations on each scale corresponded to a score >10 for distress, >2 for depression, >7 for anxiety and, >10 for somatization.

A third section recorded participant's history of domestic violence, sexual abuse and alcohol abuse by their spouse.

Participants completed the self report questionnaire in Jamaica and Trinidad, the data collection process was conducted almost simultaneously. Individuals who were illiterate, possessed sensory deficits or other disabilities, but were willing to participate were assisted by the investigators if found suitable for participation. The questionnaire was thoroughly explained, read to them, and on indication of their understanding were invited to participate.

Analysis was conducted with the use of the Statistical Program for Social Scientists (SPSS). Frequencies of symptoms reported by participants were calculated. The relationship between somatization and the presence of a female somatizing relative, domestic violence, depression, anxiety, and distress were examined using T-tests and chi-square tests. Between countries, comparisons were also examined using chi-square tests.

OUR FINDINGS

Elevated somatization was reported by 27.5% of the sample. 30% had elevated scores for distress, 26% for depression, 10.5% for anxiety, and 15.5% gave a history of domestic violence, 7.5% reported stigma and 9% had a history of sexual abuse. This is represented in figure 1.

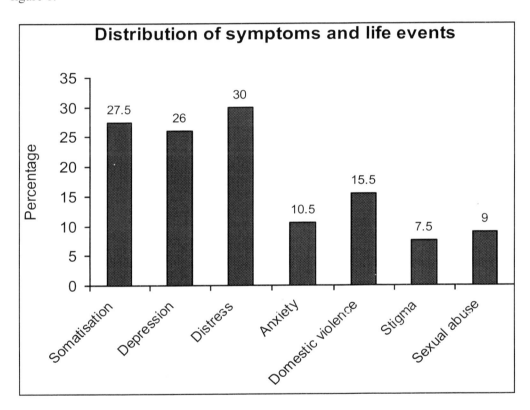

Figure 1. Distribution of symptoms and life events, N=200

Somatization

Overall, 27.5% of the sample or 55 persons reported high somatization. Higher rates of elevated somatization were found in the Trinidadian sample (60%) compared to the Jamaican cohort (40%). See figure 2. However the difference between the two countries was not significant (Chi-square (1) = 3.034, p = NS)

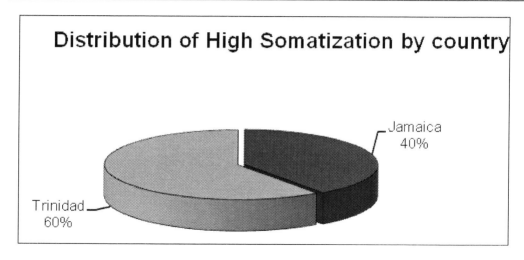

Figure 2. Distribution of high somatization by country, N=55

Somatization and depression

A greater proportion of individuals with depression had high somatization scores than those without. Chi-square analysis revealed that a significant moderate relationship exists between depression and somatization, there was a P value of .000 (Chi-square (1) = 45.580, p<0.05). Hence, high somatizers were more likely to suffer from depression.

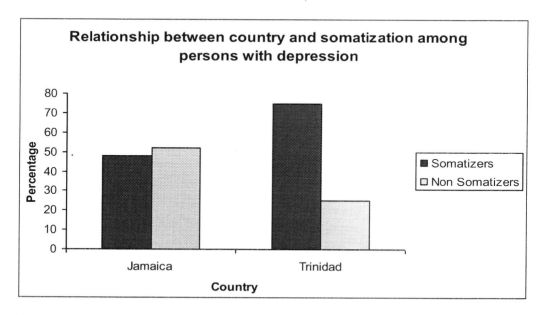

Figure 3. Somatization and depression by country

An analysis of differences by country also showed that the proportion of somatizers in Trinidad who have depression is much higher than the Jamaica sample. In the Trinidad sample, 21 out of 27 (75%) persons with elevated depression scores were somatizers as compared to 12 out of 25 (48%) in the Jamaica sample. See figure 3. Chi-square analysis revealed that a moderate relationship does exist between depression and somatization for the Trinidad sample (Chi-square (1) = 4.96, p<0.026).

Somatization and anxiety

Somatizers were more likely to also report high anxiety (71.4%) than non somatizers (28.6%) (see figure 4). Thus, somatizers are more likely to report high anxiety. Chi-square analysis revealed a significant relationship between somatization disorder and anxiety for the entire sample (Chi-square (1) = 22.710, p<0.00). No significant country differences were observed.

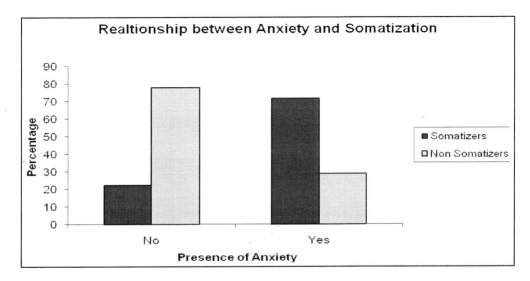

Figure 4. Relationship between anxiety and somatization.

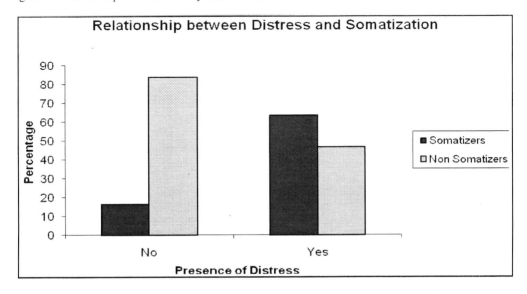

Figure 5. Relationship between distress and somatization

Somatization and distress

High somatization was more commonly reported among persons with high distress. From Figure 5, it can be seen that 63.3% of persons with distress are also somatizers as compared to 16.4% of persons with low distress. A moderate relationship exists between somatization disorder and distress (Chi-square (1) = 28.691, p<0.00). No significant country differences were observed.

Somatization and domestic violence

A greater percentage of persons reporting domestic violence had high somatization scores (45%) as compared to those who had not experienced domestic violence (24%). See figure 6.

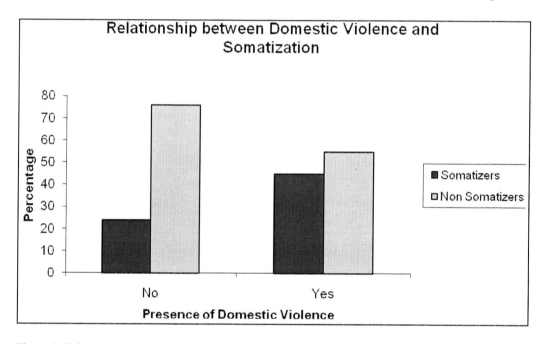

Figure 6. Relationship between somatization and domestic violence

Of the 31 persons who reported exposure to domestic violence, 12 were from Trinidad and 19 from Jamaica. Among these, a greater percentage of Trinidadian women had elevated somatization scores than Jamaican women (64.3% (9 out of 12 persons) versus 35.7% (5 out of 14 persons, (see figure 7). Chi-square analysis for individuals who responded "yes" to being a victim of domestic violence indicates a stronger relationship between domestic violence and elevated somatization in Trinidad than in Jamaica. A significant statistical relationship does exist and the strength of this relationship is a moderate one (Chi-square (1) = 7.04, p<0.05).

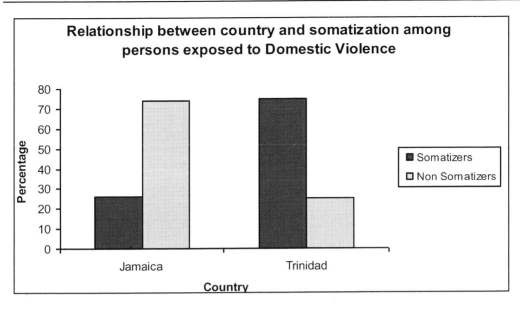

Figure 7. Relationship between country and somatization among persons exposed to domestic violence

Somatization and relative with somatic symptoms

Approximately forty two percent (41.9%) of persons with a female relative who has somatic symptoms reported high somatization scores as compared to 21.9% of persons with no female relative with somatic symptoms. See figure 8. Thus a greater proportion of those with female relatives with somatic symptoms were likely to have elevated somatization scores. A statistically significant relationship was found between somatization disorder and having a female relative with somatic symptoms, (Chi-square (1) = 9.391, $p<0.002$. No significant country differences were found.

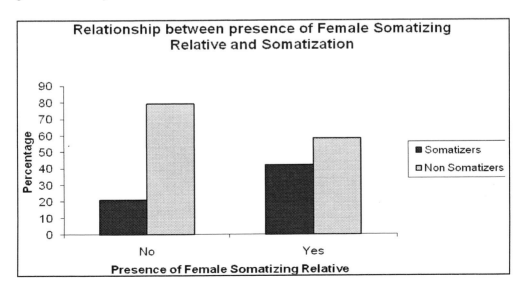

Figure 8. Relationship between somatization and female relative with somatic symptoms.

Somatization and stigma

Overall, most people do not associate somatic symptoms with stigma as 92.5% of the sample stated that they disagreed with the assertion that they were weak or worthless for experiencing somatic symptoms. Among those that do hold stigma however, 60% reported high somatization as compared to 25% among those who did not report stigma. See figure 9. A weak but significant relationship was found between persons feeling that they are weak or worth less than others if they have somatic symptoms and the presence of somatization disorder (Chi-square (1) = 8.591, p=0.03). No significant country differences were found.

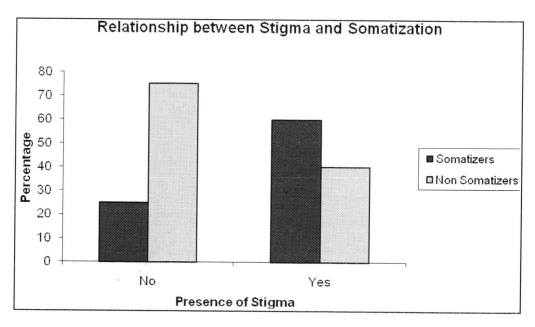

Figure 9. Relationship between stigma and somatization

DISCUSSION

The results from this study showed an overall prevalence of 27.5% for somatization across Trinidad and Jamaica. This is somewhat higher than the average of 19.7% reported by Gureje et al [13], but also well within in the range of 7.6 to 36.8%. This supports findings that Asians may somatize more often than some ethnic groups (e.g. Caucasians) [21]. While Trinidad accounted for 60% percent of these high somatizers and Jamaica the other 40%, this difference was not found to be significant. High somatization was also found to be significantly associated with reports of elevated distress, depression, and anxiety. Persons who yielded high scores on these symptoms were also more likely to be somatizers than those with low scores. This finding is also consistent with those reported in the literature. As suggested by numerous studies somatization disorder has high co-morbidity with depression and anxiety [7,18,20,26,35]. Price [36] has stated that in the United States of America the depression rates for women ranges between 20% - 25%. In this study the elevated depression rates (26%) are on the high end of this range. Ustun et al [37] has also stated that there is a significant relationship between somatic symptoms and overt psychological expression of distress. Thus the clinical picture of co-morbid symptomatology among Asian Caribbean women seems to reflect that found among other ethnic groups and societies.

No country differences existed between high somatization and elevated distress, depression and anxiety. This finding suggests that although national cultural differences exist between Trinidad and Tobago, these do not influence the report of symptoms associated with somatization, distress, depression or anxiety. Thus, the pattern of these symptoms among Asian women in Trinidad and Jamaica are similar. This may be explained by the cohesive retention of many aspects of Indian culture among its Caribbean descendants. Caribbeans of East Indian descent have retained many aspects of their culture (including food, dress and religion) and thus concepts and expressions of illness and disease may have also been retained. The relatively high rates of somatization (27.5%) may be consistent with the Ayurvedic medical tradition that does not establish a distinction between physical and mental manifestations of illness and disease and as such facilitates subjective expressions of experiences.

As Kirmayer [15] stated, it is the particular cultural stigma associated with expressing emotional distress that will determine how that distress will be expressed. In the Caribbean, certain factors may be contributing to the levels of somatization, distress, depression and anxiety experienced by Asian women.

Approximately 15% of the sample indicated a past history of domestic violence. These women may have no other means of venting their frustration, and since they are not able to talk to anyone about their difficulties because of the stigma attached to this sort of behaviour, they easily become depressed, anxious and distressed. Women have to keep their feelings bottled up and this can be said to also be contributing to their high levels of depression. Additionally, the women may be fearful of their violent spouses and hesitant to seek help. The women live in a cultural environment where one is not encouraged to verbalize their troubles, and cannot talk to their spouse openly about issues that are affecting them. Hence, these Asian women do not have the spousal support that women of other ethnic groups have. This by itself can be contributing to their somatization and in relation to this their high levels of depression, anxiety and distress.

Another possible explanation for this occurrence is that for both countries in this study there exist very high levels of criminal activity in each country. Hence, the level of fear that exist in individual living on both islands can be said to be very high and not only for females but for the males in these countries as well. This could have contributed to the high level of anxiety that was discovered in both samples, particularly as females are more at risk for being victims of violent crimes [38]. Therefore, it can be said that they feel more vulnerable than their male counterparts and because of this increased anxiety they can be said to be feeling higher levels of distress also. Hence, lack of spousal support, domestic violence etc. can be said to have played an important part in the high levels of depression, anxiety and distress that was found in this sample.

This finding of stigma being closely related to somatization in the Asian population has also been highlighted by Kirmayer [15], who reported that Asians somatize much more than any other ethnic group and tend to stigmatize mental disorders much more than any other ethnic group. Chaturvedi et al [18,39,40] have all suggested that Asians and in particular Indians somatize their psychological symptoms into physical ones to avoid the stigma associated with a mental disorder. This stigma might negatively affect their self esteem, prestige within the community, or might jeopardize any future marriage arrangements for themselves or their children. The present study confirmed all these previous findings by these researchers as individuals thought that they were indeed weak or worth less than others if they had somatic symptoms and would rather say they have somatic symptoms that say they have a mental disorder such as anxiety or depression. For both the Jamaica and Trinidad samples the Indians surveyed answered positively to these questions. The concept of stigmatization of a mental disorder and it being more prevalent among the Asian community than their European counterparts has been described [14,17,21,22]. Hence, from the present study it can be said that not only Indians living in India, Great Britain or United States of America somatize because of stigmatization but also their decedents living in the Caribbean as well.

Another reason why stigma is an important issue for the Indians in Jamaica and Trinidad is that even though Indians arrived approximately 160 years ago to these islands a large amount of the Indian culture that was originally brought to the islands still play a significant part in the Indians living here today. This is especially true in Trinidad where [31] a large part of the Trinidad date calendar is focused around cultural events. Hence, more of the persons who had somatization disorder and thought that they were weak or worth less than others if they had somatic symptoms came from the Trinidad sample (77.8%). Therefore, it can be said that the Indians that are currently living in Trinidad are still closely tied to their ancestors in terms of some of their ideas about what contributes to a person being regarded as important in the community. The Indians in Trinidad seem to still place more emphasis on "looking good" to their fellow neighbors, whereas, Jamaican Indians do place great emphasis on this area but not as much as Indians in Trinidad. This could be because Jamaica, as mentioned has a much smaller population of East Indian decedents living on the island, hence it can be said that not as much of the culture that was brought to the island may have been retained. This could have contributed to Trinidadian Indians holding more value to not being viewed by others as weak or worth less than others if they had somatic symptoms, than Jamaican Indians. In fact, one of the authors in a visit to Westmoreland in Jamaica, noted that Indians in Jamaica were ashamed of their identity and felt that they were lower in the pecking order than Africans. This is the reverse in Trinidad.

Additional data indicated that both the Jamaica and Trinidad samples stated that they would visit either a medical doctor or a psychiatrist for somatic symptoms, but more than half of the sample chose not to state why they would visit either. This could be due again to stigma because more of the sample chose not to state why they would not visit a psychiatrist as opposed to why they would visit a medical doctor. The psychiatrist is often associated with "mad" or "insane" individuals, hence, this can be why respondents did not want to say why they would visit a psychiatrist. Also, more of the respondents thought that it would be beneficial to visit the medical doctor because the somatic symptoms were physical in nature, as opposed to less thinking that the symptoms are considered to be mental problems. Additionally, a small percentage of the sample thought that the somatic symptoms were not even serious enough to visit a psychiatrist. Hence, this supports the notion that the general population is not at all well educated about somatization disorder and any other mental illness. Their lack of knowledge does not provide them with avenues for treatment as most do not even realize that they may have a serious mental illness.

The entire idea of the pervasiveness of stigmatization of a mental disorder raises the question of having a female relative with somatic symptoms. Since Indians in Jamaica and Trinidad hold such high stigmatization beliefs about psychological illness, and this can be because of their ancestors, it brings into question whether having a female relative with somatic symptoms contributed to the beliefs currently held by Indians in this survey. A significant relationship was found between somatization disorder and having a female relative with somatic symptoms. That is, the persons who have somatization disorder in both samples also have a significant number of female relatives, in particular a mother, with somatic symptoms. The hypothesis is supported and supports previous finding by Kerry and DSM-IV-TR [7,10] that between 10% - 20% of individuals who have a first degree relative with somatization will also have or eventually develop somatization disorder themselves. This certainly will proffer discussions for a more genetic than environmental effect.

Another area that revealed important information was the concept that if an individual is exposed to abuse, and in particular sexual abuse and domestic violence, then the person is more likely to be predisposed to developing somatization disorder. A significant relationship was discovered between domestic violence and somatization disorder; hence the Indian females in this study who were surveyed and have somatization disorder also have a high degree of being physically abused by a spouse. This discovery is consistent with previous findings [26,35,41], who have suggested that being exposed to violence is a predisposing factor for developing somatization disorder. The present study found that 15.5% of the entire sample had a history of domestic violence, and when compared to global statistics, which reported that 20-50% of women at some stage in their life reported some form of domestic violence [42]. Of note, the Trinidadian sample reported a much higher level of being physically abused than the Jamaica sample. The exact reason for this was not investigated in this study but a possible reason could be that in recent years there has been a significant increase in the crime level in Trinidad and since this violent trend is emerging then this could have impacted on how individuals relate to each other in Trinidad. The question remains unanswered whether the abuse is the cause or effect.

Another reason why the Trinidad sample has a higher rate of domestic violence is that the women in Trinidad can be considered to be more submissive. Again, because of the strong Indian culture many women believe that they have to submit to their spouse or in general the male, otherwise they are not considered to be a "good" person. Therefore, if they are being domestically abused many women would prefer to accept this abuse rather than leaving, for fear that others will scorn them. Indians in a pervasive Indian community tend to be more submissive due to group culture and will therefore tolerate abuse. Unlike Trinidad, Indians in a pervasively African society like Jamaica, who will not be submissive. In Jamaica, children are left with their grandparents while the mothers are free to seek employment, unlike Trinidad where looking after children is taken as a serious responsibility by mothers. Trinidad women are therefore more dependent on the male. Most Jamaican women have to go out into the working world and earn and hence, they become emotionally stronger than their counterparts in Trinidad [43].

The increasing crime rate alone is not the only explanation of higher levels domestic violence in Trinidad, but the combination of tradition and fear of stigmatization may have also played a role. When Indians face difficulties in their lives they rarely seek help from outside sources as mentioned above, they would rather try to cope or solve the problem within the immediate family but since they may lack the knowledge of how to solve these problems they would resort to more extreme methods. Indians would not seek out help because again of the stigma attached to having mental problems and also family problems and when the frustration level builds up and there seems to be no one to help, so that the only solution may be to physically hit the person. This supports previous findings [22,44] that has suggested that Asian women were known to be isolated and suffer despair silently when cultural prohibitions prevent them from recruiting social support for intolerable domestic or economic situation.

In the face of the domestic abuse, women develop somatization disorder as a means of coping with stress, and also as a sympathy plea. If the person is sick then she will get positive attention from significant others and not be physically abused since she is now seen as having a physical illness. Bass [14] have suggested that individuals will somatize in order to have more control over interpersonal relationships, receive sympathy and attention from others and be taken more seriously. Therefore, these findings can be said to be supported by this study and the females who are being domestically abused by their spouse will somatize to gain some form of sympathy as mentioned earlier.

Research suggests that sexual abuse also predisposes an individual to somatization disorder [26,41]. However, when investigated in the present study the analysis was unreliable due to the small sample size. In the present sample only 9% admitted to sexual abuse, but still there was significant relationship between somatization and sexual abuse, hence it seems that sexual abuse is a predisposing factor for somatization disorder as suggested by the researchers mentioned earlier.

Another area of this study that revealed significant information was that more of the participants who have somatization disorder were in a common-law relationships, whereas individuals who were married or single had a significantly lower level of somatization disorder. Persons in a common-law relationship can be said to be in a more unstable relationship than their counterparts in a married union, and if one is single then they would not have to deal and cope with the problems of interacting and living with a significant other. Hence the female in a common-law union, particularly if children are involved, would have to think about and cope with the possibility that the male might one day leave and she would now be left with the total responsibility of caring for the children on her own. Also, there will be no formal divorce, and again if they break up there may be no financial support. The married female has this security, hence she is now able to cope with life stresses more adaptively. The common-law union may not be permanent and there will be a lot of switching of partners and this can prove to be stressful to the female and hence, she develops somatization disorder in an effort to deal with stress and keep that person in her life since as mentioned before persons will somatize to gain attention and even financial gain from others [14]. Hence, she is now able to have control over the interpersonal relationship with all these somatic symptoms whereas if she did not have these symptoms she may feel that she would lose the male in her life.

To help curb the problem of stigma that is having a significant impact on the Indian communities in these countries, education about somatization disorder as well as other mental disorders is very strongly recommended since it is only through education can one empower themselves and move beyond this stigma. If the stigmatization of mental disorders is stopped or at least reduced, then one can hope to also see a reduction in domestic violence, depression, anxiety and distress that faced the individuals involved in this study as well as the community at large. With proper education the incidences of somatization as well as the co morbid disorders may be reduced and a study to investigate if any change occurred after education of participants can prove to be significant. Women also need to be given the necessary education to increase awareness about the importance of not staying in physically abusive relationships. Help in obtaining skills that aid their financial problems can alleviate their need to remain in abusive situations. There are numerous benefits in educating Asian women in communities from countries such as India, Trinidad, Jamaica, United States and England.

CONCLUSION

Even though there has not been much research on the Indian community in the Caribbean region the findings of the present study support numerous other studies in their findings about somatization disorder. It has also noted high levels of domestic violence, sexual abuse, depression, anxiety and distress in the islands of Jamaica and Trinidad among the female Indians living there. These findings are consistent with many findings from studies done on Asians in other parts of the world. Therefore, it seems that once one is of East Indian descent the predisposition may be the same, among individuals who have roots in Asia. When somatization disorder was investigated there are many commonalities between the Caribbean sample and their counterparts in the United States of America, Great Britain and India. In addition, the notion that individuals in this research had somatization disorder and a significant co-morbidity with both depression and anxiety, suggest that they are in fact somatizing as no medical explanations were presented for illnesses. Thus, supportive of theories on the nature of Somatization Disorder in Asian populations.

REFERENCES

[1] Kleinman, A. Depression, somatization, and the new cross-cultural psychiatry. Soc Sci Med 1977;11:3-10.

[2] Goldberg DP, Bridges K. Somatic presentations of psychiatric illness in primary care setting. J Psychosomat Res 1988;3(2)137-44.

[3] Barsky AJ. Amplification, somatization, and the somatoform disorders. Psychosomatics 1992;33:28-34.

[4] Mai F. Somatization disorder: A practical review. Can J Psychiatry 2004:49:652-62.

[5] Mai FM, Merskey H. Briquet's concept of hysteria: an historical perspective. Can J Psychiatry 1981;26:57–63.

[6] American Psychiatric Association. Diagnostic and statistical manual of mental disorders, 3rd ed. text rev. Washington, DC: APA, 1980.

[7] American Psychiatric Association. Diagnostic and statistical manual of mental disorders, 4th ed. text rev. Washington, DC: APA, 2000.

[8] World Health Organization. Somatoform disorders: Somatization disorder. In: ICD-10: The ICD-10 classification of mental and behavioral disorders: Clinical descriptions and diagnostic guidelines. Geneva: WHO, 1992:162-70.

[9] Baron, RA. Psychology, 4th edition. Boston, MA: Allyn Bacon, 1998.

[10] Kerry S. Chronic fatigue syndrome. Long term health maintenance.   Leawood, KS: Am Acad Fam Physicians, 2002.

[11] Smith JF. Somatoform Disorders. Medical Library. [Online] 2004 [cited 2009 Oct 28]. Available from: http://www.chclibrary.org/micromed/00065690.htm/

[12] Kirmayer LJ, Young A. Culture and somatization: clinical, epidemiological, and ethnographic perspectives. Psychosomat Med 1998;60(4):420-30.

[13] Gureje O, Simon GE, Ustun TB, et al. Somatization in crosscultural perspective: A World Health Organization study in primary care. Am J Psychiatry 1997;154:989-95.

[14]   Bass CM. Somatization, physical symptoms and psychological illness. Oxford: Blackwell, 1991.

[15]   Kirmayer LJ. Culture, affect and somatization. Transcultural Psychiatr Res Rev 1984;21:159-88.

[16]   Fabrega H. Somatization in cultural and historical perspective. In: Kirmayer LJ, Robbins JM, eds. Current concepts of somatization: Research and clinical perspectives. Washington, DC: Am Psychiatr Press, 1991:181-99.

[17]   Hardin EE. Depression and social anxiety among Asians and European Americans: The roles of self-discrepancy, optimism, and pessimisn. Dissertation. Columbus, OH: Ohio State Univ, 2002.

[18]   Chaturvedi SK, Venugopal D. Somatization and somatic neurosis. Cross cultural variations. Psychiatr Online 1994:1359-7620.

[19]   Sarason I, Sarason B. Abnormal psychology. The problem of maladaptive behaviour, 9th ed. Upper Saddle River, NJ: Prentice Hall, 1999.

[20]   Saxena S, Nepal MK, Mohan D. DSM-III Axis 1 diagnosis of Indian psychiatric patients with somatic symptoms. Am J Psychiarty 1988; 145:8.

[21]   Fernando S. Mental health, race and culture, 2nd ed. Basingstoke: Palgrave, 2002.

[22]   Bhui, K. Common mental disorders among Indian and Pakistani people. Int Rev Psychiatry 2002;11:136-44.

[23]   Jablensky A, Sartorius N, Gulbinat W, Ernberg G. Characteristics of depressive patients. Acta Psychiatr Scand 1981;63:367-83.

[24]   Beiser M, Fleming JAE: Measuring psychiatric disorder among Southeast Asian refugees. Psychol Med 1986;16:627-39.

[25]   Prince RH. The changing picture of depressive syndromes in Africa: is it fact or diagnostic fashion? Can J African Stud 1968;1:177-92.

[26]   Holloway KL, Zerbe KJ. Simplified approach to somatization disorder. Postgrad Med 2000;108(6):89-95.

[27]   Farooq S, Gahir MS, Okyere E, Sheikh AJ, Oyebode F, et al. Somatization: A transcultural study. J Psychosom Res 1995;39: 883–8.

[28]   McCauley J, Kern D, Kolodner K, et al. The "Battering Syndrome": Prevalence and clinical characteristics of domestic violence in primary care. Ann Internal Med 1995;123(10):737-46.

[29]   Routh D, Ernst A. Somatization disorder in relatives of children and adolescents with functional abdominal pain. J Paed Psychol 1984;9(4):427-37.

[30]   Maharajh HD, Ali A. Recognition of cultural behaviours in Trinidad and Tobago. Internet J Third World Med 2004;1:2.

[31]   Emrit RC. The best of Trinidad and Tobago. [Online] 2003 [cited 2003 Oct 28] Available from: www.geocities.com/ronemrit

[32]   Lahmeyer, J. Jamaica: General data, Populstat. [Online] 2004 [cited Oct 28   2009].   Available from: http://www.populstat.info/Americas/jamaicag.htm

[33]   Coutsoukis P. Jamaica people 2001. [Online] 2001 [cited 2009 Oct 28]. Available from: http://www.photius.com/wfb2001/Jamaica/Jamaica_people.html.

[34]   Terluin B. De Vierdimensionale Klachtenlijst (4DKL): Een vragenlijst voor het meten van distress, depressie, angst en somatisatie. Huisarts Wet 1996;39:538-47. [Dutch]

[35]   Shaffer D. Persistent unexplained medical complaints. Behav Med Briefs 1999;8.

[36]   Price P. All About Depression: Causes of Depression. [Online] 2003 [cited Oct 27]. Available from: http://www.allaboutdepression.com/cau_01.html

[37]   Ustun TB, Sartorius N. Mental illness in general health care: An international study. Chichester: John Wiley, 1995.

[38]   Kaplan R, Sallis J, Patterson T. Health and human behavior, New York: McGraw-Hill, 1993.

[39]   Ritts V. Infusing culture into psychopathology. A supplement for instructors. Meramec: St Louis Comm Coll, 1999.

[40]   Raguram R, Weiss MG, Channabasavanna SM, Devins GM. Stigma, Depression, and somatization in South India. Am J Psychiatry 1996;153(8):1043-9.

[41]   Righter EN, Sonsone RA. Managing somatic preoccupation. Dayton, OH: Wright State Univ School Med, 1999.

[42]   Jewkes R. Preventing domestic violence. BMJ 2002;324:253-4.

[43] Miller E. Marginalization of the Black male. Insights from the Development of the teaching profession, 2nd ed. Traverse City, MI: Canoe Press, USA.1997.

[44] Beliappa J. Illness of distress. Alternative models of mental health. London: Confed Indian Org, 1991.

In: Social and Cultural Psychiatry Experience from the... ISBN: 978-1-61668-506-5
Editor: Hari D. Maharajh and Joav Merrick © 2010 Nova Science Publishers, Inc.

Chapter 29

FORENSIC PSYCHIATRY IN THE COLONIAL AND POST COLONIAL ERAS

Hari D. Maharajh

In this chapter, the concepts of common and statute laws are reviewed with respect to their application and the duties of the psychiatrist. The history, development and practice of Forensic Psychiatry in the colonial period in Trinidad are explored and later following independence during the establishment of a Mental Health Act and the introduction of the Sectorization Plan in 1975. Three case histories are presented: the first investigates liability in a mentally ill offender, the second is a Court Report intended to assess mental illness in a man charged with murder and the third examines the role of the Psychiatric Tribunal in discharge from Prison following illegal detention. Defenses available for these individuals are briefly discussed. Despite a PAHO's expert finding of human abuse in the Forensic system in Trinidad, the assessment of mentally ill offenders in developing countries with different social and cultural imperatives is no easy task.

INTRODUCTION

Forensic psychiatry is defined as a specialty of psychiatry that deals with the assessment and treatment of mentally ill offenders. This process incorporates the utilization of both common law and statute law. The terms used here are legal and not medical and are in need of further explanation in the description of psychiatric illnesses.

Mental disorder in the Mental Health Act is defined as a mental illness, arrested or incomplete development of the mind, psychopathic disorder and any other disorder or disability of mind [1]. The term mental illness includes a broad range of disorders of the mind including delirium and dementia as well as more formal forms of psychiatric disorders such as schizophrenia.

Common law refers to that body of rights, duties, obligations and liabilities recognized by the courts over the years. It is made up of principles identified by the judges and adapted and changed to meet the needs of particular cases or particular developments in our society. This is also known as case law. Under common law, powers may be used in an emergency situation to detain or briefly treat individuals with mental illness, when no statutory mechanisms or protections are in place. Actions should be performed out of necessity to protect the individual or others from potential harm. Common law also gives power to doctors to treat patients medically if their capacity to give consent is impaired and if the medical treatment required is urgent. Capacity and mental illness are not the same, and a patient can be mentally ill, but retain capacity and the right to refuse medication.

Statute law comprises the rules and regulations agreed by the authority of Parliament and implemented by the passage of Parliamentary Acts, for example The Mental Health Act of 1975 in Trinidad [1]. This Act gives powers to doctors and mental health professionals to admit and treat patients with mental illness on a compulsory basis. All patients have the right to appeal under the Act which is usually held by a mental health review tribunal. Parts of the Mental Health Act deals with the detention and treatment of patients as outlined in Section 6 [1].

Two important common law principles are the Principle of Necessity which allows members of the public and health professionals to intervene on an emergency basis to temporarily restrain a mentally ill person until appropriate action can be taken and secondly, the Duty of Care imposed on all professional staff to all persons within a hospital. Health professionals are expected to provide proper care for mentally ill people beyond the responsibility of ordinary people of the public.

DUTIES OF A PSYCHIATRIST

a) Capacity for consent

All doctors must be able to assess a patient's capacity to give consent for treatment. The patient must be able to:

- Comprehend and retain information that is material to the decision to accept or refuse treatment, especially as to the likely consequences of having or not having the particular treatment in question.
- Believe the medical advice to be true
- Be able to use the information received and be able to weigh it up as part of the process of coming to a clear decision.

b) How to assess dangerousness

Issues of safety and the mentally ill have increased public concern due to the high public profile of a small number of cases of homicide by mentally ill patients. Assessment of dangerousness is necessary in order to prevent homicide. The following key points need to be followed:

1. Current mental state:

- Is the patient showing evidence of aggressive or threatening behavior?
- Does the patient hold any abnormal beliefs that could potentially result in violence? e.g. belief that he is persecuted by someone whom he plans to harm.
- Does the patient have extreme feelings of jealousy towards his/her partner and has he/she threatened the patient in any way?
- Is the patient experiencing auditory hallucinations that are telling him/her to be violent?
- What degree of insight does the patient have into these abnormal experiences?
- How able is he/she to resist acting upon them?
- How willing is he/she to accept treatment?

2. Recent act of violence and possible repeat

- How serious was the episode?
- How bizarre was the episode?
- How potentially serious could the episode have been?
- Did the patient give any warning before hand?
- Was it provoked or unprovoked?
- Was anyone able to detect a change in patient's behavior before the episode?
- How unpredictable was the episode?
- Is the patient able to discuss the episode and tell staff why he or she carried out the episode?
- Does the patient have any regrets?
- Was the patient mentally unwell at the time?
- Was the violence directly related to his illness?

3. Previous history of violence

- Is there a previous history of violence?
- How serious was this?
- How predictable was the violence
- Was the violence associated with mental illness or did the patient do it when he was well?

4. Alcohol and drug use

- Was the patient under the influence of alcohol or drug at the time of the violence?
- Is alcohol and drug thought to be a serious contributing factor to the risk of violence in this patient
- How likely is the patient to remain abstinent?

5. *Provoking circumstances*

- Is the patient likely to re-experience circumstances or individual people that provoked previous violence?

6. *Response to treatment*

- If violence or the risk of violence is associated with mental illness, what is the likely response to initial treatment and how likely is the patient likely to comply with treatment in the long term?

C) Unfit to plead

A psychiatric defense at the time of the trial is admission of the accused into a special hospital for treatment until fit to plead.

- Unable to understand the charge or the significance of the plea or
- Unable to challenge a juror or
- Unable to instruct counsel or
- Unable to examine a witness or
- Unable to follow the progress of the trial.

D) Testamentary capacity

A person may make a will if he or she is of sound disposing mind, memory and understanding and

- Knows the nature and extent of his or her property
- Knows the persons having a claim on it and the relative strengths of their claims
- Can express oneself clearly and without ambiguity.

CAUSES OF OFFENDING

A number of psychosocial and biological factors have been associated with the causation of offenses. These are individual factors such as hyperactivity, low impulse control and mental retardation with low intelligence. Family factors including the nature of child rearing with bonding and attachment issues, young age of mothers and child abuse, dysfunctional families with parental absence or conflicts are common. In addition, parental involvement in crime and drugs, large, unstable family sizes with multiple parenting are common occurrences in family with offenders. Social factors ascribed to offending are poverty and economic deprivation, peer pressure especially influences at school and at the community levels and situational group or gang influential behaviors. The question often asked is whether there is a biological contribution to offending. The evidence based on twin, family and adoption studies, genetic and environmental interactions and molecular genetics suggests the presence of biological factors.

HISTORY OF THE DEVELOPMENT OF FORENSIC PSYCHIATRY

Many postcolonial British territories have shadowed the change of mental health legislation taking place in the United Kingdom, even after the attainment of political independence from that country. The 1976 Mental Health Law of Trinidad is a case in point, as it paralleled the 1959 English Mental Health Act.

Incorporated as part of the contractual agreement relating to indentured workers, the provision of medical services by the British colonizers became mandatory during the indentureship period in Trinidad (1845-1919). This resulted in the establishment of medical facilities and implementation of policies that were similar to those in Great Britain. As communities developed - the black slaves now being free - legislation became necessary for the maintenance of law and order. Regulated by Ordinances, services to the colonies were for the most part similar, but varied according to the ecology of diseases and the social, political and economic climates prevailing at the given time. There were however, differences among the colonies: Barbados and Jamaica had been British since the 17th century, while Trinidad became British in 1797 near the end of the 18th century. According to Seheult [2] "Trinidad (1814-1944) with its comparative prosperity stood prominently forward, among her less fortunate sisters in the Caribbean."

Prior to 1814, the practice of medicine in Trinidad was unregulated [2, 3]. In that year, a Medical Board was created by the Proclamation and vested with statutory powers to collaborate with the Government for the purpose of the control of medicine in the best interest of the community. In 1846 an amending ordinance was passed to improve the Medical Board and to better regulate the practice of the medicine, surgery and ancillary services. Under British rule, the early treatment of the mentally ill in Trinidad paralleled the management and treatment of the insane in Britain. Thus in 1849, the first ordinance was passed for custody at the Royal Gaol of insane persons charged with offences. Almost a decade later in 1858, the Belmont Lunatic Asylum was opened with forty seven inmates under the direction of a succession of medical officers with no special knowledge of lunacy. In 1882, Dr Seccombe, who had experience in the management of the insane in England, was appointed Medical Superintendent of the Lunatic Asylum, at the time housing 389 inmates. He found conditions at the Asylum so primitive that he remarked:

"It was behind the age and one would have to go back 40 years in the history of the insane to find another such institution in Britain. The defects were many and varied; the site was unsuitable and did not lend itself to major improvements; the buildings were in a state of disrepair and badly arranged; the water supply was inadequate; the sanitary arrangements presented a sad spectacle; the two sexes were not sufficiently kept apart; the bathrooms and closets were shared alike by male and females; supervision was lacking and the overcrowding was deplorable; industrial employment as a means towards mental restoration was absent, and there was little or no amusement which is generally useful in the cure of some forms of lunacy" [2]

Dr Seccombe through hard work and determination corrected many of the abuses and succeeded in having the more luxurious, comfortable and modern hospital built at St Ann's. The St Ann's Asylum was opened in 1900 with 500 residents. After twenty-six years Dr Seccombe resigned office in 1908 and his work was continued by Dr Rake. Psychiatric care was brought to a high level equal to that of Britain. In 1923 the ratio of certified lunatics in Trinidad was twenty per 10,000 of population, while in Great Britain it was thirty per 10,000.

Notwithstanding the sparkling brilliance and reflected luster of the written reports of the masters of the Colonial Medical Service, an analysis of outcome among the colonized appears to be contradictory. Following the emancipation of slavery, between 1838 and 1917, over 400,000 indentured Indians came to the Caribbean. The end of the slave trade did not precipitate the end of slavery, but the slave system was practiced in Jamaica laid the foundation on which the coolie system was later erected in other colonies. This was crucial to Trinidad and Guyana countries to which the majority of indentured workers were transported. The name had been changed, but a new system of slavery was introduced [4].

The structure of slavery persisted and in Trinidad, estates made their own arrangements with private practitioners for the medical care of immigrants. The system was changed when the India office objected on the grounds that the medical officers were servants of the planters. In 1841 the Government of India stopped the migration of workers to Guyana due to the treatment of workers on the plantations. In Trinidad, mortality rates were high, one quarter to one third of the new arrivals died in the first year. At the Lunatic Asylums the mortality rate was high as fifty percent of yearly admissions. Legal control was important to the colonizer, not so much for the protection of the workers in the sugar plantations, but for the protection of their economic investments.

During the periods of slavery and indentureship, hot houses were created within the plantations to incarcerate workers who were construed to be unwell. Terms such as vagrancy, vagabondage, maroonage and drapetomania were coined to describe workers who had developed a tendency to wander. The Africans and Creole were described as being constitutionally prone to wandering and straying and had to be restrained. Lord Harris, Governor of Trinidad, condemned the Indians for their habits of wandering and vagrancy [4]. These observations set the stage for compulsory detention in later legislative framework, both in the colonies and in later years for migrants to the UK.

Within the Caribbean, there is a tendency to invest heavily in the development of progressive, visionary and sometimes costly plans without some form of legal mechanism to ensure the implementation. Plans such as the comprehensive Lewis plan for Mental Health (1959) and the Chan Plan for the sub-division for the large Mental Hospitals into four separate hospitals in Trinidad have been all shelved [5]. The Roberts Plan (1959) and Alex Richman recommendation (1964) to set up a model ward as a therapeutic community at Bellevue Hospital in Jamaica for the purpose of training all categories of staff met a similar fate [6]. Major changes tend to follow mental health legislation.

In 1935, in an attempt to de-stigmatize patients, the name of St Ann's Lunatic Asylum was changed to Mental Hospital, and then in 1961 to St Ann's Hospital [7]. Unfortunately, in 2002 the name has reverted to St Ann's Mental Hospital. By Ordinance 12 of 1946 a Mental Hospital Board was authorized in harmony with the administration of Mental Homes in England. The latter was subsequently incorporated in the UK Mental Health Act of 1959 which advocated compulsory detention. This act was adopted and utilized until 1975 in

Trinidad and Tobago. Legal certification and commitment, regardless of the patient's rights, were forcefully instituted.

SECTORIZATION AND MENTAL HEALTH IN TRINIDAD AND TOBAGO

In the vein of a tradition of implementation of policies without public consultation, 1975 was heralded as a dawn of a new era in psychiatry in Trinidad and Tobago. Two major changes took place: in June 1975 a policy of regionalization known as the Sectorization Plan, copied from the French model, was adopted for the setting up of a Community Mental Health Programme. Trinidad and Tobago, with a population of one million inhabitants then, was divided into five sectors or catchment areas of approximately 200,000 persons. Each sector consisted of a team of psychiatrists, social workers, community nurses and paramedical auxiliaries that looked after the welfare of patients. In order to make effective this plan, a new Mental Health Act No 30 of 1975, based on the 1959 UK Mental Health Act and which had undergone several drafts since 1960, was passed by the House of Representatives and Senate and became law. A new category of mental health officers was created by the passage of this Act, and the protection of patients by the provision of a Psychiatric Hospital Tribunal.

Despite the new oil wealth of the 1970s, the Trinidad Sectorization Pogramme 'literally lost its head in 1976 when it was little more than a year and a half old' [6]. In 1974 Michael Beaubrun of Grenadian descent had acted as Principal Medical Officer of Institutions when the programme was first conceived. He provided psychiatric guidance for the implementation of the proposed plan. Unfortunately, he lost favour with the politicians and he returned to the University of the West Indies in 1976. His lack of commitment to the sectorization plan, his self-obsession and perceived ownership of programmes contributed to the failure of this community health programme. In addition, the government's neglect of the building programme and failure to provide the necessary infrastructural needs, nursing shortages and too few mental health officers, lack of cooperation by police officers to assist in the detention of the mentally ill on the grounds of lack of training, financial neglect, insufficient public relations activity and the abuse of patients at institutions further contributed to the demise of the sectorization plan. The final result was a failed sectorization plan, and draconian legislation that was heavily biased towards the needs of society rather then towards the rights or treatment of individuals. The Mental Health Act Chap 28:02 1975 [1] is a document of thirty-one pages comprising sixty-four sections in eight parts. The parts are:

- Part I: Admission and detention in psychiatric ward or hospital
- Part II: Psychiatric Hospital tribunal
- Part III: Mental Health review tribunal
- Part IV: Powers and duties psychiatric hospital director
- Part V: Approved homes
- Part VI: Admission to psychiatric ward
- Part VII: Protection of properties of patients
- Part VIII: General provisions

A cursory look at the Trinidad Act indicates that there is an emphasis on compulsory detention of the mentally ill with the removal of the civil liberties of individuals. This is not unlike the Jamaican Mental Health Act 6 of 1998. There is a striking similarity between sections 6, 7, 8, 9, 10, 13 and 14 of the Trinidad Act and section 6, 7, 8, 9, 10, 15, and 16 of the Jamaican Act. Section 15 of the Jamaican Act [8], giving unbridled authority to police officers, is not incorporated in the Trinidad Act and may be subject of abuse in Caribbean communities. Section 15 of the 1975 Act in Trinidad has been criticized as a breach of human rights. This involves admission on application of a Mental Health officer. The Act states:

> A person found wandering at large on a highway or in any public place and who, by reason of his appearance, conduct or conversation, a mental health officer has reason to believe is mentally ill and in need of care and treatment in a psychiatric hospital or ward, may be taken into custody and conveyed to such hospital or ward for admission for observation.

The person must be reviewed by a duly authorized psychiatrist within 72 hours.

ADMISSION TO THE FORENSIC WARD

A three-year analysis (1998-2000) of admissions to St Ann's Hospital utilizing Section 6 of the Mental Health Act revealed that only 3% of the approximately 1,700 admissions per year were forcefully committed. Over the three-year period, half the patients (50.6) were admitted on a voluntary status, 29.8% as urgent admissions, 16.6% by order of the Court, 1.5% medically recommend and 1.5% by Mental Health Officer Order [9]. These figures indicate that health care workers have adopted a more humanitarian approach to the admission status of patients and are supportive of a less statutory approach to patient treatment similar to what is practiced in Jamaica.

An analysis of Caribbean Mental Health Laws is confusing with respect to the 'word of the law' and 'the spirit of the law'. Gorgon and Verdun-Jones argue that the interpretation and application of the reforms retained the discretionary power of health professionals but the law seems to have had different intentions [10]. The language of the law as stated in the various Acts seems to be counterproductive. Uri Aviram [11] has proposed an interesting medical-bureaucratic model that supports a convenient compromise between the state bureaucracy and the medical profession.

The Mental Health Act, Chapter 28:02 of 1975, amended as 45 of 1975 is a document primarily concerned with the commitment, detention and control of mental patients to a chronic mental hospital [1]. Commitment means loss of freedom and possibly the imposition of treatment given, in that there is no legislation regarding consent to treatment. The Act is not client-centred but focuses on power, detention and control and does not reflect contemporary practices in psychiatry.

REVIEW OF FORENSIC SERVICES IN TRINIDAD AND TOBAGO

In 1999, Professor Arboleda-Florez, a PAHO consultant, conducted an evaluation of the Forensic Psychiatric Services in Trinidad and Tobago [12]. He reported on the perennial problems of shortage of staff, absence of training modules, absence of newer antipsychotics and overcrowding. He was critical of the slowness of the system, where patients can be kept in detention for years without any review of their legal status or the determination of the length of remand orders by the judiciary. He noted that following assessment, the accused would spend his time on the Unit awaiting the court and the haphazard extension of warrants of remand for further fourteen-day periods, without due cause. He commented on the violation of the rights of the person and sited a cause of one person who had been awaiting trial for fourteen years! Furthermore, he noted neglect or lack of interest in safeguarding the legal rights of the patients. He reported:

> For example, a Psychiatric Hospital Review Tribunal, contemplated in Section 18 of the Mental Health Act, is supposed to meet once a year to review medically committed patients and once every six months to review court ordered admissions. Yet, the Tribunal rarely meets, if ever, and consequently, nobody takes care to protect the rights of citizens who happened to be detained at the mental hospital. The same can be said about another Tribunal, The Mental Health Review Tribunal, contemplated in Section 20 of the Mental Health Act. It is not clear to discern who has an obligation to set up these tribunals or what responsibilities accrue to the Directorship of the Hospital regarding potential abuses of the human rights of mental patients.

Further mental health legislation was enacted in 1996, where part of the Tobago Regional Hospital was appointed a psychiatric ward for the care and treatment of mentally ill patients in an Order cited as the Mental Health (Appointment of Citation Psychiatric Ward) Order, 1996. In 2001 a Bill requiring a special majority for its passage in Parliament was submitted, seeking to repeal the Mental Health Act, Chap. 28:02 and to replace it with a new Mental Health Act, 2001. The Bill is divided into thirteen parts with additions of administrative law concerning the establishment of Regional and National Health Committees, legislations concerning primary or community care treatments and special provisions for the treatment and placement of children who are suffering from mental disorders. It is designed in the form and manner of the Jamaican 1998 Act.

This new Act, yet to be assented to, falls short, earning the same criticisms levelled against other Mental Health Acts in the Commonwealth Caribbean: a preoccupation with control, commitment and detention. Detention is the pillar of stigmatization; people should be persuaded to use the service to seek help when needed. A threat of detention is more than likely to prevent persons from accessing help. The law cannot always decide on the best interests of the patient and psychiatrists should not be responsible for recommending detention of patients. Detention turns psychiatrists into gaolers, not doctors. Psychiatrists should not be responsible for recommending the detention of patients. This should be a matter for a tribunal or magistrate court.

Within the Caribbean region, there appear to be more similarities than differences in the development of Mental Health Legislations. While the majority of psychiatrists find favour with a medical-psychiatric model, public policies have imposed a legalistic model advocating commitment and curtailment of civil liberties. A more humanitarian approach utilizing a medical model will enable a health worker to help a patient while at the same time preserving his civil liberties. The time has come for Caribbean psychiatrists to sit and talk and to take a more active role in redrafting the law.

Three cases are presented below: Case 1 demonstrates the interaction of law and psychiatry; Cases 2 and 3, the writing of Court Reports, and in Case 3 the application of the Mental Health Tribunal. These cases are in themselves instructive and reflect the level of psychiatric practice in the Republic.

CASE STORY 1

A 42 year-old senior staff, refinery operator of a prominent oil company was referred for a psychiatric evaluation after setting fire to his prestigious owner occupied building and was seen two days following admission to his company's private hospital. He stated that approximately one week before the incident, he was not himself and felt somewhat listless and low spirited. This he thought, may have been precipitated by a neighbour with whom he had a disagreement about an arranged marriage. After returning home on that evening, he retired into his living room and while sitting there, saw a number of enormous, grey rats 'half the length of his arm and recognized as human-eating rats' coming towards him.

He was paralyzed with fear and managed to escape from the house and ran down the street. While on the street he noticed about two hundred rats following him. Thinking that his body and clothes were contaminated with an odour that attracted the rats, he ripped his clothes off and began washing his body and clothing at a street standpipe. This caused the rats to retreat and he carefully made his way to his home using the back door to enter.

While at home he secured the premises, locking every door and window to prevent them from entering. Suddenly, the rats reappeared and began moving towards him. Now, seized by fear again, he quickly placed some newspapers on two couches on the left and right and raised a fire thinking that the smoke will get rid of these devilish animals. As the flames engulfed the couches and began spreading to other areas he saw the rats scampering away but soon realized that his own exit was tightly bolted and blocked. He then lurched through a glass window falling to the ground. He was taken to the hospital by relatives who had seen the fire and had come to his rescue.

The patient has no personal or family history of mental illness. He developed Type 1 diabetes mellitus at the age of 23 years and was treated with daily dosages of 18 units of Humulin and at times self-medicated with hypoglycaemic agents. He was aware that his compliance to medication was generally poor and irregular and recalled that he had not taken any diabetic medication over the last two weeks. He had a history of moderate alcohol intake but had stopped drinking three months prior to this incident. He denied the use of any drugs and smoked about 10 cigarettes a day.

In his personal history, his birth and development were normal with no childhood illnesses. He was a bright student and attended a well known college where he obtained his ordinary and advanced level passes. After further technical training, he was employed as a refinery operator engineer with the local oil company. He has been working now for 18 years. He is not married and lived alone in his dwelling house which was not insured. He has an established visiting relationship with a female friend in his rural village. His colleagues described him as a nice, friendly hard-working individual.

On examination, he was a thin man, unkempt and neglected with tatty clothing and edentulous in the upper jaw. He had first degree burns on his arm and neck and minor scratches from his escape from the burning house. On mental status examination he was orientated in time, person and place, cooperative, logical and coherent. There were no cognitive deficits with good anterograde and retrograde memory, judgment, insight and understanding. His intelligence was above average. There were no hallucinations, or delusions and the mood and affect were normal. There were no clinical features suggestive of epilepsy, psychosis, a dissociative state or secondary gain. The patient maintained a clear sensorium since admission.

The following investigations were done at the hospital: Full blood count was normal; HbA1C was elevated at 8.5; Urea and Electrolytes were normal; Liver function tests were within normal range as well as Renal function tests. The EEG was not indicative of a seizure disorder and ECG ruled out gross cardiac abnormalities. There were no abnormalities in calcium levels. The only abnormal finding was an increased level of blood glucose of 495 mg/dl. The glucose level two days later was 295 mg/dl after treatment with 20 units of Humulin. He was also seen by the company's endocrinologist for his diabetic status and visited by the Employees Assistance programme personnel and members of the protective services. He was seen by the author for an assessment of his competence with the view of submitting a court report.

CASE STORY 2

Kerwin Dernel, approximate age of 26 or 27, was referred to the Forensic Ward, St Ann's Hospital, Trinidad on 5th June 2008 by a Court order on a charge of murder. He was seen in the interview room at the Forensic Ward at St Ann's Hospital on Tuesday October 14th 2008 between the hours of 5:30pm to 7:30pm.

Sources of information

- Interviews with SM and AH– Senior Mental Health Nurses at the Forensic ward contemporaneously involved in the treatment of the accused.
- Letter dated 3rd October 2008 –Dr HO who states 'antisocial personality traits unrelated to any psychiatric illness with which he may have been diagnosed'. Dr HO's main concern was his removal from St. Ann's back to the prison.
- Letter dated 15th September 2008 – Dr KM, Psychologist who recorded 'low intelligence, personality disturbance, moderate score on psychopathy'.
- Please note that I have not been privy to any depositions on this patient or reports from the courts other than those referred to above.
- I have not seen a social work report which should have been attached to the file of the patient despite his long stay on the ward and the doctor's insistence that he should not be there.

- I was unable to access any other medical files on the accused despite a lifetime of institutionalizations at a home in Diego Martin, Youth Training Centre at Prison and incarceration at the Adult prison services at Golden Grove or other institutions.

Description of person charged

In my attempt to introduce myself and to state the purpose of my visit, this young, mixed, mostly Afro-Trinidad male appeared to have no interest in what I was saying and immediately began a monologue on his lifetime suffering in jail, injustices towards him and the withdrawal of his medication at the forensic unit when indeed he was sent there for treatment. 'I want medication, I am not getting any medication, they sent me here to get medication, they put me on two sets of tablets and take off one' he said. He was an aggressive man with little eye contact, an Afro hair style, missing front tooth, fairly well built with muscular arms, wearing a sleeveless red Adidas T shirt, yellow shorts and rubber slippers. He had a six inches scar on the lateral aspect of the triceps of his left hand. I saw him with an interview desk separating us and the nurses in attendance. This was not by design but the established culture of interview at the unit.

Circumstances of offence

When asked why he was at the Forensic Unit at St Ann's Hospital, Mr Dernel stated that he was sent here for treatment and lamented the poor treatment he had received in prison and now at the Unit without medication. He avoided the issue of the charge and with some pressure of speech spoke more of his personal suffering rather than his behaviour. When asked about the charge, he denied any involvement in it; 'I never kill nobody, why I in jail, if I did kill the person I would not fraid jail' When questioned about other accomplices in this matter, he said he met two other persons in prison who he never knew before. Later he changed his story saying that he was locked up with his brother and friend. A consistent finding was contradictory statements for example he had no brother of his 'own blood' and then spoke of a twin brother: 'I have a brother who is not a brother anymore' Later, on returning to the issue of the charge he said in a facetious manner 'yes I did it, I will tell the magistrate I did it.' He also denied having a mother.

Family history

Due to his approximate answers, this was difficult to ascertain from the patient himself. There was no social history available to be included in the history. From the interview, it appears as though he has a twin brother, and according to the nurses interviewed, a mother who also has rapid speech. 'My mother is not my mother, she never took care of me'. He never knew his father and had a dysfunctional upbringing. He claims he has 'a son outside'.

Personal history

When questioned about his birth and development, his standard reply was 'I don't know.' On further questioning he stated that he grew up in Maloney but could not give any time line of his movements. Later, as a child, he was sent to a home in Diego Martin and then to the Youth Training Centre in Prison and is currently at the Adult Prison seeking treatment at St. Anns Hospital.

Past history

Two years ago, he attempted suicide while in prison. No medical records were available from prison to corroborate this attempt. He mentioned that in the past he has had head injury(s) that has resulted in epileptic attacks. Scars on his body suggest an aggressive lifestyle.

Personality and behaviour

Mr Derrell said that he would kill himself, if he were to be returned to prison. The reason is that he has been beaten in prison and 'the tonkey (turnkey) paid prisoners to attack him' He was also beaten by the police 'for force instructions.' According to the nurses' report, on the ward, he demonstrates a high degree of institutional behaviour (neurosis), where he is able to emerge as leader and at the same time present himself as victim. He is manipulative, intimidating, controlling and can set up fights and is invariably involved in articles missing from patient belongings. An example of his menacing behaviour associated with intent to both humiliate and endear the staff is the presentation to them of a sharpened toothbrush on his way from the ward to the courts with the statement, 'I could have used this!' He has easy and a ready access to cannabis on the ward and this has been confirmed by positive urine testing.

Mental status examination

Mr Derrell presented as an aggressive, hostile and disinhibited man. His speech was spontaneous and plentiful and this was sustained throughout the interview. He had an extremely paranoid tone to his speech with frequent self references to his victimization by almost everyone with whom he has come in contact with. He could not recall important personal information such as the charge, the date or whether it was night or day. He was not depressed, anxious and had no hallucinatory experiences. At times he would give approximate answers-'I do not have a mother, my mother is not my mother anymore, my twin brother is not a blood brother; I am 26 years old, they tell me 27.' He gave contradictory responses, for example when asked about his plans for the future, he stated, 'When I get out of prison, I want to be a good man with a family praying to God.' Later in the interview he stated, I am not going to play the good man, I want to be a guard to watch the big boys back'.

342   Hari D. Maharajh

Cognitively, he had diminished insight, poor judgment and understanding. When asked what do you mean by, 'you can't play mas and 'fraid powder, he replied if he did kill the person, he would not 'fraid jail.'

Opinion

The findings suggest that Mr Kerwin Derrell is suffering from a condition frequently found in prisoners known as Ganser's or Ganse's syndrome. This is a disorder associated with approximate answers absurdly wrong, but almost correct. This is classified in the ICD -10 under other Dissociative disorders and the DSM-1V-TR as Dissociative disorder NOS (not otherwise stated). A dissociative disorder is defined as a disruption in the integrated functions of memory, consciousness, identity or perception of the environment.

Approximate answers are found in several conditions including malingering, mental retardation and organic brain diseases such as epilepsy. These are all possibilities in this patient. The psychologist made reference to 'low intelligence, personality disturbance, and moderate score on psychopathy' There is a history of epilepsy or organic brain disease that has not been investigated. In addition, the use of marijuana on the forensic ward further complicates the clinical picture.

It is evident therefore, that Mr Kerwin Derrell is suffering from a mental condition or mental conditions that have affected his functioning. Psychodynamically, he was brought up without a family from institution to institution which has engendered psychopathic behaviour. He may be a victim of institutionalization for which the state is liable. Again, he has access to marijuana in a government institution where he is receiving treatment. There is reportedly a history of head injury with epileptic seizures. This has not been investigated.

Legal implications

It is not possible to make a definitive diagnosis on this patient due to the absence of social and medical records and investigations. The following investigations are needed:

- Social worker report
- Institutional reports
- Laboratory tests: Complete blood count, liver function tests, renal function tests, serological testing, testosterone levels.
- CT Scan of the head
- Electroencephalography to rule out epilepsy.
- Neuropsychological assessment.

Albeit, Mr Kerwin Derrell, has a defence of diminished responsibility.

Forensic Psychiatry in the Colonial and Post Colonial Eras

CASE STORY 3

Report of an assessment of George Noreiga following a Special Tribunal Review for release from detention on September 26th, 2006.
Re:

- HCA No 2474 of 2003 George Noreiga vs the Attorney General of Trinidad and Tobago
- High Court Action No 2107 of 2005
- Court of Appeal No 65 of 2005
- George Noreiga vs Dr Rohit Doon.

Preamble

A Special Tribunal was established to review the mental condition of Mr George Noreiga in keeping with the above Court Order. The purpose of the Tribunal was to determine whether the person convicted, hereafter referred to as the prisoner, should be released from detention. The Special Tribunal chaired by Dr Rohit Doon met in its First Sitting on Friday 28th July 2006 at 10:45 AM at the Conference Room, St Ann's Hospital. Present were Dr Rohit Doon, Chairman of the Special Tribunal, Mr Sherman Mc Nichols, Chief Magistrate and Psychiatrists Nelleen Baboolal, Gerard Hutchinson and Hari Maharajh. The prisoner was examined by the Tribunal and a decision was made for further medical and psychosocial investigations following which a report will be submitted to the Chairman.

Place of interview

I saw Mr George Noreiga, a 51 year old, left handed mixed-Trinidadian, formerly of Cache Village in Moruga at the Conference Room of the Forensic Ward of St. Ann's Hospital on Monday September 25th 2006 between the hours of 10:30 AM and 12:15 PM. He was accompanied by a Staff Nurse, Shazard Mohammed, who sat throughout the entire interview and was cooperative in every way. Sources of information:

- Interview with the patient
- Verbal information from the staff nurse
- Information from the patient notes: HCA No. 2774 of 2003- George Noreiga v the AG of Trinidad and Tobago: 'Jury returned a special verdict of guilty but insane under section 66 of the Criminal Procedure Act Chapter 12:02. Detention at the State Prison by the Presidents Pleasure sec 67. Under Section 67 Order transferred to St. Ann's Hospital on 17th June 2005.'
- Letter from Solicitor General Chamber dated 16th June 2005. George Noreiga v AG- 'case not reviewed before 20th May 2004. Attended St. Ann's Hospital.'
- Letter by Dr Hazel Othello on 5th July 2005 to Minister of National Security – ' It is no longer necessary for either of these men to remain at St Ann's Hospital since

neither Mr. Noreiga nor Mr. Funrose was found to be suffering from any psychiatric illness or to be in need of psychiatric treatment at this time.'

- Letter by Hazel Othello on 26th July 2005 to Commissioner of Prison-'for reversal of ministerial Order to return to your institution'.
- Report of interview of patient by Dr Ramtahal on 21st and 28th June 2005 and report sent to Solicitor General on 27th June 2005: 'In my opinion Mr. George Noreiga suffers mild cognitive dysfunction secondary to his stroke in 1982. He has no psychiatric illness at this time and I recommend that he be released'.
- Affidavit of Dr Rohit Doon filed on December 13, 2005.

Circumstances of the offence

Mr Noreiga was in high spirits and warmly greeted me stating that he remembered me from the last interview on July 28th, but could not recall my name. He did not know why he was being seen and did not volunteer information on his offence. He was vaguely aware that attempts were being made to release him and he had to be prompted to speak of the offence.

He stated that around June 1982, at the age of 27 years he got a stroke on the right side of the body. He could not talk and did not know himself and woke up in Port of Spain General Hospital. He said that he recalled the doctor asking him if he knew where he was and he said no. He was told that he had lost weight and also had lost his senses. According to him, he was warded 'for two months and two weeks at the hospital'.

His wife Alyson Garcia Noreiga age 25 years, lived with him for eight years. She was employed at 'Tops and Bottoms' store at St James Street in San Fernando. She visited him only two times when he was in the hospital. When he returned from the hospital 'she lock off with me and told me to pack'. She left him and returned to her mother's house in Cocoyea. He moved back to his mother's house in Moruga and would visit his wife at her workplace pleading with her to return to him.

During the Christmas month of 1983, he went to her workplace at 'Tops and Bottoms'. He had sharpened a knife the night before and fatally stabbed her four times on her chest. He threw the knife in the bush and later turned himself in to the CID in San Fernando.

Family history

His father Grant Noreiga was an oilfield worker and died at the age of 61 years; his mother is still alive at age 88 and lives with his sisters in Canada. He is the fourth of seven siblings, two brothers Alvin, 48 and Carl, 71 years. His sister Pearl has died and Sylvia, 58, Lima, 46 and Zena, 45 have all migrated. He has no siblings in Trinidad. He claims that his mother and niece Dian Noreiga suffered from nerves.

Personal history

He was born in Cache Village in Moruga. His birth and development were normal. He attended St Mary's Government school until age 15 and never attended college. After leaving school he worked on the road and later he worked as a joiner making cupboards. During the time of his stroke he was employed as a welder with Texaco Trinidad. He was married for eight years and lived with his wife in a house rented for 40 dollars per month. He also had another girl friend with whom he had a child. She migrated to the United States with her son. He was shot at the age of 19 years, in 2001. He never abused alcohol or drugs but use to smoke about three cigarettes per day. He is a Spiritual Baptist and has been to the moaning ground on one occasion.

Past history

Mr Noreiga stated that while he was at Carrera, he heard voices calling his name, while he was asleep. Around 1989 while working at the Tailoring shop, he recalls visiting Dr Ghany. He also has a fungal rash on the skin for which he is being treated. His reading and writing skills are moderately decreased.

Mental status examination

Mr Noreiga appeared to be a light brown man of Spanish descent. The latter may not be a correct ethnic reference, but a local description of people of mixed ancestry with his physical appearance. He was conscious and cooperative and walked into the examination room with an ataxic gait, that is dragging his right foot, and with decreased movement of his right arm. He was dressed in a short pants and shirt and wore slippers on his feet. Despite some central balding, his hair was overgrown and I mentioned to him that he needed a hair cut.

His speech was fluent and spontaneous, but on many occasions, there was a noticeable sensory or receptive aphasia which meant that when asked questions, he had difficult in processing and understanding the question. His speech was of a magnified tone and sometimes forced due to the defect of speech sustained by a stroke in 1982.

His affect was fatuous and shallow and there were no symptoms of dysthymia, major depression, cyclothymia or suicidal behaviour. His answers were short and it appeared as though he could not elaborate on the subject matter due to defects in attention and concentration. His long term memory was intact; he was able to give an account of the circumstances of the offence in a clear and concise manner noting that this has been well rehearsed over the period of his trial. His short term memory and recall were defective and he had difficulties in recalling three objects - table, apple and pencil that were presented to him.

His functional level was of low intelligence with restricted insight and decreased judgment. He felt that if he were discharged he will return to live with his cousin who now occupied the family's home. He felt he could continue his trade as a tailor which he had acquired at Carrera. He noted that no siblings were in Trinidad, but two months following his discharge plans were being made by his sister to have him come to Canada. He was unable to think abstractly – when asked 'what do I mean by Gopaul luck is not Seepaul luck?' He smiled knowingly but was unable to articulate the meaning.

There were no hallucinations or delusions or evidence of abnormal behavior noted during his admission on the ward. He did not interact much with the other patients. During the interview, he showed little remorse or regret of the crime he had committed. He mentioned on more than one occasion, 'when she lock off with me and said to me to check myself, I ask her what I do you? I told her I had a knife and she said she had one too'.

Physical examination

His blood pressure was found to be 130/80 and sugar level by diascan 191mg/dl. The nurse indicated that he had eaten 45 minutes ago. Power was reduced on the left upper and lower limbs. There was some difficult in use of the right hand with involuntary control and past pointing. A detailed neurological examination was not done due to lack of diagnostic sets and instruments on the ward.

Findings on investigation

The following investigations were requested when the prisoner was examined on 28th July 2006. These are:

- Psychological testing – He had been assessed by Dr K Maharaj on 11th September 2006 who administered the WAIS-R (this is a test of general intelligence. Although a quantitative level was not stated by the tester, a range of dull-normal intelligence was given), MMPI-2 (this is a test of personality. The psychologist noted high scores with exaggerated profiles and noted that the prisoner fell into the faking bad category) and he surmised that the prisoner 'does not seem to have a mental disorder at this time.'
- Laboratory investigations. The following were requested: full blood count, sedimentation rate, Thyroid function tests, liver function tests, renal function tests, cholesterol, VDRL and HIV testing. These results were not in the patient files and could not be located on the ward by the nursing staff on Monday 25th September 2006.
- MRI/A of the brain done on 21st August 2006. Report stated 'focal dilatation of the posterior body and posterior horn of the left lateral ventricle immediately adjacent to extensive signal changes within the left parieto-temporal lobe. Infarct in the posterior left middle cerebral artery territory. Focal dilatation of the ventricle in keeping with atrophy.'
- EEG – no report
- SOFA – (social, occupational and functional assessment) - no report
- Social investigation of home environment pending possible discharge. No report. available.
- MMSE – A test of cognitive assessment

Opinion

Mr George Noreiga fulfills the diagnostic criteria of a Vascular Dementia coded in DSM – IV-TR as 290.4. This is characterized by

- The development of multiple cognitive deficits manifested by both memory impairment - impaired ability to learn new information or to recall previously learned information and having one or more of the following cognitive disturbances: language disturbance (aphasia), impaired inability to carry out motor activities (apraxia), failure to recognize or identify objects (agnosia) and disturbance of executive functioning in planning, organizing, sequencing and abstracting
- These deficits cause significant impairment in social and occupational functioning and represent a decline from a previous level of functioning.
- The presence of focal neurological signs and symptoms.

According to the Mental Health Act of Trinidad and Tobago Chapter 28:02 Act 30 of 1975 Section 2 p7, he is "mentally ill" or a "mentally ill person" (which) means a person who is suffering from such a disorder of mind that he requires care, supervision, treatment and control, or any of them, for his own protection or welfare or for the protection and welfare of others.

SPECIFIC DEFENCES FOR MURDER

Provocation

Provocation is a common law defense based upon the acceptance that a reasonable, even-tempered person might be so provoked that he is driven to kill. The definition of this defence is a combination of statements in S3 Homicide Act 1957 and R v Duffy (1949), All ER 932. [13] 'Where on a charge of murder there is evidence on which the jury can find that the person charged was provoked whether by things done or by things said or by both together to lose his self control, the question whether the provocation was enough to make a reasonable man do as he did shall be left to be determined by the jury; and in determining that question the jury shall take into account everything both done and said according to the effect which, in their opinion, it would have on a reasonable man'.

In R v Duffy (1949) [13] Devlin J referred to the need for evidence that the defendant at the time of the killing, had been suffering from a sudden and temporary loss of control, rendering him so subject to passion as to make him, at that moment, no longer the master of his own mind.

In the use of provocation as a defense for murder, three stages must be followed [14,15]:

- Subjective test: The first stage of the defense is to establish whether or not the accused lost his self control (a subjective test). This is a question of fact for the jury.

- "Suddenness": The second stage is to establish that the loss of self control was 'sudden'. If there is a gap in time between provocation and the killing, there will be difficulty in establishing the defense, R. v Hayward (1833) 6 C&P 157, [16].
- "Cooling Time": In R v Ibrams and Gregory (1981) 74 CR App R 154, [17] the defendants and a young woman had been terrorized by a man called a monk. They devised a plan whereby the woman would entice him into bed and the defendants would attack him. He died and the defendants were convicted of murder. Seven days had elapsed between provocation and killing.
- "Last straw": The courts are now willing to look at the history of events leading up to the defendants outburst. R v Dryden (1995) ALL ER 987 [18] and R v Thornton (1996) ALL ER 1023. [19]
- Objective test: The third stage is an objective test. Would a reasonable person sharing the characteristic of the accused have reacted as the defendant? In the House of Lord's ruling, DPP v Camplin, (1978) AC 705, [20] there was a liberalization of this defense when a 15 year old boy who was buggered by the plaintiff, killed him with a chapatti pan. He was convicted of murder since he was judged by standards of a reasonable man. The House of Lords overruled defending the harshness of the traditional "reasonable man" approach.

A number of cases suggest that issues such as: anorexia, immaturity, dyslexia, attention-seeking and battered woman syndrome can be taken into account. For example battered women: The recent decisions including R v Ahluwalia (1992) 4 All ER 894 and R v Thornton No. 2 (1996) 2 All ER 1023 [21,22] concerning battered women who kill their husbands have brought to the public's attention the defense of provocation. These defenses have failed since circumstances which induce a desire for revenge are inconsistent with provocation. Some claim that this is unfair since males react with immediate aggressive response while females are more contemplative. Although not a medical defense, provocation appears to be moving in that direction.

Diminished responsibility

The defense of diminished responsibility was introduced by S2 of the Homicide Act 1957, which provides: "Where a person kills or is party to the killing of another, he shall not be convicted of murder if he was suffering form such abnormality of mind (whether arising from a condition of arrested or retarded development of mind of any inherent causes or induced by disease or injury) has substantially impaired his mental responsibility for his acts and omissions in doing or being a party to the killing" [23]. There are 2 stages to this defense:

- To investigate whether the accused was suffering from an abnormality of mind due to retarded development, inherent causes or diseases or injury. Abnormality of mind due to external causes, such as drinks or drugs are excluded R v Gittens (1984) QB 698 [24].
- To investigate whether the abnormality is so great that it has substantially impaired the accused responsibility.

The burden of proof lies with the defense as a balance of probabilities. It should be noted that Lord Parker ruled against the trial judge in R v Bryne (1961) 2QB 369 [25] on a sexual psychopath, who had strangled a young woman. He did not allow the ground of diminished responsibility. He stated that an abnormality of the mind was simply a state of the mind that the reasonable person would find abnormal and this was essentially a matter of fact for the jury to determine. The following have been held to amount to diminished responsibility:

- Epilepsy, R v Bailey (1977) 66 Cr App R 31 [26]
- Morbid jealousy, R v Vinagre (1979) 69 Cr App R 104 [27]
- Depression, R v Gittens (1984) QB 698 [24]
- Effects of alcoholism, R v Tandy (1989) CR 350 [28]

In Trinidad, the Privy Council has recently ruled on diminished responsibility for Indravani Ramjattan, who was on a murder charge and submitted a defense of provocation. She was not acquitted. She was given the reduced sentence of 5 years for manslaughter due to battered wife syndrome.

Diminished responsibility and intoxication

Intoxication becomes a relevant factor where it amounted to chronic alcoholism in that the defendant's responsibility for his actions became substantially impaired because of his craving for drinks R v Tandy (1989) 1 All ER 267 [28] or drugs R v Sanderson (1994) 98 CR App R 325 [29]. The fact that a defendant might have been drunk at the time of committing a murder is highly irrelevant to the issue of diminished responsibility, as it will not constitute an "inherent cause".

Infanticide

S1 Infanticide Act 1938 where a woman, by act on omission causes the death of her child under the age of 12 months, but at that time the balance of her mind was disturbed by reason of her not having fully recovered from the effect of giving birth [30].

Suicide pact

S4 Homicide Act 1957. It is manslaughter, and not murder where a person kills another in pursuance of a suicide pact, that is common agreement between two or more people, having for its object the death of all of them. Note that a person who aids, abets, counsels or procures the suicide or attempted suicide of another is liable [31].

DISCUSSION

In this chapter general information is presented for psychiatrists and mental health workers in the specialty of forensic psychiatry which is often viewed as difficult and demanding, especially with the need for frequent court appearances with numerous adjournments of the same cases. Three cases are reported. Case one never reached the courts so confidentiality is needed, while Case 2 and 3 are in the public domain.

In Case 1, changes in blood glucose levels are associated with mental disorders, antisocial and criminal activities. This is more commonly seen in hypoglycaemic than in hyperglycaemic conditions. Hyperglycaemia or high blood sugar may precipitate mental disorders. This is viewed as a disease of the body which affects the mind and carries a legal defence of insanity. The most probable diagnosis of this patient at the time of the fire setting is delirium induced by hyperglycaemia. There is no formal psychiatric diagnosis other than delirium secondary to a General Medical Condition. This is supported by the absence of a psychiatric history, uneventful physical findings, normal electrolytes, hyperglycaemia due to poorly regulated Type 1 diabetes as evidenced by a high level of glycosalated hemoglobin and a spontaneous recovery.

It can be argued that a blood glucose level of 495 mg/dl is below the range to cause delirium. This level must be interpreted in the setting of a gentleman who experienced three hours of ordeal with rats that caused him to engage in an enormous amount of physical activities. This would have reduced his blood glucose levels. It is unlikely that the long standing dispute with his neighbour who had arranged a marriage for him to her niece which he had rejected would have resulted in a brief psychotic disorder. The question of liability for arson is unlikely since the defendant is suffering from a disease of the body that is, hyperglycaemia which affected the mind. He therefore has the defence of insanity. In this case, if he is charged, the defendant cannot make a plea for the defence of automatism (caused by external factors) as is normally done in cases of hypoglycaemia.

This study highlights the existence of the less commonly described hyperglycaemic delirium with far-reaching consequences of financial loss and forensic intervention. Hyperglycaemic delirium is a severe state with paranoid delusions and visual hallucinations and hyperglycaemia can lead to other severe states like hyperglycaemic hyperosmolarity without ketosis to diabetic ketoacidosis [32]. The psychodynamics of fire setting in this patient was not motivated by insurance fraud, bankruptcy, revenge or to cover up another crime. There seem to be no primary interest in the fire for the purpose of excitement or sexual arousal, release of tension or the desire to be a hero. His motives were a response to intense fear experienced from visual hallucinations of man-eating rats that chased him. There was no intent to damage property. He had intended to smoke the rodents from the house after failing to lock them out. Even in his delirious state, he made a culturally acceptable attempt to destroy the rats but got the setting wrong. In delirium, the individual responds to the abnormal perception without insight to the consequences. In such circumstances, there is no case to answer or if charged, he can plead insanity through the special verdict of M'Naughten rule.

In less developed and developing countries ample regulation of blood glucose levels by medication is a major problem. This is because of the lack of education and information about the severity of diabetes mellitus and consequently the absence of knowledge on the long-term consequences of the disease. In addition, oral medication for diabetes mellitus Type 2 and insulin preparations are less available. The daily monitoring of blood sugar levels is impractical and costly. The disease itself is coloured with cultural beliefs and local herbal treatment modalities that make control difficult.

Special care is needed for both insulin-dependent diabetes mellitus and non insulin-dependent diabetes mellitus patients and the appearance of disturbances in consciousness and behavioural changes. In this case, the delirium was preceded with vague symptoms of de-realization suggesting a deregulation of the blood sugar level. General practitioners and nurses should be sensitized to the clinical presentations of hypoglycaemia and hyperglycaemia with a view to early intervention. Blood sugar are connected with emotional instability, confusion, antisocial and criminal behaviour. Health care workers have an important part to play in maintaining social order within the criminal justice system. Few studies have investigated the association between hyperglycaemia and delirium resulting in the destruction of property by fire.

General practitioners and nurses should be sensitized to the clinical presentations of changes in blood sugar levels in diabetic patients with a view to early intervention. Blood glucose levels are connected with emotional instability, confusion, antisocial and criminal behaviour. Health care workers have an important part to play in maintaining social order within the criminal justice system. Fire setting or arson is the unlawful destruction or damage to property by fire. It is a common finding in mentally ill offenders and individuals with abnormal blood sugar levels. The latter is associated with antisocial and criminal behaviour [33]. The commonest finding is the relationship between hypoglycaemia or low blood sugar and criminality [34] and violence and reactive hypoglycaemia, that is, a tendency towards very low blood sugar levels as a reaction to being given a large dose of glucose [35]. Hyperglycaemia or high blood sugar is a less common cause of criminal behaviour and is interpreted as a disease of the body which affects the mind and is classified as insanity.

In cases 2 and 3, both individuals were charged with murder. Case no 2 was seen at the Forensic Unit at St Anns Hospital for a court report. Case No 3 was seen following the setting up of a special tribunal by the President to investigate his prolonged incarceration in prison without redress.

In Case 2, it is not possible to make a definitive diagnosis on this patient due to the absence of social and medical records and investigations. However, a number of differential diagnoses are possible. These are Ganser Syndrome, Epilepsy, Psychopathy, Mental Retardation, Personality Disorder, Cannabis related disorder and Malingering. There is sufficient psychopathology to submit a defence for Diminished Responsibility described above.

The availability of cannabis at the Forensic Unit, raises the issue of the accuracy of Court reports from that institution. In addition, it violates the rights of patients and their families to fair treatment. It is apparent that there is a security risk in housing. Forensic patients at St Ann's Hospital and the high rates of recidivism and remand put too much stress on the system. It is estimated that 18% of the admission to St Ann's Hospital is due to admission from the Courts [9].

In the present climate, The Forensic Unit at St Ann's Hospital should be transferred to Maximum Security Unit at Golden Grove where facilities were built for that purpose. This will enable better control of patients heightening the therapeutic processes where health professionals will not be viewed as goalers, reduction of drug use, and preoccupation of psychiatrists in having patients sent back to prison.

Case 3 supports the previous claims by the PAHO experts who lamented the absence of the protection of mentally ill patients in prisons and hospitals. Mr Noreiga has paid his dues to society but languishes in prison indefinitely contrary to Sections 18 and 20 of the Mental Health Act. There is overwhelming evidence from the history, examination and investigation that Mr. George Noreiga is suffering from a Mental illness despite evidence to the contrary from cited reports of two psychiatrists and one psychologist. Two of these reports cited psychopathological findings but concluded the absence of mental illness. It appears that these matters are not treated with urgency and in a frivolous manner. This patient suffered a stroke and now has a vascular dementia which will certainly affect his return to the greater society. As a consequence, the following are of concern:

- If returned to the community can the patient /prisoner live in a non supportive environment, independent of help from relatives or helping agency? It should be noted that his relatives are abroad and without insight, he thinks he can join them.
- What are the chances of re-offending again or recidivism?
- Will the state be held liable for returning an individual to the community without providing the necessary structure and amenities that is necessary for his survival in the light of moderate cognitive disability?
- What has been the outcome of persons returned to the community locally and internationally? Local findings are for the most part anecdotal, but the Jamaican repatriate programme has had extremely poor outcome.

Consideration should also be given to the fact that social programmes of half way houses and sheltered workshops or intensive social work case managements are not present in Trinidad and Tobago. It will not be without risk to return Mr. Noreiga to the community. It would be instructive to get the social work reports, the aforementioned report of Dr Ghany and the visit made by the prisoner while he was in the prison island of Carrera. In addition, the medical notes of his stay at Port of Spain General Hospital will be useful.

Mr Noreiga has benefited tremendously from his incarceration from the point of his health in that he has been confined in a sheltered environment with reduced stressful factors. If Mr Noreiga were to be discharged, a period of rehabilitation at Arima Rehabilitation centre with graded return and intensive social support and care management by social workers and other members of the health team is recommended for a duration of six months. Without supportive care his outcome will favor a poor prognosis.

CONCLUSION

The circular theory of society contributing to your illness and in return punishing you for it is not without merit. Finding the best line between the rights of individuals and the rights of society is not easy. In developing societies, it is sometimes difficult to enact legislations that have been handed down. Despite statutes on marijuana use for example, there may be more discretion to its usage in Jamaica than in Barbados. The non-abolishment of capital punishment in Trinidad and Tobago and other Caribbean islands adds a different meaning to Forensic Psychiatry with more emphasis on defenses. With a poorly established infrastructure and inadequate services in Mental Hospitals and Prisons, the assessment of mentally ill offenders is no easy task. There is a need for closer collaboration of the justice and medical systems especially in the field of mental health. Too much adversary exists.

REFERENCES

[1]   Mental health Act No 30. Laws of the Republic of Trinidad and Tobago. Chapter 1975;28:02.

[2]   Seheult R. A survey of the Trinidad Medical Services 1814-1944. Archival report. Trinidad and Tobago: Ministry of Health, 1948.

[3]   Boucaud JEA. The practice of medicine in the British West Indies. Caribb Med J 1962;24(1-4):40-4.

[4]   Tinker H. A new system of slavery. The export of Indian labour overseas 1830-1920. London: Oxford Univ Press, 1974.

[5]   Maharajh HD, Ali A. The mental health policies of Trinidad and Tobago. Bulletin of the Board of International Affairs, Royal College of Psychiatrists, 2004:13-16.

[6]   Beaubrun MH. How does the community care? An Historical review and current perspectives on health/mental health models in the commonwealth Caribbean. Keynote Address delivered at Runaway Bay, Jamaica, 1983 Apr 24.

[7]   Maharajh HD, Parasram R. Psychiatry in Trinidad and Tobago. Int Rev Psychiatry 1999;11:173-83.

[8]   Mental Health Act No.6 of 1998 Jamaica. Assented to by HF Cooke, Governor General, 25th day of March, 1997.

[9]   Maharajh HD, Ali A. Deinstitutionalization in the Caribbean: A tale of two countries. Caribb Med J 2004; 66(1): 25-35

[10]   Gordon RM, Verdun Jones SN. Mental health law and law reform in the Commonwealth: The rise of the 'new legalism?' In: Weistub DN, ed. Law and mental health. International perspectives. New York: Pergamon, 1986;2:1-82.

[11]   Aviram U. Care or convenience? On the medical-bureaucratic model of commitment of the mentally ill. Int J Law Psychiatr 1990;13: 163-77.

[12]   Arboleda-Florez J. Report on Forensic Psychiatric Services in Trinidad and Tobago. OAHO Consultant to Ministry of Health, Government of Trinidad and Tobago, 1999.

[13]   R v Duffy (1949) All ER 932.

[14]   Templeman L. Revision Workbook. Criminal Law. Old Bailey Press, 1999.

[15]   Templeman L, Mohan MT. Criminal Law. Old Bailey Press, 1997.

[16]   R. v Hayward (1833) 6 C&P 157

[17]   R v Ibrams and Gregory (1981) 74 CR App R 154

[18]   R v Dryden (1995) ALL ER 987

[19]   R v Thornton (1996) ALL ER 1023.

[20]   DPP v Camplin, (1978) AC 705

[21]   R v Ahluwalia (1992) 4 All ER 894

[22]   R v Thornton No. 2 (1996) 2 All ER 1023

[23]   S2 of the Homicide Act 1957

[24]   R v Gittens (1984) QB 698

[25]   R v Bryne (1961) 2QB 369

[26]   R v Bailey (1977) 66 Cr App R 31.

[27]   R v Vinagre (1979) 69 Cr App R 104.

[28]   R v Tandy (1989) CR 350

[29]   R v Sanderson (1994) 98 CR App R 325.

[30]   S1 Infanticide Act 1938

[31]   S4 Homicide Act 1957

[32]   Matz R. Management of the hyperosmolar hyperglycemic syndrome. Am Fam Physician 1999;60(5):1468-76.

[33] Schoenthaler SJ. The effects of blood sugar on the treatment and control of antisocial behaviour: A double- blind study of an incarcerated juvenile population. Int J Biopsoc Res 1982;3:1.

[34] Clapham B. A case of hypoglcaemia. Criminologist 1989;13:2.

[35] Virkkunen M. Metabolic dysfunctions among habitually violent offenders: Reactive hypoglycaemia and cholesterol levels. In: Mednick SA, Moffitt TE, Stack Sa, eds. The causes of crime: New biological approaches. Cambridge: Cambridge Univ Press, 1987.

In: Social and Cultural Psychiatry Experience from the...
Editor: Hari D. Maharajh and Joav Merrick

ISBN: 978-1-61668-506-5
© 2010 Nova Science Publishers, Inc.

Chapter 30

LUNACY, TIME OF THE YEAR AND ABSCONDING FROM A PSYCHIATRIC HOSPITAL

Hari D. Maharajh and Akleema Ali

Personal characteristics of patients and environmental factors at psychiatric hospitals have been identified as predictors of absconding. In this chapter we seek to establish a relationship between time of the year and absconding. All characteristics of absconders were taken over a two – year period from hospital records (N = 104). Public holidays and lunar phases were obtained through almanacs for each year; and school vacation period was determined by reference to a school academic calendar. Fridays was the most popular day of the week for absconding. Males were more likely to escape on the weekends while females tended to escape during the wet season. Christmas was the most popular holiday season for absconding. The largest percentage of absconding was at the full moon phase. It is recommended that the system of patient care should be client driven at all times and greater supervision of patients is needed on weekends, vacation periods and during the full moon phase.

INTRODUCTION

A number of predictors have been identified as contributory factors of absconding at psychiatric hospitals. These include personal characteristics such as multiple admissions, male sex, single status and younger age [1-3] and environmental factors such as stigmatization, ward settings, attitude of staff, lack of privacy, harassment by other patients and concerns about their homes and families [4-6]. To date, no investigation has been done that investigates the relationship between time of the year and absconding in a psychiatric hospital in a developing country.

In the third world setting, a number of factors have been reported that can facilitate absconding [7]. Factors can be categorized as being endemic or trigger factors. Endemic or chronic factors are those that have persisted over many years. Endemic factors such as overcrowding and acute staff shortages are common. Other factors that contribute to absconding are poor conditions, long stay of patients, abandonment, rejection and absence of visits by relatives and the lack of therapeutic and occupational activities leading to boredom and institutional aimlessness. In addition, there are improper nursing personnel 'plan of care' with the absence of standardized treatment and follow-up, incomplete documentation and handing over, irregular visits and unsatisfactory treatment by doctors on the ward, absence of basic amenities and the workers frustration resulting in the displacement of anger and aggression in the hospital setting.

Trigger factors act as precipitants and consist of occurrences such as riots on the wards for food, space or clothing, fear of personal safety due to aggression, fires, electrical outages and brutalization and the inability of the staff to defuse the situation. Other trigger factors are the transfer of staff and the admission of new disturbed patients.

Among all Caribbean islands, Trinidad and Tobago has the most public holidays. Most are at fixed dates and others vary annually. Due to the fact that it is a tropical country, Trinidad does not experience the four seasons (spring, summer, autumn and winter) typical of temperate countries. Instead there are two (2) distinct seasons: dry and wet season. The dry season (January – May) is characterized by mostly dry, hot, humid weather, while the wet season (June – December) is occasioned with heavy rains, thunderstorms and the possibilities of hurricanes.

The objective of this study is to investigate whether a relationship exists between time of the year (weekends, holidays, season and lunar phase) and absconding at St. Ann's Psychiatric Hospital in Trinidad.

Table 1. Public holidays for 1999 and 2000

1999		2000	
Holiday	Date	Holiday	Date
New Year's Day	January 1st	New Year's Day	January 1st
Eid-Ul-Fitr	January 19th	Eid-Ul-Fitr	January 9th
Carnival Monday*	February 15th	Carnival Monday*	March 6th
Carnival Tuesday*	February 16th	Carnival Tuesday*	March 7th
Shouter Baptist Liberation Day	March 30th	Shouter Baptist Liberation Day	March 30th
Good Friday	April 2nd	Good Friday	April 21st
Easter Monday	April 5th	Easter Monday	April 24th
Arrival Day	May 30th	Arrival Day	May 30th
Corpus Christi	June 3rd	Labor Day	June 19th
Labor Day	June 19th	Corpus Christi	June 22nd
Emancipation Day	August 1st	Emancipation Day	August 1st
Independence Day	August 31st	Independence Day	August 31st
Divali	November 8th	Divali	October 26th
Christmas	December 25th	Christmas	December 25th
Boxing Day	December 26th	Boxing Day	December 26th
		Eid-Ul-Fitr	December 27th

* Non-Statutory Public Holidays

OUR STUDY AND FINDINGS

Public holidays for each year were obtained through the public holidays listing within almanacs for each year. Table 1 shows the public holiday listing for 1999 and 2000. Easter and Christmas seasons were determined by reference to a school academic calendar (see table

2). The school academic calendar is issued by the Permanent Secretary of the Ministry of Education and forwarded to all school principals and supervisors. The lunar phases were gathered using the almanacs for each year and were defined as being three days preceding and three days following the specific moon date. Patients' characteristics such as gender, ward and date escape occurred and average number of nurses on duty per month was taken from hospital records over a two-year period.

Table 2. Holiday seasons as specified by school academic calendar

HOLIDAY SEASON	1999	2000
Easter	March 27th - April 11th	April 15th – April 30th
July – September (Mid-Summer) Vacation	July 10th – September 1st	July 8th – September 3rd
Christmas	December 11th – January 2nd	December 9th – January 3rd

All data was entered and analyzed by the use of SPSS (Statistical Package for the Social Sciences, Version 8.0). Data was collected along a nominal level therefore the main statistical test used was Chi-Square.

In total there were 104 escapes (N = 104) from January 1999 to December 2000. Male absconding amounted to 85% of all escapes while female escapes were only 15%. This gender difference was statistically significant, Pearson Chi-square = 49.846, df = 1, p < 0.001. The most popular (24%) day of the week for escapes to occur was on a Friday (see figure 1).

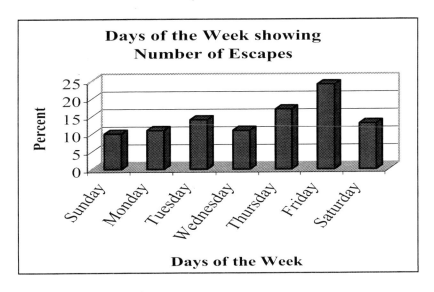

Figure 1. Escape and day of the week

Majority of escapes (77%) took place during the week while 23% took place on weekends. The finding proved significant where Chi-square = 30.154, df = 1, p < 0.001. With respect to season, 66% of escapes took place during the wet season and 34% during the dry season, which again was significant, Chi-square = 11.15, df = 1, p < 0.01. Most popular months for escapes were June (16%), December (15%) and January (14%). This result was significant, Chi-square = 27.077, df = 11, p < 0.01.

Four percent (4%) of all escapes fell on a public holiday. When the public holiday fell on a Monday, 9% of escapes occurred on the weekend (Saturday and Sunday). With regards to escapes that occurred within a particular holiday season, 75% was at Christmas season, 15% was at Easter season, 5% on Emancipation Day and 5% on Carnival Sunday. This result proved significant where Chi-square = 27.20, df = 3, p < 0.001.

Males were more likely (38%) than their female counterparts (13%) to escape in the dry season. On the other hand, females were more likely (87%) than males (62%) to escape in the wet season (see figuret 2). The relationship that existed between gender and season proved to be significant where Pearson X2 = 3.790, d.f. = 1, p < 0.05.

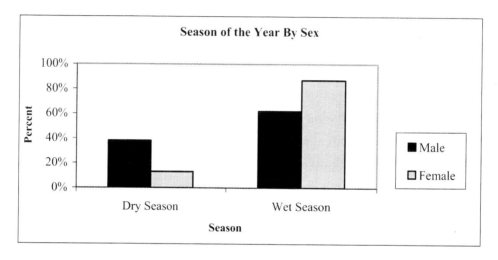

Figure 2. Escape and season of the year

Males were also more likely (26%) than female absconders (6%) to escape on the weekend (see table 3). The relationship existing between gender and escapes during the week / weekend missed significance where, Pearson Chi-square = 3.016, df = 1, p < 0.05 NS (p = 0.082).

Table 3. Escape (week/weekend) by gender

	Male N	%	Female N	%
Weekend	23	26	1	6
During the Week	65	74	15	94
Total	88	100	16	100

When escapes outside school vacation was controlled for, 48% of escapes during the July-September vacation period, 43% was during the Christmas vacation and 9% occurred during the Easter vacation. Females were more likely (43.8%) than males to escape during the school vacation period than their male counterparts (31.8%). Despite this fact, the relationship existing between gender and school vacation period was non-significant, Pearson Chi-square = .863, df = 1, p < 0.05 NS.

The cumulative mean (1999 and 2000) for number of nurses on duty per month was 459. Majority (57%) of nurses on duty per month was less than the mean. Of the 57%, 75% was at Christmas vacation, 15% was at Easter vacation and 10% was at July –September vacation.

Overall correlation between number of vacation days and absconding rate revealed a low non-significant relationship where r = .439, p < 0.05 NS (see figure 3). Further analysis on Christmas vacation revealed a perfect correlation where r = 1, p < 0.01 between vacation days and absconding.

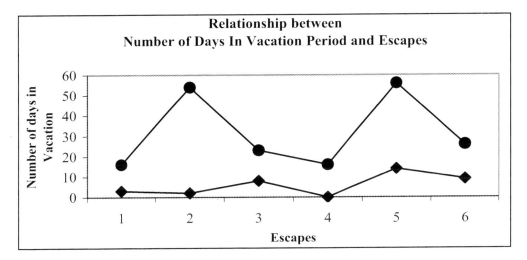

Figure 3. Escape and number of days in vacation period

The majority (37%) of escapes occurred during the full moon phase, 24% was during the new moon, 24% during the last quarter phase, and 14% occurred during the first quarter phase (see figure 4). This trend proved significant where Chi-square = 8.393, df = 3, p < 0.05. A greater percentage (41.7%) of females escaped during the full moon phase when compared to males (36.4%). There was no statistical difference between gender and all lunar phases, Pearson Chi-square = .380, df = 3, p < 0.05 NS.

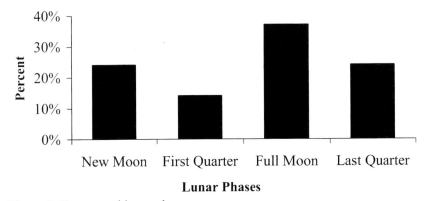

Figure 4. Escape and lunar phase

DISCUSSION

Findings indicate that there is a significant relationship between time of the year and absconding rates of patients at St. Ann's Hospital (n = 104). Seasons related both to climatic changes and festivity resulted in increased escapes. An interesting finding was that two thirds of all escapes occurred during the rainy season from June to December with peak time being the seasonal transition months of January, June and December (45%). Females were more likely to escape than males (1.4:1) in the wet season while the reverse was true in the dry season (2.9:1).

At St. Ann's Hospital peaks of hospital admission for depression have been reported for females during the months of January, June and December [8]. The concomitant increase of female escapes during these months might be explained by an increase of female admissions due to a seasonal pattern of depression. This seasonal variation does support the hypothesis that depressive episodes show a seasonal pattern in temperate countries [9-11]. Further investigation is needed in tropical countries.

The majority of male admissions to St. Ann's Hospital are diagnosed with schizophrenic disorders [12,13]. It is well established in the "social drift" hypothesis that psychiatric patients, especially chronic schizophrenics will seek out or drift to urban areas [14]. Our findings of increased escapes of male patients during the dry season and weekends can be explained by the fact that the majority of male escapes are schizophrenics who are exposed to high temperatures and overcrowding. Patients with mental illness feel more crowded than those without psychiatric disorders [15]. In addition, it has been reported that men become more hostile and aggressive in high-density environs [16].

With respect to days of the week, Fridays were the most popular day that escapes occurred (24%), followed by Thursdays 16% (see figure 1). Thursdays and Fridays are the official paydays in our setting. As the week comes to an end patients face the prospect of spending yet another weekend isolated, with family abandonment, hopelessness and despair. Another contributory factor to 'end of weekday escape' is the low level of activity at the hospital during weekends, compared to the high degree of entertainment and socialization in the community in a population well known for its frolic and festive attitudes.

The finding that males absconded during the weekend may reflect the admission diagnoses that the majority of male admissions suffered from schizophrenia and substance abuse [13,14]. As already stated these patients perceivably with a low degree of internal stimulation will seek out areas of high activity. This is in contrast to the low absconding rate during Carnival and public holidays (4%). This is an expected finding, since during these days there are planned celebrations within the hospital that the patients look forward to. In addition, national celebrations in the city of Port-of-Spain, a few miles away afford patients the opportunity to attend them through 'passes' and 'town parole'. At that time the movement of the general population is toward the city areas. Patients are therefore not tempted to return home.

The correlation between escapes and vacation period during the wet season is based on the fact that the two larger school vacations, the mid-summer break of 52 days and the Christmas break of 25 days fall within the rainy season. During these periods, children are out of school and mothers or caretakers of extended family, traditionally female, are needed at home. During these periods absenteeism among nurses are common, and many health workers go on leave to spend holidays with their children. This is supported by the findings that a 7% decrease in the average number of nurses on duty from 1999 to 2000 resulted in a doubling of the absconding rate during the same period of time.

A perfect correlation between absconding and the Christmas vacation r = 1, p < 0.01 underlines the meaning of Christmas to everyone. It is a period of relaxation of rules and regulations at the hospital where everyone seeks to be home with their families.

The highest percentage (37%) of escapes occurred within the full moon period when compared to the other lunar phases (new moon, first quarter and last quarter). Traditionally the full moon has been linked to crime, suicide, mental illness, disasters, accidents, birthrates and fertility among other things. The relationship between absconding and the lunar phases, particularly the difference in gender, needs to be investigated further.

This study identifies an association with absconding from a mental hospital to time of the year. Knowledge of the types of patients with respect to sex and diagnosis, the pattern of escapes, Fridays, vacation period of weekdays, seasonal variations and lunar phases are important parameters for planning the delivery of health care and administrative restructuring of a psychiatric hospital. These findings should be used to strengthen the structural and managerial system at the St. Ann's Hospital and the system of patient care ought to be made more robust and client driven at all times. There should be increased nursing personnel and administrators during the latter half of the year (June – December). It is imperative that hospital and nursing administrators restructure their staffing. Male wards should be supervised more closely on the weekends, while the females during the school vacation periods, and all patients during the full moon phase. In addition, it is recommended that more activity is needed during the weekend period to reduce the isolation of the patients.

REFERENCES

[1] Mueller DJ. The "missing" patient. BMJ 1962;1:177-9.
[2] Milner G. The absconder. Comprehen Psychiatry 1966;7:147-51.
[3] Antebi R. Some characteristics of mental hospitals absconders. Br J
[4] Psychiatry 1967;113:1087-90.
[5] Altman H, Angle HV, Brown ML, et al. Prediction of unauthorized absence. Am J Psychiatry 1972;128:1460.
[6] Tomison AR. Characteristics of psychiatric hospitals absconders. Br J Psychiatry 1989;154:368-71.
[7] Falkowski J, Watts V, Falkowski W, Dean T. Patients leaving hospital without the knowledge or permission of staff – absconding. Br J Psychiatry 1990;156:488-90.
[8] Maharajh H, Ali A. Escapes from a West Indian psychiatric hospital: a two-year retrospective analysis. West Indian Med J 2002;51(2):43.
[9] St Ann's Hospital. Annual Records. Medical Records Department. 1999 – 2000.
[10] Eastwood MR, Staisny S. Psychiatric disorder, hospital admission and season. Arch Gen Psychiatry 1978;35:766-71.
[11] Parker G, Walter S. Seasonal variation in depressive disorder and suicidal deaths in New South Wales. Br J Psychiatry 1982;140:626-32.
[12] Silverstone T, Romans S, Hunt N, McPherson H. Is there a seasonal pattern of relapse in bipolar affective disorders? A northern and southern hemisphere cohort study. Br J Psychiatry 1995;167:58-60.
[13] Neehall J. An analysis of psychiatric inpatient admissions from a defined geographical area over a one year period. West Indian Med J 1991;40(1):16-21.

[14] Hilwig M, Maharajh HD. Pattern of first admissions in a psychiatric outpatient clinic in Trinidad. West Indian Med J 1992;41(2):32.

[15] Goldberg EM, Morrison SL. Schizophrenia and social class. Br J Psychiatry 1963;109:785.

[16] Kamal P, Gupta ID. Feeling of crowding and psychiatric disorders. Indian J Psychiatry 1963;30:85-9.

[17] Aiello JR, Thompson DE, Brodzinsky DM. How funny is crowding anyway? Effects of room size, group size and the introduction of humor. Basic Appl Soc Psychiatry 1983;4:193-207.

SECTION SEVEN: REFLECTIONS

In: Social and Cultural Psychiatry Experience from the...
Editor: Hari D. Maharajh and Joav Merrick

ISBN: 978-1-61668-506-5
© 2010 Nova Science Publishers, Inc.

Chapter 31

THE WAY FORWARD

Hari D. Maharajh and Joav Merrick

In Jamaica, there is a proverb that says 'crocodile lay eggs, but him no fowl' meaning that things are not always the way, they seem to be. The eggs of research have been laid for many years now in the Caribbean region, well fertilized by the founding of the University of the West Indies in 1948 and annual conferences by the Caribbean Health Research Council (CHRC). Furthermore, many academics, who have studied abroad have maintained ties with their former instructors and colleagues and have partnered in conferences and research. So too, have specialty branches of Medicine, who have established their own societies and host annual conferences. Both the Medical Associations and the Psychiatry Associations in the Caribbean have done well in fostering research and through its organ the Caribbean Medical Journal have since 1938, highlighted and disseminated research findings in the region. Caribbean Governments for the most part have not been supportive of research and seem to have little interest. This is not unusual for developing regions, since research is often seen as superfluous, investing in what we already know and perceived by many to be at the top of Maslow's hierarchy.

There is no dearth of research in the Caribbean; there is however, the difficulty of bringing Caribbean findings to the forefront. In the past, theses and projects were lost for public consumption, since the major purpose was not their research contents, but their utility in matriculating for a postgraduate degree. The majority of researchers never carried the process through and left their work in obscured areas of Caribbean libraries, if perchance they had qualified for shelving. In other words, publication has been the major problem facing Caribbean writers and researchers with little opportunity to get their work on the international fora.

Over the last decade research publications from the Caribbean have moved from a trickle to a flood with water rushes from Jamaica and Trinidad. While there has been a fair amount of publications in international journals, written texts by people of the Caribbean have been few and far between. In the neurosciences, Professor Fred Hickling from Jamaica started the process with a number of text publications in psychology and psychiatry. Despite the age old criticism of 'Jamaican monopoly', his texts on psychology, psychiatry and culture represent a new movement, a landmark in Caribbean research and publication. Similarly, In Trinidad, there exists untapped potential for writing in the neurosciences with Professor Hutchinson.

It seems as though, Caribbean people have come to terms with their academic achievements and are at the watershed of a new evolutionary process of self-documentation. This should be encouraged, with the knowledge that culturally, there will always be criticisms. It is well known that in any gathering of three people in the region, there are five opinions, just as the wisdom of Israel founding father David Ben Gurion, who observed that for every two Jews there are three opinions (and we usually also say five political parties). This has given us a reputation for not only answering question with questions, but a perception that we mostly operate with conflicts. In April 2005 one of the authors (HDM) published a textbook on neurology for students, presented in twelve simple learning units, which has proven helpful for nurses, students and doctors. This undertaking was encouraging.

This book presents research undertakings from over the past fifteen years. Some are published works and have been adapted for publication in this text. It is written with the intention that the contents presented will provide a foundation on which to build. It is predicted that there will be discussions and disagreements, since we did not shy away from controversial issues in thought and practice. This will serve well for the present academic renaissance in Trinidad and Tobago and other Caribbean countries. If the goal lies in seeking truth, then it must be somewhere between what is recorded and the recesses of your own mind. The text is therefore interactive, with you being an integral part of the contents presented. The way forward is to inspire, stimulate, educate and record our own history and lifestyles as we lay claims to being developed nations. Intended to raise eyebrows, this book will make a difference, not only as a first text in psychiatry in the Southern Caribbean, but in the exposure of behaviours hitherto concealed. Students at the various Universities and institutions will be the arbiters, their views are welcomed. Let us be reminded that we cannot make an omelette without breaking an egg or even boil yam without first removing the skin.

The way forward is well enunciated in chapter 2. It is not looking into the mirror and seeing the reflections of others. It is a necessity to capture the uniqueness of the Caribbean experience, a society immersed in the supernaturalism of culture-forms of demon possession, magical realism, obeah, priestcraft and witchcraft. Supernaturalism and magical realism reflective of Caribbean societies are the controlling aesthetics passed trans-generationally through folklore and storytelling. The way forward is to articulate a Caribbean identity, self definition and experience by those immersed in a post colonial Caribbean society.

The way forward is Caribbeing psychiatry, a psychological process of unravelling the cultural tapestry of the tightly woven web of witchcraft, religion, madness and science, which can best be done by Caribbeing people themselves.

SECTION EIGHT: ACKNOWLEDGMENTS

In: Social and Cultural Psychiatry Experience from the...   ISBN: 978-1-61668-506-5
Editor: Hari D. Maharajh and Joav Merrick   © 2010 Nova Science Publishers, Inc.

Chapter 32

ABOUT THE AUTHORS

Petal S Abdool, is a resident in Psychiatry at the University of Toronto. She previously worked as a senior House Officer in the Psychiatry Department of the San Fernando General Hospital located in Trinidad and Tobago. She is a graduate of the University of the West Indies, Faculty of Medical Sciences, Eric Williams Complex Mount Hope, Trinidad. She started her postgraduate training in Psychiatry at Mount Hope and later moved to the University of Toronto, where she is pursuing post-graduate studies in Psychiatry. Also a national scholarship winner with a keen interest in research. E-mail: petal_abdool@yahoo.co.uk

Akleema Ali, BSc, is currently a Guidance Officer in the student Support Services Division of the Ministry of Education In Trinidad. In 2004, she was awarded a Commonwealth Scholarship to pursue research at the Maudsley Hospital in London. She is an excellent student with skills in research methodology and statistics.

Ria Birbal is a final year medical student who volunteered for a class project in psychiatry during her clerkship rotation.

Risa Birbal is a final year medical student who volunteered for a class project in psychiatry during her clerkship rotation.

Maria Clapperton is a final year medical student who volunteered for a class project in psychiatry during her clerkship rotation

Johnathan Jarvis is a final year medical student who volunteered for a class project in psychiatry during his clerkship rotation

Astra Kassiram, BSc, MSc, MSc completed both her undergraduate and postgraduate degrees at the Department of Sociology, Psychology and Social Work at the University of the West Indies in Jamaica. She obtained a BSc in Psychology in 1999 and a MSc degree in 2002. Following her return to Trinidad, she worked for a brief period as a counselling psychologist with the Ministry of Education. She later re-entered the University of the West Indies in Trinidad where she succesfully pursued another MSc degree in Criminology and Criminal Jurisprudence. Her interests are psychological testing, teaching and transcultural psychology. At the present time, Ms. Kassiram is employed as a lecturer with the University of the Southern Caribbean in Trinidad.

Monique Konings, MD is currently a Consultant Psychiatrist attached to the Psychiatric Unit, Mental Health care, OOst Brabant, the Netherlands. She spent a one year research fellowship at the Psychiatry Unit at Mount Hope Hospital, Trinidad where she was involved in research. Her interests are substance abuse, and transcultural psychiatry.

Katija Khan, BSc, MSc, is a PhD candidate and teaching fellow in the Clinical Neuroscience Centre at the University of Hull in England. She did her undergraduate training in Trinidad and Masters in Psychology in Jamaica. Her present interests include cross-cultural assessments, HIV/AIDS, Alzheimer's disease and dementia.

Hari D Maharajh, (pictured below) BSc (Hons), MBBS (UWI), MRCPsych, Dip Clin Neuro, LLB (Hons), CMT; FRCPsych, Consultant Neuropsychiatrist, is a Professor of Psychiatry at the University of the West Indies, Mount Hope, Trinidad. He has pursued an academic career with interests in medicine, law and social sciences. He studied zoology and chemistry at the University of Manitoba, medicine at the University of The Wset Indies, psychiatry at St. George's Hospital London, and neurology at the Institute of Neurology, London. He also read law at the University of London. In 2000 he was awarded the Chaconia Gold Medal of Trinidad and Tobago for long and meritorious service in medicine. He has published a number of scientific and popular articles and is the author of a textbook in neurology. He enjoys teaching, writing and doing research in adolescents, forensic and cultural issues. E-mail: drharim@carib-link.net

Joav Merrick, MD, MMedSci, DMSc, is professor of pediatrics, child health and human development affiliated with Kentucky Children's Hospital, University of Kentucky, Lexington, United States and the Zusman Child Development Center, Division of Pediatrics, Soroka University Medical Center, Ben Gurion University, Beer-Sheva, Israel, the medical director of the Health Services, Division for Mental Retardation, Ministry of Social Affairs and Socail Services, Jerusalem, the founder and director of the National Institute of Child Health and Human Development. Numerous publications in the field of pediatrics, child health and human development, rehabilitation, intellectual disability, disability, health, welfare, abuse, advocacy, quality of life and prevention. He received the Peter Sabroe Child Award for outstanding work on behalf of Danish Children in 1985 and the International LEGO-Prize ("The Children's Nobel Prize") for an extraordinary contribution towards improvement in child welfare and well-being in 1987. E-mail: jmerrick@zahav.net.il; Homepage: http://jmerrick50.googlepages.com/home

Rehannah Mohammed, MBBS, obtained her MBBS degree from the University of the West Indies in Trinidad in 1999. After graduaton, she entered into a postgraduate training program reading for the DM in Psychiatry at the University of the West Indies at Mount Hope.

Anushka Ragoonath, is a final year medical student who volunteered for a class project in Psychiatry during her clerkship rotation.

Rainah AK Seepersad, BSc, MSc is a Psychologist and Graduate Research Assistant. She holds a BSc in Psychology with a minor in Human Resource Management with First class honours from the Univeristy of the West Indies, St Augustine. She has recently completed a postgraduate degree, an MSc in Clinical Psychology at the University of the West Indies, Faculty of Medical Sciences, Eric Williams Medical Sciences Complex, Mt Hope. Her interests include hiking, violin playing and has recently developed an interest in research. E-mail: rainahs@hotmail.com

Kali Uppalapati, is a final year medical student who volunteered for a class project in psychiatry during his clerkship rotation.

In: Social and Cultural Psychiatry Experience from the... ISBN: 978-1-61668-506-5
Editor: Hari D. Maharajh and Joav Merrick © 2010 Nova Science Publishers, Inc.

Chapter 33

ABOUT THE DEPARTMENT OF CLINICAL MEDICINE AT THE UNIVERSITY OF THE WEST INDIES, MOUNT HOPE, TRINIDAD

The Faculty of Medical Sciences at St Augustine, Trinidad and Tobago is situated at the Eric Williams Medical Sciences Complex and comprise the Schools of Medicine, Dentistry, Veterinary Medicine, Pharmacy and Advanced Nursing Education. The Caribbean Medical School offers the Problem-Based Learning (PBL) System. This modality of learning requires student interaction in small groups supplemented by didactic lectures. The Faculty of Medical Sciences offers a choice of research-based Postgraduate degrees in the Schools of Medicine and Veterinary Medicine, which will allow interested graduates to pursue research work in areas of interest in Anatomy, Biochemistry, Physiology, Pharmacology and Public Health. The school also offers the MD by Thesis in clinical disciplines as well as professional training in Anaesthetics, Obstetrics and Gynaecology, Radiology, Psychiatry, Orthopaedics and shortly in Child Health, Internal Medicine and Surgery.

The Faculty of Medical Sciences is committed to the development of excellence in dental, medical and veterinary health research. Research priorities are determined by local and regional needs, but an international perspective remain through the development of productive research collaborations with renowned research institutions across the world.

MISSION STATEMENT

To recruit and train students as health care professionals in Medicine as well as in Dentistry, Veterinary Sciences, Advanced Nursing and fields allied to health; to meet the needs of and improve the health care delivery system for the people they serve, by striving for professional excellence throughout their career in this constantly changing world.

To contribute to the social, economic, and cultural development of the Caribbean by maintaining a Centre of Excellence, inculcating in graduates an attitude of excellence in service and research.

BACKGROUND

The University of the West Indies (UWI) was founded in 1948 at Mona, Jamaica as a College of the University of London. In that year, thirty-three students from nine countries of the British West Indies were admitted to the founding Faculty of Medicine. The University Hospital was completed in 1953 when the first graduates obtained their MBBS degree, having had their clinical training at the Kingston Public Hospital. In 1961, the University of the West Indies became an independent entity and at about that time it established two other campuses, first in Trinidad at St Augustine, and later in Barbados at Cave Hill. The University then served 15 different territories, most of which were still colonies of Great Britain.

As a result of a feasibility study on expansion and/or duplication of the Faculty of Medicine, The University accepted the need for expansion and in 1979 the Government of Trinidad and Tobago agreed to fund the establishment of the school and hospital at Mt Hope. A purpose-built facility to accommodate Medical, Dental, Veterinary, Pharmacy and Advanced Nursing Education was built on the Mt Hope site, where a Women's Hospital was already located and which was in use for that segment of the training of students in Trinidad. This complex, subsequently called the Eric Williams Medical Sciences Complex is managed by the Government of Trinidad and Tobago and since 1989 accommodates the teaching facilities of the Faculty of Medical Sciences at St Augustine for Medical, Dental, Veterinary and Pharmacy students. In 2005 the first nursing students were enrolled.

SCHOOL OF MEDICINE

The School of Medicine of the Faculty of Medical Sciences (St Augustine) located at the Eric Williams Medical Sciences Complex, opened its doors to a full 5-year teaching programme for students in 1989. Since then several cohorts of graduates have distinguished themselves worldwide and specialized in many different fields of Medicine.

MEDICAL HOSPITAL

The main Medical Hospital at the Eric Williams Medical Sciences Complex is geared to provide both generalist and specialist Medical and Surgical services. There are three (3) blocks of clinical research laboratories in close proximity to the wards. There are also generous ambulatory health care facilities, thirteen (13) operating theatres, Nuclear Medicine, CAT Scanning and other Radiological facilities, as well as provisions for specialised areas of functional analysis, Intensive Care Units, Out-Patient Clinics and Accident and Emergency Units.

WEBSITE

http://sta.uwi.edu/fms/aboutus.asp

In: Social and Cultural Psychiatry Experience from the...
Editor: Hari D. Maharajh and Joav Merrick

ISBN: 978-1-61668-506-5
© 2010 Nova Science Publishers, Inc.

Chapter 34

ABOUT THE NATIONAL INSTITUTE OF CHILD HEALTH AND HUMAN DEVELOPMENT IN ISRAEL

The National Institute of Child Health and Human Development (NICHD) in Israel was established in 1998 as a virtual institute under the auspicies of the Medical Director, Ministry of Social Affairs and Social Services in order to function as the research arm for the Office of the Medical Director. In 1998 the National Council for Child Health and Pediatrics, Ministry of Health and in 1999 the Director General and Deputy Director General of the Ministry of Health endorsed the establishment of the NICHD.

MISSION

The mission of a National Institute for Child Health and Human Development in Israel is to provide an academic focal point for the scholarly interdisciplinary study of child life, health, public health, welfare, disability, rehabilitation, intellectual disability and related aspects of human development. This mission includes research, teaching, clinical work, information and public service activities in the field of child health and human development.

SERVICE AND ACADEMIC ACTIVITIES

Over the years many activities became focused in the south of Israel due to collaboration with various professionals at the Faculty of Health Sciences (FOHS) at the Ben Gurion University of the Negev (BGU). Since 2000 an affiliation with the Zusman Child Development Center at the Pediatric Division of Soroka University Medical Center has resulted in collaboration around the establishment of the Down Syndrome Clinic at that center. In 2002 a full course on "Disability" was established at the Recanati School for Allied Professions in the Community, FOHS, BGU and in 2005 collaboration was started with the Primary Care Unit of the faculty and disability became part of the master of public health course on "Children and society". In the academic year 2005-2006 a one semester course on "Aging with disability" was started as part of the Master of Science program in gerontology in our collaboration with the Center for Multidisciplinary Research in Aging.

RESEARCH ACTIVITIES

The affiliated staff has over the years published work from projects and research activities in this national and international collaboration. In the year 2000 the International Journal of Adolescent Medicine and Health and in 2005 the International Journal on Disability and Human development of Freund Publishing House (London and Tel Aviv), in the year 2003 the TSW-Child Health and Human Development and in 2006 the TSW-Holistic Health and Medicine of the Scientific World Journal (New York and Kirkkonummi, Finland), all peer-reviewed international journals were affiliated with the National Institute of Child Health and Human Development. From 2008 also the International Journal of Child Health and Human Development (Nova Science, New York), the International Journal of Child and Adolescent Health (Nova Science) and the Journal of Pain Management (Nova Science) affiliated and from 2009 the International Public Health Journal (Nova Science) and Journal of Alternative Medicine Research (Nova Science).

NATIONAL COLLABORATIONS

Nationally the NICHD works in collaboration with the Faculty of Health Sciences, Ben Gurion University of the Negev; Department of Physical Therapy, Sackler School of Medicine, Tel Aviv University; Autism Center, Assaf HaRofeh Medical Center; National Rett and PKU Centers at Chaim Sheba Medical Center, Tel HaShomer; Department of Physiotherapy, Haifa University; Department of Education, Bar Ilan University, Ramat Gan, Faculty of Social Sciences and Health Sciences; College of Judea and Samaria in Ariel and recently also collaborations has been established with the Division of Pediatrics at Hadassah, Center for Pediatric Chronic Illness, Har HaZofim in Jerusalem.

INTERNATIONAL COLLABORATIONS

Internationally with the Department of Disability and Human Development, College of Applied Health Sciences, University of Illinois at Chicago; Strong Center for Developmental Disabilities, Golisano Children's Hospital at Strong, University of Rochester School of Medicine and Dentistry, New York; Centre on Intellectual Disabilities, University of Albany, New York; Centre for Chronic Disease Prevention and Control, Health Canada, Ottawa; Chandler Medical Center and Children's Hospital, Kentucky Children's Hospital, Section of Adolescent Medicine, University of Kentucky, Lexington; Chronic Disease Prevention and Control Research Center, Baylor College of Medicine, Houston, Texas; Division of Neuroscience, Department of Psychiatry, Columbia University, New York; Institute for the Study of Disadvantage and Disability, Atlanta; Center for Autism and Related Disorders, Department of Psychiatry, Children's Hospital Boston, Boston; Department of Paediatrics, Child Health and Adolescent Medicine, Children's Hospital at Westmead, Westmead, Australia; International Centre for the Study of Occupational and Mental Health, Düsseldorf, Germany; Centre for Advanced Studies in Nursing, Department of General Practice and Primary Care, University of Aberdeen, Aberdeen, United Kingdom; Quality of Life Research

Center, Copenhagen, Denmark; Nordic School of Public Health, Gottenburg, Sweden, Scandinavian Institute of Quality of Working Life, Oslo, Norway; Centre for Quality of Life of the Hong Kong Institute of Asia-Pacific Studies and School of Social Work, Chinese University, Hong Kong.

TARGETS

Our focus is on research, international collaborations, clinical work, teaching and policy in health, disability and human development and to establish the NICHD as a permanent institute in Israel in order to conduct model research and together with the four university schools of public health/medicine in Israel establish a national master and doctoral program in disability and human development at the institute to secure the next generation of professionals working in this often non-prestigious/low-status field of work.

CONTACT

Joav Merrick, MD, DMSc
Professor of Pediatrics, Child Health and Human Development
Medical Director, Health Services, Division for Mental Retardation, Ministry of Social Affairs and Social Services, POB 1260, IL-91012 Jerusalem, Israel.
E-mail: jmerrick@zahav.net.il

In: Social and Cultural Psychiatry Experience from the... ISBN: 978-1-61668-506-5
Editor: Hari D. Maharajh and Joav Merrick © 2010 Nova Science Publishers, Inc.

Chapter 35

ABOUT THE BOOK SERIES
"HEALTH AND HUMAN DEVELOPMENT"

Health and human development is a book series with publications from a multidisciplinary group of researchers, practitioners and clinicians for an international professional forum interested in the broad spectrum of health and human development.

- Merrick J, Omar HA, eds. Adolescent behavior research. International perspectives. New York: Nova Science, 2007.
- Kratky KW. Complementary medicine systems: Comparison and integration. New York: Nova Science, 2008.
- Schofield P, Merrick J, eds. Pain in children and youth. New York: Nova Science, 2009.
- Greydanus DE, Patel DR, Pratt HD, Calles Jr JL, eds. Behavioral pediatrics, 3 ed. New York: Nova Science, 2009.
- Ventegodt S, Merrick J, eds. Meaningful work: Research in quality of working life. New York: Nova Science, 2009.
- Omar HA, Greydanus DE, Patel DR, Merrick J, eds. Obesity and adolescence. A public health concern. New York: Nova Science, 2009.
- Lieberman A, Merrick J, eds. Poverty and children. A public health concern. New York: Nova Science, 2009.
- Goodbread J. Living on the edge. The mythical, spiritual and philosophical roots of social marginality. New York: Nova Science, 2009.
- Bennett DL, Towns S, Elliot E, Merrick J, eds. Challenges in adolescent health: An Australian perspective. New York: Nova Science, 2009.
- Schofield P, Merrick J, eds. Children and pain. New York: Nova Science, 2009.
- Sher L, Kandel I, Merrick J. Alcohol-related cognitive disorders: Research and clinical perspectives. New York: Nova Science, 2009.
- Anyanwu EC. Advances in environmental health effects of toxigenic mold and mycotoxins. New York: Nova Science, 2009.
- Bell E, Merrick J, eds. Rural child health. International aspects. New York: Nova Science, 2009.

- Dubowitz H, Merrick J, eds. International aspects of child abuse and neglect. New York: Nova Science, 2010.
- Shahtahmasebi S, Berridge D. Conceptualizing behavior: A practical guide to data analysis. New York: Nova Science, 2010.
- Wernik U. Chance action and therapy. The playful way of changing. New York: Nova Science, 2010.
- Omar HA, Greydanus DE, Patel DR, Merrick J, eds. Adolescence and chronic illness. A public health concern. New York: Nova Science, 2010.
- Patel DR, Greydanus DE, Omar HA, Merrick J, eds. Adolescence and sports. New York: Nova Science, 2010.
- Dhek DTL, Ma HK, Merrick J, eds. Positive youth development: Evaluation and future directions in a Chinese context. New York: Nova Science, 2010.

CONTACT

Professor Joav Merrick, MD, MMedSci, DMSc
Medical Director, Medical Services
Division for Mental Retardation
Ministry of Social Affairs
POBox 1260
IL-91012 Jerusalem, Israel
E-mail: jmerrick@zahav.net.il
Home-page: http://jmerrick50.googlepages.com/home

INDEX

A

abstraction, 117
academic performance, 114
academics, 29, 34, 87, 114, 365
access, 58, 59, 89, 90, 167, 242, 285, 340, 341, 342
accessibility, 131, 139, 141, 183, 199
accountability, 13
accounting, 33, 135, 193, 198, 205, 217, 229, 235, 288, 297, 299, 301
acculturation, 304
achievement, 92, 97
acid, 195, 206, 272
adaptability, 127, 128
additives, 249
adjustment, 49, 71, 72, 78, 156, 246
administrators, 361
adolescence, 143, 154, 176, 181, 209, 254, 289, 293, 294, 295, 379
adulthood, 143, 154, 175, 287, 292, 293, 294, 295
advertisements, 96
advocacy, 371
aesthetics, 18, 366
affect intensity, 181
affective disorder, 361
affirmative action, 9, 33, 46, 88, 89, 97, 114
agencies, 8, 59, 103, 183
aggression, 18, 102, 135, 158, 160, 161, 177, 219, 220, 223, 224, 225, 226, 227, 261, 270, 274, 356
aggressive behavior, 170
aggressiveness, 135, 160, 225
agnosia, 347
agriculture, 48, 299
AIDS, 113, 204
alcohol consumption, 159, 215, 217, 219, 223, 226, 239, 254
alcohol dependence, 121, 232, 234, 237, 240, 241, 242, 243, 244, 260

alcohol problems, 234, 242, 244
alcohol use, 48, 80, 115, 121, 147, 152, 214, 225, 229, 233, 238, 242, 244, 246, 247, 248, 254, 255, 268, 303
alcoholics, 154, 224, 225, 226, 229, 230, 231, 232, 233, 240, 243, 294
alertness, 274
alienation, 305
alternatives, 232
altruistic behavior, 175
ambiguity, 332
ambivalence, 2, 109, 123, 126, 127, 186
ammonia, 196
amphetamines, 257
anatomy, 164
anemia, 42
anger, 114, 165, 168, 172, 176, 356
annihilation, 133, 134
anorexia, 2, 26, 27, 84, 123, 124, 125, 126, 127, 128, 255, 348
anorexia nervosa, 2, 26, 84, 123, 124, 125, 126, 127, 128, 255
antagonism, 2, 33, 89
anthropologists, 126
antipsychotic, 35, 262, 264
antisocial personality, 339
anxiety disorder, 167, 249, 255, 292, 311
apathy, 102
aphasia, 345, 347
appetite, xiii, 249, 269, 273, 311
applications, 285
appointments, 79, 89
appraisals, 101, 105
apraxia, 347
aptitude, 20
arousal, 118, 157, 350
arrest, 32, 271
arson, 350, 351
arteries, 47

artery, 346
arthritis, 48, 246
assassination, 270
assault, 112, 158, 220, 226
assertiveness, 160
assessment, 30, 45, 121, 128, 132, 178, 180, 199, 203, 204, 209, 219, 240, 267, 329, 337, 339, 342, 343, 346, 353
assignment, 176, 284
assimilation, 132, 304
assumptions, 58, 64, 65, 89, 133, 176
asthma, 246, 252
asylum, 278
athletes, 244
atrophy, 346
attachment, 119, 159, 160, 332
attacks, 22, 48, 99, 114, 314, 341
attitudes, 59, 103, 120, 165, 179, 360
auditing, 115
authorities, 42, 139, 166, 168, 178, 252, 263
authority, 53, 101, 102, 103, 330, 336
authors, 30, 105, 135, 175, 240, 241, 259, 265, 304, 311, 322, 366
autonomy, 172
autopsy, 55, 137, 138, 145, 146, 156, 200
availability, 14, 156, 194, 203, 204, 208, 220, 242, 246, 266, 351
aversion, 233
aversion therapy, 233
avoidance, 43, 123, 127, 137, 160
awareness, 56, 63, 65, 68, 69, 70, 75, 76, 80, 99, 115, 184, 241, 242, 257, 284, 324

B

background, 2, 20, 58, 63, 102, 112, 119, 136, 160, 175, 207, 208, 262, 312
backlash, 24
bad behavior, 113
bankruptcy, 350
bargaining, 12
barriers, 70
base year, 280
basic needs, 139, 151
battered women, 224, 226, 348
beams, 139
beauty, 126, 127
beer, 213, 215, 216, 217, 218, 220, 261
behavioral disorders, 150, 325
behavioral problems, 146, 158, 246
belief systems, 59, 101
beverages, 66, 121, 215, 218, 275
bias, 30, 77, 90, 105, 229

bible, 252, 263
bicarbonate, 271, 272
bile, 175
bipolar disorder, 250, 256, 258, 265, 267, 268
bipolar illness, 250, 258
birth, 10, 79, 104, 113, 120, 138, 232, 243, 292, 298, 304, 338, 341, 345, 349
birth rate, 113
births, 160
black women, 101
blame, 36, 59, 125, 178, 287
bleaching, 88, 106
bleeding, 167
blocks, 374
blood flow, 47, 166
blood pressure, 47, 273, 346
blood stream, 245
blood vessels, 273
bloodshed, 176
body fat, 46
body fluid, 55
body image, 123, 125, 175
body weight, 48, 125
bonding, 332
bonds, 45
bone, 169
bone age, 169
bones, 169, 269
borderline personality disorder, 179, 180, 181
boredom, 115, 355
bounds, 115
boxer, 96
boys, 23, 158, 258, 291, 292, 341
brain, 10, 22, 57, 64, 77, 84, 112, 169, 225, 245, 249, 268, 342, 346
breakdown, 170, 185
breathing, 273
broadband, 191
bronchitis, 46, 249
brothers, 305, 344
brutality, 112
buffer, 134, 291
bulimia, 128, 255
bulimia nervosa, 255
bullying, 189
bureaucracy, 336
burn, 273
burning, 24, 111, 114, 135, 167, 169, 175, 187, 339
bystander effect, 187

C

cabinet members, 96

caffeine, 230
calcium, 339
calorie, 125
cancer, 48, 204
cannabinoids, 257, 259, 265, 266
capital punishment, 352
carbohydrate, 127
carbohydrates, 47
carbon, 139
carbon monoxide, 139
cardiac risk, 46, 50
cardiac risk factors, 46, 50
cardiovascular disease, 46, 49
caregivers, 51
case law, 330
case study, 121, 126
cast, 22
casting, 52, 79, 183
catalyst, 91
category a, 196
catharsis, 112
cattle, 32
causation, 27, 67, 76, 132, 145, 146, 155, 160, 161, 303, 304, 305, 306, 332
central nervous system, 269
certification, 106, 335
challenges, xiii, 25
changing environment, xiii, 7
character, 13, 56
child abuse, 117, 118, 158, 332, 380
child rearing, 332
childhood, 48, 106, 173, 175, 179, 181, 251, 288, 293, 294, 295, 338
cholera, 42, 46, 49
cholesterol, 346, 354
chronic illness, 380
circulation, 218
civil disorder, 113
civil liberties, 279, 336, 337
civil servants, 120
civil service, 270, 298
civilization, 39, 131, 141, 276
clarity, 56, 126
classes, 198, 279, 281
classification, 26, 33, 37, 122, 164, 166, 172, 196, 257, 299, 304, 310, 325
classrooms, 291
cleaning, 207
cleavages, 34
clients, 25, 97, 241
climate, 152, 351
clinical assessment, 259
clinical depression, 205

clinical diagnosis, 35
clinical presentation, 127, 256, 257, 259, 264, 265, 266, 351
clinical syndrome, 180
closure, 208, 278
clusters, 46
cocaine abuse, 272
codes, 64, 123, 132, 137
coding, 68
coffee, 252
cognitive deficit, 339, 347
cognitive deficits, 339, 347
cognitive dysfunction, 344
cognitive impairment, 120, 159
cognitive testing, 261
cohesion, 128
cohort, 3, 153, 255, 256, 258, 267, 287, 292, 297, 315, 361
coke, 274
collaboration, xiii, 4, 33, 59, 201, 202, 353, 375, 376
collective unconscious, 18, 103
college students, 128
colonization, 304
color, 11, 30, 90, 102, 103, 104
combination therapy, 125
common findings, 52, 139, 267
common law, 284, 329, 330, 347
common sense, 58
communication, 63, 81, 103, 126, 127, 243, 244, 290
community service, 54, 278, 279, 284
comorbidity, 35
compassion, 13
compensation, 96, 114, 274
competence, 339
competition, 1, 76
competitiveness, 101, 105
compilation, 4, 293
complex partial seizure, 56
complexity, 26
compliance, 258, 338
components, 13, 50, 126
composition, 7, 50, 97, 101, 104, 148, 195, 229, 236, 287, 291, 299, 301, 302, 313
compounds, 43, 139, 194, 272
compression, 267
compulsion, 177
concentration, 218, 266, 345
conception, 8
conceptualization, 18, 27, 64, 78, 84, 133, 142, 175, 304
concrete, 57
conduct disorder, 176, 251, 265
conference, 10, 12, 13, 15, 153, 285

confessions, 59, 230
confidence, 281
confidence interval, 281
confidentiality, 147, 350
confinement, 32
conflict, 2, 51, 89, 102, 104, 125, 157, 160, 162, 223, 290, 294, 310
conflict resolution, 160
conformity, 103
confounding variables, 266
confrontation, 57, 81, 178
confusion, 3, 126, 127, 166, 169, 175, 273, 274, 303, 304, 305, 351
congruence, 147, 170
connective tissue, 55
consciousness, 19, 29, 53, 57, 58, 103, 105, 107, 342, 351
consensus, 3, 60, 92, 213, 264, 294, 297, 303, 305
consent, 147, 259, 269, 330, 336
consolidation, 88
constipation, 311
construction, 20
consultants, 201, 204, 283, 311
consumers, 13, 272
consumption, 43, 167, 213, 215, 216, 217, 218, 220, 223, 239, 242, 246, 252, 254, 258, 266, 365
contamination, 137, 195, 196, 197
continuity, 268
contradiction, 33, 91
control group, 223, 224, 225
controversies, 3, 60, 245, 294
contusion, 166, 175, 176
convergence, 101
conversion, 1
convulsion, 24
cooking, 80, 186
cooling, 273
coping strategies, 131, 141, 176, 181
coronary artery disease, 47, 49
coronary heart disease, 47, 50
correlation, 68, 76, 114, 147, 216, 277, 281, 359, 360, 361
correlation coefficient, 76
correlations, 213, 215, 311
corruption, 12, 26, 111
cosmetics, 224
costs, 92
counsel, 56, 332
counseling, 125, 178
country of origin, 80
couples, 226
courtship, 23, 66, 77, 111, 117, 118, 119, 120, 121, 122, 175

crack, 272, 275
craving, 274, 349
creative process, 2
creativity, 27, 107, 109, 112, 115, 117, 173, 245, 246, 276
credibility, 79
criminal activity, 3, 112, 213, 321
criminal justice system, 121, 351
criminal violence, 219, 245, 254
criminality, 351
criminals, 113, 219, 270
critical period, 287
criticism, 7, 30, 365
crocodile, 365
cross-cultural comparison, 213, 219
cross-sectional study, 57, 79, 248
crown, 50
crying, 20, 33, 42
crystalline, 269
cultivation, 39, 253
cultural beliefs, 19, 26, 134, 160, 351
cultural differences, 33, 102, 103, 104, 284, 289, 321
cultural heritage, 80
cultural imperialism, 18, 19, 34
cultural influence, 53
cultural norms, 64, 104, 132, 140, 160, 303
cultural practices, 25, 82, 127, 151, 246
cultural tradition, 241
cultural transition, 142
currency, 259
curriculum, 29
cycles, 138, 160, 256
cyst, 169

D

damages, viii
dance, 63, 66, 90, 110, 112, 116, 117, 119, 120
danger, 198, 262, 275
dangerousness, 330
data analysis, 380
data collection, 31, 233, 314
database, 299
deaths, 46, 160, 162, 184, 187, 188, 193, 194, 197, 207, 270, 274, 361
debt, 42
decay, 252, 253, 271
decentralization, 12
decisions, 14, 40, 93, 348
defects, 51, 333, 345
defence, 97, 134, 342, 347, 350, 351
defendants, 348

Index

defense, 31, 32, 34, 36, 53, 87, 132, 265, 332, 347, 348, 349

defense mechanisms, 87, 132

deficiencies, 12

deficiency, 124

definition, 17, 19, 91, 118, 140, 166, 229, 347, 366

deinstitutionalization, 3, 277, 279, 284, 285, 286

delegates, 10

delinquency, 140

delirium, 203, 249, 265, 329, 350, 351

delivery, 208, 361, 373

delusion, 30, 254

delusions, 120, 249, 260, 265, 339, 346, 350

dementia, 203, 329, 370

democracy, 13

demographic characteristics, 3, 173, 229, 233, 294, 314

demographic data, 70, 75, 205, 247

demographic factors, 205, 230, 243, 303, 314

demographics, 168

demonstrations, 113

denial, 19, 27, 97, 123, 124, 126, 159, 160

density, 360

dependent variable, 215

depersonalization, 83, 249

deposits, 13

depressive symptomatology, 288, 292

depressive symptoms, 242, 255, 256, 257, 258, 267, 295

deprivation, 57, 67, 79, 250, 302, 306, 332

deregulation, 351

dermatology, 15

destruction, 90, 112, 114, 166, 177, 351

detection, 54, 219, 257, 270

detention, 329, 330, 334, 335, 336, 337, 343

deterrence, 220

detoxification, 263, 273

developed countries, 165, 194, 195, 257, 266, 267, 277

developed nations, 366

developmental change, 8

developmental disorder, 173

developmental milestones, 169, 170, 171

developmental process, 181

developmental psychopathology, 293

deviation, 42, 64, 132, 236

diabetes, 46, 47, 48, 49, 50, 338, 350, 351

diabetic ketoacidosis, 350

diabetic patients, 351

diagnostic criteria, 120, 267, 268, 306, 307, 347

diarrhea, 252

dichotomy, 76

diet, 46, 48, 49

differential rates, 167, 303

differentiation, 166

dignity, 136, 157

dilation, 274

disability, 102, 199, 202, 209, 329, 352, 371, 375, 377

disappointment, 24, 93

disaster, 79

discharges, 53

discipline, 32, 58, 139, 178

disclosure, 230, 265

discomfort, 96, 119, 252, 311

discrimination, 30, 31, 33, 88, 89, 90, 91, 92, 93, 94, 95, 96, 97, 99, 102, 104, 105, 106, 137, 292, 305

displacement, 356

disposition, 35, 261

dissociation, 26, 53, 64, 168, 179

dissonance, 97

distortions, 117

distress, 53, 118, 131, 138, 140, 143, 153, 163, 177, 180, 220, 290, 291, 309, 310, 311, 314, 315, 317, 318, 320, 321, 324, 325, 326, 327

distribution, 35, 67, 89, 97, 139, 218, 235, 236, 238, 239, 304, 306

diversification, 95

diversity, 1, 2, 19, 34, 63, 64, 97, 99, 104, 127, 133, 241, 313

division, 137, 231, 334

divorce, 176, 302, 324

doctors, 2, 7, 8, 9, 11, 12, 13, 14, 51, 55, 90, 91, 96, 97, 150, 161, 201, 269, 330, 337, 356, 366

dogs, 270

domestic violence, 223, 224, 226, 309, 310, 312, 314, 315, 318, 319, 321, 323, 324, 325, 326

dominance, 2, 32, 88, 101, 172

doors, 374

dopamine, 2, 51, 53, 54, 59, 60, 84, 266, 269

dosing, 35, 257

downsizing, 208, 277

drainage, 8

drawing, 19, 259

dream, 106, 275

dreams, 73, 74, 273

drinking pattern, 218

drinking patterns, 218

drug abuse, 51, 257, 305

drug addict, 140, 146, 252

drug addiction, 140, 146, 252

drug history, 263

drug interaction, 254

drug trafficking, 95, 271

drug use, 3, 42, 240, 247, 248, 250, 254, 255, 256, 259, 260, 261, 265, 271, 272, 276, 293, 298, 312, 331, 351
DSM, 19, 33, 64, 83, 122, 123, 133, 224, 242, 257, 265, 267, 268, 295, 299, 304, 306, 307, 309, 312, 323, 326, 342, 347
dualism, 58, 310
dumping, 284
duplication, 157, 374
duration, 56, 223, 224, 244, 249, 250, 257, 258, 259, 264, 265, 266, 295, 352
duties, 3, 56, 124, 204, 329, 335
dynamics, 101, 102, 106, 123, 125, 126, 127, 136, 151, 165, 168, 173, 176, 178, 179, 214, 220, 305
dyslexia, 348
dysphoria, 249, 273
dysthymia, 265, 288, 292, 345
dysthymic disorder, 312

E

earnings, 219
earth, 115, 263
eating, 24, 49, 70, 80, 123, 124, 126, 127, 128, 167, 262, 287, 293, 338, 350
eating disorders, 49, 126, 128, 167, 293
eating disturbances, 287
ecology, 302, 333
economic development, 139
economic goods, 218
economic status, 103, 104
economic theory, 217
economics, 220
editors, 14, 141
educational system, 245, 247
egg, 366
ego, 9, 14, 53, 131, 132, 249, 274, 305
ego strength, 274
ejaculation, 225
elderly, 142, 188
elders, 56, 232, 247
electricity, 22, 55
elementary school, 292
emigration, 43, 50, 91, 304
emotion, 2, 105, 166, 173, 176, 295
emotion regulation, 295
emotional disorder, 135, 176
emotional distress, 290, 309, 310, 321
emotional state, 264
emotions, 2, 17, 18, 20, 49, 53, 87, 98, 104, 157, 176, 178, 231, 257, 265
employment, 33, 67, 90, 98, 105, 138, 214, 219, 292, 323, 333

encouragement, 186
endocrinologist, 169, 339
energy, 23, 24, 47, 56, 58, 77, 110, 260, 261, 269, 287
enforcement, 110, 121, 253
engagement, 103, 123
engineering, 168
enthusiasm, 4, 7, 77
environmental factors, 30, 168, 250, 251, 257, 264, 266, 302, 303, 304, 305, 355
environmental influences, 39, 172, 305
epidemic, 48, 83
epidemiology, 142, 143, 163, 200, 291
epilepsy, 22, 24, 339, 342
equality, 91, 92, 97
equilibrium, 176
equipment, 194
equity, 98, 204
erosion, 270
estimating, 195, 219
estrogen, 250, 303
ethics, 51
ethnic background, 19
ethnic Indians, 135
ethnic minority, 35
euphoria, 249, 250, 257, 265, 274
evening, 21, 23, 127, 137, 157, 338
evil, 22, 24, 25, 52, 53, 54, 55, 56, 57, 73
evolution, 19, 30, 84, 265
examinations, 188
excitability, 274
exclusion, 80, 97, 162, 299
excuse, 1, 70, 78, 105, 115
executive function, 347
executive functioning, 347
exercise, 21, 46, 112, 113, 125, 127, 178
exploitation, 39
expulsion, 91
externalizing behavior, 150
extraction, 128
extroversion, 120

F

failure, 10, 54, 177, 187, 188, 246, 252, 284, 335, 347
faith, 23, 24, 52, 55, 73, 79, 81, 140, 159, 169, 175, 313
false belief, 30
family conflict, 125, 155, 290
family environment, 292
family factors, 152
family functioning, 126, 128, 151, 290

family history, 46, 159, 169, 261, 262, 263, 266, 338
family life, 77, 105, 110
family members, 54, 56, 158, 160, 177, 178, 231, 241, 248, 257, 259, 290
family relationships, 151, 290
family support, 243, 283
family system, 102, 136, 151, 152, 160
family therapy, 107, 123
family violence, 226
fantasy, 190
farmers, 139
fasting, 112, 123, 124, 125, 126, 127
fat, 48, 50, 74
fatigue, 325
fear, 12, 27, 41, 52, 91, 114, 125, 166, 168, 186, 226, 240, 270, 294, 303, 305, 321, 323, 338, 350, 356
fears, 102
feelings, 22, 34, 53, 78, 105, 125, 157, 168, 170, 176, 177, 287, 304, 311, 321, 331
feet, 41, 77, 112, 345
fertility, 64, 111, 113, 361
fertilization, 90, 160
fever, 46, 54, 274
fidelity, 77, 78, 119
films, 8, 17, 18, 27, 138
financial distress, 20
financial support, 324
firearms, 139, 187
fires, 356
first degree relative, 323
first generation, 39, 41
fish, 125, 126
fishing, 273
fixation, 117
flame, 263, 272
flashbacks, 249
flavor, 104
flavour, 26
flight, 126, 261, 271
flood, 202, 232, 365
flooding, 96
flooring, 273
focusing, 124, 224
folklore, 18, 26, 73, 366
food intake, 126
football, 71, 110, 169
forests, 270
forgiveness, 55, 162
fractures, 223
fraud, 66, 350
free choice, 120
freedom, 45, 59, 114, 118, 120, 122, 219, 253, 336
freedom of choice, 59

friendship, 231
fruits, 254
frustration, 176, 225, 227, 321, 323, 356
fuel, 87, 98, 219
functional analysis, 374
functional approach, 180
funding, 204
funds, 13, 204
furniture, 55
fusion, 34, 80, 106, 112, 117, 127

gait, 345
gambling, 66, 230
gangs, 271
gases, 196
gasoline, 11
GDP, 207
gender gap, 292
gender identity, 122
gene, 305
general intelligence, 346
general practitioner, 284
generalized anxiety disorder, 312
generation, 49, 55, 56, 65, 66, 104, 270, 314
genetic factors, 250, 251, 264
genetics, 46, 333
genocide, 91
gerontology, 375
gestational diabetes, 46
gift, 26, 71, 77, 78
gifted, 9
girls, 45, 59, 126, 143, 154, 158, 167, 175, 180, 258, 266, 291, 292
glasses, 261
glaucoma, 252
global village, 37
glucose, 47, 339, 350, 351
gold, 271
gonorrhea, 252
goods and services, 90
governance, 137, 269
grades, 147, 170
graduate students, 4
greed, 374
grief, 191
gross domestic product, 207
group identity, 102
group membership, 104
group size, 362
group therapy, 176, 178, 186
grouping, 9, 46, 80, 137, 302

growth, 123, 184, 286
guardian, 99, 100, 190, 256
guidance, 58, 156, 157, 171, 263, 335
guidelines, 3, 37, 138, 184, 189, 325
guilt, 27, 103, 121, 137, 160, 232, 287
guilty, 120, 133, 134, 190, 343

H

hair, 22, 102, 167, 169, 340, 345
hallucinations, 24, 57, 120, 159, 161, 203, 249, 250, 260, 263, 265, 331, 339, 346, 350
hands, 11, 25, 51, 52, 54, 167, 263, 273
happiness, 138, 261
harassment, 355
harmony, 11, 34, 107, 334
hate, 2, 11, 18, 45, 88, 113, 171
hazards, 48
HDL, 46
head injury, 341, 342
healing, 22, 24, 51, 52, 59, 67, 79, 178, 230
health care, 7, 12, 13, 29, 31, 121, 199, 201, 202, 258, 279, 287, 326, 336, 361, 373, 374
health care professionals, 121, 373
health care system, 31, 258
health effects, 379
health expenditure, 207
health problems, 47
health services, 15, 267
heart attack, 47
heart disease, 47
heat, 311
heating, 56, 263
hegemony, 17, 34, 65
height, 48, 125, 351
helplessness, 287
hemisphere, 361
hemoglobin, 350
herbicide, 156, 194
heredity, 49
heroin, 252
heterogeneity, 34
high blood pressure, 47, 48
high fat, 194
high school, 27, 152, 156, 162, 240, 287, 292
hip, 118, 277, 282, 324
hiring, 30, 94
HIV, 180, 272, 276, 346, 370
home culture, 127, 135
homicidal behaviour, 2, 157
homicide, 84, 214, 219, 220, 330
homicide rates, 220
honesty, 13, 78

hopelessness, 125, 230, 287, 360
hopes, 7
hormone, 47
hospitalization, 170, 200, 278
hospitals, 8, 12, 46, 48, 79, 157, 200, 201, 202, 208, 272, 277, 278, 285, 334, 352, 361
host, 30, 123, 127, 251, 365
hostility, 12, 20, 57, 88, 105, 135, 142, 177, 249
households, 84
housing, 89, 90, 96, 97, 105, 137, 250, 302, 333, 351
human behavior, 326
human development, 370, 375, 377, 379
human rights, 284, 336, 337
human values, 104
humility, 54, 230
hurricanes, 356
husband, 20, 21, 74, 119, 120, 121, 138, 171, 226
hybridity, 17, 19
hybridization, 19
hydrocele, 46
hydrogen, 187
hyperactivity, 158, 332
hyperglycaemia, 350, 351
hyperinsulinemia, 47
hypersensitivity, 105
hypertension, 46, 47, 49, 50
hyperventilation, 22
hypothesis, 10, 35, 189, 202, 218, 247, 323, 360

I

ICD, 19, 33, 37, 128, 310, 325, 342
ideal, 34, 114, 284, 305
idealization, 124
ideals, 57, 103
identification, 27, 33, 87, 98, 126, 152, 202, 290, 307

ideology, 230
idiosyncratic, 274
image, 14, 22, 26, 105, 176
imagery, 157
images, 2, 17, 19, 26, 52, 53, 162
imagination, 112
imitation, 155, 156, 157, 158, 184
immigrants, 35, 39, 41, 42, 43, 44, 50, 80, 102, 135, 232, 304, 313, 334
immigration, 134, 142
immortality, 124
impairments, 310
imperialism, 19
implementation, 3, 208, 257, 267, 271, 278, 279, 283, 284, 333, 334, 335
imprisonment, 253, 263

impulses, 115, 117, 118
impulsive, 115
impulsivity, 158
incarceration, 340, 351, 352
incidence, 15, 36, 47, 49, 64, 113, 127, 131, 135, 142, 158, 166, 170, 184, 193, 246, 248, 258, 268, 288, 297, 298, 305, 306
inclusion, 19, 97, 179, 299, 302, 309
income, 68, 223, 226
indentured servant, 32
independence, 3, 7, 19, 102, 160, 234, 329, 333
Independence, 10, 105, 207, 283, 356
independent variable, 215
indication, 179, 196, 314
indicators, 255
indigenous, 17, 18, 27, 29, 34, 64, 65, 78, 84, 121, 133, 135, 140, 142, 269
individuality, 32
indoctrination, 53, 161, 241
induction, 103, 165, 174, 175
industrialization, 299
industrialized societies, 278
industry, 13, 17, 18, 43, 46, 49, 77, 109, 110, 113, 271, 272, 276, 298
inefficiencies, 7
inequality, 89, 92, 94, 96, 218, 219, 221
infection, 171
inferences, 97
inferiority, 34, 287
infinite, 59
informed consent, 203
infrastructure, 352
ingest, 271
ingestion, 49, 137, 139, 156, 170, 193, 194, 195, 196, 197, 198, 199, 206, 207
inheritance, 260
initiation, 9, 242
inmates, 45, 333
innocence, 121
insane, 275, 322, 333, 343
insanity, 36, 65, 350, 351
insecticide, 194
insecurity, 34, 58, 271
insight, 137, 159, 160, 161, 261, 262, 274, 305, 331, 339, 342, 345, 350, 352
inspiration, 4
instability, 32, 151, 158, 175, 351
instinct, 87, 98
institutionalisation, 278
institutions, 3, 89, 106, 145, 166, 187, 208, 255, 271, 287, 335, 340, 366, 373
instruction, 26
instructors, 326, 365

instruments, 175, 234, 346
insulin, 46, 47, 50, 351
insulin resistance, 46, 47, 50
insurance, 350
integration, 39, 115, 255, 278, 379
integrity, 78
intelligence, 332, 339, 342, 345, 346
intentions, 89, 185, 229, 233, 234, 276, 336
interaction, 25, 88, 103, 118, 119, 123, 125, 126, 128, 178, 181, 305, 338, 373
interactions, 64, 102, 132, 260, 333
interference, 12
internalization, 103
internalizing, 103, 150, 288, 290, 294
internet, 162, 183, 184, 185, 186, 187, 188, 189, 190, 191
interpersonal factors, 111, 120
interpersonal relations, 324
interpersonal relationships, 324
interpersonal skills, 120, 260
interrelations, 164
intervention, 51, 54, 155, 173, 177, 180, 181, 189, 191, 230, 234, 238, 350, 351
interview, 65, 81, 95, 156, 171, 176, 177, 190, 203, 234, 261, 339, 340, 341, 343, 344, 346
intoxication, 139, 198, 199, 200, 213, 219, 249, 265, 349
intuition, 54
inventions, 275
inversion, 298
investment, 13, 194, 208, 277, 279, 284
iron, 119
irony, 49
isolation, 188, 302, 361

J

jaundice, 46, 55
jaw, 339
jobs, 40, 94
joints, 74, 250, 259, 261, 265, 267
journalism, 59
judges, 329
judgment, 91, 112, 249, 274, 339, 342, 345
judiciary, 337
jurisdiction, 120
juror, 332
justice, 95, 253, 353

K

kerosene, 206, 207
kidnapping, 112, 270, 303

killing, 36, 79, 135, 187, 347, 348

L

labor, 39, 40, 313
labour, 31, 36, 41, 135, 142, 219, 353
labour market, 219
land, 40, 43, 96, 104, 105, 207, 270, 279
landscape, 1, 18, 19, 29, 31
language, 17, 25, 27, 39, 58, 63, 64, 102, 105, 133, 241, 275, 276, 313, 336, 347
later life, 303
laughing, 273
law enforcement, 271
laws, 3, 20, 41, 45, 160, 253, 256, 329
lawyers, 8
leadership, 91
learning, 117, 366, 373
legal issues, 204
legend, 192
leisure, 66, 90
lending, 177
leptin, 50
liberalization, 348
liberation, 160
life cycle, 134, 142
life experiences, 183
lifestyle, 2, 39, 46, 47, 49, 82, 101, 110, 115, 126, 178, 293, 305, 341
lifestyle changes, 47
lifetime, 9, 11, 27, 234, 246, 247, 258, 272, 298, 299, 340
likelihood, 187, 233, 251
limestone, 65
limitation, 7, 152, 198, 266, 285
line, 8, 51, 54, 57, 95, 120, 121, 156, 271, 280, 341, 352
linkage, 17
liquids, 20
listening, 170
liver, 47, 120, 261, 342, 346
liver function tests, 120, 342, 346
living arrangements, 48
longitudinal study, 152, 292, 295
love, 22, 66, 71, 72, 78, 172, 223, 224, 225
loyalty, 41, 98, 103, 123, 126
luggage, 271
lying, 22, 23, 58, 66, 71, 72

M

magical thinking, 79
maintenance, 39, 325, 333

major depression, 30, 288, 292, 311, 345
major depressive disorder, 258, 264, 289, 291, 292
malaria, 8
malingering, 42, 49, 342
malnutrition, 218, 246, 252
maltreatment, 43, 181
management, 13, 25, 121, 131, 141, 165, 168, 172, 178, 201, 202, 203, 204, 293, 333, 352
mania, 265, 266
manic, 257, 258
manic episode, 258
manic symptoms, 257
manipulation, 126
manslaughter, 349
manufacturing, 262, 298
marginalization, 19, 137, 138, 155, 156
marital status, 65, 81
market, 246
marketing, 253
markets, 271
marriage, 20, 32, 45, 90, 157, 185, 223, 226, 292, 312, 322, 338, 350
masculinity, 1
mass media, 192
mastery, 165, 173, 177
matrix, 58
meals, 55, 125
measles, 46
measurement, 148, 164, 288
measures, 46, 143, 153, 163, 184, 189, 208, 218, 219, 220, 259, 271, 288, 310, 312
meat, 124, 126
media, 59, 66, 91, 113, 131, 134, 140, 156, 157, 161, 162, 163, 164, 183, 186, 187, 188, 189, 191, 284
median, 45, 298, 299, 300, 301
mediation, 107, 203
medical care, 48, 58, 334
medication, 54, 57, 59, 187, 197, 198, 199, 207, 258, 330, 338, 340, 350
melting, xiii, 2, 34, 101, 104
membership, 229, 231
memory, 18, 23, 332, 339, 342, 345, 347
menarche, 168
meningitis, 46
menstruation, 168
mental health professionals, 19, 30, 59, 162, 201, 202, 330
mental retardation, 332, 342
mental state, 201, 202, 264, 309, 331
mental states, 309
mentally ill persons, 51, 58
messages, 89, 171, 310
meta-analysis, 298, 303, 306

metabolic disorder, 46
metabolic syndrome, 46
metabolism, 250
metabolites, 266
methodology, 306, 369
middle class, 18, 25, 64, 69, 80, 125, 133
migrant population, 101
migrants, 39, 48, 50, 101, 161, 334
migration, 2, 18, 19, 31, 39, 63, 80, 284, 305, 334
military, 134, 167
milk, 55
mimicry, 114
mind-body, 310
minimum wage, 218

minorities, 95, 244
minority, 30, 31, 33, 34, 70, 95, 115
minors, 252
misconceptions, 106, 140
misunderstanding, 121, 175
mobile phone, 270
modeling, 244
models, 96, 113, 152, 168, 181, 213, 217, 250, 253, 278, 279, 283, 286, 327, 353
moderators, 189
modules, 337
mold, 379
money, 22, 25, 43, 71, 81, 171, 172, 261, 262, 270, 271
money laundering, 270, 271
monopoly, 33, 365
mood disorder, 3, 84, 107, 142, 167, 176, 245, 246, 249, 250, 251, 256, 257, 258, 264, 267, 311
moral judgment, 103
morality, 78, 124, 199, 209
morbidity, 36, 116, 122, 174, 250, 251, 258, 265, 266, 268, 295, 320, 325
morning, 21, 23, 57, 77, 111, 112, 113, 170, 262
morphine, 252, 274
morphology, 133
mortality, 42, 44, 49, 146, 194, 195, 334
mortality rate, 42, 44, 194, 195, 334
mothers, 160, 323, 332, 360
motion, 4, 13, 27, 181, 187
motivation, 126, 219
motives, 89, 94, 124, 350
movement, 11, 17, 22, 30, 31, 39, 55, 119, 139, 161, 230, 246, 251, 275, 278, 345, 360, 366
multiculturalism, 2, 101, 106, 293
multidimensional, 79
multi-ethnic, 36, 93, 101, 106, 135, 187, 240
multi-ethnicity, 101
multiple regression, 213, 215, 217

multiple regression analyses, 215
multiple regression analysis, 213
murder, 32, 41, 112, 131, 133, 161, 177, 219, 246, 255, 268, 270, 303, 329, 339, 347, 348, 349, 351
muscle spasms, 22
music, 1, 66, 70, 82, 104, 110, 111, 112, 115, 117, 118, 119, 121, 157, 166, 170, 252, 262
musicians, 112
mutation, 50
mycotoxins, 379
myocardial infarction, 50

N

nation, 12, 27, 95, 97, 114, 115, 140, 162, 190, 271, 313
nation building, 162
national security, 279
National Survey, 36, 255, 267
nationality, 67, 174, 175, 188
native population, 109, 135
natural sciences, 168
nausea, 273
NCA, 243
negative consequences, 287
negative relation, 277, 282
neglect, 74, 335, 337, 380
Nepal, 326
nerve, 274
nervousness, 22, 223, 311
Netherlands, 4, 249, 252, 254, 298, 369
networking, 246
neuropharmacology, 227
neuroses, 31
neuroticism, 48, 120
newsgroup, 190
newspapers, 184, 189, 338
next generation, 377
nicotine, 250, 259, 265
noise, 302
non-clinical population, 167, 181
normal children, 295
normative practices, 117
nostalgia, 43
nuclear family, 175, 176, 290
nudity, 113
nurses, 16, 52, 97, 204, 335, 340, 341, 351, 357, 359, 360, 366
nursing, 97, 179, 191, 201, 202, 203, 284, 335, 346, 356, 361, 374
nursing home, 201, 202, 284
nutrition, 8

O

obedience, 103, 124
obesity, 46, 48, 50
objectivity, 97
obligation, 124, 337
observations, 49, 93, 137, 173, 258, 334
oceans, xiii
offenders, 122, 329, 332, 351, 353
oil, 58, 66, 98, 206, 207, 245, 252, 267, 335, 338
old age, 249
older adults, 305
omission, 7, 257, 349
openness, 103
operator, 58, 338
opioids, 257
opportunities, 9, 11, 12, 41, 45, 88, 89, 96, 101, 137, 218, 219, 305
oppression, 88, 102, 106, 107, 275
optimism, 326
organ, 14, 365
organic disease, 202
organised crime, 220
orientation, 102
originality, 34
outpatients, 3, 257, 297, 298, 306
overweight, 48
ownership, 335
ox, 181

P

pacing, 262
pain, 126, 160, 165, 168, 171, 172, 188, 225, 246, 273, 310, 311, 312, 326, 379
paints, 175, 176
palpitations, 22, 311, 314
panic attack, 249
panic disorder, 311
paradigm, 59
paradigm shift, 59
parallel, 13, 214
paralysis, 22
parameters, 3, 250, 287, 305, 361
paranoia, 22
paranoid schizophrenia, 274, 298, 303, 304
paraphilia, 224
parentage, 9
parental involvement, 332
parenting, 151, 152, 248, 332
Parliament, 12, 91, 330, 337
parole, 360
passive, 101, 102, 113, 125, 126

pathogenesis, 15, 127
pathology, 15, 173
pathways, 36, 242
patient care, 3, 277, 355, 361
pediatrician, 169
peer group, 80, 247, 248, 251
peers, 78, 87, 189, 260, 290
penalties, 253
penis, 114
percentile, 76, 291
perceptions, 159, 188, 261
performance, 9, 95, 118, 170, 175
permission, viii, 14, 32, 147, 170, 171, 310, 361
perpetration, 223, 226
perpetrators, 88, 89, 303
personal history, 169, 170, 338
personal hygiene, 262
personality disorder, 60, 120, 158, 249, 311
personality type, 305
persuasion, 57, 114, 157
pesticide, 3, 193, 194, 195, 196, 197, 198, 199, 200, 207, 209
pests, 194
Petal, x, 131, 201, 369
pharmacological treatment, 25
pharmacology, 268
phenomenology, 58, 236
phenotype, 266
phobia, 123
physical abuse, 137, 151
physical activity, 46
physical aggression, 226, 227
physical attractiveness, 128
physical features, 133
physical health, 40, 137, 269
pilot study, 65, 305
placebo, 225
planning, 12, 145, 152, 188, 267, 279, 347, 361
plants, 245, 252, 253
plasma, 47
plasticity, 303
platform, 2
pleasure, 102, 115, 124, 177
pleasure principle, 115
plexus, 56
pluralism, 2
pneumonia, 46
poetry, 276
poison, 22, 194, 207, 269
polarization, 291
police, 11, 54, 55, 58, 95, 97, 185, 226, 250, 253, 263, 265, 270, 273, 275, 335, 336, 341
policy making, 214

policy options, 209
political leaders, 137
political parties, 87, 98, 366
political power, 91
politics, 2, 8, 14, 31, 98, 100
pollution, 302
polygamy, 80
polymorphisms, 243
poor performance, 171, 246
popular support, 59
population density, 298, 299
positive correlation, 277
positive relation, 281
positive relationship, 281
poverty, 33, 41, 44, 49, 105, 137, 218, 250, 253, 263, 269, 332
poverty line, 269
power sharing, 87, 98
prayer, 3, 52, 54, 55, 124, 136, 145, 147, 150, 152, 158, 287, 290, 291
precedents, 309
precipitation, 157
predictability, 177
prediction, 192
predictor variables, 215, 217
predictors, 136, 141, 145, 146, 152, 158, 164, 213, 214, 215, 217, 244, 255, 268, 355
preference, 9, 33, 102, 118
pregnancy, 46, 127, 137, 151, 159, 256, 293
prejudice, 1, 31, 88, 89, 106
premature death, 46, 132, 145
preschool, 158, 163, 164
preschool children, 158, 163, 164
preschoolers, 158, 164
president, 34
pressure, 47, 240, 247, 260, 261, 332, 340
prestige, 53, 147, 160, 241, 269, 291, 292, 293, 304, 322
prevention, 132, 145, 146, 152, 163, 191, 193, 203, 209, 253, 293, 371
prices, 44, 246, 252, 266
primary caregivers, 223
primary school, 158
prisoners, 341, 342
prisons, 95, 278, 285, 352
privacy, 355
private practice, 204, 284, 303
private sector, 270
probability, 146, 187
problem behavior, 290
problem drinkers, 233
procedural justice, 95
prodrome, 304

production, 4, 8, 27
profanity, 114
profits, 40, 271
prognosis, 352
program, 114, 181, 230, 231, 278, 279, 313, 371, 375, 377
project, 4, 34, 65, 147, 226, 257, 369, 371
proliferation, 3
promoter, 50, 243
propaganda, 105
propagation, 3
properties, 13, 93, 102, 252, 335
prosperity, 56, 135, 333
protective factors, 134, 135, 246, 255, 294, 303
protective mechanisms, 247
protocol, 78
psychiatric diagnosis, 64, 119, 132, 350
psychiatric disorders, 59, 64, 127, 132, 146, 163, 186, 203, 204, 234, 239, 242, 250, 251, 257, 265, 295, 311, 329, 360, 362
psychiatric hospitals, 3, 277, 278, 284, 355, 361
psychiatric illness, 63, 155, 159, 186, 249, 262, 325, 329, 339, 344
psychiatric morbidity, 84
psychiatric patients, 3, 52, 284, 326, 360
psychiatrist, 3, 22, 25, 26, 27, 35, 53, 54, 57, 59, 120, 125, 133, 170, 178, 201, 202, 204, 232, 242, 253, 262, 263, 266, 284, 299, 322, 329, 330, 336
psychoactive drug, 247, 249
psychological pain, 1
psychological problems, 49, 241, 311
psychological processes, 101
psychological well-being, 142
psychologist, 125, 170, 342, 346, 352, 369
psychology, 2, 19, 29, 84, 98, 168, 293, 326, 365, 369
psychopathology, 17, 27, 30, 32, 131, 140, 150, 158, 176, 178, 247, 251, 288, 326, 351
psychopathy, 339, 342
psychoses, 3, 35, 245, 250, 264, 265
psychosocial factors, 175
psychosocial stress, 127, 162
psychosomatic, 49, 201, 202, 223
psychotherapy, 19, 30, 107, 168, 173, 174, 175, 204
psychotic symptoms, 248, 255, 257, 265, 267, 268
psychotropic medications, 195
puberty, 120, 123, 124, 170
public domain, 186, 350
public health, 3, 8, 91, 145, 179, 189, 193, 195, 250, 257, 258, 375, 377, 379, 380
public sector, 94
public service, 97, 137, 375
pumps, 47

punishment, 32, 155, 158, 220
purification, 272

Q

qualifications, 94
quality of life, 306, 371
questioning, 92, 241, 341
quota sampling, 67
quotas, 32

R

racial differences, 88, 89
racism, 2, 30, 31, 32, 35, 42, 87, 88, 89, 95, 96, 97, 98, 99, 105, 113, 116, 133, 305
radio, 8, 91, 188, 275
radius, 171
range, 51, 53, 64, 111, 120, 127, 133, 145, 146, 155, 169, 196, 223, 224, 235, 265, 288, 299, 300, 301, 320, 329, 339, 346, 350
rape, 112, 117, 118, 119, 120, 122
rash, 55, 345
reaction formation, 97
reactions, 265
reactivity, 181
reading, 10, 26, 345, 371
realism, 17, 18, 366
reality, xiii, 17, 18, 19, 101; 112, 192, 242
reason, 9, 45, 90, 97, 105, 186, 203, 207, 220, 232, 278, 311, 322, 323, 336, 341, 349
reasoning, 186
recall, 12, 13, 288, 341, 344, 345, 347
recalling, 345
reception, 25
receptors, 268
recidivism, 351, 352
recognition, 12, 54, 93, 105, 304
recommendations, viii, 10, 94, 193, 203
reconstruction, 232
recovery, 161, 230, 231, 232, 233, 242, 244
recreation, 119, 246
recruiting, 184, 324
recurrence, 91, 295
reductionism, 51
reflection, 4, 34, 52, 246
reforms, 336
refugees, 326
regression equation, 215
regulation, 168, 177, 350
rehabilitation, 29, 201, 202, 229, 230, 232, 263, 278, 352, 371, 375
reinforcement, 53, 78

rejection, 1, 76, 78, 91, 94, 100, 120, 185, 284, 304, 355
relaxation, 2, 18, 70, 140, 232, 361
relevance, 18, 29, 30, 63
reliability, 68, 80, 147, 299
relief, 70, 77, 232, 246
religiosity, 146, 160
religious beliefs, 76, 79, 137, 140, 157, 188
renaissance, 366
repression, 53
reputation, 76, 113, 366
resentment, 45, 105
resilience, 40
resistance, 32, 46, 47, 53, 54, 160, 305, 313
resolution, 10, 78, 118, 241
resources, 186, 202, 209, 253, 273
respiratory, 46, 48, 252, 271
respiratory disorders, 48
responsiveness, 225
restructuring, 232, 246, 283, 285, 361
retention, 321
returns, 42, 43, 54, 176
revenue, 219
rewards, 140
rhythm, 117
rice, 55
rights, viii, 90, 161, 186, 329, 335, 337, 351, 352
rings, 172
risk factors, 118, 122, 140, 163, 181, 191, 199, 209, 246, 250, 255, 256
robberies, 113
rodents, 350
rolling, 22, 81, 208
rolls, 114
rubber, 40, 340
rule of law, 104, 253
rural areas, 139, 193, 205, 305

S

sadness, 125, 170, 273, 287, 311
safety, 84, 194, 302, 303, 330, 356
sales, 214, 220
salt, 47, 272
salts, 271
sampling, 31, 314
sanctions, 1, 78, 80, 134, 138, 254
satisfaction, 71, 137, 225, 226
saturated fat, 46
saturation, 242
savings, 202
scarcity, 49, 92
schizophrenic patients, 36, 84, 302

scholarship, 89, 97, 369
school authority, 262
school culture, 289
schooling, 107, 126, 263
scientific knowledge, 18, 29, 57
search, 22, 90, 119, 183, 264, 270, 273, 313
searching, 273, 275
secondary data, 145, 146, 156, 213, 215, 277, 280, 285
secondary education, 255
secondary school students, 52, 166, 247, 248, 254, 255, 258, 266, 268, 276, 294
secondary schools, 84, 116, 147, 248, 268, 272, 287, 288
security, 95, 97, 112, 113, 224, 270, 279, 304, 324, 351
security services, 97
sedentary lifestyle, 49
sedimentation, 346
seed, 39, 87, 98, 189
segregation, 88, 102, 106
seizure, 274, 339
self esteem, 42, 101, 102, 125, 261, 321
self-definition, 17
self-destruction, 134
self-discrepancy, 326
self-esteem, 175, 246, 293
self-mutilation, 166, 167, 168, 176, 177
self-report data, 67
self-reports, 259
semen, 83
seminars, 4
Senate, 335
sensation, 23, 311
sensations, 225
senses, 344
sensitivity, 27, 103, 106, 234, 273
separateness, 107
separation, 26, 43, 165, 173, 176
septum, 274
sequencing, 347
serotonin, 225, 227, 269
service provider, 165, 179
severity, 199, 244, 288, 350
sex differences, 294, 298
sex ratio, 195, 310
sexual abuse, 165, 173, 224, 309, 310, 314, 315, 323, 324, 325
sexual behavior, 110, 111, 118, 120, 121
sexual development, 168, 169
sexual deviancy, 121
sexual experiences, 223, 225
sexual offending, 122

sexual orientation, 102
sexual psychopath, 349
sexuality, 3, 118, 120, 127, 140, 168, 174
shade, 109
shame, 78, 137, 226, 311
shape, 104
shares, 4
sharing, 183, 348
shores, 41, 189, 253
short term memory, 345
shortage, 32, 43, 284, 337
shoulders, 4
siblings, 25, 55, 125, 171, 344, 345
signals, 115
signs, 223, 226, 241, 347
simulation, 184
skills, 112, 135, 177, 204, 208, 288, 324, 345, 369
skin, 22, 30, 88, 102, 103, 106, 133, 166, 168, 169, 170, 175, 176, 252, 274, 345, 366
slaves, 9, 31, 32, 40, 42, 102, 111, 114, 246, 333
sleep disturbance, 311
smoke, 171, 245, 249, 251, 338, 345, 350
smoking, 124, 252, 260, 261, 262, 263
smuggling, 245, 267, 273
sobriety, 230, 231
sociability, 127
social acceptance, 26, 117
social adjustment, 161, 246
social anxiety, 326
social attitudes, 102, 157
social behavior, 39
social behaviour, 65, 161
social class, 65, 67, 69, 77, 161, 223, 224, 272, 362
social consequences, 220, 254, 311
social context, 102, 105
social environment, 102, 303, 307
social group, 64, 102, 103, 132
social ills, 253
social impairment, 64, 132
social institutions, 101
social integration, 111, 290
social order, 351
social phobia, 83
social policy, 163
social problems, 131, 137, 140, 191, 245
social psychology, 107
social relations, 118
social relationships, 118
social roles, 292
social sciences, 84, 87, 370
social status, 78, 104
social stress, 64, 111, 133
social structure, 40, 77, 110

social support, 78, 288, 324, 352
social upheaval, 151
social welfare, 285
social withdrawal, 249, 251, 261, 287
social workers, 58, 204, 335, 352
socialization, 107, 115, 232, 246, 360
sodium, 271, 272
soil, 9
solitude, 246
somatic preoccupation, 326
somatization, 3, 309, 310, 311, 312, 314, 315, 316, 317, 318, 319, 320, 321, 322, 323, 324, 325, 326
somatization disorder, 3, 309, 310, 311, 312, 317, 318, 319, 320, 322, 323, 324, 325, 326
somatizers, 316, 317, 318, 320
sovereignty, 17, 18, 19
space, 187, 192, 356
specialists, 311
spectrum, 34, 379
speculation, 45
speech, 32, 68, 171, 260, 261, 262, 263, 266, 304, 340, 341, 345
speed, 272
sperm, 249
spirituality, 25, 146, 230, 233
spontaneous recovery, 350
sports, 1, 96, 380
spousal support, 321
stability, 160, 268, 305
stabilization, 265
staffing, 361
standard deviation, 148, 196, 235, 236, 299
standardization, 241
standards, 17, 19, 120, 157, 254, 348
starvation, 26, 126
state enterprises, 97
statistics, 46, 215, 221, 323, 369
statute, 3, 329
statutes, 131, 352
stereotypes, 87, 98, 102, 103, 106
stereotyping, 30, 121
stigma, 25, 30, 240, 242, 309, 310, 315, 320, 321, 322, 323, 324
stigmatized, 89, 105, 110, 311
stimulant, 269, 274
stimulus, 188
stock, 266
stomach, 55, 159, 187
storage, 139, 266
storytelling, 242, 366
stoves, 186
strain, 293
strategies, 3, 193, 257, 267, 271, 278, 285

strategy, 162, 168, 278
stratification, 88, 107
strength, 27, 91, 215, 229, 267, 269, 318
stress, 64, 70, 77, 125, 137, 156, 157, 246, 251, 290, 291, 304, 305, 324, 351
stress factors, 304
stress reactions, 156
stressors, 169, 205
stretching, 58
stroke, 19, 47, 344, 345, 352
subgroups, 189
subjective experience, 128
substance use, 153, 245, 255, 256, 303
substitutes, 276
succession, 333
sugar, 32, 39, 40, 42, 43, 47, 107, 120, 139, 232, 334, 346, 350, 351, 354
sugarcane, 46, 298
suicide attempters, 156
suicide bombers, 134, 140
suicide rate, 43, 44, 131, 134, 135, 136, 138, 140, 145, 149, 156, 162, 187, 188, 189, 194, 199, 207, 208
summer, 356, 360
superimposition, 1, 134, 305
superiority, 30, 34, 89, 101, 104, 105, 133
supernatural, 25, 26, 55
supervision, 55, 139, 151, 333, 347, 355
supervisor, 147
supervisors, 137, 357
supply, 253, 333
surface area, 167
surplus, 87
surveillance, 273
survival, 298, 352
survivors, 31, 32
suspects, 160
swamps, 270
sweat, 20
switching, 324
symbolic meanings, 64, 111, 133
symbolic systems, 126
symbols, 19, 26, 53, 58, 76, 90, 126, 128
sympathy, 324
symptom, 24, 47, 53, 123, 241, 266
synthesis, 51

T

targets, 101, 113, 218
taxonomy, 99
teachers, 261

Index

teaching, 9, 27, 135, 201, 202, 203, 204, 327, 369, 370, 374, 375, 377

teenage girls, 59

teenagers, 78, 251, 255, 267

telecommunications, 191

television, 55, 103, 113, 157, 159, 162, 170, 188, 192

tempo, 110, 121, 261

temporal lobe, 346

tension, 53, 92, 99, 102, 111, 165, 172, 173, 176, 177, 287, 311, 350

tensions, 20, 92, 99

tenure, 57

terminal illness, 156, 160

territory, 91, 346

terrorism, 112, 143

tertiary education, 105

testing, 55, 79, 120, 147, 152, 169, 240, 259, 264, 341, 342, 346, 369

testosterone, 342

theatre, 8, 111, 112

therapeutic approaches, 26

therapeutic community, 334

therapeutic process, 351

therapeutic relationship, 25

therapists, 155, 162, 178

therapy, 17, 19, 27, 59, 125, 127, 141, 177, 179, 186, 232, 233, 263, 380

thinking, 56, 70, 71, 79, 80, 81, 87, 88, 109, 110, 115, 257, 291, 293, 322, 338

third dimension, 58

Third World, 18, 89, 106, 122, 127, 141, 199, 326

thoughts, xiii, 18, 25, 49, 52, 53, 146, 147, 153, 164, 172, 177, 186, 188, 251, 260, 261

threat, 52, 88, 95, 160, 178, 337

threatening behavior, 331

threats, 203

threshold, 179

thyroid, 120, 261

time periods, 279, 283

time series, 214, 219, 220

timing, 295

tissue, 166, 177

tonic, 252, 274

tourism, 253, 271

toxic effect, 274

toxicity, 194, 259, 260, 264

tracking, 119, 120

trade, 39, 40, 58, 96, 119, 219, 246, 254, 269, 270, 313, 334, 345

tradition, 14, 81, 111, 133, 231, 321, 323, 335

traditional authority, 140

traditional practices, 29, 65, 76, 127, 278

traditions, 17, 231, 243

training, 9, 10, 27, 30, 55, 58, 124, 137, 155, 162, 201, 208, 334, 335, 337, 338, 369, 370, 371, 373, 374

traits, 68, 89, 142, 241, 260, 339

transactions, 252, 274

transcendence, 67, 133

transformation, 269, 275, 276, 278

transgression, 138

transition, 104, 208, 360

transmission, 180

transplantation, 204

transport, 271

transportation, 271

transshipment, 253

trauma, 22, 36, 53, 208, 224

trees, 66, 109, 139

trends, 142, 145, 156, 214, 254, 277, 285, 287, 288, 293

trial, 32, 180, 332, 337, 345, 349

triangulation, 80

tribes, 114

triceps, 340

trichotillomania, 167

trust, 14, 26, 27, 96, 271

tuberculosis, 8

twins, 255, 267

type 2 diabetes, 46, 50

typhoid fever, 46

U

ultrasound, 169

uncertainty, 257, 267

unemployment, 3, 33, 131, 138, 140, 155, 156, 213, 214, 215, 216, 217, 218, 219, 220, 221, 250, 268, 302, 305

unemployment rate, 215, 217, 219

unhappiness, 125

unions, 32, 290

Universal Declaration of Human Rights, 90

universe, 24, 60, 263

upward mobility, 91

urban areas, 80, 113, 360

urbanicity, 302, 306

urbanization, 303

urea, 120, 261

urine, 120, 257, 259, 261, 266, 341

UWI, 11, 90, 183, 370, 374

V

validation, 244

variables, 3, 67, 76, 134, 145, 147, 152, 215, 217, 223, 224, 229, 233, 234, 241, 249, 257, 266, 275, 287, 293, 303, 305
variance, 213, 217, 218
variations, 39, 132, 134, 267, 326, 361
vascular dementia, 352
VDRL, 346
vector, 10
vehicles, 114, 139, 270, 273
vein, 253, 335
venereal disease, 8, 46, 49
ventilation, 291
ventricle, 346
venue, 56
vessels, 273
veto, 94, 95
victimization, 341
victims, 88, 89, 138, 139, 186, 224, 226, 274, 303, 321
video games, 161, 162, 164
village, 43, 232, 339
violent behaviour, 161, 218
violent crime, 112, 113, 220, 321
violent offenders, 354
viral infection, 302
vision, 10, 56, 204, 278
visions, 17, 26, 73
visual images, 117
vitamin C, 65
vitamin C deficiency, 65
vitamins, 196
voice, 22, 97
vomiting, 24, 273
vulnerability, 35, 49, 131, 134, 251, 257, 266, 288, 303

W

wages, 32, 40, 44
waking, 23
walking, 4, 273
war, xiii, 59, 66, 100, 193, 195, 197, 207, 279, 280, 356, 361, 374
warrants, 30, 32, 337
waste, 25

watershed, 366
weakness, 273, 311
wealth, 4, 26, 39, 66, 104, 218, 269, 335
weapons, 112, 114, 139
weeping, 51
weight gain, 125, 127
weight loss, 123
welfare, 8, 29, 52, 263, 335, 347, 371, 375
well-being, 132, 249, 266, 371
wind, 8
windows, 22, 114
winning, 14, 89
winter, 356
wires, 171
witchcraft, 2, 17, 18, 20, 22, 23, 24, 26, 59, 73, 366
withdrawal, 66, 71, 72, 274, 340
work ethic, 70, 77
workers, 32, 40, 42, 52, 58, 137, 246, 313, 333, 334, 336, 350, 351, 356, 361
working conditions, 40, 43
working groups, 76
working hours, 80
workplace, 70, 110, 115, 137, 344
World Bank, 277
World Health Organisation, 37, 189
worms, 42, 55
worry, 237
wrists, 139, 167
writing, 158, 338, 345, 366, 370

X

xenophobia, 88, 99

Y

yang, 64
young adults, 139, 152, 157, 163, 181, 224, 254, 258, 268
young women, 124

Z

zimbabwe, 194, 200
zoology, 370